THE TAPESTRY OF CULTURE

AN INTRODUCTION TO CULTURAL ANTHROPOLOGY

Eleventh Edition

—— **MAXINE WEISGRAU** ——

—— **ABRAHAM ROSMAN** ——

—— **PAULA G. RUBEL** ——

ROWMAN & LITTLEFIELD

Lanham · Boulder · New York · London

To the memory of Daniel

Senior Acquisitions Editor: Alyssa Palazzo
Assistant Acquisitions Editor: Samantha Delwarte
Sales and Marketing Inquiries: textbooks@rowman.com

Credits and acknowledgments for material borrowed from other sources, and reproduced with permission, appear on the appropriate pages within the text.

Published by Rowman & Littlefield
An imprint of The Rowman & Littlefield Publishing Group, Inc.
4501 Forbes Boulevard, Suite 200, Lanham, Maryland 20706
www.rowman.com

86-90 Paul Street, London EC2A 4NE

Cover Image: A young girl learns the art of weaving on a hand loom, Chittangong Hill Tracts region, Bangladesh, Asia.

British Library Cataloguing in Publication Information Available

Library of Congress Cataloging-in-Publication Data

Names: Weisgrau, Maxine K., author. | Rosman, Abraham, author. | Rubel, Paula G., author.
Title: The tapestry of culture : an introduction to cultural anthropology / Maxine Weisgrau, Abraham Rosman, Paula G. Rubel.
Description: Eleventh edition. | Lanham, Maryland : Rowman & Littlefield, 2024. | Includes bibliographical references and index.
Identifiers: LCCN 2023005738 (print) | LCCN 2023005739 (ebook) | ISBN 9781538163801 (cloth) | ISBN 9781538163818 (paperback) | ISBN 9781538163825 (epub)
Subjects: LCSH: Ethnology.
Classification: LCC GN316 .R67 2024 (print) | LCC GN316 (ebook) | DDC 306—dc23/eng/20230313
LC record available at https://lccn.loc.gov/2023005738
LC ebook record available at https://lccn.loc.gov/2023005739

♾™ The paper used in this publication meets the minimum requirements of American National Standard for Information Sciences—Permanence of Paper for Printed Library Materials, ANSI/NISO Z39.48-1992.

BRIEF CONTENTS

CONTENTS

The Tapestry of Culture has been used in teaching introductory anthropology courses to several generations of undergraduate students of anthropology. Over the years, the theoretical frameworks of anthropology have changed greatly, as have our methodological perspectives; successive editions of this book have sought to reflect these changes in a student-friendly way. The authors are cultural anthropologists with extensive fieldwork and classroom experience. This collective experience, and the passion we share for the discipline, underlies our continuing commitment to communicating this material to new generations of anthropology students. This book has been revised through eleven editions to accommodate the changing intellectual needs of undergraduate students as well as the pedagogical challenges of their instructors in a wide variety of learning institutions and settings around the world.

When we think about society and culture, often we think of our own culture—the culture in which we were raised, or in which we currently live. But it is important to understand that different parts of the world are organized in very different ways. Anthropology offers a way to understand the nature of such differences. At the same time, anthropology as an intellectual discipline with changing generations of scholars, teachers, and practitioners does not exist in a vacuum, but rather responds to current social and political influences. While exploring the breadth of the human experience, *The Tapestry of Culture* also explains shifts in the discipline and the debates around them, and identifies what is still generally accepted and agreed upon by most anthropologists.

HALLMARK FEATURES

The Tapestry of Culture adopts a distinctive approach to anthropology, accommodating the history of anthropological thought as well as the various viewpoints in the field today. Although designed primarily as a textbook for undergraduate cultural anthropology courses, *The Tapestry of Culture* engages with many areas of research in human evolution, which theorists increasingly draw on to explore contemporary social and cultural norms. *Tapestry* examines contemporary cultural differences but also points out similarities that emerge as a result of comparative study. The approach also emphasizes the interpretation of language and symbols and the meaning of things in everyday life. The goal of this book is to translate the concepts, ideas, and behavior of other cultures into terms and concepts recognizable to contemporary students. Today the trend is to see ethnography as a description of a unique cultural and historical setting; however, beyond each society's uniqueness, the presence of cultural similarities is apparent and compelling. From its inception, anthropology has always been comparative. Formerly, anthropologists generalized about the nature of rules regarding residence and kinship terminology, but at present, generalizations may deal, for example, with how globalization affects labor patterns around the world, or how political movements mobilize through social media.

Contemporary anthropologists pay particular attention to the nature of ethnographic texts, and most still consider ethnography, based on field research, the heart of the discipline. While originally situated in small-scale societies, anthropological fieldwork is now conducted in urban communities, as well as online communities and corporations. We feel that one of the best ways for students to be introduced to anthropology is by reading ethnographies so that they can feel the excitement of innovative fieldworkers engaged in their work. Students gain from understanding the concepts and theories that anthropologists use in order to appreciate the differences between a society like that of the Trobriand Islands described by Malinowski in the early twentieth century, and the social lives of, for example, disadvantaged minority lesbian mothers in urban settings today. Each chapter therefore cites multiple ethnographies—both classics and contemporary works. Our goal is to provide concise and up-to-date conceptual frameworks with which to understand classic ethnographies as well as the ethnographies about globalized, complex societies, including our own, being written today. *The Tapestry of Culture* is organized so that it can be used together with the particular ethnographies that suit the instructor's interests.

We use the metaphor of a tapestry to highlight how cultures are composed of many interconnected threads, in which the whole is more than the sum of its parts. Standing back from the tapestry, one no longer sees the individual threads, but an overall design. Like a tapestry, each culture has an overall design, even though we, as anthropologists, do take it apart, study the components (by employing categories such as kinship, economics, and religion), and then examine the interconnections between them. This metaphor is far from perfect; the fit between the parts in reality is much more complicated than one overall design. There are always disjunctions and contradictions, and contestations over meaning within any one community. In today's globally connected world, the disjunctions and contradictions often obscure efforts at identifying an overall picture of a particular culture. Anthropologists, collaborating with members of communities, try to create a picture of an aspect of their understanding, in a specific time and place and from a particular perspective, described in ethnography. Therefore, we understand that culture is an analytical concept, an abstraction from reality.

Anthropology, as the study of humans and their ways of life, has the task of understanding the ways in which people bring about changes in their cultures, deal with these changes, sometimes resist them, and try to understand them. Ethnicity and ethnic identity are crucial issues in the world today. Nation-states and empires have fractured and reformulated. People of different ethnic groups and religions who lived together in one state and even intermarried are now fiercely at war with one another. Technological advances in many fields have brought about great changes in all societies, but not all participate equally in their benefits. Outsourcing and remote technologies have made many types of production and employment obsolete, but not everyone has access to the new century's employment skills or technologies. These changes in production require the rethinking of the economic and social organization of modern industrial societies. Migration and transnational families are redefining how people think about their own identities and those of their families. Global pandemics and climate change are part of everyday conversations and household strategies around the world. Electronic media have been integrated into daily lives and everyday forms of communication and information. Technology has transformed aspects of human reproduction and ideas about the human body; we now require new ways of thinking about motherhood, fatherhood, and parenting. Ideas about inequality, gender, work, and sexualities are being reformulated, with significant consequences for family organization around the world. These and numerous other contemporary issues are defining how anthropologists envision their work, locations, and activities in the twenty-first century.

NEW TO THE ELEVENTH EDITION

In this edition we have added a great deal of new material with ethnographic examples in every chapter, consistent with present-day thinking about anthropology. We have particularly strengthened the discussions of gender, inequalities, globalization, social media, health, and social movements in several chapters of the book. Although some issues have been with us since the beginnings of the discipline, contemporary commentators and critics within and outside anthropology have compelled us to confront them anew.

Chapter 1, "Anthropological Perspectives," features an expanded discussion of the evolution of hominins, drawing on recent archeological and paleontological information. We put particular emphasis on the development of language and artistic expression as evolutionary issues. We expand our discussion of theoretical perspectives in anthropological analysis to include various perspectives of environmental anthropology, political ecology, and inequality. We explore the so-called nature vs. nurture debate, as well as important social movements, climate change, globalization, and transnationalism as subjects that generate theory and methods of anthropological inquiry.

Chapter 2, "Anthropological Methods," includes an expanded discussion of the ethical aspects of fieldwork. We discuss Institutional Review Boards (IRBs) and research guidelines for anthropological research. We explore the ethics of writing ethnography and the collaboration of local community members in all phases of research planning and information gathering. We integrate issues of health, pandemics, and social media in our comparative study of weddings as rituals and performance in two different cultures.

Chapter 3, "Language and Culture," discusses the evolution and structures of spoken language. We update this chapter with illustrations of linguistic agency and code-switching. There is an extended discussion of the role language use plays in political discourse as well as multiple language use. We also focus on language loss and revitalization, using current examples of how indigenous communities using new technologies and approaches to language retention.

Chapter 4, "Who We Are: Culture and the Individual," includes an expanded discussion about childhood development and enculturation. New material explores the roles of fathers as caregivers, and the impact on families of parental migration and changes in global labor markets. This chapter also contains current discussions about genetics, behavior, and personality, and the complex relationships between socioeconomic conditions in the household, mental health, and childhood learning capacity. We also include a new discussion on nonverbal communication and body gestures as cultural messaging.

Chapter 5, "Symbols and Their Meanings," discusses contestation and debates around dominant and minority interpretations of cultural symbols. We explore theories and ethnographies that look at the cultural constructions of public and private space. We illustrate contestation over historical representation through debates over monuments and memorials. We also discuss cultural appropriation and the uses of cultural symbols within and across ethnic groups.

Chapter 6, "Ties That Connect: Marriage, Family, and Kinship," deals with the present-day role of kinship in all societies, as well as a subject of anthropological inquiry. We discuss some of the classic concepts of kinship studies through the lens of contemporary political and social issues. We expand our discussion of migration and transnational families to include the role of state policies on citizenship that establish or deny the rights of individuals to live in recognized and protected families.

Chapter 7, "Genders, Sexualities, and Life Stages" includes an expanded discussion of the cultural construction of binary and non-binary categories of gender and sexuality, as well as LGBTQ+ issues in activism, and in anthropological theory and practice cross-culturally. We explore gender and sexuality through queer studies and in postcolonial settings. We expand our discussion of gender and sexual identities to include political participation and power sharing between dominant and minority identities. We include a discussion of gender and the care economy, as related to epidemics and aging issues around the world.

Chapter 8, "Economic Organization: Production, Distribution, and Consumption," includes several new sections in light of the enormous economic changes that have taken place on a global level. We update the history of agriculture as a global phenomenon, and its role in modern globalized economies in light of climate change, land ownership, genetically modified crops, and global inequality issues in production and consumption. We describe new forms of labor activism, using social media, and explore the implications of labor practices in some sectors that link employment and technology.

Chapter 9, "Power, Politics, and Conflict," considers the roles of civil society and gendered political empowerment. The ever-changing manifestations of nationalism in conflict and postconflict settings are investigated, as are the concepts of warfare, and "fragile" and "weak" states. We include a discussion of social movements in the United States and globally, and how social media speeds up the process of communicating political messaging, as well as back-lash against activism.

Chapter 10, "Belief Systems, Rituals, and the Spirit World," discusses characteristics of religious systems and the supernatural. We distinguish between myths, legends, and folktales, with cross-cultural examples. We explore religious syncretism and the widespread online engagement of mainstream and minority religious systems. We illustrate how ritual performance enacts conceptions of the supernatural. We emphasize the ways in which religious ideologies are contested and reinterpreted by minority groups. We explore how local myths and rituals memorialize "first contact" with European explorers. These historical relationships are now being rewritten and reinterpreted in public performance and memorials to include the voices and perspectives of the victimized indigenous communities.

Chapter 11, "Spaces and Places of Creative Expression," is a newly conceptualized chapter on creative expression, its diverse forms, and its multiple audiences. Throughout this chapter, we explore how social media and internet technologies play a major role in how contemporary audiences view and understand creativity. We relate creativity and artistic expression to gender, ritual, politics, and transnational flows of film and other media. We discuss music, dance, theater, film, painting, and other performance styles as containing recognizable cultural and ideological themes, now communicated through new forms of media. We discuss the history and traditions of museums and art/artifact collecting, and how they are being resisted by, and reinterpreted through, adoption of new expressive media by traditional artists, as well as through NAGPRA compliance. We provide a brief history of the use of internet and email technologies, and the emergence of social media platforms, using anthropological contributions and perspectives on performance and creativity.

Chapter 12, "Global Health and Wellness," is a new subject in *The Tapestry of Culture*. This new chapter explores multiple perspectives of the cultural components of being physically and mentally healthy, well fed, and economically productive. We explore historical, political, and cultural issues that shape knowledge systems about disease and health, as well as public health institutions within states and communities. We illustrate with case studies the underlying theories of, and practices of, health intervention strategies. We discuss climate change and sanitation infrastructure and their relationships to health and wellness. We explore how inequalities in access to physical and mental health services create enormous burdens on individuals and communities, and how newly created interventions mobilize peers and volunteers to help address some of these issues. We discuss the critical issue of delivery of health care services to pregnant women and newborn children. We illustrate the challenges of health care delivery in conflict zones and migration settings, from the perspective of humanitarian efforts to alleviate the physical and mental traumas associated with these ever-present crises in today's world.

Chapter 13, "Living/Working in the Globalized World: Colonialism, Globalization, Migration, and Development," focuses on colonial and imperial precursors to contemporary development strategies and globalization. We document, using ethnographic sources, the ever-growing relationships as reflected in households and communities between migrant "movers" and the "non-movers" they interact with. We discuss social media, financial technologies, and remittances as forms of connection between members of transnational families. We document some of the social movements that have emerged through global dissemination of information about unsafe labor conditions, and the importance of digital technologies and media in this information flow. We explore the feminization of migration and global care and service economies, and the important role of state regulations in the possibilities of creating citizenship and recognized families in migration settings.

Chapter 14, "States and Identities: Ethnicity, Race, and Nationalism," examines and compares identity systems in contemporary America to those in other countries. We explore critical race theory, and its contributions to analyzing multiple forms of racism and discrimination. We include an exploration of the challenges of multiculturalism in contexts of nationality, ethnicity, and political representation.

We discuss the role of state sovereignty in the globalized world of international flows of capital and commerce. We illustrate ethnic parades in the United States and elsewhere as vehicles by which identity is constructed and asserted, as well as increasingly representing forms of conflict in "home" countries in new settings.

End-of-chapter material includes detailed bulleted summaries, suggested additional readings (including recently published ethnographies), and related websites. Terms defined in the glossary section are clearly identified in boldface throughout the text, and section headings guide students and instructors to the key ideas and concepts within each chapter.

ACKNOWLEDGMENTS

This new edition could not have been written without assistance from many people. First, we thank the many students in our anthropology classes who, over the years, have asked us many penetrating questions and have provided valuable insights into their understanding of the material in *The Tapestry of Culture*. We have always learned from our students and are continuously in their debt. We are especially grateful to the professors who use *The Tapestry of Culture* in their introductory anthropology courses and who have given us their comments and observations. To these individuals and all the others who have helped us in the past, we owe a debt of gratitude for raising questions that have contributed to significant improvement in the organization and clarity of this book. We thank the reviewers, Teddi Setzer, Jason Miller, and Nadine Qashu Lim, who offered many valuable comments and suggestions for the tenth edition.

To Professors Lesley Sharp, Ellen Marakowitz, Jill Shapiro, Brian Larkin, Carol Henderson, Brian Ferguson, and Barbara Worley, we owe an immeasurable debt of gratitude for their insights that have resulted in significant improvement in the content, organization, and clarity of multiple editions. To our late esteemed colleagues and teachers Alex Alland Jr. and Morton Klass, we honor their contributions to the discipline and to our professional lives.

We extend thanks to Rowman & Littlefield project editors, permissions and photo researchers, design managers, cover designers, and especially to editors Alyssa Palazzo and Samantha Delwarte for their encouragement and assistance in producing this edition. And we remember Alan McClare for his commitment and support for *The Tapestry of Culture*, and for finding us such a supportive new home.

Maxine Weisgrau received a PhD in anthropology from Columbia University. She has conducted field research in Rajasthan, India, since 1988, documenting local nongovernmental organizations and their interaction with rural communities. Her book *Interpreting Development: Local Histories, Local Strategies* (1997) explores multiple perspectives and often-conflicting interpretations of development, and the impact of shifting strategies of local and global organizations. She is the coeditor (with Morton Klass) of *Across the Boundaries of Belief: Contemporary Issues in the Anthropology of Religion* (1999). She is also coeditor of (with Carol E. Henderson) and contributor to *Raj Rhapsodies: Tourism, Heritage and the Seduction of History* (2007), an interdisciplinary analysis of the impact of Rajasthan's colonial histories on contemporary tourism encounters. She has taught both graduate and undergraduate courses in anthropology, development, gender, and women's studies at many colleges and universities. She currently holds appointments at Columbia University School of International Affairs (SIPA) and at Baruch College.

Abraham Rosman (1930–2020) received a PhD in anthropology from Yale University. His first fieldwork was with the Kanuri of Bornu Province, in northern Nigeria. He taught at Vassar College and Antioch College, and was appointed Emeritus Professor of Anthropology at Barnard College and Columbia University, where he taught introduction to cultural anthropology as well as many other graduate and undergraduate courses for many years.

Paula G. Rubel (1933–2008) received a PhD in anthropology from Columbia University. She carried out fieldwork on the Kalmyk Mongol refugees who settled in New Jersey and Philadelphia in 1950. Her doctoral dissertation was published as *The Kalmyk Mongols: A Study in Continuity and Change* (1967). She has taught introduction to cultural anthropology as well as many other courses at Barnard College and Columbia University, where she was most recently appointed Professor Emerita.

Abraham Rosman and Paula G. Rubel began their long and productive collaboration in 1971 when they published *Feasting with Mine Enemy* (reissued in 1986), a comparative study of the potlatch in six Northwest Coast societies. They conducted fieldwork together in Iran, Afghanistan, and Papua New Guinea, and in 1978 they published *Your Own Pigs You May Not Eat: A Comparative Study of New Guinea Societies*. They have also published many articles on their fieldwork and comparative research. Their later fieldwork in New Ireland, Papua New Guinea, and their research on the nineteenth-century collecting of ethnographic artifacts have been the basis for several publications. They are the coeditors of *Translating Cultures: Perspectives on Translation and Anthropology* (2003) and are coauthors of *Collecting Tribal Art: How Kwakiutl Masks and Easter Island Lizard Men Became Art* (2012) and *Aliens on Our Shores: An Anthropological History of New Ireland, Papua New Guinea 1616 to 1914* (2022), edited by Suzanne Hanchett.

Chapter 1

Anthropological Perspectives

LEARNING OBJECTIVES

- Understand how the metaphor of the "tapestry" applies to learning about culture.
- Identify multiple aspects of culture and the sub-disciplines of anthropology.
- Relate major physical and cognitive characteristics of *Homo sapiens* to those of earlier hominins.

- Recognize issues in the history of anthropology and changes in the discipline over the past 150 years.
- Apply anthropological theories and methods to contemporary global issues.

HUMANS POSSESS CULTURE, AND THAT makes them significantly different from other members of the animal kingdom. *Culture* refers to the behavior, symbols, beliefs, ideas, and material objects humans make. It is also referred to as the "way of life" of a people. Although humans have culture, they are still primates and share over 98 percent of their genetic sequences with some other members of this biological order. But the differences in genetic sequencing account for dramatic variations in humans, such as upright walking (bipedalism) and complex symbolic learning systems. Other animals have systems of communication such as calls, but no other animal has the equivalent of human language. The behavior of humans is shaped by **cultural rules** and norms. No other animal gathers and later cooks its food, eats, and shares meals according to various cultural norms the way humans do. All humans have basic needs that must be satisfied to assure biological reproduction and social reproduction, in other words, the continuity of the norms and values of the group. Basic needs include access to food, shelter, and security, and successful adaptation to the climate and environment. In human groups these goals are met through social reproduction, or learned intergenerational skills and strategies: negotiating access to important resources with others, identifying marriage partners and negotiating family formation, maintaining peace and stability, and when necessary, fighting enemies when negotiations and other strategies fail. These are universal goals that are common to all human groups; solutions are specific to individual communities.

Some anthropologists argue that we must constantly consider humans within their biological context, since only then will we be able to understand how language and culture evolved. What were the biological and ecological conditions that permitted or encouraged these evolutionary developments? In contrast, others argue that knowing the anatomical, genetic, and evolutionary background of humans tells us little when we set out to study the multiple expressions of cultural behavior and languages. To these theorists, the fact that humans are animals is less important to the study of human culture than understanding the variations in learned, communicated behavior. Debates over theories and perspectives that stress what cultures have in common, as opposed to how they differ, have been present in the discipline of anthropology since its inception over a century ago.

This debate is sometimes framed as the questions of **nature vs. nurture**—that is, what do individuals inherit in their behavioral and cognitive repertoire, and what do they learn over time by being a member of a group? The idea that behaviors are the result of biological and genetic inheritance is highly problematic. Inaccurate assumptions about the inherent characteristics of different "races" have led to centuries of discrimination and exploitation of peoples of color. "Biological or genetic explanations tend to make people nervous, and not without reason. The promotion of eugenics and racist science by leading biologists and anthropologists of the nineteenth and early twentieth century produced some deeply shameful outcomes, culminating in the Nazis' appropriation of eugenic ideals to justify the Holocaust" (Barrett and Stulp 2019: 203).

Contemporary scholars point out that the framing of "nature vs. nurture" as opposites or a dichotomy, is itself an inaccurate and biased expression of the issue. (See chapter 4 for further discussion.) Some

cultural rules

Internalized norms of behavior covering all aspects of life.

nature vs. nurture

Theories and debates about the influences of inherited and acquired characteristics.

argue that the world lacks deterministic regularities, so why should we expect such regularities to characterize human social behavior? People behave in ways that demonstrate cultural regularities. The major components of research into cultural variations—fieldwork, substantive ethnographic materials and questions, and comparative dimensions—remain relevant and important in anthropology to document the enormous range of behaviors and responses to solving human problems in varied social, political, and economic environments.

What are the concepts anthropologists today use to investigate the culture or way of life of a people, with all its variations and permutations? Each culture has an underlying logic of its own. For people from another culture, it may seem that this logic makes no sense. Variations in norms and cultural ideas may begin to make sense once we understand the complexities and variations in the way people live. The anthropologist's task is in part to "translate" cultures and their foundational ideas to make them understandable to others, as well as to people within cultures. This sometimes involves applying analytical concepts and categories that allow comparison and may aid in identifying cross-cultural differences and similarities.

Anthropologists historically focused on societies other than their own Euro-American cultures. Most people are very aware of different cultures today, as a consequence of the spread of ideas through globalization and migration, but anthropology still has a mission to perform. It is to learn more about other cultures to permit better intercultural communication so that we can better understand others. In learning about other cultures, we learn more about ourselves. The anthropologist's methods are different from those of other social scientists. Those differences influence the nature of the discipline—its concepts, procedures, and theories—as well as the outcome of inquiry.

Anthropological research involves a journey—a journey in space, a journey through time, and a psychological journey. Anthropologists attempt to suspend the judgments of their own society and its cultural rules to learn the way of life of another society, and try to tell an aspect of "its story." By doing this, anthropologists seem to put themselves in the position of being the "authority" about that society. Sometimes people in the communities anthropologist study reject this authority; some have called the gathering, analysis, and publication of information by anthropologists an "appropriation" of their culture. To avoid these conflicts, anthropologists now consult with communities and come to a shared understanding of the work they do. Over the years, journalists, novelists, and science fiction writers have been drawn to such journeys into different worlds. They may have brief encounters with individuals from other cultures, and draw conclusions about them based in part on preexisting assumptions. Anthropologists' encounters are different. They engage in long-term associations, conduct many interviews, experience scores of events, and participate in multiple rituals with other members of the community.

Humans have always moved and traveled beyond the area they called "home." This was the means by which *Homo sapiens* eventually peopled most of the earth's surface. Characteristics of one culture have always spread to other cultures. The process of globalization has brought Western products in the form of Pepsi-Cola and McDonald's menus to the

A young man with the Berber scarf in the Merzouga desert of Morocco. Among some Berber groups, men wear headscarves and women do not.

ethnocentrism

The idea that what is present in one's own culture represents the natural and best way to do things.

ethnonationalism

The desire of ethnic groups within a state to have their own nation-states.

cultural relativism

The emphasis on the unique aspects of each culture, without judgments or categories predetermined by one's own culture.

cultural universals

Cultural features that are found in all societies.

universal human rights

A doctrine that emphasizes inalienable rights of the individual over the cultural norms of the community.

most remote parts of the world, but a traveler to distant places is still impressed with the differences between cultures. Snake and insects are served in food markets and restaurants around the world; most North Americans do not consider such creatures to be food. Veiling is another cultural feature increasingly shared by many societies. In some societies women veil, but in Tuareg society (Saharan Berber people) it is the men who veil.

People in every culture think that what they eat and do is "natural," correct, and appropriate; conversely how other people act may be deemed incorrect or inappropriate. The belief that one's own culture represents the best way to do things is known as **ethnocentrism**. Ethnocentrism emphasizes the pride a group has in its cultural accomplishments, its historical achievements, the supremacy of its religious beliefs, and the virtues of its family, household, gender, and culinary practices. Ethnocentrism sometimes includes the idea that other people's (often one's closest neighbors) beliefs, customs, and practices are unaccomplished, immoral, and worthy of scorn. Ethnocentrism is at the root of ethnic conflict and **ethnonationalism**, which motivates so many aspects of political conflict today. (See chapter 14.)

Anthropology examines the world of cultural differences. It examines cultural practices within their own larger cultural contexts. **Cultural relativism** is the idea that each culture is unique and distinctive and that no culture is superior to another. This is in sharp contrast to the ethnocentric point of view. Cultural relativism is also in opposition to the concept of **cultural universals**. Given cultural relativism, how do we understand morality, that is, good and evil? On the one hand, there are those who believe that killing another human being should be universally condemned. On the other hand, there are cultural relativists who argue that killing within ceremonial or ritual contexts like headhunting and cannibalism in the past was a core feature of societies in which it occurred. A doctrine of **universal human rights** emphasizes the rights of the individual over those of the community, and condemns such killings. Those supporting universal human rights say community-supported arranged marriages, normal in some communities, violate the rights of individuals. In the United States the death penalty is accepted but is renounced by practically all other countries as a violation of the universal moral principle that no one has the right to take the life of another human being. This conflict over the death penalty becomes an international issue when the United States attempts to extradite an alleged criminal from a country that has renounced the death penalty to possibly face the death penalty here. There is an ongoing debate between supporters of a universal morality and supporters of moral relativism. Subjects like the death penalty and abortion are widely debated in our own society. Many who object to abortion as the taking of human life support the death penalty, and this represents a basic contradiction. As we shall see, such contradictions and contested views of norms and practices are found in all cultures.

In addition to understanding cultural differences, anthropologists also engage with what cultures have in common. Anthropologists utilize the **comparative approach** to compare and contrast cultures, identifying fundamental similarities of cultural patterning as well as differences. Contemporary anthropologists now routinely include globalization, climate change, shifting political borders, and forms of marginalization in documenting how access to important resources in any society is mediated by politics and socioeconomic status.

STUDYING CULTURE: ASSUMPTIONS AND DEBATES

The central concept in anthropology is **culture**, which consists of ideas transmitted symbolically and intergenerationally about the things people make, their behavior, their beliefs, and ideas. In defining culture, different anthropologists emphasize different aspects of culture, and in that sense, the concept is "contested." Some focus on culture as a set of shared ideas and meanings that people use, derived from the past and reshaped in the present. In this view, patterns of meaning, embodied in symbols and language, are the means by which humans communicate, perpetuate, and develop their knowledge about and attitudes toward life. The role of the anthropologist, then, is to grasp, comprehend, and translate those ideas and meanings so people of other groups may understand them. Others focus on how different groups may have opposing or conflicting views to those of the mainstream or dominant groups who, by virtue of their elite status, exercise **hegemony** over other groups, that is, the power to define and enforce social and legal norms.

At the turn of the twentieth century, academic anthropology was in its earliest phase; field workers treated the cultures that they studied as if they were isolated and their cultural boundaries relatively fixed. This view is now discarded, as generations of anthropologists have documented how European contact and exploration integrated virtually all indigenous communities around the world into trade networks and consumption patterns that profoundly impacted their social, gendered, political, and economic norms. Anthropologists now routinely explore culture in historical perspectives, demonstrating that groups of people have always been in contact with others, and their interactions are inevitably shaped by economic and political inequalities. At cultural boundaries, individuals are bilingual, frequently intermarry, and often join together in rituals. Change constantly takes place in all cultures, often as a consequence of contact with others or changes within the culture itself. Individuals have **agency**, meaning they are active participants in shaping and challenging norms, and are continuously involved in reworking their cultures and their traditions.

comparative approach

Comparing societies to uncover similarities and reveal differences.

culture

The way of life of a people, including their behavior, the things they make, their ideas, beliefs, language use, social organization, governance, and production systems.

hegemony

Dominance and influence of one social or political group over another.

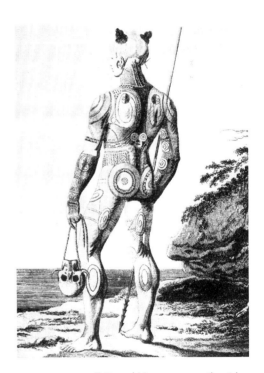

Tattooed Marquesan youth said to be holding a trophy head taken from an enemy. This image is depicted in the account of the voyages of G. H. Langsdorff published in 1813 and is therefore a European visual representation..

agency

Refers to the fact that individuals are active interpreters of and responders to their culture.

Many disciplines study the various types of human activities; the concept of culture is routinely utilized by historians, economists, sociologists, political scientists, and scholars of cultural studies. Sometimes a specific sector of human activity is imagined as if it were largely autonomous; thus, economists study aspects of the economy such as the gross national product or the stock exchange. Political scientists study how laws are enacted. Art historians study paintings and sculpture. Musicologists study songs and instruments. Religious specialists study ritual practices and scriptural texts. Anthropologists also investigate these subjects but emphasize their interrelationship to understand how people act, and in turn, how their actions and ideas shape their institutions.

Anthropology's approach uses culture as an organizing concept and stressing the interrelationships among multiple forms of cultural expression. For an anthropologist, the emphasis is on the way in which, for example, economics may affect politics as well as art. In turn, religion and economics may be examined in terms of how they affect one another. In the late nineteenth and early twentieth centuries, anthropologists focused on small-scale societies; sociology and other fields primarily explored the institutions of cities and industrialized societies. Today, anthropologists focus on how forms of inequality are embedded in economic and political change in both rural and urban communities. What were once thought of as small-scale "isolated" societies are all now part of complex nation-states integrated into global systems of migration and trade, with divisions of labor and multiple forms of inequality characterizing these systems.

cultural anthropology

The subfield of anthropology that studies variation in beliefs, understanding, behavior, and ideas in human settings.

archaeology

Examines cultures through their material remains.

physical anthropology

Investigates the physical evolution of the human body and its anatomical and molecular characteristics.

linguistics

The study of language and the relationship between language and culture.

The concept of culture unites **cultural anthropology** with anthropology's other subdisciplines. **Archaeology** examines the norms and institutions of cultures, both past and present, as expressed through their material remains. **Physical anthropology** (or biological anthropology) investigates human evolution and the relationship between the culture of humans and their anatomical and genetic characteristics. **Linguistics** is the study of language and the relationship between language and culture. Anthropological research routinely crosses these subdisciplinary boundaries. For example, an investigation into the peopling of the Pacific, that is, the migration of humans into Australia, New Guinea, and the Oceanic islands, demonstrates how all four subdisciplines may play a role in research. Genetic and linguistic differences are significant in investigating how the different cultures of the areas were transformed through time. Archaeological evidence shows when people moved into these areas and how their material cultures, resource utilization, political systems, and everyday practices changed through time. Cultural anthropology examines the way in which migration and contact inevitably brings about changes and cultural diversification for all groups.

Other disciplines utilize understanding of cultural norms to help direct and motivate social change. The World Bank and many other development agencies employ anthropologists to do research in cultural ideas and meanings to provide the important context to encourage economic and social development, adoption of new health strategies, and support for early education for all children in effective and sustainable ways. Some scholars refer to **applied anthropology**, the application of anthropological research and strategies to development and health interventions, as the fifth subfield of anthropology. (See chapter 13.)

applied anthropology

The application of anthropological knowledge and methodologies to the solution of practical problems, direct action and/or development policy.

Today, all individuals live their lives in a world of overlapping cultures. Anthropologists are equally interested in studying both change and continuity. The Dine' recognize their identity and culture as they participate in the American economy and political systems. Many are bilingual, speaking the Navajo language and English. Within the Dine' population, there is considerable cultural variation among individuals, between rural and urban communities. Some live on reservations, which are sites of active cultural assertion. Some live off the reservations and pursue education, careers, and lifestyles in urban centers. The Dine' people have always been very receptive to new cultural ideas. Sheep herding and blanket weaving were introduced by the Spanish centuries ago, at the time of their conquest of the New World. Later, the creation of silver jewelry became part of the Dine' political economy. But earlier, the Dine' people chose not to adopt the horticultural practices of their neighbors, the Hopi and Zuni. What emerges from this example is an awareness that cultural norms exist at many levels and emerge at different times, expressed through the agency and choices of the individual, the community, and the larger society or political entity.

All cultures have a certain degree of internal consistency. We call this book *The Tapestry of Culture* because the imagery of a tapestry in some ways conveys a picture of culture as integrated. Many strands, many colors, many patterns contribute to the overall design of a tapestry, just as many items of behavior and many customs form patterns that, in turn, compose a culture. This metaphor of culture as a tapestry is not a perfect one; unlike a woven cloth, culture is constantly changing over time. There are very frequently internal inconsistencies and contradictions, as will be illustrated in the following chapters. Cultures are not single, monolithic entities over time. There is variation based on regional, class, ethnic, racial, gender, sexual, and religious differences. There is also variation within these categories; people always have different perspectives on the norms of the culture they share. From each group, a researcher will get only "partial truths" about the culture. Some ethnic, racial, and sexual identity groups in America argue that they live in "different worlds" from those of cultural or economic elites, and have little in common with their beliefs, values, or worldviews.

The patterns and regularities of any culture or community never remain eternally the same but always change through time. Political and social changes, like the movement for women's rights and the #MeToo movement, have redefined gender expectations for fair and safe work and life environments. The Black Lives Matter movement has drawn global attention to racial bias in policing and criminal justice in the United States and elsewhere. Every significant technological invention—such as the electric light bulb, the telephone, the automobile, and the computer—has resulted in major changes in different parts of global culture, although never with the same speed or degree of availability for every group or community. The term **digital divide** calls

digital divide

Inequality in access to electronic devices and internet resources.

The Americas

1. Aymara – Peru
2. Cherokee – United States
3. Chillihuani – Peru
4. Crow – United States
5. Haida – Canada
6. Inuit – Canada
7. Kayapo – Brazil
8. Kwakiutl – Canada
9. Mashantucket Pequot – United States
10. Misstassini Cree – Canada
11. Navajo – United States
12. Nuchanulth (Nootka) – Canada
13. Ojibwa – Canada
14. Seneca – United States
15. Sioux – United States
16. Tlingit – United States, Canada
17. Tsimshian – Canada
18. Wapichana – Guyana
19. Yanomamo – Venezuela

Europe

20. Abkhazian – Autonomous Region of Georgia
21. Chechan – Russian Federation
22. South Ossetian – Autonomous Region of Georgia

Africa and the Middle East

23. Aluund – Democratic Republic of Congo (Zaire)
24. Ashanti (Asante) – Ghana
25. Bedouin – North Africa, Saudi Arabia
26. Igbo – Nigeria
27. Kanuri – Nigeria
28. Maasai – Kenya, Tanzania
29. Marsh Arabs – Iraq
30. Nyakyusa – Tanzania, Malawi
31. Samburu – Kenya
32. Tuareg – West Africa
33. Yako – Nigeria
34. Yoruba – Nigeria

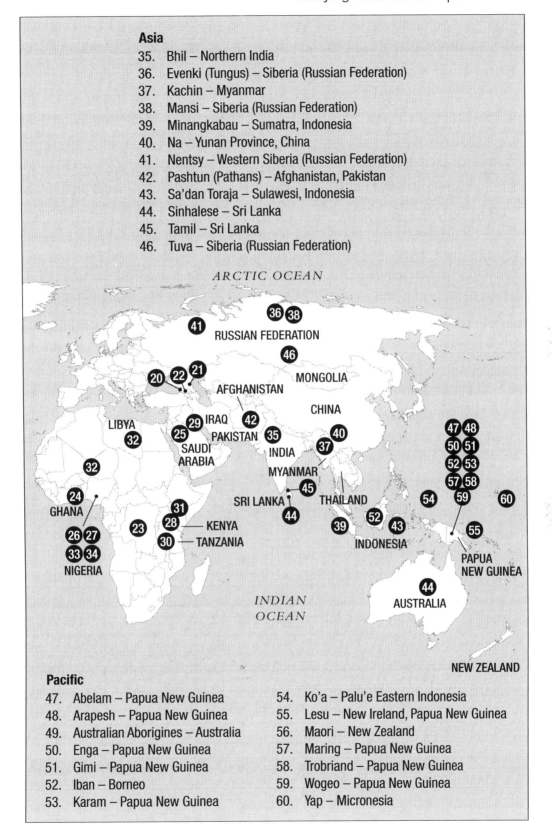

Asia

35. Bhil – Northern India
36. Evenki (Tungus) – Siberia (Russian Federation)
37. Kachin – Myanmar
38. Mansi – Siberia (Russian Federation)
39. Minangkabau – Sumatra, Indonesia
40. Na – Yunan Province, China
41. Nentsy – Western Siberia (Russian Federation)
42. Pashtun (Pathans) – Afghanistan, Pakistan
43. Sa'dan Toraja – Sulawesi, Indonesia
44. Sinhalese – Sri Lanka
45. Tamil – Sri Lanka
46. Tuva – Siberia (Russian Federation)

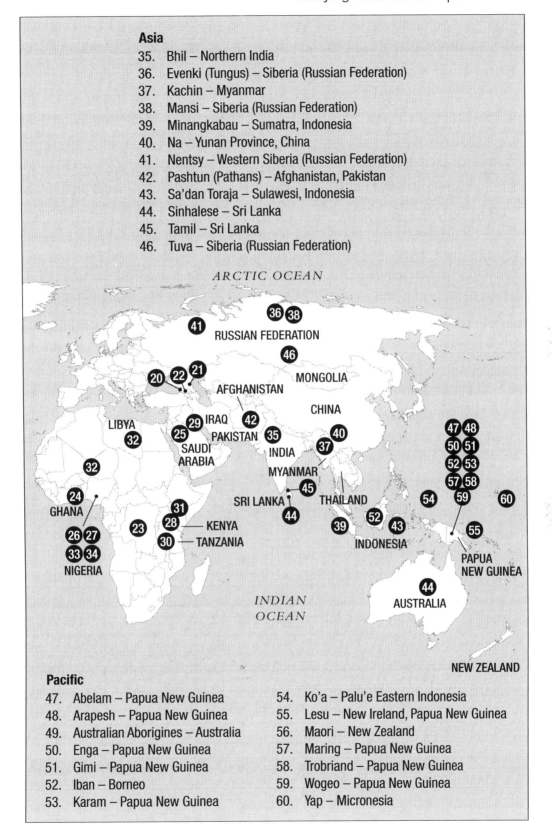

Pacific

47. Abelam – Papua New Guinea
48. Arapesh – Papua New Guinea
49. Australian Aborigines – Australia
50. Enga – Papua New Guinea
51. Gimi – Papua New Guinea
52. Iban – Borneo
53. Karam – Papua New Guinea
54. Ko'a – Palu'e Eastern Indonesia
55. Lesu – New Ireland, Papua New Guinea
56. Maori – New Zealand
57. Maring – Papua New Guinea
58. Trobriand – Papua New Guinea
59. Wogeo – Papua New Guinea
60. Yap – Micronesia

attention to the differences within states and across genders and communities in access to reliable electricity, software and hardware, and cell phone service.

Culture is learned and acquired by infants through a process referred to by anthropologists as **enculturation**. Individuals are enculturated as active agents. They internalize cultural practices but may change and transform those practices as a result of their experiences. Individuals learn another language and culture when they migrate to a new area, but the degree to which they internalize new norms may vary. This learning is transgenerational; that is, it continues beyond the lifetimes of individuals. There is some consistency of cultural patterning through time, despite the fact that culture is continually being reworked and recreated. For example, nuclear families and neolocal (forming a new residence independent of parents and other kin) postmarital residence patterns have been the household norm in American culture particularly since industrialization (see chapter 6). However, many changes have taken place that influence how individual households are configured; not everyone is raised in the traditional nuclear family, although it is still perceived to be the North American norm.

Culture is always in a dialogue between past and present. Changes occur, some of which are the result of internal developments, innovations, and inventions, while others may represent interpretations of introductions from outside. Anthropologists study the process of culture change through time by examining historical, archival, demographic, and, sometimes, archaeological data. Ideas about "tradition" in any culture can therefore be seen as the past imagined and expressed in the present. Innovators and rebels, who try to transform their societies, have a view of their society that is different from that of other members. It is an imagining of a different future, which demands that present ways of doing things be reexamined and transformed.

Culture, as defined above in all its complexity, is a distinguishing characteristic of modern humans. In other species, social behaviors and communication exist, but they are expressed primarily by instinct and are essentially uniform throughout each species. Although it was originally thought that only humans possessed culture, recent research shows that several nonhuman primate species exhibit behavior that seems to resemble culture. Chimpanzees make and use different tools to solve different food gathering problems. In Gabon, chimpanzees at Loango National Park use five different tools in sequence to extract honey from three different types of bee nests (Boesch, Head, and Robbins 2009). They use different tools to solve multiple problems; hence, they have what can be described as a tool kit. All these chimpanzee behaviors are communicated intergenerationally and would therefore seem to be learned behavior.

HUMAN EVOLUTION AND CULTURE: THE EMERGENCE OF ANATOMICALLY MODERN HUMANS

According to the principle of **natural selection**, the central tenet of Darwinian evolutionary theory, individuals within a species with adaptive physical traits are more successful in reproduction; they produce more

enculturation

The process by which cultural rules and norms are learned and acquired by individuals.

natural selection

In Darwinian evolutionary theory, the concept that genetically based adaptive traits create reproductive advantages over time, thus preserving those traits across generations.

offspring and flourish, while those with traits that are not adaptive do not pass on their genes with the same frequency. Over long periods of time and multiple generations, species evolve and adapt their physical characteristics to their environments. Cultural traits, however, cannot be explained in terms of natural selection or reproductive advantage. Many cultural norms in present-day communities are not adaptive and do not create reproductive disadvantages; yet these traits persist due to social and political influence. The cultural behavior of modern humans, *Homo sapiens sapiens*, is learned and transmitted within groups from one generation to the next; it is based on language and the capacity to manipulate symbols. Human cultural behavior is not bounded, but is infinitely expandable.

The evolution from proto-human and early human forms involved a number of significant physical changes, including the development of **bipedal erect locomotion** (upright walking), changes in brain size, and neurological reorganization of the increasingly larger brain. Paleoanthropologists, who study the evolution of the human body, analyze these changes through fossil evidence, material remains, and more recently recovery of molecular and genetic evidence. Ancient DNA and archeological remains provide evidence of evolutionary changes that contributed to the development of modern humans. More speculative analysis hypothesizes about how these anatomical and genetic changes expressed themselves in behavior, technology use and innovation, and social interactions.

Earlier **hominin** forms, such as *Australopithecus*, emerged about 4.2 million years ago. Adults averaged approximately four feet tall, and they had the anatomy and skeleton to support upright walking. They had a small brain size, and among paleoanthropologists, there is some debate over their neurological and cognitive capacities. About 3.3 million years ago, the oldest recognized stone tools appear in the archaeological record. *Homo habilis*, which appeared around 2.7 million years ago in East and South Africa, had a larger brain size than *Australopithecus* and was fully adapted to bipedalism. Until recently, *Homo habilis* (named "handy man" by its discovers) was thought to be the first stone tool maker, but there is now evidence of this technology associated with earlier forms. *Homo habilis* had a larger brain size and reorganized neural anatomy distinguishing it from other earlier species. *Homo habilis* was a scavenger, and fossil evidence suggests this food gathering technique created innovations in the way they interacted with their physical environment.

Homo erectus, associated with more sophisticated stone tool technologies and fire use in some geographic locations, appeared about 1.8 million years ago. This species is believed to be fully adapted to both walking and running upright. *Homo erectus* remains are found in Africa, Central Asia, Indonesia, and China. It is believed that this species existed for a million and a half years and migrated throughout parts of Africa and Asia. Their increased brain size and what are believed to be increased cognitive abilities helped them to adapt to different natural environments and to expand geographically to such a degree. The presence of at least one comparatively old individual who had lost

bipedal erect locomotion

The emergence of physical and cultural characteristic of anatomically modern humans associated with total upright walking on two legs.

hominin

In contemporary usage, the group that includes modern and extinct humans and other extinct prehumans such as Australopithecus and its predecessors. The group hominid includes modern and extinct humans and their ancestors, as well as gorillas, great apes, and orangutans and their evolutionary ancestors.

all its teeth supports the hypothesis that they cared for the elderly, suggesting some aspects of their social relationships.

Homo heidelbergensis emerges approximately 1.5 million years ago, and therefore existed simultaneously with *Homo erectus*. *Homo heidelbergensis* has modern human size, dentition, and shows sexual dimorphism (differences in size between adult males and females). Paleoanthropologists find evidence of complex tool manufacture and use, including spears and blades. There is clear evidence of controlled use of fire and large-animal hunting. Remains found in colder climates in northern Europe suggest that they may have built simple protective shelters and created protective garments. There is also evidence of the presence of ochre pigment, which may have been used for body decoration. There is some evidence of social behaviors associated with protection and care of helpless group members. This is inferred from a fossil finding of an individual with a skull pathology that would have created severe mental impairment; this individual lived far longer than would have been expected without care and assistance.

Homo neanderthalensis, generally acknowledged to be among the closest extinct human relatives, appears in the fossil record in Europe and central Asia approximately four hundred thousand years ago; later Neandertal sites have been identified in the Middle East. DNA has been recovered from some European Neandertals, enabling the creation of the genome sequences of this human ancestor. The presence of a very small amount of Neandertal DNA in some modern human populations suggests the coexistence of, and interbreeding between, Neandertals and other early modern human ancestors. Material remains associated with Neandertals exhibit many important symbolic traits such as intentional burial of the dead and body adornment with pigments, feathers, and deliberately fashioned shell pendants. Many researchers see in their brain and anatomical structures the beginning of the capacity for producing spoken language.

There are several theories about the chronology and circumstances surrounding the emergence of anatomically modern humans (AMHs) in the evolutionary framework. The evolutionary history of *Homo sapiens sapiens*, the subspecies that includes all modern humans, is continually reevaluated due to fossil finds of earlier groups, including Neandertals, Denisovans, and other species like *Homo longi*, recently recognized in China. Genetic analyses confirm coexistence among archaic human populations at several points in evolutionary history, as opposed to replacement of one species by another.

Upright Walking and Bipedalism: Cultural Implications of Evolutionary Change

Some scholars, in analyzing human evolution, particularly focus on the anatomical and cognitive requirements for what eventually evolved into a major hallmark characteristic of modern humans: speech capacity. "Our bipedal locomotion was a gateway to many of the unique traits that make us human. It is our hallmark . . . upright walking made us human" (DeSilva 2021: xiii).

Bipedalism freed the arms of our ancestors, and gave rise to the capacity for a full range of body-language movements and complex visual gesturing. These are the dominant features of human interaction, and the primary means of communication for our early hominin ancestors. With the use of visually based language (gestures), the brain expanded, and this resulted in a pre-adaptation for verbal language. Verbal language could only appear after the multiple anatomical features of the vocal tract necessary for production of some speech-associated sounds were in place.

Human language corresponds with the use, creation, and manipulation of symbols; it is the vehicle for human cultural expression. Its historical emergence is therefore of great interest to anthropologists, paleoanthropologists, linguists, and other scientists. The ability to create and manipulate language evolved as did brain size, vocal tract anatomy, and neurological structures. But the origin of language "remains unknown and controversial" (DeSilva 2021: 142). Fossils of anatomically modern humans appear in European and Asian sites by the Upper Paleolithic period, about forty thousand years ago. Various sites have yielded a broad range of food gathering and processing technologies, including fishing nets and fishing hooks. Portable and stationary artistic representations also make their first appearance in this period. "The increasing ability for symbolic thinking—to let one thing stand for another . . . allowed people to make visual representations of things that they could remember and imagine" (Marchant 2016). Remarkable cave paintings found in southern France depicting different species of animals are dated to about thirty thousand years ago. Carved mammoth ivory figurines found in Germany were dated to approximately the same period (Marchant 2016: 84). Discoveries of stenciled handprints and animal paintings in Sulawesi, an island of Indonesia, are at least thirty five thousand years old. Complexity of tools occurred with expansion in brain size and neurological reorganization. Simultaneous with anatomical and technological changes is the emergence of the capacity for language and symbolic manipulation. This suggests the capacity for the exchange of information between scattered groups, a feature that characterizes culture.

Meat Eating: Raw and Cooked

The brain growth and neurological specialization that leads to the anatomical capacity for language required the consumption of calories and nutrients beyond those obtained from vegetable diets. The energy released from eating meat may have facilitated this critical brain transformation. The controlled use of fire is therefore another significant element in the evolution of humans. Cooking transformed meat and fibrous vegetation into nutritious food, making it digestible and providing increased amounts of caloric energy. Once cooked, such food became a valuable resource that had to be protected as it was easily subject to marauding and theft. Preparation and protection of food, together with the formation of an extended period of female sexual receptivity, may have led to strong male-female bonds, a pattern not found among most nonhuman primates.

Cooking of food of course presupposes the control of fire. The ability to use fire and cooking are universal in human cultures. Fire use and cooking distinguished human cultural behavior from animal behavior. Cooking and distributing food to others illustrates the capacity to defer gratification, which increased as humans evolved. Human beings do not eat the minute they become hungry, nor do they immediately consume what they hunt or gather. With the introduction of cooking, humans deferred eating until long after the acquisition of food. Hunting and the gathering of vegetation are complicated multistep technologies that require the cultivation of skills, division of labor, and group cohesion. Human food production and consumption are controlled by rules. Sexual intercourse and pair-bonding are similarly subject to cultural rules; unlike most other animals, humans do not have a short period of sexual receptivity only during which they have sexual intercourse. Humans are continually receptive to sex; they therefore follow their culture's set of rules as to how, when, where, and with whom to have sex, and during which life stages it is, or is not, appropriate. These rules also form group behaviors and shared group taboos, thus engendering a sense of community identity and recognition.

CULTURAL UNIVERSALS: WHAT CHARACTERISTICS DO ALL HUMANS SHARE?

All cultures solve the basic problems of human existence: providing food, protection, and reproduction. As a consequence, all cultures share some fundamental similarities, which are referred to as cultural universals. Although languages differ, they are all characterized by certain universal features, such as the presence of nouns, possessive forms, and verbs that distinguish between the past, present, and future. Human consumption of food follows cultural rules regarding what is eaten, when, with whom, and how—with which utensils you eat, and which hand dominates. All cultures have some kind of incest taboo, though the relatives with whom they must not have sexual intercourse vary, as we will describe in chapter 6. Rites of passage, marking birth, reaching adulthood, marriage, and death, are celebrated ceremonially by societies, though not all of them recognize these life stages in the same way.

All cultures have systems of governance, religion, marriage, family, and kinship. These universal cultural categories are present in all human societies since each must deal with the problems and concerns that all humans face. Languages and cultures are structured in a particular manner as a consequence of the fact that the brain of *Homo sapiens* is organized in a certain way. The capacity for social exchange and altruism are universal in cultures, though the rules of social exchange vary from one culture to another.

Cultural Rules and Norms

Cultural norms dictate the way in which instincts and feelings are expressed; they are learned and internalized by human infants during the process of enculturation. The enormous variations between cultures are due in part to differences in cultural rules. Defining these cultural rules is like trying to identify the rules that govern a language. All languages operate according to sets of rules, and people follow these in their speech. It is the linguist's job to determine the rules of grammar that the speakers of languages are usually not aware of and use automatically. Frequently, people can tell an anthropologist what the cultural rules are. At other times, they may behave according to rules that they themselves cannot verbalize. An anthropologist's job is to uncover those cultural rules of which people may or may not be aware.

The existence of rules does not imply that speakers of a language or members of a culture speak and act in identical fashion. Each infant learns cultural rules in a distinctive manner, and every speaker of a language has distinctive pronunciation and linguistic mannerisms. There is considerable individual variation in spoken language, and it is equally present in cultural practice. Rules can be flouted, and often individuals ignore rules. Individuals are not simply recipients of culture; they are active participants in reworking their cultures and their traditions. As a consequence, there is variation in observing the rules.

Rules governing sexual behavior in terms of with whom it is allowed, as well as when, where, and how, are highly variable. For example, when Hortense Powdermaker (1933) studied the village of Lesu in Papua New Guinea, it was acceptable for sexual intercourse to take place before marriage. The marriage relationship was symbolized by eating together. When a couple publicly shared a meal, this signified that they were married and could henceforth eat only with one another. Even though husband and wife could have sexual relations with other individuals, they could not eat with them in public. In American society, in contrast, until the beginning of the sexual revolution of the 1960s, engaged couples could eat together, but sexual intercourse should not take place until after marriage. The act of sexual intercourse symbolized marriage. At that time, if either spouse had intercourse with another individual after marriage, that constituted adultery. However, either spouse could have dinner with someone of the opposite sex. From the perspective of someone in American society, the rules governing marriage in Lesu appear to be like our rules but "upside down."

Every culture has subgroups whose repertoire of cultural rules may vary. Similarly, cultural groups exhibit variability in their rules and norms. On occasion, individuals may violate cultural rules. All cultures have some provision for sanctioning the violation of cultural rules as well as rewards for obeying them. In the same way that the sets of cultural rules differ, both rewards and punishments also differ from one culture to another. Cultural rules also change over time. When many individuals consistently interpret a rule differently than it had been interpreted before, the result will be a change in the rule itself. Sometimes cultural norms concerning the rights of individuals are unequally applied; social and political movements are often based on one group's insistence that the rules and norms be extended to include the protection of all members of society.

Society

society

An organized social grouping characterizing humans and other social animals, often differentiated by age and gender.

Another concept paralleling culture is that of **society**. Culture deals with meanings and symbolic patterning, while society refers to the organization of social relationships within groups. Culture is distinctive of humans alone, although there are some primates that have what we have characterized as proto-culture. However, all animals that live in groups, humans among them, can be said to have societies. Thus a bee hive, wolf pack, deer herd, and baboon troop all constitute societies. The individual members of a wolf pack are differentiated as males and females, as immature individuals and adults, and as mothers, fathers, and offspring. Individual wolves in each of these social categories behave in particular ways. That there are resemblances between wolf and human societies should not be surprising, since both wolves and humans are social animals.

Today, there are no bounded social entities of the type that were labeled "societies" in the past. Nation-states that are independent political entities are connected to other nation-states. Nation-states are multiethnic, containing groups with somewhat different cultural repertoires than the dominant ethnicity. Although anthropologists might begin their research with groups as if they were separate entities, in the final analysis, their social and cultural connection to other such groups and to the nation-state must always be considered. These groups share cultural ideas, and still other ideas are contested, but they have some ideas in common as part of the nation-state.

Social Structure

social structure

The pattern of social relationships that characterizes a society.

social organization

Behavioral choices that individuals make in connection with the social structure.

practice

Individual choices and decision making.

social status

The position an individual occupies in a society.

social role

The behavior associated with a particular social status in a society.

The particular patterns of social relationships that characterize a society or social group are its **social structure**. Patterns of social structure are based on cultural rules. Societies or social groups may be organized on the basis of family, kinship, residential patterns, common interest, friendship, or class. These groupings have continuity through time. Social structure may be distinguished from **social organization**. While structure emphasizes continuity and stability, organization refers to the way in which individuals perceive the structure and context of any situation and make decisions and choices from among alternative courses of behavior. Organization emphasizes flux and change and refers to variations in individual behavior. This emphasis on individual choices and decisions is also defined as **practice**. Agency, discussed previously, refers to the point of view of the individual making the choices. The range of choices people can choose from is always shaped by the social structure. The action they take as "agents" may serve to reconfigure the social structure.

In societies or social groups, individuals usually occupy more than one position or **social status** at the same time. An individual may be a mother, a daughter, an employee, and a student all at the same time. The behavior associated with a particular social status in a society is known as a **social role**. Social roles involve behavioral norms understood to be applied toward other people. Inequality characterizes many social roles, so that a father has power over children, a manager has power over workers, and a professor has power over students in her class. Social structure contains a network of social roles, that is, the learned behaviors associated with a particular position or status, and a distribution of power through that network.

ANALYZING AND WRITING ABOUT CULTURE: A BRIEF HISTORY OF ANTHROPOLOGICAL APPROACHES

To more clearly understand the work that anthropologists are doing today, as well as the results of their past research, we briefly survey the significant theoretical and methodological approaches that have informed, shaped, and focused this research. When anthropology was developing during the nineteenth century, it was envisioned as a science, patterned after the natural sciences. This image was dominant until the early part of the twentieth century. In the decades that followed, anthropology oscillated between humanistic and scientific approaches. One must also keep in mind that the framework within which Western anthropologists worked during the nineteenth and much of the twentieth century was developed within European colonial empires. European and American anthropologists, often in the service of their governments, studied non-European cultures and institutions to facilitate colonial rule.

Cultural Evolutionary Theory

The nineteenth century was a period of colonial expansion and the development of great empires by European powers. Darwinian evolutionary theory dominated both biological and cultural analysis. Social Darwinism, which proclaimed the survival of the fittest, was used to justify the domination of native peoples, as well as the exploitation of underclasses in industrial societies. During this period, the discipline of anthropology, which focused on the study of indigenous peoples of the colonies that had been established, came into being.

Generally, anthropologists of that time remained in their armchairs and libraries, studying the published accounts of missionaries and explorers. Captain Cook and travelers such as Prince Maximilian, who explored the area of the Louisiana Purchase, described the native peoples they encountered. Many of these descriptions were ethnocentric and biased. This body of literature on the multiple forms of cultural diversity encountered around the world inspired scholars to create a single, unified theory to account for this diversity in human organization. Lewis Henry Morgan (1877) and Sir Edward Tylor (1871), major nineteenth-century theorists, conceptualized **cultural evolution** in terms of stages through which all societies had progressed, with simple societies developing into increasingly more complex forms, culminating

cultural evolution

A theory that refers to the patterns of cultures presumed to continually be developing into more complex forms over time.

in their own Victorian society. In their view, some societies, namely those being encountered by missionaries and others, represented contemporary examples of earlier stages or survivals of earlier stages of social, political, and economic development.

At the beginning of the twentieth century, anthropologists recognized the weaknesses of the nineteenth-century unilineal cultural evolutionary approach, since the information on which the theories were based was found to be speculative at best as well as ethnocentric and biased. The characteristics of Western societies, such as monogamy, state structure, and monotheism, were arbitrarily selected to represent the highest forms of societal development. As more ethnographic data were collected, based on fieldwork by trained anthropologists, it was clear that not *all* societies had passed through the same evolutionary stages. Fieldwork revealed that monogamy and monotheism were found in societies other than the "most evolved." Nineteenth-century evolutionary theory based on universal stages is largely discarded by academics. Most cultural anthropologists feel that "meta," or all-encompassing, theory obscures the unique political, social, and economic aspects of communities on which they now focus.

Franz Boas and Cultural Relativism

Franz Boas studied the natural sciences in German universities before immigrating to the United States in 1886. His fieldwork in the Baffin Islands in the late nineteenth century, and somewhat later with a variety of Northwest Coast societies, influenced his thinking about cultural differences. After learning local languages, he came to respect the significant differences among cultures in their language structure, material production, and mythological systems. He came to understand that all cultures and languages were equally distinctive and complex in different ways. This emphasis on uniqueness came to be referred to as cultural relativism or **cultural particularism**. He stressed that anthropologists should first concentrate on learning about and documenting the history of the development of societies before drawing comparative conclusions. This became known as **historical particularism**. He urged his graduate students to master the four fields of anthropology and apply them into their fieldwork and analysis. Boas also studied migration policy and racial categories in the United States, leading him to challenge these categories as biologically fixed and inherited, and instead to see them as fluid and politically determined. His emphasis on cultural relativism came to be associated with the humanistic approach that characterized the work of subsequent generations of anthropological scholars.

cultural particularism

Emphasizes uniqueness of individual cultures.

historical particularism

Theoretical approach emphasizing each culture's uniqueness.

Functionalism

The British reaction against nineteenth-century unilineal cultural evolutionary theory took a somewhat different form. British anthropologists at the beginning of the twentieth century supplanted evolutionary theory with **functionalism**, a model, derived from biology, of society as a living organism. The basic organizing principles they used were the linked concepts of structure and function. **Structure** is a description of form and the relationship of parts to one another, whereas **function** refers to how the structure works. They rejected historical speculation and "meta" theorizing about unverifiable global and historical transformations. They used **fieldwork**, that is, the empirical field observations by academically trained anthropologists who spend a year or more working with a group of people, learning their language and observing and participating in their culture. This fieldwork was often conducted in small-scale communities of indigenous people living as subjects within the British colonial empire.

Bronislaw Malinowski, a major proponent of functionalism, was one of the originators of modern anthropological fieldwork. He spent an extended period of time doing fieldwork in the Trobriand Islands off Papua New Guinea. He identified the institutions that made up the "skeleton" of societies (i.e., their structure) and then described in detail how those institutions functioned. Malinowski saw cultural institutions functioning in response to basic human biological needs, as well as to what he called "culturally derived needs." He recognized the matrilineality of the Trobriand Islands, and its influence on all aspects of economic, political, and social life. He described in precise detail their horticultural production and ocean-going trade systems. He described planting and cultivating yams, the use of spells and ritual involved in yam cultivation, and how these yams were used in the exchange systems of fulfilling obligations to kin and political leaders.

With the breakdown of colonial empires after World War II, the functionalist theoretical framework, which emphasized unchanging societies existing in a state of equilibrium, came under attack. Anthropologists began to follow communities over time; they recorded the life stories of people as they moved into cities and went to work in mines, documenting the economic and political changes that were occurring in their lives. Others turned to archival research to document the histories of societies with which they were doing ethnographic research. A more processual model, which documents how social structures and social organization change over time, eventually came to replace anthropological perspectives that stressed "the steady state" of unchanging equilibrium.

Structuralism

Structuralism as a theoretical approach is closely associated with the work of the French anthropologist Claude Lévi-Strauss in the 1950s and 1960s. He used linguistic theory and methods to analyze culture. He noted that some sounds in a language by themselves have no meaning but are part of a larger structure that conveys meaning. In the same way, the elements of a culture must be seen in their relationship to one another as they form a structure

functionalism

The theoretical position that sees cultures as analogous to living organisms operating to maintain a steady state.

structure

A description of parts or elements of a culture in relationship to one another.

function

The way a particular unit or structure operates and what it does.

fieldwork

The hallmark research methodology of cultural anthropology. When doing fieldwork an anthropologist, to the best of their ability, participates in community activities, explores the material and social environments, and interviews local consultants about their perceptions of an aspect of their lives.

structuralism

Theoretical approach emphasizing the relationship between cultural elements.

that conveys cultural meanings. Structural anthropologists attempted to determine the underlying structure of a culture, which corresponds to the grammar of a language in the linguist's analysis, and may not be in the consciousness of the speaker. Structuralists did research on connections between kinship structure, art, mythology, ritual and ceremony, and residential patterns. Structural anthropologists were comparative in that they attempted to determine whether there were similarities in underlying structures in different cultures. Thus, this approach may group together societies that seem to be very different at first glance. Lévi-Straussian structuralism was later challenged by postmodernists and poststructuralists because its models were highly abstract and unverifiable, and ignored the roles of history and politics in manipulating these structures.

Symbolic Anthropology

symbolic anthropology

Theoretical approach emphasizing the interpretation of cultural symbols.

Symbolic anthropology, which had its efflorescence in the mid- to late twentieth century, is concerned with the interpretation of culture through its symbols, and the search for meaning embedded in those symbols. Culture is seen as a system of symbols, and the task of the anthropologist is to decipher its meanings. In the 1970s, anthropologists including David Schneider and Clifford Geertz began to focus on the tangle of interrelated meanings that cultures encode. They understood the work of an anthropologist to be a "translator" of the layers of meaning of a particular cultural phenomenon into understandable concepts and language. Clifford Geertz, in his attempt to understand the meaning of the Balinese cockfight, called this type of translation a **thick description** by which culture is viewed as a text to be read and interpreted. This emphasis on deciphering meaning has been associated in anthropology with cultural particularism and cultural relativism, both of which downplay comparative perspectives.

thick description

A methodology whereby culture is viewed as a text to be read, analyzed, and interpreted, associated with the scholar Clifford Geertz.

Focus on History in Anthropology

Anthropologists have always been concerned with the temporal or historical dimension of culture. The armchair anthropologists of the nineteenth century constructed a schema that attempted to describe the evolution of all human cultures. The students of Boas, during the early twentieth century, attempted to reconstruct the history of particular cultures by looking at the spread of culture traits. They were dealing with cultures without written histories that they could consult, and further, they were interested in what was labeled "traditional culture" as opposed to "modern culture." These efforts at reconstructing history without written records were rejected by British functionalist Radcliffe-Brown as "conjectural history." But from the time of Western contact, these cultures were embedded within a historical framework of conquest and colonialism, which many anthropologists in the first half of the twentieth century did not consider relevant. Clearly, from contemporary perspectives, what was being documented in written history, in archival and other historical sources, was written from the conquerors' point of view. As anthropologists began to pay more attention to the effects of colonialism on the people they were studying, they recognized that there were many forms of indigenous recording of events that documented the consequences of European conquest, including oral narratives and artistic production. Recognizing these as local history expanded anthropologists' understanding of the perceptions of the interactions between the colonizers and those they had colonized, and how each had reconstructed their world as a consequence of the other. **Ethnohistory** is the umbrella term for the study of archaeological, archival, and oral history materials in order to trace the histories of cultures with limited written records.

ethnohistory

Efforts at reconstructing the histories of societies with limited indigenous records that draw on archaeology, oral histories, or archives.

It is now clear that recognizing how mechanisms of control, domination, and differences in power is central to anthropology as an intellectual enterprise. The regional, nation-state, and emerging global contexts with their political and economic actors dominate contemporary anthropological analysis. One must consider how the local and global interpenetrate each other over time. It is now accepted that the methodologies of both history and anthropology are relevant to any investigation. Many anthropologists recognize the necessity to include historical processes in their cultural analysis. Abe Rosman, Paula Rubel, and Maxine Weisgrau, coauthors of this textbook, recognized the necessity of documenting the changing historical context of the society or social group they were studying. These were to be found in state archives, which in the case of Rubel's study of the Kalmyk Mongols meant going back to material three centuries old to ferret out information. Weisgrau's work in Rajasthan India (1997; Henderson and Weisgrau 2007) traces continuities between British colonial documents and contemporary ideas about development, tourism, and local constructions of identity. Anthropologists pay close attention to cultural meanings and how individuals and groups interpret changes over time. By paying close attention to real people doing real things, they take seriously the content of how different groups of people express their perceptions about the world around them.

Feminist Anthropology: Gender Identities in Theory and Practice

Feminist anthropology was inspired in part by the global women's movements of the 1960s that sought to understand how systems of patriarchy operate to create and perpetuate ideas about women in society. Equally important is uncovering the systems of ideas reinforced through multiple institutions that construct identities of men and women, and limit opportunities. Drawing on many different theoretical perspectives, feminist anthropologists sought both explanations for the origins of sexism as well as strategies to confront issues of power and inequality. Feminist anthropologists, many of whom were trailblazers in bringing women's voices to field settings around the world, also broke gender barriers in academic departments in colleges and universities. These scholars called attention to inherent biases in dividing people into binary opposites—like male and female—and attributing unquestioned power to one group and inherent characteristics to the other. These binaries obscure the understanding of how individuals actually understand their own behaviors and navigate their own spaces of power and influence. Feminist anthropologists therefore brought fresh perspectives to the practices of anthropology and fieldwork by laying bare gender bias inherent in the male-dominated discipline. Annette Weiner, in her "re-visit" to the Trobriand Islands, comes to understand the complicated productive roles of women, particularly in important political and economic rituals, that were generally ignored by Malinowski in his classic studies. While admiring of Malinowski's superb ethnographic documentation of Trobriand life, Weiner (1988) understands how her own identity as a woman ethnographer and her ability to recognize women's achievements, enhances the overall understanding of women's activities and contributions to the operation of political and economic institutions.

Postmodernism in Anthropology

postmodernism

Refers to a contemporary point of view that is opposed to making universalizing generalizations in anthropological thinking, and encourages interdisciplinary analysis.

ethnography

Written description of an aspect of a community or group of people, usually based on fieldwork, participant observation, and consultant interviews.

Beginning in the 1980s and 1990s, anthropology, along with other social sciences and humanities, underwent a number of theoretical and methodological reassessments, which are collectively referred to as **postmodernism**. Postmodernism in anthropology found fault with generalization and claims of a scientific approach. This perspective also calls attention to ethnographers bringing along their own cultural categories with them into the field. Anthropologists are now aware of how their own cultural categories frame their observations and research. The idea that an anthropologist could encompass in written accounts or **ethnography** the totality of another culture was abandoned and replaced with James Clifford's approach that ethnography always documents "partial truths" or particular perspectives (Clifford 1986).

Some scholars have seen ethnography, the written and published product of the dialogue between informant and fieldworker, as not sufficiently representative of the variety of points of view or ideas held by individuals in the culture. They argue that different segments of a society have contesting views regarding cultural meanings and that opposing views should be represented in ethnography in informants' own words. To pay more attention to these views, anthropologists share their information with the community. Many now prefer that the informants' voices take center stage in telling their story, revitalizing the life history approach, which has traditionally been part of anthropological methodology. This is in response to the feeling that in the past, the voices of ethnographic subjects have been marginalized or displaced by the sole authoritative voice of the ethnographer, who appropriated their stories.

The role of the local consultant or informant is also related to the matter of cultural representation. Such individuals may be seen as having better understanding of the culture than an "outsider" and greater ability to empathize with the people and interpret their expression than an anthropologist who is a member of another culture. However, there are those who argue that greater empathy comes at the expense of the perspective and understanding that an outsider can bring. Often the local anthropologist is studying communities that may be in their country, but not one in which they grew up. Urban-based anthropologists may be "outsiders" to the rural agriculturalists they are researching.

This perspective encourages all anthropologists to rethink the social and political dynamics of fieldwork. It introduces **reflexivity** into researching and writing. This includes self-reflection in ethnography and documentation of how ethnographers think and feel in the fieldwork situation, as well as trying to understand how they are perceived by community members. This reflexive perspective requires the understanding that both informants and anthropologists are studying and analyzing one another. Reflexivity in fieldwork is discussed further in chapter 2.

reflexivity

Attention to one's own cognitive framework, assumptions, biases, and privileges as one researches another culture.

BOX 1.1 | "March of Progress": What's Wrong with This Picture?

Evolution's "March of Progress" as public art in Porto, Portugal.

This image, or a variation of it, is a familiar representation of the recap of human evolution often defined as the "March of Progress." It represents an outdated visualization of human evolution with several embedded assumptions that are now rejected by scholars of human evolution.

The Myth of Complexity is embedded in this visual representation, suggesting that evolution is an inevitable process of increasing complexity. The emergence of the taller, clothed, tool-bearing "man" presumably exploiting his environment with more complex technologies, is not an inevitable outcome of primate evolution. Complexity does not guarantee evolutionary success; many simpler formers of adaptation were successful for hundreds of thousands of years.

The Myth of Replacement is also apparent in this visualization. It suggests that the emergence of a new species with recognizable physical traits replaces those that have come before it. There is ample evidence for the coexistence of multiple species throughout evolutionary history. Moreover, these different groups invariably made contact and interbred with each other; we now know for example that Neandertal DNA is present a large number of modern human population groups, evidence of coexisting and intergroup mating.

This image also reinforces some myths about the dominance of males as the primary movers of evolution. Females are rarely, if ever, conceived of being part of the sequence of evolution; the activities, skills, and tools associated with the triumphant "final" image bears artifacts that were probably created by and used by women as well as men.

The realities of human evolution belie a simple, linear, "modern male humans on top" image. The realities are much more difficult to represent; these visual images however continue to remind us how assumptions about our past are often based on ideas and approaches rejected by subsequent generations of scholars.

FIELDWORK AND ETHNOGRAPHY IN THE TWENTY-FIRST CENTURY

Anthropologists today do their research with a variety of perspectives. Since contemporary approaches are so varied that no single set of assumptions is shared, nor does a single theoretical approach tend to dominate in a single ethnography. Most present-day anthropological approaches used in research do not constitute single theories in the formal sense. Postmodernist scholars encouraged anthropologists to rethink the basic concepts, premises, and power dynamics of the discipline. Many anthropologists are now interested in the political and economic roles of "subaltern," or underclass, cultures. A focus on the life of everyday people shows that they are not passive instruments of elite domination, but rather actors making decisions and choices within their understandings of the structures of constraints.

Globalization as an Anthropological Issue

globalization

The worldwide connection between societies based upon the existence of global market connections and the spread of cultural items everywhere; associated with intensive movement of people, goods, capital, technologies, and ideas.

Anthropological research clearly reveals how potent a force **globalization** has become in all places around the world and how intimately entwined the production systems and political realities of all people have become. Anthropologists continually focus on globalization and its effects on the lived experiences of participants ethnographically. For example, in Papua New Guinea, anthropologist Paige West documented the local effects of growing coffee as a cash crop and selling it to traders who come along the Highlands highway. This represents an incorporation of coffee into a worldwide network from villagers to, ultimately, your morning cup of coffee (West 2012). What is the power relationship between the traders and growers, what are the ideas associated with this relationship, and how do these affect other parts of the way of life of these people and their relationship with the several levels of politics and ultimately the Papua New Guinea state? Are those on the local scene relatively powerless, or do they actively engage in shaping these relationships? Some who use the globalization framework are interested in the way ideas and perceptions are formed and manipulated by the elites of capitalist systems to maintain class divisions through access to employment, disguising what is in reality class exploitation.

neoliberalism

The contemporary revival of classic economic liberalism that stresses the role of private enterprise in all institutions of the state and deregulation of markets and trade.

Scholars who study globalization are particularly interested in the late-twentieth-century global reorganization of capitalism, which includes the spread of the economic and political agendas of **neoliberalism** around the world. An additional focus for understanding globalization is the idea of "circulation" and exchange, though it is recognized that the circulation of products and ideas takes place in asymmetrical spaces marked by power differentials between participants (Dissanayake 2006: 29).

The Anthropocene

Anthropocene is a term originally introduced from geology, chemistry, and biology; it refers generally to the period in which human behaviors have had significant impact on the earth's ecology, climate, and global ecosystems. There is considerable difference in the way that the term has been defined, as well as when the period began. In earlier periods of theorizing about nature and culture, nature was seen as fixed, with human cultures around the world either taming it or adapting to it. With this new concept, the focus shifts to a view that human intervention in the use and exploitation of limited resources brings about changes in the environment as well as in the geology of the world. These include changes in animal biodiversity through extinction, changes in climate, depletion of water, changes in air quality, and modifications in the stratigraphy of the earth's surface.

There is debate about when the Anthropocene began and the previous geological period, the Holocene, ended. Some geologists see the two periods as contemporaneous. Although *Homo erectus*, an early hominin, utilized fire, it was not until humans used controlled fire to burn grasslands and forests in the hunt for animals that larger-scale changes in the environment began. Others cite the beginning of agriculture, approximately ten thousand years ago, when landscapes, forests, and grasslands in different parts of the world began to be significantly altered, as the beginning of the Anthropocene. Agriculturalists in China and the Amazon region built earthworks, dams, and canals, changing the nature of river systems. From the 1500s on, when European colonists moved to new environments in North and South America, Asia, Australia, and New Zealand, they brought with them the flora and fauna of their homeland. This often had a profound effect on the ecology of these colonial regions. Still others see the beginning of the Anthropocene at the onset of the Industrial Revolution, at about 1750. This brought about changes in the chemistry of the atmosphere and of the water in rivers and in oceans, the courses of rivers, and global warming. Anthropologists find the concept of the Anthropocene useful because it highlights the ways in which humans and their cultures have the effect of extracting and transforming all of the aspects of the physical, material environment around them.

anthropocene

A term originally introduced from geology to refer to the period in which human cultural behavior had significant impact on the ecology and geology of the earth.

The Material World and Culture: Environmental Anthropologies

Since its inception, the discipline of anthropology has engaged in efforts at understanding the relationship between cultures and their physical, material environments. Ethnographers have documented and theorized the many different strategies groups of people have engaged in to extract, transform, and distribute productive resources from the environment around them. Some have attempted to create theories that link the physical environment

to the emergence of social, political, and religious institutions. **Environmental anthropology** now has many sub-disciplines and perspectives, as anthropologists work with ecological scientists and climate change specialists to understand the critical challenges of environmental crises, pollution, habitat destruction, and species extinctions, and the devastating impacts of climate change. These perspectives all attempt to understand the complex relationships groups of human beings have with the environments they inhabit.

Aerial view of deforested area of the Amazon rainforest caused by illegal mining activities in Brazil. Deforestation and illegal gold mining destroy the forest and contaminate the rivers with mercury, resulting in severe disruption of and widespread violence against Yanomamo and Kayapo communities.

environmental anthropology

An anthropological specialty that documents the relationships between human communities and their environments.

political ecology

The study of the relationships between political, social, and economic resources and environmental changes.

Political Ecology: Ecosystems and Inequalities

Anthropological exploration of environmental challenges and their impacts on the lived experiences of people and communities around the world informs multiple perspectives and methodologies. As do other ecologically based modes of inquiry, **political ecology** brings multiple disciplines together to explore its primary interest: the unequal impacts of interventions in the physical environment, such as development projects, large dams and irrigation schemes, and industrialization and resulting pollution, on lifeways of communities around the world. Political ecology perspectives understand these interventions as being driven by capitalistic markets within states and see them as both disruptive and destructive to local and global ecosystems. Political ecology draws on analysis of inequality of access between different classes and identity groups in society to important and productive resources. It also references previous generations of cultural ecology scholars whose ethnographies document resource utilization patterns and drivers. Contemporary political ecology perspectives focus particularly on the inequalities embedded in capitalistic market-driven development, as well as the unequal burden of resulting environmental degradation that falls on marginalized and disenfranchised populations around the world. These scholars also demonstrate how material resources are always the subject of competition and contestation; the outcomes of these conflicts invariably reflect existing power dynamics within states and regions.

Political ecology is therefore best seen as an umbrella term for many different themes and approaches to understanding the interaction between physical environments and quality of life of individuals and groups. It is also concerned with interventions and social justice movements that address these inequalities. Scholars of social justice movements have expanded the idea of cultural ecology to explore how racial, gender, socioeconomic, and ethnic divisions in society are critically important variables in understanding how, for example, weather-related disasters, climate change, deforestation, and pandemics are experienced differently by individuals and groups within one state or community. The Covid-19 pandemic brought these issues of unequal burdens borne by the poor and marginal populations into stark focus, and this is documented by physicians, public health officials, medical and cultural anthropologists, and epidemiologists around the world (Higgins et al. 2020).

The Fieldwork Journey

The journey to another place, which we defined at the beginning of this chapter as the hallmark of cultural anthropology, is recapitulated by student anthropologists as they embark on fieldwork. This journey can involve going from one place to another, or shifting one's perspective on viewing one's own community. Lévi-Strauss, in his personal memoir, *Tristes Tropiques*, saw his own fieldwork in terms of just such a journey. His journey took him from the Old World to the New World, from the cold North to the tropical South, to communities that contrasted in every respect with his own. As in all fieldwork situations, he was first struck by great cultural differences. However, in time, Lévi-Strauss saw behind the painted faces of the Nambikwara in Brazil a humanity he shared with them. He wrote, "I had been looking for a society reduced to its simplest expression. The society of the Nambikwara had been reduced to the point at which I found nothing but human beings" (Lévi-Strauss 1961: 310). Contemporary anthropologists might amend this observation to include in their journeys not only finding human beings but also how globalization, power, and inequality shape their lives.

SUMMARY

- Humans possess culture, which makes them significantly different from other members of the animal kingdom. Humans are also primates and share almost 99 percent of their genes with other members of the biological order.

- Some anthropologists argue that the larger biological context must be considered in understanding human behavior in an evolutionary context. Others consider culture as learned-specific settings independent of the evolutionary history of the human species.

- The study of anthropology can be thought of as a journey into a different place or community where people's ideas, behaviors, and beliefs may be different from one's own.

- The belief that one's own culture represents the best way to do things is known as *ethnocentrism*. Ethnocentrism emphasizes pride in a group's cultural accomplishments, as well as a denigration of others' beliefs, customs, and practices. It is at the root of ethnic conflict and ethnonationalism.

- Cultural relativism is the idea that each culture is unique and distinctive but that no one culture is superior to any other culture.

- Some anthropologists utilize the comparative approach to compare cultures. This method identifies fundamental similarities of cultural patterning as well as differences.

- The central concept of anthropology is culture. Culture consists of the things people make, their behavior, their beliefs and ideas. Each culture has an underlying logic of its own; the behavior of people makes sense once we understand the basic premises by which they live.

- The subdisciplines of anthropology include archeology, biological or physical anthropology, cultural anthropology, and linguistic anthropology. Some anthropologists identify applied anthropology as the fifth subfield.

- Culture is learned and acquired by infants through a process referred to by anthropologists as enculturation. Individuals internalize cultural practices but may challenge, change, and transform those practices as a result of experience.

- Culture is not a single, monolithic entity. In most societies subcultures based on region, class, ethnicity, religion, and gender have differing views of their culture.

- Culture includes the use of meanings and symbolic patterning and is believed by many anthropologists to be distinctive of humans alone.

- The evolution of culture in humans was dependent on the prior development of bipedal erect locomotion, or upright walking, increased brain size, and neurological reorganization.

- The capacity for language, the creation and manipulation of verbal symbols, could only appear after anatomical features necessary for bipedalism were in place.

- Language and art both illustrate the ability of humans to create and manipulate symbols.

- Cooking by using fire to make foods in the environment was a significant development in the evolution of the human capacity for culture.

- The biological nature of the human species requires that all cultures solve the basic problems of human existence and continuity. Although cultural differences do exist, all cultures share certain fundamental similarities.

- Despite the presence of cultural rules, not everyone interprets them in the same way. Groups exhibit variability in their culture rules. Individuals may violate cultural rules, and these rules can change over time. Individuals may also affiliate with multiple groups, each with its own set of rules and norms. These are examples of intracultural variation.

- Society refers to the social relationships and differences in patterns of behavior based on sex and age within all groups, both human and animal.

- Social structure, which is composed of particular patterns of social relationships, includes social groupings that may be organized on the basis of family, kinship, residential propinquity, common interest, or class.

- Individuals occupy different positions, or social statuses; for example, an individual may be a mother, an agricultural worker and a shaman simultaneously. The behavior toward other people associated with a particular social status is the social role.

- Anthropology as an academic discipline is more than 130 years old. Its history is marked by waxing and waning of significant theoretical and methodological approaches.

- Cultural evolution, proposed in the nineteenth century, conceptualized universal stages of development through which all societies progressed, with simple societies developing into increasingly more complex forms, culminating in theorists' own Victorian society.

- By the beginning of the twentieth century, scholars noted the weaknesses of the nineteenth-century evolutionary approach to culture, including its lack of field data to support its theorizing as well as its Eurocentric biases.

- Cultural relativism, as first articulated by American anthropologist Franz Boas, rejected previous efforts to rank or range societies from simple to complex and considered all cultures and languages equally distinctive and complex.

- British anthropology at the beginning of the twentieth century also rejected evolutionary theory and adopted functionalism as a model, which derives from the biological analogy of society as a living organism.

- Structuralism sees the elements of a culture in relationship to one another as a structure that conveys cultural meanings. The structural anthropologist attempts to determine the underlying structure of a culture, which corresponds to the grammar of a language in the linguist's analysis.

- Symbolic anthropology views culture as a system of symbols, with the task of the anthropologist to decipher the meanings of the system.

- Ethnohistory uses archaeological, archival, and oral history materials to trace the histories of cultures with limited written records.

- Postmodernism in anthropology can be understood in part as a multifaceted reassessment of the discipline, its methodologies, and the writing of ethnography.

- Contemporary anthropologists focus on globalization as a cultural force in all settings, and they document local understandings of global technologies, businesses, and products

- Political ecology theories and methodologies illuminate how the impacts of climate change, pandemics, drought, deforestation, and other environmental crises are related to forms of inequality within affected societies. It also explores the global and regional impacts of these crises on the lived experiences of people everywhere.

- Contemporary analytical approaches are less unified than the theoretical approaches described above. They draw on multiple approaches and do not share a single set of assumptions as did earlier theoretical points of view.

KEY TERMS

agency, 5
anthropocene, 25
applied anthropology, 7
archaeology, 6
bipedal erect locomotion, 11
comparative approach, 5
cultural anthropology, 6
cultural evolution, 17
cultural particularism, 18
cultural relativism, 4
cultural rules, 2
cultural universals, 4
culture, 5
digital divide, 7
enculturation, 10
environmental anthropology, 26
ethnocentrism, 4
ethnohistory, 21
ethnography, 22
ethnonationalism, 4
fieldwork, 19
function, 19
functionalism, 19

globalization, 24
hegemony, 5
historical particularism, 18
hominin, 11
linguistics, 6
natural selection, 10
nature vs. nurture, 2
neoliberalism, 24
physical anthropology, 6
political ecology, 26
postmodernism, 22
practice, 16
reflexivity, 23
social organization, 16
social role, 16
social status, 16
social structure, 16
society, 16
structuralism, 19
structure, 19
symbolic anthropology, 20
thick description, 20
universal human rights, 4

SUGGESTED READINGS

Clifford, James, and George E. Marcus. *Writing Culture: The Poetics and Politics of Ethnography*. Berkeley: University of California Press, 1986.

A highly influential collection of essays reflecting on fieldwork and writing ethnography.

DeSilva, Jeremy. *First Steps: How Walking Upright Made Us Human*. Great Britain: William Collins, 2021.

A student-friendly but comprehensive discussion of paleoanthropology and the evidence for the emergence of upright walking, which eventually paved the way for the emergence of many of the hallmark traits of modern humans.

Erickson, Paul A., and Liam D. Murphy. *A History of Anthropological Theory*. 6th ed. Toronto: University of Toronto Press, 2021.

A comprehensive introduction to anthropological theory from antiquity to the present, including discussions of postcolonialism and non-Western anthropology.

SUGGESTED WEBSITES

https://humanorigins.si.edu

Smithsonian Institute/Museum of Natural History website featuring details about the multiple phases and species playing a role in human evolution, including "What's Hot in Human Origins?," news and updates on this rapidly changing field.

https://foodanthro.com/

Website of the Society for the Anthropology of Food and Nutrition. Contains articles, blogs, and new publications about the cultural and political analysis of eating and cooking practices around the world.

https://www.discoveranthropology.org.uk/

A website operated by Great Britain's Royal Anthropological Institute's Education Outreach Program. Provides easily accessible information, webinars, activities, and resources for those interested in learning more about British anthropology, history, and fieldwork.

Chapter 2
Anthropological Methods

LEARNING OBJECTIVES

- Understand the methodologies and political dynamics of anthropological fieldwork.
- Recognize dilemmas and ethical issues fieldworkers face engaging in participant-observation and ethnographic writing.
- Appreciate the multiple aspects of reflexivity, reciprocity, and translation in fieldwork and ethnographic writing.

- Discuss how American weddings are adapted by couples to suit their goals for a public ritual.
- Suggest similarities and differences between contemporary American and early twentieth-century ethnographic representations of Canadian First Nation wedding rituals.

The methodology used by mid-nineteenth-century anthropologists involved examining the information collected by others: Euro-American travelers, explorers, missionaries, and colonial officials who visited or lived for a time in other parts of the world. These "armchair" anthropologists focused on what they presumed to be the evolution of all cultures throughout history as their theoretical framework. After the turn of the century, fieldwork by professionally trained anthropologists who lived among the people, observing them firsthand, learning their language, and participating in their ceremonies and daily lives, became the defining methodology for cultural anthropology.

FIELDWORK

Franz Boas was the first person to carry out what we would call "anthropological fieldwork." In 1883–1884, he worked among the Inuits of Baffin Island in the Canadian territory of Nunavut. He first familiarized himself with the literature on the area, including accounts of voyages of discovery and missionary descriptions of Inuit ways of life. He learned the Inuit language from missionary wordbooks and grammars. His research problem was to examine the ways in which the Baffin Islanders migrated over the terrain and subsisted in the region. He traveled by dogsled from village to village and lived in people's igloos. Shortly after this, Bronislaw Malinowski was the first British anthropologist to conduct extended fieldwork, in the Trobriand Islands of Papua New Guinea.

How does one gain perspective on another society? The answer for contemporary anthropologists, as it was for Boas and Malinowski, is to step outside the web of their own cultural world and closely examine another, often vastly different, way of life. For contemporary anthropologists, this can mean traveling to another country or entering a different community in one's own culture. But before entering that "other cultural world," anthropologists today must develop a set of research questions to be posed and consider the methods to be used to answer them. This is referred to by some as a **research design**. However, these questions are frequently transformed as the field research proceeds. The contemporary anthropologist must also apply for funds to do the research, sometimes from private foundations, academic institutions, or from government agencies. Before beginning field research, present-day anthropologists become acquainted with the research area by doing a literature review, reading whatever has been published on the geographic area as well as on the proposed research questions. They consult archives, census data, colonial-era records, and other published information before the fieldwork begins, as well as during and after field research to gain historical perspectives.

The heart of fieldwork is **participant observation**—living among other people, learning their language or lingo, and coming to understand what is important to them. It includes living in their housing and eating their food, on their mealtime schedules. This is how one learns about the everyday life of the people. Fieldworkers celebrate birth rites, and they mourn at funerals.

research design

Identifying key research questions and methodologies for fieldwork projects.

participant observation

The anthropological method of collecting data by living with other people, learning their language, and understanding their culture.

If possible, the local language is mastered before going to the new community. Very often, arrangements for fieldwork involve negotiations with various authorities and community members to get informed consent on the proposed research. When first immersed in a different culture, fieldworkers experience **culture shock** upon recognizing that their own framework is not "natural," because other people do things differently. At first, as anthropologists learn about this new culture, they are in the position of a child in that culture who slowly learns appropriate behaviors and social norms.

Participant observation involves an inherent contradiction. A participant operates inside a culture, while an observer is like a stranger, looking in from the outside. On the other hand, observers are expected to remain detached and to record what they observe and hear. As Hume and Mulcock note, "[T]he practice of ethnography also assumes the importance of maintaining enough intellectual distance to ensure that researchers are able to undertake a critical analysis of the events in which they are participating" (2004: xi). Learning about another culture is very different from objectively analyzing and interpreting it. Since the anthropologist is interacting and participating with other people, it is impossible to be completely objective or detached; fieldworkers form intimate friendships with community members that often last lifetimes.

Participant observation is difficult to carry out because it involves this basic paradox. It remains an ideal that is never completely realized. Participation in another culture means attempting to view things from the "insider's" point of view. This means experiencing the concepts and ideas that order that world. When anthropologists do fieldwork, they bring with them their own cultural categories, ways of seeing things, and personal values. They try to avoid allowing these to color their perceptions. Paying attention to one's own cognitive framework as one operates in another culture is called "reflexivity." "Contemporary ethnography . . . attempts to be reflexive, that is to say it is conducted in full awareness of the myriad limitations associated with humans studying other human lives" (O'Reilly 2005: 14). This means being aware of the fieldwork context, the nature of the power relationship between "researcher and researched," the effects of colonialism and postcolonial sociopolitical arrangements, the question of whose voice or voices are to be represented in the research, and finally, how the ethnography is produced. Reflexivity involves understanding that the final written ethnographic text contains the author's style and is the result of writing, editing, and translating experience and discussions into a written narrative

In addition to observation, anthropologists gain information by interviewing individuals, who are referred to variously as **informants**, interlocutors, collaborators or local cultural **consultants**. These interviews are usually open-ended, meaning that when the informant is stimulated by the anthropologist's questions to go beyond them, following different "information paths," the anthropologist follows along. These contrast with interviews based solely on pre-prepared questionnaires or surveys, which can be distributed to many people and returned to be coded and analyzed. To the anthropologist

culture shock

Effect upon the observer of encountering a cultural practice different from one's own.

informants or consultants

Individuals in a community who provide information, insights, and guidance to an anthropologist.

today, community members are fieldworker-colleagues. They increasingly learn what the fieldworker is interested in exploring and also gain a certain amount of knowledge about anthropology. Anthropologists routinely share observations, information, and findings with community members, who often begin to understand their own culture from an anthropological perspective. In their interactions, anthropologists and the community members they interview are, in a sense, operating in an area of communication between their two cultures.

The personal relationship between anthropologist and informants is a complex one. A **key informant** for Abe Rosman while he was doing fieldwork among the Kanuri was the District Head, a titled aristocrat much older than the fledgling anthropologist, whom he adopted as fictive kin. This relationship was crucial for the fieldwork since many people trusted the anthropologist and were willing to talk to him as a consequence of this patron. However, given this connection, other sources of information were closed to the anthropologist because those who had such information were in opposition to or belonged to another faction of the community.

Fieldwork involves reciprocity on the part of anthropologists; however, the nature of what the anthropologist returns to informants is highly varied. In rural as well as urban areas, the anthropologist with a vehicle often reciprocates by becoming chauffeur for the entire community, as Paula Rubel did for the Kalmyk Mongols with whom she worked in New Jersey. Frequently, anthropologists become partisans, taking on the causes of the community as advocates in the media or becoming expert witnesses for them in the courts. When legal conflicts arose between Native American groups concerning land ownership, anthropologists who had done research with the Dine' advocated their side of the case, while those who had worked with the Hopi researched the case from their point of view.

Anthropological fieldwork involves a whole series of ethical considerations. Fieldwork **ethics** includes being open and honest about the research, obtaining informed consent from participants, disclosing what they are studying and producing, and honoring confidentiality. An anthropologist must be aware that participation in interviews and being included in published work may potentially create jeopardy or harm for local participants. Avoiding this harm is a crucial aspect of ethical concern. Some ethnographers protect the identities of local participants by using aliases or only first names for individuals and obscuring the exact location of the research.

Fieldwork involves the anthropologist in a moral dilemma. It could be said that anthropologists use community members for their own ends, since the anthropologists return home with the information gathered. The analysis and publication of this information in a dissertation, article, or book helps the career of the anthropologist, but in what way does it help the people whose way of life has been recorded? Often, research done by anthropologists in the past may be of use to communities today. For example, some communities have found that ethnographies are of value as written records of traditions and political conflicts. Such information often proves important for pursuing

key informants

Individuals with whom the anthropologist forms a personal, ongoing relationship and who serve as mentors and cultural consultants.

ethics

The rules and practices that protect the rights of participants in fieldwork and research.

claims regarding land rights and intellectual property such as the knowledge of local herbs and medicines. Many anthropologists around the world are working with local advocates to communicate information to a wide audience on the negative impacts on local communities of state-sponsored infrastructure projects like dams, roadways, and natural resource extraction. The impacts of climate change are best explored by working with members of local communities to document changes in resource availability and food supply. Anthropologists today invariably include in their research the impact of migration and globalization as part of the lived experiences of community members.

The anthropologist performs multiple kinds of **translation**. First, there is the translation from the local language to the anthropologist's written language. Problems usually arise because the terms in the local language are never exactly equivalent to the concepts in English. For example, when property passes from one generation to the next before the death of a member of the senior generation, as among the Kwakwaka'wakw of the West Coast of Canada, this is sometimes translated as "inheritance" in the ethnographic literature. However, the definition of inheritance in English presupposes the death of the member of the senior generation, so this is not an accurate translation of the Kwakwaka'wakw concept. Another challenge is to translate the cultural categories of the society being studied into the language of anthropology, that is, the conceptual framework being set forth in *The Tapestry of Culture*. The basic assumption of this kind of translation is that cultures have characteristics in common, above and beyond those aspects that are unique. Comparative research, using anthropological concepts, tests out assumptions about cross-cultural comparisons and verifies them (or disproves them) using ethnographic data.

Writing daily in a journal or field diary is critical to the ethnographic research process. The researcher writes down notes during discussions with informants containing general observations and, when given permission by the informant, records and then transcribes the content of interviews. "Writing up" involves pulling together everything known about a category (disputes, marriage, households, betel-nut chewing, cockfighting, inheritance, etc.). These are overlapping categories. For example, cockfighting in Bali involves religion as well as politics. This stage is still description. But anthropology is more than description; interpretation is equally important. Interpretation involves moving beyond the descriptions and meanings provided by community members. In the Kwakwaka'wakw marriage described below, some of the participants blackened their faces as they would for warfare; the anthropologist interprets this to mean that warfare symbolizes an aspect of marriage. The two sides were in an antagonistic relationship with one another, and in the future, they would compete for the children of the marriage to become members of their respective groups. This anthropological analysis attempts to illuminate the structure and meaning of cultural events, which may not be expressed by community members themselves.

In the past, anthropological fieldworkers investigated societies that were small, both in scale and population size, where it was believed that all the

translation

The multiple forms of explaining the meaning of words, ideas, symbols, and norms from one cultural setting to another.

community

An organized social unit.

spheres of human activity could be explored by a single investigator. Some anthropologists selected islands for study, whereas others selected a village or a neighborhood on which to concentrate and from which they generalized about the culture. Each of these is sometimes referred to as a **community**. The community may be perceived by its members as being bounded, in the sense that they concentrate their interactions within it. The analysis of interaction of the community with other communities, and with social and political institutions outside the immediate vicinity and even beyond the borders of the state, are of critical importance to contemporary observers.

ANTHROPOLOGY MOVES TO THE STUDY OF COMPLEX SOCIETIES

Anthropologists now recognize that no single community could be considered representative of, for example, India, France, or Japan. **Complex societies** are heterogeneous and culturally diverse with regional, class, occupational, religious, and ethnic differences. Such diverse groups have communities of their own that may become units of analysis for anthropologists, who must keep in mind that what is happening locally is always related to what is happening on a broader national or international level.

complex societies

Heterogeneous, culturally diverse societies with regional, class, gender, occupational, religious, and ethnic differences.

Anthropologists working in complex societies also focus on particular issues such as rural-urban migration or the effects of a mine or factory closing. They may study corporations, school boards, or medical research laboratories. The focus of analysis is dictated by the problem, which may be evident in a farming community, a labor union, an online community, or a social movement. In the United States, for example, an anthropologist might focus on some aspect of American culture, like the multiple perspectives in the debate over abortion or differing perspectives among and within racial and ethnic populations in a town or city.

Earlier, anthropologists tended to work in areas where their own states had established colonial empires or political dominance. American anthropologists studied Native Americans, and British and French anthropologists worked in British and French colonies in Africa and parts of Asia. Some of the communities or positions of power that anthropologists in the past assumed were indigenous categories were, in reality, colonial or imperial constructs. After first contact with Europeans, small-scale societies and even indigenous states were increasingly brought under the jurisdiction of larger political entities, typically European colonial empires. Colonial administrations replaced indigenous units based on geographic boundaries to govern more efficiently. At first, anthropologists paid little attention to the colonial administration of which they were a part. Today they study the historical process and contemporary impacts of how local populations were identified, categorized, and incorporated into colonial empires and postcolonial nation-states. Surrounded by new borders and included in new states, these groups have been transformed into ethnic groups, sometimes speaking different languages, often in conflict with one another. Industrialization and globalization have made small-scale societies part of interconnected world systems of labor allocation, production, and consumption, and anthropologists now investigate how they have responded to these changes.

As previously mentioned, anthropologists are increasingly concerned with being self-reflexive, or self-aware, by informing the readers of their ethnography about the experiential aspects of the fieldwork, not just the anthropological conclusions of the field research. In some ethnographies fieldworkers' experiences are at center stage, and they focus on how they came to know a particular social world, not on that world itself. The way of life of the people being studied may become secondary to the fieldworker's feelings and experiences. These ideas about the ethnographic enterprise have had an impact on the field, if only to make anthropologists more explicit about what they are doing when they do fieldwork. The anthropologist also reveals how the various aspects of fieldwork, and other types of research related to the project at hand, are translated into conclusions in the written form of ethnography, to clarify conclusions reached about the social world that the anthropologist has chosen as a subject of research.

Anthropologists often come from academic institutions in powerful Northern industrialized nations to conduct research in Southern countries. The initial relationship in the field may be perceived in terms of dominance and subordination, or power differentials, between anthropologists and community members. Often, anthropologists and informants use one another. Sometimes anthropologists are recognized by informants to further their political ambitions by providing information about and sometimes access to local power brokers or political leaders. Informants may see the anthropologist as exploiting them by "taking away" their myths, rituals, and traditions, and erroneously representing and portraying them to the outside world as violent people or helpless victims. All these factors may influence the nature of the information that is obtained and must be considered when field data are being analyzed.

As noted earlier, in addition to fieldwork, anthropologists utilize other techniques to collect data, such as historical and archival information, as well as data from archaeological and linguistic investigations and census materials. Research on a culture's past, sometimes referred to as the "ethnohistorical approach" or "historical anthropology," has become particularly significant as anthropology has moved to a processual model that includes the historical transformation of social relations and political institutions when analyzing present-day dynamics.

Increasingly, the social reality that an anthropologist chooses to study is "deterritorialized," and is explored in **multisited ethnography**. This becomes particularly important when an ethnographer is documenting the integration of local communities and processes with globalized production and marketing. For example, in Andrew Walsh's (2012) ethnography about sapphire mining and ecotourism in Madagascar, he interviews multiple different participants involved in the mining and tourism sectors, from local religious and political leaders, miners and gem brokers, and tour guides in

multisited ethnography

An ethnography that draws on information and informants in various locations, often across borders and over different time periods.

informed consent

The right of participants in research projects to be fully informed about the nature of the research, potential risks, and liabilities of participation.

Madagascar, to the government officials who regulate these industries. He talks to the gem polishers, jewelry designers, and stone setters in multiple locations around the world who all participate in the transformation of rocks from Madagascar into jewelry marketed to Northern consumers.

BOX 2.1 | Institutional Review Boards and Anthropological Research

Institutional Review Boards (IRBs) are committees in colleges and universities that provide guidance and oversight for research involving human and animal subjects in multiple disciplines. IRBs advise anthropologists in creating research methods that assure that the risk of participation by informants is minimal and that their rights are protected. The federal government mandates these provisions for all research funded directly or indirectly from government sources. Even when federal funding is not involved, most academic institutions review human and animal research projects for compliance before the research proceeds.

Specific rights of participants in anthropological research include that they be clearly informed about the project and its research methodologies prior to agreeing to participate voluntarily. This is known as **informed consent** and is usually acknowledged by participants in writing. The right of confidentiality of data collected is also protected; research proposals should contain procedures to assure informant confidentiality. The safety and well-being of individual research participants and informants should be anticipated in the research proposal. Guidelines include strategies for protecting the psychological and physical well-being of participants, especially of "vulnerable subjects" such as pregnant women, children, prisoners, the elderly, or people with any form of diminished capacity.

The American Anthropological Association (AAA), in its multiple statements on the principles of professional responsibility, stresses the overall obligation of all anthropologists to protect the confidentiality and well-being of their informants. The organization recommends that if those obligations cannot be assured, the research should

not be pursued. The AAA guidelines are generally accepted by all anthropologists "but not without debate, discussion, challenges, and recommendations for revision to make these guidelines more (or less) compatible with both national and international formal ethical principles and guidelines" (Whiteford and Trotter 2008: 7).

Ethical principles in anthropology and other social sciences apply to research design, data collection, and ethnographic writing. These principles and procedures continue to evolve over time; revisions are often prompted by new situations or pedagogical approaches within the disciplines. For example, many undergraduate anthropology departments now encourage students to do independent research, often in conjunction with community-based engagement or study abroad. Some colleges and universities require that undergraduate research proposals be submitted to their IRB for approval. Others require that project proposals and final projects demonstrate knowledge of, and compliance with, IRB ethical guidelines and procedures. Since the global Covid-19 pandemic, there has been renewed interest among anthropologists for "non-contact" research. This may involve using video and recording technologies as well as content analysis of online interactive sources. There is broad consensus among faculty and administrators that anthropology students at all levels be familiar with ethical principles and standards that assure that no harm will result to any informant as a result of participating in all forms of ethnographic research, and that procedures for assuring this protection be integrated into proposals, fieldwork, and ethnographic writing situated in the United States or abroad.

STUDYING RITUALS ACROSS TIME AND SPACE: THE COMPARATIVE APPROACH

Anthropologists have studied marriage patterns and related rituals since the inception of the discipline; we discuss anthropological perspectives on marriage and family formation in detail in chapter 6. Here, however, we discuss weddings and related rituals as separate and apart from the study of marriage and family; we employ a comparative approach by contrasting contemporary American wedding norms with Kwakwaka'wakw marriage rituals as recorded by Franz Boas. Referred to by Boas as the Kwakiutl, they are now the Kwakwaka'wakw, meaning "Kwak'wala speaking," Canadian indigenous First Nation of the western coast of British Columbia. Both settings illustrate how weddings are significant **rites of passage**, events that mark the transition of participants from one stage of their life cycle to another as well as events of economic and political significance. Wedding rituals have great cultural significance to the participants, as well as the kin groups and communities who observe and share in the events. Wedding rituals therefore are social texts that communicate and reinforce important aspects of shared cultural identity to participants and viewers. In examining marriage in these two very different societies, we will demonstrate how weddings illustrate different themes in Kwakwaka'wakw society at the turn of the twentieth century and in contemporary American society. Nevertheless, as shall be seen, there are also some fundamental similarities. In both societies, extravagant spending and opulent gift exchanges at weddings are ways of expressing social status and acquiring prestige.

In Boas's time, the aim of some anthropologists was **salvage anthropology**—that is, recording as much of the traditional culture as possible before it disappeared. As a consequence, his descriptions omitted the fact that the Kwakwaka'wakw at that time were part of the larger Canadian economic and political systems. The blankets they distributed in the ceremonies described below were purchased from the Hudson's Bay Company trade store. Enormous amounts of material goods involved in the ceremonies were obtained with money earned from working locally in canneries and from employment in Victoria, British Columbia, and elsewhere.

The description of the Kwakwaka'wakw marriage below was based on accounts collected primarily by George Hunt as well as some participant observation by Hunt (Boas 1955, 1966). Boas trained Hunt to be a field

In this circa 1900 photo of a wedding procession by Edward L. Curtis of a Kwakwaka'wakw of the West Coast of Canada, the groom's party arrives by canoe at an early stage of a marriage. A crest belonging to the groom's clan decorates the front of the canoe. Curtis's photographs are important and artistic legacies of ethnographic representation but are now critiqued by contemporary scholars because some were staged and included artifacts supplied by the photographer.

rites of passage

Communal rituals held to mark changes in status as individuals progress through their culturally patterned life cycle.

salvage anthropology

In Boas's time, the term applied to the gathering of ethnographic information about disappearing and threatened cultural practices.

researcher and to record texts in phonetic transcription in Kwak'wala, the language of the Kwakwaka'wakw. Although Hunt's mother was Tlingit, another tribe on the Canadian Northwest Coast, his father was Scottish; he grew up at Fort Rupert, British Columbia, and was fluent in Kwak'wala and English. Boas organized the data into a description of the marriage rite, which remained unpublished until after his death in 1942. It describes the marriage rites of the children of chiefs that occurred in the late nineteenth century. It blends the events from multiple actual marriages into a general description of the rites.

There were multiple stages to a Kwakwaka'wakw marriage spread over several months. The first stage was the beginning of negotiations between the parents of the young people, sometimes even without their knowledge. Messengers were sent by the groom's side to the bride's father requesting the bride in marriage. They were rewarded with blankets, and returned to the groom, who also gave them blankets. That night, the groom went to eat in the bride's house, sitting next to her. The bride's father told the groom that he expected to receive hundreds of blankets as the bride-wealth payment. After the groom's father assembled the blankets, they were piled in front of the door of the bride's father's house. The groom's father, accompanied by several chiefs, then went to the bride's house. The blankets were handed over to the bride's father, and he expressed his thanks. Several months later, at the next ceremony, the men of the groom's **numaym** (the Kwakwaka'wakw term for kin group) and those of other numaym blackened their faces and dressed like warriors as they went to the bride's house with the final payment of blankets. Her doorway was protected against the "invading warriors," who often had to run a gauntlet of flaming torches or go through a ring of burning cedar bark soaked in oil.

Then the chiefs from the groom's side made their traditional wedding speeches. In these speeches, the chiefs called upon their supernatural powers, which had come from ancient mythological times and were passed down through their families. These powers were said to be used to "move the bride." Each chief received a payment of blankets for (as the Kwakwaka'wakw say) "the weight of his breath," referring to the speech that was delivered at the wedding. Their combined breaths acted as a weight upon an imaginary scale used to move the bride. A high-status bride deserved more powerful speeches, or "breaths," to move her to the groom.

After the last of the chiefs had spoken, the ceremony of giving out the blankets brought by the groom's side for the bride's side took place. After the bride's side piled up two hundred blankets alongside the bride, a chief from the bride's side said, "Come to your wife and take her into your house with these two hundred blankets as her mat." The bride then walked to the groom's side and was led to the seat she was to occupy. In the evening,

numaym

Cognatic descent group of the Kwakwaka-wala, native people of the Northwest Coast.

The speaker for the chief distributes blankets at a Kwakwaka'wakw wedding potlatch photographed in 1894.

distinguished young men from the Kwakwaka'wakw tribes sang love songs and led the bride and groom back to his father's house. The groom sat alongside his new wife, and this part of the marriage ceremony came to an end.

Sometime later, usually after a child was born to the couple, the wife's side prepared to make a large return of goods to the husband's side, which Boas refers to as the "repurchase of the wife" by her own numaym. The Kwakwaka'wakw refer to this as "payment of the marriage debt." Since the wife's group was the "receiver" of the marriage potlatch (an elaborate ceremony of collection and redistribution of valuables) from the groom's group, it was under an obligation to make payments in return. This return at another potlatch consisted of objects referred to in Kwakwaka'wakw as "trifles" or "bad things." From the list of items described by Boas and Hunt, trifles and bad things meant just the opposite. The return was far more than what the wife's father had received.

The "repurchase" rituals for a wife were normally not held until after the birth of a child. When the wife had been repurchased by her father, she was free to return to him unless her husband purchased her for the second time. This would be followed by a second repurchase by her own group. These exchanges of property via potlatches could take place up to four times, after which the wife's rank was so high, because of the goods expended in successive repurchases, that she could "stay for nothing." The families of both groom and bride respectively increased their rank and prestige with each potlatch and its transfer of goods.

Analysis of the ritual of marriage among the Kwakwaka'wakw reveals that it embodies many of the central themes in Kwakwaka'wakw culture. The Kwakwaka'wakw emphasis on rank was reiterated again and again throughout the course of the marriage potlatch. The high rank of the bride demanded that there be large payments for her. At the

Contemporary Kwakwaka'wakw bride and groom's wedding cakes depict clan images. People around the world adapt their wedding rituals to reflect their identities and priorities.

same time, such payments enhanced the rank of the giver, the groom's kin group. In the Kwakwaka'wakw marriage, we also see that marriage is a symbolic form of warfare. Warriors from the groom's side come to "capture" the bride. Marriage and warfare are similar in that the two sets of affines, or kin by marriage, are in opposition to one other and in competition. Since one's wife comes from what is in the marriage symbolically the "enemy" side, there may be implications for husband-wife relations and for gender relations generally. The groom's side compensates the bride's side, by paying "bride-wealth." Just as the payment of "blood money" recompenses the side in a feud that has suffered a loss, bride-wealth payment pays for the "capture" of the bride.

American White Wedding Gowns and Rituals

As the above descriptions illustrate, Kwakwaka'wakw marriage rituals had kinship, economic, religious, political, aesthetic, and performative dimensions. In urban societies, in addition to the variegated nature of social groupings, there are complex political economies and institutional specializations involved in executing marriage rituals. Many contemporary American weddings are referred to by scholars as "white weddings," a reference to the expected color of bridal attire, as well as to the elaborate rituals, food, drink, entertainment, and expenditures that constitute the event (Jellison 2008). When one examines weddings in America, one finds a wedding industry that provides information and supplies: wedding magazines, wedding boutiques, wedding planners, and multiple businesses that provide distinctive commodities and specialized services. Like Kwakwaka'wakw marriage rituals, American weddings also involve a series of rituals marking a critical rite of passage. American weddings and marriages are political events as well; a marriage after all is a contract creating a new and legally recognized entity, hence the necessity for a marriage license granted by the state in which the ritual takes place. In American society, some people still refuse to marry in the eyes of the state but commit themselves to each other through public ritual attended by members of their families and communities. One unique aspect of contemporary American weddings as ritual is that the couple usually plans them in detail, sometimes years in advance of the actual event.

The following discussion, drawing on multiple ethnographic and media sources, outlines general historical trends and descriptions, supplemented with ethnographic description of a particular wedding ritual based on observation and interviews with the participants. Elaborate wedding practices in contemporary America encode many heteronormative, gender, ethnic, and class norms. But the persistence of these wedding norms and their adoption by all ethnicities and minority groups shows that rituals accommodate multiple forms of identity, as well as illustrating changes in participants' expectations and priorities.

American fascination with the subject of weddings is illustrated in part by its visibility in multiple forms of media. Internet, print media, and television coverage of celebrity weddings invariably result in high viewer ratings and increased media consumption. Weddings feature prominently in the narratives of broadcast and cable television; wedding gown shopping and wedding preparation are major themes in scripted and reality broadcasts and streaming service programming. Many wedding-related media concepts quickly pass into general recognition and usage; the term "bridezilla," also the title of a reality television show documenting escalating prewedding demands of brides-to-be, is now defined in the online Oxford English Dictionary as "A woman thought to have become intolerably obsessive or overbearing in planning the details of her wedding." The internet is filled with etiquette guides, wedding event schedulers and planners, recommendations, fashion sources, and increasingly, information specifically targeted to relatives and friends of brides and grooms. The film *Father of the Bride*, based on a popular 1948 novel, was a hit in 1950, successfully remade in 1991, and newly produced in 2022 featuring a Hispanic American couple, demonstrating the popularity over several decades of stories about weddings and the families participating in them.

These forms of mass media are "cultural documents" used in part to assemble the description below. Media materials are now understood to be texts, or representations, of cultural subject matter. This means that when documenting contemporary American wedding rituals, we must be clear about our sources of information and their perspectives. The media are a rich source for research on the culture of weddings; anthropologists supplement media coverage with their observations and insights, as well as use the work of historians and other social scientists.

Generally the American white wedding prominently features a costly, formal wedding gown ensemble for the bride purchased exclusively for this one occasion; formal attire for the groom (usually rented); a religious or spiritual ceremony attended by family and friends; and multiple attendants also wearing specially purchased or rented garments and accessories. The ceremony, attended by a pre-confirmed list of family members and friends, is generally followed by an elaborate meal in a specially selected location and, at some point in the future, a honeymoon trip for the newly married couple. The wedding rituals are preceded by smaller gatherings that tend to be "single gender" events honoring either one or the other future spouse. One or more "showers," usually hosted by friends, are occasions of gift giving to a future spouse in support of the household being established after marriage. Bachelor and bachelorette parties, attended by a small group of friends (usually the wedding attendants) are also generally single gender events that provide an opportunity for the respective soon-to-be spouses to bid farewell, often raucously and with inhibitions lowered by excessive alcohol consumption, to their unmarried lifestyles.

These wedding norms symbolize social status, relationship commitment, and the transition into adulthood; although associated with dominant, heterosexual norms in American society, different genders, identity groups, classes, ethnic groups, and religious communities in America embrace and adapt "white wedding" styles and rituals. Wedding gowns and other

Western-style formal attire for participants and elaborate reception meals have been integrated into the wedding rituals of many different cultures around the world. Spurred by the recognition of marriage rights in the United States and elsewhere, sexual minorities embrace and adapt white wedding rituals as powerful symbols of the public recognition of their relationships, marriage, and family formation.

Contemporary scholars who study and analyze weddings globally encourage seeing them simultaneously as representing cultural norms as well as providing spaces by which individuals and couples contest these norms with innovations. While wedding rituals provide "commentary on gender, status, national identity, and the social good, these things are not social 'givens' but objects of contestation" (Kendall 1996: 19). This perspective focuses simultaneously on continuities in ritual while also paying close attention to the perspectives of participants and the decisions they make concerning who is, and what events are, included or not included in their wedding rituals. These variations provide commentary on contemporary perceptions of general norms and expectations around wedding rituals while simultaneously illustrating how participants contest or resist these norms with their own innovations throughout pre-wedding and wedding ritual celebrations.

White Wedding Gowns and Rituals: A Brief History

The practice of a bride wearing a white gown for her wedding ceremony is a relatively recent phenomenon; this fashion innovation is widely attributed to Queen Victoria of Great Britain. Prior to Victoria's 1840 wedding to Prince Albert, royal and elite brides wore embellished dresses in a range of colors, including black, brown, or gray. "Following this grand event, many white Western middle-class brides imitated Victoria and adopted the white wedding gown. By the turn of the century, white had not only become the standard but had also become laden with symbolism—it stood for purity, virginity, innocence, and promise, as well as power and privilege" (Ingraham 1999: 34).

The white gown and elaborate, expensive wedding celebrations quickly became a staple for late-nineteenth-century and early-twentieth-century elite American brides. "Upper middle class and elite weddings might be marked by lavish consumer expenditure, but weddings of middle-class, working-class or rural men and women were more likely to be a blend of carefully selected purchases and home craft or entirely homespun affairs" (Dunak 2013: 18). The economic depression of the 1930s, and the draft of hundreds of thousands of men into the armed forces before and during World War II did not discourage American marriages but did discourage elaborate and expensive wedding celebrations.

The end of World War II and the beginning of postwar prosperity of the 1950s marked a major transition in the economy and family lives of many

Americans. Wartime austerity and pessimism were replaced with postwar optimism and economic growth; jobs and housing opportunities in newly emerging suburban communities created mobility and aspirations for a growing, mostly white American middle class. "The market and the media contributed to the shift in the American mindset. The rapidly expanding consumer economy presented Americans with a vast array of consumption opportunities as they returned to a peacetime world . . . the home, and the suburban home, in particular became a staple adult fantasy. A couple would marry, find a home, and fill that home with children and goods" (Dunak 2013: 22). Peaceful, prosperous, postwar America reinforced household economic division of labor along gender lines; newly married women were encouraged to give up paid work outside the home and seek personal satisfaction as mothers and homemakers in suburban households.

In mid-century middle-class America, marriage and weddings were encouraged and promoted in this increasingly consumer-driven economy. Marriage was recognized as the defining moment in the transformation of both men and women into adult, responsible family members with their respective economic and social roles in nuclear families. Weddings are increasingly thought of as the domain of the bride and groom's decision making. "National media and a renewed wedding industry shaped the wedding and standardized the . . . style of celebration, further cementing the 'normalcy' and indicating the desirability of the marital state. Such influences often replaced the authority of ethnic, familiar, or local culture" (Dunak 2013: 25).

For many of its images and products, the mid-twentieth century wedding industry drew on the new technology of television to deliver powerful messages directly into the American home. The weddings of Britain's Queen Elizabeth II and American actress Grace Kelly, who at her marriage became Princess Grace of Monaco, instantly delivered to an eager audience resplendent images of royal princess brides in long white wedding gowns, jeweled headpieces, and elaborate veils, accompanied by multiple attendants—all taking place in public, religious settings. In the United States, the White House weddings of Tricia Nixon, Luci Baines Johnson, and later her sister, Lynda Bird Johnson (daughters of President Richard Nixon and Lyndon Baines Johnson), were widely covered by American media, explicitly linking these celebrations to America's version of princess brides. The British royal weddings of Lady Diana Spencer to Prince Charles, eldest son of Queen Elizabeth II in 1981, Catharine Middleton to Charles's eldest son Prince William in 2011, and American actress Meghan Markel to Charles's younger son Prince Harry in 2018 were major media and consumer events. They each established fashion and consumption patterns emulated by brides around the world.

Media coverage of and commentary on all these elite weddings have stressed the connection between the "princess bride" (whether real or imagined) and the wedding ensemble she wears. Celebrity gowns and accessories are instantly duplicated by manufacturers and marketers and are quickly made available in department stores (the primary venue of bridal gown shopping throughout the mid- to late twentieth century), specialty independent

British Prince Harry, Duke of Sussex, and Meghan Markle, Duchess of Sussex, after getting married in Windsor, England, in 2018. Meghan Markle's dress and accessories, like those of other royal brides, were reproduced by "fast fashion" wedding suppliers and marketers around the world immediately after photographs became available.

bridal stores and national chains, and on the internet. The wedding supplier industry, estimated to represent about $62 billion in sales in the United States in 2022, includes wedding planners and consultants, who guide couples into renting venues and hiring catering specialists, florists, musicians and photographers, jewelers, and transportation suppliers, and choosing wedding gift retailers. The global Covid-19 pandemic drastically impacted the number of wedding celebrations and their size throughout 2020 and 2021, creating a significant drop in revenue for all these wedding-related industries. Thus new, normalized "traditions" and aspirations of bridal dress and elaborate wedding ceremonies, along with a new set of cultural meanings associated with them, are created while simultaneously being perceived as long-standing and "timeless."

An elaborate wedding of the pre-pandemic twenty-first century represented a substantial financial investment; a survey of 16,000 American couples married in 2014 concluded that the national average of wedding budgets was $31,213, up from $29,858 in 2013. This figure excluded the honeymoon but did include the engagement ring, wedding rings, wedding gown, groom's attire, musicians, photography, food, beverages, venue expenses, wedding cakes, transportation, favors, and the rehearsal dinner (The Knot 2014). This expense (double in parts of the Northeast but lower in parts of the Midwest and Southeast) raises questions relevant to analyzing wedding celebrations around the world: How are these costs divided up between different participants, different individuals, and different kin groups based on their relationship to the bride and groom? Answering this question reveals some important shifts in the perception of financial obligations related to weddings, as well as changes in the demographic profile of American brides and grooms.

Wedding couples in the twenty-first century are older than they were previously; the current generation of brides and grooms tends to be in their late twenties or early thirties and have been employed and living outside of their parents' homes for many years. They may have been previously married and are planning second or "encore" weddings. They are economically self-sufficient, as well as socially and sexually experienced; they are making their own decisions and choices for their wedding rituals. Today's couple is rarely transitioning from exclusive residence in their parents' home to setting up a new first household after marriage.

The historical etiquette guideline of the bride's parents paying for all the wedding expenses is now rarely applied; in 2010 the president of the Association of Bridal Consultants stated that only about 10 percent of weddings are now wholly paid for by the bride's parents and that a third of weddings are financed by the bride and bridegroom alone (Ellin 2010). But paying for wedding rituals remains a kin-based obligation. Couples rely not only on the bride's parents, who have traditionally borne most of the burden, but also on contributions from the bridegroom's parents, stepparents, grandparents, aunts, and uncles. Wedding etiquette guides continue to cite familial obligations and suggest the groom's family be responsible for engagement and wedding rings, groom and groomsmen attire, rehearsal dinner expenses, officiant's fee, and wedding party transportation costs. These conventions and guidelines do not, however, always eliminate conflict and dispute over payment for weddings; bitter disagreements between brides, grooms, and family members over the number of guests and how to divide the payment of wedding expenses often mark the planning process, and in extreme cases threaten the marriage's even taking place. Disputes over and consequences of financial decisions, including debt incurred to finance wedding expenses, may linger far beyond the conclusion of the festivities of "that special day."

Wedding Ritual Variations: Marriage Equality and an American Wedding

Rituals are generally understood to be the enactment of repetitive behaviors that have important and shared symbolic meanings for the participants and observers. Their meanings derive in part from fulfillment of expectations and associations with tradition and history. Wedding rituals, particularly, enact shared community ideas about gender, family formation, and life-cycle status. Weddings are also revealing "texts" by which to illustrate how rituals invariably change over time; these changes become increasingly significant and meaningful to both participants and observers. This duality of ritual, containing aspects of both change and continuity, is important in understanding how weddings are made meaningful to diverse communities that do not conform to the middle-class, heteronormative, white communities from which these traditions historically arise.

One example of the many forms of diversity of wedding rituals is wedding ceremonies of people who self-identify as same sex. State-recognized marriage for same sex couples in the United States was affirmed by various state legislatures and court rulings in the first decade of the twenty-first century, and by the Supreme Court in 2015. This has not ended social and legal challenges to marriage equality from some religious and political groups. Nor did many same sex couples wait for "official" state sanctioning to marry; commitment ceremonies and marriage rituals attended by families and friends symbolized and publically confirmed the enduring nature of their relationships prior to legal recognition (Dunak 2013: 152).

In June 2011 in New York State, the Legislature passed the Marriage Equality Act, providing full legal and civil recognition of same-sex marriages. In October 2011, New York City residents Ellen and Alicia celebrated their wedding, with a religious ceremony and wedding reception attended by over

120 people (among them Maxine Weisgrau). At the time of their wedding, they had been in a committed relationship for over twenty years and were the parents of two teenage sons. They both were prompted by the legalization of marriage status in New York to have a wedding, or "the full deal," as Alicia remarked. They began planning their wedding as soon as the marriage law was changed in New York, particularly encouraged by one teenage son to have a "big wedding." Ellen reveled in all the fantasy elements involved in her "big day"—the dress, the hair, the makeup, the reception—experiences she'd always wanted. "We had not done any kind of domestic partnership or other commitment ceremony before getting married; we wanted the full and real deal."

As long-term partners with grown children, they were known to their extended families and a large network of friends as a close couple and family; they both expressed, however, that the wedding was an opportunity to publicly acknowledge this commitment to each other and to their sons. Ellen said in recollecting the wedding, "It also felt very intimate and meaningful to be surrounded by people who knew us so well, and maybe especially knew us as a couple and family. There was definite excitement in being a newly minted married couple, something that was really almost unimaginable when we met [in 1990]." The wedding was also an opportunity, therefore, to honor the support of their friends and family throughout their relationship. Alicia said that in planning the event, "We wanted to talk about our gratitude that our family was always behind us, and that the state was barely catching up with how forward-looking they had been all along." They both described the event as a "mid-marriage wedding" marking a close relationship and family that had been formed two decades previously.

As busy professionals and parents with only four months to plan their wedding, they first prioritized obtaining the venue. They sought a location that would be easily reachable by most of their guests who lived in the New York City area, and one that had a large, unencumbered space for dancing and musicians. They selected an event space in a Brooklyn, New York, park that had ample inside and outside space, both of which were used on the mild October day of their wedding. Both brides selected formal white wedding gowns, purchased on different days at a bridal specialty chain store in Manhattan in one day of shopping. Alicia was accompanied by her mother and a wedding attendant; Ellen was accompanied by the same wedding attendant on her shopping outing. Neither of the brides saw each other's dress before the ceremony. They arranged for the catering online and by phone. Ellen remarked, "We are probably the only wedding couple ever who did not do a taste testing! I just relied on Internet reviews of this caterer," and they both met him and his staff for the first time at the wedding venue the day of the celebration. Alicia's mother contributed to the expenses for the food; the couple paid for all the remaining expenses with credit cards that were still being paid off three years later.

For both Ellen and Alicia, the music at their wedding was a major consideration. Alicia is a world-renowned professional Klezmer musician (Eastern

European Jewish music traditions); all the musicians who performed at the wedding were esteemed colleagues and friends. Ellen is an accomplished amateur vocalist with a lifelong passion for singing. They both wanted their wedding to be a joyous experience that included music and dancing reflecting their respective Jewish Eastern European and Slovakian/Austrian heritages and wedding traditions.

Although neither is religiously observant in daily life, the couple wanted to represent their backgrounds, Jewish and Catholic, in their wedding ceremony. Ellen felt that it would be unlikely that a Catholic priest would share officiant duties at their wedding; they decided that a Jewish scholar known to Alicia and a minister (a family member) would both officiate at the ceremony. Ellen remarked, "I always feel the need to make a clear demarcation between Christian and Catholic. These choices were not perfect for me, but it was the best we could do. Both officiants were very open to what we wanted, and they couldn't have been more cooperative."

Their religious ceremony featured many aspects of Jewish wedding tradition; after some discussion between them, the couple agreed to having a chuppah, or wedding canopy, as the focal point for the ceremony. The chuppah was covered with a tablecloth their family has used at several holiday gatherings and was held up in each of its four corners by their wedding attendants, sons, friends, and family members. They each wrote their own vows that were deeply meaningful, particularly as witnessed by family and friends when recited under the chuppah. The ceremony was interspersed with musical performances and poetry readings by friends and family members. At the conclusion of the marriage ceremony, they each enacted the ritual of "breaking the glass," a near-universal culmination of Jewish weddings that is historically the exclusive role of a male groom. The recessional was particularly joyous, as Alicia requested the musicians play both Jewish wedding songs and the polka, a favorite of Ellen's Slovakian and Austrian relatives.

Both brides at Ellen and Alicia's "white wedding" chose traditional gowns and accessories.

At the conclusion of the wedding ceremony, family and friends made brief speeches honoring the brides and their family. These speeches included many different themes, but all honored the enduring nature of their relationship as well as the importance of the couple's sons and other family members as participants in their wedding day. While some speeches addressed the legal significance of marriage equality, they all acknowledged that Ellen, Alicia, and their sons were a close family whose commitments to each other were being honored that day.

Throughout the multicourse reception meal, there were continuous interludes of live music, singing, and dancing, in which all guests were encouraged to participate. The music and dancing, led by the Klezmer performers, was particularly joyful, and included multiple polka interludes. The traditional carrying of the brides on elevated chairs held up by wedding guests and paraded around the reception room was one of the highlights, as it is in many other Jewish cultural-inspired weddings. The meal culminated with the cutting of a multi-tiered wedding cake, decorated with fresh flowers and topped with two brides in white gowns. A performance by Ellen of an "American standard" love song composed in the 1930s, "You Go to My Head," accompanied by the musicians, was particularly moving for Alicia. In recollecting the most memorable parts of the event, they both expressed their joy at seeing all their friends and family members surrounding them and their sons with good will and joy. Said Alicia, "Walking down the aisle with the beautiful music, looking at the faces of so many people from my life, all there together for us—it all felt incredibly sincere and moving." In a separate interview Ellen expressed the same theme: "Just walking in and seeing people watch us walk down aisle . . . I was very emotional during the ceremony; more than I thought I would be."

With such a significance placed by both Ellen and Alicia on the presence of family and friends at their wedding, they questioned the motivations of some who were invited and chose not to attend. One family of distant relatives did not respond to their invitation, despite the request for a timely RSVP. Members of this family had expressed disapproval of their relationship in the past, although they later sent a card expressing support for the marriage. Alicia observed that it was unclear what motivated their actions and whether they changed their minds about supporting the marriage. Ellen noted that one of her cousins who attended the wedding initially questioned her on why they felt they needed to get married. "She and her family came to the wedding and at the end of it she apologized because she said she totally understood why and regretted that she'd wondered about it. That felt good." Ellen also commented that some self-identifying lesbian friends with whom she discussed the wedding were supportive of their personal decision but were not into marriage from a political perspective. "One lesbian couple we knew did not come to our wedding; probably scheduling but I also think they had political views that turned away from marriage."

The Comparative Approach

Earlier we noted that fieldwork and participant observation were the hallmarks of anthropological methodology. In the same manner, the comparative approach has been important to the discipline. What does a comparison of the Kwakwaka'wakw and American weddings reveal? In comparison to the Kwakwaka'wakw wedding, in an American wedding, the focus is almost exclusively on the marrying couple. American weddings are less a matter of two kin groups establishing a relationship, as was the case in a Kwakwaka'wakw wedding, and more a matter of bringing together and displaying the couple's personal networks of friends and colleagues. At the Kwakwaka'wakw wedding, marriage is a matter of relationships between kin groups. It is symbolized by the witnessing by an enormous audience of the capture of the bride by warriors of her husband's numaym, who "move" her to her husband's group.

In America the couple is the center of all wedding activity, though other individuals from their respective families as well as friends and relatives play some part. This emphasis on the couple themselves echoes the importance in American culture of the newly formed family as autonomous and separate from other families. The Kwakwaka'wakw wedding, on the other hand, was a **total social phenomenon** in which the entire community was involved and in which elements of economics, politics, and political maneuvering concerning transfer of a whole series of privileges as well as property were at issue. In the American wedding, economics are involved, in that goods and services were purchased, there were many expenditures, and guests all brought gifts for the brides. The Kwakwaka'wakw marriage itself was an institution for transfers of large amounts of property. Religion is involved in the American wedding, in that an officiant oversees the event and the couple chooses to include rituals associated with religious traditions. Similarly, in the Kwakwaka'wakw marriage, the recitation of myths linking people to their ancestors plays a large part in the unfolding of the ceremonies. In a Kwakwaka'wakw marriage, the whole underlying structure of Kwakwaka'wakw society is played out. In contrast, in America, there is more institutional separation through the creation of a wedding supplier industry, and a wedding focuses on the public recognition of the couple and their nuclear family.

total social phenomena
Large-scale rituals that integrate all aspects of society—economic, political, kinship, religion, art, etc.

There are obvious differences, but also some interesting similarities that should be recognized. In both Kwakwaka'wakw and American societies, weddings are public ceremonies witnessed by others. In both instances, guests attend the ceremony and communally partake in the supplied feast. They perform the function of publicly participating in, as well as witnessing, a rite of passage. In both societies, prestige is communicated by the size of the outlay, which in turn relates to the social status of the families involved. The more lavish the display, the greater the standing of the hosts and their families. Northwest Coast indigenous ceremonies have been described by anthropologists as **potlatches**, elaborate rituals marked by distribution and redistribution by the hosts of locally significant goods; they are displays of conspicuous consumption and gift giving. Potlatches serve social and political functions, especially to highlight and reinforce the economic and social status of the hosts. Elaborate American weddings, with their norms of payment, repayment, gift giving, and distribution of food and gifts, can similarly described as potlatches. Participation by guests creates a joyous celebration as well as establishing claims for reciprocity.

potlatch
A large-scale ceremonial distribution of goods found among the indigenous peoples of the Northwest Coast of North America.

SUMMARY

- The defining methodology of anthropology is fieldwork conducted through participant observation, which involves an inherent contradiction because one is at the same time an observer outside the culture as well as a participant within it.

- Culture shock is the realization of all the implications of the fact that other people do things differently and one's own culture is not "natural."

- The fieldworker learns how to view things from consultants' points of view, that is, according to the concepts and ideas that order their world but also make their own observations.

- The anthropologist gains information from people referred to as "informants," "cultural consultants," or "local experts," who eventually become fieldworker-colleagues.

- Participant-observation is the heart of fieldwork. It involves living with other people, learning their language or lingo, and participating in local events to whatever extent possible as a community member.

- Anthropologists are increasingly engaging with ethical and moral considerations in designing and executing fieldwork-based research.

- Fieldwork involves reciprocity in the sense that informants provide information, and the anthropologist gives various forms of assistance, including acting as an advisor for the group in legal matters.

- The anthropologist engages in different kinds of translations, not only from the language or dialect of informants to the anthropologist's own language, but also translation into the concepts and categories of anthropological analysis.

- Ethnography is the translation of fieldwork observations into a written narrative form, involving editing, organizing, and all the other techniques necessary to create a written version of multiple forms of data and experiences.

- Reflexivity suggests the self-awareness of the possibilities and limitations of the fieldwork process, including understanding the historical, political, and economic relationships between the researcher and community.

- The unit of analysis for anthropology in small-scale societies was the community. As anthropology has shifted to complex societies, the unit of analysis is now dictated by the research question selected.

- Many of the now-classic twentieth-century ethnographies were written about local communities during colonial and imperialistic periods of domination; ethnographers were invariably trained in the countries of the rulers and were writing about the colonized "others."

- Contemporary ethnography makes fieldwork procedures and methodologies explicit, including informing readers about the experiential aspects of fieldwork and how the data are used to make generalized conclusions.

- In addition to fieldwork, anthropologists utilize other sources such as historical and archival information, as well as data from archaeological and linguistic investigations and census materials.

- Rich, detailed ethnographic descriptions, applied in the comparative approach, reveal certain basic similarities between American and Kwakwaka'wakw weddings, along with the differences in symbolic meanings.

KEY TERMS

community, 38
complex societies, 38
consultants, 35
culture shock, 35
ethics, 36
informants, 35
informed consent, 40
key informants, 36
multisited ethnography, 39

numaym, 42
participant observation, 34
potlatch, 53
research design, 34
rites of passage, 41
salvage anthropology, 41
total social phenomena, 53
translation, 37

SUGGESTED READINGS

Robben, Antonius, and Jeffrey A. Sluka. *Ethnographic Fieldwork: An Anthropological Reader*. Malden, MA: Blackwell Publishers, 2007.

A collection of articles, both historical and contemporary, regarding how fieldwork is conducted.

Sanjak, Roger, ed. *Mutuality: Anthropology's Changing Terms of Engagement*. Philadelphia: University of Pennsylvania Press, 2015.

A collection of essays by distinguished anthropologists that draw on personal and professional histories. They describe their collaborative fieldwork, community-based projects and consultations, and advocacy with fieldwork communities.

Taylor, Steven J. *Introduction to Qualitative Research Methods: A Guidebook and Resource*. Hoboken, NJ: John Wiley & Sons, 2016.

Detailed descriptions of all the phases of the research process illustrated with examples of completed research projects.

SUGGESTED WEBSITES

https://www.firstvoices.com/explore/FV/sections/Data/search/?query=Kwakwala&page=1

Information on and links to further resources on contemporary Kwakwala language and culture.

https://www.americananthro.org/ethics-and-methods

The official website of the American Anthropological Association offers numerous resources and blogs accessible to students and non-members. The link above leads to multiple resources and blogs that explore ethical guidelines principles and controversies in the anthropological methods.

Chapter 3
Language and Culture

LEARNING OBJECTIVES

- Recognize the components and characteristics of spoken languages.
- Understand how the histories of languages and language groups are reconstructed.
- Review the evolutionary implications of speech in anatomically modern humans.
- Explore the politics of language use, language loss, and revitalization.
- Explain how linguistic agency expresses identity, affiliation, and resistance.

LANGUAGE AND CULTURE ARE LIKE two sides of a coin. Language is a part of culture, yet it is more than that since language is the means through which culture is communicated, expressed, and learned. As human cultures developed, some means of communication—a spoken language and sometimes a written form—also developed. Only humans have the capacity for learning language and manipulating it. In any language, a limitless number of possible ideas can be constructed and used. This allows humans to communicate an infinite number of new cultural ideas and symbolic meanings from one generation to the next, and to constantly express new thoughts and ideas and discard others. Because of this, human spoken language is significantly different from any other system of communication. Language classifies things; it classifies actions; it classifies our experiences. Objects and events are ordered by language into categories of time and space. Languages are constantly changing, adding new concepts and ideas, and eliminating older norms and rules. No language therefore can be thought of as "pure" and "unchanging"; so the methods used for understanding language in many ways are similar to those for understanding culture.

THE EVOLUTION OF SPOKEN-LANGUAGE CAPACITY

There is no doubt that animals have the capacity to communicate with one another, from honey bees that use an elaborate dance to communicate the presence of a new food source, to monkeys, chimpanzees, and other primates who have developed call systems to communicate the presence of predators. Some primates have been taught sign language in captivity by human caregivers, with whom they seem to communicate by responding to simple questions and performing limited tasks on command. However, human communication, in contrast to animal communication, is very complex: it is both verbal and nonverbal, uses arbitrary symbols, has words with meanings, can transmit cultural ideas, involves spontaneous usage, turn-taking, the double layering of sounds and words, reference to objects and events not present, and the presence of structure and creativity (Workman and Reader 2004: 229–30). In no animal communication system are all these criteria present, nor do communication systems of any other primate seem to involve grammar of any sort.

According to many scholars, the presence of language gives humans a selective advantage since information can be conveyed efficiently and with detail. In other words, natural selection seems to have favored the capacity for language. A number of hypotheses have been offered regarding the "why" of language evolution, that is, why the capacity for language developed. But no single explanation seems to answer this vexing question. Noam Chomsky (1998) has famously argued that there is an innate cognitive basis for human language present at birth and that all babies are predisposed to language learning and acquisition (which we shall discuss in detail in the next chapter). However, Chomsky does not propose that these mechanisms are the result of natural selection but that "the language organ evolved for some other purpose and was co-opted, or adapted for its current purpose" (Workman and Reader 2004: 259). The genetic basis for this "innate disposition" has not yet been ascertained, although researchers working with the language disorder known as "specific language impairment," the result of a damaged gene, see this as a demonstration of the presence of a series of genes relating to this innate capacity. Neuroscientists and others who study speech capacity stress the complexity of human speech, in that it involves simultaneously anatomical capacities, with actions and skills drawing on neurological, anatomical, and social systems. The neurological, anatomical, and sensory coordination required for human speech challenges the idea that any one genetic mutation could account for the presence or absence of such a highly complicated human skill.

The complexity of human speech also complicates questions about when the capacity for language began to evolve. Some have argued that Homo erectus, which appeared in Africa some 1.8 million years ago, had some of the neurological and cranial capacity for nonverbal communication and may possibly have had a proto-form of verbal communication, on the basis of the presence of two areas of the brain associated with language in modern humans. Neandertals are seen by some as being capable of formulating some discreet speech sounds based on the anatomical features of their vocal tract and cranium. Others claim that the full complex of anatomical, cognitive, and cultural capacities associated with human language only appeared with Homo sapiens. Understanding all the aspects of language evolution is one of the "great mysteries of our species." Resolving this intriguing mystery in the future will require coordinating discoveries from a multitude of disciplines, including animal behavior, paleontology, neurobiology, archaeology, and genetics (Hauser et al. 2014: 10).

THE STRUCTURE OF LANGUAGE

Like culture, spoken language is patterned; the units of language that carry meaning are two-sided. One side consists of physical characteristics that make up the word. These characteristics consist of sounds transmitted through the air, which emanate from one person and are received by another. The other side consists of the word's meaning or what it stands for. For example, the word tree in English is made up of a particular series of sounds—t/r/e—and what it stands for is depicted in figure 3.1.

The same object is referred to as arbre in French and Baum in German. The connection between any combination of sounds that make up a word and its meaning is arbitrary—that is, there is no intrinsic and natural connection between the sounds of a word and its meaning. The same meaning is conveyed by a different combination of sounds in each language. Occasionally, there is limited connection between sound and meaning in a specific language system, as occurs in English words that imitate natural

Fig. 3.1 *The combination of phonemes and morphemes for the same object in different languages conforms to the linguistic history, rules, and norms of a particular language.*

phonemes

The smallest units of sound that are distinguished from each other in any language.

allophone

A variant form of a phoneme.

phenomena, such as buzz and hiss. But these are also symbolic and are expressed in different ways in different languages.

Phonemic Structure

Discreet sounds are the building blocks of every language. Multiple anatomical components of human speech, including the tongue, lips, soft and hard palate, and larynx and vocal cords, create the capacity for producing hundreds of basic sounds. Every language has a much smaller number of basic sounds, usually between twenty and forty, which are used in various combinations to make up the units of meaning. These basic sound units are called **phonemes**: units of sound in a language that create contrast but have no meaning. All languages are constructed in the same way; from a small number of phonemes, arranged in different ways, an infinite number of words can be produced. For example, the English word pin differs in meaning from pan since /i/ is a different phoneme from /a/. If /s/ is added to the beginning of the word, the result is spin, a word with a totally different meaning. Thus, the same phonemes in a different order produce a word with a different meaning. You may have recognized that the /p/ in pin is different from the /p/ in spin. If you hold a sheet of paper in front of your mouth and pronounce "pin" loudly, the paper will flutter because the /p/ in pin is aspirated (air is blown out of the mouth). Pronounce spin, and the sheet of paper remains still, because the /p/ in spin is not aspirated. The two spoken forms of /p/ are said to be **allophones** of the same phoneme. They are variant forms of the single English phoneme /p/. They vary because of the different phonemic contexts in which they are found.

The phonemes of a language form a structure or system. The phonemes of English can be divided into vowels and consonants. For a native speaker, English consonants seem independent and unrelated to one another. However, let us examine some English consonants:

t	d
p	b
f	v
s	z
k	g

When one makes the sounds /t/ and /d/, the tongue, teeth, and lips, which are called the points of articulation, are in the same position for both. This is also true for the other paired sounds on the two lists—/p/ and /b/, /f/ and /v/, /s/ and /z/, and /k/ and /g/. There is a relationship between the group of consonants in the left-hand column and the group of consonants in the right-hand column. The consonants in the column on the left are all pronounced without vibrations of the vocal cords. They are voiceless consonants. The vocal cords vibrate when those in the right-hand column are pronounced. These are called voiced consonants. The distinction between voiced and voiceless consonants is one of the several kinds of distinctions characterizing English phonemes. All these features organize the set of English phonemes into a structure and serve to differentiate each phoneme from every other. Their use is unconscious; we cannot intentionally make our vocal cords vibrate. In English, phonemes differentiate words like *pin* and *pan*. Phonemes themselves do not carry meaning; their function is to form words in combination with other phonemes (and morphemes), and to differentiate these words by meaning.

Morphemic Structure

The smallest units of language that have sound and carry meaning are called **morphemes**. Morphemes are not equivalent to words because some words may be broken into smaller units that themselves carry meaning. For example, the word shoemaker may be subdivided into three separate morphemes: shoe, make, and -er, each contributing its own meaning to the word. Each of these morphemes is in turn made up of phonemes. Some morphemes, like shoe, can stand independently. These are called "free morphemes." Others, like -er, meaning "one who has to do with," are always found bound to other morphemes (as in *speaker*, *singer*, and *leader*) and are referred to as bound morphemes. Sometimes two or more forms of a morpheme have the same meaning. For example, the plural morpheme in English /s/ has different spoken forms with the same meaning in different environments: /s/ as in cats; /z/ as in dogs; and /es/ as in busses. Every language has its own morphemic structure and characteristics, and specific "rules" for adding forms of morphemes to phonemes forming recognizable symbols. These rules are unconsciously absorbed as children master the language around them.

morpheme

The smallest unit of a language conveying meaning.

Syntax and Grammar

The **syntax** of a language is the set of rules by which larger speech units, such as phrases and sentences, are formed. English, like all other languages, has rules about the order of words in a sentence, but unlike some other languages, in English, word order creates meaning. In some languages, morphemes convey the part of speech being formed by the word, so a speaker is expressing whether the word is the subject of a sentence or an object of a verb or

syntax

That part of grammar that deals with the rules of combination of morphemes.

preposition. With this kind of system, word order does not convey the meaning of the sentence. In English there are few bound morphemes to express total meaning: therefore word order is significant in conveying meaning. For example, the two sentences below use the same forms for verbs and nouns, subjects and objects; word order is therefore critical in conveying meaning:

The boy hit the ball.   The ball hit the boy.

The ways in which a language indicates singular and plural are also part of its syntax. The complete description of a language is known as its **grammar**. This includes the phonology (a description of its phonemic system), the morphology (a description of its morphemic system), and the syntax. In addition, a complete description of a language would also include a **lexicon**, or dictionary, that lists all the morphemes and their meanings.

Linguistic Relativity

European expansion and colonialism intensified the encounter between speakers of languages unrelated to Indo-European, the language family whose languages were spoken in Europe. Early linguists thought (incorrectly) that the newly discovered languages, like those spoken by Native peoples of North America, could be analyzed in terms of the same grammatical categories used to analyze English, French, Italian, and other Indo-European languages. These linguists were ethnocentric in their approach and termed languages "advanced" if they were spoken by people who were perceived to be "civilized" by European cultural standards. Hunters and gatherers were said to speak "primitive" languages. It became evident to Franz Boas, and later to others, that there is no relationship between technology, culture, and language complexity. All languages known to linguists, regardless of whether the society has writing, are equally complex. This is known as **linguistic relativity**. It parallels the concept of cultural relativity. Furthermore, Boas convincingly demonstrated that it was necessary to analyze each language in terms of its own structure and functions.

Linguistic Universals

Earlier, we pointed out that anthropology uses the comparative method to investigate cultural similarities and cultural differences. Linguistics adopts the same approach. The differences and similarities between languages are immediately apparent, and the similarities point some scholars to hypothesizing the universals in human language systems. Among the broad conclusions of this approach are that all languages have vowels and consonants, nouns and verbs, and some form of negative construction. Another route of inquiry is based on Noam Chomsky's concept of a universal grammar, a "language faculty," which he hypothesizes is based on the underlying cognitive structure of the

---

grammar

The complete description of a language, including phonology, morphology, and syntax.

lexicon (or dictionary)

The complete description of all morphemes and their meanings in a language.

linguistic relativity

A point of view that emphasizes the uniqueness of each language and the need to examine it in its own terms.

human mind. While the first approach is empirical and inductive, the second is highly theoretical and deductive.

Language, Cognition, and Understanding

There is a close and intimate relationship between language and experience. Boas recognized that in the Kwak'wala language of some Northwest Coast native communities, the speaker must indicate how she or he knows about an action other individuals are performing. For example, in the sentence

"The lady was washing clothes,"

Kwak'wala makes the following distinctions: Did the speaker actually see the lady washing clothes? Did the speaker infer that she was washing clothes from the sound that was heard? Did a third party tell the speaker that she was washing clothes? Kwak'wala language speakers make distinctions that indicate how the speaker knows the information. These distinctions are part of the grammar of the language. The Kwak'wala grammar also includes forms by which speakers specify how they acquired the information they are imparting. English does not have this feature as part of its grammar, though this information may be provided by speakers, if they wish to give it, with additional words. In all languages, grammatical rules are generally used unconsciously. Language speakers may not be able to articulate these rules, but they learn them along with all the other components of linguistic competence.

People speaking different languages have different ways of organizing what they experience. Thus Kwak'wala speakers always attend to how they receive information because this is necessary in conveying information to others. One can imagine the comparison between the precision of a Kwakiutl witness at a court trial and the lack of specificity of the equivalent English-speaking witness at the same trial. This illustrates the relationship between language and the organization of experience. Conceptualizations of the world are seen, to a great extent, to be based unconsciously upon the language usage of a community. While these are clear to native speakers they may be misunderstood by nonnative speakers, who must rely on translations. As is clear from the above example, translation into another language is often incomplete and does not always capture the nuances of the original linguistic expression.

Ethnosemantics

There is a close connection between the way language is organized and the way culture is organized. This can be seen most clearly by examination of a specific cultural domain, such as the organization and classification of the world of animals, the world of plants, or the system of colors. In all languages, there is a set of terms used to refer to animals. The world of animals is separable from other domains in the world. It is distinct from the domain of plants, though they both are alive, in contrast to the inanimate world of rocks and soil. People using different languages will sort the world of animals in ways different from our own. For example, the system developed by Swedish scientist Carl Linnaeus (1707–1778), which is the Linnaean system, is used in Euro-American animal classification. This system groups human beings, bats, and whales into one category, mammals, on the basis that they are all warm-blooded, suckle their young, and have hair. Whether these animals fly, live on the land, or swim in the sea is not important. The categories are hierarchically organized into successively more inclusive groupings from species to genus to class and are in accord with Darwin's evolutionary classifications.

Other peoples use different criteria for their animal classifications. The Karam of Papua New Guinea distinguish birds from other animals in their language. However, the cassowary, a flightless bird like an ostrich, which stands over five feet tall, is not placed in the category of birds (where we place it). Rather, the Karam place it in an anomalous category. Unlike birds, it does not fly. It walks on two legs and is seen as related to humans. When anthropological linguists study Karam language and culture, they collect the meanings of all animal terms and the categories in which the Karam place them and must then try to determine the reasons why the Karam sort and classify animals in this way. They ascertain the distinctive features the Karam employ when they classify forms such as the cassowary. Each language employs its own cultural logic in making classifications. The anthropological investigation of classification and its cultural logic is known as **ethnosemantics**.

In this general discussion of ethnosemantics, we have shown the way in which the concept of distinctive features is used. A common way of distinguishing two categories from one another is for one of the categories to possess an attribute that the other category lacks. In the Linnaean classification, mammals are warm-blooded animals while reptiles are not. Thus, one might say that the category of mammals is the "plus" category. This is a distinction biologists make. The linguist Roman Jakobson makes a similar classificatory distinction, which he called **markedness**. He called the category in which the attribute was present the "marked" category, and the category in which it was absent, the "unmarked" category. Jakobson pointed out that in linguistics, the unmarked category is the more general and inclusive of the two. For example, in English, we use the words lion and lioness. The marked category is the word lioness (-ess is added to lion, thus marking it female). Lion includes lioness, as in the sentence "The lion devoured its prey." The presence of marked and unmarked categories is considered to be another universal characteristic of language systems.

Sociolinguistics

To obtain information about a language, contemporary fieldworkers observe and record many examples of speech. These examples are analyzed to obtain a picture of the grammar, or its underlying structure. **Sociolinguistics** deals with the analysis of speech and its social functions. Recently, anthropological

ethnosemantics

The anthropological investigation of indigenous systems of classifications.

markedness

The linguistic process whereby a category (the marked category) is distinguished from a larger, more inclusive category (the unmarked category) by the presence of a single attribute.

sociolinguistics

The study of aspects of language that express status and class differences as understood through language use and practices.

linguists have been interested in a more integrative way of understanding how language organizes social life. Language is an integral part of the construction of social life; it also provides a window on social process. Language forges shared cultural understandings and acts as a medium of social exchange and connection between people. Linguistic choices create affiliations between cohorts of speakers, as well as distinctions between them and others. In chapter 1, we discussed the concepts of social structure, social organization, and agency. **Linguistic agency** emphasizes the capacity for individual choices in language use, in that individuals have some control over the choices they make in their own speech patterns. The speech pattern used by influential individuals, however, can provide the initial force for an individual's, or community's, language change.

In Uttar Pradesh, India, girls and women learn basic literary skills in informal settings, as local social norms discourage them from traveling to and attending schools, which may be several kilometers away from their villages.

linguistic agency

The capacity of language speakers to make choices about the forms and styles they use in everyday speech.

Gender and Speech

In many societies, there are distinctions in the speech patterns of genders; gender distinctions in linguistic communication styles can create misunderstandings and lack of communication (Tannen 2001a). As infants and young children learn their language and their culture, they are simultaneously learning age and gender-specific behavior, as well as forms of speech. Gender in speech analysis is now understood as "[g]enders . . . conceptualized as plural, with a range of femininities and masculinities available to speakers at any point in time" (Coates 2004: 4). In a survey of differences between masculine and feminine communicative competence (meaning grammar and appropriateness of usage) in a range of linguistic settings in Great Britain, Coates noted that masculine speakers tend to dominate the conversation in a variety of different environments by interrupting, by controlling the topics of the conversation, and by becoming silent. In contrast, feminine speech style uses more tentative speech and more linguistic forms associated with politeness, and makes greater use of minimal responses (like "uh-huh") to indicate support for the speaker. In single-sex conversations, a different pattern emerges. Whereas masculine style tends to stress disagreement or ignoring each other's utterances, feminine style in conversations with others is collaborative, melding or blending their talk. They tend to talk about people and feelings, rather than about things. In contrast, men pursue a style of competitiveness, individual assertion, and power, and discuss current affairs, travel, and sport (Coates 2004: 128). These different styles sometimes result in miscommunication in public areas between the sexes. Females in positions of authority may be perceived as less powerful and assertive than their male peers because of the speech patterns they use.

More recently, the relationship between language and sexuality in the linguistic tactics of gay men has also been the subject of research. Droschel asks: "[H]ow do a sample of British and American gay men negotiate and construct their sexual identities through their knowledge and use of gay slang?" (2007: 118). She demonstrates the way in which the growth of heterogeneity in the gay community has resulted in a diversification of vocabulary use with the development of different linguistic subsets. She focuses on the way in which "gay individuals explore and constantly recreate the lexical system in order to construct their identities" (2007: 137).

African American Vernacular English

African American Vernacular English (AAVE)

Speech patterns and norms adopted in some settings that demonstrate identity and community affiliation.

Differences in language usage in the United States parallel regional and class, as well as racial and ethnic differences. The speech of the African American community, referred to in the past as Black English (BE) but now referred to as **African American Vernacular English (AAVE)**, in contrast to Standard English (SE), is the subject of much scholarly research and debate (Rickford 2006). AAVE was originally viewed by standard-English speakers as the result of mistakes and deviations from SE, interpreted as deficits in the cultural behavior of its speakers. This view has now been replaced with understanding AAVE as a consistent, patterned form of communication used intergenerationally by a community of speakers.

Originally, it was believed that African languages and cultures were completely destroyed by the experience of slavery. However, today scholars have challenged this opinion and have come to the conclusion that the African heritage continues to exist in African American language and culture. Rickford suggests that AAVE may have originated from contact between African slaves and white settlers as "a simplified fusion of English and African languages—from which Ebonics evolved. Native to none of its speakers, a pidgin is a mixed language, incorporating elements of its users' native languages but with less complex grammar and fewer words than either parent language" (1996: 89). (See below for more discussion of pidgin languages.)

Linguists now recognize that AAVE should be viewed as a language system in itself, analyzed without reference to other dialects or speech patterns. Sociolinguists generally agree that language is an important aspect of the construction of cultural identity. But they also note that language acceptance and perception are widely contested issues. While sociolinguists acknowledge AAVE as a patterned, consistent, and infinitely creative linguistic form, its differences from standard English are often judged by non-specialists as "lazy English" or "slang." Educators are increasingly aware of the necessity of recognizing the patterns of AAVE and helping young students navigate the differences between their speech patterns and those of SE. Today AAVE plays a role in the construction of African American identity in a multicultural America. But people recognize that both AAVE and SE are necessary to improve one's life chances, since lack of SE competence may harm one in school and in the workplace, while absence of AAVE deprives one of status within one's ethnic group. In recent years, there has been an increase in the interest in multiple language patterns of African Americans and other under-represented minorities. Language agency and code-switching are illustrated by African American college students who choose lexical, phonological, and grammatical features of AAVE in some contexts in order to reinforce their affiliations with their peers (De Bose 2005: 139).

Selecting vocabulary and/or grammatical variations from different languages in a single conversation is referred to as **code-switching** or by some linguists as "code-mixing." This form of language accommodation is usually associated with bilingual speakers and listeners who are members of the same-language community, and illustrates linguistic agency as well as an awareness of the linguistic history of self and others in the conversation. Language accommodation can also be a means of identification with an ethnic or racial group other than one's own, as in the use of urban-styled hip-hop language in White youth culture. Cutler (2010) studied the use of hip-hop language and style by four foreign-born teenage informants who self-identified as White and were raised in predominantly White neighborhoods. "The role of Black America (and AAVE) as a key frame of reference in hip-hop culture . . . suggests that the emergence of local hip-hop language style is indeed a case of conscious identification with another group as well as a desire to project local distinctiveness" (Cutler 2010: 249). Although the informants demonstrated variation in their use of AAVE and other urban minority linguistic norms, they all internalized variables of hip-hop speech patterns to such a degree that they were identified as non-White by a significant proportion of peer-aged listeners. This demonstrates the ability of speakers to mobilize language agency in making conscious and concerted efforts to communicate affiliation with a group other than one's own. "Furthermore, this sort of accommodation emerges from a complex, long-term identity project . . . showing that individuals can accommodate to the speech of another group in the absence of systematic contact" (Cutler 2010: 264).

code-switching

The use of one or more languages or speech styles in conversation.

LANGUAGE CHANGE AND HISTORICAL LINGUISTICS

As noted in chapter 1, cultures are continually undergoing some degree of change. As language is a part of culture, it too is always changing. Of course, during one's lifetime, one may not aware of linguistic change, except for changes in vocabulary, particularly slang words and expressions. If we compare our language usage today with that of the language of Shakespeare's plays, the extent to which English has changed over the past centuries is obvious. It is apparent that present-day **dialect** differences represent developments, or language changes, from a single earlier form of the language. How do such dialect differences arise in the first place? **Speech communities** are made up of members of a group within a society who interact and speak

dialects

Variations within a single language between one speech community and another.

speech community

A group of people that interacts and speaks frequently with one another.

frequently with one another. One speech community that is very similar to a neighboring speech community will develop slight differences in pronunciation or vocabulary, differentiating it from its neighbor. As these differences increase, they become the basis for greater dialect differentiation. Dialect differentiation, over time, leads to further divergence and eventually to the development of two separate languages.

For example, English, Dutch, German, and the Scandinavian languages compose the Germanic language family—all descended from a common proto-language called Proto-Germanic. These European languages, along with other European and Asian languages, such as Persian, Hindi, and Bengali, form a large family of related languages called the Indo-European language family. All these languages are descended from a common ancestor, Proto-Indo-European. Where was this ancestral language located geographically? Recent research that combines linguistics with archaeology locates the original ancestral language in Anatolia (present-day Turkey) about 8,700 years ago. The earliest branches, Hittite and Tocharian, split off from Proto-Indo-European at this time. According to Renfrew, Indo-European languages were spread by the earliest farmers who migrated from Anatolia into Greece and the Balkans, bringing with them agricultural technologies and the Indo-European language (Atkinson and Gray 2006: 102).

A second large migration, referred to as the Kurgan expansion, occurred around five thousand years ago from the Ukrainian area, leading to the divergence of the Slavic, Germanic, Italic, and Celtic subfamilies. Since the Proto-Indo-European speakers had words for beaver, otter, birch, and aspen, and used euphemisms for the ritually important bear, they must have lived in a temperate climate—like that of the Ukraine. Other Indo-European speakers moved south into Iran and southeast into India, resulting in the diversification that produced other branches of Indo-European. Not all languages spoken in Europe are part of this family. Finnish and Hungarian belong to the Finno-Ugric family, while Basque is completely unrelated to any other language, and is called a "language isolate."

For languages where written records have existed for millennia, the historical sequence of language development is verifiable. Languages thought to be related are studied using the **comparative approach**. This can be illustrated with an example from the Germanic languages. The English word dance has as its equivalent the German word Tanz, and the English word door has as its equivalent the German Tur. These forms have the same meaning, and their phonemic structures are similar but not identical. These pairs are referred to as **cognates**. The initial *d* in English regularly corresponds to the initial *t* in German. These two forms represent modern divergences from the original phoneme in Proto-Germanic. This is just a single example of the many sound correspondences to be found between German and English.

As a result of their earlier association with small-scale societies, anthropologists have studied the spoken languages of indigenous peoples around the world. These indigenous languages did not have a written form. In the same manner as the European languages, these languages are organized in terms

comparative approach

Comparing societies to uncover similarities and reveal differences.

cognate

In linguistics, words in two different languages that resemble one another and demonstrate that the two languages are related to each other.

of language families, utilizing the concept of cognates and the comparative method. Some of these language families are very large, encompassing many languages, whereas others may be very small or may even be isolates, like Basque. Recently, linguists have shown some relationship between language families like Indo-European and Uralic, Altaic, Eskimo-Aleut, and Chukchi-Kamchatka, placing them in a single super-family, Eurasitic. The objective of this research is to try to show the historical relationships between language families and the way in which different language groups developed as Homo sapiens spread out from Africa and migrated across Europe and Asia. The aim is eventually to create a model of proto-languages from which other languages developed.

Languages also change as a result of **diffusion**, or borrowing from speakers of one language by speakers of another language. This may be the borrowing of words, sounds, or grammatical forms. Contact and borrowing come about in a number of different ways, some of them peaceful, others not. An excellent example of language change as a consequence of military conquest occurred after the Norman conquest of England (AD 1066). The Norman invaders, the conquering class, were speakers of an earlier version of French, while the subjugated English spoke Anglo-Saxon, a Germanic language that was the precursor of English. The English borrowed a series of terms referring to different kinds of cooked meat from the language of the French. The cow (Saxon), when cooked, became beef (boeuf in French); calf (Saxon) became veal (veau in French); sheep (Saxon) became mutton (mouton in French); and swine (Saxon) became pork (porc in French). The French words for the cooked versions have been incorporated into English.

diffusion

The process by which a culture trait that originates in one place spreads to another.

Contact Languages: Pidgins and Creoles

European exploration and colonization of many parts of the world brought indigenous language speakers into contact with European languages. This sets into motion linguistic processes that result in new contact languages, referred to as **pidgins** and **creoles**. Pidgins are created by contact conditions, like trade, that require the development of a "makeshift" language to enable communication between two or more language communities (McWhorter 2005: 11). The most important characteristic of pidgins is that for all speakers, they are second languages. Governed by rules, they have vocabularies and grammars that are simpler than either of their source languages. They are sufficiently different from their source languages so as not to be mutually intelligible with them. Creole languages have their origins in the mixture of two languages as the result of contact or conquest. But over time they become stable and are learned by children as first languages. Gullah, the language spoken on the Sea Islands off the coast of Georgia, is considered by some to be a creole, structurally related to the creole languages that developed on some Caribbean islands where English was the colonial language (Rickford 2006: 28).

pidgin

A lingua franca that developed when people speaking different languages but no common language needed to communicate with one another.

creole

A stable language resulting from contact situations that is acquired by subsequent generations as the native language.

Several varieties of pidgins developed in the Pacific region out of nautical and trade jargons used during the nineteenth century. These have since become national languages. Tok Pisin is the Melanesian variety of pidgin. It originated among workers in the German colony of New Guinea, especially those from the islands of New Ireland and New Britain, who were recruited to work on German-owned plantations in Samoa. They brought the pidgin back with them on their return. Fifteen percent of the vocabulary of Tok Pisin derives from Tolai, spoken in the area around Rabaul, on New Britain, the early headquarters of the German colonial government (Lynch 1998: 223–24).

When a pidgin language is no longer a second language, it is categorized by linguists as a creole (Baker and Muhlhausler 2007: 92). For over one hundred years, Tok Pisin remained a second language for its speakers, second to their native language. However, in the twentieth century, during the postwar period, Tok Pisin began to become the primary language for families in the urban areas of Papua New Guinea, where the adults came from different language areas as a consequence of increasing rural urban migration and social mobility. Since the independence of Papua New Guinea in 1975, Tok Pisin has been the official language of the nation. Harrison notes that when he revisited the village of Avatip, on the Sepik River, where he had done fieldwork in the late 1970s, the children no longer spoke their vernacular language; Papua New Guinea Pidgin (Tok Pisin) was now their first language (Harrison 2001: 4).

Linguistic Imperialism

Linguistic imperialism, a major consequence of contact, colonialism, and imperialism, is the primary factor causing language loss and extinction. Before the arrival of Europeans in the late fifteenth century, the Pacific area was one of marked linguistic diversity. Up to four thousand languages were spoken there, most of them in Melanesia, where two million people speak (or spoke) one quarter of the world's languages. This intensive language diversity existed side by side with bi- and multilingualism. As a consequence of European colonization and language imperialism, English, French, German, or one of the pidgins (discussed earlier) became the dominant language in the respective colonial areas. A trend from linguistic diversity to monolingualism and language disappearance began. There were many changes in the indigenous languages that persisted in postcolonial states, including loss of lexical items and changes in grammatical forms. Indigenous language maintenance in new nation-states like Papua New Guinea pits multilingualism against building a national culture with a single national language. Tok Pisin (or NeoMelanesian, its more formal name) was adopted as the national language as a matter of policy. In urban areas of Papua New Guinea, intermarriage between different ethnic and language-use communities is common, and Tok Pisin is the language of the household as well as of the public arena. In rural areas, however, older people often speak only the indigenous language, while others may be bilingual, speaking the indigenous language and Tok Pisin.

In some states in the United States, there have been attempts at legislation to make English, and only English, the official language. The argument advanced for doing so, as in the case of Papua New Guinea, is that the use of one official language reinforces the notion of a single American culture and state. This represents a kind of linguistic imperialism in the face of the current multilingual diversity in the United States. Language domination is especially apparent in education and the attitude of schools toward multiple language use. We also see negotiation of the use of languages other than English in courtrooms and voting booths as well as in the private sector.

In the United States, state Voting Rights Acts require that voters have access to ballots in the languages of minority populations in excess of 5 percent of the voting district's population, based on census data. These accommodations vary by state and county and only mildly weaken the "English only" language policies of the United States.

Language Loss and Revitalization

Many linguists now predict that by the end of the twenty-first century only half of the world's 6,000 to 7,000 languages may still be spoken. The prediction of dramatic language loss worldwide has generated considerable discussion by scholars and activists about the value of linguistic diversity within states and transnationally. Discussions on language use and retention consider the political implications for the rights of minority language speakers when national languages become the lingua franca of law and education. Some rights-based perspectives include the right of continued fluency in and exposure to "mother tongues" as inalienable universal human rights. Linguistic scholars and activists explore the variable strategies and outcomes of different efforts at reestablishing linguistic competence in communities where the number of fluent speakers is dwindling.

When a language no longer has a significant number of speakers who use it intergenerationally, conversationally, and spontaneously, does that mean that the culture no longer exists? When a community is bilingual in their indigenous language and in the dominant language of the nation-state, we find that each language may have its own functions and that switching from one language to another follows predictable patterns. Even when the trend toward monolingualism progresses, and only the grandparental generation speaks the indigenous language fluently, underlying patterns of language retention may be perpetuated.

Woodbury cites an example of this type of linguistic retention in an Alaskan community. College students from Inupiaq and Yupik communities use a variety of qualifiers in written English essays to avoid sounding assertive. Circumspection is part of the way an individual should behave in

BOX 3.1 | Innovations in Language Revitalization

Performers in the Brazilian heavy metal rock band Arandu Arakuaa perform in the dress and language of the indigenous Tupi Guarani. Their lyrics document indigenous rights and struggles in Brazil and are bringing to a new audience awareness of the endangered Tupi Guarani language and culture.

Educators and scholars of language revitalization are constantly exploring new methods of bringing this issue to the attention of native communities as well the general public. Two innovations in these efforts include a heavy metal band in Brazil, and a series of graphic publications, or comic books, in Mexico.

In Brazil, the band Arandu Arakuaa produces music using traditional instruments like flutes and foot rattles and lyrics that are sung in the endangered Tupi Guarani language (Ferreira 2022). The band's founder, Zhandi Aquino, is a descendent of a Tupi-speaking family in northern Brazil. Some of the band's music is exclusively in the Tupi language and, when translated into Portuguese, poetically explores the struggles of the Tupi and other indigenous tribes in Brazil for survival, especially through control over their traditional lands and ways of life. Aquino combines his love of music with his connections to the Tupi Guarani language and culture and hopes to contribute to the national dialogue over the hundreds of endangered languages in Brazil. Videos of Arandu Arakuaa are available on YouTube with Portuguese subtitles that help introduce the music, language, and struggles of Brazil's indigenous peoples to the Brazilian public.

In Mexico, the comic book *Ar Metlaloke* (*The Tlaloques Hunter*) describes the adventures of Tlaloc, a tempestuous deity important in the belief system of the Ñäñho people of central Mexico (Gerry 2021). The graphic publication is written in Hñäñho, the language of the Ñäñho people, and translated into in Spanish and English. This publication and others documenting and recording Hñäñho have been produced in collaboration with sociolinguist Ewald Hekking and community members. Working with Severiano Andres de Jesus, a bilingual native of a Ñäñho community, they produced a grammar of the language and a bilingual dictionary. Hekking has also created a virtual course for teaching Hñäñho. Graphic novels and comic books are especially compelling to children, who respond enthusiastically to their recognition of sounds, characters, and images on the printed page unavailable in Spanish language sources.

their native culture (Woodbury 1993). This way of nativizing a replacement language is fragile and tentative as it is likely to disappear under pressure from the mainstream community. Woodbury concludes that while we cannot assume that a culture has "died" when language diminishes, a fundamental way of organizing the surrounding world eventually disappears because it simply cannot be translated into the words and phrases of the dominant language. According to Woodbury, "Loss of a language leads to an unraveling, or restructuring, or reevaluation of cultural tradition" (1993: 14).

Some Native groups are maintaining and rejuvenating their languages by developing language materials using the phonetic alphabet to teach the language in school settings. They use interactive computerized, digital, and online technologies for language instruction. Other forms of electronic mediation in language revitalization include radio and television broadcasting using minority languages. Scholars studying language-activism movements identify the differences in the understanding of language renewal between scholarly linguists and language activists. "Local language activists and professional linguists may hold divergent views on what it means to 'have' a language and, therefore, of what should be revitalized to begin with" (Eisenlohr 2004).

The use of electronic media for language revitalization highlights important differences in the processes of acquisition of language competence and maintenance in community and family and those settings requiring "mobilization of material and political resources" (Eisenlohr 2004: 25). Production and dissemination of digital language resources may require financial support from state and nongovernmental organizations for widespread community access to hardware and software. Community members may not all share the same goals or values around broadcast and digital content to be included, which often draws on English-language models for teaching or broadcast media. Advantages cited by activists in the use of digital and broadcast technologies is that their content can respond quickly and inexpensively to local input, thus enhancing their ability to mobilize community ownership, use, and support.

Language, Power, and Policy

As all of the above discussions illustrate, language use is always politically important and often represents policy decisions about language usage. These policies govern the use of languages in schools, in political discourse, and in the media. Policies of language usage are related to national identity movements in newly emerging nation-states. In the (former Soviet) Republic of Kazakhstan and in the Kyrgyz Republic, Russian is still spoken by the majority of these states' populations, a legacy of the Soviet-period educational and political institution building. Both of these former Soviet republics are promoting the use of their national languages as part of identity-building initiatives as independent states. To this end, all candidates for president in recent elections were required to submit to language competence tests to demonstrate their fluency in the written and spoken Kazakh and Kyrgyz languages in their respective countries. In the Kyrgyz Republic, these tests were televised. In both cases, the field of potential candidates was reduced when candidates were determined by the election commissions to have failed the Kazakh and Kyrgyz language competence examinations.

Political policy and power are involved when a government selects a particular language as a national language from a number of options. Political leaders in newly independent India in 1948 faced the need to establish language policy that reconciled India's linguistic plurality with widespread official use of English, the language of India's colonizers. The language diversity of India is widely acknowledged by linguists and politicians alike; the enumeration of this diversity also depends on political policy. Dasgupta notes that the 1961 census mentions 1,642 languages; the 1971 census reported 221, and the 1981 census 106 languages (2003: 25–26). Prior to independence from Great Britain, the primary language issues on the subcontinent were linguistic diversity and the relative statuses of Urdu, Hindi, Sanskrit, and English. Urdu use is associated with Muslims in South Asia, but spoken Urdu is generally understood by Hindi speakers. Hindi written in Devanagari script is the language associated with the northern part of India (often referred to as the Hindi belt) and followers of Hinduism. In southern India, unrelated languages such as Tamil, Kanada, and Telugu were also spoken. With the simultaneous partition of India, Pakistan, and East Pakistan in 1947, the new Indian government focused on a national language policy that favored Hindi and Hindustani (the spoken form of Hindi associated with many northern Indian states) using Devanagari script and English, already widely in use in legal and administrative systems.

The challenges faced by the Indian government in 1947 were similar to those of other newly independent states: debates around a national language and the use of the colonial language as well as the status and official uses of minority languages (Brown and Ganguly 2003: 3–5). The status of English in India was debated widely in the post-independence period; there were practical considerations for its retention in that it provided, unlike any of the Indian languages, an internationally recognized language of science, technology, law, and business. The counter argument was that a newly independent state could not establish its own identity until it abandoned a foreign colonial language and adopted one of its own (Brass 1994: 161).

The use of Hindi as a national language was challenged by its limited regional distribution in the southern half of India. Selection of Hindi would have hampered non-Hindi speakers' access to civil service positions, education, and many other economic and social benefits of citizenship. The Tamil-speaking states of the south of India were strongly opposed to this; in some parts of India, this opposition led to violent demonstrations between opposing sides of the language debates. However, compromises were instituted in the 1950s and 1960s. The final one included "the joint use of Hindi and English in Parliament, for the use of Hindi as the language of communication between the Center and the Hindi-speaking states and for the use of English for communications between the Center and non-Hindi-speaking states. However, the [language] Act and the overall compromise also contained multilingual elements, particularly on the matter of the languages of examinations for entry into the Indian Administrative Service and other Union services" (Brass 1994: 167). It is widely recognized now, however, that knowledge of the English language provides great advantages to people throughout India for employment in both national and international businesses. Although official school policy still maintains Hindi or Tamil mediums of instruction, people of all socioeconomic strata seek out private schools and tutorials instructing children in English.

World Englishes and the Spread of English

The English language spread over the world in multiple waves. It was first carried by English-speaking immigrants to what are today the United States, Canada, South Africa, Australia, and New Zealand. Different versions of the English language are spoken in all these countries. These differences were brought about through the process of dialect formation. The second spread of English was the consequence of England's colo-

Signage in some commercial settings in China uses both English and local languages, as in this announcement of the opening of a new outlet of a coffee chain in a Tianjin shopping mall.

nial expansion to parts of Africa, South and Southeast Asia, and the Caribbean. English is spoken today in countries such as Nigeria, Ghana, Kenya, Tanzania, South Africa, India, Pakistan, Bangladesh, Malaysia, and Singapore.

Linguists have emphasized two somewhat contradictory processes. On the one hand, in the context of Britain's colonial empire, the spread of English is an example of linguistic imperialism, which produces a hierarchical ordering of the speech of colonial "masters" and that of indigenous speakers. As Pennycook points out, "There are . . . continuing relations of global inequality . . . of economic, political, military, communicative (communication and transport), cultural and social imperialism—and the global spread of English" (2001: 61). English, however, is the language of global commerce. People throughout the postcolonial period learned the language for practical economic reasons, rather than having been forced to learn English by their colonial masters. English, the former colonial language, was selected by the African National Congress for use in its struggle against apartheid in South Africa (Ricento 2006: 4). In postcolonial South Asia, learning English served several different functions. Fluency in English among the educated classes has enabled India to be in the forefront of the computer and outsourcing industries. English was also useful in other areas. It served as a medium of communication when people spoke mutually unintelligible indigenous languages; it was a method of gaining further education; it helped in legal and administrative areas; and finally it enabled entry into English literary genres such as English literary journals, newspapers, and political journals (Bhatt 2001: 531–32). The last point, however, is a source of controversy. Is it better for writers from former colonial areas to write in colonial languages (English or French) or in their indigenous language or dialect? World-famous writers such as Salmon Rushdie, Chinua Achebe, or V. S. Naipul have chosen English as their medium of expression. The language of hip-hop/rap, a part of American urban youth culture, has also spread to other parts of the world.

Many linguists have adopted a point of view that stresses that the context in which English is learned and spoken is uniquely different in different areas. The context in which English is learned in India is different from that of Nigeria or South Africa, so that in each of these areas a different variant of English is spoken. Instead of referencing the spread of the same form of English throughout the world, linguists speak about many World Englishes. Bhatt states that "nonnative English speakers thus created new, culture-sensitive and socially appropriate meanings—expressions of the bilingual's creativity—by altering and manipulating the structure and function of English in its new ecology" (2001: 534). He provides an example from the English that is spoken in India. There is a device in English known as "the tag question" to turn a statement into a question, such as: "He said he would come home early, didn't he?" In Indian English, such tag questions are transformed into: "You are going home soon, isn't it?" Politeness in verbal expression demands that the "you" and "he" forms be replaced by what is called an undifferentiated tag—"isn't it?" In the tag question example above, the way in which English is used by Indians is shaped and modified by Indian social structure.

Linguists who have adopted a World Englishes perspective—meaning that there are many forms of English, and not a single correct one with incorrect subservient variants—are aware that their view carries a political agenda with it. The external threat to indigenous languages that is posed by the spread of English is countered by the idea of "language rights," that is, "the right to identify with, to maintain and to fully develop one's mother tongue(s)" (Pennycook 2001: 63). Simultaneously, English competence is seen as a skill that people believe will best connect them and their children to the economic and social benefits of the increasing reach of globalization around the world. Learning English is therefore highly valued; whether and how it will be modified in the manners we have described above is an ongoing question.

SUMMARY

- Language allows humans to communicate cultural ideas and symbolic meanings from one generation to the next in a cumulative fashion, and to constantly create new cultural ideas.
- It is not clear when this human complex of speech and cognition emerged in human evolution.
- Every language has a small number of basic sounds, called phonemes, usually between twenty and forty, which are used in various combinations to make up the units of meaning.
- Phonemes do not carry meaning but function to differentiate words in terms of their meanings.
- The units of language that carry meaning are called "morphemes."
- The rules by which larger speech units, such as phrases and sentences, are formed compose the syntax of a language. The complete description of a language is its grammar.

- All languages are equally complex and share the same functions and basic structures. This is known as linguistic relativity.

- There is a close connection between the way language is organized and the way culture is organized, as seen in the systems of classification of the world of animals, the world of plants, or the system of colors.

- Sociolinguistics analyzes the social functions of speech and the agency of individuals in making choices about speech use.

- Different genders and age groups have different roles in society and differences in speech patterns.

- The speech patterns associated with urban African Americans, referred to as AAVE, has its own distinct phonology, morphology, and syntax and is not an incorrect or incomplete version of English. It constitutes an important marker of gender, life stage, and ethnic identity.

- Code-switching or code-mixing occurs when bilingual speakers use vocabulary and structures from both languages in conversation. These are examples of language accommodation and linguistic agency.

- Dialect differentiation over time may lead to further divergence and eventually to the development of two separate languages.

- Using the comparative method, scholars of linguistic history explore languages thought to be related to each other and that derive from a shared proto-language. The original homeland of the speakers is determined from the words for plants, trees, and animals in the proto-language.

- Aspects of language are continually borrowed by speakers of one language from another as the result of contact with new groups of people or through media.

- New languages, known as pidgins and creoles, developed when colonization brought European languages into contact with indigenous ones.

- English has spread over the world as a result of emigration, conquest, and the dominance of the language in global communications. The result is that there are many forms of English subsumed under the category "World Englishes," not a single correct one.

- Colonialism and imperialism have linguistic implications; during colonial rule and in postcolonial states local and indigenous language use is often discouraged, in hopes of replacing several different languages and dialects with one national language.

- Some human rights advocates claim that continued fluency in and exposure to the language of one's community is a basic human right. Many indigenous communities around the world are using different methods to assure that current and future generations have knowledge of their traditional languages.

KEY TERMS

African American Vernacular
  English (AAVE), 66
allophones, 60
code-switching, 67
cognates, 68
comparative approach, 68
creoles, 69
dialect, 67
diffusion, 69
ethnosemantics, 64
grammar, 62

lexicon, 62
linguistic agency, 65
linguistic imperialism, 70
linguistic relativity, 62
markedness, 64
morphemes, 61
phonemes, 60
pidgins, 69
sociolinguistics, 64
speech communities, 67
syntax, 61

SUGGESTED READINGS

Ahearn, Laura M. *Living Language: An Introduction to Linguistic Anthropology.* Malden, MA: Wiley-Blackwell, 2012.

> Introduction to the study of language in social contexts around the world through the contemporary theory and practice of linguistic anthropology.

Campbell, Lyle. *Historical Linguistics: An Introduction.* 4th ed. Cambridge, MA: MIT Press, 2021.

> A student-friendly text on the history of languages and the methods for the study of language history and change.

Perley, Bernard C. *Defying Maliseet Language Death Emergent Vitalities of Language, Culture, and Identity in Eastern Canada.* Lincoln: University of Nebraska Press, 2011.

> An ethnographic study by a member of this First Nation that examines the role of the Maliseet language and its survival in Maliseet identity.

SUGGESTED WEBSITES

https://nonverbal.ucsc.edu/

> This website explains multiple forms of nonverbal channels of communication, illustrating the meanings of how something is said, which is often more important than the words alone, or what is said.

http://www.linguisticsociety.org/issues-linguistics

> The website of the Linguistics Society of America contains this link (among others) to a discussion of contemporary linguistic approaches to gender, educational diversity, and ethics in linguistic research.

https://www.endangeredlanguages.com

> The website of the Endangered Languages Project explores multiple resources related to endangered languages around the world, including recordings and recent efforts at language revitalization.

Chapter 4

Who We Are

Culture and the Individual

LEARNING OBJECTIVES

- Understand the variations in parenting and alloparenting strategies.
- Explain the relationship between learning one's language and learning one's culture, values, and norms.
- Understand debates about "nature," "nurture," and the role of social environments in human behaviors.

- Explore theories about enculturation, socialization, and personality variation.
- Discuss how anthropologists study mental illness and wellness using cross-cultural perspectives.

WHAT ARE THE WAYS IN which individuals born into a particular society learn its culture, its language, and the behaviors that individuals in that culture consider appropriate? How does the human brain learn and store cultural knowledge? What is the relationship of individuals to their culture and the range of personality and behavior variation within cultures, and what are the ways of dealing with individuals whose behavior is outside the norms of their culture? This relates to how mental illness is defined in particular cultures and how innovators and rebels, whose societies sometimes consider them mentally ill, are viewed.

How babies learn to recognize significant individuals, respond to their voices, and then form words and more complex thoughts to communicate with them has been of interest to developmental psychologists for over a century. Some twentieth-century linguists and psychologists focused on the speed with which human children acquire linguistic competence as well as the decline of this ability in adulthood. This is evident to any college student trying to learn a second language in a foreign language class. Rapid childhood language acquisition skills are universal; all human babies in all cultures have the ability within two to three years of birth to recognize and navigate the language being spoken around them. While learning language they are simultaneously learning cultural norms, behaviors, and categories communicated to them by their caregivers. The universality of these learning skills in human babies suggests that these are innate capabilities present at birth. They are widely believed to be the result of the physical heritage of babies, most particularly the brain, its neuro-anatomy, and sensory organs of all human newborns.

Species-wide characteristics in humans raise questions about the evolutionary history of those traits. Scholars in the discipline of **evolutionary psychology** (also known as "sociobiology") try to understand the adaptive significance of these skills throughout human evolution. They may compare the skills and abilities of human babies to the newborns of other species. It is obvious by comparing newborn human babies to newborn foals or deer, for example, that other animals are born with skills to navigate their environments that human babies do not have. Within hours of their birth these four-legged animals can stand, be mobile, locate their mothers, and begin feeding. Human babies are totally dependent on caregivers for a much longer period of time before they have comparable mobility and coordination.

This basic observation identifies the extended period of dependence of human babies and toddlers as opposed to other species. Prolonged dependence suggests to physical anthropologists that human babies are "born too soon," as opposed to other animals, who express the capacity for physical mobility and contact with those around them simultaneously with birth. These human deficits are, however, compensated for with other skills. The capacity for human babies to bond with those around them in an intense and sustained way helps assure protection from others, which facilitates their physical survival. Evolutionary psychologists and physical anthropologists generalize about how inherited physical characteristics that facilitate the capacity for social communication confer adaptive advantage; these advantages also help assure survival into adulthood as well as the passing on of these traits to future generations.

evolutionary psychology

The application of Darwinian principles of natural selection to attempts at understanding the evolution of cultural norms.

PARENTING AND ALLOPARENTING

Uniquely human social skills and traits are seen in the behaviors between babies and caregivers. Sarah Blaffer Hrdy (2009) argues that a critical factor in understanding the evolutionary history of prolonged dependence is to recognize that both human infants and their biological mothers, unique among other species, have evolved multiple strategies for social behavior that help assure the survival of helpless, highly dependent infants. Hrdy suggests that humans are uniquely "cooperative breeders" in that human mothers share care responsibilities with others in their social group to a degree unknown in other species, even our closest primate relatives. Chimpanzee and gorilla mothers are the sole caregivers of their infants and jealously guard contact between their infants and others. Humans welcome the participation of "allomothers," or other mothers, and in virtually all cultures and communities, encourage the sharing of the care of their infants with trusted members of their social group. Simultaneously, babies have evolved social skills that help them bond with those around them, such as the ability practically at birth to grab onto a finger of a caregiver, and at a very early age to make eye contact and smile. The communication skills of both mothers and infants assure the survival of highly dependent babies to get them through the very long period of dependence on others for food, protection, and the time needed for acquisition of more complex and symbolic skills. Acquiring speech, communication techniques, and cultural knowledge in this protective environment eventually enables babies and toddlers to navigate their environment independently.

Fathers as Caregivers

The role of fathers as providers and caregivers, in both evolutionary perspectives and contemporary ethnographic settings, is now the focus of research on alloparenting. "Unlike most mammals, human fathers cooperate with mothers to care for young to an extraordinary degree. Human paternal care likely evolved alongside our unique life history strategy of raising slow-developing, energetically costly children, often in rapid succession" (Gettler et al. 2020). Assumptions about paternal roles in raising children often generalize the impacts on families of "present" or "absent" fathers. More recent approaches to understanding paternal contributions go far beyond this simple binary and explore how fathers contribute to the lives of their children in a variety of household structures. In some settings fathers may tend to spend less time in direct contact with their children than do mothers or allomothers, but the quality of their interaction is significant to language acquisition and social **enculturation**. Scholars who study the nature of these interactions focus on the outcomes of these differences between the styles and content of fathers' and mothers' language communication with children; fathers tend to use more challenging language and complex sentence structure with their children, and may use more "rough and tumble" play than other caregivers (Gettler et al. 2020: 149).

enculturation

The process by which cultural rules and norms are learned and acquired by individuals.

Migrating Parents and Global Labor Markets

Understanding alloparenting strategies and their effects on the developmental outcomes of children is significant in the context of contemporary global migration and transnational families. These are important issues throughout the world, especially in areas that privilege maternal out-migration as well as both male and female participation in global labor markets. In a study of Caribbean families with migrating parents, Nelson (2020) observes that most theoretical models of household parental strategies assume a two-parent household and tend to pathologize a single-parent setting. But where systematic ethnographic study is carried out, anthropologists have documented that alloparenting, or extramaternal care, is an integral aspect of human childrearing (Nelson 2020: 355). In the Caribbean, maternal out-migration and alloparental practices are motivated by employment opportunities abroad that are not available domestically to well-educated Caribbean women. The surrogate parents to children whose mothers work abroad are usually maternal kin, often grandmothers; the children who remain at home experience great variation in, and long-term effects of, being raised by surrogates. "The dynamic aspect of the care practices enacted by these transnational families reveals the behavioral flexibility that has been integral to human survival" (2020: 355).

There is of course great disruption in the lives of children whose biological mothers and/or fathers migrate abroad to pursue work not available locally. The working mothers abroad invariably send remittances (financial transfers) to the caregivers at home. They often supplement this with regular shipments of material goods, clothing, new technology, and health supplies. These regular packages signal to the alloparents and the children that their mothers remain committed to their children's well-being. "But the separation from one or both parents has consequences to the psychological well-being and educational outcomes of these children. Boys especially may suffer from educational deficits and poor performance in school. Even after reunification or as adults, these people may feel a continuing sense of abandonment and lack of trust in their relationships" (Nelson 2020: 365).

WHAT IS HUMAN NATURE? NATURE, NURTURE, AND BEYOND THE DICHOTOMY

The evolution of social skills and behaviors in human beings is a subject of tremendous interest to scientists as well as to the general public. Studying the species-wide evolutionary heritage of human behavior involves a deep knowledge of the evolution of the human brain as well as genetic evidence. It also involves conjecture and inference, especially in the areas of social behavior. As the **human genome** is more fully explored, questions about the genetic origins of disease and physical characteristics are slowly being uncovered. In the popular imagination, this often leads to curiosity about "the gene" for psychological expression and behavior, or "the genetic nature" of these phenomena. This presents scholars with important challenges in explaining what

human genome

The complete set of DNA codes in a human cell.

is known, and what is not known, about genetic expression, human behavior, and intergenerational inheritance of genetic characteristics. One major challenge in the study of what is presumed to be "human nature" is to assure that characteristics attributed to all human beings are not just those cultural norms of the scientists doing the studies and/or the audiences who read these studies (Henrich, Heine, and Norenzayan 2010). Another challenge is to assure that methodologies and outcomes are not influenced, consciously or unconsciously, by political biases and preexisting expectations of the readers and researchers.

Research on genes and behavior overwhelmingly shows that behavior and cognition in individuals is invariably the result of both "nature" (inherited characteristics) and "nurture" (the totality of the environment within which an individual exists). Most behavior is influenced by many genes, and is therefore polygenic. "There are lots of genes, each can affect many characteristics, and the effect of any one gene frequently depends on the other genes it is associated with" (Hosken et al. 2019: 2). In addition, the environment within which a person's genetic inheritance is being expressed plays an enormous role in their behavior; environmental factors include family, nutrition, socioeconomic status, and access to important resources like education and a stress-free environment. "Traits are produced in a [human] individual by complex interactions that make it impossible to cleanly assign the outcome to genes or environment" (Barrett and Stulp 2019: 205).

It is now evident that genetic heritage is not fixed and immutable throughout a person's lifetime. Intergenerational socioeconomic status is itself a driver of both genetics and behavior, and is recognized to be a major feedback influence on genes, health, and behavior. **Epigenetics** recognizes how environmental factors impacting an individual can affect the person's biological processes, such as cell division, which will in turn create modifications to genetic material that may impact behavior or phenotype expression. These genetic changes alter the physical structure of DNA and may be expressed through changes in gametes, or eggs and sperm cells, over the course of a person's lifetime.

epigenetics

Genetic changes that take place during an individual's lifetime as the result of environmental influences.

Evidence now shows that unborn babies in the last trimester of pregnancy respond to familiar sounds and can distinguish their mother's language from foreign languages hours after birth.

HOW CHILDREN LEARN TO COMMUNICATE

The environment into which a child is born plays a critical role in what and how the child subsequently learns. As we have discussed previously, learning the language (or languages) spoken in the parental household is a basic component of the child learning the norms and variations of their culture. Language learning begins even before the child is born. Recent advances in research techniques have shown that a fetus can hear

The use of "baby talk" or "motherese" by parents and caregivers is a global phenomenon. Adults around the world speak more slowly and exaggerate pitch and tone when they speak to babies. This special communication style plays an important part in language learning by engaging babies' emotions and highlighting language structure.

and differentiate voices from other sounds, such as music or white noise filtered through amniotic fluid, as early as the last trimester before birth. Auditory stimuli elicit changes in fetal heart rate and in motor responses such as kicking. Since it has been shown that newborns immediately identify their biological mother's voice, it is clear that this recognition is learned prenatally, when the fetus learns to recognize its mother's intonation and styles of verbal tones and stress. At four days or earlier, newborns can discriminate phonemes and perceive well-formed syllables as units. They can distinguish the difference between the rhythmic characteristics of mother's language and other languages. Between six and twelve months, infants lose the ability to perceive nonnative speech contrasts as they move to master the sound structure of their own speech community.

Parents and caregivers use a special language in our society in their interactions with their infants. In some cultures, parents may speak to the fetus. In this speech style referred to as "motherese," the parent stresses patterns within words and sentences. Repetitions and rising intonation are used to attract the infant's attention; high pitch and exaggerated tones engage infants in speech production. The rhythm pattern, not word meaning, attracts the attention of the infant. This demonstrates that social interaction plays an important role in encouraging infant communication. There is considerable variation cross-culturally in the extent to which parents and other adults modify their speech for children or even speak directly to children, yet children still learn language; hence language development does not depend exclusively on the existence of a single caregiver.

Between two and three months of age, during which time the baby is learning to create sounds, the infant produces sounds that are nonlinguistic; between four and six months, its sound production consists of vowel- and consonant-like sounds (these sounds may go beyond the native language, but when not heard often, they are dropped); from seven months onward, other vowel and consonant transitions like "da-da" are produced; by ten months, the infant's native tongue begins to affect the types of sounds produced; just past the first year meaningful word production usually begins.

The building of infant vocabulary relates to external factors such as gender—girls tend to produce language earlier than boys because girls' brains mature somewhat faster. Parental linguistic competence, socioeconomic status, education, social competence, and attitudes toward child rearing are also factors that relate to the way parents interact linguistically with the child. Although infants do not produce comprehensible words until between twelve and twenty months, they can understand words before that point. It has recently been shown that children as young as fourteen months can also learn the connections between words and objects (Diesendruck 2007: 271). By twenty-four months, toddlers can produce fifty different words. At

BOX 4.1 | "Old Enough!"

In 2022 Netflix began streaming episodes of a Japanese reality show that has been seen on Nippon TV since 1991. The short episodes, averaging around fifteen minutes, show the progress of toddlers, some as young as two years old, attempting to run household errands on their own, navigating public streets and engaging with shopkeepers and strangers without direct supervision. There are off-camera safety supervisors following the child, a narrator tracking the child's progress, and an audience reacting to the child's successes and failures in each episode. The series has been viewed in Europe and Asia since its inception over three decades ago.

"The show's popularity in Japan is a reflection of the country's high level of public safety, as well as a parenting culture that sees toddlers' independence as a key marker of their development" (Ueno and Ives 2022). According to a child development expert in Japan, the show illustrates the typical norms of raising children in Japan, which can appear to be surprising to viewers in North America. These norms include early adaptation of managing daily tasks for the household, as well as in school.

The episodes explore the behaviors that are encouraged to actualize the cultural norms of responsibility to others and independence in executing these responsibilities. They also represent the perception in Japan of the safety of neighborhood streets. But not everyone supports the concepts and ideas behind these episodes. One father expressed that it was painful to watch his two-year old attempt, and fail, to do errands encouraged by the child's mother. Some critics point out that the contemporary perception of the safety of streets outside the home is overestimated by many, and that the series originated in a time of lower crime and greater safety on the streets. Others question the fee paid to the family as a source of possible coercion in getting the children to perform errands on camera.

The series, and reactions to it, certainly illuminate differences in the values that are communicated to children in different countries around the world. And it has generated debate in Japan about how toddlers should best learn these values in a changing public safety environment.

first, single words are used to designate whole concepts and categories; for example, the use of the word *dog* for all four-legged animals. Learning the meanings of words does not occur in a vacuum. Cognitive development and social constraints (i.e., aspects of the child's social environment) all play a role in language learning. "[F]rom as early as 12 months of age, children themselves actively monitor meaning—relevant social clues that others exhibit, and put these clues to work to guide inferences about reference and meaning" (Baldwin and Meyer 2007: 100).

Infants begin to detect the use of word order and verb tense from seven to eighteen months of age (Gerken 2007: 184–85). A study presented 10.5-month-olds with normal English sentences and those in which determiners and nouns were reversed. The children listened longer to the unmodified sentences, suggesting that they were able to tell the difference between the two. This shows that English-speaking children soon learn the importance of word order in their language. Although sentence production at two years is rudimentary, the child has already become sensitive to complex grammatical forms and the nature of word order. It is clear, however, that sensitivity to grammar is greater than production of grammatical form. Grammatical speech, in the form of word combination, can begin with as few as 50 to 150 words.

Word order is an integral part of syntax. Nouns, either as subject or object, refer to things; verbs refer to actions. Children at age three years or so begin using sentences and become aware that word position in the sentence (i.e., grammar) determines meaning (semantics). As grammar is learned, the precise meaning and use of different verbs are learned, and mistakes are made less and less frequently. Some studies have revealed cross-linguistic differences in the development of the use of nouns and verbs. Children usually learn nouns first, except when learning non-Western languages such as Chinese, Korean, Tzotzil, and Tzeltzal, in which verbs are more salient in communication (Tomasello and Bates 2001: 59).

The socioeconomic status of the household in which the child is mastering language skills is the result of forces outside of the control of household members. Studies in cultural variation and language acquisition support the conclusions of language socialization researchers who currently work in poverty contexts in the United States and elsewhere. They stress that household learning environments are related to macropolitical economic process resulting from colonialism, postcolonial institutions, and globalization. Their work "continue(s) to confirm that there is no single best pathway for linguistic and cultural learning; instead they show how these practices are shaped by cultural differences and preferences, as well as by historical, political, economic, and social constraints" (Paugh and Riley 2019: 3036–307). They also demonstrate "that exposure to alternative language ideologies, communicative strategies, and childrearing practices can lead to children developing into resilient members of speakers for their community even in contexts of extreme structural inequality" (Paugh and Riley 2019: 307).

Learning Cultural Norms

Sociocultural information is encoded in the organization of conversation and behavior, and from earliest infancy, children acquire cultural knowledge as they are involved in observation and interactions. Children learn language from those surrounding them, those who care for them, and those with whom they interact; they also learn social roles, politeness and deference toward elders, autonomy, assertiveness, and initiative. Children learn the appropriate ways to operate successfully in the all-important reciprocity and exchange activities in which they are involved. They learn cultural values and what is appropriate behavior for a child in their culture. In Kaluli society in Papua New Guinea, for example children learn that autonomy and assertiveness are valued in their culture; Samoan children learn that deference toward elders is valued. Japanese children learn that indirectness and circumscribed behavior are valued rather than directness (Schieffelin and Ochs 1996).

Particular forms of language as they relate to correct forms of behavior in each society are taught to children. Children raised in Chillihuani, a Quecha-speaking village in the highlands of Peru, grow up in very marginal living conditions where "specific behavioral norms centering on respect are necessary to make society work and assure survival" (Bolin 2006: 151). This is an egalitarian society in which children at an early age are "introduced to a culture of respect . . . to other people and the deities but [also] . . . to all forms of life" (2006: 33). Children are raised in a permissive atmosphere and at a young age are "introduced to the unwritten law of reciprocity, the hallmark of Andean life" (2006: 152). They grow up within an extended family and participate in adult activities, learning through observation in an environment where children are treated with respect and take on work tasks when they feel ready for them. The norm of reciprocity is found in a great many other societies as well and is introduced in different stages of the life cycle.

Self-reliance is more valued in some societies than in others. It is inculcated in the young infant through the process of **enculturation**. Before World War II, self-reliance was encouraged and fostered in both American infants and German infants, but after World War II, in America, an ideology of parental protection replaced this. American mothers never leave infants alone and rush to pick them up when they cry, believing that if they were to

---

BOX 4.2 | Who Are the WEIRDEST People in the World?

Research on human behavior and psychology has historically assumed that there are fundamental universal processes that can be identified as shared by all humans, and that a theory or conclusion drawn by experimentation can be applied across different population groups. Anthropologists have long supported the view that most behavior derives from cultural norms and culture-specific forms of enculturation. This debate was highlighted in a highly influential article published in 2010 in the journal *Behavior and Brain Sciences*, with the intriguing title "The Weirdest People in the World?" (Henrich, Heine, and Norenzayan 2010). The article analyzes the methodologies of hundreds of psychological and behavioral studies, and concludes that their findings are drawn from a highly specific group of subjects: people from Western, educated, industrialized, rich and democratic societies (WEIRD), and most specifically, American college undergraduates.

This evidence has important implications for thinking about the generalizability of psychological research findings and human variation. "The findings suggest that members of WEIRD societies, including young children, are among the least representative populations one could find for generalizing about behavior—hence, there are no obvious *a priori* grounds for claiming that a particular behavioral phenomenon is universal based on sampling from a single subpopulation" (Henrich, Heine, and Norenzayan 2010: 61). In other words, it is theoretically unjustified to claim universal psychological characters, or make statements about human nature, based on research of one group that is highly unusual when compared with the rest of the world's population.

The authors of the article conclude with their "vision for the future of scientific efforts to understand the foundations of human psychology and behavior," including collaborative large-scale interdisciplinary research with international participants, using long-term data and multiple indicators and research strategies (Henrich, Heine, and Norenzayan 2010: 122).

These suggestions do not discourage research into cultural variability but will serve to enhance its legitimacy and applicability, important characteristics in research addressing issues of human diversity, interaction and understanding in our globalized world.

do otherwise, the child would feel abandoned and not develop a secure sense of attachment. In contrast, German mothers may leave an infant alone while they go out shopping, and will not rush to pick up crying children. They want the infant to be enculturated into a sense of independent self-reliance and are concerned lest the child become "spoiled." At ten months of age, German infants expect less attention from their mothers than do American infants. These differences in child-rearing practices between Germans and Americans begin during the first year of life and are part of each culture's concepts of moral virtue (Levine and Norman 2001: 91). German concepts of "self-reliance" contrast with the American precept of parental protection given freely.

Different cultures emphasize different relational values in their child-rearing practices. While some emphasize assertiveness and self-reliance, others emphasize just the opposite—that the child must learn its appropriate subordinate position in relation to its elders. Some cultures stress the need to foster the close attachment between parent and child, and others teach the child to keep one's true feelings from others. It is apparent that each culture favors a certain set of personality traits. To achieve this, children are brought up to behave in culturally desirable ways.

Nonverbal Communications

Sign languages are not universally understood. Across the globe, more than three hundred sign languages are formally recognized. Also, it is now apparent that a country's spoken tongue does not dictate which sign language is used by the deaf and hard of hearing communities in a particular linguistic environment. Like any linguistic system, sign language is taught and learned using a symbolic system understood by the community of speakers.

In addition to verbal language use, we communicate an enormous amount of information through nonverbal communication, which includes facial expression, tone, gestures using arms and hands, body posture and position, distance, touching, and gaze. Nonverbal communication is equally important to communication as verbal language use. Body gestures are often used to supplement verbal forms; they can be used to emphasize emotional content when using language. Think about the many different ways and forms of nonverbal communication you might invoke, for example, when communicating to someone else your displeasure at their lateness for a social engagement. The simple statement in English "You are late" can be articulated in many different ways that nuance the meaning of the statement. The emphasis could be placed on "you," signaling that the other was late and the speaker was not. The emphasis could be on "late," communicating displeasure at the lateness. Foot tapping, obvious looking at a watch or clock, and gestures, such as pointing at the other person, communicate the speaker's displeasure.

Body gestures are also used to replace language in many different settings and are referred to as "emblems." Emblems may be used when speech will not be heard, as in a crowd, or when spoken forms are inappropriate. The so-called peace sign, or making a V with two fingers with the palm facing

outward, communicates multiple meanings in Western cultures around ideas of reducing or eliminating conflict. The use of "secret handshakes" and complex repertoires of body movements and upper-body touching communicate both greeting and shared-group affiliation. Direct gaze, of which eye contact is one example, in Western cultures, communicates honesty or candor in the speaker's verbal community. But in many other cultures, it is disrespectful to look directly into the eyes of an elder or superior.

These examples of nonverbal communication illustrate that they are culturally situated and symbolically understood as part of a culture-specific communication repertoire. Some cultures encourage the use of hand and arm gestures to emphasize verbal content; others discourage it as inappropriate expression in public. Touching and space between speakers is also symbolically shaped, and is therefore culturally constructed. The meaning and interpretation of touching and body closeness during speech may also be gender specific; these gestures may be appropriate when people of the same gender are in conversation, but not appropriate across genders. Sometimes people mistakenly believe that nonverbal forms of communication are universal and will be understood by everyone in the same way. This is not so, and as these examples illustrate, can often lead to misunderstanding and lack of communication. Gestures that are welcoming in one culture may be inappropriate, rude, or hostile in another. Learning the nonverbal forms of communication and their meanings are part of learning the cultural environment of specific communication systems.

Learning Gender Roles

Gender roles and appropriate behaviors are also acquired during the socialization and language acquisition processes. If boys are expected to be more assertive than girls in a particular culture, they are taught by the individuals around them to express themselves in that way. Their assertive use of language reflects this gender difference. Research shows that in preadolescent years, some American girls become less confident and more deferential; however African American girls may become more assertive and self-sufficient (Rogoff 2003: 192).

In the Middle East and North Africa, differentials in gender treatment begin at birth, when there is greater celebration of a boy's birth, and he is subject to more intensive and prolonged nurturing than is a girl. By the age of five to seven, "parents increasingly instruct their children about the behaviors appropriate for boys and girls and begin rewarding compliance and punishing deviance more seriously" (Gregg 2005: 204). By this time, girls spend much of the day helping their mothers, taking care of younger children, while boys are less supervised and often teased into competition to

Gender roles and expectations are learned and negotiated through everyday activities. People share cultural norms across generations, as well as modify their expectations and behaviors, often subverting and redefining gender roles.

facilitate assertiveness. In most parts of the world, since young children are more often in the company of women, young boys and girls usually help with female activities. After early childhood, boys move away from the home to be in the company of other boys, while the gender role of girls begins to parallel that of women.

For Australian parents and children, male and female gender roles are mutually exclusive. The chores performed at home are primarily complementary and not overlapping, with fathers and boys concerned with outdoor activities, such as tidying the yard, washing the car, and working on the periphery of meal preparation; mothers and girls are concerned with tasks inside the home. Furthermore, in play situations at school, "girls felt comfortable emulating home settings, where they were familiar with the rituals and positions involved. The boys, on the other hand, were more comfortable exploring the boundaries of socially acceptable behavior and developing the skills they felt they would need as adults to work outdoors and outside the home" (Lowe 1998: 209). It is apparent that children enter school with gender roles already clearly defined, being aware of the complementarity of roles. Observation of the interaction of children in play settings in school reveals that they enact male domination of space and language and female submissiveness (1998: 214). In many cultures, some educators now include deliberate efforts, in their organization of classrooms and class activities, to make children aware of the possibility of roles that are more egalitarian in nature rather than those roles that suggest male dominance and female subordination.

CULTURE AND PERSONALITY

Not only do individuals in a society learn a language and a culture, but they also learn its values, beliefs, and norms, and how to behave in a way that is consistent with these values and norms. They learn which values are negotiable or flexible, and which ones ought to be nonnegotiable. There are many different components to thinking about learning cultural norms, and to understanding individual personalities and inevitable variations within any group. In today's world, multicultural identities are increasingly commonplace as people migrate and grow up in social environments different from the ones into which they were born. In much the same way that people linguistically code-switch (that is, make choices about language use depending on their perception of the context and environment) people can understand multiple cultural frameworks simultaneously and make choices about self-presentation according to their perceptions of the context.

Anthropologists often distinguish between ideas about "person" and "self." These are not absolute or bounded concepts, and there are many different ways to understand these concepts. To generalize, the concept of person (or **personhood**) focuses on an individual in social life, and includes all the behaviors, roles, and expectations in that person interacting with others as defined by the multiple institutions in the social environment. Concepts of **self** focus on the individual's awareness of themselves as a unique

personhood

Culturally constructed concepts of the relationship of individuals to others.

self

An individual's own sense of identity and self-awareness.

individual, and how an individual negotiates the multiple presentations of their personhood.

Personality refers to traits and behavioral characteristics of an individual that people use consistently in different contexts and situations and that are believed to be relatively stable throughout a person's life. Personality differences account for the inevitable variation between people within any one group. In all societies, people exhibit individual personality differences as a result of their upbringing and particular life experiences. Although individuals have a certain personality that is more or less stable over their lifetime, this is not to say that individuals never change. An individual's personality can change, sometimes through experience or through one's own efforts.

Although there is a range of personality types in every society, in any one society there is a preponderance of individuals with a particular kind of personality that often reflects the adoption of specific values and norms of that group. Personality types differ from one society to the next. The attempt to characterize the personality types that are dominant in different societies goes back to ancient times. Tacitus, a Roman historian of the first century AD, tried to capture what was distinctive about the personality characteristics of the Germans as a people. Throughout history, such characterizations of different peoples have been made, often during times of conflict or conquest when generalizations about the personality of an enemy are used as propaganda or in military strategy. One must always be wary of stereotypes based on prejudice, as distinguished from characterizations based on data and observations.

We have discussed how children acquire and learn the rules of their own culture. In the process, the particular personality characteristics favored in that culture are also stressed. Through the process of enculturation, children learn not only the rules of their culture, but also, as noted earlier, the values of their society. In addition, they increasingly become motivated to act according to those values. The motivations that have been built in during the enculturation process are what lead most people to conform to those rules. To act otherwise—to violate rules—may produce guilt in the individual, or a desire to avoid punishment and sanctions. Understanding that human beings process cultural norms individually through their cognitive skills has inspired the blending of anthropological with psychological theories. Contemporary approaches in psychological anthropology focus on exploring personality development and traits cross-culturally, using rigorous methodologies that will account for conclusions based on ethnographic and psychometric data, and not preexisting ideas or assumptions.

While the person may be conceived of in different ways in various cultures, there are some concepts that can be applied cross-culturally. These features are present in the early stages of the process of psychological development. Developmental psychologists are of the opinion that the boundedness of self and self-motivation are found in children in all societies. During the enculturation process in some societies, such as Java's and Bali's, a different notion of self is inculcated. All infants share boundedness and act as autonomous entities who are in contrast with others. However, as children develop in some non-Western cultures, they learn to suppress this autonomous self.

personality

Relatively stable characteristics that form an individual's unique character.

Anthropologist Clifford Geertz (1972, 1974) examined differences in personhood in Javanese, Balinese, and Western societies. Rather than putting himself in the place of "the Other" or conducting psychological tests, as did earlier psychological anthropologists, Geertz preferred to analyze the series of symbolic forms that people in a culture use to represent themselves to themselves and to others. He began his analysis with the Western conception of the person, which he described as "a bounded, unique, more or less integrated motivational and cognitive universe, a dynamic center of awareness, emotion, judgment, and action organized into a distinctive whole and set contrastively both against other such wholes and against its social and natural background" (Geertz 1974: 126).

The Balinese view of the person is as an appropriate representative of a category, rather than a unique individual. People attempt to mute individual personal characteristics and to emphasize, in contrast, features of status. Geertz, who frequently used a dramatic or theatrical metaphor to describe Balinese culture, likened Balinese persons to a cast of characters. In Bali, the face itself is considered a mask. Geertz's point is that the Western concept of the person as an autonomous, bounded entity operating in one's own way vis-à-vis other like entities is not shared by other cultures. Since Geertz is a cultural relativist, who emphasizes the unique features that differentiate cultures, he also views personhood as being distinctive for each culture.

Differences in the conceptualization of the self in different cultures are expressed in language. To use the proper linguistic forms in Javanese or in Japanese, speakers must know their relationship to the listener (or receiver). Misperceiving the relationship and using the wrong or impolite form is a disgraceful act. Thus, the speaker must know certain information—for example, whether the person being addressed is a professor, is of a higher social class, or is older than the speaker. Relative age is always a factor—one is either a younger sibling or an older sibling. One must always use the appropriate form of address. In discussing the Japanese concept of the self, scholars usually stress that it is basically relational—the self constantly viewed in relation to others (higher or lower, more respectful or less respectful, older or younger). In contrast, the American self is bounded (rather than relational), autonomous, and individualistic (Brown 1996: 47–48). As the anthropologist Dorinne Kondo observed, when she conducted field research in Japan, "I was always defined by my obligations and links to others" (Kondo, cited in Brown 1996: 47). East Asians tend to show a predominantly interdependent mode of being where the self exists in relation to others. Because it is necessary for Japanese children to learn the complexities of the social structure and their place in relation to all others within that structure, learning the proper forms of linguistic expression may take hard work and years of training. Middle-class North Americans primarily exhibit an independent mode of being that does not emphasize dependence on others. This is also learned by children as they age, and is encouraged through household and educational environments.

Ewing discusses how the self is constructed in a transnational situation. A woman of Turkish descent born in the Netherlands, Ewing moves between the culture of her Turkish homeland and the culture of the Netherlands.

She is the daughter of a Turkish guest-worker whose family has established permanent residence in the Netherlands yet maintains close ties with Turkey (Ewing 2000: 97). Identity is no longer a matter of giving up "old ways" and an old identity and becoming modern, but something more complicated. Even though young people born in the Netherlands, where their parents are guest-workers, live in predominantly Turkish communities and go to schools that exclusively serve immigrant populations, these young people are nevertheless influenced by Dutch and European media, and have a very different vision of the self and gender relations than is operative in the communities of their homeland. Ewing describes a young Turkish woman, a professional with a business school education and a career, who had been in an arranged marriage with her mother's sister's son, an uneducated assembly line worker in a pillow factory. She had lived a compartmentalized existence: although now part of a professional cosmopolitan world, she had been engaged at age eleven and married at eighteen within her Turkish world, which she had visited every summer as a child. Her sense of self in these two worlds was significantly different, though as she got older she resisted the arranged marriage and being engulfed in Turkish culture and identity, in which girls and women are subservient to the will of their parents. Her parents eventually won out, though a factor in her decisions was her desire to be identified as a "good girl" within Turkish culture (Ewing 2000: 107). Eventually, however, she ran away from her husband and was able to get a divorce and make a settlement with him and her parents, giving her the independence and professional identity she so vigorously sought (Ewing 2000).

Social Status and Personality

In all societies, people are minimally differentiated according to age and sex. Individuals who make up a society occupy different social positions, different statuses in the society. Beyond this, there are many other bases for differentiation. Individuals who occupy different statuses within the same society are likely to have different personality characteristics. For example, shamans in a society will have somewhat different personalities from others in the same society. The Big Man, a type of political leader, which we discuss in chapter 9, has a somewhat different personality from his followers. These differences in personality characteristics result from individual differences in socialization. There are two ways to view this relationship between social status and personality. In the first view, individuals with certain kinds of personality characteristics will gravitate toward those social roles or occupations that suit their personalities. For example, in our own society, individuals who are self-confident, assertive, and willing to take risks often gravitate toward entrepreneurial activities in the business world. Others, with personality traits such as a tendency to intellectualize and a curiosity about the world but a sense of uneasiness in dealing with other people, are more likely to become scientists and to do laboratory research.

People moving into particular social roles may undergo personality changes brought about by the demands of the role. A classic example of this is

Thomas à Becket (ca. 1118–1170), who, as chancellor of the British exchequer in the twelfth century, was a free spirit, who caroused and drank with King Henry II. When Becket was appointed Archbishop of Canterbury by the king, he proceeded to behave according to that role. He changed from a frivolous, pleasure-seeking individual to the committed defender of a moral cause who chose martyrdom at the command of his former friend, the king, rather than betray his principles.

Rebels and Innovators

From time to time, individuals renounce or challenge important aspects of their own culture and propose a radically different way of doing things. They may be considered mentally ill or criminals by the members of their society. But when they are successful in attracting followers and in overthrowing the old order, they are called "innovators" and "revolutionaries." These individuals are often central in bringing about changes that result in significant transformations. Their conceptualization, which may come to them in the form of an intellectual vision or a different vision for the future, may result in new norms or ideas about society being adopted.

The typical personality type of the well-adjusted individual in all cultures incorporates the motivations and values of the culture. Such an individual will want to do the things considered desirable in the society and will not think of changing them, and is very different from the rebel and innovator. The rebel, therefore, should differ in personality in some significant way from the typical person. Erik Erikson (1969) explored the relationship between successful rebels, their early life experiences, and their cultures in a series of biographical case studies of Martin Luther and Gandhi. Erickson emphasized the psychological characteristics of innovators, as these relate to the cultural setting within which these individuals lived, and their effect on history. Erikson has stressed the significance of these individuals to the historical process of cultural change. This approach might be seen as influencing some contemporary historians who create psychohistories of political leaders to help account for their strategies and political actions.

A demonstrator in the Palestinian Territories invokes the legacies of Mahatma Gandhi of India, Martin Luther King Jr. of the United States, and Nelson Mandela of South Africa—globally recognizable innovators of political change through nonviolent strategies.

EMOTIONAL EXPRESSION AND CULTURAL NORMS

The socially constituted person, as distinguished from the individual self, is a concept with a long history in anthropology. Individuals learn to perform a repertoire of social roles, and those roles constitute a major component of the social person. Each society has its own conception of which emotions people can appropriately express and when they can be expressed. Although the form in which emotion is expressed varies from one culture to another, certain aspects of emotional states, such as happiness and grief, are universal and largely innate. However, the ways in which emotions are expressed and interpreted are culturally determined and are inculcated during early childhood. "In a cultural context with an individualistic orientation like Germany, caregivers tend to view themselves and their children as independent and autonomous . . . and a child has the right to display such a negative feeling in the relationship if the cause of the emotion justifies such a reaction. . . . In a cultural context with a collectivist orientation like Japan, an interdependent self-construct is held in high esteem . . . and the expression of negative emotions . . . is undesirable" (Holodynski and Friedlmeier 2006: 209–10).

Emotion is expressed through gestures such as facial expressions and bodily movements. It is also asserted through various levels of language (i.e., intonation, nouns, and phrases). Wierzbiecka presents an interesting series of contrasts between Anglo-American and Polish attitudes toward emotions and their expression (1999: 240ff). For example, Polish culture values the truthful expression of one's feelings, saying and showing what one really feels, in contrast to Anglo-American culture, in which a display of good feelings is valued even if one does not necessarily feel that way. For Americans, this is coupled with the suppression of bad feelings, which may damage one's image and be unpleasant for other people. Americans are seen as smiling all the time even if it does not express how they feel. Wierzbiecka argues that Americans are being deceptive when they hide their true feelings behind polite language ("Have a nice day"), while Poles are simply honest. One might also conclude that for Americans it is not appropriate to present a picture of bad or insincere feelings about other people or their ideas, but this is not a matter of "lying." Among the Swat Pathans of Pakistan, to allow one's enemies to know one's true feelings is to show weakness, so one must therefore always hide feelings and emotions and present oneself as even-tempered and not show anger (Barth 1959). It is thus clear that there is cultural variability regarding the circumstances under which total truthfulness should be expressed.

Our examples illustrate how societies vary in the nature of personhood, the self, and the expression of emotions. We saw that Americans view each individual as an autonomous entity who operates in opposition to other similar entities. In contrast, the Japanese self operates more in relation to others, and this position is not autonomous, but relational. This is consistent with the general distinction made between individualism and collectivism. As Mascolo and Li note, "[I]ndividualist (most Western) cultures are those that emphasize individuals as separate, autonomous self-contained entities. In contrast, collectivist cultures (most non-Western cultures) place primary value on group orientation, the goals and needs of others, and readiness to cooperate" (2004: 1). Although they fall within the collectivist category, Balinese selves are different in still another way—they are always playing a part, a role, as in a drama. Faces are like masks used to portray emotion of the role rather than the person's true emotions. While European Poles and Germans are straightforward regarding the expression of emotions, one can say that Americans, along with South Asian Pathans, do not reveal their true feelings to others in everyday conversation. In these various ways, the self in different cultures is expressed in dissimilar ways.

Culture and Mental Illness

If, in mainstream American society, a man said one day that a spirit had come to him and told him that it would protect and watch over him throughout his life as long as he followed certain commands and obeyed certain taboos, a psychiatrist might say that he was having visual or auditory hallucinations. However, adolescent boys among the Crow Indians were expected to go on a vision quest to seek such a spirit. Earlier, seeing visions was very common among the Crow, as well as among many other Native American societies that also had the vision quest as a rite of passage. What is regarded as a symptom of mental illness in one society may be merely one aspect of normal, even highly valued, psychological experience in another.

mental illness

In anthropological terms, posits normal, expected, and acceptable behavior in a culture as a baseline; deviance from this baseline is abnormal behavior or mental illness.

The anthropological definition of **mental illness** takes the expected and acceptable behavior in a culture as a baseline and views deviance from this baseline as abnormal behavior or mental illness. Seeking a vision was expected, valued behavior for Crow boys, and they might undergo pain, stress, and deprivation until the vision came to them. But having visions of spirits are not generally expected behavior in American society. Someone who sees them and hears them is said to be exhibiting abnormal behavior. Similarly, belief in the powers of witchcraft is widespread; individuals who believe that someone was practicing witchcraft on them would have these claims recognized. There is a growing recognition among medical practitioners in the United States who serve ethnically diverse communities that a patient's spiritual belief in spirits or witchcraft may sometimes cause physical symptoms as well as behaviors. Individuals who seek medical care complaining of physical pain or emotional anguish that they believe originates from curses or witchcraft may be treated by both Western medical interventions and culturally appropriate religious or medical practitioners.

This approach to behavior and mental illness is essentially a relativistic one. Nevertheless, anthropologists who study forms of mental illness cross-culturally use certain general categories. They distinguish between disorders caused by brain damage and behavioral disorders, in which there is no apparent brain damage. The latter category is subdivided into psychoses, such as schizophrenia, depression, and paranoia, and neuroses of a variety of types. Grief, the emotion that accompanies bereavement, is experienced in all societies. In many different cultures, depression as an emotion or affect seems to be experienced in a similar manner. Depressive illness has a psycho-physiological syndrome of behaviors that can be recognized by clinicians cross-culturally. The cultural meanings of depressive illness and the cultural expression of the symptoms differ from one culture to another. Universal aspects of other mental illnesses, such as schizophrenia, neuroses, and personality disturbances, have also been recognized. However, these illnesses are also culturally shaped. Variations in their manifestations are related to social, economic, technological, religious, and other features of the societies in which they are found that shape cultural concepts of self and others.

In a cross-cultural study, anthropologists interviewed people in the United States, Ghana, and India who were diagnosed by psychiatrists in their countries with serious psychotic disorders including schizophrenia. The interviewees all reported having heard voices (auditory hallucinations) during their illness. The researchers asked questions about the voices, including what caused them, whether they recognized the source, and whether the voices were distressing or comforting. The researchers found variations from person to person within each national setting, but also found some general characteristics within each group. "In general the American sample experienced voices as bombardment and as symptoms of a brain disease caused by genes or trauma. They used diagnostic labels readily. . . . None of the [American] sample reported predominantly positive experiences, although half reported some positive dimensions to the voice-hearing." (Luhrmann et al. 2015: 42). Only one American respondent reported knowing the identity of the voice, which they generally saw as a negative and dangerous intrusion into their private lives. In the Indian sample, most respondents reported hearing the voices of parents, spouses, or other kin. "These voices behaved as relatives do: they gave guidance, but they also scolded" (2015: 42). In Ghana, the majority of respondents associated the voices with positive experience, originating from God or other spirits. One respondent reported hearing voices from demons but that God's voice spoke louder (2015: 43). The researchers conclude that this cross-cultural study affirms theoretical approaches to comparing basic concepts of self cross-culturally. The researchers concluded that "the point this research makes is that relationships with others are more salient to the ways non-Westerners (certainly South Asians and Africans) interpret their experience than they are to Westerners. We believe that these social expectations about minds and persons may shape the voice-hearing experience of those with serious psychotic disorder" (2015: 42–43).

Universally recognized stressful situations, like feeling grief, fear, or anxiety, are found to produce different patterns of emotional responses in different cultures. **Culture-bound syndromes** are patterns of aberrant behaviors associated with specific localities or societies. Amok is a mental syndrome found in Malaysia and Indonesia; a feature of amok is that the victim becomes violent to others while in a temporarily deranged state, experiencing complete amnesia of the attack afterward. Some researchers consider amok a disease specific to these particular cultures, while others consider it a form of depression psychosis produced by extreme stress, which is culturally determined. We get our expression in English "to run amok" from this mental syndrome of Southeast Asia. It has been pointed out that amok occurs in societies in

culture-bound syndrome

Manifestation of behaviors identified as specific to a culture or culture area.

BOX 4.3 | Psychiatry and Culture

For decades, cultural anthropologists have documented "culture bound syndromes"—the manifestation of behaviors in societies that appear by Western diagnostic criteria to be mental illness specific to cultures or culture areas. Anthropologists and mental health practitioners study these culture bound syndromes for their particular interests in understanding and treating mental disorders. More generally, these syndromes raise important questions about the cause and treatment of mental illness.

Some Western psychiatrists are moving toward the understanding of many mental disorders as having biological and organic causes with pharmacological solutions. This would suggest these disorders are universal in manifestation, categorization, and treatment. **Ethnopsychiatry** applies cross-cultural study to the diagnosis and treatment of mental illness. Culture bound syndromes suggest that environment and society influence how people respond to mental stress, manifest mental disorder, and potentially respond to treatment. Understanding mental illness cross-culturally is further complicated by the global use of the *Diagnostic and Statistical Manual of Mental Disorders* (*DSM*), revised and published regularly by the American Psychiatric Association. The *DSM*, in its last two editions, included culture-bond syndromes and recommendations for their treatment. Psychiatrists and psychologists are increasingly analyzing cultural issues and mental health interventions; they are recognizing the value of drawing on traditional healing techniques and practitioners in conjunction with Western psychiatry. The Western recognition of the possibilities of these complementary approaches is becoming ever more vital as the result of global patterns of migration and immigration.

The following case was documented by Dr. Juan Mezzich, a psychiatrist at the Mount Sinai School of Medicine in Manhattan, who is originally from Peru (as described in Goleman 1995). "The

patient seemed psychotic, complaining in a listless ramble, 'My soul is not with me anymore—I can't do anything.' Seriously disturbed, she had been taken to a psychiatric hospital by her relatives. . . . [T]he problem had begun when she got bad news from her native Ecuador: an uncle she was close to had died unexpectedly." Dr. Mezzich understood that her symptoms corresponded with a syndrome known in Latin American cultures as susto, or loss of the soul. "In facing the tragic news, the soul of the patient departs with the dead person, leaving the person soulless. In our psychiatric terms, we would say she was depressed."

He devised a treatment for her that drew upon his understanding of her background. "Instead of just giving her antidepressants, I tried an approach based on Hispanic culture." In Ecuador, family members would expect to have a mourning ritual to help the person assimilate the loss; Dr. Mezzich encouraged duplicating the ritual in New York. "[W]ith her family, we organized a sort of wake where everyone talked about the loss of her uncle and what it meant to them. The wake was quite powerful for her . . . within a few meetings, including two with her family, her symptoms lifted and she was back participating fully in life once again" (in Goleman 1995).

Practitioners around the world are identifying the multiple ways their psychiatric patients seek out diagnosis and treatment from traditional indigenous practitioners, as well as psychiatrists and psychologists if they are available in their communities. Many psychiatrists are now encouraging the cultural understanding of mental disorders in all clinical settings, including Europe and the United States. Nasser encourages the "deeper acknowledgement that far more mental illnesses might be cultural than we currently think. After all, commonly cited Western syndromes like chronic fatigue syndrome or multiple personality disorder are unknown in many countries, and yet the 1994 [*DSM*] includes no British or

(Continued)

BOX 4.3 | Psychiatry and Culture (Continued)

American syndromes in its 'culture-bound' category" (Nasser 2012: 7).

Diversity of treatment for all forms of disease and mental disorders is widely practiced but not always recognized for its cultural importance. An American may seek out a religious practitioner for healing prayer or the laying on of hands to treat illness, while simultaneously taking drugs and engaging in medical treatment to relieve symptoms. These approaches should be recognized as combining the use of healers and concepts of wellness and illness, and culture-bound syndromes, in our own culture.

which individuals may go into a trance. While in a trance they perform "stereotyped behavior, which allows the release of repressed feelings" (Azhar and Varma 2000: 171–72). A suggested explanation for amok in Malaysia is that it may be an extreme expression of aggression in a society that strictly prohibits such expression. Symptoms similar to amok have also been reported in the United States (2000: 173). The explanation for the occurrence of amok in Southeast Asia may also account for students "running amok" and attacking classmates and teachers in American schools and then killing themselves.

Latah is another syndrome found in Malaysia. Its symptoms are a startle reaction, after which the individual falls to the ground and performs compulsive imitation of words, gestures, and acts. The person may also utter obscenities. Winzeler (1995) indicates that latah occurs in societies in which there is familiarity with trance states and that practice shamanism. The identification of latah and amok in Malaysia was much more common in the past than today. These categories of mental syndromes have been replaced by diagnosis of depression, hypochondriasis, and anxiety, which are now treated with locally significant therapies that include the use of the Quran (Azhar and Varma 2000: 184). These forms of behavior are recognized as abnormal by the peoples of the cultures themselves, and they use what they determine to be the appropriate terms to describe them and remedies to address them.

The belief in witchcraft and sorcery in some societies is not in and of itself deemed to be an indication of mental illness. However, in Algeria, a sick person is believed to be possessed by *jinn* (spirits), and this is considered to be a form of "madness" (Al-Issa 2000: 103). This condition is often considered to be the result of sorcery. People believe that someone, motivated by envy, will use the "evil eye," so that the victim's behavior and desires come under the control of supernatural beings. The marabout, a saint and healer, is one type of traditional therapist who treats such patients. According to Al-Issa, "Exorcism consists of conversing with the evil spirit through the patient to convince him to leave" (2000: 104). The use of traditional therapists such as the marabout are on the increase in Algeria. In Iraq, Kuwait, and Tunisia, such therapies are illegal because they are associated by the governments with underdevelopment and backwardness, in contrast to modernization (2000: 104).

ethnopsychiatry

The application of cross-cultural variation to the diagnosis and treatment of mental illness.

As discussed above, mental illness from an anthropological perspective is behavior that is different from the cultural norms in a particular society. It is important to differentiate deviant behavior that represents mental illness from deviant behavior that does not. Not all those who violate the rules of a society are, by definition, mentally ill. Some are criminals, some are rebels, and some are innovators. The specific responses to these variations are another aspect of cultural norms embedded in ideas about mental illness and wellness. Behavior that departs from the psychological norms may be used by authorities to silence or imprison those who resist the sociopolitical system around them. In Soviet-era Russia, political reformers were often labeled by government officials as mentally ill. "After 1905 the police began to place politically dangerous individuals in mental hospitals" (Brown 2007: 291). After "glasnost" and the dismantling of the Soviet empire beginning in 1989, this practice of politically motivated punitive psychiatry and forced incarceration became a subject of debate in Russia and elsewhere.

Cross-Cultural Study of Mental Illness and Wellness: Twenty-First-Century Challenges

Cross-cultural studies of learning and behavior are increasingly informed by a necessity to rigorously explore methodologies and assumptions to assess what can be accurately claimed as part of human nature, and what forms of behavior and understandings are culture specific. This dichotomy is, however, being questioned as we increasingly acknowledge the spread of ideas as an inherent part of globalization. This globalization lens is being applied to diagnosing mental illness and its treatments, including medications prescribed to alleviate its symptoms around the world. Journalist Ethan Watters (2010) explores how the Euro-American concept of mental illness as the result of brain chemistry imbalances has been exported around the world; it is adopted by local psychiatrists and psychologists who are trained in these theories and the use of medications as therapy. This has resulted in a shift in diagnostic terminologies used around the world to conform with those originating in the United States and other Western countries. He documents the example of the parameters of anorexia, an eating disorder associated with Western teenage girls, being increasingly applied in the local media in Hong Kong to local cases of eating disorders, which are described in the press as the same as American-based anorexia characterized by "fat phobia."

Watters illustrates this and other examples of the dramatic increase over time in the adoption of American diagnostic categories abroad, with important consequences for diagnosis and treatment. "Western ideas do not simply obscure the understanding of anorexia in Hong Kong; they also may have changed the expression of the illness itself. As the general public and the region's mental health professionals came to understand the American diagnosis of anorexia, the presentation of the illness in [one physician's] patient population appears to transform into the more virulent American standard. . . . New patients appeared to be increasingly conforming their experience of anorexia to the Western version of the disease" (Watters 2010: 2). More broadly, the notion of "disease" as applied to mental disorders triggers a variety of responses that draw from biomedical disease models, including medication to treat the symptoms; the possibility of the diagnosed person being separated and isolated from others; the reliance on medical specialists for diagnosis and treatment; and the social stigma of a mental disease diagnosis. This contrasts with alternative cultural models for dealing with mental disorders, which include maintenance of social and familial ties and the use of local practitioners and strategies such as invoking religious rituals. This may not cure the patient, but it does keep them within the social group and reduces the stigma associated with the symptoms. (2010: 7).

SUMMARY

- Human babies are totally dependent on caregivers for an extended period of time. Social and linguistic skills that enhance their ability to bond with those around them are probably evolutionary adaptations.

- Sociocultural information is encoded in the organization of conversation, and from earliest infancy, children acquire knowledge as they are involved in such interactions.

- Self-reliance, a characteristic that is valued more in some societies than in others, is inculcated in the infant through the process of enculturation.

- Gender roles are also acquired along with socialization and language acquisition.

- Not only do individuals in a society learn a language and a culture, but they also acquire an appropriate idea of personhood and self that is characteristic of their culture.

- In the process of acquiring language and learning the rules of their culture, individuals are inculcated with the particular personality characteristics favored in that culture.

- What is regarded as a symptom of mental illness in one society may be merely one aspect of normal, healthy life in another.

- One view of mental illness is that universal psychopathological disease categories (such as schizophrenia and depression) are manifested in different kinds of behavior from one culture to another. The opposing view is that universally stressful situations produce different kinds of responses in different cultures.

- The emotional endowment of humans is universal and largely innate. However, the way in which emotion is expressed and interpreted is determined culturally.

- Every culture has a concept of the self, though the conception of the person varies from one society to the next.

KEY TERMS

culture-bound syndromes, 97
enculturation, 81
epigenetics, 83
ethnopsychiatry, 98
evolutionary psychology, 80

human genome, 82
mental illness, 96
personality, 91
personhood, 90
self, 90

SUGGESTED READINGS

Eller, Jack D. *Psychological Anthropology for the 21st Century*. New York: Routledge, 2019.

A textbook exploring the history of psychological anthropology, and contemporary issues in the discipline.

Fadiman, Anne. *The Spirit Catches You and You Fall Down: A Hmong Child, Her American Doctors, and the Collision of Two Cultures*. New York: Farrar, Straus and Giroux, 2012.

An exploration of the conflicts between a Hmong family and the hospitals in California, where they reside, over the treatment and care of their child who was diagnosed with epilepsy.

Mahler, Sarah J. *Culture as Comfort*. Boston: Pearson, 2013.

A comprehensive, accessible discussion of the neurological, cognitive, and social factors involved in learning one's culture.

SUGGESTED WEBSITES

www.neuroanthropology.net

A website devoted to multiple aspects of information to enhance understanding of the intersection between culture, brain, and body.

https://www.bbc.com/future/family-tree

A website that features discussions of parenting and child-rearing techniques from around the world.

https://www.genome.gov

The website of the U.S. National Human Genome Research Institute, which describes research and results in analyzing genomic advances "to improve health for all humans."

Chapter 5

Symbols and Their Meanings

LEARNING OBJECTIVES

- Understand the symbolic use of metaphor and metonym, and the two-sidedness of symbols.
- Recognize the multiple meanings of food and eating cross-culturally.
- Explain how group identities are established and reinforced through symbolism.

- Discuss the symbolism of domestic and public spaces, and the politics of monuments and memorials.
- Explore debates about cultural appropriation.

symbols

Words, objects, actions, or concepts recognized within a group suggesting other concepts and often invoking strong sentiments.

THE BEHAVIOR OF PEOPLE IN a culture is framed in part according to a set of **symbols** or cultural ideas. This component helps constitute the overall design of the tapestry of their culture. To understand people's economic, political, and social behavior, one must understand the system of cultural meanings that permeates these institutions. In their day-to-day actions, people create and convey cultural meaning as they enact their culture. How they walk, how they dress, and how they talk all convey cultural meaning. When people change their behavior, the meaning also changes. One must "read" cultural symbols like texts to understand the meaning of cultural behavior. (See the description of symbolic anthropology in chapter 1.)

The analysis of symbols deals with the meanings of words, actions, and objects in a culture. In addition to involving meaning, symbols are also expressive and convey emotion. This is especially true with regard to symbols in art, religion, and politics. As noted in chapter 3, language itself is a system made up entirely of symbols. All symbols, like the morphemes of language, operate as if they are two-sided coins. On one side are the physical characteristics, and on the other side are the meanings, or what the symbols stand for. Symbols and their meanings guide people's actions and also motivate such actions. Furthermore, people's behavior itself has symbolic meaning to those who observe it.

There are many ways to study symbolism anthropologically. One is comparative—to examine a particular symbol and the different meanings that are attached to it in various cultures. We will explore the symbolism of food to illustrate how its universal presence is understood very differently in different cultures. Another approach is to begin with the thing symbolized and the different symbols used for it within a culture. For example, within one culture, a clan (a type of kin group) may be symbolized by, among other things, land, the spirits of the dead, or a totemic animal. It is, however, important to note that within any one culture or society, there will not always be consensus on the meanings of symbols. While the symbols may be readily recognized, not all people interpret symbols in the same way. Debates in the United States about the presence of the Confederate flag and Civil War memorials illustrate this point. To some, the Confederate flag symbolizes the recognition of a period of Southern history that created an alliance of states that battled the Union for autonomy during the Civil War. To others, the Confederate flag symbolizes the glorification of slavery, racial segregation, and opposition to the civil rights of African Americans. This is just one example of the necessity of interpreting symbols within their social, political, and economic contexts, as well as recognizing that the meanings of symbols are subject to contestation and renegotiation over time.

CATEGORIES OF SYMBOLS

metaphor

An analytical concept in which one idea stands for another because of some similarity they seem to share.

Metaphor, a kind of symbol, is an important analytical concept used by anthropologists in the study of symbolic systems. A metaphor is an idea that stands for another set of ideas. The meaning of the metaphor is the recognition of the connection between the metaphor itself and the "something else" it represents. In the Native Canadian Kwakwaka'wakw marriage ceremony, discussed in chapter 2, many of the activities described were also characteristic of warfare, such as blackening faces, dressing like warriors, and running through a gauntlet of fire to demonstrate courage. Among the Kwakwaka'wakw, marriage rituals are metaphorically a form of warfare. Warfare is an apt metaphor for marriage among the Kwakwaka'wakw because the two sides compete with each other. The competitive aspect in the marriage ceremony is also seen in the potlatch, which pits one side against the other in accumulation and redistribution of valued goods.

In American society, games are often used as metaphors for life. Games involve struggle and competition. Sometimes you win and sometimes you lose, but games must be played according to a set of rules. Games demand from the players the demonstration of strategic ability, risk taking, stamina, and courage—virtues in American culture. The expression "playing hardball" is widely used in written and spoken English to stand for a strategy in business or politics that embodies bold competition, struggle, and some element of uncertain outcome. This expression is so much a part of English speech that its origins as a sports metaphor are generally ignored.

Metaphors create the connection between two unrelated things; they are used in all forms of language and art to communicate abstract ideas. William Shakespeare created one of the most famous metaphors in the English language: "All the world's a stage, and all the men and women merely players" in his play *As You Like It*. If we slightly modify the lines to read "All the world is like a stage" and "all the men and women are like players" we have created similes, a form of metaphor that compares two unrelated things with the use of a connecting word such as "like" or "as."

Another type of symbol is a **metonym**. Like a metaphor, a metonym is also based upon a substitution of one thing for another, but in this case the symbol standing for the "something else" is one of several parts that constitute the "something else." Thus the monarch can be referred to as the head of state, and the crown or throne can stand as a metonymic symbol for the monarchy. The capital of any type of government can be referred to as the seat of government. In each case, a part has been taken and used to stand as a symbol for the whole and for speaking for the whole, as in "The White House issued a statement. . . ."

One category of symbols, **public symbols**, constitutes a cultural system for society. Many of these cultural symbols are known and recognized by all members of the society, although different groups may have different interpretations associated with them, as discussed above. Some symbols are more esoteric and may be known only by a small group; knowledge of the symbol may in fact be the basis of mutual recognition of group membership, such as a secret handshake or form of greeting. Individuals also create symbols out of their own experiences, symbols that are not commonly shared by others. These are known as **private symbols** and are the symbols of our dream life and fantasies. In the creative process, artists, novelists, or filmmakers use private symbols. The process of interpretation of artistic works by the public and by critics involves trying to decipher what the private symbols of the artist

metonym

The symbolic substitution of one of the constituent parts for the whole.

public symbols

Symbols used and understood by the members of a society.

private symbols

Personal symbols related to an individual's unique life history.

mean. We will discuss how the creative artist uses private and public symbols further in chapter 12.

THE SYMBOLISM OF FOOD

We examine the symbolism of food to show how a symbol may have various meanings attached to it in different cultures. From the utilitarian or materialist perspective, food is ingested by humans to release its energy needed by the human body to grow and sustain life. It is made up of calories, protein, fats, minerals, and carbohydrates and is introduced into humans by processing, chewing, swallowing, and digesting. These aspects of food are equivalent to the physical manifestations or sounds that make up a word. Not going beyond this aspect of food in terms of one's investigation of symbolism would be like analyzing words without considering their meanings.

Eating is a metaphor for sexual intercourse in a great many societies. Why is one a metaphor for the other? What do the two actions have in common? These two acts are completely different physiologically; nevertheless, they are tied together in their symbolic significance. "To hunger for" is a metaphor for sexual desire. Among the Mehinaku of the Amazon region, having sex is defined as "to eat to the fullest extent. . . . The essential idea is that the genitals of one sex are the 'food' of the others" (Gregor 1985: 70). In a different part of the world, among the Lardil of Mornington Island, Australia, "there is a strong identification between food and sex, sexual intercourse and eating" (McKnight 1999: 23). In discussing eating practices among Americans, Lukanuski has pointed out the same equation and intertwining of eating and sex (1998: 114).

Eating is sometimes a metaphor for marriage. In many New Guinean societies, like that of Lesu, on the island of New Ireland in the Pacific, and that of the Trobriand Islanders, marriage is symbolized by the couple's eating together for the first time. Adolescent boys and girls freely engage in sexual intercourse without commitment to marriage and without any gossip or criticism from the community. But eating together constitutes a public announcement that they are now married. Eating together symbolizes their new status as a married couple. Earlier, in our society, it was just the reverse. One could dine publically without signaling a commitment to marriage, but engaging in sexual intercourse was a symbol of the intention of marriage.

In other New Guinean societies such as Wogeo's, if a man eats with a woman, then she is considered to be like his sister and he cannot marry her. Here, eating is equally symbolic but has the reverse meaning. Instead of marriage, eating symbolizes a brother-sister relationship—those who cannot marry. Among the Na of China, sexual intercourse is forbidden among close consanguineous relatives. The Na say, "Those who eat from the same bowl and the same plate must not mate" (Cai 2001: 125).

In some New Guinean societies, the nuclear family is not the unit that eats together, as is the case in American society. Men take their meals in the men's house, separately from their wives and children. Women prepare and eat their food in their own houses, and take the husbands' portions of food to the men's houses. This pattern is also widespread among Middle-Eastern and South-Asian societies, where men usually eat with other men and women with other women and children, after serving male family members; husbands and wives usually do not eat together. This is the case among the Marri Baluch of western Pakistan, where the family arranges marriage between parallel cousins, and husbands never eat with their wives. But in adulterous relationships between a Marri Baluch man and woman, illicit eating together symbolizes their love for one another. In Lesu, the symbolic meaning of eating is exactly opposite from its meaning among the Marri Baluch. In Lesu, marriage is symbolized by a man and woman sitting down and eating together, but a woman never eats with her lover. Gendered patterns of food preparation may be reversed in public or ritual settings; in rural Rajasthan at community-wide rite of passage feasts, men prepare and serve the food to their guests. In these events food preparation and service symbolizes male hospitality and group solidarity.

In many societies men prepare food and eat with other men in public events, as in this inter-village gathering in rural Rajasthan. This reverses the traditional domestic norms in households of women preparing food and men being served first.

Recognition of the metaphoric connection between eating and sexual intercourse can also help explain some other cultural rules that have to do with taboos against eating certain things. In some societies, members of a clan are not allowed to eat the animal or bird that is their totemic ancestor. Since they believe themselves to be descended from that ancestor, it would be like eating that ancestor or eating themselves. Among the Abelam and the Arapesh of Papua New Guinea there is an incest-like prohibition involving food: eating the totemic animal is seen as a form of incest, comparable to having intercourse with a person from one's own clan. The Arapesh express it in the form of a well known saying:

Other people's mothers
Other people's sisters
Other people's pigs
Other people's yams which they have piled up
You may eat,
Your own mother
Your own sister
Your own pigs
Your own yams which you have piled up
You may not eat.

The pigs that a person raises are considered his children, and the owner of a pig is referred to as its father. The Arapesh explicitly recognize the symbolic connection between eating and sexual intercourse, as evidenced in the prohibition against eating one's own pigs and yams and the prohibition against incest with one's sister and mother. In Arapesh, the taboo against eating one's own pigs and yams compels social groups to exchange their pigs and yams with other groups, resulting in ongoing exchange relationships and alliances with those groups (Rubel and Rosman 1978).

In some societies around the world, it would be unthinkable to eat with one's enemies. Eating together, or commensality, symbolizes goodwill and peaceful relations. What happens when enemies accidentally find themselves together for one reason or another? The Pathans of Swat, Pakistan, place great stress on hospitality, which is symbolized by giving food and drink. Even if the host learns his guests are enemies, with whom he would normally not share food, the rules of hospitality dictate that as guests they must be fed. When the guests are ready to leave, the host escorts them to the border of his territory, where his obligations of hospitality end, and he is free to treat them like enemies.

The association between food prohibitions and sociopolitical rank is found in the rules of commensality that dictate whom one may eat with and accept food and water from in the caste system of India. A caste system consists of ranked groups, each with a different historical economic specialization. In India there is an association between caste and the idea of ritual pollution transmitted through food, water, or physical contact. Because of the fear of pollution, orthodox Brahmans and other upper-caste individuals may not share food with, eat from the same plate as, or even accept food from an individual from a lower-ranking caste. In modern India, ignoring traditional inter-caste rules of commensality symbolizes an individual's progressive and secular perspective on caste relations.

Food has a great many meanings in present-day American society. For example, regions are symbolized by different foods. Grits, fried chicken, barbecue, black-eyed peas, collards, and mustard greens represent the cuisine of the South. Some foods, like the Big Mac and Classic Coke, which symbolize America, have become international and can be found, adapted to local preferences and food restrictions, in almost every part of the globe. The multiethnic nature of America today is symbolized by widespread availability of ethnic foods and ingredients, such as pizza, bagels, pita bread, and sushi, as well as regional spices and condiments, all of which are on the shelves of supermarkets in small towns as well as large cities. This illustrates that some forms of diversity of ethnic identities have become increasingly prominent as symbols of American identity.

SOCIAL GROUPS, SOCIAL CATEGORIES, AND THEIR SYMBOLS

In the previous section, we selected something tangible, food, and then discussed the various meanings attached to it in different cultures. Group identity may be symbolized in a number of other ways in addition to cuisine. For example, a social group such as a clan may be represented by a **totemic animal**, with pictorial representations of the animal being used to signify that clan. The Kwakwaka'wakw, as well as other Native Peoples of the Pacific Coast of Canada, painted the specific totemic animals of their groups on the facades of their houses and carved these animals on the elaborately decorated "totem" poles standing in front of their houses or in prominent places in their communities. As in many other societies of the world, personal names given to members of the group were the property of the entire group. When people died, their names returned to the pool of names, to be used again when a child was born. There was also the belief that a name carried an identity, and that identity was perpetuated through the names handed down from generation to generation. In this way, individual identity was linked to clan identity since, to the outside world, the name symbolized membership in the group.

In general, the clan as a social group may be associated with particular spirits, including spirits of the clan ancestors, who are said to dwell in specific locations in the clan territory. The spirits and the territory represent the clan. Strangers crossing into their territory or hunting in it are in danger from the spirits that protect it. In such a situation, in which the land symbolizes the continuity of the social group (the clan) from mythical times to the present, the land could not be sold by clan members for money without destroying the identity of the group itself. Thus, an animal, painting, carving, name, or territory stands as a symbol of the group.

Animal forms are often used to symbolize social groups such as birds, fish, and bears. One may ask why animals are used to stand for people. Although the animal world exists apart from the human world, people use the animal world to talk metaphorically about the human world. In American culture the world is seen as a jungle or referred to as an animal farm. Though the world of animals and the world of people are very different, there are links between them. The world of animals is divided into species; the world of people into social groups. Societies use the different characteristics of animal species to make systems of classification of animals, such as those discussed in chapter 3. Classification systems differ from one society to the next because each society may single out different characteristics upon which its classification is based. In a society with clans, each clan is different from the others, just as the animal species representing it differ from one another. This is why differences among animals are used to express differences among groups of people.

Sometimes society is conceptualized as being divided into halves, which may be symbolically represented as higher and lower, sun and moon, or right side and left side. The Yafar of New Guinea think of the two parts as male and female. Each village is divided into two sides, one side referred to as "male" and made up of several clans, and the other side referred to as "female" and

A Kwakwaka'wakw hand-carved display of clan totems, or symbols of animals, birds, and other beings of significance to families or regions.

totemic animal

An animal from which members of a clan believe themselves descended and with whom they enact a special symbolic relationship.

| BOX 5.1 | Cultural Exchange/Cultural Appropriation |

Cultural appropriation is broadly defined as "the use of one culture's symbols, artifacts, genres, rituals, or technologies by members of another culture—regardless of intent, ethics, function or outcome. . . . [It] is inescapable when cultures come into contact, including virtual or representational contact" (Rogers 2006). Debates around specific examples of cultural appropriation involving sports teams, fashion, and body adornment invariably become viral events, quickly drawing millions of responses and comments on the internet. At its most basic, it is the result of one group of people becoming aware of and adopting the symbols of another culture; critical reflection on the process reveals that it is inevitably also about a dominant culture commodifying aspects of a more marginal group of people. It is therefore important to understand the cultural politics of this process, and evaluate

how it operates in a world that puts groups of people instantly in contact with others.

Cultural appropriation is often debated in the media and on the internet, partly because the term is often used without being accompanied by definitions or discussions. It is therefore open to interpretation and invariably often-acrimonious debate. Appropriation inevitably involves cultural exchange, but this exchange rarely takes place between two groups at equal levels of power. Cultural dominance, the appropriation of elements of a subordinated culture by a dominant culture, invariably occurs without reciprocity, permission, or compensation (Rogers 2006: 474). Exploring individual experiences of cultural appropriation through this framework of ethical considerations and political inequality helps illuminate the passions and debates around this issue.

cultural appropriation

The adoption of symbols or practices of one group of people by another more dominant group.

also comprising several clans. In rituals, men of the male half of the village use objects conceptualized as male and associated with plants designated male, while men of the female half of the village use ritual objects that are female and connected to female plants (Juillerat 1996). The two halves are considered to be complementary, as are male and female.

SYMBOLIC MEANINGS OF SPACE

Public spaces and cultural expectations about them make important symbolic statements about gender, social groupings, and social relationships. Patel (2010) illustrates how class and gender differences in India are "experienced in and through place" in her ethnography of women call-center workers in Indian cities. Patel discusses how "space matters, particularly in terms of the social construction of identities" (2010: 3). For example, in India, Dalits (formerly known as Untouchables) were barred from entering some Hindu temples or other sacred places because of the low status assigned to them by orthodox practices of caste identity and behavior. In addition, menstruating women are forbidden entry to Hindu temples in India and elsewhere because of the belief that their presence will contaminate the purity of sacred spaces. "In this context, a temple is far from a neutral space. It marks people as pure or impure, as compatible with the sacred or essentially profane. Who belongs in a temple is determined by multiple categories such as age, gender, religion, and class" (2010: 3).

The symbolic construction of public spaces, particularly urban spaces and urban infrastructure at night, in India normally excludes women; traditional gender norms bar proper and virtuous women from being out of their homes at night, on streets or in transit. Despite this, educated, middle-class women are attracted to call-center work because of its relatively high wages, which are welcomed by their household members. However, due to international time differences, they must work the night shift to accommodate the call-centers' American and European clients' daytime work schedules. These Indian women are therefore now entering the "nightscape" by traveling to and from work during times when these spaces are considered appropriate only for males, or for women presumed to be engaging in prostitution or other illicit behaviors.

This violation of the gender-appropriate norms of public space creates extreme forms of social and physical jeopardy for these women. They are subjected to gossip about their activities from neighbors who disparage their comings and goings during the night. In addition, despite their financial contributions to their households, they often experience scorn and criticism from family members for possibly neglecting their daytime domestic responsibilities. Patel suggests that "these cultural constructions of nightscapes discipline and constrain women's aspirations" for economic mobility. "Areas perceived as safe during the day transform into spaces of danger at night, and stories about the dangers of going out at night are used to control women's mobility. As a result, women who break the rules about their place are viewed as 'asking for it' if they meet with violence, even rape, when they go out at night" (Patel 2010: 3–4). Media coverage in India of horrific acts of violence against women call-center workers serves to reinforce the constraints on women's aspirations to enter "male-only" domains of work and leisure.

Arrangements of community and domestic spaces also make important symbolic statements about social groupings and social relationships. Among the Nuchanulth, a Native community of the Pacific Coast of Canada, each of the large plank houses in the winter villages in which they lived in the nineteenth century represented a social group. The floor plan of the house was divided into spaces that were ranked with respect to one another. The place of honor, the left-rear corner of the house, was occupied by the owner, who was the highest-ranking person in the house, with the highest title, and his family. The next most important man and his family occupied the right-rear corner of the house; the third most important man and his family occupied the left-front corner of the house; the fourth most important man and his family were in the right-front corner; the least important titled man lived with his family on the left-hand side of the house. Untitled commoners and their families lived in the remaining spaces along the sides of the house. Each location had its own hearth. The floor plan of the house was like a seating plan according to seniority. There is archeological evidence of this type of house with its status divisions going back at least two thousand years. However, with demographic decline and the incursion of the cash economy in the late nineteenth century, a new pattern developed in which related nuclear families

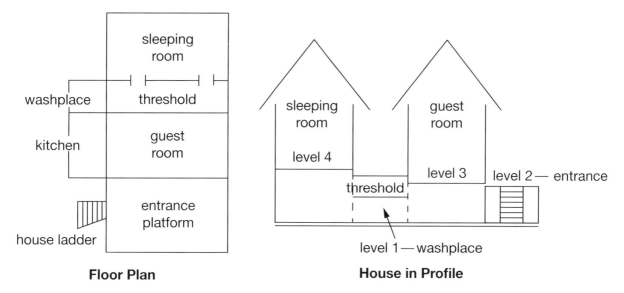

Fig. 5.1 *Thai house floor plan*

lived in single family dwellings clustered behind the large houses that were now used for "sociopolitical rituals . . . [and were] transformed into potlatch houses" (Marshall 2000: 102).

In a peasant village in northeastern Thailand, space in a house is divided to symbolize rules about marriage and sex. The sleeping room is the most sacred part of the house. First cousins, with whom sexual relations and marriage are not permitted, may enter that room but may not sleep there. More distant relatives, whom one may marry, are not allowed to enter the sleeping room and must remain in the guest room. Tambiah (1969), who has analyzed the Thai material, also relates categories of animals and their edibility to relatives whom you may and may not marry. First cousins, whom you cannot marry, are equivalent to your own buffalo, oxen, and pigs, which live under the house. You may not eat them and must give them to other people. More distant relatives, whom you can marry, are equivalent to other people's domestic animals, which you can eat. Since social space symbolizes degree of social relationship, and edibility also signifies social relationships, the meaning of social space is also related to edibility.

In Mexico, the meaning and layout of domestic space is organized around a patio, or courtyard. Rooms for sleeping, dressing, talking when the weather is inclement, cooking, and storage open onto the patio, where all kinds of domestic activities, such as socializing, child play, bathing, and doing laundry, take place. Individuals do not have separate bedrooms. Children often sleep with parents, and same-sex siblings share a bed, emphasizing familial interdependence. Rooms in Mexican houses are locations for multiple activities that, in contrast, are rigidly separated in the United States. The households of Mexican Americans in Los Angeles represent a transition between Mexican and American usages. According to Pader, they "blur the lines between the U.S. coding system, with its emphasis on greater bodily privacy and the individual, and the Mexican system, with its emphasis on sharing and close daily interconnection" (1993: 130–31). As Mexican-American children mature, they change their ideas about family, become more individuated, and desire their own beds and bedrooms.

In many Euro-American societies, individuals have their own private spaces for sleeping, reflecting the premium placed upon privacy and individuality. People feel that others should not intrude into one's own space. When a teenager closes the door to her room, this is a sign that parents and siblings should not enter. This is in contrast to other societies, in which space is communal and has a different meaning. When space is communally shared by a group, that group may have shared responsibilities, such as pooling income, caring for children or the elderly, or paying a dowry or bride price.

BODY SYMBOLISM

The human body is often the basis for metaphors. A common way to symbolize social groupings and social relationships is to use the human body metaphorically. Roman historian Tacitus (ca. 56–117 AD) wrote that among Teutonic tribes in early European history, close and distant relatives were symbolized by close and more distant parts of the body, reckoned from the head. The father and mother were symbolized by the head; brothers and sisters were at the neck; first cousins at the shoulders; second cousins at the elbows; third cousins at the wrists; and fourth, fifth, and sixth cousins at the knuckles and finger joints. At the cutoff point of kin were seventh cousins, who were called "nail relatives." Individuals beyond seven degrees of relationship were not considered kinsmen.

The internal skeletal structure of the body is also used as a metaphor for the internal structure of society. For example, among the Mongols the word *bone* was used for *clan*, and the aristocracy was referred to as *White Bone* to distinguish them from commoners, who were referred to as *Black Bone*. A slightly different metaphor is used by the Riff of Morocco, who refer to their clan as a *vein*. Just as the Mongols used a skeletal metaphor, the Riff use the metaphor of blood vessels to represent the interconnection between the branching parts of their society. Americans use the metaphor of blood to represent kinship. In thinking about the biological facts of conception, we can see that the sperm from the father and the egg from the mother, which unite to form the new individual, have nothing to do with blood. Yet Americans say that the blood of their fathers and mothers flows in their veins. "Blood" is a symbolic way of talking about American kinship and relatedness.

Sharp illustrates some of the ways in which "the human body is a symbolically charged landscape" in her analysis of organ transplantation (2001: 112). Organ donation and procurement, an emotionally charged area, have generated a complex set of "symbolic renderings of the body, death, and mourning." Once it has been determined that brain death, the point considered to be the death of the self or the individual, has taken place, "harvesting" of the viable organs from a body still otherwise functioning can take place if the donor's kin have given their approval. To the transplant specialists, donors become dehumanized, and their organs have become "sophisticated, replaceable mechanical parts" completely separated from the identity of the donor (2001: 115). Donated organs are not paid for at present; however, because of the shortage of such organs, the suggestion has been made that a system of payment be instituted. Informal and unofficial systems of organ procurement may involve payment or even involuntary removal of organs from marginal groups of people; these types of organ transactions are officially banned in many countries. Organs are treated as if they were commodities, like other commercial medical goods that are bought and sold today (such as blood, sperm, and ova). In an effort to mask this commercialization, the donor kin are encouraged to regard the transplanted organs of their loved ones as continuing to live in the bodies of unknown recipients, a life after death, so to speak. The donated organs are seen as a "gift of life," and transplant personnel use various strategies to accomplish the "veiling of procurement" (2001: 118).

The identity and life history of donors were originally kept secret, as were the circumstances of their death, violent or otherwise. In some countries this information is now shared with donor and recipient families, who may meet and honor the donors' generosity and continuing legacy of "life." The message of the transplant professionals is "a greening of the body, a form of 'semantic message' that foregrounds the goodness associated with donation while simultaneously denying transplantation's more disturbing reliance on death and organ retrieval" (Sharp 2001: 120). Using logos associated with ecology, such as butterflies, trees, and foliage, on stationery, pamphlets, lapel pins, rings, T-shirts, posters, and bumper stickers shifts the emphasis from death to life. The use of agricultural metaphors is pervasive (e.g., organs are said to be harvested or transplanted through grafting). Some hospitals and organ-procurement organizations have established "donor gardens" and "donor trees," which are decorated by recipients of donated organs at ceremonies (2001: 125). Interestingly, the kin of the donors reject such symbolism and imagery since it dehumanizes and depersonalizes their deceased loved ones, and have begun to make donor memorial quilts similar to the AIDS memorial quilts, in which each panel commemorates a loved one who had given the "gift of life." Metaphors are used throughout the transplantation process to transform death into life.

Symbolism of Body Decoration

People all over the world decorate their bodies with a wide variety of permanent and temporary embellishments, all of which communicate meanings. The symbolic messages conveyed by body decoration range from statements about social, economic, or political status and class, and the different phases of a life, to the sacred and profane. Body decorations must always be examined within a cultural context that may change over time in order to decode their meanings. For example, Maori tattooing, performed with a chisel-like implement by a revered and highly paid expert over a period of years, was a very significant aspect of Maori culture up to the nineteenth century. Today, Maoris use the same tattoo designs for ceremonial purposes, but they are

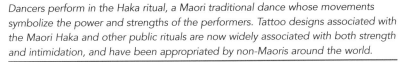

Dancers perform in the Haka ritual, a Maori traditional dance whose movements symbolize the power and strengths of the performers. Tattoo designs associated with the Maori Haka and other public rituals are now widely associated with both strength and intimidation, and have been appropriated by non-Maoris around the world.

American boxer and actor Mike Tyson displays his interpretation of these symbols through facial tattoos.

applied with pigment that can be removed when the ritual is complete. Many tattoo designs, originally associated with one culture are now widely copied and displayed by performers, athletes, and other people who are using these symbols in their own symbolic ways.

Tattooing or modification of the skin is a form of body modification. As such, it is part of a larger category and related to other symbolic practices such as knocking out the incisors (which occurs among some east African societies), cutting off a finger joint (practiced by some Plains societies), or circumcision. The simplest form of skin modification is scarification, a very widespread custom that occurs typically at initiation. A child, female or male, is symbolically "born again" through rites of initiation, which confer tribal status. Scarification, therefore, symbolizes a transformation from nature and one's unblemished skin, to culture, with its tribal markings. The *moka* facial tattooing of the Maori and the total body tattooing of the Marquesans unquestionably use the body to communicate symbolic ideas about the courage of the individual who has gone through the painful ordeal typical of initiation (Atkinson 2003: 52).

Body decoration, or body modification as it is sometimes called, is widely practiced in modern American society. Tattooing and piercing are popular ways of embellishing the body. Hewitt sees a parallel between the transformation of the body and the symbolism of religious conversion since such self-alterations communicate acts of self-transformation, ways of creating a new identity, or expressing one's individuality or affiliation with a particular alternative subcultural group (1997). Body tattooing with a hot needle, originally associated with the exoticism of the circus in America, became popular with lower-class and blue-collar workers at the beginning of the twentieth century. In the 1950s, there was a tattoo renaissance as a new, safer technology was introduced. Clients with more income and better education often design their own tattoos, making the tattoos symbols of self-expression and self-identification. Various types of body piercing are now popular; piercing has moved from a countercultural symbol of identity to become a trend and a fashion, represented in mainstream cultures. The popularity of temporary, removable forms eliminate the pain of their application, and also some of the meaning associated with endurance and strength. Tattooing and body piercing, which once symbolized marginality in America, have been partly transformed into practices that symbolize that the bearer is trendy and hip, and is conforming to norms of groups or occupations with which they affiliate.

THE SYMBOLISM OF SPORTS

As noted earlier, games in a culture are often metaphors for life. Sports in American society are children's games played by adults, but they are much more than just games. They make symbolic statements about the society, which explains their enormous popularity. In American team sports, such as football, individual achievement, which is often seen as a highly desirable cultural characteristic of Americans, is subordinated to team effort. Football is an exclusively male activity in which male bonding ties individuals together in a collective effort. In this aspect, it is similar to male initiations in other societies, in which a ritual binds them together into a male peer group. In his analysis of American football "Into the Endzone for a Touchdown," Alan Dundes examines the folk speech involved in football and observes that "American football could be a ritual combat between groups of males attempting to assert their masculinity by penetrating the end zones of their rivals" (1978: 86). He likens football, which he sees as a form of symbolic homoerotic behavior, to the initiation rites of aboriginal Australia, which also have a homoerotic aspect. The male bonding of American football sets males, the participants, against females, the outsiders. This would also explain why many sports teams expressed strong feelings that the presence of female reporters, but not male reporters, in their dressing rooms was completely inappropriate. In their eyes, these women were intruding into a male ritual space. The team aspect of football is also a recapitulation of the value of teamwork, pulling together for a common goal.

When a sport that originated in one culture spreads to another culture, it may take on a completely different set of symbolic meanings. With the expansion of the British Empire, cricket moved into the colonial areas that the British conquered, and today is played enthusiastically in Asia, Africa, the Caribbean, and the Pacific region. During the colonial period, it personified the essence of British colonialism. In fact, the expression "not cricket" means not acting like a proper Englishman and refers to stretching the rules. Nowhere is cricket played in a more spirited fashion than in the Trobriand Islands, where it was introduced by English missionaries at the beginning of the twentieth century. Over the years, the Trobrianders transformed the English version of the game, which represented colonial domination, into a

BOX 5.2 | The Symbolism of Sports Mascots

American Indian images and names are commonplace as symbolic representations of sports teams, used widely by schools, colleges, and professional sports franchises throughout the United States. As the result of pressure from Indian advocates and civil rights groups, the practice is now being challenged in the courts, as well as in "the court of public opinion." The practice of using Indian images on sports and product logos goes back to the nineteenth century and is widely acknowledged, by both opponents and supporters of the practice, as rendering to Indians one-dimensional characteristics. Proponents of the continued use of these images claim they are honoring Indians with these images; a small number of tribes have encouraged their continued use to keep Native Americans visible and prominent in popular activities.

Critics argue that these images and the rituals that go along with them perpetuate racist stereotypes about Indians in America. "'Every time the Atlanta Braves do their tomahawk chop . . . we are no longer successful businessmen, doctors, soldiers, co-workers or neighbors,' says Cynthia Connolly of the Little Traverse Bay Bands of Odowa Indians in Michigan. 'To the fan, we exist only in the 1800s as a warrior culture'" (Potenza 2014). Advocates for changing the symbolic strategy of sports teams argue that these caricatures and stereotypes of Native people are harmful, and negate the personhood and achievements of Indians in contemporary America. In 2005, the National Collegiate Athletic Association (NCAA) encouraged member teams to either stop using these names and images or obtain permission from tribes to continue their use. Baseball and football teams, from major league national clubs to college and high school sports teams are reevaluating the use of mascots that represent a particular ethnic group.

cultural creation that has a multiplicity of meanings in their own Trobriand culture. In contrast to English cricket, in which all the players wear white, in Trobriand cricket, the players dress in the traditional regalia for warfare, and each team may have up to forty players. The cricket game is usually part of the competition when one village challenges another to a *kayasa*, a competitive period of feasting and exchange of yams. Magic that was used in warfare, which was outlawed by the colonial authorities, is used during the cricket game since the game of cricket is symbolically like warfare as well as a competitive exchange. When the bowler pitches the ball, he recites the magic formula that was formerly used to make a spear hit its target. In Trobriand cricket, the home team always wins. The symbolism of Trobriand cricket may be seen as more like that of a competitive exchange—first you "win," then I "win"—than the way sports are played elsewhere, that is, to decide the "ultimate" winners. The symbolism of warfare characterizes other aspects of culture in other societies. In chapter 2, we saw symbolism of warfare being used throughout the Kwakwaka'wakw marriage ritual.

UNIVERSAL SYMBOLS?

It can be argued that certain symbols are found universally and carry similar meanings in all cultures. Colors are frequently associated with emotional states and sometimes with other meaningful messages as well. In American society, red means danger and is used for stop signs in traffic control. Green is the complementary color to red and is used to symbolize the opposite of red. Since traffic lights, like all symbols, are arbitrary, the question of whether they might have originally been put forth in reversed manner, so that red meant go and green meant stop, could be asked. These symbols are part of the larger category of color symbolism in American society; as the "red-light district" signifies prostitution and other illicit activities, it seems unlikely that the traffic light colors could have been reversed. The question of whether red has the same meaning in other cultures cannot be assumed and should be systematically explored. In Europe and North America, black is the color of mourning; at a funeral, people wear black clothing. In contrast, white, the color of wedding gowns, symbolizes purity and virginity. A bride wears white when the relationship is established and black if the relationship is terminated by the death of her husband. In India, the color symbolism for death and mourning is exactly the opposite; there, white is the color of death and mourning, so mourners and widows wear white clothing. Throughout Asia brides wear red, and not white, which would be considered inauspicious and inappropriate for a wedding. It is therefore clear that the meanings of colors vary from one culture to another.

Other symbols have been suggested as ones that have universal meaning. Hair is one of these. As noted earlier, long hair can be a symbol of rebellion when everyone else is wearing short hair. In several widely separate cultures, long hair, especially unkempt long hair, is a symbol of sexuality. Short hair symbolizes restraint, while a shaved head often indicates celibacy, although today it has other meanings as well. The symbolism of hair is quite overt. We are not dealing here with private symbols of the type referred to earlier in this chapter but, rather, with a culturally accepted and widely understood symbol that is appropriated by individuals and groups to communicate to others their adherence to, or rejection of, a particular social or political perspective.

SYMBOLS, POLITICS, AND AUTHORITY

Just as families, lineages, and clans can be represented by things such as totems, houses, space, and personal names, so too may an entire nation be represented by an array of symbols. The combat between symbolic animals—the eagle and the bear—was used by political cartoonists to portray the conflict between the United States and the former Soviet Union during the Cold War period beginning in the early 1950s. In the same way, two buildings continue to represent the United States and Russia; news reports often indicate that "the White House says this" and "the Kremlin says that." National flags, anthems, and food also symbolize nations. Acts that damage or destroy a flag are said to be "desecrating" it and are powerfully negative statements about the country the flag symbolizes.

Symbolism is deeply embedded within the public presentation of politics and political perspectives. Desecration of a flag or even suggestions to change the design of a flag usually provoke outrage. Flags and other political symbols have a more complex series of emotional qualities and ideas associated with them than other types of symbols. They are associated with the solidarity of the groups or nations the symbols represent. The tricolor flag and "The Soldier's Song," which had inspired the Sinn Fein of Ireland in their struggle for independence from Britain, became the official symbols of the Irish Free State after it achieved its independence from the United Kingdom and its separation from Northern Ireland with its large Protestant population in 1922 (Morris 2005: 38ff).

In contrast, Northern Ireland, which remained part of the United Kingdom, though it had its own parliament, emphasized this continued connection by having the British flag, the Union Jack, as their most important symbol, which served to distance Northern Ireland from the Irish Free State. These highly charged political symbols played an important role in the development of Irish national identity, though at the beginning there was no unanimity about them on the part of all the political parties in what became the Irish Free State. At first, some were upset that the symbols of Sinn Fein, which had played such an important role in the fight for independence, were selected as representing the Irish nation rather than the symbols of other political parties or movements. The symbols of Northern Ireland reiterated their continued relationship with the Crown, while the symbols of the Irish Free State represented their independence and separation from Britain.

If authority is represented by a series of symbols, opposition to that authority is symbolically represented by an inversion of those symbols. In the 1960s in the United States, men in authority had short hair. Young men created a symbol of opposition when they allowed their hair to grow long. If authorities have short hair, then long hair is a symbol of opposition to that authority. During the seventeenth century, the Cavaliers of Charles I of England wore their hair long, while those who opposed them, the Puritans led by Oliver Cromwell, wore short hair. The Puritans' hairstyle became the focal symbol of their opposition, and so they were called Roundheads. These examples relate to the general principle that those who oppose the established authority will select as their symbol something that is the reverse of the symbol of those in authority. Political symbols may seem trivial, but, in reality, people will fight to retain them. People's identity or concept of self as members of a group is powerfully bound up with such symbols. To deny or reject them is to deny one's identity and worth.

Hair length throughout history communicates ideas about gender, class, and group affiliation. In many societies, women's hair length symbolizes their beauty and sexuality. Its visual presence in some cultures is discouraged by keeping it uncut and covered; noncompliance can be disciplined, as in contemporary Iran. This woman in Turkey is protesting the arrest of women in Iran for not covering their hair with ritually approved clothing. She is cutting her own hair in public to symbolize her support of Iranian women who are being forced to cover their hair at all times.

PUBLIC MEMORIALS AND MONUMENTS: CREATING AND CONTESTING SYMBOLS OF HISTORY

Monuments and memorials are used in public spaces to commemorate people and events of the past, but their durability (often

fashioned of stone and metal) is designed to be reminders of aspects of history to people in the present. They are usually large and expensive to produce and have historically been produced by (and financed by) governments; they therefore often represent the official, or dominant, narrative of history. Their creation and placement in public spaces is a symbol of what this dominant narrative claims are important to remember from the past. They represent choices made in political contexts about which people, values, and ideas should be remembered; their power lies in contemporary resonance with and recognition of these values in the present.

Contemporary social activists often target public monuments because the values they represent no longer are celebrated by people who do not share its vision of history. The valorization of certain individuals or events is often challenged as not being representative of an inclusive vision of history. This contestation has become part of contemporary dialogue in many parts of the United States, where the Black Lives Matter (BLM) and other social movements have protested the presence of public monuments recognizing Confederate generals of the American Civil War. In 2020, many monuments honoring Civil War military leaders were attacked, vandalized, and eventually removed because they were no longer considered appropriate symbols to honor in the present. For example, after weeks of protests over the murder of African American men by police, a statue of Albert Pike in Washington, DC, honoring an officer of the Confederate States Army, was toppled by protesters and removed from its place of display in the nation's capital.

Public memory is influenced not only by the presence of monuments and memorials, but also by their absence. Therefore, activists representing marginalized people whose historical presence has been ignored by official narratives are increasingly demanding memorials be created to recognize them through public symbols. The contribution of women, gays and lesbians, noncommissioned soldiers, and ethnic minorities to the American military is now being recognized through the display of official-built memorials and more ephemeral symbols. The widespread use of a red poppy to recognize the sacrifice of hundreds of thousands of soldiers during World War I now honors the war dead and all veterans throughout the United States and Europe. Whatever form they take, symbols of history and memorialization invoke emotions and draw the viewer into the experience of history and memory. Contemporary constructed memorials tend to be simplified in their presentation by the use of plain shapes and forms to make a more abstract statement that individuals can react to, with their own understanding and emotional experience coming to the forefront of the experience.

Public memorials in prominent places invoke strong emotions through their design and placement. Many memorials honoring the deaths of people in war and political violence follow the design introduced by Maya Lin for the Vietnam War Memorial in Washington, DC, in 1982—a simple yet moving presentation of the names of people killed and injured. Mourners are encouraged to interact with the memorial by creating rubbings of the names of loved ones.

SUMMARY

- Symbols and their meanings are crucial to understanding what a culture is all about.

- The term *metaphor* refers to the relationship in which one thing stands for something else, as eating does for sexual activity.

- *Metonym* refers to a part of something standing for the whole, such as the crown that stands for the political authority of the queen or king of England.

- Symbols are two-sided—the physical properties of the symbol as distinct from what the symbol stands for.

- There will not always be consensus on the meanings of symbols within one society. Different groups will interpret symbols differently based on their histories and relationships with other groups.

- Debates about cultural appropriation focus on the unequal status between the cultures that adapt the symbols or others, and the culture from which that symbol has been appropriated.

- Food has many different meanings in different cultures. Understanding the symbolism of food is an important way of understanding relationships between different groups of people within society.

- Group identity may be symbolized in a number of other ways in addition to food consumption and commensality.

- Public spaces and cultural expectations about them make important symbolic statements about gender, social groupings, and social relationships.

- Arrangements of domestic space within households also reveal cultural norms about kinship, social groups, and their relationships.

- Political authority and factions are readily identifiable by, and invoke emotions through, their symbols, such as flags or anthems.

- The interpretation of the human body and its processes has different meanings in different cultures.

- Sports in American society contains a wide variety of symbols that make statements about gender, achievement, and values.

- Different cultural domains, such as kinship, economics, political organization, and religion, are all imbued with symbolic meaning. To understand how these institutions work, one must understand the symbols and the varied cultural meanings through which they are organized.

- Public monuments and memorials are increasingly being understood around the world as representing a dominant vision of history that excludes the roles of marginalized people and their contributions to historical events.

KEY TERMS

cultural appropriation, 110   public symbols, 105
metaphor, 104   symbols, 104
metonym, 105   totemic animal, 109
private symbols, 105

SUGGESTED READINGS

Morton, Paula E. *Tortillas: A Cultural History*. Albuquerque: University of New Mexico Press, 2014.

A social and cultural history of the significance of tortillas, a dietary staple in Mesoamerica, in religious, social, and political life.

O'Neill, Barry. *Honor, Symbols and War*. Ann Arbor: University of Michigan Press, 1999.

Examines the role that symbolism plays in international relations and conflict resolution. The importance of the symbolic expression of national honor is also considered.

Womack, Mari. *Symbols and Meaning: A Concise Introduction*. Walnut Creek, CA: Altamira Press, 2005.

A general work on the various aspects of the study of symbolism.

SUGGESTED WEBSITES

https://tatring.com/tattoo-ideas-meanings/Hawaiian-Tattoos-And-Meanings-HawaiianTattoo Designs-And-History

A website detailing explanations of Hawaiian and Pacific Island tattoo symbols and blogs from tattoo designers and users.

www.symbols.com

An online encyclopedia "that contains everything about symbols, signs, flags and glyphs arranged by categories such as culture, country, religion, and more."

https://theconversation.com/what-is-cultural-appropriation-and-how-does-it-differ-from-cultural-appreciation-162331

An online discussion of the distinctions between cultural appropriation and cultural appreciation, using recognizable examples from popular culture.

Chapter 6
Ties That Connect
Marriage, Family, and Kinship

LEARNING OBJECTIVES

- Understand the principles of marriage prohibitions, incest taboos, and marriage payments.
- Analyze multiple types of postmarital residence patterns and their subsequent effects on the composition of households over time.
- Using different types of descent systems and kinship terminology systems, reconstruct how they form identities.

- Explore the relationship between globalization and family formation.
- Discuss multiple ways in which state policy impacts family and childbirth decision making, and bestows rights and citizenship through marriage and family law.

WHAT IS "KINSHIP"? HOW CAN we identify kinship in America and elsewhere? In our society, we have families and a network of relatives beyond the family. In all societies, people who are related to one another by some form of kinship constitute a family, while people who live together under one roof form a household. The members of a household may not necessarily all be related by kinship to one another. Family and household units, therefore, may not coincide.

Households in America typically consist of two generations, parents and unmarried children; elsewhere three- or even four-generation families, including grandparents, married children of one gender, and grandchildren, may be the norm. Larger households integrate the care of young children and the elderly so they may have no need for daycare centers and nursing homes. Small, independent two-generation families are associated with the individualism characteristic of American society, though we will see later on that today American families are more diverse. Ethnic groups in complex state-based societies often use the notion of "brotherhood" or kinship to claim "we are all brothers." This collective view of brothers can be contrasted with the individualism of our own society, which pulls married brothers apart after marriage, each favoring his own immediate family.

In the societies anthropologists studied earlier, most of daily life was organized on the basis of kinship relationships. In these societies, all religious, economic, and political behavior took place within the context of a social structure based on kinship. This is why the study of kinship was considered so important in anthropology. Even with increasing industrialization and globalization in so many parts of the world today, kinship continues to be central. "Many societies still think in terms of lineages, affinal alliance systems, residence rules, and marriage payments, while virtually all are still organized in families of some sort and use kin terms to identify and classify relatives" (Parkin 1997: ix–x).

Our discussion of marriage, family, households, and kinship terminology illustrates cultural norms found in a variety of societies. Through time, cultural rules and norms are frequently transformed. Historically, before the advent of colonialism and accelerated culture change, when small-scale societies had less contact with one another, rules of kinship in these societies were more obvious. Today, kinship and kin groups continue to be significant in people's lives, whether they remain in their rural villages or migrate to expanding cities like Lagos in Nigeria, or Port Moresby in Papua New Guinea. Until recently, it was widely believed that kinship relations would be replaced by state institutions in capitalist industrial societies and would diminish in importance over time. Current ethnographic research on kinship and family reveals just the opposite. Relatives may not be living in the same country, but they still maintain regular contact by phone, e-mail, and social media.

MARRIAGE

All known societies recognize marriage. The ritual of marriage marks a change in status for the participants and the acceptance by society of the offspring. Marriage, like all other things cultural, is governed by rules that, as will be seen, are connected to one another. Just as the rules vary from one society to another, so does the ritual by which society recognizes and celebrates the marriage. In an American wedding, each spouse repeats the ritual formula "With this ring, I thee wed." In the Kwakwaka'wakw wedding described in chapter 2, the bridegroom came as a member of a feigned war party to capture the bride and take her from her father's house. At both weddings, large numbers of guests are present, serving as witnesses to the marriage, signifying that marriage is a group ritual witnessed publicly.

Marriage Prohibitions

All societies have rules about whom one can and cannot marry. These rules are directly related to the incest taboo, which is found in all societies and is therefore a universal concept. The incest taboo that forbids sexual relations between categories of kin also necessarily forbids marriage, since marriage almost always includes sexual access. Almost universally, forbidden categories include mother and son, father and daughter, and brother and sister. The **incest taboo** also forbids sexual relations and marriage between certain categories of close relatives. Since sexual partners cannot be sought within the immediate family because of the incest taboo, they must be sought elsewhere.

In many societies, there are people with whom one can have sexual intercourse but whom one cannot marry. Marriage prohibitions, therefore, are wider in scope than the prohibitions against sexual intercourse. Both the incest taboo and prohibitions against marrying certain close relatives have the effect of compelling individuals often to seek sexual partners and mates outside their own group. There is great variation from one society to another in the rules regarding which categories of relatives one is forbidden to marry. Within the United States, there is variation in the laws regarding which relatives one may not marry. Some states permit marriage between first cousins while others prohibit it; still others prohibit marriage between second cousins. There are a few striking examples of marriage between members of the immediate family that violate the universality of the incest taboo. Among the pharaohs of ancient Egypt, as well as among the royal lineages of Hawaii and the Incas in Peru, brothers and sisters married. In each instance, the ruler had to marry someone equal in rank; marrying a sibling guaranteed the equivalence in rank. But what was permitted to royalty was not acceptable for other groups in society.

incest taboo

Prohibition of sexual relations between certain categories of kin.

Exogamy and Endogamy

Marriage within a designated group is called **endogamy**, and marriage outside the group is called **exogamy**. For example, in rural Rajasthan, marriages are generally jati or caste group endogamous, and village exogamous. The rule of exogamy, like the incest taboo, requires that members of the group seek spouses outside the designated group, such as lineage exogamous. A rule of exogamy is frequently conceptualized as an extension of the incest

endogamy

A rule requiring group members to marry within their own group.

exogamy

A rule requiring group members to marry outside their own social group.

taboo in that the same term may be used for both. Among the Trobriand Islanders, the term *suvasova* is used for the incest taboo and is also extended to forbid sexual relations and marriage with women of one's own larger kin group or dala, all of whom are called sisters. A rule of endogamy requires individuals to marry within their own group and forbids them to marry outside it. Some religious groups have rules of endogamy, though these are often violated when marriage takes place between people of different religions. In rural India, marriages are caste endogamous but village exogamous. Rules of exogamy create links between groups, while rules of endogamy preserve separateness and exclusivity, and are a means of maintaining group identity and preserving group assets.

Sister Exchange

sister exchange

A marriage pattern in which two men marry each other's sisters, perpetuated across generations.

Since a rule of exogamy requires that spouses come from outside one's group, relationships are created through marriage with other groups. From the male perspective, a man cannot marry his own sister, so he gives his sister to someone in another group. According to the basic principle of exchange, something given must be returned with its equivalent. If a man accepts another man's sister, he must therefore return his own sister as the equivalent. A number of societies have a rule requiring that two men exchange sisters; anthropologists refer to this as **sister exchange**. If a man does not have a biological sister, he returns a woman for whom he uses the same kinship term that he uses for his sister. Feminist anthropologists have argued that this form of marriage could just as easily be conceptualized as brother exchange. However, where men are dominant in a society, this is seen as sister exchange from the local point of view. When Margaret Mead went to study the Mountain Arapesh in New Guinea, she asked why they didn't marry their own sisters, expecting a response indicating revulsion at the very thought. Instead, Mead's informant stated, "What is the matter with you anyway? Don't you want a brother-in-law?" (Mead 1950: 68). This is because one hunts, gardens, and travels with one's brother-in-law, among the Arapesh. Thus marriage creates a connection between husband and wife as well as alliances between brothers-in-law.

Marriage Payments

bridewealth

Payments of goods or services made by the groom's family to the family of the bride.

dowry

Goods that are given by the bride's family to the groom's family at marriage.

In many societies marriage involves a transfer or exchange of property. Sometimes, payments are made by the groom and his family to the family of the bride, as occurs among the Kwakwaka'wakw. This payment is known as **bridewealth**. In other instances, the bride brings property with her at the marriage. This is known as **dowry**, and goods are moving in the opposite direction from bridewealth payments. In societies that practice sister exchange, there may be an option to give bridewealth if one does not have a sister to exchange. However, it is also common to find sister exchange accompanied by the payment of bridewealth, so that groups are exchanging both women and bridewealth payments. In China, prior to the Communist revolution, both bridewealth and dowry were paid at marriage.

Bride Service

Sometimes the groom exchanges labor for his bride in lieu of the payment of bridewealth. When the groom works for his wife's family, this is known as **bride service**. In the Old Testament, it is described how Jacob labored for seven years in order to marry Leah, and then another seven years to marry Rachel, Leah's younger sister, thus performing fourteen years of bride service for his father-in-law. Bride service as practiced by the Yanomamo of the lowlands of Venezuela involves labor exchange; for a period of time, the groom lives with the bride's parents and hunts for them. Since the Yanomamo also have sister exchange, one might say that during this period of bride service, they really are practicing brother exchange. However, since men determine whom women will marry, the Yanomamo do not conceptualize this as two women exchanging their brothers. After the period of bride service is over, the husband takes his wife back to his group and resides there with their children.

In Mali, a dowry of ritually valued cola nuts and other gifts from the groom and his family is proudly displayed by the bride (far right) to female family members and friends.

bride service

A custom whereby the groom works for the bride's family before marriage.

monogamy

Marriage with only one spouse at a time.

polygamy

Marriage system with plural spouses, either husbands or wives.

polygyny

Marriage in which one man has more than one wife recognized at one time.

sororal polygyny

The marriage of a man to several sisters.

polyandry

marriage system in which one woman has several husbands at one time.

Number of Spouses

Some societies practice **monogamy**; that is, permitting only one living spouse at a time. Having multiple living, recognized spouses of either gender is referred to as **polygamy**. Sometimes men are allowed more than one wife at a time. This is known as **polygyny** and is practiced in many societies and religions. Sometimes a man marries several sisters; this practice is known as **sororal polygyny**. In the societies in which it occurs, it is usually explained by the fact that sisters have a good relationship with one another, and this will help overcome the inevitable jealousy that arises between co-wives. On the other hand, many people, such as the Trobriand Islanders and the Kanuri of Nigeria, explicitly forbid sororal polygyny. The Kanuri explanation for this prohibition is that the good relationship between two sisters should not be undermined by the unavoidable friction that arises between two co-wives. This clearly demonstrates that whatever rules are in effect, the people will offer an explanation for their existence that is perfectly rational and obvious in their eyes.

An alternative and less common form of marriage is known as **polyandry**, in which one woman may have several husbands. In almost all cases,

A Nyinba polyandrous family in northwest Nepal. The eldest husband is to the left, sewing clothing; the youngest husband is to the right. The woman on the left is their common wife, holding their youngest daughter. The girl on the right is their oldest daughter; leaning against her is the family's only son.

fraternal polyandry

A form of marriage in which a woman is simultaneously married to several brothers.

serial monogamy

The practice of marrying a series of spouses, one after the other.

levirate

A rule whereby the widow of a deceased man must marry his brother.

sororate

The custom whereby a widower marries his deceased wife's sister.

a woman marries several brothers; this is known as **fraternal polyandry**. Today, among ethnic Tibetans in northwest Nepal, the ideal form of marriage is fraternal polyandry, in which the eldest brother is the primary husband and nominally the father of all the children, whether or not he is the biological father (Levine 1987). Anthropologists refer to having plural spouses in general as *polygamy*, in contrast to the term *monogamy*, a system that recognizes only one living spouse at a time. Because of the frequency of divorce and subsequent remarriage in the United States, it is sometimes said that Americans practice **serial monogamy**. The state criminalizes having more than one legally recognized spouse at a time, but some people have numerous living spouses, one after the other.

Levirate and Sororate

The exchange of a woman for another woman or the exchange of a woman for bridewealth is an indication that marriage is a significant concern of the kin groups of the marrying couple. A further demonstration of this is found in the customs of the **levirate** and the **sororate**. Under the levirate, if a man dies, his widow then marries one of his brothers, thereby continuing the relationship between the two kin groups established by the first marriage. In the levirate, a woman marries one brother after the death of another brother, while in fraternal polyandry she is married to two brothers simultaneously. When a deceased wife is replaced in the marriage by an unmarried sister, this is known as the sororate. It resembles sororal polygyny, but in the sororate, a man marries two sisters serially, the second after the death of the first. This practice illustrates the kinship concept of equivalence of siblings, in which one same-sex sibling can be substituted for another.

Dissolution of Marriage

Stability of marriage varies from one society to another. Almost all societies provide a means for the dissolution of a marriage. Divorce is invariably more complicated after children have been born to the couple. Where bridewealth has been paid, it may have to be returned if the wife leaves her husband. This may be difficult to achieve if the bridewealth, paid several years before, has been spent, dispersed, or consumed. Some anthropologists have argued that the higher the bridewealth payment, the more stable the marriage and less likely a divorce, since it would require the return of bridewealth, which may be difficult in such societies. Others have said that frequency of divorce and stability of marriage are related, not to the amount of bridewealth but to the degree of incorporation of a wife into her husband's family or kin group. Among the Manchus of Manchuria, who conquered China in the seventeenth century, the wife went through a fire ceremony in front of the hearth in her husband's house. This ritual served to conceptually incorporate her permanently into his kin group. In contrast, the Kwakwaka'wakw paid bridewealth to the bride's family. At a subsequent ceremony, the bride's family paid a large amount of goods to "repurchase" her, thereby reiterating her membership in the kin group of her birth. Among the Kwakwaka'wakw, the wife is never incorporated into the husband's kin group. The husband must make a new bridewealth payment if he wishes her to continue to be his wife. The bridewealth and repurchase payments symbolize how two people may be joined in marriage and yet retain an identity in their own kin groups.

Postmarital Residence

The location in which a couple lives after the marriage ritual is governed by cultural rules, referred to as **postmarital residence rules** (see figure 6.1). The nature of the postmarital residence rule determines the composition of the household after marriage.

The postmarital residence rule in American society is that the new couple forms an independent household, referred to as **neolocal residence**. When you have neolocal residence, you have **nuclear families**, with households usually consisting of parents and children. Breaching a social rule brings sanctions. In America, if a newly married couple lives for an extended period with the family of either the husband or the wife, it is usually because of economic hardship or the couple's student status. Gossips will make snide comments about the lack of adult independence of the couple, since they continue to live as though they were children in their parents' home.

A common form of postmarital residence is followed when the newly married couple lives in the household of the groom's parents. This is known as **virilocal residence** (also

postmarital residence rule

A rule that states where a couple lives after marriage.

neolocal residence

A rule of postmarital residence in which the newly married couple forms an independent household.

nuclear family

A family consisting of a husband, wife, and their unmarried children.

virilocal residence

A rule of postmarital residence whereby the newly married couple resides with the relatives of the groom.

Fig. 6.1 *Postmarital residence patterns*

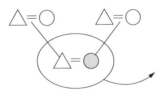

A. Neolocal residence

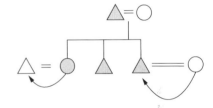

B. Virilocal residence
(patrilineal)

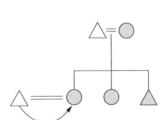

C. Uxorilocal residence
(matrilineal)

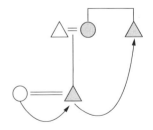

D. Avunculocal residence
(matrilineal)

△ = male

○ = female

△=○ = marriage

△ ↷ = person moves

sometimes referred to as *patrilocal* residence). With a rule of virilocal residence, the wife is incorporated, to a greater or lesser extent, into the household of her husband's kin, since it is she (the bride) who must leave her own family. The groom merely remains in his household as part of the virilocal extended family.

Less frequent is the case in which the newly married couple lives in the household of the bride's parents. This is called **uxorilocal residence** (also referred to as *matrilocal* residence) and results in an uxorilocal extended family. In this instance, it is the husband who must be incorporated into his wife's family. In the past, in some Pueblo societies of Arizona and New Mexico that had a rule of uxorilocal residence, the degree of incorporation of the husband into his wife's family was so slight that the wife could divorce him simply by leaving his belongings on the doorstep.

Still another rule of postmarital residence is the arrangement in which, after marriage, the wife joins her new husband, who is living with his mother's brother rather than with his own father. This is called **avunculocal residence** and results in the avunculocal extended family. This rule of residence involves two separate and distinct moves. The earlier move occurs when a man, as an adolescent, leaves his father's house to live with his mother's brother, from whom he will inherit later in life. The incorporation of the young man into the household of his mother's brother is associated with matrilineal descent, discussed below. After the marriage, the wife joins her husband at his mother's brother's house. The Trobriand Islanders have an avunculocal rule of postmarital residence, particularly important for people in chiefly clans.

Sometimes a society will have a rule of residence stating that after marriage, the couple can opt to live either with the bride's family or with the groom's family without establishing an independent household. This is called **bilocal residence**. On Dobu, an island near the Trobriands, the married couple spends one year in the bride's village and the following year in the groom's village, alternating in this manner between the two villages every year. Among the Iban of Borneo, however, a choice must be made at some point after marriage between affiliation with one side or the other, and this choice becomes permanent.

There is also the rare postmarital residence rule in which husband and wife live with their respective kin, apart from one another after marriage. This is known as **duolocal residence**. The Ashanti of Ghana, who traditionally lived in large towns, have this form of postmarital residence. Husbands and wives live in the same town, but not in the same household. At dusk, one could see young children carrying the evening meal prepared in their mother's house to their father's house for their father to eat.

As we have noted above, the rules stating where a couple should live after marriage result in different types of households (figure 6.2). In the Ashanti example just discussed, the family unit of husband, wife, and children live in two separate households. With neolocal postmarital residence, as exists in America, the family that is formed is the nuclear family. The nuclear family is generally a two-generation, independent household that operates autonomously in

---

uxorilocal residence

A rule of postmarital residence whereby the newly married couple resides with the relatives of the bride.

avunculocal residence

A form of postmarital residence in which the bride goes to live with her husband after he has moved to live with his mother's brother.

bilocal residence

A form of postmarital residence in which husband and wife alternate between living with the husband's relatives for a period of time and then with the wife's relatives.

duolocal residence

A postmarital rule of residence in which husband and wife live with their respective kinsmen, apart from one another.

economic affairs, in the rearing and education of children, and in other phases of life. After marriage, children will establish their own nuclear families.

What happens when there are plural spouses, as in societies that practice polygyny or polyandry? Among the Kanuri of northern Nigeria, where polygyny is practiced, only a small proportion of men actually have more than one wife. However, in these polygynous families, each wife must have her own house and hearth. The husband must visit each wife in turn, at which time she cooks for him, and he must stay the night with her. Though he may favor one wife over another, he should treat them equally. A man's house and those of his wives form a single walled compound or household. Even though they have separate hearths and separate houses, they are all under the authority of the husband, who is the head of all the households. Such a household might also include servants belonging to the head of the household. In polyandrous societies, like Tibet, a woman and her several husbands, usually brothers, live in the same house and form a single household with all their unmarried offspring.

When several related nuclear families of three or more generations live together in the same household, they form an **extended family**. When there is a rule of virilocal residence, the household consists of an older married couple, their married sons and wives, and the unmarried children of both the older couple and their married sons. Their married daughters will have left the household to join the households of their husbands. The center of this type of extended family is a core of related men. Their in-marrying wives come from different places and are not related to each other. Uxorilocal

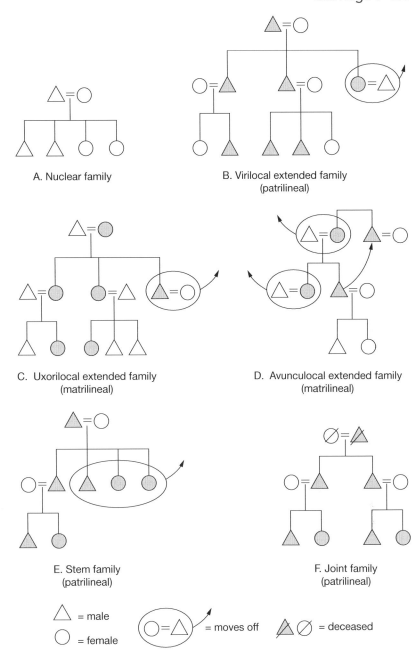

A. Nuclear family

B. Virilocal extended family
(patrilineal)

C. Uxorilocal extended family
(matrilineal)

D. Avunculocal extended family
(matrilineal)

E. Stem family
(patrilineal)

F. Joint family
(patrilineal)

△ = male
○ = female
○=△ (circled, arrow) = moves off
△ ⊘ = deceased

Fig. 6.2 *Household and family types*

extended family

Three or more generations living together in a single household.

postmarital residence results in extended families of a very different sort. In this case, a core of related women remains together, and their husbands marry into the extended family. With avunculocal residence there is once again a core of men forming the basis of the extended family, but this core of men is linked through women.

In the ethnographic literature, the most extensively documented extended family is one that consists of parents and married children of brothers, their spouses, and their children. An extended family consisting of parents and only one married son and his family per generation is known as a **stem family**. It occured in parts of rural Ireland where the amount of land inherited is small and cannot be profitably subdivided. Only one son, typically the youngest one, inherits the land, while his older brothers go off to the cities, become priests, or emigrate abroad. Another type of extended family is the **joint family**, which includes brothers and their wives and children, who stay together as a single two-generational household after the parents have died.

DESCENT SYSTEMS

The kinds of family groups that we have just described are based on both kinship and residence. Beyond the family, there are groups based upon shared kinship or descent, though members need not live in the same place. Family type and residence rules are the building blocks for such descent groups. For example, societies with virilocal residence and virilocal extended families usually have patrilineal descent groups. Membership in these groups is based upon presumed descent from a common ancestor. These groups are sometimes called "clans." Descent determines not only group membership but also rights to property and inheritance.

Patrilineal Descent and Matrilineal Descent

Societies have rules that determine whether the child belongs either to the mother's or the father's kin group. A rule that states that offspring belong to their father's group is called a **patrilineal rule of descent**. This means that children belong to their father's group, the father belongs to his father's group, and so forth, as illustrated in the diagram (figure 6.3). A daughter belongs to her father's group, but her children do not. Children share common identity with only one of their four grandparents; however, the other three grandparents are still their relatives and kinsmen. As one goes back through the generations, ties of kin relationships form a web of kinship. A rule of descent carves out of this web of kinship a much smaller segment, which comprises the members of one's own group. These descent groups continue to exist through time, beyond the lifespan of individual members, as new generations continue to be born into the group. In most societies that have patrilineal descent systems, though certainly not in all, marriages are exogamous, and one must marry outside one's own group.

---

stem family

A two-generation extended family consisting of parents and only one married son and his family.

joint family

A type of extended family in which married brothers and their families remain together after the death of their parents.

patrilineal rule of descent

A rule stating that a child belongs to his or her father's group.

A **matrilineal rule of descent** states that children belong to the group of their mother, not that of the father. The Trobriand Islanders have such a rule of descent. Among the Trobrianders, as in all matrilineal societies, the continuity of the group is not through a man's own children but through those of his sister.

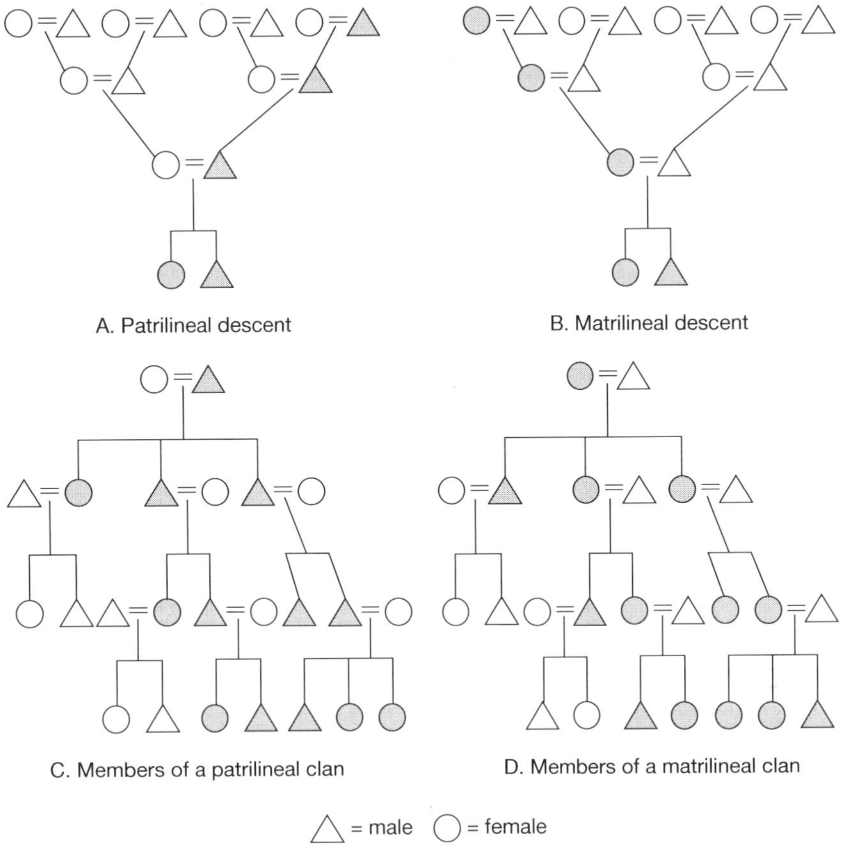

Among the Trobrianders, children belong to the group of their mother, sharing common substance with their mother and other group mates. The father is considered an affine, a relative by marriage only, in contrast to a consanguine, a blood relative. For a child to be conceived, the Trobrianders believed that

A. Patrilineal descent

B. Matrilineal descent

C. Members of a patrilineal clan

D. Members of a matrilineal clan

△ = male   ◯ = female

Fig. 6.3 *Descent and clan membership.*

an ancestral spirit from the mother's clan had entered her womb. Since the creation of a child is not seen as the result of the merging of substance from mother and father, they did not believe that sexual intercourse had anything to do with the conception of a child. The father, by repeated acts of intercourse, nurtures the child and molds the child so that the child resembles him in appearance. But this has nothing to do with the conception of the child in the first place, which is all the doing of the maternal ancestral spirit of the mother's group. The child therefore cannot be claimed by the father's group. Though the Trobriand father is a very important nurturing relative, he is still considered unrelated to his children, as are all the members of his maternal group.

Unilineal Descent Groups: Their Structures and Functions

One can see the different ways in which descent groups are structured when one looks at the way in which political leadership is inherited (figure 6.4). In patrilineal societies like that of the Mongols, inherited leadership is usually structured in the following manner: it passes from father to son and from brother to brother. Leadership in matrilineal societies, like that of the Trobrianders, is handed down from mother's brother to sister's son or from

matrilineal rule of descent

Unilineal descent rule stating that a child belongs to his or her mother's group.

A

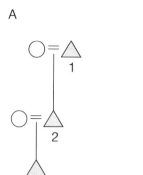

B

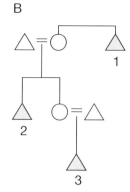

Fig. 6.4 *Passage of political leadership in a patrilineal society (A) and in a matrilineal society (B).*

cognatic descent

A rule of descent in which individuals have the choice of belonging to either their father's or their mother's group, to determine different rights or statuses, or they may have particular rights by virtue of membership in either group.

brother to brother. In a matrilineal society, a son can never directly inherit a position of leadership from his father. In such societies, although the line of descent goes through women, the women themselves are rarely the political heads of their communities. One may contrast the nature of the relationship of a man to his father in patrilineal societies and to his mother's brother in matrilineal societies. In patrilineal societies, a son will replace his father in the position of leadership and is often perceived of as a competitor and antagonist of his own father. His mother's brother, who is not in his group, is often a source of support. In contrast, in matrilineal societies, a sister's son will succeed to the position of leadership held by his mother's brother. The relationship between these two parallels that of the father-son relationship in a patrilineal society.

In the relationship between father and son in a matrilineal society, all the elements of antagonism and potential conflict between them are removed. In societies with **cognatic descent** groups, like that of the Kwakwaka'wakw, a man can succeed to political leadership by virtue of descent through his mother or through his father; thus he can be the heir of either his father or of his mother's brother. While in unilineal societies, the father-son relationship is the opposite of the mother's brother-sister's son relationship, this opposition does not occur in cognatic societies. The optional nature of the descent rule permits the possibility that brothers may be in different descent groups. Among the Kwakwaka'wakw, it frequently happens that two brothers are in different numayms or descent groups, which can even fight each other. In patrilineal and in matrilineal societies, which are unilineal, this can never happen, since brothers are always in the same group.

Clans

clan

A social group based on presumed common descent but not necessarily common residence.

Matrilineal or patrilineal **clans** are still present in societies today. Members of a clan claim a common ancestral origin, which is claimed but cannot not demonstrated. Some of the activities of clans concern rituals. For example, the matrilineal clan of the Trobrianders serves as host at the ceremonial distribution (sagali) accompanying a funeral when a member of their clan dies. Ritual objects and spells are owned by clans. Clans also have political functions and may compete with one another for power and political positions and may even fight with one another. Each clan has some kind of leadership, almost always male, to organize these political activities. The chief (the leader) of a Trobriand clan directs the accumulation of large amounts of food to be given away at a Trobriand sagali. Finally, what has frequently been seen as the most important function of the clan is its ownership of land. Members of a clan have the right to use its land by virtue of the fact that they are born into the clan. Clan members may work together at tasks, such as building a communal house or canoe, which benefit the clan as a whole.

The common ancestor from whom all the members of a clan believe that they are descended is sometimes conceived of as an ancestral or clan spirit. This ancestral spirit may be thought of as having a nonhuman form, perhaps that of an animal. In that case, all members of the clan are thought of as having a special relationship to that animal, and they may be forbidden to eat it. Such an animal is called the **clan totem**, and, as noted in chapter 5, it is a symbol that represents the clan and could be graphically represented, as depicted in the totem poles. Patrilineal clans have similar functions.

The clan is frequently referred to by anthropologists as a **corporate descent group.** Like a corporation, it has an existence independent of its individual members. Clan members die and new ones are born, while the clan continues to operate through time. A corporation owns property and so does the clan. However, anybody can buy stock in a corporation and become an owner, but membership in a clan is restricted to certain kinds of kin, as defined by the rule of descent.

In some societies, you belong to a clan simply because your father or your mother belonged to that clan. Other people with whom you cannot trace a relationship of kinship also belong to your clan. Anthropologists say that descent is stipulated in such a clan system. Where **stipulated descent** is found, there are no lengthy genealogies, and people usually remember back only to their grandfathers' generation. Where long genealogies are kept, written or oral, members of a clan can trace their kinship back to the founding ancestor of the clan and in this way to every other member of the clan. Anthropologists call this **demonstrated descent**. In societies where clans include large numbers of people living dispersed over a wide area, each clan may in turn be divided into smaller units, referred to as subclans.

Lineages

Within clans with demonstrated descent, there are smaller units referred to as **lineages**. Sometimes all the people in the society believe themselves to be descended from a single ancestor. This founding ancestor may be historical or mythical, or a little of both. The kin groups are related to one another in an extensive genealogy. The Bedouin Arabs of Cyrenaica in eastern Libya are an example of such a society. They are nomadic pastoralists who keep herds of camels and sheep in the desert areas of their territory and cows and goats in the wooded plateau areas. All the Cyrenaican Bedouin alive today consider themselves descended from the single ancestor Sa'ada, who heads the genealogy (figure 6.5). Sa'ada was the mother of two sons who are said to be the founding ancestors of the two largest groups of tribes—Baraghith and 'Aqqara. The genealogy in the diagram represents the set of ideas that the Cyrenaican Bedouin use to talk about how they are related to one another and how their group is related to all other Cyrenaican groups. The genealogy is like a branching tree, extending out to its many twigs. Several twigs, or lineages, are part of a branch, and several branches, or groupings of lineages, are part of a larger limb. The larger limb represents a still larger grouping of

clan totem

An animal from which members of a clan believe themselves descended and with whom they enact a special symbolic relationship.

corporate descent group

A kin-based group based upon common descent that owns a form of property collectively.

stipulated descent

A social unit, such as a clan, in which all members consider themselves to be related, though they cannot actually trace the genealogical relationship.

demonstrated descent

A system of descent in which kinship can be traced by means of written or oral genealogies back to a founding ancestor.

lineages

Unilineal descent groups in which descent is demonstrated.

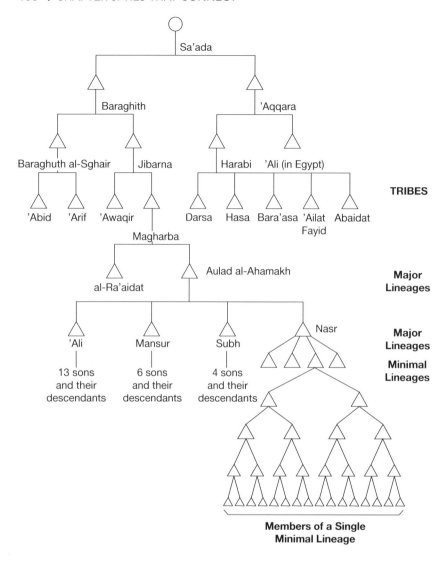

Members of a Single Minimal Lineage

Fig. 6.5 *Genealogy system of the Cyrenaican Bedouin*

lineages. This kind of descent system is called a **segmentary lineage system**. Groups at all the levels of segmentation are referred to as "lineages." This kind of system is found in societies with patrilineal descent, such as the Cyrenaican Bedouin. The constant branching out represents levels of segmentation. The branching out of the genealogy also has a close relationship to the occupation of geographical areas. The two groups of tribes, descended from each of the sons of Sa'ada, occupy the eastern and western halves of Cyrenaica. Lineages descended from brothers a few generations back graze their herds on lands adjacent to one another. Lineages that are further away genealogically occupy lands farther apart. In political action, lineages closely related to one another unite to oppose a threat from a more distantly related lineage. The Pashtuns who straddle the border between Afghanistan and northwestern Pakistan, where fighting has been taking place for years, have a segmentary lineage system, as do the Somali in Africa. (We will discuss the current situation of the Pashtuns in chapter 14. In chapter 9 we examine how segmentary lineage systems operate politically.)

segmentary lineage system

A descent system, typically patrilineal, in which the largest segments are successively divided into smaller segments, like branches of a tree.

moieties

A grouping based upon descent in which the entire society is divided into halves.

Moieties

Another kind of grouping based on descent is one in which the entire society is divided into two halves, which are referred to as **moieties**. Moieties may be based upon a patrilineal or a matrilineal rule of descent. Sometimes in societies with moieties, a village site was divided in half, each half being occupied by the members of one moiety. As noted in chapter 5, the two parts of a moiety are often referred to in oppositional terms, such as *left* and *right*. The Abelam of the Sepik River area of New Guinea have patrilineal moieties referred to simply as "us" and "them." Among the Tlingit of the Pacific Coast of northern Canada and Alaska, the two moieties are known as Raven and Wolf and are based on matrilineal descent. Moieties are usually composed of several clans.

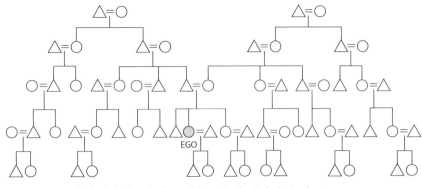

Ego's Kindred   With Ego at the center, the Kindred extends out to include Ego's siblings, first cousins, second cousins, and even more distant relatives not included in the above diagram.

Kindreds

The descent groups examined above are all based on a rule of descent from a single common ancestor and are said to be ancestor-oriented. Kindreds, on the other hand, are reckoned in an entirely different way (see figure 6.6). People are at the center of their own web of kinship. Anthropologists

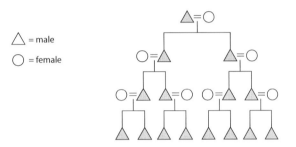

△ = male
○ = female

The Patrilineal Descent Group   In contrast to the kindred, the clan is ancestor-oriented.

Fig. 6.6   *Kindred and descent group*

refer to the individual at the center as the ego, and the relatives who make up that web of kinship constitute the ego's **kindred**. The kindred includes relatives on both the ego's mother's and father's sides. Individuals who are descendants of the ego as well as the ego's ancestors and everyone descended from those ancestors are included in the ego's kindred. The kindred is **ego-oriented**. The kindred as a unit does not own land or any other property; it only has coherence as a group around the ego at its center. Societies that do not have **unilineal descent groups** but do have kindreds are known as **bilateral societies**. On an occasion such as the American wedding described in chapter 2, the kindreds of the bride and groom attend. If any of the first cousins of the groom (for instance, his father's brother's son) get married, a different set of relatives will be present, though there will be an overlap with his kindred. This overlap occurs since the two egos share a certain set of relatives.

RELATIONS BETWEEN GROUPS THROUGH MARRIAGE

As we mentioned earlier, sister exchange occurs when a rule of exogamy compels one group to give its women to another group in marriage, receiving the women of the other group in return (figure 6.7). Arapesh men state that they marry their sisters from outside the group in order to obtain brothers-in-law.

kindred

A kin group from the perspective of a particular individual, or "ego."

ego-oriented group

A kinship unit defined in terms of a particular "ego" as designated on a kinship chart.

unilineal descent group

A kin group, such as a clan, in which membership is based on either matrilineal or patrilineal descent.

bilateral societies

Societies with kindreds but without unilineal descent groups.

BOX 6.1 | The Na: A Society without Marriage or Fathers

A Na mother and child, from Yunnan Province, China. The Na are an ethnic-minority society with a matrilineal descent structure in predominantly patrilineal China.

The Na are an ethnic group in Yunnan Province, China, not far from the Chinese border with Myanmar. A Chinese ethnographer has described their society as one in which marriage is absent. Consequently, families have neither husbands nor fathers (Cai 2001). The Na acknowledge that sexual intercourse is necessary for procreation to occur, and they consider that the substance of a child comes solely from its mother, as the Na are strongly matrilineal. A Na child belongs to its mother's lineage, and kinsmen are counted solely through its mother. The father has no social role since he is not considered a relative. There is no kinship term for him or for any members of his matrilineage.

Na rules about incest are very strict. No woman may have sexual intercourse with a relative, that is, with anyone matrilineally related to her. The strongest incest taboo concerns brother and sister. Na brothers and sisters cannot speak about sex or make any allusions to physical intimacy. In Na households, only one sex at a time can watch TV in the village because, if sexual flirtation should occur on the TV, both sexes should not be watching it together.

The Na, a minority group, are under strong political and legal pressure to adopt Han Chinese social practices; however, the Na try to cling to their own cultural ways. Cai Hua, the ethnographer, who is Han Chinese, questioned them closely about such matters as "jealousy between lovers," adultery, and illegitimacy, and the Na told him that these things do not exist in their culture. These subjects are the characteristic "problems" of patrilineal societies such as the Han Chinese, since such societies are obsessed with doubts about who the father is. According to local informants, these issues are absent in their community.

affinal link

Connections between kin groups established by marriage.

alliance

A linkage between kin groups established through marriage for the mutual benefit of the two groups.

In general, marriages not only create links between brothers-in-law but also serve to create linkages between their respective kin groups. Groups that give women to, and receive women from, one another also exchange goods and services such as bridewealth, bride service, and other kinds of services at rites of passage after children are born from the marriage. These links between kin groups established by marriage are called **affinal links**. During warfare, kin groups frequently use these affinal ties and turn to their in-laws for assistance. For this reason, marriage is the basis for what is referred to as **alliance**. Although affines may be in opposition to one another and may even fight one another, the concept of alliance is nevertheless used by anthropologists to refer to these linkages between kin groups established by marriage.

In American society, marriage is presumed to be based on the decision of the bride and groom to get married. Parents and other individuals may be nominally involved, but there are few cultural rules that guide their involvement. In other societies there are rules stating that one should marry someone from a certain category of relative. These rules have the effect of continuing alliance over time between groups of affines. When groups continue to exchange sisters over generations, women of one's own group are always marrying into the group from which wives come. This marriage pattern, sister exchange, is also referred to as a system of **reciprocal exchange** (figure 6.7). In such a system, the prospective husband and the prospective wife will already be related to one another. Since their parents are brother and sister, they will be what Americans refer to as "first cousins."

Anthropologists generally categorize two kinds of cousins (from the ego's perspective): **parallel cousins** are the children of the mother's sister or father's brother, and **cross cousins** are the children of the mother's brother or father's sister (figure 6.8). In a system with reciprocal exchange, parallel cousins, who are members of one's own group, are frequently called "siblings." Therefore they cannot marry. Cross cousins are never in one's own group but rather are members of the other group with which the parental groups have been intermarrying. These cross cousins are known as **bilateral cross cousins** since they are simultaneously the mother's brother's children and the father's sister's children. Sister exchange, continued over the generations, is in effect marrying one's bilateral cross cousin. The Yanomamo of southern Venezuela have such a marriage system of **direct reciprocal exchange**. A Yanomamo man must marry a woman whom he calls by the kinship term for female cross cousin (suaboya), and this term is at the same time the term for wife. The terms for husband and male cross cousin are also the same. Female parallel cousins among the Yanomamo are called by the same term as sisters. If a Yanomamo man has no biological sister to return to the man who gave him his wife, he returns a "sister" who is his parallel cousin.

Each of these two marriage rules produces a different structure of alliances among groups, and both are different from the kind of alliance produced by bilateral cross cousin marriage. Marrying one's cross cousins, either mother's brother's daughter or father's sister's daughter, begins with a rule of exogamy stating that one must take a wife from outside one's group. By specifying which relatives one should marry, different patterns of alliance among groups are created.

Some societies, particularly those deriving from the Middle East, have a preferential marriage rule that is structurally opposite to this rule of exogamy. The rule states that a man should marry his parallel cousin, in this case, his father's brother's daughter. Since the societies of this area, like the Bedouin of Cyrenaica discussed above, are all patrilineal in descent, this marriage rule results in endogamous marriages. The Riff of Morocco, who have this marriage rule, say that they prefer to hold onto their daughters and marry them within their own group to avoid becoming entangled in alliances with

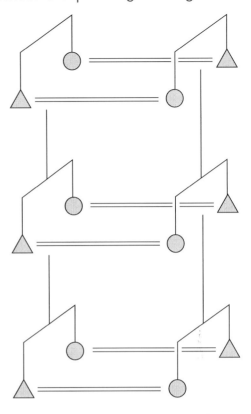

Fig. 6.7 *Sister (reciprocal) exchange*

reciprocal exchange

A type of exchange system in egalitarian societies in which marriage partners and material goods of equal value continue to be exchanged over generations.

parallel cousin

The offspring of two brothers or of two sisters.

cross cousin

Offspring of one's mother's brother and one's father's sister.

bilateral cross cousin

Offspring of opposite-sex siblings through both the mother's and father's side.

direct reciprocal exchange

A continuing exchange of equivalence between two parties creating relationships over time.

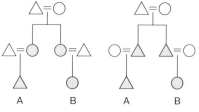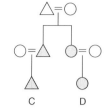

Parallel Cousins   A and B
are parallel cousins to each other.
They are the children of two
sisters or of two brothers.

Cross Cousins   C and D
are cross cousins to each other.
They are the children of a
brother and a sister.

Fig. 6.8 *Parallel and cross
cousins*

kinship terminology

A system of linguistic
designations and groupings for
those related, by descent or
marriage, to an individual.

**new reproductive technologies
(NRTs)**

Manipulation of egg and sperm
to create fertilized eggs and
viable fetuses through scientific
technology; includes the use
of surrogate mothers and/or
genetic donors.

terms of reference

The kinship terms used to refer
to a relative when speaking to
someone else.

terms of address

The kinship terms used when
talking to a relative.

Fig. 6.9 *American kinship
terminology*

other groups. When looked at across
generations it becomes clear that in
patrilineal societies with a preferential
marriage rule of patrilineal endogamy
maintains the inheritance of the assets
of the group in one lineage.

KINSHIP TERMINOLOGY SYSTEMS

Each society in the world has a set of words used to refer to relatives called **kinship terminology**. Kinship terminology is a subject that has a long history in anthropology, and a regularity of its patterning was first hypothesized by Lewis Henry Morgan in 1877. Studying kinship terminology is vital to the anthropologist in gaining insights into how societies operate. Some scholars critique the anthropological study of kinship as privileging the biological rather than social models of family formation. The study of kinship as creating social, and not biological or genetic categories of relatedness, has been revitalized by the widespread access to **new reproductive technologies (NRTs)**, same sex marriages, and adoption (Levine 2008).

There are two kinds of kinship terms, **terms of reference**, that is, the terms used to refer to other people, and **terms of address**, which are the terms one uses when talking to the person. Since languages differ, terms are not the same from one society to another. Most Americans accept their own kin terminology as being the "natural" way of classifying relatives, as do members of all other societies. Both a father's brother and mother's brother are referred to as uncle in American usage. Uncle is also used to refer to a mother's sister's husband and father's sister's husband. Though the term uncle is used for these four relatives, two of them are classified as "blood" relatives (also an American kinship concept) on different sides of the family, while two are relatives by marriage, or affines. Each of these four relatives is related to the "ego"—the designation of perspective on a kinship chart—in a different way, but American kinship terminology ignores these differences and groups them under one term. Anthropologists diagram American kinship as depicted in figure 6.9. The Yanomamo have a very different way of categorizing their relatives. They use the same term for both a father's brother and mother's sister's husband, while they use a different term for a mother's brother and father's sister's husband. The Yanomamo kinship terminology is diagrammed in figure 6.10.

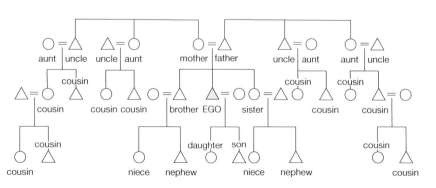

You can see that the two societies sort the terms for kin in different ways. For the parental generation, both the Yanomamo and Americans have four terms. The Americans use father, mother, aunt, and uncle; the Yanomamo use haua, naya, yaya, and shoaiya. In the

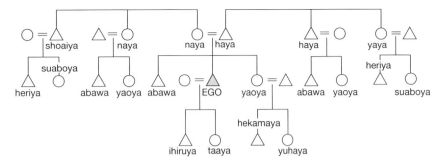

Fig. 6.10 *Yanamamo kinship terminology*

Yanomamo system, a father's brother and mother's brother have different terms, whereas in American society the same term, uncle, is used for both. Conversely, the Yanomamo classify a father and father's brother together, while American terminology uses different terms. In the American ego's own generation, there is a single term, cousin, for all the children of uncles and aunts. This term is unusual in that it is used for males and females in American English; many European languages retain the gender distinction for male and female cousins to the ego. The Yanomamo are also consistent in their usage. The children of all relatives called by the same term as *father* and *mother* are referred to by the terms for *brother* and *sister*. This means that parallel cousins are grouped with siblings. In contrast, the children of shoaiya, who are the ego's cross cousins, are referred to by terms different from *brother* and *sister*, suaboya and heriya. These kinship terminologies are different because each is related to a different type of social structure, and different rules of residence, marriage, and descent.

The American and Yanomamo kinship terminologies conform to two basic types of kinship terminology. American kinship terminology is classified as "Eskimo" (consistent with mid-nineteenth-century terminology) since it is identical to that of the Inuit in the pattern of organization. Its major characteristics are that it distinguishes between the generations and it distinguishes **lineal relatives** from **collateral relatives** (figure 6.11). Lineal relatives are those in the direct line of descent: in American kinship, designated as grandfather, father, son, grandson, grandmother, mother, daughter, and granddaughter. The **Eskimo-type kinship terminology** emphasizes individual nuclear families, and it is found in societies with a particular cluster of characteristics, such as neolocal rules of residence, kindreds, bilateral descent, and the absence of unilineal descent groups. Although Inuit and American societies differed in subsistence pattern and environmental setting, the pattern of organization of kinship terms and other kinship features was determined by anthropologists to be similar.

The kinship terminology of the Yanomamo is classified as "Iroquois." The **Iroquois-type kinship terminology** distinguishes between father's side and mother's side. However, the difference between lineal and collateral relatives is ignored; father

lineal relative

A relative in the direct line of descent.

collateral relative

A relative not in the direct line of descent.

Eskimo-type kinship terminology system

American kinship is an example of this type of kinship terminology system.

Iroquois-type kinship terminology system

A type of kinship system found among the Yanomamo.

Fig. 6.11 *Lineal and collateral kin*

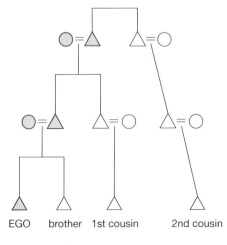

EGO   brother   1st cousin   2nd cousin

△ = lineal relatives

△ = collateral relatives

and father's brother are classed together, as are mother and mother's sister. Generational differences are always recognized, as in Eskimo-type terminology. The social structure with which this terminology is usually associated is one in which one's own kin group is distinct from the kin group from which one's mother came. The group from which one's mother comes is the same group into which one's father's sister marries. In other words, the Iroquois terminology goes with sister exchange, which is the type of marriage pattern the Yanomamo have. This is an anthropological explanation for why, in Yanomamo, the term for father's sister's husband is the same as that for mother's brother, and the term for mother's sister's husband is the same as that for father's brother. Female cross cousin is classed with wife and male cross cousin with brother-in-law. In every generation, "sisters" are exchanged between the two groups, and the kinship terminology reflects this. Iroquois terminology is associated with virilocal (which the Yanomamo had) or uxorilocal (which the Iroquois had) residence, but not with neolocal residence. Instead of independent nuclear families, extended families are present. This type of terminology system is also generally associated by anthropologists with unilineal descent, but not with cognatic descent or bilateral kinship reckoning. Iroquois is by far the most common type of kinship terminology found in the world. It should be noted that societies that are classified as Iroquois kinship terminology may not have all these social structural features, but only some of them. The Iroquois themselves had matrilineal descent and did not have sister exchange.

Besides Eskimo and Iroquois terminologies, four other major types of terminologies were identified by anthropologists by the mid-twentieth century. The **Crow-type kinship terminology**, found, for example, among the Trobriand Islanders, is almost always associated with matrilineal descent groups, avunculocal residence, and extended families. Unlike Eskimo and Iroquois terminologies, the same term may be used for members of different generations. **Omaha-type kinship terminology** is the mirror image of Crow. It is associated with patrilineal descent groups and, like Crow, ignores generational differences in some terms. The terminology system with the fewest terms is the **Hawaiian-type kinship terminology**, in which only generation and gender distinctions are made. It is usually associated with cognatic descent groups. It has been found in association with some societies, like the Hawaiian, that have complex political economies. The kinship terminology systems identified by anthropologists designated as **Sudanese-type kinship terminology** are characterized by distinguishing each category of kin by a different term. Sudanese-type systems also distinguish birth order, using different terms for elder and younger kin of the same category. Each kin term therefore communicates a large amount of information symbolically.

Some anthropologists have been critical of the use of the anthropological concepts for analyzing kinship as presented above. Critics see the use of this set of analytic concepts as the imposition of Western social science categories on indigenous cultures and categories. Instead, they prefer to utilize only the local categories that the people in each society use to conceptualize kin relationships. Kinship analysis always begins with indigenous categories; these

Crow-type kinship terminology system

Matrilineal descent system associated with avunculocal residence and extended families.

Omaha-type kinship terminology system

Associated with patrilineal descent groups and ignores generational differences in some kinship terms.

Hawaiian-type kinship terminology system

A type of terminology system that distinguishes between people by generation and gender only.

Sudanese-type kinship terminology system

A terminology system in which each category of kinship is distinguished from all others by the use of different terms.

can, however, be carefully translated into anthropological concepts to make possible any cross-cultural comparisons.

The kinship variables discussed so far in this chapter, including number of spouses, degree of incorporation of spouse, type of descent rule, kinship terminology, and structure of descent group, do not operate independently. They fit together into the particular cultural patterns; field studies enable us to test out these comparisons, as well as identify variations and uniqueness. The use of symbols and their visualization in diagrams conceptualizes and communicates these patterns. Ethnographic study and fieldwork allows anthropologists to compare the two-dimensional rendering of kinship terminologies in charts and symbols to the complexity and often-changing realities of social norms "on the ground."

Fictive Kinship

People also rely on social relationships made by means of ritual observances, which create a new set of kin known in English as **godparents**. The English labels for these relationships use kinship terms such as father, mother, daughter, and son, plus the prefix—"god." This is not simply an extension of kinship, but a different kind of relationship, which uses kinship as a metaphor. **Fictive kinship** is found in many parts of Mediterranean Europe and in Latin America. It also occurs among the Italian and Hispanic populations in the United States. The ritual occasions upon which **godparenthood** is established are baptism, confirmation, and marriage, at which the godparent serves as a kind of sponsor. This relationship is frequently established between individuals of different classes for social, political, and economic reasons. In peasant communities, for example, a patron who is a wealthy or powerful member of the community and probably a landowner may serve as godparent to the children of clients who are economically and politically dependent upon him. In the relationship between godparent and godchild, the godparent is expected to protect and assist the godchild, while the godchild honors the godparent, just as the patron receives support from the client when it is needed and the client receives favors from the patron. For example, among the Quichua-speaking Otavaleno of the Ecuadorian Andes, **compadrazgo** has not been squeezed out by the expansion of capitalism, as some anthropologists in the 1960s had predicted. These indigenous people have become prosperous weavers and traders. They now select compadres at the marriage or confirmation of their children to extend their handicraft business by connecting with sweater-factory owners, transport operators, and shopkeepers with whom they do business (Colloredo-Mansfield 1998: 52).

godparents/godparenthood

A fictive kinship relationship using marked kinship terms to reflect social privileges and responsibilities.

fictive kinship

Social relationships in which unrelated individuals use kin terms to establish and recognize their relationships. Oftentimes, the relationship is established by ritual observances.

compadrazgo

Ritual godparenthood found in Mediterranean Europe and Latin America.

Kinship in the Contemporary World

Kin groups based on unilineal descent continue to exist; they take on a variety of roles, even long after the emergence of complex societies and states. For example, after a devastating earthquake in Turkey, which occurred in the summer of 1999, forty people, self-identifying as members of the same clan, traveled six hundred miles from their home to try to rescue five trapped relatives (Andrews 1999). They brought their own equipment, including jack-hammers, drills, electrical equipment, generators, and lights. This illustrates that members of a clan sometimes feel it absolutely necessary to come to the aid of fellow clan members in distress.

In China, after Mao took power and a Communist system was initiated throughout the mainland, a series of laws were promulgated to obliterate the traditional social structure with its extended families and clans. However, "familism and its value system still greatly affect the behavior of the Chinese everywhere [today]" (Yuen et al. 2004: 5). After 1949, the Communist government sought to eliminate what they referred to as "feudal culture." They prohibited lineage activities of all kinds as well as the practices of geomancy and divination. Villagers could only go surreptitiously to their ancestors' tombs to sweep them out and pay their respects. Ancestral halls were either burned or turned into meeting houses or residences, and genealogical records were destroyed (2004: 29). Arranged marriages were discouraged, although they still continued to take place with the help of matchmakers.

In 1978, China embarked on major economic and social reforms. The government allowed traditional lineage activities to be revived, including the holding of lineage meetings and more public ancestor worship and offerings. Ancestral halls that had been destroyed were rebuilt, and genealogical records reconstructed (Yuen et al. 2004: 33). Young people sought to choose their own spouses, but some parents still used matchmakers to arrange marriages for their children. In conclusion, these authors state, "Traditional Chinese culture and the ideas of modern society are not completely incompatible; nor are conflicts between them inevitable" (2004: 198).

The Transnational Family

The transnational family is defined exclusively in terms of social connections and exchanges of resources, without continuous co-residence or shared households. Structurally, it may be made up of kin, fictive kin, and friends carrying out newly created roles. Its coherence and connections spanning multiple geographic locations have been greatly facilitated by the global reach of airplane travel, the internet, email, and social media. For example, the nature of a funeral has changed for transnational families. One family, scattered over five continents, can go online to hold a "Zoom" wake following the death of a relative; a family member can deliver a eulogy online while the rest of the family watches it on their computer screens.

The transnational family of the twenty-first century is the consequence of complex migration patterns and motivations. "Some [people] move on their own volition, while others are forced to travel. Some are looking for jobs and relatively higher wages, others—particularly refugees—are looking for a safe place to settle, while some others could be going in search of an adventure, a pilgrimage, an education, or self-actualization" (Cohen and Sirkeci 2011: 87).

Scholars studying contemporary migration globally increasingly focus their research on both the migrant experiences and the impact of migration on those in their families and communities who stay behind.

Economic migrants, both men and women, leave their families in Asia, Africa, and Latin America to travel within their countries from rural to urban centers, or cross borders to find work. They leave husbands or wives, children, and other family members at home, and send financial **remittances** or payments from their wages or enterprises to help support those back home. The "transnational capitalist class" of business people, professionals, technicians, and other skilled and educated individuals seek and find employment in the United States, Europe, Australia, the Middle East, and Canada. Ease and speed of transportation, and advances in telecommunication, have made it possible for individuals to maintain continuing connections with families and communities wherever they are located.

Levitt describes the multifaceted nature of these connections between migrants and non-migrants from Miraflores in the Dominican Republic and a community in Boston, beginning in the 1960s (Levitt 2001). She describes Miraflores as a "transnational village" with characteristics that derive from the multiple kinds of connections between migrants and those who stay behind. "Migrants' continued participation in their home communities transforms the sending-community context to such an extent that nonmigrants also adapt many of the values and practices of their migrant counterparts, engage in social relationships that span two settings, and participate in organizations that act across borders" (2001: 11). In addition to the flow of economic remittances between Miraflores and Boston is the equally important flow of social remittances: "ideas, behaviors, and social capital flow from receiving to sending communities" (2001: 11). These include ideas about gender norms and political strategies, as well as economic and material mobility that profoundly influence decision-making in Miraflores "Once this process has begun, daily life in the village is changed to such an extent, and migrants and non-migrants often become so dependent on one another, that transnational villages are likely to endure" (2001: 11).

Transnational migration is increasingly being recognized as having gendered implications, as both men and women are equally represented now in migrating populations globally. The expectations, experiences, and challenges of migrating women are different from those of migrating men. For example, Filipino women migrate to Northern and Middle Eastern countries to work as domestics or care givers or in health care industries. These women may be separated from husbands and children for many years. In such cases, fathers try to pass on the care, giving responsibilities to daughters and women in the extended family, when the mother is the migrant (Parrenas 2005: 118). When Filipino men are the migrants, they are fulfilling their traditional roles as breadwinners, and the family they leave behind is also affected by their absence. Financially motivated migrations of women from Southern to Northern countries provide services and childcare for middle-class and wealthy families. Equally important is considering the impact of migrating

remittances

Money, consumer goods, and information that flow regularly between migrants and "non-movers" in their families and home communities.

family members on those who do not migrate and continue to maintain residences and family obligations back home (Romero 1997). In the Filipino families studied by Parrenas, the children note that, despite the economic contributions their migrating parents made to their households, they would rather not have grown up in a transnational family.

Kinship in America Today

Americans think that a child receives half of its "blood" from the mother and half from the father, while more distant relatives have smaller shares of that blood, depending on the degree of distance. People think that such relationships can never be terminated because "blood"—the symbolic carrier of the relationship—is always present. On the other hand, relatives through marriage, or affines, are considered to be different. These relationships are established by people making choices. In English, affines are designated "relatives in law." Relationships that are made by marriage can also be terminated by people through divorce. When this happens in American kinship systems, the divorced in-law may no longer be considered a relative.

As a result of the availability of new reproductive technologies, or NRTs, including in-vitro fertilization, embryo transplantation, and the use of gestational surrogates, Americans have begun to rethink the meaning of kinship in their own culture (Inhorn and Birenbaum-Carmeli 2008). If women who donate their eggs and men who donate sperm are paid, this represents a commodification of reproduction, involving the purchase and sale of these genetic materials. This creates ethical dilemmas for many people who value the idea of the "gift" of body parts, as in organ transplantation. These dilemmas have been more pronounced due to the exploitation of people forced by economic or political circumstances to sell body parts and fluids for an increasingly globalized and only nominally regulated high-demand marketplace.

Reproductive processes formerly seen as creating ties of kinship through "shared blood" or other substances between father, mother, and child clearly become much more complicated by these new technologies and practices. The meanings of motherhood and fatherhood have been reconfigured by these NRTs. When in-vitro fertilization takes place, conception may result from an egg from the would-be mother and sperm from the would-be father being brought together in vitro, using laboratory technologies. The developing embryo may then be implanted into the uterus of a surrogate for gestation. If the sperm and the egg come from unknown donors, who is the father—the man who has provided the sperm, or the man who has acted as the father in raising the child? Who is the mother—the egg donor? And if the embryo is carried and delivered by a surrogate, is she the mother?

One small step in answering these complicated questions is to distinguish between genetic, gestational, and social parenting. The genetic mother contributes the ovum and genes. The gestational mother provides the uterus in which the baby comes to term and from whose body the baby is born. The social mother rears the child, often from the moment of birth. Likewise the genetic father can be distinguished from the social father. These distinctions may be invoked in custody or child-support cases. In California in 1998, an appeals court heard a complicated child-support case (*Buzzanca v. Buzzanca*) involving a couple who used anonymous egg and sperm donors and a gestational surrogate to produce a child. They separated and divorced immediately after the birth of the child. The ex-wife sued her former husband, who had no contact with the child, for child support. He refused to pay on the basis that he was not a parent to the child, as he had no biological, genetic, or social relationship with her. The California appeals court hearing this case ruled against him and stated that the decision of two people to have a child defines them as legal parents; the methods by which the process proceeds are irrelevant. In this case, the parental relationships were established when conception was initiated; that relationship exists even when there is no genetic relationship between parents and child. The former husband was therefore determined to be a parent and required to pay child support.

In two other cases, ethnicity and race, which are culturally constructed, entered the picture when an African American woman wanted the donor egg to come from an African American, and an Italian American woman wanted a donor egg to come from her Italian American friend, who would also provide the gestational setting for the fetus (Thompson 2005: 166–67; see also Carsten 2004: 177). In these cases the "origin" of ethnicity and race and their transmission from one generation to the next is called into question. Increasingly, children conceived by artificial insemination are seeking the identity of their donor fathers, who are often medical students who had donated their semen merely to help infertile parents. If the women who donate their eggs and the men who donate semen are paid, this represents a commodification of reproduction. What formerly had been seen as a natural tie of kinship and "shared blood" between father, mother, and child is clearly much more complicated by these new technologies.

There are now a large number of diseases that are attributed to genetic inheritance, and consequently there is increased emphasis on acquiring family medical histories from biological parents and now from sperm and egg donors. It has therefore become important to some individuals that they know about their biological and genetic parents as well as the extended network of other biological relatives. Throughout most of the twentieth century when children were adopted in America, records were sealed by the courts and knowledge of their biological parentage was kept from the adopted children. Given the American cultural norm that biological blood ties to parents can never be severed, one can readily understand that such children, now adults, often feel the need to know who their biological parents are. Today, adoption in the United States has become an open process in most states and under most circumstances; the adoptive parents may establish a relationship with one or both of the biological parents even before the child is born.

BOX 6.2 | Fertility Rates and Public Policy

The overall population growth rates of countries around the world have historically been associated with population-control strategies; overpopulation is considered by economics and demographers to create dangerous pressures on resources, state services, and economic productivity. The adoption of ante-natal, or strong population control policies in China in the 1970s, the "One Child Per Family" policy (later revised to allow two children per household and reversed in 2022), was effective in rapidly controlling population growth but was viewed by many scholars as being based on multiple human rights violations. Public resources were used by India during the 1970s to provide incentives to poor people to undergo permanent contraceptive procedures; they too were criticized for targeting women's reproduction for surgical intervention and unfairly targeting rural poverty-stricken populations. Repressive governments are also criticized for using birth restrictions selectively to target religious or ethnic minorities. Many countries in the industrial world in the twenty-first century are facing what economists and policy makers consider to be dangerous decreases in overall population, below the targeted replacement fertility rate of two children per couple. China's population has declined to 1.3 children per woman, far below the replacement rate. The government announced a policy in 2022 encouraging three children. But women in China are now resisting having more than one child, mirroring the trends in other industrialized countries. The United States is experiencing its lowest birthrate in decades, most pronounced among women in their twenties as they delay childbearing to prioritize education and careers. This trend is mirrored in many other industrialized countries around the world, including Japan, Korea, Greece, Germany, Italy, and Finland, among others. While global population control remains a priority of international policy makers, individual states grapple with the impact of falling birthrates over the longer term. These include an increasingly larger percentage of elderly retired people, whose care requires increasing economic support, and a decrease in the percentage of working people who are contributing to the growth of the economy and social security or retirement funds. Pro-natal policies encouraging population growth are being instituted in many countries, which include cash incentives for births, and increased child-care and medical services at low or no cost. Other incentives include universal paid leave for parents after the birth of a child, income tax benefits, and child-care services in the workplace. These benefits may have some immediate small impact on birth rates, but analysts point out that they are very costly for states and may not provide the lasting environment to encourage families to increase their fertility. Lyman Stone, a research fellow at the Institute for Family Studies, concludes that "any pro-natal policy agenda will have to be about more than just a child tax credit. It's vital that policymakers also think about how they can remove obstacles to marriage, facilitate access to decent housing, and accelerate completion of education—all vital elements in the modern economic life cycle leading up to childbearing. Without such a broad approach, pro-natal efforts will involve spending a great deal of money without a lot of results to show for it" (Stone n.d.).

Family formation in the contemporary world increasingly has a globalized framework. The scale of transnational adoption has greatly increased, and is a manifestation of globalization (Howell 2006: 12). Another manifestation of contemporary globalization is "reproductive medical tourism." Some Southern countries with increasingly sophisticated and privatized medical infrastructures are attracting Westerners seeking reproductive services, including in-vitro fertilization, egg donation, and surrogacy, offered at much lower costs than in their home countries. Both foreign adoptions and NRTs are subject to the shifting policies of states concerning their own cultures and norms of appropriate, and legal, forms of family. The policies in the supplying countries may conflict with those of the countries in which seekers of these services reside. While these policies are designed to protect the rights of their citizens, they may create legal jeopardy for perspective parents crossing borders to create families.

VARIETIES OF AMERICAN FAMILIES

Until the mid-twentieth century, the usual family type for Americans was the nuclear family, which lived neolocally after marriage. Families that included three generations were an exception. As Americans married later and later, single-individual households became more prevalent. A variant on this form is the household consisting of several unrelated young people, both men and women, who live together for financial reasons. Another household form consists of one or both grandparents and grandchildren. This occurs when the parents of the children are unable to care for them. Grandparents assume custody and responsibility instead of the state (Hayslip and Hicks Patrick 2006).

The high rate of divorce and the subsequent remarriage of divorced spouses have created the **blended family** or **stepfamily**. In blended American families, the stepfather is more likely to be living with and raising young children than the biological father, though the latter often continues to be involved in child-rearing and child support. The modern stepfamily includes a variety of sibling relationships, categorized as full siblings, half-siblings, and stepsiblings. Relations with in-laws and grandparents of the stepfamily are highly varied. In contrast to the Cinderella story and creation of the myth of the "evil stepmother," adolescent stepchildren often report that they experience less conflict with residential stepmothers than do adolescent children with their biological mothers in families without divorce (Mason 1998: 98).

The marriage-equality movement has redefined American views on marriage and the family, as well as contributed to the debates around defining parentage. Same-sex couples now have the right to marry legally in the United States and create families through adoption and/or by accessing NRTs. Although some states prohibit lesbians and gays from adopting children, independent adoption is a route followed by same-sex couples in states where this right is supported. Other alternatives are assisted-reproduction procedures like accessing donated egg or sperm, in-vitro fertilization, and surrogacy contracts with women who carry the child to term. The legality of surrogacy contracts is being challenged in many states in America, adding an element of legal vulnerability to this route for all couples. NRTs are increasingly available, although very costly and usually not fully covered by medical insurance. This option often provides some biogenetic relatedness, although it might be to only one parent, which "would automatically trump other forms

blended family or **stepfamily**

A family created by the divorce and remarriage of spouses and the combining of parents, stepparents, stepsiblings, and half-siblings.

In many countries in North America, South America, and Europe, marriage equality for all citizens is legally recognized. There are approximately eighty countries that do not recognize same-sex unions; even in countries that recognize the marriages, there may still be restrictions against adoption of children and other forms of discrimination.

of relationship and attachment" were legal disputes over custody to arise (Sullivan 2004: 43–44). Male couples choosing to become parents may use a surrogate mother, who is impregnated with the sperm of one of the partners, or they may adopt or foster a child. Overseas adoption is an option to same-sex couples, although it is also an expensive and time-consuming alternative vulnerable to shifts in state policy and public sentiment in the countries where adoptions of local children are being arranged.

Class, race, and ethnicity are important variations in understanding access to NRTs, family formation, and community norms. Analysis that problematizes these variations has been largely absent in the scholarship on same-sex families thus far. In her study of "lesbian identity, gay and lesbian family formation, and Black family life," Moore (2011) points out that lesbian mothers and their families are "invisible" both in their own communities and in the scholarship that studies gender, sexuality, and family. "The overarching theme [in this scholarship] is gay sexuality, not sexuality and race. . . . Past research has . . . taken for granted the middle-class and upper-middle class status of its subjects. . . . If we allow 'lesbian families' to mean 'White middle-class lesbian families,' and if we do not fully 'race' ourselves and our subjects, we cannot de-center the White gay subject as the norm, and we reify the myth that 'Black people aren't like that.' We also continue to perpetuate unidimensional understandings of the experience of creating and maintaining openly lesbian families and relationships" (2011: 2–3).

Moore's informants become parents intentionally or by partnering a woman with children. She cites the example of one couple, where each gave birth to a child. "Each woman adopted the other's biological child shortly after birth, so they are the legal parents of all three children. The boys call them both 'mommy' or, if they need to distinguish between them, by their names" (Moore 2011: 144). Moore's informants continually position their race, sexuality, class, and gender into a single intersectional conversation about their identities and families. "The exploration of family formation in the context of Black lesbian experience highlights for some women the fine line between maintaining images of respectability that shield Black women's sexuality from criticism, and revealing and affirming their autonomy through the expression of sexual freedom" (2011: 216). Studying parenthood of people in same-sex unions from an intersectional perspective that includes their gender, class, race, and ethnicity "offers new insights . . . to all scholars interested in the importance of ideology and identity" (2011: 217).

Kinship, Class, and Ethnicity

As ethnicity becomes an increasingly significant factor in social and economic status in American life, the U.S. Census Bureau is documenting the family organization of different ethnic groups. A comparative study documents some household norms of several ethnic minorities, including Dine', Inupiaq Eskimos of Alaska, Korean Americans, and Latinos (Schwede, Blumberg, and Chan 2005). The Dine', living on their reservation in the Four Corners area of the Southwest, still maintain their matrilineal descent system and have a fluid residential unit revolving around a grandmother, whose daughters and their families live in her house or adjacent to it, sharing meals, daily chores, child care, and resources, including income. It is a fluid unit in that some male and female members spend time working in the border towns because of unemployment on the reservation (Tongue 2005: 66).

In contrast, among the Inupiat, 78 percent of the households studied consisted of grandparents and their grandchildren, with the middle generation, mostly women, at school or work in another community. There are many single adult men, living with a parent or grandparent, who continue to participate in subsistence hunting and fishing. Local family units, an aggregate of related households, in effect a social network, continue to cooperate as a single domestic entity and in subsistence activities (Craver 2005: 109ff). Hispanics from Mexico and El Salvador living in Virginia identify the nuclear family as the ideal and the norm in their countries. After migrating to the United States, due to economic conditions, they live in complex households. These consist of extended families with a mix of spouses, children, adult siblings and their spouses and children, parents, and parents-in-law. The term hogar, implying emotional closeness, kinship, and shared domestic function, is used for such a unit.

MARRIAGE, MIGRATION, AND STATE POLICY

Throughout this chapter, we have discussed marriage rules, family organization, residence patterns after marriage, forms of descent and descent groups, and other aspects of kinship in multiple societies and cultures, ethnic groups, and classes. It is important to keep in mind that these family norms are often created by, and enforced through, state policy. The state has the power to recognize (or not recognize) the legality of marriages, the dissolution of marriage, and therefore the legal and social status of spouses and offspring. Civil law determines which marriages will be recognized and offered protection as well as regulation under the law. Increasingly, as the result of cross-border migration and residence, issues of citizenship determination and related rights are negotiated by individuals and family members based on their country of residence, where one or both spouses may not be fully recognized citizens. "[M]igration law governs non-citizens, including foreign spouses. It demands from them conformity to a set of culturally specific practices and norms regarding romantic love and marriage" (Macklin 2022: 263). In some states, divorce of a migrated couple may result in the loss of residency and employment rights for one spouse. This often puts women at a disadvantage and may compel them to stay in abusive or unhappy marriages. This is just one example of understanding how intimate decision making between marriage partners has a third participant: the state.

SUMMARY

- Kinship plays a fundamental role in weaving the tapestry of culture in all societies. The way in which American society conceptualizes relatedness and household norms is just one example of many known structures around the world.

- Marriage rules and prohibitions, family and household organization, residence patterns after marriage, forms of descent groups, and kinship terminologies are all important aspects of kinship in contemporary societies.

- Societies have rules about those one can or cannot marry. Incest taboos forbid sexual relations and marriage between certain categories of close relatives.

- Marriage to someone within one's group is called "endogamy" and marriage outside one's group is called "exogamy."

- Societies have rules regarding number of spouses and postmarital residence rules, which result in the creation of a variety of types of families. The general term for having plural spouses is polygamy.

- Rules of postmarital residence govern where a newly married couple resides. These rules symbolize important values in a society beyond those immediately related to marriage and household.

- A family is generally defined as people who are related to one another by kinship. A household consists of people who live together under one roof. Family and household units may not coincide.

- Societies that state that a child belongs to the father's clan have a patrilineal rule of descent. Societies that state that a child belongs to the mother's clan have a matrilineal rule of descent. These societies, where group membership is determined through either the mother's or the father's lines, are referred to as having unilineal descent groups.

- Each society in the world has a set of words used to refer to relatives. This is called "kinship terminology."

- Terms of reference are the terms used to refer to other people in conversation; terms of address as the terms one uses when addressing this person.

- Kinship terminology in different societies reflects the pattern of descent, family type, and marriage found in those societies.

- Fictive kinship relationships are social relationships in which the individuals involved use kin terms to establish social and ongoing relationships that mirror the ties and obligations of kinship. Oftentimes, the relationship is established by ritual observances.

- Anthropological interest in the study of kinship now includes the expression of relatedness in globally situated political and social settings, including transnational families and clan-based economic institutions around the world.

- Americans have their own cultural ideas about kinship, which are currently being rethought in light of new reproductive technologies, surrogate parenting, genetic inheritance of disease, stepparenthood, adoption, and marriage equality.

- The stepfamily, or blended family, is one result of the high rate of divorce and subsequent remarriage of divorced spouses. These marriages may also create three-generation families, with varying degrees of closeness to siblings, in-laws and grandparents.

- New reproductive technologies (NRTs) are challenging ideas about motherhood and fatherhood, and what defines the relationship between parents and children. Court rulings and family-formation technologies increasingly put the emphasis on the social relationships that define families, not biological or genetic similarity.

- New forms of family and family formation invigorate the study of kinship and relatedness by anthropologists. These studies are increasingly taking place in transnational settings as people travel across borders to work, marry, or bring children into a marriage. Principles and norms of kinship intersect with state law and ideas about citizenship, and therefore continue to be important to families all over the world.

KEY TERMS

affinal links, 138
alliance, 138
avunculocal, 130
bilateral cross cousins, 139
bilateral societies, 137
bilocal residence, 130
blended family, 149
bride service, 127
bridewealth, 126
clan totem, 135
clans, 134
cognatic descent, 134
collateral relatives, 141
compadrazgo, 143
corporate descent group, 135
cross cousins, 139
Crow-type kinship terminology system, 142

demonstrated descent, 135
direct reciprocal exchange, 139
dowry, 126
duolocal residence, 130
ego-oriented group, 137
endogamy, 125
Eskimo-type kinship terminology system, 141
exogamy, 125
extended family, 131
fictive kinship, 143
fraternal polyandry, 128
godparents/godparenthood, 143
Hawaiian-type kinship terminology system, 142
incest taboo, 125
Iroquois-type kinship terminology system, 141

SUGGESTED READINGS

Craig, Sienna R. *The Ends of Kinship: Connecting Himalayan Lives between Nepal and New York*. Seattle: University of Washington Press, 2020.

An in-depth field study of the impacts of transnational migration between the Mustang region of Nepal and New York City. The author documents the depopulation of Mustang, as well as the relative "invisibility" of Nepalese migrants in New York City.

D'Aoust, Anne-Marie, ed. *Transnational Marriage and Partner Migration Constellations of Security, Citizenship and Rights*. New Brunswick, NJ: Rutgers University Press, 2022.

An edited volume of ethnographic essays illustrating how marriage and partner migration have become the object of state scrutiny for control and exclusion in several states around the world.

Sreenivas, Mytheli. *Reproductive Politics and the Making of Modern India*. Seattle: University of Washington Press, 2021. Open-access edition: https://doi.org/10.6069/9780295748856.

The author explores debates about marriage, family, and contraception and demonstrates how concerns about reproduction surfaced within a range of political questions—about poverty and crises of subsistence, migration and claims of national sovereignty, normative heterosexuality, and drives for economic development.

SUGGESTED WEBSITES

www.umanitoba.ca/faculties/arts/anthropology/tutor/

An interactive guide to general information regarding kinship and social organization, with ethnographic examples.

https://familysearch.org/

"The largest collection of genealogical and historical records in the world." A free-access website of family genealogies compiled and maintained by the Mormon Church of Jesus Christ of Latter-day Saints.

United Nations Population Division, https://www.un.org/development/desa/pd/.

The Population Division of the Department of Economic and Social Affairs conducts demographic research, supports intergovernmental processes at the United Nations in the area of population and development, and assists countries in developing their capacity to produce and analyze population data and information.

Chapter 7

Genders, Sexualities, and Life Stages

LEARNING OBJECTIVES

- Understand non-binary cultural construction of gender and sexuality.
- Recognize the economic and political impacts of the construction of gender and sexuality.
- Explore shifting gender categories and the cultural meaning of terms denoting identities.

- Assess life stage categories as social constructions; explore age-grades and other types of age-based groupings.
- Compare concepts of aging and care giving in America and elsewhere.

WHEN IMAGINING THE HUMAN BODY, it is very challenging for most people to abandon the Euro-American cultural norm of categorizing it as having one of two genders. This "binary" model of gender is deeply ingrained in our thinking about how anatomical characteristics get mapped onto expected behaviors and norms. Anthropologists and biologists are increasingly aware of gender differences between individuals as being a complex package of multiple variables that are enacted in a spectrum of behaviors, norms, and choices, independent of anatomy and genetic makeup. When we think about gender as being culturally constructed, not biologically mandated, we recognize that it is performed in many different ways in different contexts. And gender being culturally constructed calls attention to the multiple possibilities in individual behaviors and cultural norms that shift and are reimagined over time. This is very similar to how anthropologists envision age groups. The behavioral differences between, and expectations of, senior citizens or retirees in the twenty-first century and those of fifty years ago are dramatic, especially in how they think about the period after retirement and the activities associated with it.

Ideas about gender are part of every society. They are so normalized in cultural knowledge that they are symbolic shorthand for much more complex ideas. In American society, justice is symbolized as female and death as male. In German culture, death is also male, but so is one's homeland or "fatherland." However, for Russians, the homeland is one's motherland. Perceptions of gender and age differences are universally the basis of social and economic roles. In some societies, one gender may weave cloth or plow fields, whereas in other societies, all genders may work at computers or serve in the military.

Senior citizens in American society may sometimes live in communities where children are not allowed to live, while in other societies, aged parents are revered members of the family and accorded the best living arrangements in the household throughout their lives. Ideas about age often influence ideas about gender and sexuality; in some societies, older women are afforded power and privileges they do not have when they are presumed to be sexually active and of child-bearing age (Lamb 2000: 15–16).

Relations between the genders in human societies throughout the life cycle are also culturally patterned. The nature of this patterning forms a powerful motif in the tapestry of culture. Analytic concepts about gender, sexuality, and age categories in the social sciences draw in part from past ideas about the human body and social categories based upon it. These ideas often derive from colonial-period observations of "natives" recorded as social "fact" about "others." An awareness of the sources and histories of these ideas, counterbalanced by local people articulating their own visions, are included in most ethnographies about life stages and gender today. Many of these works combine research into historical sources in archives with fieldwork, interviews, life histories, and participant-observation.

THEORIZING GENDER AND SEXUALITY

Definitions that satisfy everyone in all disciplines for contested terms are difficult to formulate; some social scientists agree on most of the following distinctions. **Sex** is a label assigned at birth based on observation of the anatomical composition of genitals. Later in life, it is associated with observation of secondary sexual characteristics (breast size, hair distribution, body fat, etc.). This label does not necessary conform with an individual's perception of their own identity and may be contested and changed over a person's lifetime. **Gender** is the culture-specific set of behavioral, ideological, and social meanings constructed around the interpretations and understandings of biology and anatomy. If a person's sex changes over the course of their lifetime, their gender designation and behaviors will probably also change. **Sexuality,** or sexual orientation, refers to emotional, romantic, and erotic desires. The term **cisgender** is used to denote someone whose self-perception of gender matches their assigned sex at birth; **transgender** applies to a person whose perceived gender is different from their sex assigned at birth.

Understanding the ways in which gender roles are culturally and historically constructed is central to anthropological theory and practice. Americans historically perceive gender differences as natural, biological distinctions from which ideas about social roles derive. Behavior, dress, and demeanor are viewed by most Americans as determining membership in one of two gender categories, which are perceived to be fixed. This construction of a binary distinction between male and female as biological, gendered, and sexually normative categories is associated with Western-derived religious and cultural systems. The binary construction is associated with a **heteronormative** cultural vision that privileges heterosexual behaviors in cultural, family, and legal norms. This political and cultural privileging can lead to discrimination against, and the punishment of, people who do not conform to these binaries. Violence against gay and transgendered individuals is one consequence of the widespread adherence to binaries of gender and sexuality. Incarceration and violation of legal and civil rights of people engaging in same-sex activities are tragic legacies of the enforcement of binary gender and sexual norms in law and culture. The binaries of male-female, masculine-feminine, and homosexual-heterosexual continue in the fabric of American life but are challenged by the voices of LGBTQ+ individuals and activists. Cross-cultural and historical studies illustrate a wide range of gender and sexual identities and practices beyond these simple binaries, or what is referred to as gender pluralism "through time and space" (Peletz 2006: 309).

Until the mid-twentieth century, anthropologists, mostly male, focused primarily on male roles and male informants in their field research. In doing so, they were unconsciously reflecting the cultural bias of their own societies, which emphasized the significance of male roles in public institutions; they sometimes projected these gender ideologies onto the societies they were studying. Due in part to feminist movements throughout the second half of the twentieth century, many anthropologists of all genders began to pay attention to how work and status were actually distributed in societies they studied, without making assumptions about that distribution. Anthropologists now focus on the cultural construction of gender and how the performance of these roles relates to other patterns including politics, economics, law, and

sex

Biological and anatomical composition of genitals and related secondary sexual characteristics.

gender

The culture-specific set of behavioral, ideological, and social meanings of constructed biological and anatomical differences.

sexualities

Erotic desires and the practices associated with them.

cisgender

Gender self-identification that corresponds with the sex category assigned at birth.

transgender

A form of self-identification indicating gender affiliation different than sex assigned at birth.

heteronormativity

Cultural perspective that privileges male and female heterosexual identity in conceptualizing social and family norms.

BOX 7.1 | Gendered Pronouns under Scrutiny

The use of gendered pronouns in English is increasingly being challenged because of embedded assumptions of binary gender and sexuality. Anthropologist Tom Boellstroff illustrates, for example, that the personal pronouns "she" and "he" in English do not denote all the ways people identify themselves. He further describes how English pronouns do not all mark for gender; "you" does not indicate gender, but English users are perfectly comfortable with its gender ambiguity. "Language isn't just a set of labels to identify things. It shapes how we see the world and is a way of acting in the world. Nor is it static: It changes with shifting times. We must now intentionally transform English to make it gender inclusive" (Boellstroff 2021). These transformations have historic precedence; in English, "thou" as a singular form of the plural "you" has been replaced, but it has retained its plural meaning. So we say "You are late" when addressing an individual; we do not say "You is late." English language users automatically accommodate this historical change in second-person pronouns and understand the meaning through context.

Gender-rights advocates are now calling for replacing the gender binary-based pronouns "he" and "she" with the gender neutral "they." When given the option, many individuals now request the use of "they" as a self-designating personal pronoun as opposed to "he" or "she." "Some complain that *they* is plural, but we have no trouble with *you* as both a singular and plural pronoun" (Boellstroff 2021). But this shift does not come without its own complications; "From a feminist perspective, one possible concern is that epicene [gender neutral] *they* could become a new masculine generic pronoun, erasing the impact that can be made by using *she* as a generic term instead of he. However, generic *she* hasn't been inclusive for many people (such as many queer women, Black women, and others historically excluded from full womanhood)" (2021).

Many languages have no gendered pronouns; some languages have more gendered pronouns than English and mark nouns and adjectives with gender. So there is no universal conceptual reason to use gender in pronouns. Shifts in usage, grammar, and syntax occur in every language; this is a commonplace characteristic of any language context. What sounds "wrong" or ungrammatical can become normalized quickly as the change appears in media and in general usage.

human rights. In studying these issues, anthropologists are also highlighting the way that individuals and groups resist and reinterpret these norms to create productive and fulfilled lives even in situations where aspects of their identities clash with religious and social norms.

Many anthropologists, particularly since the 1960s and 1970s, have developed research strategies to historicize and analyze constructions of female identities in colonial and postcolonial settings. As discussed in chapter 1, feminist anthropology in its many forms may combine inquiry with activism in that it seeks to both explore and address inequality based on gender. Feminist anthropology has evolved along with the other perspectives discussed in previous chapters; influenced by postmodernist theorizing of the 1980s, feminist anthropologists challenge the essentialist reading of all social categories and representations, particularly those of "men" and "women." They document the lived experiences of women in relation to hegemonic or dominant systems of knowledge, including those that normalize cultural ideas about race, science, medicine, religion, and political participation.

Feminist anthropologists cultivate methodologies to explore and theorize women's experiences in all societies, while documenting multiple ideas of male and female in the theories and practices.

In parallel fashion to the examination of female roles in society, it is necessary to understand the nature of **masculinity** as a series of cultural constructions "whose basis is not biological—even though the cultural construction is based on biological differences—but constructed, designed, agreed to, and upheld by a system of beliefs, attributes, and expectations" (Connell 1995; Ramirez 1999: 28). This masculinist perspective challenges the association of the concept of gender exclusively with women's roles in society. Masculinist perspectives explore the diversity of male constructions of norms and behaviors, especially as differentiated by race, class, and ethnicity. Both masculinist and feminist perspectives identify forms of exploitation and marginalization that result when a person's identities and behaviors do not conform to the dominant, hegemonic norms in society.

masculinities studies

Exploration of the variation in what constitutes masculinity within as well as between societies.

Sexualities and Identities

The study of contemporary sexualities explores how they are constantly being made and modified in particular sociopolitical and historical environments (Peletz 2011; Sinnott 2010). Foucault demonstrates this in his depiction of how the modern Western idea of binary sexuality arose in a specific European historical and social context (Whitehead and Barrett 2001; Brittan 2001: 53). Within recent years, anthropologists and others consider the spectrum of variations in gendered identities and sexualities. **Queer studies** theorizes and explores the construction of multiple forms of sexual identity in their cultural contexts and stresses the lived experiences of people who self-identify as lesbian, gay, bisexual, transgendered, queer/questioning, and/or intersexed/inquiring as reflected in the now widely used acronym LGBTQ+ (Boelstroff 2007).

queer studies

Theorizes and explores the construction of sexual identities in their cultural contexts.

Originally focused primarily on male homosexuality, ethnographic studies inspired in part by queer studies perspectives now explore, among other subjects, gay and lesbian family and parenting, gender reassignment surgery, and gender ambiguity. Queer studies in anthropology documents and theorizes local experiences and understandings of identity, as opposed to enumerating and describing multiple practices in different societies. Boellstorff states, "[T]he problem with a logic of enumeration is that . . . it presumes that concepts name preexisting entities and relations, rather than asking how the social is produced and sustained through acts of representation, including scholarly and activist representation" (2007: 19). Scholars link queer theory and gender-variation inquiry to postmodernism and postcolonialism (Hawley 2001; Boellstorff 2007). This research clarifies the distinction between hegemonic Euro-American ideas that often originate in colonial histories, and the ways in which local communities identify and recognize categories of gender and sexual identities.

For example, historically documented examples of gender diversity in North American history are identified with Native American Plains societies.

The term berdache, of French derivation, was originally used by Europeans to identify men who lived in socially recognized relationships with other men; this term and its association with male social behavior appears throughout twentieth-century literature on gender. Scholars now recognize that there were also women in these societies who dressed like men and assumed male roles, who constituted an additional gender category (Roscoe 1998). The term *berdache* is rejected by Native Americans and scholars alike, as it is associated with Western European categories of sexuality not relevant to Native American historical ideologies. The terms two spirit and two spirited are generally preferred, although they too are inadequate to capture the wide range of gender variances they encompass (Lang 1998: xiii).

Roscoe describes a number of examples of Native American women who lived, and were acknowledged, as male warriors. He notes that Cheyenne female warrior chiefs "dressed like the male members of the Hohnuka, or Contrary society, who fought wearing only their breachcloths" (Roscoe 1998: 75). Some of these Cheyenne female warriors sat with the Chief Council, and their opinions had weight. Similar cases occurred among the Pend d'Oreille and Flathead Indians, both from Montana, as well as the Crow and the Blackfoot. Running Eagle, a female warrior of the Blackfoot in the early nineteenth century, became a legendary figure in American journalism. Her story was reprinted and given new meaning in 1984 as a positive image for young women today. The Dine' also recognized female nadleehi, or transgendered individuals. Today some Dine' self-identify as nadleehi. Others self-identify with terms such as LGBTQ+ and may be unfamiliar with the nadleehi tradition (Thomas 1997: 162, 169).

Hijra

In India, communities of individuals born as males who transform their identity into a female gender category.

People who self-identify as Hijras in Mumbai, India, are increasingly politically active, obtaining access to employment, benefits, and all rights of citizenship.

Anthropologist Serena Nanda, who has studied **Hijras** in India (Nanda 2000), cautions against romanticizing or idealizing what appears to be non-Western cultures' "seemingly positive valuation of sex–gender diversity, the latitude they allow for the expression of gender variation or the integration of alternatively gendered individuals into society. . . . [A] positive or tolerant attitude toward gender diversity in the past does not necessarily translate into acceptance of gender diversity in the present" (2000: 4). The documentation of the lifestyles of Hijras of India illustrates this conclusion (Nanda 1999; Reddy 2005). Hijras, "neither man nor woman," are born as males and transform their identity (sometimes with genital surgery, always as dressing and living as females) into a new gender category. The representation of Hijras in a growing body of media and ethnography focuses mostly on their social self-representation.

Individuals living in a community of Hijras share religious ideologies, ideas about honor and respect, gender performance expectations, and lineage reckoning (Reddy 2005). Hijra identity also draws in large part on an idealization of asceticism; their own sexuality is therefore only one small part of a larger and complicated set of shared norms and ideas.

Hijras have been identified in South Asian history for centuries; their traditional ritual role has been to sing and dance at Hindu weddings and ceremonies following the birth of a son. These are highly auspicious occasions in Hindu society, and the presence of Hijras symbolizes their ritual power. Today, however, they "are generally regarded with ambivalence; social attitudes include a combination of mockery, fear, respect, contempt, and even compassion. . . . Hijras have the power to curse as well as to bless, and if they are not paid their due, they will insult a family publicly and curse it with a loss of virility" (Nanda 2000: 36).

The social status of Hijras has declined in recent history. Their social position and ritual roles were valued and regularized during precolonial periods of Indian history. British rulers in nineteenth-century India abhorred their practices of surgical manipulation of genitalia, adoption of female dress and roles by men, and their association with prostitution, resulting in the criminalization of their practices (Reddy 2005: 26–28). In contemporary India, Hijra participation in weddings and birth ceremonies has been dramatically curtailed by an overall decline in participation in the rituals of the past. To compensate for loss of ritual income, some Hijras engage in sex work, a practice that is frowned upon by many Hijras as inauthentic practice, creating status divisions and hierarchies within Hijra communities (Reddy 2005: 2). Despite the ideological recognition of the "third gender" in the history of South Asian religious traditions and Hijra participation in public rituals, the lives of contemporary Hijras are often marked by poverty, marginalization, and multiple forms of discrimination. Hijras in India today, inspired by global discourses and some changes in Indian law recognizing the rights of sexual minorities, are becoming politically active and visible, claiming their legal as well as economic rights to participate openly in all aspects of Indian society.

Identities and Political Participation

As discussed throughout this chapter, gender and sexual identities are constructed and enforced through political and legal, as well as social and cultural, norms. Many groups that have historically been marginalized in the political process recognize the necessity for visibility in, and representation of, all minority identities in the national and local political process. Political participation includes a wide range of activities, from running for public office to working for political candidates, voting, and engaging in legislative and legal activism. Equal participation and leadership in political and public life of all identity groups are essential factors in mainstreaming all interests in public discourse.

Balanced political participation and power sharing between identity groups creates an environment where issues and minority interests receive attention and political visibility. Identity does not, however, guarantee political decision making; there are conservative women leaders, for example, who have supported political policies that did not enhance the position of women in their countries. And male-led governments can set family-friendly policies and progressive social policies. However, various UNWomen reports show growing evidence that women's leadership in political decision making processes improves the likelihood of gender and family support in legislative agendas. For example, research on *panchayats* (local councils) in India discovered that the number of drinking water projects in areas with women-led councils was 62 percent higher than in those with men-led councils. In Norway, a direct causal relationship between the presence of women in municipal councils and childcare coverage was found. Likewise, sexuality-based discrimination by political institutions motives marginalized groups to vote and protest their living and working conditions, as it does for the Hijras in India in the twenty-first century.

Reproduction and Culture

Perceptions of biological and gender differences contribute to local understandings of reproduction and childbirth. Some societies perceive female sexuality and reproductive abilities as dangerous; this danger may be projected onto the local understandings of reproduction, childbirth, and medical practice. These local interpretations result in rituals and practices that regulate contact with the female biological functions of menstruation, conception, and childbirth.

Menstrual blood is a substance that, perhaps more than any other, is associated with femaleness; menstrual taboos are cultural expressions of the way in which some observed differences between men and women and their participation in reproduction are understood. Ideas about the effects of contact with menstrual blood tend to be part of a male-dominated vision of society that is, by virtue of the authority of male perspectives, often shared by women as well. These female substances can be empowering to women, and are associated variously with love potions, ritual calendars, and in metaphors of creation and production. Menstrual blood can be used symbolically in harmful ways in witchcraft and in a positive fashion in the manufacture of love charms (Buckley and Gottlieb 1988: 35).

In Wogeo, an island off New Guinea, gender differences are based

Signs at the entrance of a Hindu temple in Bali request all visitors to dress appropriately and menstruating women to not enter.

on the belief that men and women live separately in two different worlds. But realistically, men and women must come together to reproduce the society as well as to carry out the usually complementary social and economic roles upon which their society depends. Men control politics and power. Associated with these ideas about the separateness of the sexes is the belief that sexual intercourse is polluting to both sexes and that menstrual blood is harmful to men. While women menstruate naturally, in Wogeo the men incise their penises to rid themselves of the bad "menstrual" blood (Hogbin 1996 [1970]).

In contrast to Wogeo's, other societies downplay gender differences. The Wana on the island of Sulawesi, in Indonesia, conceptualize gender relationships very differently from the people of Wogeo. They minimize the differences between male and female, seeing male and female as almost identical anatomically. Husband and wife are believed to be equally involved in procreation. The Wana say that the man carries the child for the first seven days of gestation and then puts the child into a woman's body. It is believed that, in the past, men menstruated. Men's menstrual blood is said to be "white blood" and to contain the essence of humanity, which solidifies in the womb as a fetus (Atkinson 1990: 75–76).

Many societies restrict women's activities and opportunities on the basis of beliefs about the impurity of their bodies. The Mansi are a hunting and gathering society on the eastern slopes of the Ural Mountains in Siberia today. Mansi married women belong to a "'strange' clan different to that of her husband" (Fedorova 2001: 227). Women in that society are subject to a series of complex taboos that "stem from beliefs regarding the allegedly harmful essence of women related to their 'impurity'" (2001: 227). These taboos require a woman to move to a special dwelling during menstruation and immediately before childbirth. After the birth, the woman stays in the menstrual house for two or three months. The wife could not expose her face to her husband's male kin. She could not touch the religious idols in her husband's home, though after her marriage and her move to the husband's house, she was supposed to be protected by "his domestic gods" (2001: 233). During the Soviet period, education and modernization brought about a weakening of these taboos. Since the collapse of the Soviet system, many Mansi are said to be returning to "their old ways."

In America, the history of childbirth practices and the "medicalization" of childbirth contain important ideas about gender and medical practice (Davis-Floyd 2003). In the nineteenth century, American women gave birth in the home, which, as we noted, was identified as a female sphere. At the beginning of the twentieth century, with the increasing professionalization of medicine and the growth of hospitals, the medical profession, then male-dominated, took control over the process of giving birth, and by the 1930s more births occurred in hospitals than at home. Under these conditions, birth was defined as a medical procedure, and the female reproductive process was taken over and placed in the hands of male physicians.

With the significant changes in gender roles in our society, this process is being reversed. There are more female physicians now, as well as midwives and other birth attendants. Interest in natural childbirth has brought about changes, and home birth is a possibility that some women and childbirth attendants advocate. Genetic counseling and the use of various birth control techniques have also been seen as giving women more choices and greater control over reproductive decision making. However, some scholars suggest that the availability of these technologies does not really empower women but, rather, increases the control of technology and medical practitioners over women and their reproductive processes (Rapp 1993, 2000).

Reproduction and the social constructions of male and female bodies are subjects that have attracted renewed anthropological attention recently, as discussed in chapter 6. One focus of this literature is ethnographic analysis (often by female scholars and ethnographers) of the multiple ways women understand and use the taboos and spatial norms of menstruation and childbirth practices. The segregation of women who are menstruating or giving birth in special houses or restricted spaces has been widely noted by ethnographers for decades. In many cases it can result in unhealthy and unsafe conditions for women subject to these spatial taboos. The documentation of women's understandings of these forms of segregation expands analysis to include women's agency in enacting their social responsibilities and in protecting their husbands, children, and communities. The social segregation of women may create opportunities for them to spend time with their peers and young children, exchange stories and information, and cultivate alliances among other women, unsupervised by their husbands and elders. Listening to the voices of women creates an understanding of menstrual taboos and segregation beyond a simplistic reading of menstruation as polluting. "[I]deologies of pollution should be the beginning, not the end, of ethnographic analysis. Women's own views of a patriarchal ideology can offer alternative readings of that ideology, sometimes affording women a form of personal resistance to a degrading cultural script, or allowing them to reinterpret it entirely" (Gottlieb 2002: 383–84). In many places around the world, there is a growing recognition that menstrual taboos and lack of appropriate supplies and facilities inhibits young girls from attending school while they are menstruating. Addressing these concerns is now a top priority of education and gender advocates around the world.

Gender segregation in public places is a normalized practice in many cultures, as in this café in Tripoli, Libya.

WORK AND GENDER

In all societies, economic roles are based on cultural constructions of gender creating norms around the division of labor. The difference in productive and household roles between men and women is not the result of their physiological differences. A specific task may be associated with men in one society and with women in another. As we have noted above, milking herd animals (cows, goats, sheep), for example, may be a female task in some societies and a male task in others, as is also the case with making pottery and weaving cloth. Men's productive tasks invariably have greater prestige, even though women's work, such as horticulture and collecting plant foods, may provide the bulk of subsistence. This is an example of **gender stratification**. Whatever the productive role of men, it is that role that the culture values. In America and in other industrialized countries, women have become lawyers, stockbrokers, and judges, economic roles formerly reserved for men, and men are now in formerly exclusively female roles, such as nurses and airline attendants. However, even when there is gender integration, gender stratification may remain. For example, in many countries where women are entering the medical profession in almost equal numbers as men, the areas they specialize in, such as pediatrics or obstetrics and gynecology, are not as highly valued or financially remunerated as the specializations that continue to be associated with men, such as surgery or orthopedics.

In chapter 5 we discussed the ways in which space takes on different symbolic and gendered meanings. Because women have traditionally been identified with mothering, the hearth, and the home, they are therefore associated with the domestic realm. Men, in contrast, are identified with the public realm. Ethnographic and historical analysis shows that this distinction is not always the case. Malagasy women conduct the haggling that takes place in agricultural markets, while in some West African societies, women control the marketplace entirely. Comparative studies illustrate the dominance of women traders in markets in Java, South India, Ghana, Morocco, and the Philippines (Hefner 1998; Seligmann 2001).

Restrictions on women's activities outside their homes are often associated with patriarchal societies. Some women in Middle Eastern and South Asian societies follow traditions of modest dress or covering when interacting with some males of their household and unrelated men outside their home. Veiling, or covering some parts of the face and body, has become the object of attack from Western feminists because it is seen as an infringement upon women's human rights. Others see this position as ethnocentric since it ignores the particular cultural meanings of veiling. This perspective also ignores the voices of women who understand veiling as facilitating culturally appropriate ways in which they can safely and comfortably pursue their educations and careers, and actively engage publically in political and religious activities (Abu-Lughod 2002).

What constitutes appropriate economic and social roles for men also changes through time in all societies. We need to recognize that "masculine" is a contested and culturally constructed term, and there is considerable variation in what constitutes masculinity within as well as between societies (Morgan 2001: 223–24). Gutmann, in his study of the working-class neighborhood of Santo Domingo, a colonia founded on the outskirts of Mexico City, focused on the dramatic transformation of what it means today to be

gender stratification

The comparative ranking of economic and political activities associated with men and women in any society.

Boys and young men who pursue ballet and other forms of dance are increasingly fighting for equality and opportunities. They continue to face bullying and widespread stigma due to gender stereotypes about masculinity and homophobia around this highly skilled and physically demanding performance art.

male and female (2000). Both men and women in this community say that there used to be a lot of macho men, but they are not so common today. Older men still divide the world of men into machos, meaning men of honor who responsibly provide for their families, financially and otherwise, and mandilones, meaning female-dominated men (2000: 162). The latter are seen as being bossed around by women and undependable. The term machismo is negatively associated with wife beatings, sexual infidelity, consumption of alcohol, gambling, abandonment of children, defiance of death, and bullying behavior in general (2000: 164).

Younger married men see themselves in a new category, "nonmacho." The macho label may be rejected by the man who helps his wife and does not beat her, the latter (i.e., beating one's wife) being a characteristic of the macho man. This is clearly a divergent "cultural trajectory." Ideas about machomexicano and la mujerabnegada, the self-sacrificing woman, are now regarded by many working-class men as "pejorative and not worthy of emulation." Younger men rarely claim the title of macho, the model of aggressive masculinity since machos do not spend time with their children, cook, or wash dishes (Gutmann 2000: 172). For Mexican men in this colonia today, masculinity has shifting meanings, and this has been the case historically as well.

Gender and the Care Economy

"Care work" is part of every family and household around the world. We all give and receive care on a daily basis; it is part of the basic human necessities that all people, no matter what their age or health, need to survive and flourish. Care work encompasses a wide range of services, and can be paid or unpaid, through the formal sector of the economy, where it is a taxed-wage activity, or the informal economy, where it is not taxed or recorded nor is reflected in national economic statistics. It includes, but is not limited to, child care, elder care, education, healthcare-related services, and domestic services. The care sector is a major component in all economic systems; the global **care economy** is expected to double by 2030, driven in part by anticipated growth globally in life expectancy and need for elder care. The vast majority of care work is performed by women and is either unpaid or is provided through the informal economy. Globally, women healthcare workers and child care workers account for 90 percent of these services, without the protection of minimum wage or workers benefits. Often this work is provided by undocumented female workers and thus is rendered invisible to

care economy

Delivery of paid and unpaid care in domestic settings and understanding its value, sources, and practitioners.

governments and labor advocates and is further undervalued as a resource and service sector.

Research resulting from the Covid-19 pandemic made clear the critical importance to households and families of caregiving; without it, some household members could not work, go to school, and provide their family members with vital sources of income. This research also verified what labor advocates have documented for decades—that the burden of care work falls unequally on the shoulders of women, whether or not they are employed outside of the household. This burden is reflected in the "double" or "triple" work days of women who are income earners in their households, provide healthcare support and services to the young and elderly of their household, help children with homework, shop and prepare food, do laundry and clean, and provide assistance to all other household members in preparing for the next day's activities. It is estimated that globally, during the Covid-19 pandemic, in excess of 64 million jobs held by women were lost, resulting in over $800 billion in lost income in 2021 (Oxfam America 2021). As the pandemic progressed, women reported leaving their jobs due to the necessity of providing fulltime care to those who were ill or vulnerable in their households. Young women and girls often leave school because of the necessity for care in their families. And women often report that they ignore their own health and safety to engage in work and risky employment to provide income or care for their families. It is also clear that the burden of supplying care globally falls heavily on women of color, minority women, and those of lower socioeconomic status, adding another level of inequality to the care economy.

Economists and advocates globally are recognizing the necessity for creating policies and strategies that fully value care work and address the inherent inequalities in its distribution and burdens. These are issues of vital importance to care recipients, workers, employers, and policy makers. UNWomen suggests following the "5Rs" framework in understanding paid and unpaid care work and for gender equality, empowerment of women, and social justice in the care economy, and to provide a policy framework for meeting the Sustainable Development Goals (SDGs) around safe and equitable work by 2030. "The 5R framework for decent care work includes recognize, reduce and redistribute unpaid care work, and reward and represent paid care work by promoting decent work for care workers and guaranteeing their representation, social dialogue, and collective bargaining" (UNWomen 2022). This strategy stresses the necessity of putting the care economy into a global setting and addresses the workers and activities in the care economy through the frameworks of gender equality, globalization, global health, and climate change stressors.

Gender and Industrialization

In America and other industrial societies, economic, spatial, and behavioral separation of the sexes was present until the beginning of the twentieth century. Ginsburg (1989) points out, however, that in preindustrial America, the home was basically the workplace for both men and women. With increasing industrialization during the nineteenth century, men were drawn into factories and businesses, while some classes of women remained in the home, an essentially female domain. Women were identified as having an ideology of nurturance and domesticity, despite the fact that women routinely worked in domestic services, stores, and factories for wages. Politics, law, businesses, banks, pubs, and so forth, were male bastions; so too were the social clubs where mentoring, business negotiations, and alliance building were carried out.

At the beginning of the twentieth century, women who challenged the male exclusivity of economic and political activity formed Suffragist movements and began to agitate for the right to vote, which had previously been denied to them. Suffragettes were perceived as troublemakers and law-breakers, and were ridiculed in the media for being socially disruptive and not knowing "their rightful place" in society. World War II brought many women into the workforce, and since that time, ever-increasing numbers of women have become part of the American labor force. It took the feminist movement of the 1970s and affirmative action legislation to begin to raise political consciousness and bring about transformations that we see today. As women have moved into occupations such as law and medicine, formerly occupied almost exclusively by men, society at large has come to accept women as well as men in those roles. In this way, gender norms have been transformed by law and cultural practice. As this has occurred, gender expectations about work in the domestic realm have changed as well, as family members renegotiate the domestic responsibilities of cooking, cleaning, and child care. However, gender-based economic disparities continue, as women generally receive lower wages than men for the same work, and are still rare in upper levels of corporate management and political leadership.

The changes in gender roles described above do not assume an inevitable progression, nor do they assume that these changes will equally affect all members of society in the same ways. Anthropologists have described all sorts of changes affecting gender roles in different parts of the world in recent decades. Many women in parts of the Middle East and Asia have left their traditional domestic domains to go to work outside the home with varying consequences. For example, in Hong Kong in the 1970s, in families in which fathers were unemployed or underemployed, daughters went to work, becoming semiskilled factory workers (Salaff 1995). Their incomes played a prominent role in the household economy, though their personal gain was limited. There was some loosening of family ties, and they were freed from household duties and received small amounts of spending money. Their marriages were no longer arranged, and they could choose their own spouses. However, core family values of paternal rule and filial obedience were still maintained.

Variations in the nature of manhood in American settings are revealed in an examination of masculinity in various types of workplaces. Meyer, in a consideration of masculine culture on the automotive work floor during the three decades from 1930 to 1960, sees two polar forms, or ideal types, as operative during that time, which were a continuation from the nineteenth century (2001: 15). "Respectable manhood," which was related to the craft tradition, was characterized by a tempered and channeled masculinity in which mental and physical skills were used in an evenhanded fashion. In contrast, "rough manhood" related to the tradition of unskilled labor characterized by risk taking, physical strength, and disorderly behavior. Others have also associated this rough masculine culture with construction workers and steelworkers. In the urban industrial centers of the United States and Canada, many of these steelworkers self-identified as Iroquois; they transformed the masculine warrior ethic into the daring required to walk the steel beams as skyscrapers were being constructed. As Meyer points out, under industrialization and semiskilled mass production, workers blended and merged elements of these two types, the respectable elements being fed by high wages and economic stability, while in auto plants "boy-like playfulness on the shop floor . . . [and] drinking, fighting and gambling" retained aspects of the rough male identity (2001: 19).

We have considered the changing economic and domestic labor of different genders in a number of societies. From these multiple examples, it is clear that the policies of states, as well as the forces of economic and social change, impact women differently from men. Political policy and practice often specifically target women's behavior, education, work, and public participation in establishing social and economic norms. It is also well documented that the achievements obtained by middle- and upper-class women in many societies are not paralleled by similar attainments elsewhere in society. Our culture's definition of manhood historically included: a repudiation of the feminine; the necessary acquisition of power, success, wealth, and status; being strong and reliable in a crisis; never showing your emotions; and exuding manliness and aggression (Kimmel 2001: 278).

As many economies shift from manufacturing to service industries, gender expectations also shift. When a woman's earning power exceeds that of a male partner, the "stay at home dad" becomes the primary caregiver to children. Supporting and maintaining a nurturing role by fathers after divorce or separation is an encouraged norm. "Stepping up" to the social and economic responsibilities of fatherhood is part of the construction of masculinity. The quest to prove one's manhood is a lifelong endeavor. While male dominance is often culturally equated with male sexuality, ideologies of male and female are being transformed away from dominance toward more egalitarian economic and social relationships between men and women.

LIFE STAGE CATEGORIES

Aging is a continuous process; however, the way in which this continuum is divided varies from society to society, as well as over time within a single society. Every society has terms for different age groups and related rituals that mark the transition from one life stage to another. In our own society, for example, we traditionally used terms such as infant, child, adolescent, adult, and senior citizen to identify major social categories and transitions. We now recognize more age categories, including toddler, tween, teenager, baby boomer, empty nester, and so on. In America many of our life stages reflect economic and institutional transformations over the past century. For example, the teenage life stage, between adolescence and adulthood, is marked by physical maturity, mandatory schooling, and economic dependence. It is

BOX 7.2	What's Up With Teenagers? The Continuing History of "Nature versus Nurture" Debates

For over a century, scientists and anthropologists have studied and debated the relationships between biological and anatomical characteristics of the human body, and their expressions in behavior. Sometimes referred to as "nature vs. nurture," these debates address whether human behavior is the result of learning cultural and social norms from the external social environment (nurture) or the result of genetic, anatomical and biological inheritance (nature). One particular aspect of human experience, the physical changes that take place in both boys and girls during puberty, was the focus of Margaret Mead's classic ethnography, Coming of Age in Samoa (1928). She set herself a daunting research challenge: "What we wish to test is no less than the effect of civilization upon a developing human being at the age of puberty" (1928: 6). She concluded that the behavioral upheavals associated with teenage-years in America were largely absent in Samoa, due to vast differences in childhood socialization and cultural norms in these two cultures.

Inquiry in the United States into why teenagers act impulsively and often dangerously continues. More recently, research on teenage behavior has shifted from the effects of hormonal changes on behavior to brain development and neurological changes during one's lifetime. One result is the observation that the development of frontal lobes and their full connection to neural transmitters does not occur until a person reaches their mid-twenties. The frontal lobes control "the brain's executive functions. They're responsible

for planning, for self-awareness, and for judgment" (Kolbert 2015: 84). Another section of the brain, the nucleus accumbens, is a pleasure-seeking center that is implicated by some researchers in risky behaviors, especially around peers, in the pursuit of sexual and other pleasurable activities. This center is at its largest in teenagers and shrinks during adulthood. These brain systems probably provided an evolutionary advantage to adolescent primate males millions of years ago, giving them behavioral tools to pursue mating aggressively and discourage competition from other males. But these behaviors are no longer adaptive, or necessary, in contemporary social settings, creating an evolutionary mismatch between adolescent brain physiology and adaptive behaviors (Kolbert 2015).

There is, however, a strong cultural component to the manifestation and management of adolescent behaviors. In contemporary America, one consequence of these anatomical phases of the adolescent brain may be risk taking in automobile driving among teenagers, who have the highest level of car accidents and fatalities among any category of drivers. Law and social policy addresses this by restricting teenage access to a driver's license, alcohol, and firearms. These policies will not be relevant in other societies, where risk-taking behaviors among teenagers express themselves in different normative activities. Understanding what Mead called "civilizations," and what we now refer to as "culture," continues to be relevant in understanding and managing teenage behavior.

often accompanied by sexual awareness, rebellion, and parental conflict. In rural communities in America a century ago and in many contemporary agricultural societies this life stage does not exist in this form; adulthood begins immediately with physical maturity, often accompanied by marriage, parenting, and adult economic and social responsibilities (White 1994).

AGE GRADES AND AGE SETS

When age categories are formally named and recognized, and crosscut the entire society, they are referred to as **age grades**; the members of one age grade constitute an **age set**. In a number of pastoralist societies in Africa, formalized age grades have importance in expressing ethnic and group identity through ritual and social organization. In early- to mid-twentieth-century scholarship on age-grade systems, they are often described exclusively from the male perspective. For example, the male age-grade system of the Nyakyusa of Tanzania was documented by Monica Wilson (1977) based on fieldwork conducted in the 1930s. Age mates, as they matured, joined to form a new village; at 10 or 11 years old, boys built huts and established a village at the edge of their fathers' village, returning to their mothers' huts for meals and to assist their fathers in agriculture. At about age 25, the boys, now young men, married and brought their brides to live with them virilocally in the new village. Once in a generation, a great ritual was held, with administrative power and military leadership handed over by the older generation to the younger. The retiring old chief reallocated all the land and selected a headman for each new village. Therefore, all over Nyakyusaland, Wilson stated, there were three kinds of age-grade villages. They consisted of villages of grandfathers retired from leadership positions but who still performed certain ritual functions; villages of the fathers, who ruled and were responsible for defense and administration; and villages of the sons, who, when necessary, fought under the leadership of men of their fathers' generation.

Under the pressure of economic change, the Nyakyusa have been moving away from their traditional age villages. When men migrate from their homes for wage labor, they leave their wives with their mothers in intergenerational households. Furthermore, personal economic advancement creates conflict with the traditional value of sharing assets between members of an age village (Wilson 1977). This situation is in contrast to that of the Samburu, a pastoral society in Kenya that retains its age-grade system. Although some

age grade

Categories of individuals of the same age that are recognized by being given a name and that crosscut an entire society.

age set

A group of individuals of the same age that moves as a unit through successive age grades.

Maasai young man dancing and singing during the public ceremony of transition into a new age set for young boys and girls in Tanzania.

Samburu have moved to towns, many of them still retain their cattle herds. Ethnographic research among the Samburu concludes that they continue to rely on the male age-grade and age-set system as "indicators of men's roles (and the prestige associated with each) and referred to the centrality of livestock to their identity" (Straight 1997: 76).

Recent scholarship explores the participation of both women and men in shaping and transforming African pastoral practices and gender norms (Hodgson 2000). Analysis of historical sources and fieldwork among the Maasai of Kenya and Tanzania (Hodgson 1999, 2001), documents shifts in the practices and meanings associated with age grades, in part by exploring the sources from which these ideas emerge. Outsiders writing about the Maasai generally represent them as archetypal pastoral male warriors and as "immutable icons of traditional Africa" (Hodgson 1999: 121). These sources select and exaggerate only one "of a range of masculinities cross-cut by generation . . . shaped in relation to each other as well as to Maasai feminities" (1999: 125). Historical and contemporary representations in part shape the Maasai's own shifting visions of masculinity and gender and ethnic identity. "Through their [own] accounts, we learn that a dominant masculinity is less a construction than a production, and thus always in tension, always relative, and always a site of mediation and negotiation" (1999: 144).

Drawing in part on published accounts from the 1890s to the 1930s, Hodgson describes the often-ignored responsibilities of women among Maa-speaking pastoralists in this literature. "In general, men and women had distinct roles and responsibilities in the organization of the pastoral production system premised on mutual autonomy and respect, but shared common goals in furthering the interests of their homestead" (Hodgson 1999: 125). Women were important participants in the pastoral economy as milk managers and traders, and in caring for young and sick animals. They bartered milk and animal hides with neighboring communities. As caretakers of ritual and prayer, they were responsible for the well-being of people and livestock in the community. "Women also played important roles in the rites of passage which marked the transition of men from one age grade to another" as well as in enforcing important food and sex taboos (1999: 128). Through their songs, they "regulated and commented on men's behavior . . . they used songs to mock and ridicule men who failed to live up to the standards" (1999: 129) of particular age grades, thus articulating and enforcing ideas about masculinity. "As they aged . . . their respect and authority inside and outside the homestead . . . increased. Women felt deep pride in their identity as pastoralists, and as Maasai" (1999: 125–26).

The Maasai age set was a group of boys and men who together moved through the ritual and spatial rituals, who were circumcised together, and were known by a shared identifying name (Hodgson 1999: 126). As younger uncircumcised boys (ilayiok), they herded calves and small animals, and later cattle. "They endured physical hardship, hunger, and derision as their parents and siblings worked to toughen them for the circumcision which would mark their transition to adulthood" (1999: 126). Hodgson points out that the focus of most of the published accounts of Maasai age grades is invariably the attainment of the next chronological male age-grade status of ilmurran ("literally 'the circumcised ones' . . . a word most often glossed as warriors" [1999: 126]). As ilmurran they enacted the ideals of communal interests and shared masculine values; they were always in the company of one or more age-set members. They protected the interests of the community, accumulated livestock, and learned to manage their herds and pastoral economy. Although not permitted to marry in this life stage, they could cohabit with unmarried girls, and continued to intermittently live with and eat with their mothers. Ilmurran could not progress to the next stage, ilpayioni, or junior elders, until the circumcision and initiation of another ilmurran age set. As ilpayioni they could marry, reside on their own homesteads, become parents, and consolidate their political and economic power. This stage emphasized individual interests as opposed to the communal values of ilmurran, and often placed older men in conflict with their actual and classificatory sons.

According to Hodgson, in contemporary Maasai communities, "age sets are still an organizing principle of masculine subjectivity and social relations and their fundamental apparatus has remained much the same: male circumcision is still a prerequisite to becoming an adult man, each age set is still given a unique name, and men advance from age grade to more senior age grade together. But the experience, attitudes, and practices of being an age set member have changed" (1999: 142). These changes are mediated through their understanding of economic and political relationships within Maasai communities and the institutions of colonial and postcolonial states. Change is expressed by the Maasai in part through "the contradictions produced by their encounters with modernity" (1999: 144), including government policies of containment, economic and agricultural development projects, education, religious conversion, and most recently, with international tourism.

Where previous generations of elders rejected schooling and literacy in Swahili as characteristics associated with outsiders, that is, non-ethnic Maasai, currently education for men (and increasingly for women) is being embraced for its potential in providing access to employment, political alliances, and development resources. "Whatever their current survival strategy, Maasai men of all ages now assert a very modern dream: for the village, they want a hospital, a good school, a grinding machine, more cattle medicine, a better road, and cheap public transportation to the nearby district headquarters" (Hodgson 1999: 143). This vision of modernity is continually renegotiated by men and women within the community through their understandings of forces outside the community. "Ethnohistorical analysis through the prism of masculinity demonstrates . . . that modernity is never a totalizing process, but that the contradictory structures imposed by modernist interventions can be appropriated, reshaped, and even transcended by local people in novel, if painful ways" (1999: 144).

Aging, Retirement, and Care

It is currently estimated that the percentage of the world's population over sixty will rise to 22 percent by 2050 (World Health Organization 2016). This global trend is attributed to advances in medicine that have both prevented many major diseases throughout people's life times and addressed, through treatments and surgical interventions, health problems that a generation or two ago would have been fatal. This lengthening of life spans around the world (although not distributed equally across all countries or within socio-economic groups) has intensified discussions in many different disciplines about the resources for, and types of care available to, the aging, especially those in their eighties or nineties, whose independence and overall health may diminish as they age further.

Anthropologists are particularly interested in these questions, as ideas about aging and care are culturally constructed. "[A]ging is not a uniform process, but rather one profoundly shaped by local environments, access to resources, and social relations. The experience of those who survive into old age are shaped by the social roles available to elders, the depth and breadth of social support available to them, and their access to economic resources" (Buch 2015: 278).

Global economic and demographic changes are altering elder-care policy and strategies around the world. Women continue to carry the responsibility of care to the aging "through their roles as wives, daughters, daughters-in-law, and domestic servants" (Buch 2015: 278). But women are also increasingly entering formal labor markets as full time wage-earners, reducing the amount of time they can devote to unpaid family care. The global trend of urbanization and out-migration from rural communities is creating neolocal two-generation households where extended, three- or four-generation households were once the norm. The elderly can therefore no longer assume that younger household members will provide attention and care as they age. Women migrants from Southern countries provide care for the elderly in Northern countries; although their labor is indispensible, they occupy the lower-status positions in the care economy. Many countries are facing a dramatic lowering of birth rates in the current generation, greatly diminishing the size of households and reducing the number of family members who can provide care to the elderly. These global forces are creating the need for all states to examine policies and resources allocated to elder care, as well as for people around the world to anticipate how elderly members of their families will experience their aging life stages.

In North America, significant changes have taken place in the construction of the category of senior citizen. Social Security, pensions, and improvements in medical care have made postretirement lifestyles a twenty-first-century institution. By law, there is no longer a mandatory retirement age and therefore no longer a clearly defined point at which an American moves into the category of retired senior citizen. The movement toward early retirement, which characterized the 1980s and 1990s, seems to be passing; the trend now is for people to continue to do some type of work while accessing Social Security and pension benefits. This financial security allows some Americans to "age in place" while others, upon their retirement, migrate elsewhere or move to retirement communities. Those Americans who are relocating after retiring are usually younger, more affluent, and healthier than their peers

Many retirement communities are self-contained and focus on leisure activities (Riekse and Holstege 1996: 252). These communities, whose residents must be over fifty-five years of age and which do not allow children to live there, resemble a Nyakyusa village of grandfathers as described above. Retirement communities are sometimes built around religious affiliation or ethnic identity. They may also be constructed on the basis of social class. Some of them consist of mobile homes, whereas others contain condominiums or private homes.

Among South Asians and East Asians in the United States, the phenomenon of **step immigration** is growing. As middle-class, professional immigrants establish themselves in new locations and professions, they reunite their parents with their families. This economic security is not always valued by the now elderly who are uprooted from their longtime homes and communities and introduced to a new cultural setting without familiar patterns of language, food, and socializing.

As a result of **chain migration**, when earlier migrants attract later ones from the same community, clusters of individuals having long-term relations develop. A Finnish-American retirement community of this sort exists in southeast Florida, though very few other Finns live and work in this area (Stoller 1998). The community began to develop in 1940 when Finnish Americans living in New England and the Midwest, particularly Minnesota, first came to this area to retire. Some members of the community are second-generation Finnish Americans, while others were born in Finland and came to the United States after World War II. This is not a planned retirement community, like the ones described above; rather, it consists of residents scattered through a large metropolitan area and linked through informal networks and organizations. The ethnic identity manifested by the Finnish Americans in this community is the basis for informal ties and the development of solidarity and support among these older people (1998: 289).

Retirement communities are not exclusive to the United States. They have begun to be established in Japan, "which famously has the oldest population in the world" (Buch 2015: 284). Traditionally, elderly parents lived with the family of one of their children in the extended family form known as dokyo. In rural areas, a large percentage of senior citizens still live this way, while in the urban areas this is no longer the norm. Fuji-No-Sato is an example of a community, or "life-care" facility, located near Tokyo, which is also an upper-class summer resort area (Kinoshita and Kiefer 1992). Those desiring to live there purchase a right to live in the community rather than an apartment. They must be sixty years of age, live independently, and pay an endowment fee when they move in and then a monthly operating fee. This community includes primarily individuals who remain there fulltime, though a quarter of the individuals use their apartments as second homes. The well-educated inhabitants are from the middle or upper-middle classes. Since the community is an unfamiliar, unstructured, newly constituted social situation with few guidelines for behavior, people's relationships are primarily formal in nature, which characterizes Japanese behavior in such unstructured situations.

step immigration

Process by which a younger generation of immigrants reunites with their relatives in their new countries of residence.

chain migration

When earlier migrants attract later ones to the same community, resulting in residential clusters of individuals having long-term social and economic relationships.

Expectations about caregiving for the elderly often reflect gender and social norms within society. In some agricultural societies, in the absence of pensions and state support for the elderly, people are financially dependent on their children, who are in a sense their "Social Security." In rural communities of northern India that are organized around agricultural production, with patrilineal descent and virilocal postmarital residence, married sons are expected to care for their elderly parents in the household they inherit from their father. This contrasts with contemporary America, where care of elderly parents often becomes the responsibility of adult daughters; in families with an unmarried adult daughter, there is a strong expectation that she will become the primary caregiver of elderly parents. As India becomes increasingly industrialized and urbanized, traditional extended households with virilocal residential patterns are also being modified. Neolocal postmarital residence is increasing as a younger generation leaves family farms to find occupations in towns and cities. Housing and "step up care" in non-kin settings, commonplace in North America and Europe, are now emerging as a normalized option for "aging in place."

In summary, we note an explosion of scholarly interest on the part of social scientists and historians about the human body over the past decade. It is a rare book or journal article in anthropology that does not theorize or provide a local perspective on an aspect or function of the human body as a social, historical, or cultural construction. The interest in contextualizing gender, age, sexualities, reproduction, life stages, physiology, the unborn, reproductive technologies, organs, even the very boundaries of life and death, as cultural issues, is new in some ways, and familiar to anthropologists in others.

New theories, vocabularies, and methodologies encourage looking at ideas about various aspects of the body as historically contingent, normalized through political and legal discourses. Understanding science as containing cultural norms and ideas calls into question the authority of a single body of knowledge about the natural world. The rejection of meta-narratives, or a universalizing explanation, for sociopolitical phenomena is now a basic part of the anthropological approach. It is now based on understanding the historical and cultural logics that create systems of knowledge through the documentation of local voices, histories, and ideas.

SUMMARY

- Gender and age are common bases for distinction between social roles in every society.

- Categories based on age and sex do not simply build upon biological differences. The perceptions of age as well as anatomy and gender differences are defined by culture.

- Feminist anthropologists explore how conceptions of gender result in forms of inequality. The perspective of masculinist approaches also challenges assumptions about "maleness" in society.

- Masculinity, like femininity, is a series of cultural constructions that are not based simply on biological differences. It is constructed, designed, and upheld by a system of beliefs and attitudes.

- Anthropologists distinguish between sex, which is physical anatomical differentiation, and gender, the culture-specific ideas constructed around the understanding of these differences, and sexuality, the expression of romantic and erotic attractions.

- Sexuality is increasingly understood as being a wide spectrum of behaviors and preferences, with cultural recognition, but not always legal validation.

- Some societies recognize "third," "fourth," and more genders, and accommodate in their societies people who live these lifestyles.

- The cultural expressions of the biology of childbirth and menstruation vary from society to society.

- Childbirth practices and rituals are especially revealing of gender norms and constructions of female identity and normative expectations in society.

- In all societies, economic roles are based on cultural constructions of gender. Appropriate economic roles are subject to change and renegotiation over time.

- Gender and industrialization are of increasing importance in the anthropological studies of capitalism, globalization, and transnationalism.

- Affirmative action legislation and social movements have brought about transformations in the occupational and legal expectations of people around gender and sexual identity.

- Every society has terms for different age groups, but the number of terms varies. In American society, we use such terms as infant, toddler, child, adolescent, adult, and senior citizen.

- When the age categories are formally named and recognized and crosscut the entire society, they are referred to as age grades. Some societies with age grades for boys and men have complementary forms of life-cycle categories for girls and women.

- Age sets refers to the group of individuals who move through their age grades together.

- Retirement communities, populated entirely by aging individuals and couples, are becoming more commonplace in many societies around the world.

- As the population ages globally, there is an increased interest in understanding and analyzing the dynamics of, and policies for, the care of aging members of society.

- Anthropological studies of gender, sexuality, and aging theorize and document the wide variety of social practices by privileging local voices and interpretations.

KEY TERMS

age grades, 173
age set, 173
care economy, 168
chain migration, 177
cisgender, 159
feminist anthropology, 160
gender, 159
gender stratification, 167

heteronormativity, 159
Hijras, 162
masculinity studies, 161
queer studies, 161
sex, 159
sexuality, 159
step immigration, 177
transgender, 159

SUGGESTED READINGS

Boellstorff, Tom. *A Coincidence of Desires: Anthropology, Queer Studies, Indonesia.* Durham, NC: Duke University Press, 2007.

Comparative discussion of case studies, drawing in part on the author's extensive fieldwork in Indonesia, exploring the relation of sexualities to nationalism, religion, and globalization in Southeast Asia.

Kavedzija, Iza. *Making Meaningful Lives: Tales from an Aging Japan.* Philadelphia: University of Pennsylvania Press, 2022.

A detailed ethnography exploring how the growing cohort of aging men and women in contemporary Japan understand their own lives and negotiate the conflicting values of independence and the need for care as they age.

Knauft, Bruce. *The Gebusi: Lives Transformed in a Rainforest World.* 4th ed. Long Grove, IL: Waveland Press, 2016.

Kinship, marriage, gender, sexuality, and religion in a rapidly transforming community in Papua New Guinea.

SUGGESTED WEBSITES

www.who.int/topics/gender/en/

The website of the World Health Organization includes multiple entries on international health issues from a gendered perspective.

https://lgbtlifecenter.org

The website of the LGBT Life Center, an alliance of several LGBTQ+ and HIV-AIDS communities, providing information on health and wellness, rights, and resources empowering individuals, families, and communities with education and advocacy.

https://www.sexualrightsinitiative.com

The website of the the Sexual Rights Initiative, a coalition of national and regional organizations based in Canada, Poland, India, Egypt, Argentina, and South Africa that work together at the United Nations to advance human rights related to sexuality.

Chapter 8
Economic Organization
Production, Distribution, and Consumption

LEARNING OBJECTIVES

- Compare the production and consumption characteristics of hunter-gatherer, horticultural, pastoralist, agricultural, and market systems.
- Understand the gender and hierarchy components of production systems.
- Analyze the social and political implications associated with various economic and distribution systems.

- Relate the labor and consumption patterns of markets to globalization in contemporary economic relationships around the world.
- Document culture-specific interpretations of, and adaptations to, contemporary globalization.

maximizing

The concept in economic anthropology whereby individuals are seen as interpreting economic rules to their own advantage.

globalization

The worldwide connection between societies based upon the existence of global market connections and the spread of cultural items everywhere; associated with intensive movement of people, goods, capital, technologies, and ideas.

political economy

The interrelationships of political and economic structures.

distribution

The manner in which products circulate through a society.

ECONOMIC ORGANIZATION IS THE WAY in which a society, in a regularized fashion, goes about providing the material goods and services it needs to reproduce itself. Economic organization is a cultural construction that operates according to sets of cultural rules. Patterns of production and consumption are similar to other aspects of culture. Individuals may interpret the rules to their own advantage; in economic terms, this is known as **maximizing**. Human and animal labor, technologies, and resources are brought together for the provisioning of society. Historically in small-scale societies, economic behavior operated to a large extent within the context of the kinship structure. In such situations, rules governing who owns the resources, how work is organized, and who consumes the products, were governed by kinship rules. As societies were incorporated into states, economic behavior was separated from the realm of kinship, and economic institutions became separate systems. Today, some say the world can be understood as a unified economic system as a consequence of **globalization**. The societies discussed in this chapter are all embedded in states, involved in the global system in one way or another.

Economic issues are central to how people live in the contemporary world. Economic decisions always have political implications, and political decisions likewise have economic implications, as reflected in the term **political economy**. In this chapter, we will consider economic organization and access to important resources in terms of production, **distribution**, exchange, and consumption. In the next chapter, economic issues will be discussed within the context of political organization. The global production and consumption systems of the contemporary world are also discussed in chapter 13, "Living/Working in the Globalized World: Colonialism, Globalization, and Development."

production

The process whereby a society uses the tools and energy sources at its disposal and its own people's labor to create the goods necessary for supplying itself.

technology

That part of culture by means of which people directly exploit their environment.

PRODUCTION

Production is the process whereby a society uses the tools and energy sources at its disposal and the labor of people and domesticated animals to create the goods necessary for supplying society as an ongoing entity. **Technology** is that part of culture that enables people to exploit their environment. Technology encompasses the manufacture and use of tools according to a set of cultural rules. Tools relate to and impact other aspects of culture. Artifacts have important symbolic meanings with economic implications. Elaborate yam houses and canoes in the Trobriand Islands are significant symbols of chiefly power as well as examples of production technologies.

Hunting and Gathering

For the greatest time of their existence on earth, some five million years, humans and their ancestors subsisted by a combination of hunting wild animals; gathering roots, seeds, and plants; and collecting sea life along the shores. These ways of exploiting the natural environment are referred to by anthropologists as "foraging" or "hunting and gathering." They represented "a mode of existence characterized by the absence of direct human control over the reproduction of exploited species and little or no control of . . . the behavior . . . of food resources" (Panter-Brick, Layton, and Rowley-Conwy 2001: 2). Hunting and gathering as a subsistence base represented an amalgam of social traits including egalitarianism and a relatively loose attachment to the group as a consequence of mobility, enabling rapid adaptation to changing circumstances.

By the early twentieth century, when anthropologists began to do systematic fieldwork, they discovered that societies dependent primarily on hunting and gathering were found in a wide range of environments. The Inuit of the Arctic region, the indigenous people of the Ituri Forest in Zaire in Central Africa, the San (or Bushmen) of the Kalahari Desert in southern Africa, and the Washo of the Great Basin on the California-Nevada border are examples of societies that formerly depended exclusively on hunting and gathering for their subsistence. Despite the environmental variations, several generalizations can be made about their mode of subsistence. All of these societies had very low population densities. The availability of the plants and animals they depended on fluctuated according to the seasons. Migratory animals were absent for much of the year and then present for a short time in superabundance. Similarly, wild nuts, fruits, tubers, and seeds ripened during a particular time of the year, at which point they needed to be harvested. They often processed resources at special-purpose field camps and brought these processed resources back to their home base to be stored for future use (Rowley-Conwy 2001: 41). To deal with variations in availability, hunters and gatherers typically had to exploit all the resources present in their environments. Variation in the diet of hunters and gatherers relates to geographical location and climate. The degree of dependence on vegetable food generally declines as one moves farther from the equator. The percentage of meat rises until one gets to the far north, where meat constitutes almost 100 percent of the diet (Kuhn and Stiner 2001: 103–4; see also Jenike 2001). There is more diversity nearer the equator, where birds, small mammals, and reptiles complemented the vegetable diet.

Originally, technologies for obtaining and processing the proteins and vegetables hunted and gathered utilized natural materials taken directly from the environment, such as stone, bone, wood, and animal hides. Other technologies are regularly obtained through barter, trade, or purchase from sedentary groups with whom hunter-gatherers are regularly in contact. They have an intimate knowledge of the environment, including animal behavior and

A Saan Bushman hunter in southern Africa. Modern hunter-gatherers continually adapt their technologies and food-gathering practices to changes in their environments. Around the world, contemporary hunter-gatherers face state-enforced restrictions to land and resources that threaten their traditional cultural and productive practices.

the growing patterns of plants. For example, the Inuit hunted seals in many different ways, depending upon climatic conditions, seasons, and seal species. Every part of the animal was used for food or the manufacture of clothing, shelter, utilitarian implements, and ritual objects. In hunting-and-gathering societies, there were no specialists whose only occupation was to make tools. Everyone made or obtained their own tools. Children were taught how to manufacture and use tools as part of their socialization.

Task differentiation was primarily believed to be between gender and age groups. It was long assumed by scholars of hunting and gathering societies that men hunted and fished. Women were believed to have gathered plants, collected shellfish, manufactured and repaired clothing and shelter materials, processed and prepared food, and cared for children, elders, and the disabled. Scholars now believe that this strict gender-based division of labor was not necessarily fixed in all hunter-gatherer communities. Archaeological evidence in many parts of the world shows women buried with hunting tools, suggesting that they participated in these activities and were well respected for them (Venkataraman 2021). Children began to learn these tasks at a young age, and by puberty assumed adult productive roles. Successful hunters and fishermen, who excelled at their tasks, were accorded respect and prestige, and their advice was often sought. Hunting-and-gathering societies tended not to have social class divisions based on the accumulation of resources or goods. Nor did they usually rank individuals as higher or lower in social status, except by gender.

Contemporary hunting-and-gathering populations around the world suggest how earlier groups functioned and flourished. Hunters and gatherers were not isolated, as they traded with other hunters and gatherers. They began to have long-term exchange relationships with settled agriculturalists and pastoralists of the same or different ethnic groups once these other modes of production developed. For example, prior to the political upheavals and genocidal civil wars in Rwanda in the 1980s and 1990s, the Twa were hunters who were part of a hierarchical, caste-like structure. They exchanged the products of the hunt with Hutu agriculturalists and Tutsi pastoralists. Archeological evidence supports the antiquity of this kind of interaction. Dobe San sites on the edge of the Kalahari Desert show remains of ceramics, iron, and cattle from the eighth to the eleventh centuries, evidence of trade with a variety of other societies in the area for products they did not themselves produce (Layton 2001: 297).

egalitarian society

A system whereby, in theory, productive resources and positions of status and leadership are available to all members of the group.

Although most hunting-and-gathering societies were **egalitarian**, the Kwakiutl and other Northwest Coast societies of British Columbia were an exception because of the presence of ranked differences. Their environmental resources were so rich, particularly in sea life, that they were able to support a much denser population than is usual in hunting-and-gathering societies. They had permanent winter villages with wooden plank houses, though they migrated from these villages at other times of the year to exploit particular resources. They had fulltime craft specialization. They inherited titles and chiefly positions. There are several reasons for this series of differences between Northwest Coast societies, and hunting-and-gathering societies in other parts of the world. The rich environment of the Northwest Coast provided both mammals and birds; many species of edible plants; numerous varieties of fish, shellfish, and sea mammals; and finally, but importantly, the several species of salmon that annually spawned in the rivers. The preservation and storage of this wide range of products enabled them to produce and maintain large, permanent village communities. The development of large, oceangoing plank canoes among the Nuchanulth, for example, who lived on the west coast of Vancouver Island, off the southwest coast of Canada, enabled social interchanges and exchange of goods to take place over wide areas.

Contemporary Hunters and Gatherers

Hunting and gathering as an economic endeavor and a way of life still continues today. The environment is still an important source of subsistence for people in Alaska, northern Canada, and Siberia. But even in these areas, it is always combined with other kinds of economic activities, in mixed economies (Hitchcock and Biesele 2000: 6). Foraging provides subsistence as well as **market**-oriented items to be sold for cash, which is used to purchase manufactured items. This modified mode of subsistence is always integrated, to a greater or lesser degree, into national and international economies. People who still pursue a hunting-and-gathering mode of subsistence do so as a part-time endeavor and use such modern tools as rifles, steel traps, and snowmobiles. Today, foragers depend on human labor, are closely attached to the land, have common property resource-management systems, and have a worldview that combines nature with spiritual phenomena (2000: 7). Since mineral and petroleum deposits have been found in some areas where foragers traditionally lived, they have had to cope with the problem of commercial development of these resources, while promoting conservation and the survival of their ecosystem. Although the Kwak'wala and Nuchanulth still fish, their catch of halibut or salmon goes to canneries or the fish market. Then it can be sold locally, or it is sent to other parts of the world as they are now an integral part of the Canadian economy and beyond that, the world economy. Most of the food they eat is purchased at stores with money they have earned. Among the Tlingit of the Canadian Northwest Coast, subsistence fishing is done in a different location from commercial fishing, and seal hunting is still pursued, remaining an important sector of their community economy (Dombrowski 2001: 85, 105; Thornton 2008).

Animal rights groups that are against "large-scale industrial" harvesting of seals, particularly harp seal and hooded seal pups in the North Atlantic, put Native peoples in conflict with Euro-American environmental activists. These groups argue that the Inuit should use traditional technology and should restrict use of the products of the hunt to subsistence only. The Inuit argue that their tradition centers on maintaining a way of life in the same

market

A place where goods are exchanged for money, or a type of economic system whereby all goods and services are valued by and exchanged for currency.

environment as in the past. To be Inuit today means to maintain traditions, such as sharing the products of the hunt within kinship networks. Traditional religious beliefs and practices are maintained within an economic system that includes modern hunting equipment as well as other products of current technology. They sell part of their harvest to purchase store-bought items. In an even further extension of globalization into the Inuit hunting-and-gathering economy, the Inuit sell the right to hunt walruses to trophy hunters at thousands of dollars apiece. Inuit guides lead the trophy hunter up to the walrus, dispatching it with one well-placed shot, carefully avoiding the tusks and the head, which the hunter takes. The Inuit crew butchers the carcass in the traditional manner, to be stored and eaten throughout the winter by community members (Chivers 2002).

Some groups of Australian Aboriginal people, who were hunters and gatherers, hold communal title over access to and use of biological resources, that is, the plant and animal species used for food and medicines. Their "traditional knowledge" of Australian plants has been used in the commercialization of those plants, often without recognition for the contributions of Australian Aboriginal people. Smokebush, which grows in western Australia, has recognized healing properties. The western Australian government gave the US National Cancer Institute a license to collect these plants, which were later found to be useful against the HIV virus, and this discovery was patented by the Institute. Subsequently, Amrad-Victoria, an Australian pharmaceutical company, was given a worldwide license to develop the patent, and later to develop the anti-AIDS drug. The Australian Aboriginal people were not acknowledged financially or otherwise "for their role in having first discovered the healing properties of smokebush" (Biber-Klemm et al. 2006: 97). To prevent this injustice from occurring in the future, the Australian government developed a model contract to be used in negotiations over access to traditional knowledge in which benefits are shared. It is their attempt to integrate indigenous customs into their modern legal system.

Land access rights are a critical issue for indigenous peoples around the world. For example, the contemporary owners of the land comprising the Kakadu National Forest in Australia's Northern Territories are the direct descendants of people who have lived in the area for fifty thousand years. Some of them live in the park while others live nearby. The park land is owned by twelve clans. "Historically, tourism has been seen as an intrusion and the traditional owners have mostly been passive beneficiaries . . . via shared ownership of tourism properties and as beneficiaries of land rent payments and a share of park fees provided for in park lease agreements" (Wellings 2007: 94). Today, they are interested in participating in ecotourism to generate more income for employment opportunities for young people so they can remain on their traditional land. Culturally based tourism is seen as maintaining interest in and the valuing of their cultural heritage as well as passing it on to their children (Layton 2001).

THE INTRODUCTION OF AGRICULTURE

The domestication of plants and animals emerged around the world in different locations some 8,000 to 10,000 years ago. **Agriculture** depended upon the development of a new body of information and technologies by which human beings acquired greater control of the environment and, in turn, transformed it in much more significant ways than had been done by hunters and gatherers. Social groups were tied to territories differently than they had been with hunting and gathering. Small kin-based groups settled permanently and intergenerationally on the same property over which they claimed ownership rights. With a shift to agriculture, social groups utilized a smaller area, and population was more dense and concentrated in hamlets and villages. Agriculturalists operate on the basis of a seasonal cycle, especially where there is a marked climatic difference between winter and summer or rainy and dry seasons. The agricultural year is usually divided into planting time, growing time, and harvest. Even when they are under the threat of starvation, agricultural people must restrain themselves from consuming all the seed produced, or they will have no crop during the following year. The factors to be considered in an examination of different economic systems based on agriculture include how people utilize their labor, how they work the land, how they use water resources, what they grow, and whether their crops are for their own subsistence or for sale in the market.

Agriculture

Grain cultivation system characterized by permanent use of land, owned and worked continuously. Agricultural production requires access to animal and/or or mechanical traction, use of seeds, fertilizer, and a water delivery system.

Horticulture

Horticulture is based upon crops that are grown in gardens through vegetative propagation, using a part of the plant itself, rather than through the planting of harvested seeds. Systems of production based on horticulture vary in terms of the number of crops grown in a garden, the length of the fallow period, and whether the water necessary for plant growth is controlled. A continuum of New Guinea societies reflects greater and greater complexity of horticultural techniques for cultivating gardens and achieving higher crop yields and more permanent gardens. The simplest form of horticulture, known as **swidden**, or **shifting cultivation**, involves making gardens by clearing land by burning, and planting the garden in the ashes, which act as a fertilizer. Because the soil is rapidly exhausted, a new garden must be planted in a new location every few years. Gardens contain many kinds of plants on a single plot. A digging stick was often the only tool used. This type of horticulture is supplemented by hunting and the collection of wild plants.

horticulture

A form of cultivation in which crops are propagated in gardens.

swidden or **shifting cultivation**

A type of horticulture in which new gardens are made every few years, when the soil is exhausted.

The most complex forms of horticulture in New Guinea are found in the mountains of the central highlands. There, people like the Enga use a variety of labor-intensive techniques. The gardens may be used for a generation or more. Clans own land used for hunting and fishing, while arable land within clan territory is owned by individual families. Each garden consists of a regular series of mounds formed from soil and mulch, separated by ditches, and used only for sweet potato cultivation. These single-crop gardens are

Sugarcane harvesting in South Africa. An example of horticultural production, sugarcane stalks are propagated by planting sections of harvested stalks into the ground. Similar horticultural techniques are used to produce tubers like yams and potatoes.

separated from mixed gardens in which most other crops are grown. The yields from the mounded gardens of the Enga are considerably greater than the yields from the basic type of horticulture described earlier. The Enga number over 150,000, so there is considerable pressure for land, and Enga clans may fight one another over it. Horticultural systems depend upon rainfall for water; however, root crop cultivation can also involve systems of water collection and control. The Dani of the Grand Valley in western New Guinea have used dams, ditches, and drainage systems to turn a natural swamp into a productive cultivation area.

Just as hunting-and-gathering peoples have intimate knowledge of the plant and animal species that they utilize, horticulturalists display an extensive knowledge of soils, food plants, and cultivation techniques. This practical know-how is frequently combined with ritual practices performed during the process of production. In general, in societies with horticulture, clans own the land they cultivate. Individual families, that is, members of the clan owning the land, plant and harvest from their own plots.

Grain Production

In the more temperate areas of several continents of the world, agriculturalists use swidden agriculture to grow maize in the New World, millet and sorghum in Africa, and rice in Asia. In preparing fields for growing grain, the same technique of cutting down trees and burning off brush is used, as in swidden horticulture. There is also a long fallow period after several plantings. The only source of water is rainfall. Agricultural societies in much of Europe and Asia growing grain depended on a technology that involved crop rotation, the use of the plow drawn by draft animals, and animal manure as fertilizer. Wheat, rye, and barley were the predominant crops. The use of draft animals required raising additional crops such as hay to feed those animals.

Grain agriculture is dependent on the use of irrigation systems. An enormous amount of organized labor was required to create the necessary artificial environment of lakes, ponds, dikes, ditches, and terraces that made up the irrigation systems. The advent of such systems in Mesopotamia and early Imperial China was associated with the development of powerful central governments, urban civilizations, and states. Increased productivity per acre of land, the basis for increasing cultural complexity, depended on several factors. Establishing elaborate irrigation systems initially required great outputs of forced labor; maintaining them also requires a large amount of labor. The crops on which people subsisted also vary in terms of their storage potential, which affects how a crop surplus will be utilized. Technology is also an important factor in grain production. Steel axes and machetes are more efficient than stone axes. Animal labor is more efficient than human labor,

BOX 8.1 | The Agricultural Revolution: Did We Inherit a Terrible Mistake?

Approximately ten thousand years ago, production of domesticated grains and plants began appearing in parts of the Middle East, South Asia, China, and Central America. Sometimes referred to as the "Neolithic Revolution," agriculture developed independently in many different ecological environments around the world. Debates over how these processes originated and, even more intriguingly, why, occupies a significant place in anthropological literature. "The simple fact is that we do not yet have a good grasp on the causes for the origins of agriculture. The how and the why of the Neolithic transition remain among the more intriguing questions in human prehistory" (Price and Bar-Yosef 2011: S168).

What is known is that the advent of agriculture set into motion a series of social, political, and environmental transformations that dramatically altered the physical landscape and sociopolitical environments of people around the world. Agriculture turned a world of hunter-gatherers into mostly settled cultivators, living in communities of increasing population density, organized into stratified classes of economic specialization, under despotic rulers of centralized states. These settled cultivators worked longer hours than their hunter-gatherer ancestors, suffered from diseases and forms of malnutrition unknown in hunter-gather communities, and were tied intergenerationally to land subject to the destructive forces of periodic droughts and floods. Skeletal evidence from early agricultural settlements demonstrates the human cost of the transition to agriculture. Paleopathologists, who study the remains of ancient people, document shrinking height, decreasing life expectancies, malnutrition from loss of variety in the diet, and evidence of injury and degenerative bone diseases caused by intense physical labor. All this evidence prompts Jared Diamond to call agriculture "the worst mistake in the history of the human race" (Diamond 1987). Citing studies of contemporary Kalahari Bushmen, African hunter-gatherers, Diamond says, "It turns out [the Bushmen] have plenty of leisure time, sleep a good deal, and work less hard than their farming neighbors" (1987: 118).

The agricultural revolution set into motion a series of political and social innovations that are present worldwide today. "Besides malnutrition, starvation, and epidemic diseases, farming helped bring another curse upon humanity: deep class divisions. . . . Only in farming populations could a healthy, nonproducing elite set itself above the disease-ridden masses" (Diamond 1987: 120). As is evidenced in contemporary agricultural communities, these class divisions are accompanied by gendered divisions of labor and profoundly inequitable landowning practices. Patriarchal descent systems in agricultural communities, through customary law, exclude wives and daughters from inheriting land, which tends to be controlled by related males across generations.

Contemporary agriculture, including intensification of crop yields through the use of high-yielding varieties of wheat, corn, and rice, has greatly reduced the risk of starvation in many parts of the world. It has boosted the economies of developing states that export cultivated commodities into a globalized agricultural production-and-consumption system. And as is evident from social movements around the world, the social and political arrangements of agriculture and land inheritance can be changed through law and social policy. Women and girls can have greater control over land ownership and rights to agricultural decision making. Access to education, loans, credit, and supporting legal institutions reshapes gender relationships in agricultural communities. Poor and marginal farmers can resort to legal and political support in protecting their rights to land and water. Equally important to the quality of life and productivity of contemporary agriculture around the world are the challenges created by climate change, massive water usage

(Continued)

BOX 8.1 | **The Agricultural Revolution: Did We Inherit a Terrible Mistake? (Continued)**

and chemical fertilization, and the increasing emission of carbon dioxide associated with agriculture and large-scale animal production. This is a global challenge, highlighted by the adoption by all member states of the UN of the 2030 Sustainable Development Goals, which focus in part on the critical necessity of developing programs, technologies, and information systems that address the sustainability of contemporary agricultural systems.

---

except in places of high population density, such as China. Machines and the mechanization of agriculture, as well as the use of chemical fertilizers, as has occurred in the United States and elsewhere, increases productivity but also creates challenges due to the degrading of the water supply and ecosystem.

Agriculture in Today's World

Each technological advance in food production produced its own set of problems. Mechanized agriculture, for example, has resulted in overproduction and the need to store vast agricultural surpluses; the use of chemical pesticides has led to widespread pollution of soil and water. In the United States, fewer farms grow more and more food; what was once a family farm has become a corporation and may even be listed on the stock exchange. Around the world, agricultural land is being purchased by foreign and national elites to consolidate and maximize commodity production, causing small landholders to lose access to their lands. Increasingly this process is taking place across borders, as agricultural production companies in Northern countries buy up land for export commodity production in Africa and Asia.

Throughout the world, people in rural areas have been affected by the penetration of globalization and new international division of labor. There is an international flow of goods and of technological information and new political forms that serve as challenges to local ways of life. Climate change and dramatic changes in rainfall and water supply challenge agricultural production around the world. Drought destroys agricultural production in some parts of the world while, simultaneously, massive flooding and unpredictable rainfall have the same effect elsewhere. Globalization of agriculture creates changes in landownership patterns and local political structures. As communities and producers become integrated into larger systems of labor supply, production, and distribution, inequality between producers, distributors, and marketers inevitably results. But local people have responded in a variety of ways to empower local producers to produce and market commodities that are consumed in the global North. In the New Guinea highlands, subsistence horticultural practices are supplemented by the extensive cash-crop export production of coffee, while in the lowlands and the Bismarck Archipelago, coconuts are grown for oil to manufacture soap marketed to consumers for its natural properties.

Among the Asante, an ethnic group with matrilineal descent dominating the forest area of Ghana in West Africa, both men and women actively farm. Men grow cocoa, a cash crop that is exported. Both men and women participate in commercial food production for Ghanaian cities and to provide food, including tomatoes, cassava, eggplant, plantains, and yams, for those farmers who specialize in cocoa and other cash-crop production (Clark 1994: 253–70). There are also centers where food crops, locally produced, are marketed. Women dominate the farming and trade of food crops and control the marketplaces. The flexible market system with its many marketplaces also provides a market for secondary crops and craft products that are "fallback" options for the periods when crop production suffers. Women farmers, suffering from gender disparities in resource allocation, restricted from the planting of cocoa, and discouraged from expanding their farms, have diversified into food processing and trading (1994: 259–60). Female farmers and traders gain income from trading and marketing and are able to demonstrate their personal autonomy in the agricultural and commercial sectors.

ANIMAL DOMESTICATION AND PASTORALISM

Historically, the domestication of animals is associated with agriculture. A wide variety of animal species was domesticated, most of which furnished traction, meat, and milk. Some animals, such as the horse, donkey, bullock, and buffalo, were also used for transportation. The hair of others, such as sheep and goats, was woven into cloth. In the New World, the first significant animal domesticates were llama and alpaca. The animals were selectively bred to enhance those characteristics that make them more controllable and more useful to humans, and to eliminate unwanted characteristics. Humans have shaped the biological characteristics of these animals through the process of domestication. At the same time, pastoral societies adapted to the needs of their animals, particularly in the migration cycle. However, as we shall see below, pastoralism is very often at odds with state policy and enforcement of border restrictions.

Societies that are completely dependent upon their domesticated animals are known as **nomadic pastoral societies**. Only rarely do they cultivate. Nomadic pastoral societies, with one or two exceptions, were found in the in arid zones. Sheep, goats, camels, horses, cattle, yaks, water buffalo, or reindeer constituted

nomadic pastoralists

Societies dependent upon herds of domesticated animals.

Pastoralists maintain herds of animals that must migrate regularly for access to grazing and water. In contemporary states, pastoralists face increasing obstacles to maintaining this productive system, especially due to political borders and privatization of land. In the Negev Desert region of Israel, pastoralists compete with massive utility-generating plants for access to land and water.

the basic herd animals for these societies. In most cases, one or two types of animals formed the basis for herds. Nomadic pastoralists depended on their herd animals for a range of products. Daily yields of milk and milk products such as cheese were central to their diet. From earliest times, the pastoralists exchanged live animals, wool, and milk products with sedentary people for essential commodities such as tea, sugar, and flour. Since wealth was measured in numbers of animals in the herd, pastoralists were loath to kill animals for their meat alone; therefore, this was done only on special occasions.

The animal species upon which particular nomadic pastoral societies depends relates to the nature of the environment. Some species, such as camels, are best adapted to arid desert areas, and others, such as horses, to well-watered grassy plains. Some animals can withstand extremes of temperature, while others cannot. Some, such as goats, do best in steeper mountain environments, while others, such as water buffalo, can live only in flat, swampy lowlands. Nomadic pastoralists migrate in a regular annual pattern from one place to another to find grazing lands. The community and its herds might move from summer to winter pasturage or from wet to dry locations. In their seasonal movements, they resemble hunters and gatherers, particularly those who hunt large herds of migratory animals, such as the caribou. However, there is a crucial difference in that hunters follow the migratory herd wherever the herd goes in its natural migration, whereas the herds that belong to the nomadic pastoralists follow the people who herd them.

Nomadic Pastoralism in Today's World

Most nomadic pastoral societies have undergone great changes under political pressure from national governments (Humphrey and Sneath 1999). As a result of wars, revolutions, and famines, their way of life has been transformed. Sheep and goat herders in Iran no longer migrate with their herds. Instead, they move their animals and their belongings from one pasture site to another by truck, rather than using traditional draft animals such as camels or donkeys. They need not even set up camp near a water source, since tank trucks bring water to wherever they set up camp, which may even be next to a highway.

The homeland of the Marsh Arabs became a major battleground of the Iran-Iraq war in the 1980s and was a center of military activity during the Gulf War of 1990–1991. Attempts were made to forcibly settle the nomadic groups of Iran by various political regimes in Iran beginning in the 1920s and continuing to this day. Their access to grazing and migrating routes may be restricted by the discovery of mineral and petroleum resources on these lands.

The Nentsy of Siberia remain a nomadic pastoral people, dependent on reindeer herding in western Siberia, in an area of tundra in the Arctic where agriculture is not possible. After the Russian Revolution in 1917, they were collectivized, but only to a degree, since the Soviet officials allowed the Nentsy to keep private herds. After the collapse of the Soviet economic system in 1989, their economy reverted to privatization and regional economic marketing. Many other reindeer pastoralists in Siberia have undergone economically difficult times after the Soviet collapse, but the Nentsy have thrived. They sell the meat of the reindeer, as well as the antlers, which are used to make medications that are believed to "strengthen the human immune system . . . increasing strength, improving the blood, and building masculine virility" (Stammler 2005: 306). China and Korea are the primary markets for these products. The sale of reindeer meat is a source of income, permitting Nentsy families to buy flour, tea, fuel, and guns and ammunition for hunting. Although the Nentsy are active participants in an impersonal market economy, they still retain their own emphasis on communal reciprocity and exchange. Wealthy families with large herds of reindeer continue to provide leadership for the Nentsy as a whole, and families are strongly dependent on others for labor and food.

THE ORGANIZATION OF WORK

How is work organized and labor recruited in a particular social order? The organization of work in a society sometimes relates to the nature of postmarital residence and the formation of kinship groups in that society. Cooperative endeavors in which people work communally serve to reinforce the social solidarity of the group. When the most important subsistence tasks are traditionally performed by men, the residence pattern after marriage tends to be virilocal, whereas when the tasks are performed by women working together, the postmarital residence pattern tends to be uxorilocal. Chiefs were frequently instrumental in organizing certain kinds of production. For example, Trobriand chiefs organized the activities of their clan members in building canoes and creating new gardens; Kwakwaka'wakw chiefs organized the members of their numaym when they built a new house.

The division of labor in productive tasks is culturally determined in all societies, as noted earlier. In hunting-and-gathering societies, division of labor between men and women privileged male production. Often the gathering activities of women provided the bulk of the calories on which the group subsisted. The products of the hunt brought back by the men, however, represented the most highly valued food. Hunting was a more prestigious activity than gathering, reflecting the relative gender stratification of productive roles. The productive tasks assigned to men in one society may be assigned to women in another. In some New Guinean societies, such as the Tor's, women cut down the sago palm to get its pith, while in other societies, such as the Abelam's, men do this. In American society today, there are many tasks that men formerly performed exclusively that are now performed by women; the opposite is also true.

Within both male and female domains, some work tasks are done individually and others in cooperative groups. The hunting of herd animals, such as caribou, by the Inuit was carried out communally. However, for animal species that tend to move individually, hunting was done on an individual basis. Gathering and collecting by women also tended to be done on an individual

Remote work from offsite locations is growing in popularity for employers and workers. During the Covid-19 epidemic, remote work allowed skilled and professional workers to continue to be employed and collect salaries during quarantine periods. Hourly or freelance remote workers are attempting to organize the "gig economy" of short-term workers to obtain comparable benefits and job protections as those offered to onsite employees.

basis. Myanmar's (Burmese) women, who work together at the different tasks involved in the manufacture of silk, sing collectively as they work. It would seem that working communally is more pleasurable than when each person goes off to work by himself or herself. In our own society today, many people now work as freelancers or consultants out of offices set up in their homes, maintaining contact with large, multinational companies through computerized internet technologies. During pandemic periods and resulting "lockdowns," an increasing number of people around the world are faced with the challenges of conducting their work and schooling in isolation, through telecommunication. These options are often not available to some groups of workers, such as medical personnel and foodservice workers, putting these workers who are forced by economic necessity to work "face to face" at increased levels of risk for exposure to contagious diseases.

Where the mode of subsistence is crop cultivation, both men and women may be involved in planting, weeding, and harvesting. In New Guinean societies, a clear distinction is made between certain crops such as bananas and sugarcane, which are referred to as male crops, and other crops, such as sweet potatoes, grown by women, referred to as women's crops. When plows and mechanized agricultural implements are introduced, the whole range of agricultural tasks usually becomes the domain of men. Women, if they are involved in agricultural tasks at all, are limited to growing vegetables in subsistence gardens. In nomadic pastoral societies, the task of herding and moving the camp is in the male realm, while women milk the animals and manufacture milk products.

The Organization of Work in Contemporary Societies

All of the examples of economic production we have discussed thus far coexist in states that all participate in the global system of capitalist industrial production. Capitalism, and its social and political components, was famously studied and critiqued by Karl Marx and Fredric Engels in a vast corpus of publications. Capitalism is of interest to anthropologists because of its global dominance, particularly since the collapse of the Soviet empire, and its spread into virtually every corner of the world. Capitalism at its most basic is a system of production in which products and services are produced for profit. Labor, raw materials, and distribution all have a cost; the difference between these costs and the selling price of products is profit. In theory, this system of production exists in the domain of supply and demand and private enterprise. The history of the rise of capitalism, and particularly during the period of the Industrial Revolution in Europe and the United States in the nineteenth century, is associated with urbanization and the presence of factories in cities. Labor for these factories was, and continues to be in some parts of the world, supplied by migrants from rural communities, displaced by the contraction of agricultural employment.

The spread of colonialism throughout the nineteenth century is associated in part with European countries' quest for raw materials, labor, and markets for their industrial production. The contemporary spread of global capitalism continues to be associated with labor migration and the gendered division of labor. It is characterized by the alienation of the worker from control or decision making over what is being produced. The global system of capitalism has replaced "brick and mortar" factories, where all labor and raw materials came to one place and products are produced on automated assembly lines. These factories are now often replaced with a globally diffused system of production of the components of final products. They are produced and assembled in different locations around the world, utilizing vast supplies of low-priced labor and low-cost, often unregulated and unsafe, assembly facilities. (See chapter 13 for further discussion of Fordist and Post-Fordist production.)

Capitalism is also associated with multiple transformations of family farms from the agriculturally based extended intergenerational families to mobile, two-generation families that can easily move to new locations for adults to find work. In today's globalized capitalism, this migration to seek work is often characterized by different family members migrating to different places in search of wages, which are shared with nonmigrating family members as remittances. In many societies in the world today, more and more women are leaving their homes for full- or part-time wage work. They may migrate from rural to urban communities for factory work or other wage labor, or migrate to other countries where service economies have developed that are highly dependent upon the labor of migrant women.

How does globalization of work operate in a transnational setting? One example is the outsourcing of customer service, financial services, and technical support to call centers in India. Employees in these centers also do telemarketing calls, trying to sell banking and financial plans, computer hardware, and other products. Transnational labor subcontractors provide the workers with language training to "neutralize" their accents and speech patterns. Each worker is assigned a Western-sounding name. There is a predefined script the worker must follow. Because of the twelve-to-sixteen-hour time difference between India and America, Indian workers must work night shifts (Patel 2010; Mirchandani 2004). This transforms their usual lives, providing access to well-paid jobs for both men and women, as discussed in chapter 5. Call center work is highly desirable since workers are paid relatively high wages, although they know they are receiving much less than an American or European worker doing the same work would receive. The workers express dissatisfaction with the dehumanizing nature of the scripting and the routine. However, they do not want the subcontracting system to end because this work promises new forms of economic mobility.

DISTRIBUTION

Patterns and structures of distribution have been transformed over the past century in many societies. However, as we have pointed out in several examples earlier in this chapter, societies drawn into the global market retain traditional exchanges and ritual obligations of gift-giving to their kin and affines today. Systems of distribution or exchange illustrate who gives what to whom, when, where, and how. In every society, the system of distribution is determined by the operation of cultural rules and the way in which individuals in the system interpret them. Even where distribution of goods is carried out in markets, the concepts of supply and demand are culturally constructed. Certain general principles apply universally to systems of exchange; they may be broken down into three components: giving, receiving, and returning. When an object is offered, the process of exchange begins. It may be accepted or declined. If the object is accepted, then its equivalent must at some point be returned. The acceptance creates a relationship through time, until the return is made. The acceptance of something offered constitutes the assumption of an obligation to return—recipients place themselves in debt to the givers. If such indebtedness continues for a long period of time or if goods go repeatedly in the same direction and are not returned, the recipients become inferior in their own eyes, as well as others, and the givers superior. Anthropologist Marcel Mauss (1954) recognized that giving, receiving, and returning create links; exchange may be the basis for seeking assistance, obtaining goods and services, and creating alliances. Although exchange may be perceived primarily as an economic phenomenon, in fact, it is frequently linked to the political structure and differences in rank, hence the utility of viewing these conjointly as components of political economy. All the exchange systems we will discuss in the following have been penetrated to a greater or lesser degree by industrial market exchange and globalization.

Distribution in Egalitarian Societies

The simplest type of exchange system involves two sides of equal status in continuing exchange with each other. The two sides could be two parts of a village, two clans, or two moieties. This type is referred to as "reciprocal exchange." When one host group gives to several groups simultaneously, a more complex system of exchange develops (figure 8.1). The Maring of the New Guinea highlands have such a system of economic distribution or exchange (Rappaport 1984). The distributive system is part of a religious ceremony referred to as the **kaiko**, which extends over many months. A group of closely related patrilineal clans serves as hosts of the kaiko. The guests at the kaiko come in groups from the surrounding territories. The host group has intermarried with

kaiko

A lengthy Maring religious ceremony.

these neighboring groups and is allied with them in times of war. Guests come brandishing their weapons and singing war songs, and hosts and guests dance in an aggressive display demonstrating the symbolic relationship between warfare and exchange. The aggressiveness is present despite

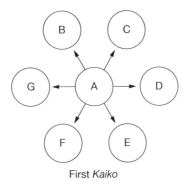

First *Kaiko*

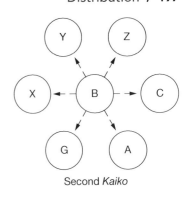

Second *Kaiko*

Fig. 8.1 *Maring* kaiko *exchange*

the fact that guests and hosts intermarry, are allied to one another, and distribute food and valuable goods to one another. Cooked pork from many pigs is distributed at the final kaiko event. Each of the guest groups, who come from a wide area, will in the future hold its own kaiko, at which it will fulfill its obligations to make a return. All the groups are relatively equal in status. The host group is invited in turn to the kaiko that each guest group will hold in the future. Despite the fact that the Maring are involved in plantation wage labor and grow some coffee for sale, they continue to hold the kaiko up to the present (LiPuma 2000: 197ff., 202).

Systems of Exchange in Societies with Flexible Rank

There are societies in which rank differences, which are an integral part of the political structure, play a significant role in their systems of exchange. Here we will be dealing with societies in which the rank of individuals and groups is not permanent, but is constantly subject to modification. The Kwakwaka'wakw wedding potlatch, described in chapter 2, was a kind of distribution in which rank and rank differences were central to the exchanges. Theoretically, every person in society holds an inherited rank position, associated with a name owned by their numaym, or cognatic descent group. However, rank can be raised through potlatching or lowered by the absence of potlatching.

The guests who come to a potlatch serve as witnesses to the event, for example, the succession to chiefly power, and receive goods for this service. The guests, affines of the hosts, are seated according to their rank and receive goods in that order. The guest numayms must at some future time reciprocate by making a return potlatch. Kwakwaka'wakw potlatches were sometimes described as if the motivation for them was competition and the desire to shame one's rivals. One must hold a potlatch in order to raise one's rank, but one needs equally high-ranking competitors to challenge.

By the end of the nineteenth century, the Kwakwaka'wakw were involved in the Canadian cash economy. Hudson Bay blankets, powerboats, sewing machines, tea cups and saucers, and other goods from the Euro-Canadian economy purchased with wages began to be distributed at potlatches. Like

sagali

A large-scale funerary ceremonial distribution among the Trobriand Islanders.

urigubu

A Trobriand harvest gift given yearly by a man to his sister's husband.

kula

An exchange system of the Trobriand Islands—involving one kind of shell valuables moving in a clockwise direction and another kind moving in a counterclockwise direction—that links the Trobriand Islanders to neighboring islands.

other societies being drawn into the world system, the Kwakwaka'wakw were using wages and manufactured products in their traditional ceremonial distributions. As early as 1895, the Canadian government made its first attempt to outlaw the potlatch. Such large-scale distributions and the destruction of property went against the Protestant ethic and the modern Canadian capitalist economy, which missionaries and government officials thought the native population should emulate. However, potlatches continued to be held in secret. The prohibition against holding a potlatch ended in 1951, and large-scale potlatches have subsequently been held by many Northwest groups.

In the Trobriand Islands, three different types of exchange systems were described in detail in multiple books and articles by Bronislaw Malinowski (1935, 1961): **sagali**, **urigubu**, and **kula**. The Trobriand Islanders are horticulturalists. The Trobrianders have matrilineal clans, avunculocal residence, and father's sister's daughter marriage (see chapter 6, figures 6.1 and 6.2). Trobriand funerary rites include the mortuary sagali, a distribution to the clan of the wife of the dead chief in exchange for all the funerary services provided by clan members. The second type of exchange is a distribution of yams called urigubu, which occurs after every harvest. Marriage initiated this annual payment of yams, the urigubu, by a man to his sister's husband (see figure 8.2). The urigubu yams are displayed in a yam house that is built by a man's brother-in-law, who will be giving him the yams. Yams for urigubu represent the prestige of the giver as a gardener and as a kinsman fulfilling an obligation. But these yams are consumed by households other than that of the producer. To market economists, the most rational, economically efficient system would be for everyone to grow and then eat his own yams. The urigubu distribution system of the Trobrianders makes sense only in terms of their social system. The urigubu is paid to the husbands and fathers of the matrilineal lineage for carrying out the important social role of father. Malinowski referred to urigubu as economic tribute for chiefs since they took many wives, up to twenty or more, given to them by village headmen in their districts. With so many brothers-in-law, the chief accumulates many yams after each harvest, which he then redistributes as rewards to his followers on the various occasions for feasts (Malinowski 1935). In addition, at harvest time, there are competitive yam feasts, called kayasa, between villages. The game of cricket played by the Trobrianders, adapted from their observation of European colonialists, is part of the competitive kayasa being held between villages.

Kula, another type of Trobriand exchange, links the Trobriand Islands with a circle of other islands that are different culturally and linguistically (Malinowski 1961). Trobrianders considered these islands dangerous places because warfare and cannibalism were endemic in precolonial times (see figure 8.3). The goods exchanged in the kula are two kinds of shell valuables—red shell necklaces, which move clockwise around the circle of islands, and white armshells, which move counterclockwise. The exchange of shell valuables in the kula created alliances between individuals living in potentially hostile areas. While the kula exchange, with its elaborate ceremony, is being carried out, direct barter of food, pottery, and other manufactured utilitarian objects is also taking place between the kula visitors and their hosts.

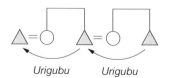

Urigubu   *Urigubu*

Fig. 8.3 *Trobriand* urigubu *ritual payments*

This barter, which does not take place with kula partners but with others on the island, involves the exchange of items that are scarce or absent in one place but not another. The Massim area, before extensive contact with Europeans, was an area of chronic warfare; the precontact kula exchange system alternated with warfare, and the kula system described by Malinowski operated as it did because of European pacification (Keesing 1990: 152).

These exchange systems, though modified, continue to operate among the Trobrianders today, who are now citizens of Papua New Guinea. A recent description of kayasa on Kaileuna indicates that it is now a contest among men of a village to see who can grow the most yams. The kayasa organizer uses this as a means of increasing his prestige. Chiefdomship is still a matter of **ascribed status**, derived from the lineage into which one is born, but **achieved status**, such as that derived from success in competitive events such as the kayasa is also an important element in becoming a chief (Schiefenhovel and Bell-Krannhals 1996: 249). Visitors come to the final stages of the ceremony as witnesses. Urigubu is also a matter of competition since men gain prestige from giving large amounts of urigubu. Though today they travel in fiberglass boats and are Christians, "in many respects the Trobrianders of today seem to have stepped from the pages of their famous ethnography" (1996: 236).

Although the Trobrianders and Kwakwaka'wakw have different modes of production, both have flexible rank systems. They both produce economic surpluses. Distribution of goods at potlatches and at sagali serves to enhance one's rank and prestige. Goods are given to chiefs by their followers in their kin groups as a kind of **tribute**, which is redistributed on ceremonial occasions. When the chief serves as a host at such a ceremonial redistribution, he validates his claim to high rank. The acceptance of the redistributed goods by

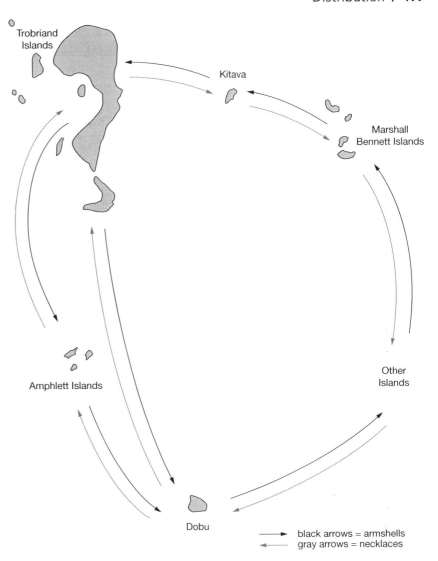

Fig. 8.3 *Trobriand kula ring exchange system*

ascribed status

An inherited position in the social structure.

achieved status

Position in a social structure dependent upon personal qualifications and individual ability.

tribute

Presentation of objects of value by people of lower status to those of higher status.

the guests means they recognize this claim. Rank in these societies is flexible in that the more one distributes, the higher one's rank becomes.

Systems of Exchange with Fixed Rank

When rank differences are permanent, the nature of exchange is significantly altered. In such systems, elites are distinguished from commoners, lords from vassals, patrons from clients, and high castes from low castes, as occurs in India. The groups in such systems differ not only in rank and prestige but also in the access they have to important economic and political resources, known as **social capital**. Societies with fixed rank systems have groups that are economically specialized and have a relatively fixed division of labor. These systems of economic distribution always symbolically emphasize the inferiority of vassal, client, commoner, and low-caste individual, and the superiority of aristocrat, lord, patron, and high-caste individual. When superiors give to inferiors, the act is seen as generosity or philanthropy. When inferiors give to superiors, it is considered tribute. No matter how much tribute the inferiors give, it does not raise their status; it merely further enhances the prestige of their superiors. At the same time, the greater generosity and continual distributions of the superiors enhances their status, not that of the recipients. Objects exchanged in these systems derive their cultural meanings solely from the status of the giver, whether the goods move up to a higher-ranked individual or down to a lower-ranked individual.

Caste in India

In India, castes were historically endogamous, specialized occupational groups within which individuals intermarried. In rural communities, all the castes form a system in which members of the various jati (local caste designations) historically performed services for one another. This system ties lower caste groups to the labor needs of upper caste groups through intergenerational obligations based on ritually enforced connections between the groups. The jati are hierarchically ordered, based on their presumed purity or pollution. Though Indian castes are relatively fixed in rank, jatis often renegotiate their placement within the system. Today they quite frequently attempt to change their position with respect to other groups. This may be the result of new technologies and new products routinely introduced into both urban and rural communities. Steel and glass implements diminish the need for potters to create clay cups and plates. In cities throughout India, washing machines are replacing the labor of dhobis, the jati of clothing and linen washers and pressers. As we noted in chapter 5, jati members may give up food and drink practices that associate them with low caste ranking, as well as abandon traditional economic practices that are perceived as polluting. Recognition of these changes in status requires the adoption of new behaviors by the entire jati, such as the abandonment of polluting economic activities like tanning or

social capital

Relationships, skills, and resources enabling an individual's or group's maximal participation in society.

hauling carcasses. It also requires the recognition of these jati-wide changes by upper caste groups (Weisgrau 1997: 30).

Where rank differences in the social system are fixed, we find economically specialized occupational groups that are tied together in an interdependent system of economic exchanges. Economic subsistence in these societies is dependent upon exchange. Distributions in egalitarian societies serve to create and maintain ongoing social relations between groups that are equal in status. In societies with flexible rank, distributions allow different groups to improve their rank. Distributions in societies with fixed rank maintain the status of some groups over others. The different types of exchange systems we have discussed are all related to particular types of political and social organization. This why many anthropologists prefer to identify these political ranks and economic exchange systems as aspects of political economy, reflecting the interrelationship between the two.

Barter

Barter is a type of distribution that conforms in part to principles of exchange. It involves direct, immediate exchange, always of different services or objects. As a consequence, barter does not create ongoing relationships. It usually involves goods and commodities that each party does not have in its own environment. Occurring within a context governed by cultural rules, it includes haggling and bargaining. The most common reason given for using barter, rather than cash, is that the buyer simply doesn't have cash. Money may be in short supply due to underemployment or no income at all. Currency and financial institutions may be mistrusted and avoided. (Humphrey 2002: 77). Barter also eliminates any "paper trail" of the transaction, circumventing the reporting of these transactions to government tax authorities. Unlike the simple form of barter in which exchange is immediate—like the yams exchanged for pots, which occurs alongside kula exchange—**delayed exchange** barter depends on trust, since the return isn't made until sometime in the future and depends on some degree of trust. In the former Soviet Union, this required working and exchanging within a community and having a powerful and successful boss who protected the participants from the authorities (2002: 18). This is particularly important when this economic activity is marginally criminal.

barter

An exchange of unlike objects or services, without the use of currency.

delayed exchange

The return of goods or of marriage partners between groups; the delay in exchange demonstrates a degree of trust between the exchanging parties.

THE MARKET SYSTEM

The term *market* has two meanings. The first refers to the location, or site, where food commodities and craft items are bought, sold, or traded. The second meaning characterizes an entire economic system based upon the determination of prices by the supply and demand for the products. Markets can be local or global. This is the exchange system with which Americans are familiar. Perhaps the most distinctive feature of market exchange is that the buyer need have no social relationship with the seller nor face-to-face contact. The relationship between buyer and seller has its basis solely in the fact that the seller has something that the buyer wants or needs and is willing to pay for. The basic premise of a market system is to make a profit, which means to buy cheap and sell for more than you have paid. Market transactions are not determined by social relationships, but social obligations may emerge from ongoing local economic relationships.

A market system depends on the presence of currency. Societies that did not have market systems did not have money in the usual sense of that term. Money serves a number of purposes. With a market system, money can be used as a standard of value because any commodity, service, or labor can be expressed in terms of its monetary worth. But most important, money can serve as a medium of exchange whereby one commodity can be converted into money and then that money can be exchanged for any other kind of goods or services. The money used in our society can be exchanged for anything that is for sale. The valuables discussed in connection with ceremonial distribution, such as the armshells and necklaces in the kula, are objects that have value only in particular situations. The restricted use to which such valuables are put is in sharp contrast to the many purposes that money serves.

Markets served to connect peasant communities with the economy of urban areas. One kind of market structure links a number of different communities to a central market town. In addition to its subsistence activities, each of these communities may specialize in a different craft activity, such as weaving, manufacture of pottery, or manufacture of tiles. In some places markets are held in different villages and towns on successive days of the week. In places like the Golden Triangle area of Myanmar (Burma), the Five Day Market moves between five different villages during the week. The sellers are primarily women from different tribal villages who come to the market in their tribal dress to sell garden crops and food. Manufactured products such as sneakers, shoes, shirts, jackets, and baby clothing are also sold. The same items are sold in all the villages that make up the Five-Day market. The buyers on a particular market day are from the villages surrounding that market. These kinds of marketing structures define a connected region.

The Market Economy and Globalization

The market economy, as Collins notes, "is a dynamic economic system that is accumulative and expansive. Once established, its tentacles spread and envelop peripheral societies both in industrial nations and in those at the margins" (2000: 1). This spread of the market system is referred to today as "globalization." This has several implications for production and consumption; it means not only the penetration of entrepreneurship, technology, technological knowledge, and the capitalist mode of production, but most recently also the development of multinational corporations and movement of capital, technology, people, and goods to, as well as from, most places in the world despite national boundaries or different currencies. International treaties such as the

North American Free Trade Agreement (NAFTA) and the creation of the European Economic Union have an important effect on the movement of products, capital, ideas, and labor around the world. Although NAFTA and other trade agreements have the potential to integrate the economies of exporting and importing countries, there is a backlash from labor in producing countries who see

The Five Day Market by Inle Lake, Myanmar. Every fifth day, hill-tribe people come down from the mountains to buy and sell their goods. Producers and customers in rotating markets are often women.

these agreements as facilitating offshore production, thus creating the danger of their losing employment as a consequence (Cook 2004: 267ff.). The British "Brexit" vote in 2016 to leave the European Union was widely interpreted as nationalist backlash against being incorporated into labor migration and production systems over which Great Britain had little control.

In a market economy, labor also operates according to the laws of supply and demand. Workers go to places where employment is available. Sometimes, a US industry like electronics manufacturing loses out to foreign competition, or the company becomes multinational, outsourcing the manufacture of its products to a country where labor costs are low. In this case, the US workers in that industry are expected to retrain themselves for other work. Most of the world today operates as a unified market. However, what is good for workers manufacturing sewing machines in the modernized economies of Taipei or Hong Kong creates hardships for workers who have lost their jobs as a result of the closing of a plant manufacturing sewing machines in Elizabeth, New Jersey, or automobiles in Flint, Michigan.

With the development of the global system, differences in the cultural settings of capitalism and market economies in different countries sometimes cause miscommunication and misunderstanding. Aiwa Ong details how foreign enterprises wishing to do business in Shanghai must "indigenize" their operation by replacing foreign expatriate managers with local staff who come with technical training but must be inculcated with "company and Western business culture" (2006: 169). Some people even believe that if a few bribes or kickbacks are necessary to conduct business, then bribery is not immoral, especially if the bribes are given to individuals outside the United States. Similarly, for South Korea, "[c]ulture has been an important driver for ICT [information and communication technologies] . . . which has become a convenient means to enrich this social norm [of word of mouth communication among the many groups to which they belong] by forming numerous communities" (Lee 2007: 123).

The world system of money and markets has penetrated producing societies physically distant from sites of consumption. In Papua New Guinea and other Pacific states, globalized market production coexists with local recipro-cal and generalized exchange. Sometimes, as on the island of Tanga in Papua New Guinea, Westernization, or modernization, and its attendant goods become a separate category, bisnis, in opposition to kastom, that is, those traditional practices continued from the past (Foster 1992).

The market principle, which is based upon the law of supply and demand, assumes that little exists that cannot be purchased with money. However, in American society, other kinds of exchanges continue to coexist alongside the market system. We have cultural rules about reciprocal gift exchange between relatives and friends who are considered equals. People who give gifts expect to be reciprocated, at some future time, with gifts that are roughly equivalent. American rules do not require the recipient to return like for like, as the Abelam do. Americans often bring gifts when invited for dinner at another person's home. It is appropriate to bring wine or flowers but not considered appropriate to bring a pound of ground sirloin or to give the hostess a twenty-dollar bill.

Capitalism and the market economy also involve other kinds of "gifts." Gift exchange as we have just described it is different from the case of the congressmen who receive gifts from constituents or lobbyists and who are exchanging these "gifts" for influence, since the purpose of such gifts is dif-ferent. The givers of these gifts will have influence in the setting of rules and the passage of legislation favorable to their businesses. Under capitalism, the giving of large monetary gifts can thereby serve to undermine government lawmaking. The line between legal contributions and illegal gifts to facilitators in exchange for influence is often an indistinct one. What one person may call a gift, another will call a bribe.

CONSUMPTION

In its most general sense, *consumption* means the way in which people use goods that they have obtained. As with other aspects of culture, consumption is determined by cultural rules. There is a relationship between the consump-tion of goods and the nature of the social system as well as the system of cultural meanings within which it is embedded. In the small-scale societies anthropologists formerly studied, food and other material goods were con-sumed in relation to subsistence as well as in the context of ritual. In many instances these goods were grown or manufactured and used within the local community. But we also saw how yams as urigubu were ceremonially moved from one Trobriand community to another. In this example, goods manufac-tured in one place were ceremonially distributed and then taken to be utilized elsewhere. This distribution includes products originating in far-away loca-tions, but easily integrated into local systems of value.

commodity

A product grown or produced for sale in a national or global market.

With the development of complex modern industrial society came the notion of the consumer. Consumers used goods referred to as commodities, which are manufactured by someone else. **Commodities** were sometimes further subdivided into goods required for subsistence and luxury items whose acquisition was usually related to high rank or elite status. Recently, anthropological focus has shifted to the way such commodity consumption is mediated by global capitalism, which produces commodities in various places all over the world that become incorporated into the local scene. Consumption may communicate social differentiation. The material goods one possesses or wears mark one's identity. These material goods define a consumer's lifestyle.

Sometimes religious beliefs dictate the nature of product consumption. A visit to Lancaster, Pennsylvania, or Shipshewana, Indiana, the location of Amish communities, will immediately demonstrate the way in which their religious beliefs have influenced the use of horse and buggy rather than car and pickup truck and the wearing of very modest clothing, blue or black in color, rather than the latest fashion. They still farm and depend on the products of their fields and herds and carefully control the commodities that enter their world as well as what is excluded based on their interpretation of their religious beliefs.

The Changing Nature of Consumption

Today, consumption and consumerism in Southern countries are often directly related to consumption in the Northern industrialized world. We know that clothing plays a significant role as a consumer item in Northern countries. Styles for both women and men change, if not seasonally then yearly. What is in fashion one year is discarded the next. Though clothing is a commodity, its purchase represents an expression of the self. What happens to this clothing when it is discarded? In the United States, some of it ends up in Salvation Army stores to be reused by people who usually cannot afford what is in fashion. Other items may end up in "resale stores" to be purchased by frugal members of the middle class. However, much of it ends up being sold abroad by dealers. Clothing, shoes, hats, belts, and the like, for men, women, and children, as well as linens and towels, may end up as far away as the bazaar in Chakhcharan in the middle of Afghanistan or in markets in Zambia, in Africa. They are recommodified and reconceptualized in their new context. In Zambia, this clothing, discarded by Westerners, is referred to as salaula and perceived as a very desirable commodity. Salaula means "rummaging," which describes the process whereby buyers select the garments they want to purchase from the opened bales of secondhand clothing that come to Zambia as a consequence of the large international secondhand clothing trade. In Zambia as elsewhere, this clothing also represents self-identity, as well as well-being (Hansen 2002: 225). Zambian economists show that this secondhand clothing industry has had a negative effect on the domestic clothing industry and thus on textile production in Zambia. This creates economic hardships for textile workers and producers, and does little to meet environmental sustainability goals in fashion manufacturing.

Food is another important object of consumption, the examination of which reveals much about cultural structure and cultural representations. For most of human existence, basic foods came from no more than a dozen miles away. This is in contrast to today's far-flung international trade in food, in which tomatoes can move from Mexico to Canada and rice from India to the United States. The use of canning, freezing, and other preservation methods has made it possible for the volume of food moving from continent to continent to greatly increase (Mintz 2006). But these global systems of food production have placed enormous strains on the resources required for massive global agricultural systems. Climate change, shifts in rain patterns and water availability, and the use of chemical fertilizers challenge the sustainability of these agricultural production systems. The use of genetically modified products that are better adapted to long-distance transport is often rejected by consumers and farmers alike. There is now a countermovement in many areas of the world to encourage the production and consumption of locally produced foods instead of products produced in remote areas and transported to local store shelves and restaurants across borders. Agricultural communities now pay close attention to the sustainability of agricultural systems and its impact on other ecological and environmental patterns.

Earlier studies of modernization and modernity assumed that when industrializing people adopted the use of money and began to purchase clothing, computers, canned food, and other items of Western manufacture, the result would be global homogenization of material. These goods often came to stand for becoming modern, and people could, by the use or nonuse of such objects, signify Americanization and Westernization, or a conscious rejection of such identification. Frequently, material goods that have been accepted are re-contextualized. Sometimes, objects used in the past have come to stand for a nostalgia for that past and a continuity of identity. The passion many Americans have for collecting toy trains, metal lunch boxes from the 1950s, and antique baseball cards derives from that same sense of nostalgia for the past, loss of youth, and remembrance of a more tranquil period in the nation's history. There is a now a robust market for such items; they have become commodities.

SUMMARY

- The economic organization of a society governs how that society goes about providing the material goods and services it needs to reproduce itself. Economic organization is a cultural construction and operates according to sets of cultural rules.

- For most of their time on earth, humans subsisted by hunting wild animals and gathering plants, an economic system long since superseded by other systems. This way of life still continues today for a small group of people but is always combined with other kinds of economic activities.

- Horticulture is based upon crops that are grown in gardens through vegetative propagation, using part of the plant itself, rather than through the planting of seeds.

- Swidden, or shifting cultivation, is employed by horticulturalists to clear land by burning forest or bushland. This also provides fertilizer for the crops.

- Grain agriculture was dependent on elaborate irrigation systems and organized labor. It produces storable surpluses that are used to support fulltime specialists, social and political hierarchies, and gendered division of labor.

- Societies that are completely dependent on domesticated animals are known as nomadic pastoral societies. A series of economic and political factors have significantly transformed this way of life.

- In all societies, there is a division of labor based on gender and age.

- In societies with flexible rank, distribution and redistribution rituals like potlatches are the means by which the ranking of groups is raised or lowered.

- The global spread of capitalism has had a dramatic effect on all types of production and subsistence patterns, as well as labor, production, and consumption around the world.

- In egalitarian societies, exchange takes place between groups of equal status and is therefore reciprocal. Systems of exchange in societies with flexible rank establish and reinforce positions of status. Societies with fixed rank systems have groups that are economically specialized; systems of economic distribution symbolically emphasize rank and hierarchy.

- The term market has two meanings. The first refers to location, or site, where food commodities and craft items are bought and sold. The second characterizes an entire economic system based on the determination of market prices, that is, in terms of supply and demand.

- The globalized market economy has not eliminated cultural variation in production, labor, and consumption patterns.

- In its most general sense, *consumption* means the way in which people use goods they have obtained. As with other aspects of culture, consumption is determined by cultural rules.

KEY TERMS

achieved status, 199
agriculture, 187
ascribed status, 199
barter, 201
commodities, 204
delayed exchange, 201
distribution, 182
egalitarian society, 184
globalization, 182
grain agriculture, 188
horticulture, 187
kaiko, 196
kula, 198

market, 185
maximizing, 182
nomadic pastoral societies, 191
political economy, 182
production, 182
sagali, 198
shifting cultivation, 187
social capital, 200
swidden, 187
technology, 182
tribute, 199
urigubu, 198

SUGGESTED READINGS

Kingsolver, Ann E. Tobacco *Town Futures: Global Encounters in Rural Kentucky*. Long Grove, IL: Waveland Press, 2011.

An ethnography of the author's home community of historically small tobacco farmers in rural Kentucky. This study is an exploration of how seemingly isolated communities are connected through capitalist practice and globalization.

Li, Tanya Murray. *Land's End Capitalist Relations on an Indigenous Frontier*. Durham, NC: Duke University Press, 2014.

Long-term ethnographic description of indigenous highlanders in Sulawesi, Indonesia, who privatized their common land to take advantage of a booming international market for cacao.

Mills, Mary Beth. *Thai Women in the Global Labor Force: Consuming Desires, Contested Selves*. New Brunswick, NJ: Rutgers University Press, 2006.

Ethnographic analysis of the extensive migration of rural women to urban centers in Thailand to work in factories and sweatshops producing goods for the global economy. The author documents the dramatic changes that take place in these women's lives as the result of new labor patterns that link them to the products and production systems of global capitalism.

SUGGESTED WEBSITES

www.openair.org

A website that surveys various types of open-air markets and vendors in different parts of the world.

http://www.farmingfirst.org/

The website of Farmingfirst, global coalition of organizations advocating sustainable agricultural production and water use in food production.

https://www.fao.org

The website of the Food and Agriculture Organization of the United Nations, containing extensive documentation of the challenges facing contemporary agricultural producers resulting from climate change and sustainability issues.

Chapter 9
Power, Politics, and Conflict

LEARNING OBJECTIVES

- Understand the concepts of politics, political organization, power, authority, and influence.
- Distinguish between informal leadership, headman, chieftainship, and state structures.
- Provide examples of how ethnicity, alliances, and factions operate within states.

- Recognize variations in feuding, warfare, and peace-making.
- Explore the symbols and strategies of resistance to state power employed by human rights and justice activists around the world.

WHAT IS POLITICS? WE ARE all familiar with politics in action: political parties and factions jockeying for power, and the global expressions of political alliances and conflict. Political scientists have defined politics over the years by proposing variations on the title of Harold Lasswell's 1936 book *Politics: Who Gets What, When, How*. Subsequently, scholars have added "where" and "who cares?" to this compound definition of politics. Lasswell's framing of politics emphasizes that power is a strategic resource that not everyone has access to; the later additions of "where" and "who cares" emphasize the competition over power, social capital, and the inequality of their distribution in political systems.

Does politics always involve the use of power? In American society, "to get an offer you cannot refuse" represents the exercise of power in many different contexts. It may be a way of forcing people to do something they do not want to do, or getting a competitor to retire from competition. How do power and politics operate in different societies? What are the political opportunities open to minorities and non-elites in resisting and reshaping the power of the state? These questions help form some definitions and concepts in all political systems and provide a framework for understanding contemporary movements for racial, gender, ethnic, religious, and regional equality.

CONCEPTS IN POLITICAL ANTHROPOLOGY

Power is the key concept used in defining political organization. Power is the ability to command others to do certain things and to get compliance from them. A Yanomamo **headman** does not have the power to compel others to act in a particular way, whereas a Trobriand **chief** demonstrates his power in a whole range of activities. Power is distinguished from **authority**. When power becomes institutionalized, we say it has been transformed into authority. This means that there is a recognized position, or **office**, whose occupant can issue commands that must be obeyed. It is apparent that the Trobriand chief has authority as well as power, which derives from his chiefly office, and his commands are to be obeyed. The Yanomamo headman holds a recognized position or office, but since the headman has no power to compel people to obey him, he has no authority. Nevertheless, he is a leader since others will follow him if he is able to influence them. **Influence** is the ability to persuade others to follow one's lead. Followers will continue to support him, and he will have influence over them as long as they have confidence in his leadership ability. When leadership is not vested in a formal institutionalized position and is based solely on influence, as is the case of the Yanomamo headman, loss of confidence means loss of followers and loss of an individual's leadership position. Influence represents informal power, in contrast to the power vested in formal political positions.

A distinction is also made between **government** and **politics**. *Government* refers to the decisions made by those in office on behalf of the entire group in carrying out common goals. This may involve going to war to maintain the defense of the group, a decision a president or prime minister must make. It also involves dealing with the day-to-day matters of law and order. Thus, the

power

The ability to command others to do certain things and get compliance from them.

headman

A leader of a group with no power or authority and with no fixed rule of succession.

chief

The leader of a society with fixed positions of leadership.

authority

An institutionalized position of power.

office

A recognized political position.

influence

The ability to persuade others to follow one's lead when one lacks the political authority or power to command.

government

The process by which those in office make and implement decisions on behalf of an entire group in order to carry out commonly held goals.

politics

The competition for political positions, economic resources, and power.

Trobriand chief carries out important governmental functions. For example, when he decides to hold a competitive kayasa with another village, he organizes the production of those under him. The chief initiates the overseas kula exchange and is the owner of the canoe used. *Kula* deals with overseas relations between Trobrianders and other peoples, in effect, foreign affairs. In contrast, among the Yanomamo, the consensus of the whole group is what is important, even though they have a headman as their leader.

Politics involves competing for power. Politics concentrates on the manipulation of people and resources, the maneuvers intended to enhance power, the rise of groups that compete for power, and the development of political factions with differing points of view. Politics emphasizes opposing points of view and conflict, that is, divergent rather than common goals. Of course, in all settings, those vying for power in the political arena usually claim that they are operating for the common good and not just on behalf of their political party or faction.

Politics also operates among both the Trobriand Islanders and the Yanomamo and is clearly illustrated in exploring rules and norms of succession in political office. All political systems have rules and norms that regulate the transfer of authority or power to ensure stability and continuity over time. When a Trobriand chief dies, the choice of a new chief is open to political maneuvering and competition among the individuals in the group of people eligible to succeed. These candidates must demonstrate their political abilities to followers who are their fellow subclansmen. At this point, potential claimants to the chiefly office make promises and point to their demonstrated skills in organizational leadership and their wealth. The man who is recognized as the new chief now has the authority to govern and assumes the appropriate Trobriand symbols of political authority. Politics is also constantly present among the Yanomamo, since headmen regularly face the potential opposition of those who also aspire to leadership in their village. Even the decision to hold a feast may be the basis for political maneuvering. A rival for the position of headman may try to organize a feast. He tries to convince others in the village that this is a wise decision politically. If he succeeds in enlisting the support of the majority of the villagers, then he has in effect become the new headman. If he can mobilize only partial support, he will come to lead his own faction in the village, and he may try again in the future. He may also fail to get any support, in which case he retires to the sidelines and sulks. Anthropologists refer to a position that depends on personal qualifications and individual ability as an achieved status, in contrast to an ascribed status, which one inherits.

Classic ethnographic description of politics presumed it to be associated with men; more recent discussions document the roles women play in political systems. In her study of Trobriand politics and ritual, Annette Weiner (1988) discusses the role of women's activities in Trobriand politics and their control over important forms of wealth. Women manufacture skirts made from banana leaves and create bundles of banana leaves, which are used as payment to mourners after a death. "It is an activity that deeply interpenetrates the economics and the politics of men. The political presence of Kiriwina women necessitates studying Trobriand society from a perspective sensitive to the complementary efforts of women and men" (1988: 27). Although Malinowski discussed the status of women in Trobriand society, he ignored their economic and political contributions. Weiner suggests that this was consistent with the anthropological approach to these issues in Malinowski's time; women were seen as peripheral to these "male" activities, and their contributions were not explored ethnographically or theoretically. "No one recognized the activity that is central to women's position and power in Trobriand society. Yet it is activity that deeply interpenetrates the economics and the politics of men" (1988: 27).

FORMS OF POLITICAL ORGANIZATION

A form of authority and leadership has always existed in all human societies. The forms of political organization that we describe characterize smaller-scale societies, and illustrate variations on the concepts of authority, influence, power, and succession. It is important to acknowledge, however, that the primary form of contemporary political organization is that of the state. Other forms of organization and leadership operate within states; political autonomy and the operation of local political systems are invariably regulated by the states within which they are embedded.

Informal Leadership

informal leadership

A type of political organization in which there is no single political leader but rather leadership is manifested intermittently.

In the simplest form of political organization, leadership was manifested intermittently. This type of organization may be called **informal leadership**. The Iglulingmiut, an Inuit group of eastern Canada, formerly had this form of political organization. The name given to the group means "the people" (miut) of Iglulik, who were all those living in the area. There were no fixed political offices, and a number of men, but never women, exerted leadership in certain situations. These temporary leaders, whom Kurtz calls "episodic leaders," did not have the power to compel people to obey them (2001: 460). Generally, people who were respected made decisions, adjudicated disputes, and represented the community in discussions with outsiders (Hitchcock and Biesele 2000: 19). There were winter villages along the coast, consisting of kin-related families, though not the same ones every year, exploiting ocean resources. The men of influence and leadership in the winter village were the "boat owners," the senior males of the kin units that owned the boats used to hunt seals. The hunting of caribou in the summer, done jointly by several families, was conducted under the leadership of a man with hunting expertise. At the end of the hunt, the families scattered, and the leader was no longer a leader. Leadership operated only through influence, and different men exercised their influence in those areas in which they had special knowledge or ability. This kind of political organization was found only among peoples whose subsistence was based exclusively upon hunting and gathering, accompanied by periodic migration and temporary larger settlements in resource-rich areas.

Band Organization

Some hunting-and-gathering societies had a form of political organization known as **band organization**. The Yanamamo, described above, are one example of having a band organization. Some bands had a fixed membership that came together annually to carry out joint rituals and economic activities. The Ojibwa—hunters and gatherers in the forests of the eastern Canadian subarctic—lived in small groups of related families that moved from one hunting area to another during most of the year. In the summertime, the whole band frequently came together on the shores of a lake and remained as a unit for the summer. The men with influence were leaders of the group. Although fluid in its membership, the band had more cohesiveness than societies with only informal leadership. The band acts as a unit under the recognized leadership of a headman, though that leadership is based on influence, not on authority.

band organization

An egalitarian type of social group that may come together annually for a period to carry out joint rituals and economic activities.

Big Man Structure

The **Big Man structure** represents a greater delineation of the leadership position than that of band organization. As leadership becomes more clearly defined, so does the group of followers (Kurtz 2001: 47–48). In Melanesia, the Big Man takes the initiative in exchanges with other groups. In contrast, ordinary men fulfill their obligations in exchanges with affines and kin and contribute to what is accumulated by the Big Man of their group, as described in Abelam exchange ceremonies in chapter 8. The Big Men organize their group's production and are the distribution nodes in the exchange system. The Big Man derives his power from his direction of the ceremonial distribution of the goods accumulated by his group and the decisions he makes in the redistribution of goods within his own group.

Big Man structure

An achieved position of leadership in which the group is defined as the Big Man and his followers.

The Big Man also directs a range of other activities. The Abelam Big Man organizes the labor involved in the production of long yams for exchange, but he also acts as the ritual expert since he alone knows the magical spells that make the yams grow so long. On behalf of his entire group, he maintains sexual abstinence for the whole growing period. Artistic ability as a carver or painter of designs is also a desirable characteristic in an Abelam Big Man, but the most important characteristic is his ability to produce the long yams on which the prestige of the entire group depends. Throughout New Guinea, the oratorical skills of the Big Man are essential since he must deliver speeches at ceremonial distributions as the representative of his group. The Big Man should also show prowess in feuding, though his involvement is usually in the organizational area. Since women cannot be near any phase of the growing

An Abelam political leader wearing emblems and ornaments signifying that he is recognized by his community as a Big Man.

chieftainship

A type of political organization in which fixed positions of leadership are present along with a method for succession to those positions.

primogeniture

A rule of succession whereby the eldest child (usually but not always male) inherits the position of power.

or exchange of long yams among the Abelam, they cannot be Big Men.

The position of Big Man is an achieved status dependent on personal qualifications and individual ability. As he ages, a Big Man may no longer be able to carry out all the activities necessary to maintain his influence in his group. In that case, his leadership position may be challenged. Competition between challengers involves political skills and maneuvering. Although, in a patrilineal society, the Big Man's son may have an initial advantage, he will not automatically become a Big Man himself if he lacks the necessary abilities and support. A man who has leadership qualities, although he may be from another family in the clan, may surpass the Big Man's son in gaining followers and, in time, be recognized as the new Big Man.

Although women have influence and play an important role in exchange in many societies of Melanesia, they rarely occupy the Big Man position. The women of the island of Vanatinai in the Coral Sea, one of the islands in the kula ring, are an exception. The term that literally means "giver" is a gender-neutral term referring to Big Men and Big Women (Lepowsky 1990). These Big Women are central nodes in the exchange of goods and valuables. They lead kula expeditions, organize mortuary feasts, and orate at ceremonies.

Chieftainship

The introduction of fixed positions of rank and a method of succession characterizes a **chieftainship**. In this form of political organization, individuals as well as the kin groups of the descent system are ranked with respect to one another. The Trobriand example exemplifies this type of organization. The chief does not merely exert influence over others but has real authority, which means that he has the power to enforce his decisions. Power and authority are vested in the chiefly office, and whoever occupies that position exercises authority and has power. In chiefdoms, which are ranked societies, the chiefly position is restricted to certain high-ranking individuals. Among the Kwak'wala speakers of the Northwest Coast, who also have a ranked system and chiefs, the oldest child, regardless of gender, inherits the chiefly position through **primogeniture**, inheritance to the oldest child. Though a female may inherit the chiefly name, a male kinsman usually carries out the duties of the office. In chieftainships, there is a hierarchy of other political positions that are ranked with respect to one another. The Trobriand chief heads a district with villages whose headmen give their sisters to the chief as wives, and who therefore pay urigubu in tribute to the chief. These village headmen are the chief's affines, or brothers-in-law; they are not of the chiefly subclan, but are from other subclans lower in rank than the chief's.

The political economy of chieftainships is a more complex redistributive system than that associated with the Big Man structure. In a chieftainship, because there are more levels of political organization, villagers give to their village headmen, who in turn give to the chief. This is exactly what happens at a Trobriand kayasa, when two villages compete with one another. Yams are presented to the chief by the heads of the two villages. The chief later redistributes what he has received in feasts to reward the villages in his district for various services. Chiefdomships have been identified archeologically in various parts of the world such as Chaco Canyon in North America and the early Bronze Age settlements in Denmark (Earle 2002: 16, 50).

The State

Archaeologists have been interested in the conditions that produced the earliest states that arose in Egypt, Mesopotamia, the Indus Valley, China, Mexico, and Peru. The state differs from the other types of political organization in a number of significant ways, one of which is a difference in scale. Though some states may be quite small, the state has the potential for encompassing millions of people within its orbit. It is organized on a territorial basis, made up of villages and districts rather than on the basis of kinship and clanship. Exceptions to this generalization are found in some extant monarchies as well as in the seven Arab states bordering the Persian Gulf, where patrilineal descent systems create both social and governance institutions (Alsharekh 2007). In the state we find social stratification, rulers, aristocrats, commoners, and various low-status groups. All those under the control of the state are its citizens or its subjects. States invariably encompass within their borders small-scale societies as well as multiethnic populations who speak different languages and are culturally different from one another.

The state is governed by a ruler whose legitimate right to command others is acknowledged by those in the state. Many of the early states were theocracies; that is, the ruler was head of both the religious hierarchy and the political state at the same time. In many indigenous states, the ruler was not only the political symbol but also the religious symbol of the whole society. A bureaucracy carries out the administrative functions of the state. The bureaucracy grows in size and complexity as the state expands. Customary law becomes formalized into a legal code. The adjudication of disputes by the leader grows into a court system, which enforces its decisions through the police. The tribute given to the chief is transformed into taxes paid to the state, which support the growing bureaucracy and infrastructure. The state expands by conquering neighboring peoples, who become culturally distinct subject peoples, and whose territories are incorporated within the state.

The way in which an indigenous state functioned in the twentieth century can be seen from a description of the empire of Bornu, the Kanuri state on the borders of Lake Chad in northern Nigeria. This state was studied by Abraham Rosman in 1956 (Rosman 1962, see also Cohen 1971), when it was still under British colonial rule. When the British entered the area at the turn of the twentieth century, they resurrected the partially collapsed indigenous state structure and governed through the Shehu of Bornu, the traditional head of state. This highly stratified society included the royal family, aristocratic families, commoners, including village farmers, and slaves. Only the Shehu could grant aristocrats titles, which sometimes came with land, including entire villages. Enslaved people were war captives and their descendants, who became the personal property of the Shehu.

Prior to the arrival of the British, the empire of Bornu was located at the southern end of a strategic caravan route that led from the Mediterranean Sea across the Sahara to the populous states of West Africa. Caravans brought manufactured goods from Libya and returned there with slaves, ivory, and other raw materials. Muskets, introduced through the caravan trade, were monopolized by the state. The army of Bornu, completely controlled by the Shehu, had generals who were slaves of the Shehu. The army defended the borders of Bornu from incursions by other states, particularly Bornu's enemies, the Hausa states to the west. As a result of conquest, non-Kanuri people permanently became part of the empire of Bornu. In the fourteenth century, Islam spread to Bornu, following the same path as the caravan routes. Islam was adopted by the entire population when the ruler of Bornu converted. Judges trained in the Qur'an and in Islamic law were appointed by the Shehu to hear criminal cases. The Shehu and his appointed district heads heard and arbitrated civil cases involving personal and family disputes. The Kanuri believed that persons in authority at every administrative level up to the Shehu must be available every day to hear the disputes and complaints of their people.

Under British colonial rule, Kanuri officials of the indigenous state structure, including the Shehu, carried out the actual administration of districts, applied customary law, and collected the taxes under the supervision of British officials. This is an example of the British colonial policy of indirect rule (see chapter 13). These activities were directed by a British lieutenant governor who resided in the provincial capital. Real authority was in the hands of the colonial masters. Under British pacification, the Kanuri army had been disbanded. After Nigeria gained independence in 1960, Bornu became a province within the new state.

Kanuri horseman in Agadiz, Niger. A dominant ethnic group in Nigeria, Niger, Chad, and Cameroon, Kanuri horsemen supported and protected local leaders until they were forced by the colonizing British to disband their armies.

WAR AND PEACE

Going to war is one of the most important decisions made by those in positions of authority. Warfare, feuds, and revenge seeking between social groups are resorted to when there are no mutually acceptable means of resolving conflicts peacefully. **Feuding** is defined as hostile action between members of the same group, and warfare as hostile action between different groups. Feuds, conducted according to rules, involve collective, not personal, responsibility. When feuds occur, revenge can be taken against any member of the group. In a segmentary lineage system, it is difficult to tell the difference between feuding and warfare because subclans within the same clan may fight each other on one occasion but come together as a single clan when fighting another clan. It is then hard to say which is feud and which is war.

According to Otterbein, warfare first emerged when humans began to hunt, and early hunters attacked competing groups of hunters. Foragers who were primarily gatherers of domesticated plants became peaceful, sedentary

feuding

Hostile actions between people of the same group.

BOX 9.1 | Is Warfare Inevitable?

For several decades, anthropologist R. Brian Ferguson has studied the documentation of warfare in "tribal societies, ancient states, recent civil wars, archaeology, biology and culture, and primatology." This "deep dive" into thousands of accounts of warfare and theoretical frameworks within which these cases are presented leads him to propose twelve concise and key conclusions about human warfare (Ferguson 2023). His twelve points on warfare are summarized below.

- Our species is not biologically destined for war.
- War is not an inescapable part of social existence.
- Understanding war involves a nested hierarchy of constraints, that creates the context for each event that includes general characteristics of economic and political conditions.
- War expresses both pan-human practicalities and culturally specific values.
- War shapes society to its own ends.
- War exists in multiple contexts historically, ecologically, and across political typologies.
- Opponents are constructed in conflict; groups that previously co-existed peacefully are created into enemies.

- War is a continuation of domestic politics by other means, often being the culmination of differences of interests, disagreements, long discussions and debates.
- Leaders favor war, because war favors leaders. The actions of both tribal communities and states include war decisions made "at the top" that may enhance a political leader's position.
- Peace is more than the absence of war. Settling conflict requires sustained political and financial support for multiple efforts and strategies.
- When war exists, gender roles and schema are adapted to war making.
- War shapes masculinity and masculinity shapes war.

An important observation to be drawn from this research is that despite the antiquity of warfare and its global distribution, humans are not biologically destined for warfare. This is particularly important because of a large body of literature created by sociobiologists and primatologists claiming that warfare is an inevitable outcome of human, species-wide characteristics.

agriculturalists. Once city-states emerged, warfare based on battles and sieges developed (2004: 10–11, 61). Evidence for warfare in the archeological record is found "in the form of skeletal evidence of violent death, the relocation of habitations to defensive sites, changes in weapons technology and the like" (Kelly 2000: 148). A number of comparative studies reveal that hunters and gatherers tend to be relatively peaceful; they resolve disputes by the disputants going their separate ways and getting out of one another's way. Warfare involves collective responsibility. In cases of collective responsibility, all members of the perpetrator's lineage, clan, or tribe are held equally responsible. Earlier, we have called this type of collective responsibility "feuding" when it takes place within a group, and "warfare" when it is between groups.

Warfare operates according to cultural rules, like all other forms of cultural behavior. Peacemaking is also governed by cultural rules. Anthropologists have attempted to comprehend warfare as it operated in small-scale societies in order to try to understand it in today's complex societies. Unfortunately, by the time anthropologists went to do field research, those small-scale societies that they studied had been conquered and pacified and were under colonial rule or were parts of **nation-states**. It is only from field descriptions of societies in Amazonia and New Guinea, where warfare continued despite contact with Europeans and colonial rule, that we have some understanding of indigenous ideas about warfare, its causes, and how it was conducted. There is also ethnohistorical data on how warfare was conducted by Native Americans during the early period of European colonization.

One of the fullest accounts of conflict in a small-scale society is that of the Yanomamo in Amazonia (however, some details of these accounts are now contested by other anthropologists). Chagnon (1983, 1997) describes how there are several levels of hostility among the Yanomamo, though hostilities could terminate at any level. The chest-pounding duel, which can arise from accusations of cowardice, stinginess with food, or gossip, is halfway between a sporting contest and a fight. It can take place between two individuals of the same village or, at a feast, between the men of two different villages. The next, more intensive level is the side-slapping contest, whose provocations are the same. The third level is the club fight, usually provoked by arguments over women. It can also take place within or between villages. Two men attack one another with long wooden clubs. These contests end when one opponent withdraws. The most intensive kind of hostility is the raid, conducted by one village against another, which one could define as warfare. Villages that have a history of being enemies raid one another to take revenge for past killings. Women are frequently captured in the course of a raid and become another reason to continue to raid. Preemptive first strikes may take place even after a feast because the Yanomamo say that you can never trust another Yanomamo.

Periods of warfare alternate with periods of peace for the Yanomamo and "peacemaking often requires the threat or actual use of force" (Chagnon 1997: 7). The Yanomamo ceremonial dialogue, or wayamou, is a ritual that takes place as a way of making peace when relations between villages that normally have close ties are deteriorating or when people from more distant,

nation-state

An autonomous state associated with national identity.

potentially hostile villages come to visit. Stylized body movements, rapid speech, and particular rhetorical features, such as metaphors, metonyms, repetition, and incomplete sentences, are utilized. Goods are often requested, which will be returned when the present hosts of the feast are invited to a feast at some future time.

Anthropologists and other social scientists have explored possible explanations for warfare. Most find unsatisfactory the frequently offered explanation that warfare is due to instinctive human aggression. Warfare is prevalent at certain times and not others, and under certain conditions and not others. The task of the anthropologist is to explain why warfare occurs when and where it does. Proposing a universal human aggressive instinct cannot explain this variability. In a recent reanalysis of all the historical and ethnographic data on the different Yanomamo groups in both Venezuela and Brazil, Ferguson argues that "the actual practice of war among the Yanomami is explainable largely as a result of antagonisms related to scarce, coveted and unequally distributed Western manufactured goods" (1995: 8). He claims that before Western contact, warfare was limited or absent among the Yanomamo (1995: 75). When Western goods were introduced, access was unequal, leading to conflict between different Yanomamo groups and increased warfare. Peters, the ethnographer of the Xilixana Yanomami of Brazil, sees an abundance of steel goods in their area and considers the reasons for warfare to be avenging sorcery and revenge in general (Peters 1998: 216–17). Koch (1974) offers another kind of explanation for warfare as it occurred in small-scale societies, like that of the Jale in New Guinea. He claims that warfare breaks out when no third party exists to settle disputes. In his view, war is just another means of dispute settlement. Anthropological explanations for warfare must be distinguished from those of the combatants. The Yanomamo themselves say that they go to war to avenge a previous killing and as a result of conflicts over women (Lizot 1994).

Many of the points made about warfare in small-scale societies are also applicable to complex societies. The motives of those who carry out the war, both the soldiers and the planners, are different from the causes of war as seen by analysts. For example, the United States declared war on Japan after Pearl Harbor was bombed. Americans explain the war as a result of Japan's aggressive act. A disinterested analyst might explain the war as a result of the fact that Japan, an increasingly more powerful and industrializing state, needed to expand its sphere of influence to obtain more raw materials, such as oil from Indonesia (then the Dutch East Indies).

Materialist or ecological explanations of warfare seem to be as applicable to modern complex societies as they are to small-scale societies. The desire to obtain more land or other important strategic resources, such as fossil fuels and mineral wealth, has often caused warfare in modern times. Sometimes modern states carry out preemptive strikes, that is, attacks on the enemy when they believe that the enemy is about to launch an attack. Yanomamo villages also carry out preemptive strikes even when they are not under attack to prevent other villages from attacking them first.

In a recent study, Fry notes that many societies have an antiwar, anti-violent ethos including those as diverse as the Mehinaku and Wauja of the Amazon, the Sami of Norway, and the Lepcha of the Himalayas (2006: 18, 19, 58). Fry claims that "the view that humans are fundamentally warlike stems much more from the cultural beliefs of the writers than from . . . data" (2006: 20). He concludes that though humans engage in warfare, they have a strong capacity for peace (2006: 246).

The Anthropology of Violence

The focus on what has come to be known as the "anthropology of violence" began with the shift in anthropology to a consideration of cultural life from the subjective point of view. As Scheper-Hughes and Bourgois note, "Violence itself defies easy categorization . . . [but one can speak] of a continuum of violence. . . . The social and cultural dimensions of violence are

---

BOX 9.2 | **Women, War, and Peace**

There is growing recognition among advocates, scholars, and policy makers that armed conflicts have profound gender implications; conflict impacts women and girls differently than it does men and boys. Civilian women have been the targets of systematic sexual violence by enemy combatants for centuries, as a military strategy designed to demoralize and destabilize families and society in war-torn settings. During conflict, women bear multiple responsibilities of maintaining the health, nutrition, and education of children and the well-being of elders, as well as being the breadwinners of households when men are in combat. In postconflict peace treaties and economic recovery programs, the needs of women and children are often ignored in an effort to provide economic and social rehabilitation to male former combatants.

The assumption that sees conflict, peace-making and diplomacy as exclusively male domains is being challenged through new international frameworks and gendered perspectives on peace, conflict, and security. Beginning in 2000, the UN Security Council passed a series of resolutions identifying and integrating women's experiences into international peace and security. These include recognizing conflict-related sexual violence as a tactic of war as requiring swift justice and peacekeeping response to hold perpetrators at all levels of military and political power accountable. Later Security Council resolutions set goals of building gender-integrated peace-keeping forces and treaty negotiation teams to assure that women's priorities are recognized throughout postconflict resolution. Economic recovery in postconflict areas is being framed to address the vulnerabilities and labor needs of women and households both during conflict and in recovery plans. UN member states have committed to building national and local capacity to meet these goals in part by increasing the number of women in the judiciary, in diplomacy, in the military, and in peace-keeping and police forces. These goals are challenging international organizations, states, and local communities, as well as activists and other civil society actors, to recognize that the concept of peace is not just a cessation of armed conflict, but also to address its impact on both combatants and civilians throughout society.

what give violence its power and meaning" (2004: 1, 2). The anthropology of violence also includes a concern with the "culture of terror" and "torture" and how these are used to establish "hegemony," or the domination of one group over another (Taussig 2002: 172–73). This focus is on the way in which political narratives "are in themselves evidence of the process whereby a culture of terror was created and sustained" (2002: 179). Competition between groups over political power and resources and the suspension of traditional values and relationships may result in genocide.

There are those who link conflict to violence, seeing violence as "an assertion of power or a physical hurt deemed legitimate by the performer and some witnesses" (Schröeder and Schmidt 2001: 3). This is a broader conceptualization, which includes what we have considered under warfare, above. Other perspectives explore the category of violence as subjective, and focus on the role played by memory, as for example, in the connection between wars and prior conflicts (2001: 3, 9). Narratives and public memorials keep alive the memory of former wars and conflicts.

Terrorism has been used as a political strategy for centuries. In the twenty-first century, it has become a subject of daily discussion in the media. Police and other officials scrutinize crimes against people and property on every continent as they are occurring to determine if they are in fact acts of terrorism. Although each act of terrorism has its own ideological and political context, there are some general characteristics that differentiate terrorism from other forms of violence. Terrorism involves the use of illegal violence against people or property with the goal of intimidation or coercion of governments and civilian populations. Terrorism is employed by clandestine or underground individuals or groups for political or ideological reasons. The victims of terrorism, often civilians, are not the political actors targeted by other forms of political violence, such as assassination. The violence and destruction of terrorism are intended to produce widespread fear and intimidation in the general population.

When terrorism creates collective large-scale violence, it generates "massive trauma" and the reshaping of cultural identity (Suarez-Orozco and Robben 2000: 1). The reactions of Americans to the coordinated terrorist attacks on September 11, 2001, and the deaths of nearly three thousand civilians brought about a rethinking of themselves and their cultural identity. These were encoded into cultural narratives such as stories, books, television programs, and documentaries. It is an example of how violence "penetrates people's psychic constitution" (Gampel 2000: 59) and redefines concepts of security and national identity. The refugee crisis in 2016 resulting from civil wars in Syria and elsewhere ignited debates around long-held values of inclusiveness and diversity. Throughout Europe and North America, expansion of immigration is challenged by political conservatives who articulate the fears associated with opening borders to immigrants and refugees from war-torn and economically devastated countries. Some right-wing politicians mobilize fears about national security to justify the exclusion of refugees and immigrants of specific religions and countries of origin.

terrorism

Acts of violence perpetrated against property and civilian populations, usually by non-state actors, designed to destabilize and demoralize perceived enemies.

More centrist and liberal political discourses encourage immigration based on the economic and cultural contribution migrants make to ethnically and religiously diverse states.

Law and Social Control

law

A system of conflict resolution and criminalization practice.

At various points in this chapter, we have touched upon the subject of **law**. Anthropologists have been interested in the way disputes have been settled in the small-scale societies they have studied. In the absence of any written legal codes or formal courts before which lawyers argued cases, anthropologists in the field listen to and record the manner in which disputes were aired and conflicts resolved. By doing this, they try to get at the rules, what constitutes proper behavior in light of those rules, what is the acceptable range of deviation from the rules, what is unacceptable behavior, and how it is dealt with and punished. The legal principles or bases upon which disputes are resolved were frequently not explicitly verbalized by the people. They emerge only through the analysis of specific cases, from which anthropologists have abstracted the legal principles that are the basis for decision making.

Societies without written legal codes had a variety of ways to settle conflicts or disputes. Sometimes the two parties thrashed it out themselves; the solution might be a fair one, or the stronger party would force the weaker to capitulate. Sometimes each side mobilized support from people with whom they had economic relationships. Song contests might be held in which an audience decided the winner (as among both the Inuit and the Tiv of Nigeria), or the disputants might simply disperse (which is what the Hadza of Tanzania did). Interestingly, today, since the Inuit have moved into permanent settlements, personal communications broadcast over the radio, received by a large audience, have some of the same characteristics of the song duel (Briggs 2000: 120).

mediator

A third party brought in to resolve conflict between two parties.

Some societies have an authority who, as a third party, acts to resolve disputes and either decides the case on its merits or plays the role of a **mediator**. Such authorities may be political leaders or judges who have the power or influence to force the disputants to accept their decisions or recommendations. The legal principle applied in a particular case becomes the precedent, or legal principle, applied to future cases. The idea of system-wide application is what makes it a principle of law rather than simply the political decision of someone in authority. When a legal decision is made after a violation of the law, some sort of sanction must be applied, possibly the use of force. Social sanctions may result if the community punishes someone by shunning or shaming them publicly. Other methods of social control include gossip and accusations of witchcraft. Informal negotiations, without recourse to state institutions, also occur. Ruffini describes the way in which shepherds in Sardinia employ negotiations between the parties, mediation, or arbitration using "kinship, ritual kinship, patron–client relations, neighborhood, and friendship bonds [to settle the dispute]" (2005: 133).

In state-based systems of law, a distinction is made between civil law and criminal law. **Civil law** deals with disputes over money, property, or family, disputes in which society acts as an arbitrator. For example, if a car stops short on a highway and your car plows into it, the owner of the car will take you to civil court and sue you for damages to his or her car. **Criminal law** deals with crimes, such as theft, assault, and murder, which are considered offenses against society as a whole. The wronged party in a crime is not allowed to punish the offender himself; the accused perpetrator is tried in criminal court. Property and family disputes in small-scale societies rend the fabric of the social structure, and they are dealt with as actions against society as a whole. Often no distinction is made between civil and criminal law in indigenous legal systems.

Anthropologists today have widened their scope of investigation of legal systems to include the processes of social and political change in state policy. "Anthropologists now consider the socio-legal aspects of the modern state in two very different milieus: the nonstate but organized subfields which exist within nation-states, and the transnational or global fields that criss-cross and transcend states, some of them official and some unofficial" (Moore 2005: 1). **Civil society** is the general term for organizations and institutions that provide citizens of a state with opportunities for organizing and creating alliances around particular issues, independent of business institutions or government. Civil society includes labor unions, nongovernmental organizations, and voluntary clubs and associations. For example, Merry studied the way three nongovernmental entities in Hilo, Hawaii, responded to violence against women (2005: 249ff.). This global system has many "players," and various institutional structures in different nation-states are involved in creating international trade regulations. A new form of "global legal pluralism" has developed to regulate this global market of production (2005: 218ff.).

Law is also associated with morality and value systems. When viewed as a series of statements of what constitutes proper behavior, the law differentiates right from wrong, good from bad. In the American legal system, some of our laws represent, in effect, the continuation of ancient religious commandments, such as "Thou shalt not steal." For most individuals, laws of this sort have been internalized; the enforcer of the law may be the person's own conscience.

LAW IN POSTCOLONIAL STATES

Many postcolonial states integrate various forms of customary law into the legal codes for their nations. The concept of **legal pluralism** refers to the relationship between indigenous forms of law and the state law that developed in colonial and postcolonial societies. Legal pluralism may also be used to describe the situation that develops when people migrate from one country to another. This has occurred in France when Muslim people from Algeria and other parts of North Africa migrated there with their Islamic culture and

civil law

The part of a legal system that regulates family and property issues.

criminal law

The part of a legal system that determines and punishes criminality.

civil society

Nongovernmental organizations and institutions that provide opportunities for organizing and creating alliances around particular issues, labor unions, religious organizations, and voluntary clubs and associations.

legal pluralism

The coexistence of indigenous and postcolonial systems of law.

Throughout India, women are increasingly demanding their rights as citizens to benefits and to political participation. Access to voting is especially demanded, as is seen in this voting rights awareness rally in the state of Rajasthan in northern India.

sovereignty

The ability of a group to determine their own laws and practices that will be recognized by other groups.

Islamic legal ideas. There are two possibilities—either the migrants submit to the hegemony of the French legal system, or the French legal system takes into account some aspects of Islamic civil law. During the colonial period, Islamic law had already been codified in accordance with the French legal system in both Egypt and Algeria, so migrants were familiar with European procedures. For example, the legal systems in Syria, Jordan, and Morocco require that civil marriages or the civil registration of a marriage takes place before the Muslim religious ceremony.

Native Americans in North America frequently engage in legal battles with federal and state governments as well as with non-Native Americans. They assert their hunting and fishing rights, their rights over land promised them in treaties, the freedom to pursue their own religious practices, or their rights to tribal cultural objects now in the hands of various museums. These cases represent an affirmation of Native American **sovereignty** clashing with the sovereignty of the United States. This confrontation can be seen, for example, in cases involving the use of Native American sacred sites. In the past, tribal people have been discouraged from using the courts to protect their freedom of religious expression because legal doctrines often equate such customary religious expression with fringe nonindigenous religions, which mainstream Americans regard with great skepticism (Carrillo 1998: 277). In 1978, Congress passed the American Indian Religious Freedom Act, which was designed to protect Native American religious expression. Although this act was supported in principle, the courts do not always uphold Native American claims. For example, evidence provided in *Lyng v. Northwest Indian Cemetery Protective Association* described how a road construction project invaded sacred sites that were significant in the belief systems of Native people of northwestern California. Native American litigants sought to stop the project, but they lost their case in court (1998: 7).

In another case, Zuni claimants won the right to pass through privately owned land during their regular quadrennial summer solstice pilgrimage from their reservation to the mountain area they called Kohlu/wala:wa in northeastern Arizona (*U.S. on Behalf of the Zuni Tribe v. Platt*, in Carrillo 1998: 318). The pilgrimage is believed by the Zuni to be to their place of origin and the home of their dead. The trek, which takes four days and is 110 miles long, has consistently covered the same territory. The Zuni lost control over the ancestral land the pilgrimage traversed in 1876, when it passed into private non-Native ownership. To the Zuni, the pilgrimage continued to be the fulfillment of a religious obligation (Meshorer 1998: 318). In its decision, the court deemed that the defendant who purchased the land was aware that the pilgrimage had been taking place and went across his property, that such usage was "actual, open and notorious, continuous and uninterrupted," that "such use was known to the surrounding community," and that the Zuni believed that their crossing was a matter of right (Carrillo 1998: 318). The court ordered that the Zuni be granted an easement over the land for twenty-five feet in either direction of the route of their pilgrimage for a two-day period every four years during the summer solstice.

As has happened in many parts of the world, the European forms of social control that were introduced during colonialism did not completely replace the older indigenous forms, but existed side by side with them. In Ghana, a police force was established soon after conquest by the British. The British colonial government curtailed the authority and jurisdiction of the indigenous political leadership. Jurisdiction over all criminal and civil cases was vested in a Supreme Court, with colonial district commissioners dealing with lesser offenses. Post-independence governments modernized the police force and expanded the court system when the level of crime rose.

According to Abotchie, "traditional modes of crime control such as trial by ordeal . . . has persisted side by side with modern methods of crime control" (1997: 7). Many people still believe in the traditional deities and express fear of them. As a consequence, traditional forces serve as a greater deterrent to criminal activity than do modern police methods and the fear of imprisonment (1997: 116–19). The Ghanaian police are seen as corrupt and unreliable. Supernatural forces, however, are inescapable, and their penalties are more severe. Though lineage leaders and chiefs have lost their politico-legal authority, their "religious functions, and [the] sanctions of the lineage head and the chief, however, remain effective . . . ; besides, both rulers still hold themselves accountable to the supernatural forces" (1997: 128). It is evident that earlier forms of social control have continued despite the introduction of modern political and legal forms and police practices.

Nation Building in Postcolonial States

After the colonial period, newly independent states in Africa, Asia, and Latin America were often organized on a European governance model. The Western, European idea of state development had global influence, but not everywhere. For example, in the Islamic Republic of Pakistan, "Islam constitutes the moral-symbolic language of Muslim politics" (Verkaaik 2001: 347). But there are varieties in Islamic interpretation, which range from the strict fundamentalism of the Wahabi regime in Saudi Arabia to the modernist interpretations that inspired the founders of Turkey. However, in today's postcolonial world, there is a challenge to the state and state power as the sole locus of territorial sovereignty and cultural legitimacy. Ethnic separatism, the globalization of trade and capital movement, and the migration of immigrants and refugees challenge state hegemony. Demands upon new states by ethnic or religious groups for autonomy or independence are countered by supranational organizations that in part protect state sovereignty, such as the UN, the World Bank, NATO, and the European Union.

Colonialism and the emergence of new nation-states in Africa and Asia have brought about great political changes. The newly emerged states of Africa and Asia were successors to colonies that were arbitrarily carved out by the colonial powers, without regard to the boundaries of indigenous political entities. These nation-states tried to develop a national culture to unify the new nation. Traditional forms of leadership and politics were transformed as they were integrated into the state systems of these new nations. Today's postcolonial nation-states contain culturally diverse populations; precolonial states in Africa, such as the kingdom of Ethiopia and the Zulu, Bemba, and Ganda states, were also multiethnic in their composition (Lewis 1999: 58ff.).

After independence was gained, in many countries, powerful non-state affiliations were seen as a problem to be overcome in forging a new national identity. However, these affiliations do not die; rather, they are transformed and then maintained as ethnic, regional, or religious difference. Although the ideology and vocabulary of ethnicity are recent, the members of an ethnic group have returned to a conceptualization of themselves as all related by bonds of kinship. When the state developed, the kinship links tying a community together were de-privileged to state institutions, only to return as an ideology when ethnicity has become important. Ethnic differences become the basis of political competition in nation-states. The drive to establish a national culture may be (or is often seen as) an attempt by the dominant and most powerful group or the numerically superior ethnic group to establish its culture as the national culture.

All the indigenous societies we have described that were part of colonial empires are now encompassed within the boundaries of modern-day states. The Trobrianders, Abelam, Maring, and Enga are all part of the nation-state of Papua New Guinea, where today both Big Men and chiefs run for the office of representative in the New Guinea Parliament or for the position of councilor in the local District Council. In the Trobriands, in particular, despite involvement in national politics, Trobriand chiefs are still strong and "hold the reins in their hands, much to the dismay of the national administration and missions" (Schiefenhovel and Bell-Krannhals 1996: 236). But "The Trobrianders . . . have an interesting mix of ascribed chieftainship, and men who achieve their rank and influence by merit" (1996: 249). Those who run for office often act like Big Men in their political activities. When Trobriand chiefs are elected members of the Papua New Guinea Parliament, they continue their chiefly control over community affairs.

Today, the Yanomamo are to be found in both Venezuela and Brazil. They have been in indirect contact, via trading networks, with the outside world for a very long time (Ferguson 1995). When missionaries arrived in numbers in the 1950s, they established themselves in an area "by giving away vast amounts of goods" (Rabbens 2004: 93). In the mid- to late 1980s, some forty thousand miners, armed with guns and airplanes, attracted by the discovery of gold, invaded Yanomami territory. Cassiterite (the basis for tin) was also sought. At least 15 percent of the Yanomami populations died of new diseases to which they had no resistance, or as a result of conflicts with the miners (2004: 12). The invasion of miners and others has resulted in the introduction of venereal diseases and the birth of mixed-race children who will no longer have rights as Yanomamo (Rohter 2002). Many villagers have moved to mission stations, where the power over their access to healthcare, employment, and schooling is in the hands of the missionaries.

The Kayapo and other Brazilian Indian groups headed by a new generation of leadership have become strong advocates for the protection of the territory of indigenous groups against the mining, hydroelectric, and forestry industries. International human rights groups such as Amnesty International and the U.S. Congressional Human Rights Caucus have helped indigenous groups in this endeavor (Rabbens 2004: 23). Davi Kopenawa Yanomami is a Yanomami leader who gained international attention. He spoke eloquently in 1992 before the General Assembly of the United Nations at the opening ceremony for the International Year of Indigenous Peoples. He also acts as a bridge to Yanomami villages, trying to bring together village leaders to discuss the cessation of feuding and internal warfare in order to move beyond the confines of the villages to unite as a single people and concentrate on common endeavors such as the improvement of medical care and education for the next generations (2004: 120ff.).

EMPOWERMENT

At the beginning of this chapter, we talked about *power* as the ability to command others and *authority* as the institutionalization of power. **Empowerment** has been used variously to refer to actions by the people to get what they want, populist action, revolt from below to subvert those in authority, and the devolution of power to place it in the hands of marginalized groups or subalterns. Using the ideas of Foucault (1972) about the way in which power is vested in **discourse**, one can say that with empowerment, the marginalized gain a political voice. When successive African states gained their independence, empowerment of the African populace was a primary policy. Globally, this concept is now used to call attention to the rights and needs of all minorities to have equal voice with other groups in economic and political participation.

India has initiated many programs that emphasized empowerment and development of all its citizens. A nongovernmental group in Uttar Pradesh, the Mahila Samakhya, sought to "empower low-caste poor rural women, through collective consciousness-raising and mobilization to challenge caste, class, and gender oppression, engender social change, and develop themselves and their community" (Sharma and Gupta 2006: 14). Since Indian officials emphasized "legal procedure," application filing, and the ability to write, the staff and clients of this program were trained to learn these skills. Being able to read and write meant "empowerment" to the nonliterate clients. Demands for village development, such as digging a well or constructing a road, had to be in writing to the local level bureaucrats, and literacy enabled the members of the group to follow the "paper trail" of their request (2006: 14, 16).

empowerment

The ability of groups or individual to identify and achieve their political, social, and economic rights and goals.

discourse

An institutionalized way of thinking or speaking about a subject that comes to be the normalized and accepted worldview through political processes.

POLITICS IN CONTEMPORARY STATES

Many political anthropologists focus their research on the emergence of the modern state. States, identified by recognizable borders, are invariably heterogeneous and include members of several different cultural, religious, and ethnic groups. The nation, or nation-state, developed in Europe with the rise of nationalism, which assumed that a people who had a culture and a language should constitute a separate political entity. The concept of nation-state links an ethnic ideology with a state organization. Ethnonationalism refers to the desire on the part of a minority ethnic group in a multiethnic state to have its own nation-state.

neo-nationalism

The emergence and assertion of newly formed nationalist movements, particularly in new states formed from the former Soviet republics.

The term **neo-nationalism** has begun to be used by European anthropologists to describe the reemergence of nationalism at the end of the Cold War "under different global and transnational conditions" (Banks and Gingrich 2006: 2). This form of nationalism is a reaction to the enormous increase in transnational migration. The strength of the neo-nationalist position is evidenced by the voting strength of the right-wing parties in many western European countries. These neo-nationalist movements have been vocal opponents of admitting large numbers of refugees coming into European countries, a result of civil wars and economic upheaval in the Middle East and Africa.

In the former Soviet Union, there had been efforts to develop a "Communist" culture, but this became, by and large, an attempt to Russify the distinctly different central Asian and Caucasian peoples who were part of the Soviet state. This policy was met with opposition but little overt conflict because of Soviet suppression. Under the policy of glasnost, which opened up Soviet society, ethnicity and nationalism reasserted themselves, and many republics (including the Baltic States, Moldavia, Ukraine, Tadjikistan, Kazakstan, Kyrgyzstan, and Uzbekistan) became politically independent. For the non-Russian republics, this meant moving out from under the domination of Russian culture. These independent states now have the challenge of defining themselves as nations, and states such as Georgia are dealing with internal ethnic minorities along with the presence of Russian minorities. The collapse of the Soviet Union was soon followed by the requests from now-independent countries such as Latvia and Lithuania to join NATO for security advantages resulting from this alliance.

The election of Vice President Kamala Harris, President Biden's running mate in 2020, represents a series of "firsts" in American politics. She is the first female vice president, as well as the first African American/Asian American vice president. Globally, women continue to be underrepresented in government and national politics; gender parity in politics is an elusive goal in all but a handful of governments.

Under the Soviets, the Kazakhs, an ethnic minority, were forced to transform their economic and political institutions to conform to Communist ideology. With the collapse of Communism, the newly created republic of Kazakhstan reverted to a different political structure that included a parliament and a president. However, in the 1990s it soon became a totalitarian state. In addition, during this time, the earlier form of political organization based on clans and on kinship that the Soviet authorities had attempted to suppress

was also resurgent. Although a considerable Russian minority remained after "independence," Kazakh ethnicity and the Kazakh language were emphasized in the new state. According to Schatz, "clan and umbrella clan genealogies experienced a revival as traits that distinguished ethnic Kazakhs from the non-titular [Russian] citizens of independent Kazakhstan. . . . In short, genealogical knowledge was understood to be axiomatic (even if it required reviving in the 1990s) [to establish Kazakh identity]" (2004: 117). Clans rose in importance and streets and schools were named after clan-based heroes (2004: 118). Opposition between clans became a major feature in the local-level politics of Kazakhstan. Patronage networks were also based on clan identity. Old clan politics and the new parliament-president political organization combine with conflicts over control of oil and other natural resources. This makes Kazakhstan an important actor in the world's energy markets.

Although this is the postcolonial period, nation-states in Europe that have been in existence for hundreds of years may still exhibit tribalism, meaning they identify with a particular group likened to a tribe and exhibit ethnic differences in ways similar to postcolonial nations in Africa and Asia. The southern area of Belgium, Walloonia, where French is spoken, has been in conflict with the northern area, where Flemish, a Dutch dialect, is spoken. The conflict concerns not only language but also control over economic resources. Each of these areas of Belgium now has its own legislature and regional executives, and the central government includes a fixed proportion of ministers from each group.

Factionalism

One of the recurring themes in the study of local-level politics has been **factionalism**. One aspect of political factionalism is related to the way national politics play out on the local level. Leaders of factions vying for power may build their followings in a number of different ways, depending upon the structure of the community. The faction consisting of the leader and his followers resembles the Big Man and his followers. Like the Big Man, the leader of a faction is in opposition to other faction leaders. The faction leader vies with other leaders to attract followers, as does the Big Man. There is an exchange relationship between the faction leader and his followers, as there is between the Big Man and his followers, and both types of leaders need to continue supporting and rewarding followers in order to hold onto their followers. When the leader in either case loses power or dies, the faction or group of followers dissolves. In this aspect, factions contrast with political parties, which continue to exist though individual leaders may come and go. However, within political parties in the United States, factions may be found on the local-community level, where party leaders and their supporters compete for control of the party apparatus at that level. In nation-states, factionalism may be based on alliances created by religious or ethnic background. In such situations, factionalism may be transformed into religious or ethnic conflict (Eller 1999).

factionalism

Local groups building support under a powerful individual or idea vying for influence locally and within state systems.

Warlords

warlord

A militarized Big Man; he and his followers are structurally similar to a faction.

Today, the term **warlord** is frequently used with reference to leaders in Afghanistan, Somalia, and Myanmar (Burma). A warlord and his followers are structurally similar to a faction and its leaders. A warlord is like a militarized Big Man. One warlord may be a military commander with an extensive regional following and the ability to use his personal prestige to secure benefits for his followers. Warlordism has become a growing phenomenon in contemporary international politics, particularly in Afghanistan (Rich 1999a, 1999b). Following the election of President Karzai in 2002, General Dostum, a leader of Uzbeks in Afghanistan, continued to operate outside President Karzai's sphere of influence and range of control. Karzai, who is Pashtun, needed to keep General Dostum and his Uzbeck followers as supporters of his newly formed government. When elections were held in Afghanistan for a new president in 2014, Ashraf Ghani was elected; his running mate was General Dostum, who was elected vice president. Despite his official position as vice president of Afghanistan, Mashal reports that Dostum "turned back to his [warlord] roots and raised a private militia" to fight the Taliban and other warlords in a land dispute (Mashal 2015). Ultimately, these efforts to maintain a cohesive state ruled by elected national officials in Afghanistan failed in 2021. When President Biden withdrew American troops, who were attempting to help build an Afghan police and military to support state building, the Taliban rapidly took over the fragile infrastructure, and the elected national officials left the country.

Some warlords and their groups are the consequence of the post–Cold War disappearance of "superpower hegemony," subsequent to which, multiplicities of ethnic and other loyalties emerged to become the basis for these new groupings of warlords and followers. Warlords are often present in **fragile states**, where the government lacks legitimacy or capacity to meet security and economic needs of its citizens, or in **failed states**, where the government has no legitimacy to function on behalf of its citizens, nor in relationships with other states. Warlords are often involved in the illicit trade of opium and other narcotics, as well as in the arms trade, all of which have become completely globalized. The emergence of mercenary armies, a new kind of "warrior class," is also associated with warlordism, which serves to undermine "the authority of conventional governments" (O'Brien 1999).

fragile state

Term applied to a government that lacks legitimacy or capacity to meet security and economic needs of its citizens.

failed state

Term applied when a government is perceived to have no legitimacy to function on behalf of its citizens, nor in relationships with other states.

PATRON-CLIENT RELATIONSHIPS

patron-client relationship

A hierarchical relationship in which the superior (the patron) acts as an intermediary and protector of the inferior (the client) vis-à-vis the national government.

The **patron-client relationship**, discussed in chapter 6 in connection with "godparenthood," a fictive kin relationship, also has important political dimensions. In the past, patrons (frequently economic and political elites) played roles as intermediaries between the peasants of a village and the provincial or national government. Problems with tax collectors and the court system brought clients to their patrons, who were always of a higher class, for assistance. Because of their wide social contacts with their social equals in the towns and cities, patrons could help clients whose social contacts were limited to their own villages. Although there were no links of actual kinship between patrons and clients, ties between the families of patron and clients were perpetuated over generations. Patrons as landlords and clients as tenants were distinguished by their differential access to land and by their class differences as gentry and peasants. These social and economic differences were the basis for a difference in political power. Patron-client relationships are usually superseded when opposition between socioeconomic classes serves to separate and oppose them.

Today, a form of patron-client relationship continues to be important in the political economy of Bangladesh. At first a homeland for Bengali Muslims and a province of the Islamic republic of Pakistan, Bangladesh became an independent nation in 1971 after a bloody civil war. An earlier class structure of commoners and nobility has been replaced by a system based on land ownership, wealth, education, and power, through which a hierarchical network of interpersonal patron-client relationships operates (Kochanek 1993: 44). In rural communities, this system is reinforced by economic forces, such as scarcity of credit, land, tenancy contracts, and employment opportunities, along with political factors, such as the need for protection. The concept of daya, meaning "grace" or "blessing," constitutes the cultural underpinning of the reciprocal patron-client relationship. Individuals feel that they have the moral right to demand food and subsistence from those "well placed." The well-placed individuals, who acquire their prosperity from a higher moral authority, are expected to give generously to their clients. The patrons who distribute the goods are expected to be authoritarian and to be feared and obeyed (1993: 45).

This pattern of patron-client relationship has extended beyond the rural area and has come to dominate not only the whole of the Bangladesh political process but the business community as well. Although Bangladesh has formal legal, constitutional, and administrative governmental structures, these have come to be monopolized by a "traditional pattern of patron–client relationships based on tadbir, a process of personal lobbying" (Kochanek 1993: 251). Policy making and implementation always require personal connections. The business community is characterized by the same pattern, with primary emphasis on personal relationships. Businessmen often obtain exemptions from rules and other kinds of business benefits by manipulating the regulatory system and the administration of policy, using their personal connections. Patron-client relationships, from the countryside to the capital, are a way of life in Bangladesh.

The concepts we have discussed in this chapter can be applied to American society as well. The operation of leadership in terms of power and exchange; the politics of empowerment, bureaucracy, and administration; and the emergence of leaders through political maneuvering, factionalism, police corruption, and patron-client relationships are relevant to political situations in American politics. Factions representing different political positions and coalitions operate at every level of our political system. They may coalesce around individuals or around an issue, such as equal rights for women or discrimination against minorities. Ethnic politics are as active today in American cities as they are in any nation-state in Asia or Africa.

Political Economy

At the beginning of this chapter, we noted that political organization and economics are intimately interwoven and that this interrelationship is referred to as "political economy." What are the ways in which the forces of production shape the culture and political organization? As shown throughout this chapter, the various types of political organization are associated with different forms of distribution and often different forms of production. For example, chieftainship is interwoven with a redistributive system, as described in chapter 8, in which surplus goods are funneled into the central political position, that of the chief, and are distributed on ceremonial occasions to other chiefs, who in turn redistribute them to their followers. The chief maintains political authority by controlling and disbursing economic goods, while the economic system is dependent on the establishment of fixed positions of authority. Markets are always associated with state structures. The state as a political system, as we have pointed out, operates on a territorial basis beyond the level of kinship and clanship. The less personal relationships of production and consumption are in accord with this type of system.

Political economy promotes a regional and cross-border perspective. As we pointed out, systems of ceremonial exchange such as the Trobriand kula demonstrate how societies with differing political systems were joined in a regional system of ceremonial exchange and barter. A focus upon political economy also reveals the way in which, for example, capitalist forces of production in Latin America have shaped the way of life of politically and economically oppressed people. An emphasis on political economy exposes global divisions of labor, illustrating how different groups of people around the world have been unequally drawn into globalized systems of labor, production, and consumption.

POLITICAL RESISTANCE AND GLOBALIZATION

Throughout this chapter, we have indicated how symbols are used to express power, rank, and authority. In the context of the modern state, symbols become a powerful means of constructing ethnic identity, and they are mobilized to express ethnic and religious conflicts as well as class and race struggles. Around the world in the twenty-first century, symbols are instantly recognizable statements of resistance to exploitation and marginalization. The globalization of all forms of media and widespread use of social media facilitate the rapid spread of symbols, images, and social movements around the world. Raising the three middle fingers with palms outward has been adopted as a symbol of resistance to authoritarian regimes in Thailand and Myanmar; it is believed to have been inspired by the use of this gesture in multiple installments of the *Hunger Games* films, widely viewed particularly by younger people around the world. In Argentina, women's rights activists wore green scarves to symbolize their support of a widespread equality movement that culminated in the legalization of abortion in 2021. Activists in other parts of

Latin America and throughout the world have been inspired by the symbols and accomplishments of the *Marea Verde* or Green Wave Movement.

The Black Lives Matter movement in the United States was galvanized by the death of Eric Garner in 2014 and many other African American men killed in police actions. Garner was killed by police officers in a tragically mishandled attempt at arrest for a minor offence; one police officer was filmed kneeling on Garner's throat despite his multiple cries of "I can't breathe" before he lost consciousness. Global media coverage of this event and its aftermath has resulted in the adoption of two very potent political symbols of resistance to police brutality in multiple settings around the world: kneeling on one knee and a raised hand clenched in a fist. These symbols provide instant recognition in the media of what has become a global movement protesting police brutality and other forms of racial injustice around the world.

SUMMARY

- Power, the key concept in defining political organization, is the ability to command others to do certain things and to get compliance from them. When power becomes institutionalized, it has been transformed into authority, with a recognized position whose occupant must be obeyed.

- Anthropologists refer to a position that depends on personal qualifications and individual ability as an achieved status, in contrast to an ascribed status, which one inherits.

- In the simplest form of political organization, leadership was manifested intermittently while band organization had a more fixed membership that came together annually to carry out joint ritual and economic activities. The position of Big Man was dependent on personal qualifications and individual ability. The political economy of chieftainships is a more complex redistributive system with more levels of political organization.

- The state differs from the other types of political organization in scale. It is organized on a territorial basis, rather than on the basis of kinship and clanship. In the state we find social stratification—rulers, aristocrats, commoners, and various low-status groups.

- Feuds conducted according to rules involve collective, not personal, responsibility, so revenge can be taken against any member of the group. Warfare is hostile action between different groups. The task of the anthropologist is to explain why warfare occurs when and where it does.

- The legal principles or bases upon which disputes are resolved emerge only through the analysis of specific cases. *Law* is a cultural system of meanings that the anthropologist must interpret.

- A political or criminal faction consisting of the leader and his followers resembles the Big Man and his followers.

- After independence was gained in many new nation-states, tribalism was seen as a problem to be overcome in forging a new national identity.

However, tribalism does not die but is transformed and maintained as ethnic differences, which then become the basis for political competition.

- The concepts of political organization—the operation of leadership in terms of power and exchange, the politics of empowerment, bureaucracy and administration, political maneuvering, factionalism, police corruption, and patron-client relationships—are all relevant to political situations in American society.

- Protest movements around the world adopt symbols and forms of representation that are immediately recognizable and generate solidarity, due in part to widespread use of social media.

KEY TERMS

authority, 210
band organization, 213
Big Man structure, 213
chief, 210
chieftainship, 214
civil law, 223
civil society, 223
criminal law, 223
discourse, 227
empowerment, 227
factionalism, 229
failed states, 230
feuding, 217
fragile states, 230
government, 210
headman, 210

influence, 210
informal leadership, 212
law, 222
legal pluralism, 223
mediator, 222
nation-state, 218
neo-nationalism, 228
office, 210
patron-client relationship, 230
politics, 210
power, 210
primogeniture, 214
sovereignty, 224
terrorism, 221
warlord, 230

SUGGESTED READINGS

Chirot, Daniel. *Contentious Identities: Ethnic, Religious, and Nationalist Conflicts in Today's World*. New York: Routledge, 2011.

A concise and accessible discussion of why ethnic and religious diversity within states sometimes (not always) becomes violent conflict.

Simpson, Audra. *Mohawk Interruptus: Political Life across the Borders of Settler States*. Durham, NC: Duke University Press, 2014.

Combining political theory with ethnographic research among the Mohawks of Kahnawà:ke, a reserve community in what is now southwestern Quebec, this ethnography examines their strategies to articulate and maintain political sovereignty throughout centuries of settler colonialism.

Vincent, Joan, ed. *The Anthropology of Politics: A Reader in Ethnography, Theory, and Critique.* Malden, MA: Blackwell Publishers, 2002.

A survey of historic and contemporary ideas that deal with political anthropology.

SUGGESTED WEBSITES

http://www.discoveranthropology.org.uk/about-anthropology/specialist-areas/politicalanthropology.html

The website of the Royal Anthropological Institute's Educational Outreach program, contains links, blogs, and recommendations on readings and films on contemporary issues in political anthropology.

http://what-when-how.com/social-and-cultural-anthropology/political-anthropology/

An online tutorial on the history of political anthropology, basic concepts, and bibliographies.

https://www.un.org/development/desa/indigenouspeoples/

The website of the United Nations division of Economic and Social Affairs for Indigenous Peoples contains multiple studies and publications documenting sovereignty issues, human rights movements, resources struggles, and development strategies of indigenous peoples around the world.

Chapter 10
Belief Systems, Rituals, and the Spirit World

LEARNING OBJECTIVES

- Identify the characteristics of religion and religious systems.
- Understand the difference between magic, science, and religion and how these categories of human experience help in the analysis of belief systems.
- Explore syncretism and religious change in the context of globalization.

- Understand how ideas about the supernatural are communicated through ritual and storytelling; that these ideas change over time; and that they adapt to new forms of communications technologies.
- Analyze the multiple uses and meanings of fundamentalism and its political expression in different national and globalized contexts.

MANY PEOPLE IN THE WORLD believe in an order of existence beyond the observable universe, that is, in the supernatural. For example, the Trobriand Islanders believe that when a person dies, his or her spirit splits in two. One part goes to live on the island of Tuma in the village of the dead, to remain there until it is reincarnated in the spirit of a newborn child. The other part of the spirit haunts the favorite places of the deceased, and its presence is frightening to the villagers still alive. They are even more afraid of sorcerers, especially flying witches, who are thought to have caused the death in the first place. Beliefs in sorcery, spirits, and witchcraft are widespread. One can ride along a country road in England and see a billboard announcing an impending meeting of a local witches' coven to be held the following week. Meetings of American witches' covens are also announced in the media. Popular television programs feature teenage witches, individuals with the power to communicate with ghosts, and the "living dead" around us.

From the secular, or nonreligious point of view, empirical explanations of the observable world are considered scientific. Explanations that do not depend on empirical evidence but instead rely on strongly held beliefs in nonempirical or supernatural forces are categorized as religious. However, people consider their spiritual culture heroes and the ghosts of their ancestors to be absolutely real, no less real than the physical world around them.

Religious phenomena involve the use of symbols that evoke powerful emotional responses. One has merely to consider the difference between water and holy water and the emotional response evoked in Catholic ritual by the latter. Symbols that evoke strong feelings are found throughout cultures in domains considered religious and those considered secular or nonreligious. Political symbols, such as a flag or a national anthem, produce strong shared emotions. Religious symbols are often employed to amplify the emotions of political rituals and intensify nationalist sentiments.

Religious ideology, supported by law, invariably normalizes gender roles. Family composition and marriage norms are informed by religious doctrine, as are the appropriate roles and behaviors of women and men in both public and private life. Sexuality is a concern of all the world's religions; ideology defines appropriate behaviors and contexts. These norms are also encoded in legal codes regulating both civil and criminal law. Religion is invoked to maintain the status quo of social divisions or mobilize people around collective action confronting the status quo. It can also provide the basis for resistance to societal norms and mobilize action around environmental protection, social justice, and cultural change. Efforts at religious conversion were a major characteristic of European colonial regimes and continue to be a factor in today's geopolitics of influence. Religious ideology not only motivates individual and group behavior but is also invariably encoded to various degrees in national identity and state policy. Religion can justify war or inspire peace; it can encourage inclusion or justify exclusion. Considering these multiple ways religion functions in human societies, it is not surprising that there is considerable debate among scholars about defining it.

RELIGION STUDIED/RELIGION DEFINED?

Religion is traditionally defined by anthropologists as the cultural means by which humans deal with the supernatural, but many humans also believe that the reverse is true—that the supernatural deals with humans. In this interaction, the supernatural is usually seen as powerful and human beings as weak. In another approach, religion is defined in terms of a pool of elements that tend to cluster together. They include a belief in a single or multiple dieties or spiritual beings,

Throughout India, people maintain household shrines containing images of important deities worshipped by the family. Household members interact with these images, providing daily offerings to them during prayer.

with whom humans can interact; a moral code believed to emanate from extra-human sources; the human ability to transcend suffering; and rituals that involve humans with the extra-human (Saler 1993: 219). The "spiritual beings" and the extra-human of Saler's definition can be equated with what we call "the supernatural." Klass (1995; see also Klass and Weisgrau 1999: 1–4) argues that defining religion in terms of the supernatural reflects a Eurocentric assumption about the separation of the "natural" and "supernatural" realms of existence. He therefore defines religion as "that instituted process of interaction among the members of that society—and between them and the universe at large as they conceive it to be constituted—which provides them with meaning, coherence, direction, unity, easement, and whatever degree of control over events they perceive as possible" (Klass 1995: 38).

A system of religious belief is found in every culture and is therefore generally acknowledged as a cultural universal; beliefs and practices, however, vary between communities and practitioners. This universality has prompted scholars to question what it is about life, and the world in which that life is lived, that compels humans to propose that the world is governed by forces beyond their empirical observations. Religion fulfills multiple kinds of human needs. One is the need to understand; this is the need for explanations and meanings. The second is the substantive need to bring about specific goals, such as rain, good crops, and health, by carrying out religious acts. The third is the psychological need to reduce fear and anxiety in situations in which these are provoked. Emile Durkheim (1965) and his followers saw religion as the means by which society inculcates values and sentiments necessary for the promotion of social solidarity and the society's ultimate survival.

Recent explanations for the universality of religion involve what is referred to as the **cognitive science of religion**. This approach examines religious phenomena as related to the evolution of the human brain and its capacity to process and categorize information. Boyer (2001) claims that religious symbolism and representations are constrained cognitively by the universal properties of the mind-brain: "Religious concepts are probably influenced by the way the brain's inference systems produce explanations without our being aware of it" (2001: 18). He suggests that the universality of religious

religion

The cultural means by which humans interact with the supernatural or extra-human domains.

cognitive science of religion

Examines religious phenomena as a result of how the human brain has evolved over time to process and categorize information.

experience is best understood by questioning "what makes human minds so selective in what supernatural claims they find plausible" (2001: 31). Other scholars of religion and cognition investigate neurophysiological and neurobiological manifestations of religious phenomena such as trance and meditation; some cite the role played by the evolution of the temporal lobe of the brain in these expressions of religious ideas, emotions, and practices.

Anthropologists who study religion document how different groups of practitioners within any one religious system interpret ideology, ritual, and everyday practice. There is a growing recognition that women and men interpret their religious ideologies and practices differently. Many of the world's religions exclude women from some areas of practice and authority. This exclusion has often silenced women's voices in public debates about doctrine and dogma. The heteronormativity associated with many religions has also silenced the voices of LGBTI participants and marginalized or banned them from mainstream religious practice. Ethnographers that associated religious dogma and practice exclusively with male authority reinforced gender marginalization in anthropological studies of religious practice. Their resulting ethnographies focused exclusively on male heterosexual voices and interpretations. Inspired in part by feminist and LGBTI rights movements, anthropologists now understand that the interpretations and practices of religion are never a unitary, single, or unchanging perspective, and must include the voices of multiple groups of participants and practitioners.

RITUAL: APPROACHING THE SUPERNATURAL

Generally speaking, human beings approach their conception of the supernatural by carrying out ritual acts, usually involving a combination of speech and patterned behavior that alters the emotional state of the participants. Recording and analyzing rituals and theorizing about their meaning and underlying belief systems has engaged anthropologists since the inception of the discipline. Some scholars analyze ritual primarily as the enacting of belief systems about the composition of the world—putting religious beliefs into practice. Others focus on the social solidarity of ritual practices as particular groups of people enact shared experience.

ritual

Patterned or repetitive performance that symbolically communicates values and ideas to both participants and observers.

Ritual is also understood as a performance that symbolically communicates values and ideas to both participants and observers; these values include communicating appropriate gender roles and behaviors and the appropriate behaviors of subordinates to those superior to them. Ritual does not simply mirror society and culture but helps shape its defining features. Ritual can also challenge the existing order. Today, rituals are seen as dynamic, ever responsive to the changing aspects of modern and postmodern life. Experimentation and the emergence of new rituals have become important foci of anthropological research. Anthropologists study the performative aspects of ritual and are interested in how participants constitute ideas about themselves through their actions. However, there is often a tension between the traditional rules of ritual and innovation or experimentation in actual performances; not all people will agree with the value or ideology being articulated by new approaches to ritual.

The anthropologist's goal in documenting and studying contemporary rituals is to understand the meaning of the ritual and its subjective aspects as encompassed in the participant's point of view. A single intellectually satisfying definition of ritual is elusive because of the multiple aspects of personal and group experience, meaning, symbolism, expression, and functions enfolded in its performance. The following ethnographic examples illustrate some of the types of rituals described by scholars and discuss various approaches to their analysis.

Hortatory rituals consist of exhortations to the supernatural to perform some act. In the event of a shipwreck, the captain of a Trobriand canoe would exhort the supernatural powers to send the marvelous fish to guide the drowning victims to a friendly shore. The Trobrianders have a native term for this category of exhortation. The term means "by the mouth only." Prayer, involving words only, differs from hortatory ritual in its method of approach and intent. Prayer emphasizes people's inferior position to all kinds of gods since they beseech the gods to act on their behalf.

Sometimes the deities can be approached by the practitioner entering a self-induced or drug-induced **trance**, an altered state of consciousness associated with the performance of ritual. The Yanomamo inhale the hallucinogenic substance **ebene** to induce a trance and enable contact with the spirit world. In the trancelike state produced by the drug, individuals may hallucinate that they are flying to the spirit world. Sometimes trances may be induced without the use of any drugs. Many North American Native societies practice the **vision quest**, in which a person, through starvation, deprivation, and sometimes bodily mutilation, attempts to induce a trance in which a supernatural being visits and thenceforth becomes a guardian spirit and lifelong protector.

Trance states are also interpreted by anthropologists as performative vehicles that unconsciously give "actors license for actions and expressions not available to them in their 'ordinary' state" (Bourguignon 2004: 557). Many scholars who study trance states in religions explore the prevalence of women performing these rituals. While men are generally the exorcists in such religions, women often evidence possession and enact the presence of the spirits (2004: 557). "Acting out the identity of spirits in ritual possession trance offers women an acceptable, and consciously deniable, way to express unconscious, forbidden thoughts and feelings, particularly in situations of social subordination" (2004: 558). In a possession trance state, women in social systems who have otherwise been socialized to subordination have temporary access to power by acting out the personalities and roles of the spirits. They are held blameless for their actions in these states and may even be elevated in status as a result of this experience.

The supernatural world in some societies can be appeased through tribute and gifts. The widespread sacrifices and offerings of live animals, food, vegetables, incense, and even money are a way of approaching the supernatural

hortatory rituals

Exhortations to the supernatural to perform some act.

trance

An altered state of consciousness associated with the performance of ritual.

ebene

Hallucinogenic substance used by the Yanomamo.

vision quest

The search for a protective supernatural spirit through rituals that may involve starvation and deprivation.

by bearing gifts. Since the relationship between humans and the supernatural emphasizes the subordination of the humans, people can only hope for supernatural support in fighting wars; in warding off misfortune, sickness, and death; and in providing fertility in exchange for their gifts.

RITES OF PASSAGE

Rites of passage are communal ritual ceremonies that publicly mark the changes in status an individual or group experiences through the progression of the life cycle, as it is culturally constituted. The beginning and end of life are always marked by some kind of ritual. In addition, one or more points between birth and death at which one's status changes, such as a girl's first menstruation or marriage, may be marked with a public ceremony. Some cultures emphasize a biological or chronological event, such as the onset of menstruation or a significant birthday, in their rites of passage. Other milestones, such as the first fish caught or a child's first haircut may be marked through ritual ceremonies. An example of the cultural determination of such rites is demonstrated in the variation in the age at which a male child is circumcised and the presence or absence of this practice around the world.

Van Gennep (1960), in his classic analysis of rites of passage, pointed out that all such rites involve three stages. The first stage marks the separation of the individual from the category or status previously occupied. Next is a period of transition in which the individual is in a kind of limbo. During this period, the individual is frequently secluded from the rest of the society. Victor Turner (1967: 93–111) has characterized this period as a particularly sacred one, a **liminal period** in which the individual is literally "in between," no longer in one status and not yet in another. Liminality may be quickly resolved by reincorporation, such as the assumption of adulthood after a bride's wedding, or extended, as in the permanent "outsider" status of religious practitioners who live their lives outside mainstream society. The last stage is reincorporation, in which the individual is ceremonially reintegrated into society, but this time in the new status. Frequently, this three-stage process is represented by means of the metaphor of death and rebirth. The individual in the former category "dies" and is "reborn" or "born again" into the new category. In the reincorporation stage of the ceremony, the person is often given a new name and puts on a different type of clothing, marking the birth of a new person.

Rites of passage generally reflect gender divisions within society; the Arapesh of New Guinea celebrate several different kinds of rites of passage that separate male and female initiates and symbolically convey the social norms and expectations for each group. Though the Arapesh have a patrilineal rule of descent, they believe their blood comes from the mother while the father contributes the semen. When one's blood is spilled, the mother's group must be recompensed by the payment of shell valuables. This principle underlies all rites-of-passage ceremonies, as well as other aspects of Arapesh

liminal period

The in-between stage in a rite-of-passage ceremony when the individual has not yet been reincorporated into society with their new status.

culture. After the birth of a child, the child's father "pays for the blood" by giving shell rings to the child's mother's brother. Through this act, the child now belongs to the father's group, though the mother's lineage is still said to "own" the child's blood. At puberty, several boys are initiated at the same time to transform them into "men." The rites involve isolation from females, with whom the boy has spent most of his time, and the incision of the boy's penis. He is also introduced to the secret male Tamberan Cult, where he learns that the Tamberan spirit is the sounds of the drums and the flute secretly played by the men. This information is kept from women and children. During initiation, the boy is reborn as a man. At the end, he is reincorporated into society as a man, at a feast made by his father to honor the boy's mother's brother. Finally, now a man, he goes on a trip and meets all his father's trading partners, signifying public recognition of his new status.

Rites of Passage in American Culture

A variety of rites of passage characterize American culture, with its multiethnic complexity and religious diversity. These include circumcision rites, baptism, various coming of age rituals for adolescents and teenagers, graduation and wedding ceremonies, the retirement party, and various types of funerals. The same stages of separation, transition, and reincorporation can be seen in these rites of passage as in those of other cultures. Just as the Arapesh payment of shell rings marks the entry of the child into his or her father's patrilineal group, circumcision, baptism, and naming ceremonies perform the same function of moving an infant or child into a recognized life-stage of society.

Many of the rites of passage described above involve some form of violence to the body of the initiates; tattooing, scarification, male and female circumcision, starvation, and other forms of physical mutilation are found in rites of passage around the world. For decades, anthropologists have documented physical ordeals associated with initiation; contemporary theorists are now focusing on this near-universal aspect of religious ritual. Whitehouse suggests that the intensity of the memory of the violence of initiation rituals serves psychological and sociological functions. The memory of the initiation, because of the pain and intensity of emotions surrounding it, is imprinted on the brain as long-term memory (Whitehouse 2000). He contrasts the information transmitted through this memory of episodes of intense physical experience ("imagistic") with the kind of religious information transmitted through scripture, sermons, or other forms of religious instruction ("doctrinal"). "The doctrinal mode, which relies on semantic memory, is more sober, organized, and verbal; the 'imagistic' mode, which relies on episodic memory, is more emotional and personal, and ideas are conveyed nonverbally to a much greater degree" (in Laidlaw 2004: 4). This analytic approach includes pain and violence inflicted on the human body during initiation rituals into a theory of religious beliefs and practices.

Rites of Intensification: Practice and Politics

rites of intensification

Communal rituals celebrated at various points in the yearly cycle.

Another major category of ritual—**rites of intensification**—is celebrated communally at various points in the yearly cycle, such as spring, fall, or the winter and summer solstices. They may also be held annually, to mark the contemporary interpretation of an historical event. These rituals are designed to bring collective harmony to a community by memorializing or marking a significant event or series of events that are acknowledged by multiple identity groups. Often they mark a historical event that is recollected in the present; thus they have important political and social messages that might not be interpreted in the same way by all participating groups. While the functions of these rituals are to create a collective experience of unity, their outcomes do not always conform to this ideal.

Among the Wogeo of Papua New Guinea, when an event of importance to the whole community takes place, such as the appointment of the official heir to the chief, a rite of intensification known as a warabwa is held. The nibek spirit monsters are summoned. The community as a whole sponsors the warabwa and hosts many villages in the celebration. The climax of the ceremony is a great distribution of food, including pork. One of the occurrences at a Wogeo warabwa is a free-for-all, at which the rules regarding the respect relationships between certain categories of relatives are suspended, and they may insult and humiliate each other without sanctions.

The suspension of rules in this case serves, in a negative fashion, to emphasize the rules of the group. The rites allow the expression or release of tension in a ritual context that could not be permitted in the everyday course of events. A similar reversal of everyday behavior occurs in North and South American cultures at Mardi Gras, just before Ash Wednesday, which marks the beginning of Lent, the forty-day period of penance leading to Easter. Mardi Gras rites, marked by great exuberance and extravagant behavior, contrast with the restraint and somberness of Lent, which follows. The celebration of Holi in Hindu cultures is another example of public exuberant behavior that reverses, for one day, the usual behaviors of social order. In northern India, this religious festival is celebrated each spring, in part by people throwing colored powders and colored water on each other; usually-submissive wives playfully confront their husbands and other relatives to whom they generally show respect and cover them with water and powders. In rural communities in Rajasthan, lower-caste men reverse the usual norms of inter-caste behavioral norms by flinging powders, waters, and animal dung at upper-caste men, actions that would not be tolerated on any other day of the year.

Thanksgiving, a national holiday in the United States, is a rite of intensification invoking the survival of the Plymouth Colony in Massachusetts in 1621, historically attributed to, in great part, the contributions of Native Americans. Presidents Washington, Jefferson, Adams, and Madison all issued proclamations declaring national days of "thanksgiving" for various military and political events. Thanksgiving as a national holiday is currently celebrated on the fourth Thursday in November; it was established by Abraham Lincoln with a presidential decree in 1863. To Lincoln and nineteenth-century

Americans, Thanksgiving recognized potential threats to national unity, including the Civil War and the influx of immigrant populations (Siskind 1992). Today, most Americans participate in a Thanksgiving meal and, by their participation, give thanks in a way that is mostly secular; the religious aspect, if present, may involve saying an appropriate prayer at the start of the meal.

This American rite of intensification demands that particular foods be eaten to symbolize Thanksgiving. Turkey, not lamb chops or meatballs, symbolizes this celebration, although it is unlikely that turkey was actually part of the Pilgrims' celebration. Native Americans are part of this historical reconstruction and are believed to have contributed to the survival of the Pilgrims. Although it is widely believed in mainstream American practice that they were part of the first Thanksgiving celebration, today Native Americans do not celebrate the day as a rite of intensification; for them the event is remembered as part of the conquest of Native America by Europeans. It is an opportunity to gather with relatives, cook indigenous foods, and reflect on historical representation of Native-indigenous relations. Some Native Americans call Thanksgiving a "day of mourning"; others see it as an opportunity to reinforce their cultural heritage and communicate cultural resilience to the younger generation.

Many anthropologists document how local myths and beliefs structured the interaction between indigenous peoples and their first contacts with European explorers. "First contact stories" and their memorialization provide historical justification for European exploration and colonization, and they attempt to reinforce myths of national identity. Reenactment rituals now give voice to the perspectives of those who were conquered and colonized by including indigenous accounts and perspectives. While history has privileged the accounts of explorers and their historical relationships with the monarchs and governments who supported their voyages, indigenous peoples now enact contact stories from their perspectives using their own oral and written histories.

For example, a reenactment of the landing of Captain Cook in 1770 off the Great Barrier Reef of Australia takes place in Cooktown annually. Cook's landing "had been historically performed and remembered as a moment of possession; the place where he came ashore and allegedly claimed Australia for His Majesty King George III" (Ward 2020: 5). In several decades of reenactment, Cook "was the hero and the founder; the [Indigenous] Guugu Yimithirr were marginal. They were on the periphery of the stage, and once the flag was raised they became the backdrop to the performance" (2020: 7). A collaboration between indigenous Australians and non-indigenous residents of Cooktown over several years resulted in the rescripting of the annual commemorative performance. Indigenous perspectives of the events are now an equal part of the public storytelling; the visibility of the indigenous perspective is a corrective to a one-sided history portrayed in these public rituals, and is also creating new opportunities for reconciliation between these two groups of Australians. "Community members . . . began to use the encounters in 1770 as a platform to publicly discuss more difficult histories of Indigenous and non-Indigenous relations, which facilitated new understandings of these relations in the present" (2020: 5).

STORIES ABOUT THE SUPERNATURAL WORLD

We have explored how people attempt to explain the unknowable by constructing a supernatural world; they also talk about that world. They tell stories about supernatural creatures. They create myths about the origins of the world and of people and their social groups. They relate these myths to subsequent generations about how the world was created, and how they came to the place in which they dwell. They tell stories about recent events, sometimes reinventing facts and attributing motivations to individuals or groups who may or may not have been involved. These different types of stories may deal with universal themes, such as birth, growing up, male-female relations, and death. They may also reflect more recent themes of the distrust of media, government, or large corporations. They therefore are revised and changed over time, to be relevant to contemporary issues, identity groups, and prevalent anxieties.

Myths, legends, and folktales are all types of stories containing some elements of the supernatural. They represent a continuum; there may be overlap in their content. These are Western categories, but they provide a comparative framework for organizing the vast array of this material. **Myths** deal with the remote past, often with the time of the origin of things, both natural and cultural. Myths often describe how the physical features of the world and its people were created, how fire was discovered and cooking began, and how crops were domesticated. As the time period becomes less remote, myths may become **legends**, which are thought to have some basis in historical fact. **Folktales** deal with an indeterminate time, which, in European folktales, is indicated by the standard opening "Once upon a time." To the tellers as well as the audience of these stories, they create an acceptable universe that include spells, prophecies, talking animals, and impossible manipulations of the progression of time. The boundaries of these three categories are very fluid, and the distinctions are often those made by the analysts and not necessarily audience members. For example, in a recent volume, African Myths of Origin, Belcher notes, "In this collection of stories the historical element regains its importance . . . the stories could be called 'traditions of origin.' . . . They describe cultural origins for the people involved . . . [and] have been handed down from one generation to another, although always with changes and adaptations to keep them relevant to their contemporary audiences" (2005: xiv).

While myths are about extraordinary, superhuman heroes or gods, the characters in fairy tales are ordinary mortals (Purkiss 2000). Fairy tales of European origin were originally transmitted orally, and consequently they changed as the centuries went by, as all oral literature does. They began to be recorded in writing in the late seventeenth century, and were then codified

myths

Stories set in the remote past that explain the origin of natural things and cultural practices.

legends

Stories about heroes who overcome obstacles set in familiar historical contexts.

folktales

Stories about fanciful creatures set in indeterminate times that impart morals or lessons.

by the Grimm brothers during the nineteenth century. Recent research has revealed that the fairy tales recorded by the brothers Grimm, such as that of Little Red Riding Hood, have their origins in Medieval Latin literature (Ziolkowski 2007: 4–5). Fairy tales perform an important function in that they are "among our most powerful socializing narratives. They contain enduring rules for understanding who we are, and how we should behave" (Orenstein 2002: 10).

A fairy tale such as "Red Riding Hood," up until the nineteenth century, was "a bawdy morality tale, quite different from the story we know today" (Orenstein 2002: 3). There have been changes in the meanings of the characters, and although the wolf has always signified evil, in the earlier adult version Red Riding Hood was an unchaste woman. As audiences of recorded versions of these stories expand, their images and narratives reflect the tastes and demands of contemporary audiences. Many European-derived fairy tales are now familiar around the world and are part of global contemporary popular culture. Film, animated, and theatrical versions are viewed enthusiastically by audiences around the world.

Legends about the founding and history of Hawaii are today being used "to reinforce a tourist-oriented image of Hawaii . . . an ongoing 'process of cultural construction' . . . situated in the preoccupations and negotiations of the present, . . . where every teller engages with the past and interprets it so as to affect listeners or readers" (Bacchilega 2007: 30). The use of myths and legends for consumption by tourists is widespread in Pacific island tourism economies, and elsewhere around the world. Some analysts note the negative impacts of the appropriation of local voices by outsiders or elites in this process of "marketing" local myths and legends to tourists. Others cite the potential of objectification and simplification in narratives and visual displays, leading to stereotypical representations of Native peoples, disembedded from history and political process. While it is unlikely that these practices of representation will be abandoned, advocates suggest that their negative representations can be mitigated by the presence of multiple local voices in the creation of tourism narratives, visuals, and any other forms of cultural representation (Baron 2010).

ANALYZING MYTHS: HISTORICAL AND CONTEMPORARY VIEWS

The people of Wogeo of New Guinea have a myth that tells how the flutes that represent the nibek spirits came to be (Hogbin 1996). As is typical, this myth takes place in the distant past when the cultural heroes who created everything in the world lived. Two female heroes dreamed of making flutes. They cut two sticks of bamboo and bored a hole in each, forming flutes that immediately began to play. They were overjoyed with the self-playing flutes. When they went to work in the gardens, they blocked the holes to prevent the flutes from playing. An adolescent boy then stole the flutes from the two women, and tried to blow them, causing the women to return. On seeing that the boy had stolen the flutes, the women told him that the flutes would never again play by themselves. Since a male had stolen them, no female could ever look at the flutes. The women told him that it would be hard to learn to blow the flutes, but, in order to become men, boys had to make the effort. The two women then left the island of Wogeo in disgust. They eventually settled on Kadovar and Blupblup Islands, off the mainland of New Guinea. These places are the only locations where bamboo for flutes can currently be found.

Various theoretical approaches have been proposed to explain the existence of myths. One views myths as literal history. Such an approach would interpret the Wogeo myth as evidence of an earlier period of matriarchy, when women controlled those aspects of society that men now control. Interpreting myths as literal history is discredited by some historians, while archaeologists sometimes find material remains that echo the mythical events.

Malinowski saw the necessity of analyzing a myth in relation to its social and cultural context. To Malinowski, myths were charters or guidelines for how and what people should believe, act, and feel. Just as our Declaration of Independence states that all men are created equal, a body of myths lays out ideals that guide the behavior of members of a culture. Malinowski's approach to myth as charter explores the Wogeo myth as justifying contemporary Wogeo cultural facts. There is a men's cult focused upon the men's house where the sacred flutes are kept. Women are kept away from the men's house and are never allowed to see the sacred flutes. Malinowski would see the Wogeo myth as providing the justification and rationale, or charter, for men's performing certain ritual and ceremonial roles from which women are excluded.

A Freudian psychological interpretation of the Wogeo myth would see the flutes as masculine objects, clearly phallic symbols. The myth signifies conflicts and fears between men and women. Whereas individuals express unconscious fears and anxieties in symbolic form through dreams, myths are seen as reflecting the collective anxieties of a society, and giving cultural expression to these anxieties. Freud considered certain repressed anxieties and frustrations to be universal characteristics related to human psychological growth and development. The universality of Freudian interpretations is challenged by historians and anthropologists; Freud's theories derived from nineteenth- and early-twentieth-century European patriarchal and nuclear family norms that focused on boys' relationships with their fathers, who are figures of authority and discipline. In matrilineal societies, these relationships are structured in a different way, and the forms of conflict present between fathers and sons do not exist as they do in patriarchal systems.

Lévi-Strauss pursued a large-scale, detailed analysis of myths from North and South American Indian societies (1963, 1971). To Lévi-Strauss, myths provide explanations for contradictions present in a culture that cannot be resolved. The Wogeo myth emphasizes the separation of women from men after men obtained possession of the flutes. In Lévi-Strauss's terms, the myth attempts to resolve the contradiction between the ideal of keeping males and females apart and the need for them to come together to reproduce society through sexual intercourse. Like all other myths, this myth fails to provide a permanent solution to this contradiction.

Most anthropologists analyzing myths today would agree that myths must always be understood in connection with other cultural facts. In Wogeo, interpreting the aphorism "Men play flutes, women bear infants" is important to understand in the Wogeo context. Male and female are seen as separate but complementary. Women bear children as part of a natural biological process. Flutes are cultural objects manufactured by men. Hence, women are associated with natural things, and men with cultural things. In Wogeo life, each sex should be separate. However, in order for women to bear children, as they should, the sexes must come together. This is the only way that society can reproduce itself. By means of the various ceremonies of boys' initiation, boys are symbolically separated from women, being reborn from the nibek spirits as men. Women dreamed, and then made the flutes, which played by themselves during a time when men and women were not separate. The myth also says that, at one time, women were superior to men, bearing children, and having the flutes as well. The present domination of men rests upon their having stolen what was once women's. When men took control of culture, they were able to dominate women. Ultimately, the myth is about the origins of culture and the tension inherent in male-female relations.

There are echoes of the same theme of tension inherent in male-female relations in ancient Greek mythology. Both the Amazons, superhuman women who controlled their society, and the Fates, women who, through their weaving, determined the destiny of all humanity, are taken to be evidence in the myths for a matriarchal stage of society. A recent reanalysis of Greek myths concludes, "If there ever was a time when women ruled the world, or even served as the central focus of a civilized society, Greek myth does not record it" (Lefkowitz 2007: 186). Lefkowitz notes that in Greek myths, women are seen as advising male rulers, and even taking over some of their responsibilities. These Greek myths tell us about contradictions in ancient Greek society. As we can see, the universal theme of male-female relations is handled in similar ways in very different societies.

American Myths, Legends, and Folktales

One may pose the question: How does contemporary American culture articulate its myths, legends, or folktales? Myths deal with the remote past and with superhumans who created the world, the people in it, and all their material objects and cultural institutions. In stories about how American culture was forged and about its origins in the continental United States, legendary figures abound. Some were historical people, such as Billy the Kid, Davy Crockett, Daniel Boone, Kit Carson, Annie Oakley, and Buffalo Bill. Stories about their lives became legends, but some legends about them had no basis in fact. Other heroes, who are the subjects of folktales, such as Pecos Bill, John Henry, and Paul Bunyan, probably never lived. The setting for all these legends was the expanding American frontier. The stories demonstrated how these people (real and imagined) conquered obstacles in expanding the frontier. They were scouts who led the wagon trains across the Plains. They were explorers who opened up the rivers to settlement and commerce. They were railroad builders who laid the steel track across an expanding nation. They were the sheriffs and marshals who enforced American law. In these legends, the theme is a characteristically American one—the conquest of the frontier by individuals and the settlement of the land.

As often occurs in legends, American heroes assert the claim of a people to their land. This, of course, totally ignored and overrode the older claims of the Native American groups who were on the land first and were forcibly expelled or exterminated in battle. Their myths and legends recount tales of valor and bravery honoring their heroes who resisted this expansion and represented their people as brave warriors or in negotiations with the American government. In the next chapter, we will explore how these themes continue to be reflected in films, television programming, and other forms of popular culture.

While the legends of Paul Bunyan and other tall tales are indigenously American, many folktales and fairy tales told in America are largely derivative, having come with people from other countries. Joel Chandler Harris was a journalist and also a writer of short stores and the Uncle Remus tales. It was "his studies into folklore, and his writing of the tales told to him by American Blacks . . . that made him one of the nation's leading folklorists" (Brasch 2000: xxii). As a young man, Harris worked for a publisher who owned a plantation worked on by enslaved people. While sitting in the cabins of the enslaved workers on the plantation, he learned about their culture and heard their language and their stories, which he later transformed into the Uncle Remus stories. Brer Rabbit, a central character in the stories, is clearly a **trickster** figure, with his trickery, deceit, and deviousness. He and the other animals in the stories represent transformations of the animals with which the enslaved workers, who came from West Africa, were familiar. Portraits of the rabbit as a trickster also appear in the tales of the Creek, Natchez, and other southeastern Native American groups. Scholarly analysis has shown that some of the elements of these African-derived tales were borrowed by Native Americans, who were often in close contact with enslaved peoples throughout American history.

trickster

A common motif in folktales cross-culturally, an animal character that is conniving and sneaky, and occasionally but not always outsmarts others.

RELIGION, HISTORY, AND SCIENCE

To many people the distinction between religious, historical, and scientific systems of knowledge and explanation is not readily apparent. Ongoing debates about the teaching of the theory of evolution in American public schools demonstrate the conflicts between religious and scientific explanation. Based on the Old Testament book of Genesis, Judeo-Christian belief states that God created the universe, the earth, humans, and all species of life on earth. The seventeenth-century clergyman Bishop Ussher determined for Christians that creation occurred in the year 4004 BC Until the late nineteenth century, this was the accepted belief about creation in the Western world. In the mid-nineteenth century, Darwin proposed his theory of the evolution of species based upon empirical evidence from comparative anatomy, geology, botany, and paleontology. This scientific theory proposed an alternative explanation for the development of all the species in the world and the appearance of human life on earth. For a time, both religious and scientific explanations of creation competed with one another.

Today, many people in America express a belief in a creationist approach to human origins, broadly generalized as the belief that each of the species on earth was created and placed here by God as spelled out in the Book of Genesis. In reality there are multiple versions of **creationist belief systems**, among them Flat Earthers, Geocentrists, Young Earth Creationism, and Progressive Creationism, all of which hypothesize models of species and geological diversity based on varying interpretations of biblical and scientific sources (Scott 1999). Creationists in the United States have challenged the exclusive teaching of Darwinian scientific evolution in public schools and have argued, in courts, on school boards, and in state legislatures, that both creationism and evolutionary science should be taught to public school students as alternative theories for the origins of life on Earth. In 1987, the Supreme Court determined that teaching creationism in public schools was unconstitutional because it advanced a particular religious perspective. Proponents recast creationism into **Intelligent Design (ID)** theories, which in various versions accept some of the scientifically proposed theories for the age of the earth and its biological complexity but require the presence of deistic agency for the creation of the earth and its life forms and extinct forms like dinosaurs (Ross 2005). For many who accept Darwin's theory of evolution, religious ideology continues to be important in their personal worldview.

Observations of the world are the basis for scientific knowledge for people in all societies. The Trobrianders, when they constructed outrigger canoes, used their empirical knowledge and were capable of accurately predicting wind currents and the displacement of objects in the water. However, they had no scientific explanation based on empirical evidence for why the wind blows or why storms come up; in these unpredictable realms, they resorted to supernatural explanations. They tried to control the wind through the use of wind magic (Malinowski 1974). In American society, people regularly resort to nonscientific explanations. Scientific knowledge cannot at present determine why some people contract illnesses while others do not. If disease strikes, a patient may seek out religious intervention, such as faith healing or the "laying on of hands" while simultaneously aggressively pursuing medical treatment.

Science, magic, and religion are all ways of understanding the natural world. Magic and religion differ from science in that what is unexplained by science in the natural world is explained in magic and religion by recourse to the concept of the supernatural. **Magic** is based on the idea that there is a link between the supernatural and the natural world such that the natural world can be compelled to act in the desired way if the spell is performed as it should

creationist belief systems

Theories of human history based on interpretations of religious sources.

Intelligent Design (ID)

Theories of speciation and geological history that accept some scientifically proposed evolutionary models but require the presence of deistic agency for the creation of the earth and its diverse life forms.

magic

A system based on the belief that the natural world can be compelled to act in the desired way through human intervention.

science

A system of knowledge based on empirically determined connections between aspects of the natural world that will regularly result in predictable outcomes.

be. **Science**, on the other hand, is based on empirically determined logical connections between aspects of the natural world that will regularly result in predictable outcomes. Hypotheses concerning these logical connections are subject to change if new empirical data suggest better hypotheses. Science is based on empirical knowledge obtained through the five senses, whereas the defining feature of religion is acknowledgment of the supernatural, a belief that "transcends the reality amenable to the five senses" (Lett 1997: 104). The religious explanations and scientific explanations that we described above coexist and are not necessarily mutually exclusive.

CONCEPTUALIZING THE SUPERNATURAL

People who believe in any religion see the supernatural world as inhabited by a variety of superhuman creatures, agents, and forces whose actions will bring about good fortune or misfortune, rain or drought, famine or fertility, health or disease, and so forth. The natural world serves as a model, though not an exact one, for people's conceptualizations of the supernatural. It would be too simplistic to say that the supernatural world is simply a mirror image of people's life on earth. Nevertheless, there is a relationship between the social structure of a society and the way in which its supernatural world is organized. Similarly, the power relationships in the supernatural world are related to the kind of political organization found in society.

spirits

The general term for those that populate the supernatural realm.

The **spirits**, the general term for those that populate the supernatural realm, may be grouped into types using English terms to describe them. This is seen by some scholars as the imposition of Western or English-language concepts on non-Western indigenous categories. These terms therefore represent an English translation and not an exact equivalent. Spirits of the dead may be categorized chronologically in relation to the living, as ghosts of the recent dead, ancestor spirits of remote generations, and the ancestral spirits of the ancient past, who were group founders in mythological times. In societies with totemic clans, founding ancestors may be represented as animals. This belief in nonhumans as ancestors directly links the identity of human groups with particular animals or birds, and is usually accompanied by prohibitions against killing and eating the ancestral, or totemic, animal by group members.

deity

A spirit perceived as having human characteristics as well as supernatural power.

Some believe that all animal and plant species have both physical and spiritual components. The natural world is then seen as having its spiritual counterpart. Natural forces such as rain, thunder, lightning, wind, and tides may also be seen as spirits themselves, as motivated by spiritual beings, or as controlled by deities or gods. If the spirit is directly perceived as having human characteristics as well as supernatural power, then it is referred to as a god or **deity**; the population of gods and deities recognized by a society is a **pantheon**. The relationships between the gods of a pantheon are frequently conceived of in human terms. The gods may show jealousy, have sexual intercourse, quarrel, kill each other, and generally live much like human beings. Human characteristics are also attributed to ghosts and ancestral spirits in many societies. Any particular combination of different kinds of spiritual

pantheon

The population of gods and deities recognized by a society.

entities may be found in a given society. The supernatural world conforms to its own logic. Often people identify with an ideological system such as Judaism, Christianity, and Hinduism, and still maintain beliefs in ghosts, witches, and spirits of nature as parallel systems.

RELIGIOUS SPECIALISTS

The supernatural is often approached indirectly, through intermediaries who have access to it because they possess some special gift. Many have been through extensive training or are believed to have inherited esoteric knowledge or ability. Religious specialists, found in all societies, often have a primary function, such as curing illness or predicting the future. The English-language labels for these specialists—diviner, oracle, magician, shaman—usually refer to that specific function, though the translation of the indigenous terms for these specialists may not be exact. Religious specialists may operate on a full- or part-time basis; this distinction is generally linked to the sociopolitical system of the society being described.

Historically, in small-scale societies, a **shaman** was usually the only religious specialist. These part-time specialists used their powers primarily to diagnose illness, cure illness, and sometimes cause illness as well (Townsend 1997). They also had other functions, such as divining the future.

Shamanism in contemporary Siberia is found among the Buddhists of the Buryat Republic, and in Tuva, an autonomous, Turkic-speaking republic in the geographical center of Asia, both of which are part of the Russian Federation. Tuvan shamans are healers dealing with various diseases and with the loss of the soul. They treat the sick by holding séances, which begin at nightfall and last until dawn, during which the shaman contacts the spirits and "voyages" to the three worlds: the subterranean, the celestial, and the middle world of humans (Kenin-Lopsan 1997: 110). The shaman employs spirit-helpers, animals ranging in size and power from bears to moths, and these spirit-helpers are artistically portrayed on wands, which the shaman employs in the ceremony. In addition, the Tuvan shaman wears a decorated coat and boots, and uses a drum and a rattle.

The Tuvan shaman may also be called in to divine the location of game for a hunter. A childless couple may seek help from the shaman to "summon the soul" of an unborn infant to their home, a felt yurt (Kenin-Lopsan 1997: 127). Kenin-Lopsan, a Tuvan ethnographer who collected many poetic chants, or songs, performed by Tuvan shamans, pointed out that these songs were a major form of Tuvan artistic expression and served to keep the Tuvan language

shaman

Part-time ritual specialist who, depending on the cultural context, diagnoses and cures illness, causes illness, and divines the future.

An early twentieth-century Tlingit shaman wearing ritual paraphernalia shakes his oyster-catcher rattle at a person presumed to be using supernatural powers to cause harm.

alive. Tuvan shamans employed the "throat singing" for which Tuva is famous. In this special kind of singing, they imitated the languages of their animal spirit-helpers (Kenin-Lopsan 1997: 132–33). Tuvan shamans may be female or male. Tuvan shamanism was outlawed during the Soviet period, but has been revived in the post-Soviet era. Shamanistic practices continue to be an integral part of Tuvan culture, and today, in particular, are part of their ethnic identity; Russian, European, and American tourists travel to Siberia seeking encounters with "shaman gurus" (Kehoe 2000: 19). Instead of being replaced by scientific theories of curing, shamanism has actually undergone a present-day revival (Winkelman 2000; McClenon 2002). These authors suggest that as a cross-cultural experience, such as New Yorkers studying shamanistic practices of Latin America, it provides a mechanism for stepping outside one's self, to take a journey to another land, to return in a reborn form, and thereby to acquire a new self-awareness.

Shamanism has taken on a modern appearance in contemporary societies in Asia. Before Korea began its rapid industrialization, shamanic rituals were held in response to life-threatening illnesses and to promote the health, harmony, and prosperity of small farming families. These families were primarily rural in outlook, though they were tied to urban commercial markets (Kendall 2001: 522). In the 1970s, Korea embarked on a course toward modernity. Government policy stressed that shamanism "deluded the people" and fostered "irrational" beliefs (Kendall 2001: 29). In popular practice, however, shamanic rituals aimed at "reconciliations between the living members of the household and their gods and ancestors who appear . . . in the person of costumed shamans." These rituals were increasingly accepted as part of "national culture" because they were considered ancient Korean traditions. Today these same shamanic rituals have spread from the rural farmers to a new class of small-businesspeople and entrepreneurs living in the cities who are holding ceremonies to ensure success in their business enterprises as well as to cure their illnesses. For those engaged in high-risk enterprises, business is precarious. and success or failure seems arbitrary and beyond their control. Thus, "doing well by the spirits" is important. Since financial distress and worry can often lead to illness, it is understandable that these ceremonies serve multiple functions (Kendall 1996b: 516–18).

Diviners are part-time religious specialists who use the supernatural to enable people to make decisions concerning how they should act in order to have success. Archaeological remains suggest that the Chinese many millennia ago used the cracks in tortoise shells to foretell the future. They also used **geomancy**—the interpretations of the future from cracks in dried mud—and other fortunetelling devices. Diviners use many different methods to gain their information; chickens or other animals are killed and their entrails inspected and interpreted to determine what action to take in the future. In our own society, many people seek help to divine what their future holds for them. Fortunetellers in storefronts in many cities, large and small, as well as at rural county fairs are paid to read palms, tea leaves, and Tarot cards, and to look into crystal balls to see the future. The services of astrologers, who

diviners

Part-time religious specialists who manipulate the supernatural to enable people to succeed in specific undertakings.

geomancy

The interpretation of the future from physical objects.

foretell the future from the positions of the stars, are sought out by Americans of all religions and classes; former White House chief of staff Donald Regan claimed that then-First Lady Nancy Reagan, wife of President Ronald Reagan, regularly sought out the services of an astrologer in scheduling public appearances to protect her husband's safety.

Since there is a logical connection between curing illness and causing it, in many societies the same specialist sometimes performs both functions. Anthropologists define **sorcery** as a set of these skills that are learned, whereas other people are born with a propensity toward **witchcraft**. Witchcraft and sorcery involve the use of supernatural means to cause bad things to happen to one's enemies, or to the enemies of individuals who engage the services of a sorcerer. These enemies may be outside one's own group or may be someone within one's own group with whom there is conflict. Kwakwaka'wala shamans could use sorcery against enemy groups. Among the Trobrianders, as noted in chapter 9, the people of a district feared that their chief would use sorcery against them if they went against his commands. These examples illustrate how sorcery can be used as a means of sociopolitical control.

Accusations of witchcraft are usually made in such a way that they reveal the cleavages in a society. Douglas (1991) compared witch trials of sixteenth-century England and the accusations of witchcraft among Yao villagers from Malawi in the 1950s. She concludes that witches are generally people on the less powerful side of a power conflict. They are accused of antisocial behavior or libeled by their accusers. Women are particularly vulnerable to charges of witchcraft in societies that practice virilocal postmarital residence patterns. Bhil women, a group designed as a Scheduled Tribe in Rajasthan, who marry into their husbands' villages, are strangers to their husband's community. If they become widowed and especially if they are childless, they lose their fragile ties to their communities of residence. Accusations of witchcraft against them may be used by their husband's kin to undercut potential claims to inheriting an interest in their husband's property. Contemporary Indian civil law supports widow inheritance, but in practice few Bhil women invoke these claims through the courts. "Her status as an outsider—and a witch—may be brought to bear particularly if it is in the interests of her husband's patrilineage to drive her out of the community, or at least the realm of respectability, in cases of dispute over property and inheritance" (Weisgrau 1997: 130).

Magic, witchcraft, and sorcery all involve the manipulation of the supernatural. Magicians direct supernatural forces toward a positive goal—to help individuals or the whole community. In parts of Melanesia, part-time religious specialists carry out magical rites to bring rain, promote fertility in the gardens, and ensure successful fishing. The garden magician among the Trobrianders is one of the most important people in the village. He recites his magical spells and performs his rituals at every stage of the process of growing yams, and what he does is seen as being as essential to the growth and maturation of crops as weeding and hoeing. He officiates at a large-scale ceremony involving all the men of the village that takes place before any gardening begins. He carries out specific rites at the planting and weeding and

sorcery

The learned practices of magic, usually for negative purposes.

witchcraft

A form of magic or manipulation practiced by individuals presumed to be born with this ability.

in assisting the plants to sprout, bud, grow, climb, and produce the yams. Since the garden magician must perform rites before each stage of production, through his spells he acts, in effect, to coordinate and regulate the stages of work throughout the entire village (Malinowski 1935). Each village has its own special system of garden magic, which is passed on by matrilineal inheritance, so a sister's son succeeds his mother's brother as garden magician.

Magical practices have always coexisted with formal religious doctrine in many societies. The belief in "the evil eye" operates in many European societies in the same way as witchcraft. If misfortune occurs, it is assumed to have happened because of the use of the evil eye by some enemy. People believe that it is dangerous to praise a child as beautiful, strong, or healthy, since this will create jealousy on the part of others and cause them to invoke the evil eye. Various kinds of magic, including protective devices and verbal ritual formulas, are used to ward off the evil eye. Among the Basseri, a nomadic pastoral society of Iran, a mirror is placed on the back of the horse on which the bride is taken to her groom, since a joyous occasion such as a wedding is likely to promote envy on the part of some onlookers. The mirror is used to reflect the evil eye back to its sender. Communities of believers around the world, despite their religious affiliation, recite magical spells to ward off the evil eye, wear charms and religious medals to bring good fortune, and adorn their homes and vehicles with religious symbols to serve as protection against harm. These are all forms of magic practiced today.

Historically, with the emergence of class divisions in states, religion became more elaborate and differentiated as a separate institution. In contrast to the shaman and the magician, who operate as individual practitioners and part-time specialists, **priests** are fulltime religious practitioners who carry out codified and elaborate rituals, and their activities are associated with a shrine or temple. The body of ritual knowledge, which is the priest's method of contacting the supernatural, must be learned over a lengthy period of time. Archaeological data on Mesopotamia reveals that in societies that were the forerunners of full-fledged states, there was a single figure that was both the political and religious head of the community, and there was a priestly class supporting the ruler. Subsequently, as the state evolved, there was a separation of political and religious positions. The class of religious specialists was but one of a number of stratified classes in an increasingly more hierarchically organized society.

Priestly classes were intimately associated with development and control of the calendar in the early civilizations of the Maya and the Aztecs, and in Egypt and Mesopotamia. It is not known whether priests invented the calendar, but it was used for determining when communal religious rites should take place. In these early civilizations, the priesthood seems also to have been associated with scientific observations of the heavens. In ancient Egypt, the flooding of the Nile was absolutely regular; its onset could be dated 365 days from the last onset. The development of a solar calendar, in place of the more widespread lunar calendar, enabled the flooding to be predicted. The development of this solar calendar depended on astronomical knowledge about the positions of

---

priests

Fulltime religious practitioners who carry out codified and elaborated rituals based on a body of knowledge learned over a lengthy period of time.

the sun, moon, and stars. The ability to predict natural phenomena, such as the yearly flooding, was associated with priestly proximity to the supernatural. This knowledge was closely guarded by the priests, and other groups were forbidden access to this information. This control over critical information in turn gave the leader great power over other classes.

RELIGIOUS SYNCRETISM: RELIGIONS AND THEIR ADAPTATIONS TO CHANGE

All religions believe that their rituals have been practiced since time immemorial; in reality religious institutions all respond to changing conditions and are influenced by other belief systems. The term **syncretism** refers to the integration of cultural traits into existing cultural practices. As we've documented, people practicing all religions wear amulets to ward off the evil eye, seek advice from fortunetellers, and go to faith healers to be cured by the laying on of hands. Various earlier pre-Christian beliefs, including belief in local spirits, were incorporated into Christianity as it spread through Europe. In America, this process has produced new forms of Christianity and Islam, for example, Mormonism (Church of Jesus Christ of Latter-day Saints), Christian Science (Church of Christ, Scientist), and the Nation of Islam.

syncretism

The integration of ideas and newly adopted practices in cultural practices.

BOX 10.1 | Religion and the Covid-19 Virus in the United States

Gallup, Inc., has been conducting public opinion polls in the United States since 1935; the Gallup Poll conducts daily telephone interviews with people on a wide variety of subjects, including patterns of religious beliefs, institutional membership, and regular attendance. Their polls in 2020 documented significant shifts in self-reported religious affiliation and formal membership between 2000 and 2020. Although some of the decline may be attributed to the Covid-19 epidemic, observers believe these declines may represent more significant and permanent levels of religious organization affiliation, especially among younger generations.

The Covid-19 pandemic had significant impacts on religious practice. "The abrupt cessation of in-person worship in churches, synagogues and mosques around the country [due to Covid-19] is one of the most significant sudden disruptions in the practice of religion in U.S. history" (Newport 2020). Religious adaptations to new conditions is not, however, a new concept. In the United

States, religious entities have been using "new" methods of communication to reach and increase their audiences—first radio, then television; and, in recent years, well before the current crisis, online technologies.

It is unclear what the long-term impact on religious attendance will be when social distancing mandates are removed; this will probably take years to determine. But people have indicated that the pandemic had an impact on the overall faith. "Close to 20% of Americans interviewed between March 28 and April 1 [2020] said their faith or spirituality has gotten better as a result of the crisis, while 3% say it has gotten worse" (Newport 2020). More people reported that their overall mental health, diet and exercise got worse, not better, during the epidemic. "But the fact that almost one in five Americans report that their faith or spirituality has gotten better as a result of the virus situation suggests the possibility of some sort of religious renaissance" (Newport 2020).

Sometimes entirely new religions, such as Scientology, emerge. Although the forms of religious expression may change, the functions they fulfill for their followers remain constant.

In the United States, we have also had a period of religious transformation and innovation, which began in the 1970s following the demise of the counterculture movements of the "flower children" of the 1960s. These alternative religious movements are sometimes referred to as **New Age Movements** or New Religious Movements. Nontraditional religious movements have a long history in the United States. Some of these groups, for example, the Shakers, are only minimally present today, while others, the Mormons, for example, continue stronger than ever. In recent years, the immigration of many non-Westerners, Buddhists, Muslims, Hindus, and others into our now multicultural, pluralistic society have introduced still other religious belief systems into the mix. Many of the New Religious Movements are cultural transplants representing groups of Asian and African origin. These New Religious Movements are seen as "different responses to the failure of mainline religious traditions to provide a meaningful moral context for everyday life" (Bromley 1998: 330).

Westerners disillusioned with their own religious institutions have turned to alternative belief systems categorized as "neoshamanism." As Atkinson notes, "[Shamanism] presents . . . a spiritual alternative for Westerners estranged from Western religious traditions" (1992: 322). Neoshamanism claims to be nonhierarchical in comparison with traditional Western religions, emphasizes self-help, and links participants to nature. Consequently, it is appealing to seekers of alternative religious experiences who are disillusioned with the ideologies and restrictions of the major religions.

Witchcraft has existed in America, in one form or another, from the seventeenth century on. There have been periodic infusions from Europe as its popularity waxed and waned. Although witches today see themselves as the reborn victims of witch-hunts in past centuries, in fact, there have been no accusations of witchcraft paralleling those in sixteenth-century England and seventeenth-century Salem (Orion 1995: 52). The flowering of what has come to be known as the "neopagan" religion, or Wicca, began in the 1960s. Wicca in America is democratized, individualized, highly creative, and inventive. Its major focus has been to disown, by lifestyle, word, and philosophy, the religious and political ideas that dominate the rest of American society (Orion 1995). Wicca is therefore a pointed rejection of Christianity: it is both pre-Christian and the object of Christian persecution.

Wicca rituals usually involve the sacred circle, formed of individuals whose constant circular movement generates a cone of energy directed to specific tasks to better the earth. This is also seen as a form of therapeutic "healing magic," releasing and dissipating "maladaptive emotional states" for the individual as well as for the earth by creative energy. Wicca celebrations mark the solstices, equinoxes, and key occasions of the agricultural year, as well as biweekly Sabbaths. They also have come to include rite-of-passage ceremonies,

New Age Movements

Alternative, small scale, and/or new religious movements.

such as Wiccaning, the blessing and presenting of infants to the pagan spirits; girls' and boys' puberty rites or initiation; handfasting, the tying together of the hands of the couple at a ceremony to signify trial or permanent marriage; and ritual preparation for death. The Wicca pantheon has the Mother Goddess, giver of life and incarnate love; the Sun; and the Moon at the core. In addition, magical beliefs from ancient Egypt, Greece, Babylonia, and the Jewish Kabbalah, as well as Celtic, Druid, Norse, and Welsh pagan beliefs, have been included in some iterations. Women usually enjoy a special status, and the person of the high priestess is venerated.

The stone circles of Stonehenge in England regularly attract Wiccan and other alternative religious followers to celebrate seasonal rituals marking solstice transitions.

An emphasis on feminist spirituality, which developed as an offshoot of radical feminism in the 1970s, influenced Wicca and the American neopagan movement and gave rise to the "American Goddess movement." It is an eclectic movement with "beliefs and practices that are becoming increasingly idiosyncratic . . . dynamic, [with an] increasingly diverse form of popular religiosity that has emerged among women" (Gottschall 2000: 60). In southern California, for example, Goddess believers gather to celebrate summer and winter solstices and pagan holidays such as Hallomas and Lammas as large public rituals with belly dancers, drummers, poets, and vocalists (2000: 61–62). Goddess worshipers see their practice of Wicca religion as challenging the patriarchal religious framework that characterizes the major world religions.

CYBERSPACE AND RELIGION

One can go on the internet, click on the Digital Avatar site, and the cyber version of a Kali temple welcomes you with the image of the god Siva. A menu of worship experiences appears from the mystical utterance of Vedic praise, which affirms the totality of creation, to meditation while watching a mystical, rapid alteration of Siva images. Alternatively, one can follow the Tweets of the Pope, or find a Facebook page for any religious affiliation. All the major religions in the world, as well as newer religious groups, recognize the vast global audience they reach in cyberspace and through social media (Mahan 2014). Most Protestant denominations have their own websites. Christian sects in America have a long tradition of preaching their beliefs, first in churches, then on radio and television and now on a large variety of websites with streaming video links. Muslims use websites to announce prayer times in a host of cities. American Buddhism, Tibetan Buddhism, and Zen Buddhism are well represented online, as are sites for Hindu temples and gurus such as Sri Sathya Sai Baba. Even the Amish in Pennsylvania, who do not use cars but ride in horse-drawn carriages, have a website, as do neopagans who are "revising customary neopagan rituals for a virtual environment . . . and designing new ones for cyberspace" (Brasher 2001: 87, 88). The global reach of internet websites creates transnational communities of religious followers, and may be used to share political as well as religious views across borders.

There are links to "cyberheaven," where one can memorialize one's deceased relative with a picture and brief tribute to that relative. This is part of a category of sites not connected to any one religious group; these sites allow individuals to utilize a website as a virtual sacred place, or preach their own religious ideas and create their own rituals. Cyberspace has also become the location for apocalyptic and messianic websites, as well as those devoted to religious satire. The internet, in theory, provides equal opportunity for both mainstream and alternative voices to represent their perspectives; Brasher suggests that online religious activity "could become the dominant form of religion and religious experience in the [twenty-first] century" (2001: 19).

The intersection of religion and the internet is undeniable, and has been reinforced during some of the outbreak periods of Covid-19 and other communicable diseases. But the nature of that intersection is debated; scholars are only recently exploring the implications of cyberspace and the human-technology interface for religious belief systems. "Boosters of the Internet in its earliest days saw the 'information superhighway' as it was dubbed, as having a utopian potential to revolutionize social relationships. . . . It soon became evident that in many ways, the Internet mirrored existing social relationships" (Henderson 2007: 62).

While the internet presents the possibility of endless streams of information about both traditional and nontraditional religious practices, access to this information is mediated by familiar forms of market capitalism: "A user's access to websites reflects his or her computer's operating system and software. . . . Not all search engines gain access to all sites. An individual user's preferred search engine, or browser—and different versions of this—determines search outcomes" (Henderson 2007: 68). The "digital divide"—the lack of access to computers and internet technology for some—remains a global reality; access tends to be high among elites and the middle class and much lower among more economically and socially marginalized groups.

Cowan (2005b) identifies major differences between online interactive ritual and "real life" experiences.

Contemporary religious institutions adapt to an online presence. All religions worldwide modify and change ideology and practice over time to meet the changing communication and worship practices of followers, as is demonstrated in this tweet by Pope Francis.

Pope Francis ✔
@Pontifex

...

Poor people are not "outside" our communities. They are brothers and sisters whose suffering we share, in order to alleviate their difficulties and marginalization, so that their lost dignity might be restored, and to ensure their necessary social inclusion. #EndPoverty

7:30 AM · Oct 17, 2022 · TweetDeck

1,394 Retweets **66** Quote Tweets **7,554** Likes

Online, rituals are text-based rather than experiential; instructions and responses are read and typed. The ritual environment is imagined or reproduced in two dimensions rather than experienced; the use of a candle, for example, as a word or computer image as opposed to rituals experienced through sight and smell on an altar, will result in very different responses. The practice of religion, Cowan argues, is not likely to be replaced by online experience. "While we may interact with each other through the computer, we do not live 'life on the screen.' Indeed, throughout our online experience, the offline world constantly impinges; it continually reminds us of its presence and its power" (2005b: 262).

POLITICS, RELIGIONS, AND STATES

In today's world, religion plays an extremely important role in politics. In a sense, we have come full circle. When states and civilization began, political and religious institutions were intertwined. This connection between politics and religion has been widespread throughout history and in different societies and is a characteristic of contemporary politics around the world. For example, today, political parties in Europe often have religious labels, such as the Christian Democratic party in Germany. Civil war in Sri Lanka was mobilized around the two major religions in the country: Buddhism and Hinduism. Former American president George W. Bush regularly and publicly discussed his religious identity as a "born-again Christian" and the effect of his religious ideas on national and international policy formation. Many Republican candidates in American election campaigns explicitly reference their religious identity among their credentials, and how their religion related to their visions of national and international policy.

The label **fundamentalism** is widely and often ambiguously applied to an ever-widening range of political and religious ideologies. This term historically "connotes an attachment to a set of irreducible beliefs or a theology that forestalls further question" (Nagata 2001: 481). It is now attached to a wide range of religious and political movements in both scholarly and journalistic sources; its very ambiguity often invokes emotional responses in the reader. Nagata (2001) identifies some characteristics of its use in multiple sources; it is invariably used to describe an "other" and is rarely a term of self-identification in religious or political discourse. Through general usage, "fundamentalism" invokes a religious perspective; however, it is also used to describe a wide range of political ideologies including ultranationalisms, extreme ethnic chauvinisms, as well as often-violent movements for linguistic and cultural purity (2001: 493). Fundamentalism, wherever it is found, is characterized by a certainty of its principles, focus on difference rather than shared interests with others, a rejection of relativism, and "a retreat from ecumenism and dialogue" (2001: 494).

Violence and conflict perpetrated in the name of religion are widespread phenomena in the twenty-first century. Chirot (2011) analyzes many of these forms of conflict around the world and sees the role of religion as embedded

fundamentalism

A range of political and religious ideologies generally connoting a set of beliefs accepted as irreducible that forestall further inquiry or debate.

in broader issues of ethnicity and nationalism in pluralistic states. Some examples of ethnic conflict mobilized around religious identities originate in claims for sovereignty or power; "ethnic and nationalist wars can amount to the same thing" (2011: ix). These forms of conflict often result when the two sides in the conflict over power and political dominance identify as different religious groups. "Looking, for example, at the Catholic-Protestant conflict in Northern Ireland in the late twentieth century, it is evident that it had almost nothing to do with theological disputes, but was really between two different ethnic groups that spoke the same language, lived in the same state, but rarely intermarried or socialized with each other" (2011: x). There is no inevitability to conflict between religious groups; people of different religions can coexist in the same communities for centuries until these identities and loyalties are mobilized around political or factional objectives.

WHY RELIGION?

Much of religious behavior has an instrumental goal; that is, the individual has some particular goal in mind when the religious ritual is performed. Those who carry out the rites and perform the spells desire to produce results, such as stopping a storm, bringing rain, or ensuring fertility for their crops. The Inuit shaman contacts spirits to find out where hunters should go to find prey. The Trobriand garden magician recites the particular spells that will make the yams grow. In many cultures, women perform religious rites to help them become pregnant. For example, in Poland, Catholic women go to the tombs of Catholic saints; Orthodox Jewish women in Israel go to the tomb of Rachael, in Hebron, with the same goal. The motives and goals in all these cases are to bring about specific results—to make natural forces and natural processes respond to human need.

Ritual practices have particular effects that the individual or groups of participants may not be aware of. These are different from the conscious goals and purposes of the participants themselves. American baseball players use magic rituals and formulas in areas of the game most fraught with uncertainty—hitting and pitching (Gmelch 1971). Reducing anxiety for the pitcher or the hitter and giving the individual a sense of confidence, even if it is false confidence, improves performance. Anxiety is reduced for the Korean businessman after he goes through the performance of a shamanic ritual. He feels more confident as a consequence. However, one could argue that anxiety itself has important functions in dangerous situations. Under such circumstances, adrenaline should be flowing and all of one's senses should be alerted to potential danger. When a person is faced with uncertainty in possibly dangerous situations, alertness to the real dangers and confidence in one's ability to cope with the situation are the most desirable mix and can be brought about by performing some magical or religious ritual.

Predictions of social scientists in the mid-twentieth century that economic development and modernization would result in global secularization have not come to pass. Religious ideology and identity dominate national and international policy. They shape the outcome of elections and motivate invasion and military action. In pluralistic states worldwide, religious identity continues to be the basis of discrimination and violence against minorities. In the twenty-first century, it's impossible to think about contemporary states and geopolitics without thinking about the religious identities of those in and out of power.

SUMMARY

- Religion is generally defined as the cultural means by which humans deal with the supernatural; some religious systems integrate the supernatural realm into their overall system of beliefs about the world in general.

- Religion fulfills certain universal functions, such as the allaying of anxiety; explanatory functions, which answer such questions as why humans came to be on earth and the meaning of life; and expiatory function, in which individuals are assisted with guilt and misfortune.

- Humans attempt to understand and at least influence or control through a belief in the supernatural what is otherwise uncontrollable and unexplainable, and by doing this, they alleviate anxieties about their helplessness in the situation.

- In terms of its explanatory function, religion is to be distinguished from science in that the latter is based on observations and the former on belief.

- Magic and religion differ from science in that what is unexplained by science in the natural world is explained in magic and religion by recourse to the concept of the supernatural.

- Societies have a variety of ways of conceiving of the supernatural and telling stories about this realm. These conceptualizations are directly related to the ways in which their societies are organized, and are reinforced through national ideologies and practices.

- Myths, legends, and folktales all include some form of supernatural elements that provide guidelines for valued cultural behavior.

- Myths deal with the remote past, often with the time of the origin of things both natural and cultural, and are associated with the sacred.

- Legends are stories that combine the supernatural with some historical context.

- Folktales deal with an indeterminate time and combine stories that imbue animals and humans with superhuman powers with a moral or lesson for contemporary listeners.

- When transmitted orally, each telling of a myth, legend, or folktale is a performance. When they are written down or filmed, they become part of a culture's creative legacy.

- The population of gods and deities recognized by a society is a pantheon. The relationships between the gods of a pantheon are frequently conceived of in human terms.

- In some societies, such as those of Native Americans who lived on the Plains, individuals go out alone to seek a vision of an animal spirit, which then becomes their protector and guardian spirit throughout life.

- Priests are fulltime religious specialists. Classes of priests are associated with economic specialization that characterizes both ancient and modern states.

- Part-time religious specialists such as shamans, witches, and diviners, coexist with fulltime religious specialists in contemporary states.

- Often, people believe in a monotheistic religion such as Judaism, Christianity, and Islam, and still maintain beliefs in ghosts, witches, and spirits of nature as parallel systems.

- Generally speaking, human beings approach the supernatural by carrying out ritual acts, usually involving a combination of speech and patterned behavior that alters the emotional state of the participants.

- Secular or nonreligious rituals, and rites of intensification, may be used to present, as well as resist and rewrite, narratives of history to include previously unheard versions and perspectives.

- Rites of passage are found in all societies; they recognize and mark the transition of life stages, as well as enforce gender norms associated with each life stage.

- All religions adapt to the environments of their practitioners; religious syncretism conceptualizes how religious practices incorporate new ideas in new settings.

- Although religion is invoked in political movements and in sites of conflict, there is no necessity of conflict between different religious groups. Long periods of coexistence can be interrupted with outbursts of political discourse that encourages conflict and competition between religious groups.

KEY TERMS

SUGGESTED READINGS

Mahan, Jeffrey H. *Media, Religion and Culture: An Introduction*. New York: Routledge, 2014.

   A discussion, with detailed case studies from around the world, of religious content in the media, and new forms of religious voices using websites, social media, TV, and print media.

McCleary, Thimothy P. *The Stars We Know: Crow Indian Astronomy and Lifeways*. 2nd ed. Long Grove, IL. Waveland Press, 2012.

   This ethnography explores how Crow Indians have blended empirical observation and analysis with religious symbolism. Systematic observations of the stars, sun, moon, and planets shape the principles of Crow values and ethics.

Rouse, Carolyn Moxley. *Engaged Surrender: African American Women and Islam*. Berkeley: University of California Press, 2006.

   An ethnography exploring the lives of African American women in California who convert to Islam. They articulate their religious conversion from the perspectives of racism, capitalism, theology, and faith in their daily lives.

SUGGESTED WEBSITES

https://sar.americananthro.org/

   The website of the Society for the Anthropology of Religion, a section of the American Anthropological Association. This website contains references and resources, including an extensive list of recently published ethnographies focusing on the practice of religion in contemporary America and around the world.

http://www.history.com/topics/thanksgiving

   Video content and discussions, historical myths, and realities about Thanksgiving celebrations in America.

http://www.thefuneralsource.org/trad01.html

   A compendium of funeral practices and traditions for various groups in the United States and in other countries.

Chapter 11

Spaces and Places of Creative Expression

LEARNING OBJECTIVES

- Identify various forms of creative expression and their audiences.
- Understand how creativity relates to other aspects of culture, including gender, ritual, religion, politics, and social organization.

- Explore how art and digital media operate in the representation and contestation of identities.
- Discuss the role of social media in challenging political and cultural norms.

IN MANY PARTS OF THE world, art, myth, and performance are interdependent. Similar concepts can be expressed in spoken and written words, in actions, and in visual forms. The interconnection between performance, myth, creative expression, and ritual, as discussed in the previous chapter, illustrates this point. Music, dance, theater, and film are considered performing arts because their creation and subsequent performance evokes emotion in an audience, and they can be evaluated in terms of both aesthetics and competence by that audience. In contrast to painting and sculpture, music, dance, and cinema are like spoken language in three important aspects. All three unfold through time. Every sentence, every musical composition, every dance, every scene has a beginning, a middle, and an end. This is not true of a painting or a carving, which has no beginning or ending and for which the dimension of time is irrelevant. Once made, films, paintings and sculptures continue to exist. Musical compositions, theatrical events, and dance performances were once considered ephemeral; the performance of the piece dies away when it has been completed. But these distinctions become blurred when recording technologies are considered.

In many societies, masculine and feminine are differentiated spheres of expressive activity. Some forms of performance and creativity may be dominated by masculine performers while others are the exclusive domain of feminine styles. The genre or type of performance, the style of the performance, and the location of the performance may vary by gender. The expectations of the audience often include gender and sexuality norms in performances; these expectations are often undermined by explicitly "gender bending" creative performance. For example, the history of painting and sculpture for hundreds of years in the European centers of production was dominated by a tradition of masculine producers representing cultural ideals of heterosexuality, masculinity, and representations of the feminine body. In the twenty-first century, feminine, non-binary, and transgendered creators demand their spaces and voices of self-representation, previously silenced in heteronormative artistic production, be visible in all forms of media.

The recording of previously ephemeral performances, on film and more recently using video technology on cell phones and other handheld devices, is a modern phenomenon. These performances now exist in multiple sites on the internet, giving them an existence throughout time. This is just one of many examples of how digital media is transforming the understanding of the production and display of creative arts. In today's world, the creation of a piece of artwork or a film, a museum exhibition or a public performance, is interdependent with communication about it, and the reactions to it, on electronic media. Some forms of creative experiences are lived exclusively through the internet and social media. Streaming services on the internet like Netflix and Amazon Prime are now also producers of cinematic content, produced to be viewed exclusively on internet streaming services, bypassing movie theaters and traditional systems of film distribution.

Anthropology is often said in part to make "the familiar strange" or to explore the multiple meanings and constructions of aspects of everyday life that are often taken for granted. Electronic media and communication are familiar and omnipresent globally. Anthropologists are exploring the impact of the internet and of social media in the production and consumption of all forms of traditional expression (by artists, writers, filmmakers, museum curators), and by individuals using new forms of expression (e.g., TikTok postings and Facebook pages, internet pages, and streaming services). Where previously the audience for performances and art exhibitions was limited to ticket holders in one location, audiences and viewers are now everywhere an electronic device and a Wi-Fi signal are available.

Anthropological and ethnographic approaches to these everyday phenomena with which so many people engage on a daily basis give us an opportunity to explore their components and cultural dynamics. These approaches emphasize how digital technology penetrates everyday life, but not what its boundaries are with "the real world."

The term **virtuality** captures the essence of the "huge swaths of human activity [that] have migrated to where we work, play, study, love, rear children, form relationships, take care of ourselves and essentially, *exist* through digital technology" (emphasis in original) (Nardi 2015: 16). The concept of virtuality includes the collective activities that involve multiple digital technologies, including but not limited to the internet, video, podcasts, games and online worlds, podcasts, and databases. The use and understanding of the internet has changed dramatically over the course of past two decades; its various components are now deeply embedded within contemporary lives. It is something new, with no historical parallel, that has to be understood on its own terms (Boellstroff 2012). This perspective provides a window onto how users of these technologies produce and consume creative output in a variety of different forms around the world.

virtuality

Collective activities that have been normalized through digital technologies.

ART AS COMMUNICATION, EXPERIENCE, AND RESISTANCE

Children worldwide now integrate electronic devices and social media into their daily activities. Experts are unsure of the long-term effects on childhood socialization of many hours of online communication instead of more traditional forms of childhood play and face-to-face interaction.

The kind of production that the Western world labels "art" is not a universal one. Objects that were formed in non-Western settings to meet local utilitarian needs were frequently embellished and decorated; if they are displayed in Euro-American museums or sold in galleries, they are referred to as "tribal art." In reality these objects were produced for aesthetic or emotional reasons, or to communicate a message of identity or group membership. Artistic production is a mode of communication; it communicates information, thought, and emotion. Dance and gesture, poetry and music, painting, sculpture, and architecture are all part of this system of visual communication.

On the Northwest Coast of the United States and West Coast of Canada, masks, totem poles, sculpted house posts, painted house fronts, decorated ceremonial bowls, and other objects include designs that represent particular clans. These designs depict the mythological ancestors of the clan, such as the wolf, the grizzly bear, the sea

bear, the raven, the eagle, and the killer whale. The message conveyed is that the created object represents the kin group. Objects are created for use at rituals, for example, the masks worn by participants at the wedding potlatch described in chapter 2. During such rituals, stories recounting the adventures of the mythological ancestor will be told, or the dance or song associated with that myth will be performed. These performances also communicate emotion. The emotion may be awe, as is the case when statues represent powerful supernatural spirits. It may be terror, as invoked by Poro masks from West Africa. It may be mirth and pleasure, as when masked dancers carry out their antics or when satirical performances caricature pomposity.

Art in the Western world traditionally was produced for "consumption"—to be viewed, sometimes purchased, hung in museums, galleries, and homes, or to be performed in concerts before large paying audiences. In the societies that anthropologists first studied, art was embedded in all aspects of culture. Ritual performances employed art, and the meanings that the art communicated related to the meaning of the ritual and the mythology associated with it. But today Australian indigenous artists and artists from the Northwest Coast use nontraditional techniques (silkscreen prints or acrylic paints) embodying traditional styles of art, which is exhibited and sold in galleries around the world. Artists of the Tiwi Islands are distinguishing themselves in the global art marketplace from other artistic communities by rejecting the use of acrylics and canvas and using only naturally occurring local sources for their pigments. "They are also using traditional wooden combs to apply pigments to paper, board or linen, much as it was used to paint their ancestors' bodies" (Perlez 2016). Native American artists are using new creative techniques, such as creating their images in glass, adding new dimensions to their own representation of traditional mythic and ritual figures.

Today, art is found in public parks, on streets, and on buildings and is spontaneously produced on any surface available to an individual looking for a medium of creative expression. Painted murals on buildings or other public surfaces provide a visual reminder of important people in communities that are not included in official narratives of history or representation. These murals and other forms of public art give voice to creative people and their messages of resistance to the political and artistic control by dominant society. Sometimes these counterculture artists and their creations become recognized by traditional arbiters of art and creativity, and their works become part of the artistic establishment. In this process, the mainstream definition of, and audience for, artistic creation is transformed, creating new markets for the consumption of new art forms.

Major artists now recognized by the international art market, like Banksy (a pseudonym for an unidentified artist) and Keith Haring, began their careers as graffiti artists in New York City. They put their images on any surface they could find, often using subway stations or trains themselves as their "canvas" and dodging law enforcement as they created. Their works were discovered by art galleries and museum curators, and now command great sums of money for purchase on the art market. But they continue to see themselves as subverting and resisting the norms of artistic commodification; Banksy created a work in 2018 that automatically shredded itself after being auctioned for over $5 million.

These contemporary innovations in creative production are important reminders that artistic media are always changing. Forms of creative expression and the sites of production and consumption are all fluid backdrops against which to discuss historical and contemporary approaches cross-culturally, to understand the content and contexts of creative expression, and most importantly to recognize their meaning to the people who create them and the audiences who see and react to them.

ART AND ARTISTS

One approach to the cultural understanding of artistic production focuses on the style of an individual artist and the features that are characteristic of a particular artist. Sometimes the art style of a village, city, or region can be identified. It is more frequent to refer to the art style of a single society and/ or a time period. Contemporary Northwest Coast artists, such as the remarkable Haida carver Bill Reid, use the traditional content and the distinctive style of Northwest Coast art but add their own individual quality to it. The style of each artist is therefore different, as is the case for European and American artists. The sculpture in bronze by Bill Reid, patinated to look like argillite and titled *The Spirit of Haida Gwaii*, exemplifies the combination of traditional themes from Haida mythology with the genius of a creative artist. It is displayed in a public urban setting outside the Canadian Embassy in Washington, DC. A second version of the full-sized sculpture, *The Spirit of Haida Gwaii, the Jade Canoe*, is now on display in the International Terminal at Vancouver International Airport. The public display of Bill Reid's work recognizes the skills of the Haida artist and the association of the Haida with Canadian identity, as well as the artistic traditions his work represents.

"The Jade Canoe" sculpture of the Spirit of Haida Gwaii, *by Haida artist Bill Reid, located in the Vancouver International Airport; a second version is displayed prominently outside the Canadian Embassy in Washington, DC. These public displays of Haida mythological figures underscore Canadian recognition of the indigenous communities throughout Canada and the contributions of their contemporary artists.*

Within the cultural context and in the community in which art is produced, the creativity of the individual artist is usually recognized and rewarded, and the names of superior artists are known and recognized. However, some art became anonymous, with no artist's name attached to it when it was extracted from its original cultural context and transformed into objects displayed in Western museums. Contrary to the traditional assumptions of Western art historians, the creators of weavings, carvings, and paintings were well known in the communities in which they lived and produced. Anthropologists today attempt to determine who the artists were who created many of the masterpieces now found in Western museums. These efforts are often successful, as

in the case of Olowe, a carver who died in 1938, considered by many to be the most important Yoruba artist of the twentieth century. Although he was famous in Nigeria, ethnographers and collectors of the time paid no attention to the identity of this outstanding carver (Walker 1998: 91).

PERFORMANCE AND CREATIVITY

Originally, myths, legends, and folktales were transmitted orally, and each narration was an ephemeral performance involving a teller and an audience. These stories were retold from generation to generation, to the awe and amusement of successive audiences. Each time a story was retold, it came out slightly differently. Variations were introduced, different episodes were included, and, eventually, different versions of the same story developed. Stories usually traveled from one society to another over a wide area, and in each of these societies a somewhat different version of the story could be found. Anthropologists collect as many versions of a single story told in a particular setting as they can. By comparing these different versions, they are better able to ascertain the meaning of the story. In similar fashion, the same and related stories in different societies over a wide area are collected and compared by anthropologists.

When we shift to an examination of the performance aspects of myths, legends, and folktales—which are, in effect, oral narratives—the factor of creativity enters the picture. Huntsman points out that the different pre-sentations of the same story move from a veneration of "tradition" to a celebration of individual "creativity" (1995: 124). The narrators have a wide latitude to elaborate and embellish a story as long as they include what their listeners expect. Specific geographic place names "'ground' the narrative as an account of events that happened at known, named places" (1995: 154). These place names must be narrated accurately, but they may actually change over time as borders and maps are redrawn. Storytellers tailor their narrative performances to their audiences as well as demonstrating their personal storytelling abilities.

Consideration of the performance aspects of oral narratives over time raises questions about the continuities and changes of such accounts. For example, the ghost narratives of the Cook Islands, or *tupapaku*, recount stories about spirits in animal form, which are deeply rooted in Polynesian history. They have come to include stories about cows, pigs, dogs, goats, horses, and cats—recently domesticated animals—as spirit vehicles. As Clerk notes, tupapaku accounts "have never been separated from the life of the community as a whole. They have adapted consistently to new circum-stances, incorporating new experience, yet maintaining a continuity with traditions of great antiquity" (1995: 173; see also Alexander-Frizer 2008: part 3). The balance between continuity and change also characterizes many other aspects of culture. As we noted for the potlatch in previous chapters, although people now give away power-boats and tea sets instead of elk skins, the organization of the potlatch remains the same. The contents of myths, tales, and rituals change much more rapidly than does their underlying structure.

When oral narrative is recorded in written form, the stories may form the basis for the literary tradition of the society. The legends of King Arthur and the Knights of the Round Table ceased to be stories told by bards, or professional storytellers, and became published literature. The fact that the story is now written down does not mean that it will not continue to change. It may be rewritten by different writers and may change with each publication and transformation to different media. The characters, motifs, and central themes of these stories have been used by poets, novelists, dramatists, and filmmakers in their own works, transforming the content and medium of storytelling yet retaining key elements of the King Arthur legends.

Anthropologists emphasize the relationship between artistic production and other aspects of culture. In our discussion of the visual arts in small-scale societies, we saw that art was not produced simply to be admired but was integrated with other aspects of culture. The same is true of music, film, and dance. In fact, when anthropologists first began to study dance, they were more interested in the cultural context of the dance than in the dance itself.

BOX 11.1 | Dance as Healing and Political Resistance

Around the world, dance is a space for community building and identity building. In Martinique, an island in the Caribbean Sea, practitioners of *bélé* "celebrate their African forebears and carve out spaces where they can incite conversations and action around individual and collective identity, expression, and healing through dance" (Lewis 2021: 2). A former French colony, Martinique is now a department of France, and residents of the island have the same rights as French citizens. But during the period of colonial rule, the French government tried to eradicate local traditions in the name of modernization. "The trauma of assimilation in the ensuing decades has led to documented mental health problems within the Martinican population" (2021: 2).

Bélé is a drum and dance tradition found throughout the Caribbean; each community has its own music and dance styles. It is believed by researchers to have originally been based in part on European ballroom dances and integrated African movement, dance styles, and music. Bélé in Martinique "is known to have retained and successfully integrated African elements more than

any other version. . . . To dance and drum bélé is to resist assimilation and to reclaim health, connection, and well-being" (Lewis 2021: 2).

Anthropologist Camee Maddow-Winfield, who is documenting the bélé resurgence movement, associates it with political activism and resistance to the history of French cultural assimilation in Martinique. "For many bélé activists, speaking Creole, dancing bélé, and playing the drum were not allowed when they were growing up. Bélé was associated with the poor, rural working class. . . . Many people I interviewed . . . said they were inspired and motivated to learn more about aspects of their heritage that had been systematically discouraged" (Lewis 2021: 4). Maddow-Winfield states that bélé is particularly empowering for women, "who are empowered and feel a sense of affirmation through bélé that they say contributes to their healing and well-being. . . . It's a form of therapy and self-care—not just because you're moving your body and getting physically fit, but spiritually and emotionally, it's a space where a lot of transformation happens" (Lewis 2021: 5).

There is a great range of ritual and ceremonial settings in which music and dance play important roles. Birth, initiation, weddings, and funerals are typically occasions for music and dance. The two weddings described in chapter 2 both include music and dancing, as well as the performance of elaborate rituals. These two examples illustrate the contrasting ways in which performances function in the two societies.

The dances and songs performed at the Kwakwaka'wakw wedding were owned by the numayms of the chiefs who performed them, as were the crests on the masks worn by the performers, in contrast to the dance music played at the American wedding by a hired band, disk jockey, or the wedding participants themselves. We must now also consider who has the right to perform a piece of music or dance and who owns it. There is a great range of variation regarding the degree of specialization involved in the performance of music and dance, even within societies. Sometimes songs and dances are privately owned and may be performed only by their owners. There are dances that may be performed or observed only at a particular stage in life, such as dances for a male initiation. Films and videos may be legally duplicated or "pirated" and sold unofficially, in some places, illegally.

Both weddings include rituals, music, dance, and what in the Western world would be called "theater," all of which come together in a performance, or performing arts. The discussion of the performing arts involves not only an examination of the forms and the rules that characterize the particular genres, or styles, but also how they are acquired; the degree of mastery necessary; the nature of the interpretation in the particular performance; virtuosity, that is, the level of mastery of the performer; and whether audiences understand and appreciate what they are experiencing.

Panpipes of the Aymara of Peru have transformed from an indigenous rural ethnic marker, to a Peruvian national symbol, to a staple of the global marketplace for international music. This Peruvian panpipe player is performing in the New York City subway system.

Music

While the functions of music and dance are similar to those of the visual arts, each is characterized by a different kind of structure. The elements of music are sounds, and their characteristics are pitch and duration. Sounds produced consecutively constitute melody, while sounds produced simultaneously form harmony. The basic concepts for analyzing the structure of music, which varies from one culture to another, are often immediately recognizable and can be attributed to a particular genre. For example, the very distinctive rhythms and instrumentalization of reggae music is immediately recognizable and attributed to Afro-Caribbean musical artists.

Music is a form of communication. The music at an American wedding conveys a message. When a bride, dressed in white, marches down the aisle, the audience silently repeats the words "Here comes the bride, all dressed in white" and immediately recognizes the significance of the traditional wedding processional music. Music also plays a role in funerals and memorials. In these instances, music can convey the emotions of grief and sadness better perhaps than any other medium and is felt collectively by the participants. Because music is a powerful vehicle for expressing emotions as well as ideas, it can be a central mechanism for symbolizing cultural unity and highlighting cultural differences.

The style of playing panpipes (a group of pipes bound together, each one emitting a different note) among the Aymara, the indigenous people of highland Peru, was distinctive of their culture. From the 1920s on, it has had an interesting diffusion, which reveals the nature of asymmetrical power relations in Peru (Turino 1991) as well as the globalization of recorded international music. This musical style among the Aymara, who were the clients of mestizo patrons living in the town of Conima, was characterized by ad hoc musical ensembles organized in an egalitarian fashion playing music in several different traditions at various kinds of fiestas. This was in keeping with the emphasis on equality and on group solidarity in Aymara communities. Aspects of Aymara culture, such as the panpipe tradition, began to be selected as symbols to stand for Peruvian national identity. In this process, however, the panpipe tradition of the Aymara was transformed into one with fixed membership, regular rehearsals, the maintenance of performance quality, and change in the nature of the harmony. This transformation took place in the town of Conima, and the changed musical form was later brought to Lima and other cities around the world when the newly organized group traveled there to perform. During the 1970s, by which time Lima was swollen with rural migrants from the highlands, the panpipe tradition from Conima began to be performed by migrants who had heretofore been ashamed to perform their music in the city because of social prejudice against Aymara Indian culture. Radicalized middle-class students in the city also began to perform the panpipe music and subsequently brought it back to the rural towns from which these students had come. Panpipe music is now a staple in the global international music market. Young Aymara people in the villages, increasingly influenced by national and global cultural movements, now ignore the majority of indigenous musical instruments and community traditions in favor of the widely recognized panpipe movement. This example illustrates the way in which an indigenous musical tradition is altered in form when it moves to an urban and global environment and it comes to symbolize national culture. It is then brought back to the countryside, where it displaces earlier musical forms.

Dance

Dance has been defined as those cultural practices that "formalize human movement into structured systems in much the same way that poetry formalizes language" (Kaeppler 1985: 92). A formal description of the structure of dance would include the steps, spatial patterns, relationships to music, interaction of participants, and their postural positioning. Beyond the description, the focus of anthropological analysis of dance is on its cultural setting and its meaning. Dances, like other forms of performance art, encode particular cultural messages. They may be visual manifestations of social relations, or they may be part of a visual aesthetic system. Westerners frequently isolated the formal movement aspects of rituals and ceremonials as dance, neglecting the role such movements played in the total social phenomena within which they were performed. In doing this, they were utilizing a Western categorization, since dance, for the most part, has become performative entertainment, disassociated from ritual and ceremonial.

Until recently, dances were performed guided only by memory of previous performances. Now there are systems of dance notation that are analogous to written language. Ethnomusicologists and anthropologists, when they studied music and dance in small-scale societies, were studying a tradition transmitted orally and by performance. In these societies, music and dance, like oral literature and folktales, were taught and passed on without benefit of written notational or recording systems until the intervention of outsiders.

Dance can also enable individuals to assume "exotic new identities" through social dancing or through professional immersion in dance careers (Shay 2008: 1). In the United States and Canada, such a phenomenon took place during the 1960s and 1970s when multiculturalism and the search for ethnic roots and identities became important. Shay notes, "During this post 1950s period, literally millions of mainstream [North] Americans . . . [became interested in] . . . various exotic dance genres: . . . Balkan dances of various ethnicities, Latin American dance traditions such as the samba, tango, . . . a wide variety of Asian genres . . . like Chinese opera, Balinese, Cambodian, Javanese classical traditions, and Middle Eastern dance genres of various types but particularly belly dancing which alone attracted over a million women by the 1980s" (2008: 12). What happens to these dance forms as they are transmitted from one culture to another? Several studies describe these transformations. For example, "the tango was commodified and colonized in an uneven movement from the developing world to the First World" (Savigliano in Shay 2008: 41). Asian and Middle Eastern dance forms in which myriad Orientalist images abound are "(mis)appropriated and perpetuated in performances" (Shay 2008: 31). The appropriation of dance forms can move in the reverse direction as well. As Shay notes, "Belly dancers in Egypt between the 1930s and the 1970s frequently appropriated movements, costumes and other elements for the dances from Hollywood films" (2008: 31).

Tango performers at an outdoor dance festival in Uruguay. Tango music and dance styles are believed to have originated in Argentina and Uruguay in the late eighteenth century among European immigrant communities and African enslaved populations. Originally associated with lower-class communities and temporarily banned by the Argentina authorities to prevent its spreading in the nineteenth century, its popularity as a music and performance style has spread worldwide, adapting local styles and preferences in each setting.

Urban Legends: Stories on the Internet

Urban legends, a form of storytelling, are highly dependent on the use of electronic media for their creation and rapid dissemination. An urban or contemporary legend can be defined as "a story in a contemporary setting (not necessarily a city), reported as a true individual experience, with traditional variants that indicate its legendary character. . . . [The stories] typically have three good reasons for their popularity: a suspenseful or humorous story line, an element of actual belief, and a warning or moral that is either stated or implied" (Brunvand 2000: 6). There is a very broad range of such legends, and clearly some drop out as others begin to be told. Harding notes, "Urban Legend and conspiracy theory blend neatly together" (2005: 110); many contemporary urban legends comment on real events, but attributing causes and motivations to national and global conspiracies.

Organ-theft narratives constitute urban legends, that is, "a body of beliefs which can be summarized thus: organized criminal groups engaged in the organ trade are using large-scale kidnapping and murder, preferably of children, in order to supply human organs to a vast network of professional but criminal medical personnel, who practice clandestine transplants, bring huge profits to themselves and to those in the trade" (Campion-Vincent 2005: 3). They include stories about the pseudo-adoption or purchase of the babies of poor women: babies destined to be cut up and used in organ transplants, children kidnapped for their eyes, or tourists kidnapped for their kidneys (2005: 4, 13, 25). Despite the fact that organ transplants are a life-giving and legitimate medical procedure, hostile attitudes toward medicine and the actual fact of a modern and highly exploitative trade in organs have made the accusations and human rights abuses in these stories "more plausible" (2005: 38).

Electronic and broadcast media play key roles in the development and dissemination of urban legends, which lends a further aura of truth to the story. People confidently claim that these stories are true because they "saw it on TV" or "saw it on the internet." Koven points out that "television programs not only draw upon urban legend material for their stories but also, by retelling these legends, redistribute these stories to new generations" (2008: 69). Brunvand observes that "the stories do tell one kind of truth. They are a unique, unselfconscious reflection of major concerns of individuals in the societies in which the [urban] legends circulate" (1998: 146).

Frank (2015) describes multiple forms of "fake news" that now regularly circulate on news media, the internet, and social media platforms. These may be deliberately satirical, consciously created by news parodists to appear to be accurate reportage in traditional media, but consciously parodying its format, style, and language. Other forms of fake news are designed to spread stories that the tellers believe to be either true or possibly true, with the understanding that there is an audience of listeners who will accept them as accurate. To folklorists, false news is a new form of legend (Frank 2015). In analyzing these new forms of legends, scholars believe that the truth or accuracy of these stories is not as important as the hopes, fears, and anxieties they express to

urban legends

Stories about contemporary events purporting to be factual that circulate widely and with variation.

believers. In this sense, the urban legends of contemporary media are no different from the myths we discussed earlier, which also deal with such major concerns.

CINEMA AND GLOBAL FLOWS

Cinema has become a globalized, capitalistic commodity, purchased through individual performances, but increasingly recorded and owned, first on film, then on video and disks, and now streamed on internet sites. Films produced in Hollywood have, throughout the twentieth century, been viewed by, and influenced, groups of people around the world. French, Italian, and British filmmakers have interacted with generations of screenwriters and directors throughout Asia, Africa, and the Middle East. Scholars have more recently documented other flows of cinema viewing and production originating in non-Western centers of film production. "Bollywood" films, a prodigious genre of cinema originating in the production studios in Mumbai, India, are hugely popular throughout South Asia and among South Asian diaspora communities around the world. Bollywood films usually focus on love stories, and feature exuberant dances and songs. This has created a secondary global phenomenon of fashion, dance clubs, dance schools, and live performances inspired by the performance styles and costumes of Hindi films (Morcom 2015) performed in transnational communities. More recently, Bollywood films have engaged with social justice issues and feature themes of gender equality and the challenges of caste and class participation in the political and economic transformation of contemporary India.

Bollywood films also found enthusiastic audiences in parts of Africa throughout the 1960s and 1990s. "[M]ainstream audiences in Africa, especially female audiences, loved Indian films. Even though they didn't understand the words they would end up knowing the songs by heart from seeing the films over and over again, and they loved the dances and the intrigues of the sentimental melodramas that were easily deciphered from the images alone" (Barlet 2010). Brian Larkin's ethnographic studies document the popularity of Indian films among ethnic Hausa in northern Nigeria. "When I first visited Kano, the major city in northern Nigeria, it came as a surprise, then, that Indian films are shown five nights a week at the cinemas (compared with one night

Bollywood films, produced in India, have a wide following in Asia and Africa, as well as among South Asian diaspora populations worldwide. Originally portraying escapist romance and dance spectacles, contemporary Bollywood films now address themes of gender equality, social justice, political corruption, and communal conflict.

for Hollywood films and one night for Chinese films) . . . and that most video shops reserved the bulk of their space for Indian films" (Larkin 1997: 406). "The popularity of Indian film in Nigeria highlights the circulation of media within and between non-Western countries, an aspect of transnational cultural flows that has been largely ignored in recent theories of globalization." Larkin suggests that Hindi-language films, which prominently feature romantic and sexualized stories of love affairs between unmarried men and women, engage Hausa youth with "forms of tradition different from their own at the same time as conceiving of a modernity that comes without the political and ideological significance of the west" (1997: 407). These films have, however, generated controversy and public debate; the films are, according to some critics, "corrupting Hausa youth by borrowing from Indian films foreign modes of love and sexual relations" (1997: 407).

The popularity of Bollywood films throughout Africa is now being eclipsed by films produced in "Nollywood"—the now-booming Nigerian film production center. "Nollywood generates about 2,500 movies a year, making it the second-biggest producer after Bollywood in India, and its films have displaced American, Indian, and Chinese ones on the televisions that are ubiquitous in bars, hair salons, airport lounges, and homes across Africa" (Onishi 2016). The new popularity of Nollywood films is attributed to their dealing with political, economic, and social issues of more relevance to African audiences such as "violence, lack of social mobility, lack of state services and protection, the burden of social customs, etc." (Barlet 2010: 142). These themes are currently being enacted by a new generation of social media users in Nigeria, who are creating their own content that enacts everyday life events. Digital media enactments create a political message that reminds the viewers and followers of these new media producers of everyday struggles of people in Nigeria (Yékú 2022) and the failures of the state to meet their demands. Subversive messages using social media often elude the scrutiny of mainstream political actors, who usually repress these messages in traditional media.

American Films, American Myths and Legends

Legends and stories are rarely created spontaneously by storytellers in present-day America. Parents may read stories to small children, and perhaps these stories may be read in required literature courses. Major themes of such stories, however, continue to be repeated, but now in the media of mass communications. Many of the same themes from legends and tales reappear in different forms of media. One has only to think of the Western-themed film to understand this point, since Westerns have become inextricably linked to American identity. The hero of the classic Western, like the heroes of American legends, is a rugged individualist who tames the frontier. But Americans now have an ambivalent attitude about "taming the frontier" by forcibly removing Native populations and replacing vast tracts of forests with agricultural and urban centers. Some may look back with nostalgia to the time when the frontier represented escape from the constraints of urban society—a time when individuals took the law into their own hands. The cattlemen who used the open range for cattle grazing fought the farmers who wanted to fence in the range and who represented a further step in the process of control over nature.

Despite the changes in emphasis of the 1960s and 1970s, "the Western's overall thrust sanctified territorial expansion, justified dispossession of the Indians, fueled nostalgia for a largely mythicized past, exalted self-reliance and posited violence as the main solution to personal and societal problems" (Coyne 1997: 3). However, the usual representation of American identity in the Western was white and male. To some extent, this picture was transformed in the late 1970s when the TV miniseries *Centennial*, based on a novel by James Michener, presented the history of a Colorado town, emphasizing the multicultural composition of the frontier and condemning the mass slaughter of the Indians by a racist army officer (1997: 184). More recently, *Dances with Wolves*, released in 1990, clearly centralizes the Native American lifeways and perspectives, which are largely absent in classic Western-themed films. But many of these themes continue to resonate in contemporary American society, particularly that of the individual's responsibility to "pull oneself up by one's bootstraps"—a direct reference to the myth of self-reliance in an earlier period in American history.

In addition to seeing Western films as contemporary versions of American legends, some analysts have examined American films as myths whose meanings encode somewhat different symbolic patterns characterizing American society. Nathanson, for example, has analyzed the classic 1939 film *The Wizard of Oz*, which continues to be remade and reshown today, in terms of the way its specific mythic properties relate to the important problems of human existence (Nathanson 1991). As Nathanson notes, "'The Wizard of Oz' may be called a 'secular myth' because, though not overtly religious, it functions in a modern ostensibly secular society, to some extent, the way myths function in traditional and religious societies" (1991: 312). The use of fantastic imagery, the inclusion of supernatural forces and beings, and the fact that it relates to basic human questions, such as where we have come from, where we are going, where we belong, and who we are in relation to others, situate it in the realm of myth. *The Wizard of Oz* is about coming of age and building new relationships and also about the meaning of home. Although the Wizard himself initially appears to be a fraud, he is the source of important folk wisdom: the qualities Dorothy and her companions are searching for—a heart for the Tin Man, courage for the Cowardly Lion, a brain for the Scarecrow, and the capacity to be grown up, for Dorothy—are to be found within oneself. The heroine, Dorothy, comes of age in the Emerald City, where she is transformed from a child into an adult, after which she is transported back to her home in Kansas.

The film was made during the Depression, a very unsettled time in America, where millions of people lost homes and jobs and were forced to migrate in search of work and shelter. Films from this period often explicitly depict the anguish of lost homes and lifestyles and the necessity for youngsters to transform themselves into responsible adults. Various American symbolic landscapes can be identified in the film, including Munchkin City (a small Midwestern city); the Emerald City (the eastern metropolis); the Haunted Forest (the wilderness, threatening and hostile untamed nature); the Yellow Brick Road (a path that pierces the wilderness and represents the unification of America as well as the freedom and hope of the open highway); and, finally, the Frontier Farm (home, order, and civilization). *The Wizard of OZ* also communicates the notion of the progressive urban setting, as set against the traditional rural countryside of the populist worldview, the ultimate resolution of the two being technological agriculture in a bucolic paradise (Nathanson 1991: 173). Kansas is the beginning, the paradise; Oz is the world in which Dorothy searches for order in chaos (the Haunted Forest). At the end of the film, she repeats the mantra "There's no place like home," and she's back in her bedroom in Kansas (Mackey-Kallis 2001: 137). This represents one of the most important themes of the film, the need to return home, having grown up. The fear of losing one's home was a particularly poignant theme in the 1930s, when the film was made, and continues to resonate with viewers in times of continuing economic inequalities and uncertainties.

The film gives mythic expression to what are seen as the deepest feelings of the American people, a nostalgia for the past combined with a hope for the future. The myth of Dorothy in Oz has been recycled in other versions of the film, including *The Wiz*, which featured only African American actors in the major roles. The original 1939 film *The Wizard of Oz* is one of the most popular of American films today and continues to be viewed in its original form on broadcast television and in multiple other formats, including multiple live theatrical musical adaptations that shift the focus from Dorothy to the "good witch" and the "bad witch" characters. A Broadway musical adaptation of the novel of the same name, *Wicked*, deconstructs the assumptions about good and evil embedded in these dichotomous figures; the play experienced a multiyear run on Broadway, attracting audiences for several years. It is also anticipated that the story will be released in film version.

The *Star Wars* film series also represents "one of the great myths of our time," combining the theme of a heroic journey with that of the eternal battle between good and evil (Mary Henderson 1997: 3). *Star Wars* is the "quintessential hero quest" (Mackey-Kallis 2001: 202, 214ff.). However, in the *Star Wars* series, filmmaker George Lucas recycled some Western themes discussed above that continue to resonate with more general American conceptualizations. At the beginning of the first *Star Wars* film, Luke Skywalker is living with his foster parents on the remote desert planet Tatooine, the frontier of civilization, which is also occupied by the Sand People, representing the uncivilized Other. Luke starts on his heroic journey of revenge after his foster parents are killed and his home destroyed. This parallels the destruction by Native Americans of frontier settlements established on Indian territory by American pioneers, who saw the area as a wilderness to be occupied and tamed, and the survivors who sought revenge. Some of the characters in the film recapitulate prototypical figures from Western-themed films:

for example, Han Solo (the loner), the quick-on-the-draw gunfighter, and Greedo the bounty hunter. The first film in the series is climaxed by a classic Western-style shoot-out with the Death Star, with the Evil Empire as the O.K. Corral (Henderson 1997: 129). The third film in the original trilogy, *Return of the Jedi*, was released in 1983. Luke, representing the force for good, returns to his home planet, now overrun by a powerful criminal and his gang, and turns out the villains. This theme in *Return of the Jedi* is a recapitulation of the themes of many of the classic American Western films. Since its original introduction, the major characters and themes have been portrayed in multiple sequels and "prequels," which explore the characters in their youth. Star Wars movies, released in movie theaters around the world, attract a massive global audience; their themes continue to engage a new generation of youthful moviegoers, extending the audience across generations.

Star Wars themes and characters have demonstrated their relevance to audiences of multiple age groups around the world. The theme of technology and its potential is omnipresent in the *Star Wars* franchise. Science fiction, in the form of literature, comic books, and film, has been the setting in which this category of themes is explored. In the multiple *Star Wars* films, intergalactic travel is an everyday occurrence, and the level of technological development is accelerated to a degree far beyond current experience, but it remains an aspirational goal that attracts global attention.

Today, many people are very concerned about climate change and global warming. The dilemma of how we will maintain our humanity in relating to technology is depicted in various *Star Wars* films. In the Empire, technology is supreme, and the aim is to turn human beings into machinelike servants to technology, suppressing their humanity. The Empire becomes a dystopia, the opposite of a utopia, a place in the future where totalitarian power and violence reign supreme (Henderson 1997: 152–53). Luke Skywalker must use his interior strength and fortitude to fight the system and put humans and their feelings and emotions in control of the machines, instead of having the machines control humans.

Another theme is the fear of militarized empires, which could be interpreted as a fear of aliens, others, or expansionist states, projected onto outer space. In the various *Star Wars* battles, the combatants are represented as good and evil; Luke takes on heroic characteristics in leading the forces of good. The *Star Wars* series echoes the King Arthur stories in that Luke grows up in "relative obscurity" and finds Obi-Wan Kanobi, his Merlin-like mentor (Mackey-Kallis 2001: 206ff., 226). These themes now have a universal resonance that appeals to *Star Wars* fans around the world. When installments of *Star Wars* are released, they are simultaneously available in movie theaters around the world. This greatly contributes to the films' profitability, not only through box office tickets but also the sale of related computer games, collateral merchandise, and collectibles. *Star Wars* fans around the world continue to embrace the spirit of the now ethnically and racially diverse cast and stories, as well as their underlying mythologies and anxieties.

COLLECTIONS AND DISPLAYS: CONFLICTS AND RECONCILIATION

Museums play a pivotal role in our understandings of art and artifact production. Many museums and public collections are explicitly self-identified as "ethnographic," suggesting their authority in cross-cultural knowledge and representation. This knowledge, and the presentation of artifacts and creative production, is deeply intertwined with colonial activities that enabled the unfettered removal of art and artifacts from communities colonized by Western political powers. Displays of these materials, which at times included human remains and burial artifacts, often reflected colonial-era thinking about which types of production were worthy of museum exhibitions, and how these artifacts and their producers were to be understood. Museum curators controlled the definitions of value and artistic expression, and were gatekeepers in defining what was "art" and who was an artist. These definitions were invariably rooted in Euro-American patriarchal biases privileging cisgender male producers and activities, and silencing the creative voices of feminine and non-binary artists and activities. Contemporary museums are now engaged in a self-reflexive reconsideration of their methods of knowledge production and forms of representation. They are actively diversifying the ethnicity, gender, and sexuality of communities represented in their collections, their staffs, and their audiences (Adair and Levin 2020).

The removal of local artifacts for display in European sites began with the Age of Exploration. The British eighteenth-century explorer Captain Cook brought back many specimens that people throughout Europe saw as representative of the way of life of the people he encountered. He also brought back Omai, a Tahitian, along with "artificial curiosities" and "natural curiosities" such as fossils, rocks, and shells. These natural curiosities found homes in the collectors' cabinets of royalty and the aristocracy. Such collections later formed the core around which, in the nineteenth century, museums such as the British Museum were formed. In the heyday of colonialism, large quantities of such objects were taken by traders, missionaries, government officials, and anthropologists from what had become parts of colonial empires. These objects were sent to museums in all the capitals of Europe, as well as to America. They are now displayed in glass cases, removed from the cultural context in which they were created and used, and reducing their contexts and creators to obscurity (Rubel and Rosman 2015).

As early as the 1930s and 1940s, the Osage and North Carolina Cherokee communities in the United States established their own museums; by the 1960s and 1970s, many other Native American communities joined the "museum movement" (Watt 2007: 70). These museums, community owned and operated, were seen as a means not only of perpetuating local perspectives on history and culture but also as "a benchmark or milestone of collective self-worth . . . 'a declaration that we are important' and culturally worth maintaining" (2007: 73). The audiences for these museums are local community members as well as academics and the general public. At the A:shiwi

A:wan Museum set up by the Zuni, knowledge production and transfer are both relevant to how the museum decides to exhibit material. Issac (2007) describes how decisions about how the exhibits are presented may be complicated by conflict between the generations. Today there are hundreds of tribal museums in the United States, as well as a national museum devoted to Native American cultures within the complex of the Smithsonian museums in Washington, DC. Tribal museums have also been established by First Nations in Canada such as U'mista, which displays potlatch material confiscated by the Canadian government in the 1920s and subsequently returned many years later (McLoughlin 1999).

The **Native American Graves Protection and Repatriation Act (NAGPRA)**, in effect in the United States since 1990, challenges the collection and display in American museums of human remains as well as some Native American objects that have religious and cultural significance. With the passage of this act by the federal government, all American museums were required to survey their collections and publish an inventory of human remains and funerary and sacred objects, along with other materials of "cultural patrimony." These inventories identify geographic origin, cultural origin, and the facts regarding the accession of the objects (Dubin 2001: 23). After the inventories were published, Native American communities could then make repatriation claims to objects for their return to the communities of origin. Even prior to the passage of NAGPRA, the Zuni had started to try to repatriate the wooden anthropomorphic carvings of their war gods, stimulated by the great increase in Native American political activity that began in the late 1960s.

Compliance with NAGPRA guidelines has been complicated by many factors; the U.S. National Park Service has "facilitated the return of about 67,000 ancestral human remains, 1.9 million funerary objects, and 15,000 sacred and communally owned objects. But remains of 127,000 Native Americans and millions of belongings from graves continue to sit on the shelves of American museums" (Nash and Colwell 2020: 226). Repatriation of culturally sensitive objects to Native communities requires that they demonstrate the connection between the artifacts and the contemporary community. This bureaucratic process is cumbersome and time-consuming. It is based, in part, on evidence that privileges concepts of identity established by the US government that may not be shared by Native communities in establishing community membership and belonging. "Yet, for the most part, NAGPRA has empowered some tribes to reclaim their heritage, and pushed museums to be more oriented to Native concerns and critiques" (2020: 229). In some cases, the repatriation has been marked with new rituals honoring the return of remains and artifacts to the community of origin. Participation in these rituals by community members as well as non-Native archaeologists and museum representatives provides opportunities for reconciliation between often-oppositional participants in the repatriation process.

Digital technology is also emerging as an unresolved factor in debates over repatriation and control over culturally sensitive materials and artifacts.

Native American Graves Protection and Repatriation Act (NAGPRA)

Federal legislation in the United States requiring the return of human remains and some cultural artifacts to recognized native groups.

American museums and educational institutions now routinely digitize their collections and archives and make them publicly available on internet websites. While this is often viewed by the institutions as a great advantage for all interested parties, it can involve conflicts over the access of these materials by people who are not members of the communities of producers. Online access to images of documents and artifacts may be as culturally insensitive to the source community as is the display of the original material. Institutions now negotiate online access and limitations to these digitized images with the originating communities in an attempt to include their sensitivities in the viewing of any culturally sensitive artifacts and images.

The current generation of Native American artists are creating new media and new forms of artistic expression that bypasses and subverts the historical traditions of display and ownership. They are claiming the right to define their own art, and to the spaces necessary to display it. They use new forms as well as new materials to express their visions of their past and present lives, and control the digital platforms on which to create and display them. They claim the voice to confront, without censorship or intervention, the violence committed against their communities in the name of expansion and "the civilizing" agenda of the American state. This is not always a clear-cut process; continuous debate and conflict arises between museum curators, gallery owners, and Native artists over what is to be created, exhibited, and seen, and under what circumstances. This debate sometimes is carried out within Native communities across different generations on social media, demonstrating a rich variety of perspectives and possibilities over contemporary representation.

THE INTERNATIONAL ART WORLD TODAY: CREATING VALUE AND COST

Traditional styles of what were small-scale societies like those of New Ireland and the Northwest Coast continue today, vibrant and alive, translated into new media. In these new forms, their art has become part of a commercial art market, exhibited in elegant galleries and sold to buyers from all over the world. The translation of a sculptural style into modern graphics has occurred not only in New Ireland, but on the Northwest Coast as well. For example, the Kwakwalawaka artist Tony Hunt is a printmaker as well as a sculptor. Indigenous Australian artists exhibit their unique paintings in art galleries from Sydney to Santa Fe. Bill Reid, the contemporary Haida artist whose public sculptures are described earlier in this chapter, also creates jewelry in silver and gold.

When tourism develops in an area, simplified versions of traditional art and objects embodying traditional motifs in new materials frequently begin to be manufactured as tourist art. In the mid-nineteenth century, the Haida of British Columbia began to carve miniature totem poles, platters, and boxes out of argillite, a soft, black, easily carved form of coal, using traditional designs for sale to traders and tourists. Argillite is a medium that the Haida had not used before European contact. Some argillite carvings portrayed Europeans, such as ship captains and their wives. What has been called "airport art" can be found from Nairobi to Port Moresby. When style and content are dictated by tourist demand, Navajo jewelry artists, for example, make crosses and Stars of David out of silver and turquoise to be sold in retail jewelry stores. These transformed art styles are the Navajo's modern interpretations of style, materials, and demand. Silver jewelry production in the American Southwest is not an indigenous art form; it was introduced by non-Navajo artisans in the late nineteenth century, drawing on Spanish traditions from Mexico and South America. Sometimes, the designs of tourist art become so popular that that their production and consumption are part of global circulation. Miniature totem poles, symbols of the Northwest Coast, are mass-produced in Japan to be sold in Vancouver; silver and turquoise jewelry, mass-produced in Hong Kong, is sold to tourists in Santa Fe, New Mexico.

The pleasure art gives the viewer, and its artistic assessment, often derives from its monetary value. Utilitarian objects are often recognized as art at a later time, when they are valued for their aesthetic beauty and referred to as "decorative arts." Furniture and other objects made by the Shakers and quilts made by the Amish are examples of this type of production. Today, the term *decorative arts* has come to include objects in current use that are admired for their aesthetic qualities, as well as antique furniture and household objects owned and used by elites from the past.

Curators' decisions on what to exhibit and critics' opinions about the quality of the art determine the financial value assigned to the artwork. Curators and critics influence which artists are favored, and selling their art, and which are not. Their decisions also determine what is to be considered as artistic production; often works produced by an individual artist or community of artisans to be sold to tourists or for local utilitarian use is not considered by museum curators to have artistic value. It is only now coming to be realized that baskets, pottery, weavings, and textiles that had social use or economic value are artistic production as well. For example, carvings or beadwork produced for sale are being recognized for their artistic value regardless of the motivation behind their production.

Much of what is labeled art is created solely to give aesthetic pleasure, to be admired, and to be assigned a monetary value. As discussed previously, this is a hotly contested and debatable issue in the display and sale of art and artifacts. What gives pleasure to one community of viewers is often deeply offensive and insulting to another community. Navigating these conflicting perspectives is an important part of the curatorial process in museums. galleries, and retail stores around the world. One step in addressing these issues is to include curators and advisors who identify as a member of the group or community whose histories, art, and artifacts are being displayed and consumed.

THE INTERNET AND SOCIAL MEDIA: ANTHROPOLOGICAL PERSPECTIVES

Many users of this book (an example of print media) cannot envision a time when the internet, the World Wide Web, and the scores of platforms that are part of daily life did not exist. But these technologies are, historically speaking, recent technological advances that are part of the broader history of computer hardware (the physical parts of computer technology) and software (instructions to the computer that are stored on it and operated by the hardware). Computer technology through the 1970s was generally used by businesses, governments, the military, and academic or scientific organizations. This technology, whose advantages were readily recognized, was very expensive, massive in size, and accessible only by a community of trained experts. The internet has its origins in the recognition that information stored on individual computer systems could be linked together and shared at little or no cost via networking technologies. Personal computers greatly reduced the size and cost of computing technology; by the 1980s, the era of individual computer access began. Simultaneously, the availability of compatible networking technologies made the linkages of businesses, government, financial institutions, and multiple forms of media with personal computer systems a reality. The now ubiquitous network World Wide Web, or www, part of the "addresses" of so many websites, is now accessible to anyone with the widely available and increasingly inexpensive hardware and software.

Connections between individuals using these new technologies enabled people to communicate through electronic mail, or email, at first on a one-on-one basis (dyadic) through networking technologies that linked users whose computers had the same networking programs. In the mid-1980s new communications technologies, such as Simple Mail Transfer Protocol (SMTP) and the Post Office Protocol (POP) further standardized how email messages were sent and received. MIME, or Multipurpose Internet Mail Extension, made it possible to include images and audio and video attachments to messages without having to know technical codes or programming. The introduction of free Webmail services (like AOL, Gmail, and Yahoo) allowed anyone with an internet connection to access their email on any computer, thus freeing personal computer users and later the users of handheld devices and smart phones from the limitations of access.

The evolution of these communication technologies moved email and other messaging technologies beyond a simple dyadic form of communication. Global networks of users use these technologies for multiple forms of commerce, political messaging, emergency alerts, and personalized communications to individuals and as well as self-selecting groups of people. The term **social media** is now widely used to refer to **internet platforms** for communicating to and interacting with a group of people; platforms are privately owned (like Facebook, now part of Meta, TikTok, or Twitter); the platform owner sets conditions for use and sharing information. And as any user of these technologies knows, there are tremendous benefits as well as social

social media

The multiple forms of electronic communication, expression, and creativity.

internet platform

A digital service that allows interactions between users.

costs associated with their use. Spam or unsolicited communication, fraud, intimidation, bullying, and untruthful messaging and images can be as easily communicated instantly around the world as can thoughtful, empathetic, and verifiable perspectives.

Anthropologists have become very interested in the necessity for, and methodologies appropriate to, the study of communication technologies in general, and more recently, social media in particular (Boelstroff 2012). The unique approach for anthropologists in these studies is to analyze social media content, to tease out meanings and ideas in postings, much as any other cultural text, as a song, recitation of a myth, or the content of a dance would be scrutinized. Social media is a relatively recent but now highly influential part of everyday life. It is interesting to many different social scientists to see how social media creates social and cultural norms and, simultaneously, how it is changing our ideas about who we and others are. This may seem contradictory, but anthropological research very often has to deal with these ambiguities. New ideas, technologies, and political and economic realities change us and our worlds, and simultaneously, we often understand these changes through the lens of our existing social and cultural norms. And finally, anthropological study of internet access and social media usage has been greatly enhanced by cross-cultural studies that explore how users in different countries and communities around the world interpret and use the same technologies but in very different ways, and to different ends.

It is important to note, however, that access to computers and internet resources is not automatically available to everyone. The concept of **digital divide** is a reminder that not all members of every community have equal access to these critical communication and informational technologies. International studies document that women globally have much less access to digital networks and related opportunities due to community gender norms. Poverty and marginalization often results in communities being underserved by electricity and digital infrastructure. And household poverty greatly limits access to cellphones, computers, and internet services.

Some contemporary studies of internet and social media focus on posing questions about whether they are useful or harmful or whether they obscure the difference between real life and online reality. As the result of global pandemics and widespread quarantines, psychologists and educators are producing multiple studies of the pedagogical effect of students learning online. Some of the important issues include whether online learning enhances or detracts from significant learning: Does online education create social and academic engagement, and can it address issues of loneliness and psychological well-being among students? These are all very important questions to confront in the contemporary world but not necessarily guidelines for anthropological study, which puts a priority on how people in communities understand these issues. In a cross-cultural ethnographic study of social media in nine different countries, the authors collectively state, "Our intention is not to evaluate social media, either positively or negatively. Instead the purpose is educational, providing detailed evidence of what social media has

digital divide

Inequality in access to electronic devices and internet resources.

become in each place and the local consequences, including local evaluations" (Miller et al. 2016: n.p.).

For example, these authors state that social media postings and their relationship to existing social groups varies considerably from site to site. In some settings, these postings create new groups and networks; in other settings, they tend to reflect pervasive influential social norms. "In our South Indian

---

BOX 11.2 | Social Media and Social Movements

The use of multiple social media sites around the world is now associated with the strategies and outcomes of numerous social and political movements. Social media creates new opportunities for social movements by providing the means of rapid communication for deliberate and coordinated action, and the capacity for communicating directly with hundreds or thousands of followers. These communications include original content, excerpts from traditional media, uniquely generated blogs and position papers, as well as video clips, music, and artwork that motivates followers and reinforces particular messages.

Recent movements, such as Occupy Wall Street (OWS), Arab Spring, and Black Lives Matter (BLM) have been organized with, and generated momentum and followers through, the strategic deployment of digital media. There are countless examples of how digital media created, mobilized, and deployed followers of social movements representing the entire spectrum of political identity, from ultra-radical to extreme right wing. In some political environments, social media can subvert or bypass political or police intervention, as new sites and technologies by tech-savvy activists are created more rapidly than their official surveillance allows.

Scholars also document the relationship between digital media with more traditional news formats and outlets. News outlets and traditional journalists can limit the effectiveness of social media communication by "ignoring, marginalizing, or undercutting their claims" (Caren, Andrews, and Lu 2020: 444). Some digital movements emerge directly as a result of what followers perceive to be an absence of their positions in mainstream media. And when traditional news reporting covers social-movement activities originating in digital media they often ignore the movement message and frame the mobilization as illegal gatherings and focus on arrests and law-and-order violations.

Digital media does not always benefit social movements. While it is very important in the rapid mobilization of followers, it can just as rapidly generate a counternarrative through tweets on Twitter and Instagram postings. Censoring of content on digital media can be accomplished in a number of ways. Owners of platforms may determine that particular content violates its practices, and may block individuals or particular postings. Governments in some authoritarian states exercise their power to block individual platforms from their citizens' access, as well as internet content and access. These contradictory forces are now apparent, and illustrate the necessity for future study of digital media and social change.

"Clearly, social media platforms are now a regular part of the activist tool kit and are central to the hybrid media environment. As such, scholars need to look beyond the novelty of social media. . . . We might ask such questions as how and to what extent activists employ some technologies and not others; how the specific affordances of each technology might provide constraints or opportunities for the mobilization and effects of social movements, and how differential, unequal access to some platforms over others might affect the trajectory of social movement mobilization among some collective groups and not others" (Caren, Andrews, and Lu 2020: 457).

field site . . . the groups that associated around social media are mainly traditional social units such as the family or the caste. By contrast, in our industrial Chinese site the floating population of migrant workers have largely lost their traditional forms of sociality, and in effect create social groups adapted to a new life spent mainly moving from city to city. Their more constant social life is actually on social media rather than offline. In some cases the more private platforms have radically changed people's lives, as in our site in southeast Turkey on which young women and men can more easily chat with each other" (Miller et al. 2016: 7). The emphasis in these studies is similar to that expressed by other scholars of electronic media. It is not about the difference between virtual and "live" experience but about understanding digital interactions as cultural productions unto themselves.

SUMMARY

- Creative expression communicates ideas as well as emotions through an aesthetic impulse.

- Music, dance, theater, and film are considered performing arts and may be ephemeral; painting and sculpture continue to exist throughout time.

- Gender differentiation is often expressed in creative expression; type of performance, style, and location may vary by gender.

- Increasingly, all forms of performance and creative expression now exist on multiple internet sites, just one example of how digital media is transforming production and display of creative arts and personal expression.

- The term *virtuality* highlights the multiple ways in which digital technology has became an integral part of contemporary expression and daily life.

- Artists around the world innovate by using new materials and techniques to create their works, which often enter into a global marketplace.

- Public spaces provide an opportunity for all kinds of artists to express their creative expression, as well as resist the traditions of limiting art to museums and galleries.

- In the past, scholars questioned whether individual artists in small-scale societies were recognized for their accomplishments. Their production was embedded in social, ritual, and ceremonial contexts.

- Ethnohistorical documentation of artistic production shows that regional and local styles, as well as the skill of individual artists, was widely recognized in their communities.

- The various arts operate within a set of traditional constraints. Yet every carver, painter, musician, and dancer adds their individual conceptualization and interpretation to the final product. It is in this aspect of art that creativity is to be found, and this creativity forms the basis for the audience's judgment of the aesthetic worth of the art produced.

- Myths, legends, and folktales were originally oral traditions. With writing, publications, film, and online sources, they are transmitted to much larger audiences and change over time.

- Music is a key part of creative expression around the world. Music forms originating in one part of the world now circulate globally through an international market for performers and genres from all parts of the world.

- Urban legends are a form of storytelling dependent on the internet and digital technologies for their transmission. They contain elements of what are purported to be real events and often express underlying anxieties about modern life.

- Various cinematic traditions have emerged in India and Nigeria. These forms of cinema circulate regionally and internationally, as does European and American cinema.

- American cinema often reflects basic themes relevant to the audience, such as climate change, political dominance, and increasing use of technology in daily life.

- In the eighteenth century, the collecting of the artifacts of the small-scale societies that anthropologists were to later study was referred to as the collection of "artificial curiosities." These privately owned artifacts, collected in colonial and imperialist settings, later formed the basis for many museum collections.

- Indigenous communities are now claiming ownership over the art and artifacts that were removed illegally from their environments. They are also claiming the right to determine how their art, artifacts, and cultural histories will be represented.

- The Native American Graves Protection and Repatriation Act (NAGPRA) was passed by the United States government in 1990 to aid in the process of the repatriation of sacred objects and human remains to the Native communities from which they were taken.

- Global tourism has resulted in the production of tourist art, the manufacture of objects by local artists to meet the demands of consumers who want a remembrance of the places they visited. Once rejected as "art," this production is now recognized as a significant form of local expression.

- The art world has become an international community of buyers and sellers as a consequence of the commodification of art and the development of a worldwide internet-based auction market.

- Social media is now an everyday part of communication, expression, creativity, and display. Anthropologists are developing methodologies to study communication technologies and social media as part of daily life in different cultural settings.

- The concept of the digital divide explores how access to computers and internet-based technologies is often limited to already socially, economically, and politically marginalized groups.

KEY TERMS

digital divide, 288
internet platform, 287
Native American Graves
 Protection and Repatriation Act
 (NAGPRA), 284

social media, 287
urban legends, 277
virtuality, 269

SUGGESTED READINGS

Nardi, Bonnie. *My Life As a Night Elf Prince: An Anthropological Account of World of Warcraft.* Ann Arbor: University of Michigan Press, 2010.

An ethnographic account, based on three years of participatory research, into the transnational community of over eleven million subscribers to the online game "World of Warcraft."

Randall, Linda K. *Finding Grace in the Concert Hall: Community and Meaning among Springsteen Fans.* Long Grove, IL: Waveland Press, 2011.

This ethnography documents the ways in which the global community of fans of the musician Bruce Springsteen functions as a social network, with shared values, beliefs, and spiritual connections.

Yékú, James. *Cultural Netizenship: Social Media, Popular Culture and Performance in Nigeria.* Bloomington: Indiana University Press, 2022.

A detailed exploration of the multiple uses and meanings of social media in Nigeria, focusing on performance and creativity as political resistance to a repressive postcolonial state.

SUGGESTED WEBSITES

www.native-languages.org/northwest

A compilation of general information about Northwest Coast art and artifacts.

www.art-pacific.com/artifacts/nuguinea/malagan.htm

A guide to the different forms of artistic production of New Ireland, Papua New Guinea.

https://www.masterclass.com/articles/nollywood-new-nigerian-cinema -explained

A brief history of Nollywood, or New Nigerian Cinema, highlighting notable films and filmmakers.

Chapter 12
Global Health and Wellness

LEARNING OBJECTIVES

- Understand why health and wellness are global issues, and how they affect all people everywhere.
- Provide theories for understanding health issues as part of the contemporary world.
- Identify the historical, political, and cultural issues that shape knowledge about disease and health.

- Explore consequences of inequality in obtaining physical and mental health services, nutrition, and clean water.
- Illustrate with case studies how policy, cooperation, and political will contribute to successful health intervention strategies.

HEALTH AND WELLNESS ARE ISSUES that everyone around the world confronts on a daily basis. Being healthy and combatting disease are part of the human experience. Everyone hopes for themselves and their family members to be well fed and cared for; if we fall ill, we hope for quick access to the medical services and supplies that will return us to health and productivity. Good health and well-being for all people are part of both national policy and global initiatives, like the United Nations **Sustainable Development Goals (SDGs)** agreed to by all UN member states in 2015. Every country has a set of policies and resources that provide healthcare to its citizens. Globally in the past fifty years, great progress has been made in eradicating or greatly reducing cases of specific diseases like smallpox and polio. But despite these documented successes, it is equally clear that enormous challenges remain within all countries. Even countries in the "highly developed" category, like the United States, face challenges in sustaining the progress already achieved, as well as addressing the multiple forms of inequality in achieving health throughout a person's lifetime.

It is now clearly documented around the world that gender, sexuality, ethnicity, race, and socioeconomic status play a critical role in how likely you are to be healthy over the course of your lifetime and, if ill, to recover quickly. Poverty is a recognized factor in poor health outcomes. Women and newborn children continue to face childbirth-related illness and premature mortality. The stress of economic insecurity is now closely linked to mental as well as physical problems. Climate change and environmental disasters are clearly implicated in cycles of malnutrition, water shortages, and health challenges. Global pandemics are part of the everyday vocabulary of the world's population. Conflict zones create devastating health challenges for civilians and combatants alike, and in addition shape migration pressures in multiple locations around the world. These are all problems that are part of everyday social and political life; identifying these problems and their solutions are part of public health policy.

Public health perspectives and solutions understand disease and appropriate interventions as part of communities and social life; these perspectives combine medical knowledge with understanding how diseases spread through human population groups as the result of social interaction with others. Public health includes medical and scientific knowledge of diseases and prevention, combined with understanding the social environments within which diseases are transmitted and may be prevented. It includes education and interventions, providing individuals with both information and medical infrastructure so they can make sound decisions about avoiding disease and modifying behaviors that are implicated with forms of illness. While the practice of medicine focuses on the delivery of care to individuals for diagnosis and treatment, public health focuses on a large number of interventions for groups of people to prevent illness and promote well-being and lifetime productivity.

Public health officials and researchers are tasked with **monitoring and evaluation**, or documenting the outcomes of intervention initiatives. They design new programs drawing on theories, techniques, and methods that have been developed by experts throughout the global

Sustainable Development Goals (SDGs)

The United Nations goals and priorities aimed at eliminating global poverty and inequality by 2030.

monitoring and evaluation

The evaluation of the outcomes of public health and development initiatives to see if programs and initiatives meet their stated goals.

health system. They clearly articulate their goals and desired outcomes, as well as how they will conform to existing ethical standards of public health research. They review professional publications for published reports of results and outcomes of similar programs. They adapt new programs by using both quantitative or statistical information, as well as qualitative data about the intervention community, and often focus on particular priorities as expressed by members of the community. Once the programs are up and running, the critical phase of monitoring and evaluation begins. This involves rigorously evaluating the outcomes of the project, using "state of the art" statistical analysis techniques. This often includes **randomized controlled studies**, where a large number of participants are objectively analyzed for evidence of change and outcomes, and compared to groups of people not participating in the specific intervention. Data are collected throughout the program intervention: at the beginning of the program to form a "baseline" of the community; mid-point and at the conclusion of the study period; and most importantly as follow-up information to indicate whether there has been sustained change as a result of the program. This rigorous process creates **evidence-based outcomes** that enable the project designers to make verified claims about areas of success and identify where more research is required. This process is now built into public health initiatives and is included in case studies of interventions.

randomized controlled studies

An objective research method for determining evidence of change as the result of a health or development initiative, comparing groups of people that did and did not participate in the intervention.

evidence-based outcomes

Claims of results of health or development initiatives that are based on the objective and verifiable gathering of data.

COVID-19, PUBLIC HEALTH POLICY, AND INEQUALITIES

The global Covid-19 pandemic, which began in 2020, illustrates how knowledge of medicine and social life combine to create public health policy. It is also important to note that even with shared medical information, groups of people, institutions, and state policy makers interpret this knowledge differently; public health policy is therefore politically and culturally constructed around concepts and forms of knowledge. It is based on many different variables and involves a balance between medicine and social costs. For example, in the United States, as the Covid-19 epidemic proceeded, important differences emerged in public health policy in educational institutions. At the outset of the epidemic, elementary schools, secondary schools, and colleges adapted to the public health recommendations for mandatory "lockdowns" of schools. After the introduction of vaccines for adults, educators and public health officials developed recommendations for reopening schools. Experts balanced the risks of contracting the virus with the social and educational costs of students being isolated from their peers and teachers for long periods of time.

Their policies also drew on the growing recognition that the Covid-19 epidemic lockdowns created a variety of mental health challenges in both the short and long term in communities affected by widespread quarantines. There was ample evidence of psychological stress resulting from disruption in the food supply chain, loss of friends and relatives, and the trauma of losing jobs and financial security (Weinhouse 2021). Policies to facilitate returning to work and school had to manage both the physical risks of contracting the highly contagious virus with a recognition of the need to manage psychological impacts of living through the pandemic on students, teachers, and administrators.

Online learning, widely adopted at the outset of the pandemic, was effective for some students but inadequate for those who flourish in the classroom. It became evident that a policy of online education did not address inherent forms of inequality among students. Not all families could afford up-to-date computers and reliable Wi-Fi connections needed for day-long internet connectivity. Nor were all apartments or houses conducive to a quiet and private setting for learning on the computer. Some high school and college students had to take over care and work responsibilities for other family members who lost their jobs or had their work hours cut as the result of the pandemic. Individual institutions made decisions about how to accommodate the presence of the virus in the population by instituting various health policies for returning teachers and students, such as requiring proof of vaccination and the use of masks indoors. A wide range of debates around these issues and different strategies reflects the American political culture, which combines ongoing negotiations between government-mandated regulations and institutional and individual choice.

DISEASE AND HEALTH

What does it mean to be "healthy"? Many people would respond to this question by saying "not being sick" or "not suffering from disease." In 1948 the World Health Organization (WHO), the division of the United Nations that focuses on global health policy, established an influential definition of health that takes a different approach. WHO proposed understanding health as physical, mental, and social well-being, not limited to the absence of illness or infirmity. Putting this definition into different cultural and political contexts illuminates many of the different public health challenges faced by different groups of people in countries around the world. Well-being is a broad concept that includes a healthy and stable physical environment, free of hunger and conflict. It also includes access to housing, clean water, sanitation, and electricity; to safe and reliable employment; and to medical and psychological care when needed.

This approach encourages public health practitioners and policy makers to broaden their mandates beyond disease treatment and prevention, to include addressing important social issues like domestic violence, homelessness, gun violence, and political conflict. This inclusive public health mandate helps to facilitate a global perspective on these issues, as people facing these challenges cross borders, impacting on the well-being of people simultaneously in multiple settings around the world. As the result of studying the transmission of Ebola, SARS, and Covid-19 variants, we understand how quickly our globalized transportation system delivers viruses from one part of the world to another. This is inevitable considering that global trade and the movement of people around the world is a defining characteristic of the global economy.

This is just one of many ways to think about how health issues in one part of the world impact others. In addition, political conflict and crisis, so prevalent in today's world, motivate the migration of people across borders. Out-migration due to instability in one country can affect the economic and social stability of neighboring countries. Floods, droughts, and natural disasters in one country create displacement and motivate migration across borders. The interconnectedness of economic and political systems around the world has never been more pronounced than it is today; challenges in one country reverberate quickly in other countries around the world. It is therefore important for all people to understand how global health systems operate around the world, and to recognize the major players and stakeholders engaged in creating well-being for all.

How to Study Global Health: Theories of Knowledge

Public health policies are created by both medical practitioners and social scientists, often employing anthropological concepts and methodologies with scientific information. **Medical anthropologists** are part of public health teams, using their unique methods of social analysis to track disease transmission and propose sustainable solutions. As we have seen in previous discussions of anthropological theory and practice, the approaches employed and their underlying conceptual frameworks undergo continual scrutiny and reevaluation. Interventions adopted in one time period and location may have seemed appropriate, while subsequent evaluation shows lack of sustainability or unintended negative consequences.

medical anthropology

The anthropological specialty that focuses on the social and cultural components of health and wellness, and the distribution of related resources.

Health initiatives developed during colonial regimes drew on paradigms and assumptions often based on unverified notions of scientific racism or inherent social characteristics of groups of people. These ideas are now replaced with social justice frameworks and the necessity for the equality in the delivery of health care. Health and wellness are understood to be embedded in social, environmental, and demographic characteristics; no one pill or intervention will solve health problems in all communities. "Effective global health leaders must consider problems from multiple perspectives. They must measure the effects of interventions and explain the meanings of those effects to diverse actors, in diverse places, and at different moments" (Hanna and Kleinman 2013: 16).

The biosocial approach combines medical and social knowledge, and understands health issues as interactions between the biological and the social world. "A biosocial approach posits that biologic and clinical processes are inflected by society, political economy, history and culture and are thus best understood as interactions of biological and social processes" (Hanna and

Kleinman 2015: 17). This requires an interdisciplinary approach to understanding how diseases are acquired, which bacteria or viruses are involved, what medications can be administered to destroy the disease on a cellular level, how the diseases are transmitted through specific human activities, which of these medications are available to whom and under what conditions, and how human behavior patterns can be transformed to prevent both infection and transmission. As has been demonstrated throughout the twentieth and twenty-first centuries, knowing the biological source of a disease does not automatically mean that it will be completely and permanently eradicated; human ideas and behaviors constantly interact with the scientific and biological knowledge of disease transmission.

The biosocial approach includes understanding society-wide issues and their relationship to wellness and disease. These structural issues are outside of the control of any one individual or group to confront. Disease risk and poverty are clearly correlated in public health literature. The persistence of tuberculosis, malaria, and waterborne diseases is understood to be closely associated with communities of high unemployment, constraints in access to education, and lack of consistent nutrition, clean water, and sanitation facilities. There is now a clear understanding emerging from biosocial analysis that psychological problems are associated with the continuous forms of stress that result from individuals and families coping with unemployment, poverty, and dangerous or unstable living conditions. Public health initiatives therefore navigate the complex worlds of science, environmental conditions, and social inequality in developing diagnoses and successful, sustainable interventions. But even when the complete range of biosocial factors is brought to bear in problem solving, unanticipated outcomes may become apparent but only after long-term study of the disease environment, as is illustrated in the detailed case study of guinea worm disease eradication in Rajasthan discussed below.

biopower

As articulated by scholar Michel Foucault, the concept of recognizing how institutions and widely held but shifting ideas related to health, criminality, and medical practices are created by state institutions to discipline and control individuals in communities.

The concept of **biopower** was articulated through multiple works of scholarship by the French philosopher/historian Michel Foucault. This concept brings together many familiar aspects of modern institutions, like data gathering, dissemination of information, and the creation of official discourse, to create strategies that control and discipline individuals in communities. Most people normalize, and accept without question, the fact that prisons and hospitals are a part of modern society. But over time we have come to reject as a modern institution the existence of debtor's prisons, which throughout many centuries in western Europe, conceptualized an individual's unpaid debt as a crime to be punished by incarceration. Foucault argues, by documenting the histories of public institutions like prisons, asylums, and mental hospitals in different periods of European history, that they are powerful mechanisms by which ideas about punishment and discipline are regularized within a society. He argues that these institutions construct definitions of, and strategies for, defining and controlling the "sane" or "insane," those who are criminal or not, those who are well or unwell. And most importantly, these ideas, which often originate in social and political conditions of the past, may continue to operate in the bureaucracies of the present, and continue to be accepted as natural and enshrined in law.

Foucault argues that modern state bureaucracies observe, gather information about, and discipline their citizens; these functions of surveillance and discipline are carried out by governmental bureaucracies. The bodies and behaviors of prisoners are controlled by rules instituted by prisoner officials. Employers increasingly have access to information about the health and wellness of their employees and institute nutritional and health policies to make them more productive. These are examples of biopower in contemporary society: the normalization of "official" surveillance of, and disciplining of, human bodies under the control of modern bureaucracies and institutions. Using the example of the outbreaks of plague in Europe in the eighteenth and nineteenth centuries, Foucault discusses the history of biopower in ways that are now very familiar to citizens of all countries in the twenty-first century. "During outbreaks of plague, for example, public health authorities developed an infrastructure of surveillance and quarantine for observing and collecting information about populations and human bodies. After epidemics of plague subsided, states continued to use this infrastructure to keep track of, and exert coercive force over, their subjects. In the modern world, Foucault posits, disciplinary power is the principal means by which governments and other coercive institutions control populations" (Hanna and Kleinman 2015: 27).

Foucault's historical approach clearly illustrates that the forms of knowledge invoked by and acted upon by governments and other institutions fluctuate over time, and therefore are constructed according to historical cultural and political norms. But their impact on the lives and the bodies of the citizens of the time is no less powerful. During colonial regimes, Western colonial rulers in Africa and Asia created censuses that drew on "eugenics" theories about racial characteristics and categories, and their intergenerational behavioral and social manifestations. In England in the nineteenth century (and transported to the British colonies), the concept of inherent criminality of groups of people based on measurement of physical characteristics and assumptions of group-wide behaviors, was translated into the category of "Criminal Tribes" of India. This designation, reified in the colonial-period Census of India, criminalized all people and their offspring so designated; they could be subject to incarceration, restrictions on their physical movement, or physical punishment merely because of this inherited identity, which was operative during British rule, but later rejected by Indian political institutions after independence.

The prominent physician-anthropologist Paul Farmer (1959–2022) was among the most influential recent public health researchers and advocates. He spent his entire career as a physician-anthropologist theorizing and documenting the manifestations of structural, persistent poverty on the lives of people around the world. He documented, and insisted on the inclusion of the analysis of, the violence and social suffering of people resulting from the systematic and devastating under-delivery of public health services around the world. For example, Farmer and his associates researched young women in rural Haiti who suffered from AIDS. These unemployed women invariably contracted the virus from men whom they saw as having higher status and income than themselves. These men invariably had multiple other sex partners, due to their mobility as drivers, tourism workers, or soldiers. The rural female partners of these men were more at risk of contracting HIV than were those women whose partners were local farmers. Neither group of women could be classified as promiscuous, a label often attributed to women suffering from AIDS. Farmer encouraged researchers to listen carefully to the life stories of these women, whose illness was just the latest tragedy to befall them because of their poverty and marginalization. He articulated the principle of **structural violence** to understand how people suffering from disease and disabilities experienced multiple misfortunes throughout their lives due to circumstances outside of their control. "At the macro level, the theory [of structural violence] underscores the political, economic, and historical forces that pattern and link material deprivation and poor health" (Hanna and Kleinman 2015: 31).

structural violence

Multiple forms of violence and exploitation that are the consequences of societal norms and institutions that regularize discrimination throughout society.

Case Study: Guinea Worm Eradication in Rajasthan, India

A water, health, and sanitation project administered by UNICEF in conjunction with the government of Rajasthan began in the late 1980s and continued through the mid-1990s in northern India. The project was well known in southern Rajasthan and was one focus of the fieldwork conducted by Maxine Weisgrau. This project represents many of the issues and challenges addressed by the theoretical and practical models discussed above; in addition, longitudinal analysis of this project provides a necessary opportunity to assess the project's goals as well its long-term impacts. Most public health project assessment is limited to its impacts and outcomes at the project-cycle conclusion, leaving unexplored long-term and unanticipated outcomes. This project also illustrates multiple levels of project inspiration, financing, theoretical frameworks, and participation.

The project's organizational infrastructure, focused goals, and large funding made it a unique aspect of the local development landscape. It was also unique in that the program was designed to be completed within a specific time period, and then phased out by 1995, consistent with "exit strategy" guidelines that govern most large-scale development programs. The reach of the program was impressive; even in most interior and inaccessible regions of southern Rajasthan, people were familiar with it, particularly with those aspects of the program that related to the treatment of Guinea worm, a previously endemic disease. The project was locally referred to as SWACH (Sanitation, Water, and Community Health); this acronym translates to "clean" or "pure" in Hindi and is recognized as such in local languages. The project was inspired in part by the declaration by the United Nations of 1981–1990 as "The International Drinking Water Supply and Sanitation Decade," a global UN initiative designed to draw attention to sanitation and water-supply challenges around the world. An extensive community health program in several districts of southern Rajasthan, SWACH was funded in part by the United Nations International Children's Fund (UNICEF); the Swedish International

Development Agency (SIDA) and the Rajasthan state government. Its budget for 1986–1990 was US$7 million; the project was to address a number of related problems within the fields of Safe Water Supply, Sanitation, and Public Health (UNICEF 1994: 1).

The prevalence of Guinea worm disease in Rajasthan, known locally as *naru*, was first and foremost among the identified problems. The parameters of the program involved a multipronged approach to combating Guinea worm disease: medical interventions for those already infected; major water infrastructural interventions including the reconfiguration of open wells and their eventual replacement with closed hand-pump systems; and a widespread educational program that provided local communities with training in sanitary and disease-preventing strategies for accessing and using water.

In many parts of the world, people lack a clean household water supply and sanitation facilities. Water must be carried (usually by women and young girls as in northern India) from remote sources. The lack of these facilities in homes and communities has a particularly strong impact on the health and well-being of women and children. WASH interventions— Water Access, Sanitation and Hygiene initiatives—are a major health policy priority in countries that confront the health burden of water-borne diseases.

Guinea worm is associated with the use of open step-wells for domestic water and agricultural use in rural communities; it was endemic in desert-prone areas of Africa and South Asia and is particularly linked to the use of open wells and other water sources. Step-wells have a series of steps built into their walls that enable the user to walk down into the water supply and extract it manually. Step-wells have long been part of the Rajasthan landscape, but are most particularly associated with poorer areas that do not have access to mechanized closed-water extraction systems. Guinea worm is a painful and debilitating disease that erodes the health of its victims in a number of ways but is usually not fatal; it therefore has not attracted the same global and medical attention of other fatal communicable diseases. The presence of the worm itself is destructive to muscle and connective tissue. If not surgically removed, the worm eventually works its way to the surface of the skin, and this eruption creates an open wound that, without medical treatment, becomes infected and ulcerated. Many village-level workers recruited for the program wept during training sessions as they described the slow, agonizing progression of the disease in their family members.

Guinea worm disease is found in arid regions of Africa, the Middle East, South America, and India, although the south-central region of Rajasthan was described by a local expert as the most affected region on earth (Cairncross et al. 2002; Joshi 1991: 33). The disease is caused by the parasite *Dracunculus medinensis L.*, which lives in open tanks, ponds, and step-wells. The life cycle of the disease is directly related to human behaviors and water-extraction techniques. The larvae of the worm are ingested by Cyclops crustaceans that also live in the well water; they are then ingested by humans who drink the infected water. When the Cyclops is digested in the stomach, larvae are released, penetrate the intestinal wall, and mature in connective tissue. The young worm migrates to the victim's extremities, where the life cycle of the disease culminates in the formation of a long adult worm, sometimes as long as two or three feet, which grows in intramuscular and connective tissue below the surface of the arms or legs. The worm eventually edges closer to the surface of the skin and erupts, causing an open wound accompanied by intense pain, irritation, and itching. Bathing the infected parts in water provides minimal relief, and in many areas, the step-well is the only available water source. In the eruption phase of the disease, worm larvae are expelled into the well water from the open wound of disease sufferers, and the disease cycle begins again when the well water is ingested by others.

There is no drug that can kill the worm inside the infected patient, nor is there a vaccine that inoculates against it. The chemical Temephos can be applied to infected well water to kill the water-borne larvae; effective use of Temephos requires a very high concentration applied into open wells repeatedly over several months. According to informants who worked in the SWACH program, this procedure was rarely carried out to indicated specifications because of inefficiencies in the program's technical and training infrastructure (Weisgrau 1997: 149–56).

Once the worm begins to grow inside the human host, the only way to cure an infected person and prevent the spread of the disease is to extract the worm just before it erupts. A local doctor, working on the SWACH team, perfected a process by which the worm is extracted physically—a dangerous and difficult process analogous to removing, through a small incision in the skin, an unbroken strand of cooked spaghetti embedded in muscle tissue. If the worm ruptures during this delicate process it releases a fatal flood of toxins and larvae into the body.

As disease transmission and control is so closely related to step-well water use, the SWACH program included both engineering and educational initiatives. The engineering phase involved removing of steps from the interior of step-wells to prevent access, and resurfacing the inside of wells, as well as installing a pulley and pail system for retrieving water. This reconstruction was designed to eliminate the possibility of Guinea worm disease sufferers bathing their feet in the well and releasing larvae during the eruption stage. The engineering and construction budget also included the funds for the installation of hand-pumps throughout the project area to supplement the use of open wells as a water source. In another phase of the project, local women were trained to maintain and repair these hand-pumps.

An extensive and integrated educational program accompanied SWACH's engineering efforts. This aspect of the program, which involved the recruitment and training of hundreds of local women, was designed to communicate information throughout the local villages about the life cycle of the disease as well as more general water and sanitation techniques. The educational aspect of the program introduced the use of double-layered straining cloths, one side green, the other white, which, if regularly used when transferring water from the well or hand-pump into household-use vessels, would supposedly strain off the Cyclops carrying the larvae, thus preventing ingestion. This procedure was eventually recognized as having questionable value. There was no convincing data to show that cloth straining was an effective method to prevent human contamination. Ubiquitous widely available green and white straining clothes were eventually replaced with a funnel and filtering system, but that was more expensive and not widely accessible. Nevertheless, the use of the straining cloth was a pivotal aspect of the village-level training program. It was unclear to local coordinators and trainers why it remained so important in the program's training aspect when its medical value was dubious; one reason for its continued emphasis was rationalized as being a reminder to people, particularly to women who access and handle water, to take constant care with their treatment of water and be aware that the water contained harmful things. The reality of the situation is that these cloths are ineffective in addressing these problems, a fact that was not effectively communicated to community members.

The primary strategy for the educational/training aspect of the program was the recruitment of village contact teams, mostly women, who were trained as educators and village-level information sources, to conduct household-by-household surveys of those ill with Guinea worm, and train household members in the use of straining cloths and other water sanitation techniques. In addition to the ongoing village-level educational activities, periodic meetings were held with coordinators and higher-level organizational staff to reinforce the local-level animators' training and communication efforts.

In the program's initial stages, local nongovernmental organizations (NGOs) were integrated into its structure, although in practice the actualization of this participation was limited. Local NGOs eventually withdrew because of conflicts between their strategies and SWACH goals. In 1992 the UNICEF medical and organizational consultants were shifted from a project office in Udaipur to the state capital of Jaipur according to plan; the program was taken over entirely by the government of Rajasthan in 1995 and phased into the state government's health program. Its local activities have disappeared from the scene, although villagers widely attribute the program with having successfully eliminated Guinea worm disease.

Contrast and Dispute Over Strategy

Maxine Weisgrau attended many SWACH meetings and training sessions throughout the district; one in particular brought into sharp focus many of the conflicts and contradictions inherent in the structure of the project. The SWACH meeting was one of several that were held in villages in the area.

Maxine recognized the woman leading the SWACH meeting—a ubiquitous and very talented organizer, speaker, and trainer from the headquarters staff of the project in Udaipur. She was assisted by two women, also SWACH employees. They were all dressed in saris and wore watches and other types of gold jewelry that distinguished them from the local community women.

The SWACH organizer led the assembled women in an enthusiastic discussion of, and songfest about, health issues. At one point during the presentation, some of the village women became restless, and one started to get up to leave. The meeting organizer stopped her, drawing unwelcomed attention to her. She was told to sit down and then stayed for the entire meeting, as did all the other local women. Only after about another ninety minutes did it become apparent that this meeting had another agenda besides local education, which explained why the women had been encouraged to remain. A large delegation suddenly arrived in one of SWACH's air-conditioned vans. Five people emerged—three Indian women dressed in saris, an Indian man dressed in a Western suit, and one European man who was identified as an important visitor from overseas. He spoke briefly through an interpreter and said, "I am only an ignorant man; like your husbands, I am ignorant. You have to show me how to do things." The women laughed as he mimed the awkward and incorrect use of the straining cloths that had been distributed to the meeting participants. The European man (who I subsequently found out was a top official of SIDA) recounted a story about his grandmother, a rural woman who taught herself to read by marking letters with charcoal on a tree stump. He concluded his presentation with an acknowledgment of the work of the all the SWACH participants and local NGOs active in the village. After about half an hour, the visiting delegation got back into their van and left. The meeting continued for another two hours, with more lectures and more songs about local health conditions that had been composed by the SWACH team based on variations of local women's folk songs. The meeting concluded with the distribution of a few biscuits and bananas to the assembled women.

At the conclusion of the meeting, a heated discussion developed between two local NGO workers and the organizer of the meeting from SWACH. The dispute between representatives of two different types of organizations encapsulated conflicts inherent in the rural development process: two approaches, two strategies, two separate philosophies, very much at odds with each other despite the deep commitment to what they were all trying to accomplish. The local NGO workers believe that if development agencies are to make change that is significant to the community, then program organizers must make a long-term commitment to that community—spending time living within it and finding out how community members think, feel, and respond. This information will then serve as the basis for programs and strategies that emanate from, and are based on, local needs, resources, strengths, and priorities.

This approach contrasts with the SWACH program, whose parameters emanated from a global health agency, based on protocols developed in Africa. SWACH's extensive financial and personnel resources blanketed the area with information. Local trainers and organizers attempted to revisit contacted villages every two months. They trained local women as volunteer animators to visit local households and communicate to their neighbors the details of the health maintenance message. The program organizers did not establish close relationships with the women in the village; this was the role envisioned for the volunteer village workers. SWACH's overall strategy was designed by medical doctors and development/aid administrators with little or no local input. The medical protocols and administrative structures were intended to be used to confront a medical problem, and to be duplicated in multiple settings quickly around the world.

The SWACH strategies approached eradicating disease as a biological and medical problem rather than a sociocultural one. The training and communications systems were designed to alter behavioral practices, but did not take in information from the communities. The project designers did not take into account, for example, the caste-based dynamics of well ownership and access. SWACH eventually commissioned and executed a study to assess local perceptions and social structures relating to water use and well ownership, but this information was compiled and completed five years after the program was instituted in Rajasthan (Deegan 1990).

The project designers and implementers had a highly specific goal: eliminate Guinea worm disease, alleviate suffering, and avoid unnecessary infections and loss of productivity. This can be accomplished, they believed, by dispensing information on the nature of the disease quickly and effectively to as many people as possible in as short a time period as possible. In 1995, Maxine returned to the area and asked about Guinea worm and SWACH. The program is part of local memory, recollected selectively and symbolically. Follow-up epidemiological studies confirmed its success, although a 2010 report indicated the presence of a scant number of Guinea worm cases in one district (Choubisa 2010). More significant, however, was the recognition in 2018 that the groundwater supply delivered by a large number of closed hand-pumps and borewells installed in the region, which were believed to provide safer water than open wells, is contaminated with high levels of naturally occurring fluoride exceeding safe consumption levels (Choubisa et al. 2018).

The SWACH program illustrates many of the strengths as well as the weaknesses of public-health development projects. As a focused attack on one medically defined local problem—Guinea worm disease—it has been declared to be successful; the World Health Organization in 2020 declared that Guinea worm has been totally eradicated from India. But from its inception, the program neglected the social and cultural contexts of the disease and water use, and it is thus an example of a lost educational opportunity that had the potential of having significant long-term quality-of-life effects, an observation made in follow-up evaluation of the project (SIDA 1998).

While the structure of the program was designed to integrate women into every level of the educational process, and a concerted effort was made to hire local women animators at the village level to be trained as hand pump repair mechanics as well as educational advisors, the wages that they were paid were considerably lower than those of men doing the equivalent work. The majority of the women who actually participated in village level SWACH activities were recruited as unpaid volunteer workers, thus perpetuating many of the local gender biases and inequities. Despite its continuous use of rhetoric about "people's participation" and local "grassroots" involvement, the program was hierarchical and centrally organized; knowledge and strategies emanated from global centers, not local communities. It was designed and structured at UNICEF headquarters in New York and New Delhi and based on a medical protocol first developed by UNICEF for western Africa; it was only minimally modified to accord with the social, cultural, and environmental complexities of water use in Rajasthan.

Health and Human Capital

Good health is, throughout the world, interconnected with a complex of socioeconomic factors. Health and wellness are part of the components of **human capital**, all the forms of knowledge, skills, and abilities that a person accumulates to enable them to be productive and financially secure over the course of their lives. Obviously, good health is one aspect of human capital; chronic illness prevents steady employment and secure wages. Health status is a factor in a child's ability to attend school regularly and to be an engaged and productive student. The costs of accessing necessary healthcare services and facilities in many parts of the world are out of the reach of parents and children. These costs can often put a household into debt and tip a working family into poverty and financial insecurity. Good health throughout a person's lifetime is dependent on sound nutrition of pregnant women and their children; it is also linked to continual access to clean water and safe sanitation systems.

It therefore becomes an issue of public health and policy to provide all communities, and all people within them, with the same forms of human capital, to enable everyone to grow up healthy, educated, and productive throughout their lives. But inequality, between countries and within countries, is recognized as the major factor that keeps some groups of people in poverty throughout their lives and simultaneously allows other groups to flourish. So providing all people with access to the basic forms of human capital are global and national priorities in economic development of states and communities around the world. From global health and development perspectives, it is important to understand the connections between health status and overall economic and social productivity.

CONFRONTING INEQUALITY: UN SUSTAINABLE DEVELOPMENT GOALS

The Sustainable Development Goals (SDGs) are seventeen interconnected global goals supported by all the member states of the United Nations; they

---

human capital

The resources, skills, and access to important social and political resources an individual can access to achieve health, education, and economic and political benefits.

are "a blueprint to achieve a better and more sustainable future for all people and the world by 2030." The goals are all focused on ending global poverty and inequality and attaining good health and well-being for all. Individual countries are creating programs and strategies consistent with their own interpretations of how to best actualize these goals. An integral part of the SDG strategies is the creation and monitoring of new forms of data that document and track the actual progress countries are making in reaching these goals. The SDGs, singly and collectively, are a form of global discourse that gives us a way of understanding contemporary development and health strategies, and how problems and solutions are envisioned to be interconnected and interdependent. The first goal, "No poverty," is connected with eliminating hunger, attaining health and well-being, quality education, gender equality, and clean water and sanitation, to cite just six of the seventeen interrelated goals.

The United Nations Sustainable Development Goals (SDGs) target multiple forms of poverty and inequality. They aim to eliminate poverty and hunger worldwide by 2030.

Health and Education

There is a clearly demonstrated connection between health and education; this connection is seen within households and across generations of household members. The education and health status of parents profoundly affects their children. Family members with responsibility for the care and feeding of children will be more effective caregivers when they are educated in basic principles of nutrition, health, and sanitation. Educated caregivers are more likely than those without education to be steady wage earners able to obtain food and preventive medical care. Educated people are generally better able to manage illness, and know where to seek out the necessary resources. Children who are malnourished or undernourished are greatly limited in their ability to attend school and, if they can make it to school, to be engaged learners.

Many studies show the connection between a mother's educational level and the health outcomes of her children. A mother's education has a direct bearing on her ability to encourage education for her children and understand the need for good nutrition, sanitation, and healthcare. Countries and communities that do not support educational attainment for all genders limit the possibilities of girls and young women to be productive and healthy, and to become the next generation of community and national leaders. An educated mother enhances the health and educational outcomes of their children.

For these and multiple other reasons, gender equality in educational is a primary goal of international, national, and humanitarian efforts

Health Disparities and Inequalities within Countries

The recent Covid-19 pandemic clearly illustrated that, even in high-income countries around the world, there were profound group inequalities in the impact of the disease. These disparities within the United States were documented throughout the course of the pandemic. At the outset of the pandemic, prior to the development of effective vaccines, older adults were at the highest risk for severe illness and need for hospitalization. A person's risk of severe illness increased with the number of their underlying medical conditions; many of these conditions are associated with a lifetime of poor nutrition and delayed medical care. People were at increased risk of hospitalization or death because of underservice by medical practitioners or inability to pay for health insurance. The Centers for Disease Control and Prevention (CDC) documented in multiple sources that some people are at increased risk of getting very sick or dying from Covid-19 because of where they live or the kind of work they do. This includes people from racial, ethnic, and other minority groups often subject to housing discrimination. People with disabilities also suffered disproportionately from severe illness and death, as they are likely to have underlying chronic health conditions, as well as barriers in accessing health care.

Income and wealth inequality were apparent during periods of quarantine and lockdown. In New York City, for example, people with white-collar jobs and higher incomes were able to work at home, remotely, and collect their paychecks. They were able to access food delivery systems and "take-out" to keep them nourished. New Yorkers with second homes outside of urban densely populated neighborhoods were able to leave the city completely and relocate to rural areas, while maintaining their incomes with online work. The strategies of these higher-income professionals were supported by so-called essential workers, or service workers who could not afford to remain at home and were at increased risk for disease exposure. Their lower and more insecure incomes required that they continue to work, often supplying delivery and other services to middle- and upper-income communities (Levin 2021).

These health-outcome disparities are documented within and between countries, and between regions and rural and urban areas. On a global scale, it is apparent that poorer people, generally with less political power, have poorer health and nutrition outcomes and access to fewer health services. They generally have less income and are employed in the informal or intermittent employment sectors, without steady wages and benefits. People with disabilities, mental challenges, and chronic health issues face systematic discrimination in accessing employment, housing, and equitable medical care, as do people who self-identify as LGBTI. It is now recognized that there are social rights, human rights, and economic costs to marginalizing large numbers of potential workers in employment sectors. Improving income-disparity inequalities within and between countries, as measured by multiple forms of data, was a major priority of international policy makers, economists, and humanitarian actors for several decades. But the devastating impact of the Covid-19 pandemic on the economies of regions and countries around the world has halted some progress in reducing levels of inequality between countries, particularly between countries of the global North and global South.

During epidemics and health-related lockdowns, there is marked inequality in the workers who can afford to stay home and those who are forced by necessity to continue to work outside the home. Low-wage and daily workers in food and service industries must jeopardize their own health to provide services in exchange for wages, even during quarantines and epidemics.

FOOD SECURITY AND NUTRITION

Ending hunger, malnutrition, and all forms of food insecurity, are increasing challenges around. the world. Despite some gains in these areas, especially in child nutrition, the Covid-19 pandemic demonstrated the fragility of the global food-production and distribution system. Food supply chains were disrupted throughout 2020–2022, which resulted in both an insecure supply and increased prices for the basic foods needed for a healthy diet. "It is estimated that the number of people unable to afford a healthy diet around the world rose by 112 million, to almost 3.1 billion, during the pandemic" (FAO et al. 2022: 8). Accounting for post-Covid-19 improvements in food production and distribution, it is projected that about 8 percent of the world's population, almost 670 million people, will still be facing hunger in 2030.

These data reflect inequalities in the ability of people to maintain a healthy, nutritional diet. Women are more likely than men to suffer the effects of chronic anemia, which creates higher death rates and increased complications in pregnancy and newborn babies' outcomes. Children in rural settings and low-income households with poor nutrition are likely to suffer from stunted growth and decreased cognitive development potential. In urban areas and wealthier households around the world, childhood obesity has reached pandemic proportions (FAO et al. 2022: 19). There are however policy recommendations that are designed to improve this global nutritional inequality. Incentives to both the public and private agricultural sectors to plant and grow nutritious foods aim at increasing the incomes of farmers, and increasing the supply of food in the global supply chain. Governments can support food and agriculture production through market price control and subsidies to both producers and consumers. Price incentives on fresh produce, that is, fruits and vegetables, reduce their price to consumers. Negative price incentives such as increased tax levels on unhealthful foods in the marketplace, like high-sugar beverages and processed foods high in sugar, salt, and calories, help address obesity and all its related medical conditions for both adults and children. These policies are already in effect in some countries around the world, and if expanded, can improve the access of people around the world to affordable, healthy, nutritious foods (FAO et al. 2022).

FOCUS ON WOMEN'S HEALTH

Public health policies often focus on the health challenges women face throughout their lifetimes, especially in low- and medium-income countries. There are a number of interrelated reasons for the prominence of this gender focus in current policy and strategy. Gender has a significant impact on health; the health of women and girls is of particular concern because in many societies they face multiple forms of sociocultural discrimination that prevent them from benefiting from health services and optimal quality of life. In many locations around the world, social norms decrease girls' access to education. Women do not have the same level of access to paid employment opportunities as men. In many societies, women's early marriage and the stress on reproductive roles create enormous social pressure to have children, especially male children. Failure to do so can create other types of sociocultural risks, ranging from family pressure to have children, denial of access to contraception, and in extreme cases, violence for failing to produce male offspring. Women are potentially the victims of multiple forms of physical and emotional violence within their households, and other forms of gender-based violence when outside their homes.

Public health perspectives recognize that these multiple forms of risk can be prevented, often with relatively low-cost but effective interventions to improve women's overall health. These interventions will help enable women and girls to actualize their right to a productive, healthy life, as well as reduce the costs to families and society more generally of illness and early death. Many of the health challenges women face are related to pregnancy and childbirth, most especially when births are not attended by trained specialists. It is also well established that a woman's health and well-being during her pregnancy will enhance the outcomes of her children's lives.

Some health and gender specialists are now advocating the adoption of integrated interventions that focus on the "first 1000 days" of a woman's pregnancy and the first year of her child. This period is understood to be a critical window of opportunity during which nutrition and health care for the pregnant woman can help prevent physical stunting, malnutrition, and intellectual delays in her child. These approaches facilitate a pregnant woman's access to a comprehensive package of services for mothers, babies, their families, and caregivers. These may include educational information about water and sanitation, including the importance of hand washing and prevention of water-borne bacteria to avoid diarrheal disease that places babies at high risk. They encourage mothers to access all available forms of vaccinations for themselves and their babies. Support for exclusively breastfeeding for the first six months of a baby's life is provided in these programs, as well as nutritional training and the use of vitamins and other nutritional supplements when available. These programs are aimed at mothers and their babies, but also include other family members, when available, to participate in the informed care of the both the pregnant woman and her newborn baby. They stress the critical recognition of the impact of a mother's health and caregiving skills on the health and growth outcomes of her children. They recognize that these inputs may not be available to a pregnant woman due to constraints beyond her control, and that she must be supported by the state and humanitarian organizations for access to these resources to assure a positive health outcome for her and her child.

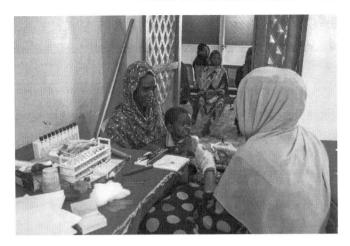

A mother brings her son for a blood test at a health facility for internally displaced people in the Abu Shouk camp in North Darfur. Humanitarian organizations attempt to deliver health services to displaced people and migrants; while designed to accommodate short-term residents, these camps are increasingly becoming long-term communities of migrant populations who are unable to find permanent housing, employment, and medical care.

Child Mortality

Globally, under-age-five mortality rates have dropped significantly since 1990; data shows significant decreases in all the regions of the world. For example, in Sub-Saharan Africa that rate of deaths per 1,000 live births dropped to 74 in 2020, as compared to 181 in 1990 (UNICEF 2021: 13). But despite worldwide progress, **child mortality** around the world continues to take a major toll: "More than 5 million children died before age 5 during in 2020 alone" (2021: 5). The most tragic part of this enormous loss of life is that much of it is preventable, and that the burden continues to fall most heavily in Sub-Saharan Africa. "The SDGs call for an end to preventable deaths of newborns and children under age 5; the global goal by 2030 is neonatal mortality rate of 12 or fewer deaths per 1,000 live births, and an under-five mortality rate of 25 or fewer deaths per 1,000 live births by 2030" (2021: 5).

The first month of life is the most vulnerable; nearly half of all under-five deaths occur during the neonatal period, the first twenty-eight days of life. Birth complications, premature birth, pneumonia, diarrhea, and malaria are the leading causes of preventable deaths of children under five. Children living in conflict settings are especially vulnerable; almost half of under-five deaths globally in 2020 occurred in conflict settings. An accurate assessment of the global situation is, however, hampered by data-gathering challenges in many countries; the capacity to gather and report good quality child-mortality statistics exists in fewer than half the countries around the world. Increasing the capacity to track and report high-quality data in a timely and reliable way is therefore another priority in addressing child mortality globally.

child mortality

Statistics that measure the rates of infant survival and death usually before the first five years of life.

BOX 12.1 | The Four Delays—Maternal and Neonatal Mortality

The Third Sustainable Development Goal is "Ensure healthy lives and promote well being for all at all ages." The first two specific targets are: "Target 3.1 By 2030, reduce the global maternal mortality ratio to less than 70 per 100,000 live births, and Target 3.2 By 2030, end preventable deaths of newborns and children under 5 years of age, with all countries aiming to reduce neonatal mortality to at least as low as 12 per 1,000 live births and under-5 mortality to at least as low as 25 per 1,000 live births." Maternal mortality remains a daunting challenge in many lower- and middle-income countries; even in high-income countries like the United States, maternal mortality is higher in communities of poverty and of primarily African American populations. It has long been recognized that these health challenges are very closely related to the ability of pregnant women to access medical services throughout their pregnancy and promptly obtain skilled medical care when needed.

One now-classic approach to conceptualizing maternal mortality in the public-health literature is the "Three Delays" framework. Maternal death can result from (1) delay in seeking appropriate medical help for a pregnancy-related emergency, (2) delay in reaching an appropriate medical facility, and (3) delay in receiving adequate care on arrival at the medical facility (Thaddeus and Main 1982). Scholars are now adding a fourth delay to this model: delay within the family and community to share responsibility for the well-being of the pregnant woman by providing food, money, transportation, or whatever assistance is necessary to counteract the first three delays. "The fourth delay" emphasizes the need for communities to mobilize around pregnancy-related emergencies and act collectively to assist individuals facing pregnancy and birth-related challenges (Macdonald et al. 2018).

Case Study: South Africa

UNICEF South Africa, working with the South African Departments of Health, Social Development, and Basic Education, along with private-sector and civil-society partners, developed an action plan for the "first 1,000 days" focusing on the specific health challenges faced by women and their newborn children. This program was part of other initiatives in South Africa that have lowered under-five child mortality by 50 percent since 2002, but the rate still remains relatively high at 42 deaths per 1,000 live births (UNICEF South Africa 2017). This compares with 37 deaths per 1,000 live births globally in 2020; data after 2020 are complicated by accounting for child-mortality figures due to Covid-19 infections throughout populations that reported data (UNICEF 2021).

Children in South Africa die from preventable causes of death, including pneumonia, HIV, tuberculosis (TB), and diarrhea; half of the children dying in South Africa are HIV positive, and one-third have severe malnutrition and are underweight. There are medications available to prevent mother-to-child transmission of HIV, but obtaining them remains a challenge for women living in rural, marginalized areas. The priorities in the program are: improved nutrition for pregnant women; delivery of medications to prevent HIV infection from mother to child; screening for TB and follow-up in medication retention; exclusively breastfeeding during the first six months of the infant's life; appropriate nutritious food and safe water for mother and child, monitoring hygiene and sanitation practices; and tracking infant growth and development (UNICEF South Africa 2017: 2).

These goals were translated into a program of services specifically designed for the South African healthcare environment. "The project created a comprehensive package of services for mothers, babies, families and caregivers. These included:

- Educating families in providing support to mothers for exclusive breastfeeding
- Scaling up infant and young child feeding programs
- Raising awareness on the importance of growth monitoring
- Expanding immunization coverage and uptake
- Training communities on the importance of handwashing with soap to prevent illness
- Ensuring that eligible households receive their child support grants and have sufficient money to buy food.
- Use of mobile health technology to deliver communications to parents and caregivers on mobile phones" (UNICEF South Africa 2017: 2).

Programs such as those developed for South Africa show that children who receive optimal nutrition during their first thousand days are likely to maintain good health, and are also likely to complete more grades at school and go on to earn more in wages as adults. These are "multi-sectoral" integrated programs that bring together multiple stakeholders, influencers, and care providers to support the nutritional and sanitation environment for pregnant mothers, their households, and their communities. They mobilize medical and technical research, and include the use of technology like mobile phones to help implement service delivery (USAID n.d.: 1).

VALUING TOILETS: SANITATION/GENDER/HEALTH

The United Nations recently declared November 19 as "World Toilet Day"; the 2021 observance campaign stressed the theme of "Valuing Toilets" to raise awareness of the 3.6 billion people around the world living without access to safe toilets and related sanitation systems. This awareness campaign helps support SDG 6, which calls for clean water and sanitation systems for all by 2030. The UN estimates that the advantages of investing in adequate sanitation-system infrastructure has multiple advantages to policy makers: "Every $1 invested in basic sanitation returns up to $5 in saved medical costs and increased productivity, and jobs are created along the entire service chain." Toilets and sanitation infrastructure are poorly managed, underfunded, and neglected in many parts of the world. It is estimated that globally, two billion people use a contaminated drinking source and that seven hundred children under five years old, who are particularly vulnerable to diarrheal diseases, die every day from unsafe water, sanitation, and poor hygiene (UN Water 2022). Unsafe or absent toilets threaten everyone's health; the absence or poor distribution of toilets in all kinds of spaces, including households, offices, public streets, and parks, and in transportation systems, leads to open or uncontained defecation and urination. In the case of poor rural areas and informal urban slums, this can be a community-wide issue. Poor sanitation contaminates drinking water sources, rivers, beaches, and other environmental assets, and is implicated in spreading multiple contagious diseases, including cholera, typhoid, and diarrheal disease, among groups of people in the entire population.

An adequate toilet facility confines excreted material and must be cleaned regularly and properly maintained throughout the year. It must be conveniently located, provide privacy and hand-washing facilities, and be accessible to all people, including those with disabilities (Hanchett 2019). To assure maximum and sustainable usage of toilets and other sanitation infrastructure, public-health advocates acknowledge the necessity of community input on the design and placement of equipment. It is now apparent that men and women, while they share the general need for clean and sanitary toilets, have different specific needs that must be met in sanitation facilities.

A toilet with a facility for hand washing per single household is the optimum goal, but there also continues to be a need in many rural and informal urban slum settlements for communal toilets that accommodate the vulnerabilities of girls and women. Open defecation puts women at risk of physical violence and psychological stress resulting from fears of violating local taboos. The need to change and dispose of menstrual products requires privacy as well as regularly maintained containers for disposal. A combination of shame and modesty often prevents women and girls from using facilities that don't protect their privacy; as a result, they resort to open defecation, despite its physical and health dangers.

Beyond the technical inputs in developing a safe, reliable sanitation system in a community, these systems must be understood within social and cultural contexts. "Every place has its own characteristics that need to be taken into account when planning or implementing sanitation programs. Culture, social diversity, geography, weather, water availability—these things and others constrain sanitation options and pose special challenges to eliminating open defecation and creating toilet security for women and girls" (Hanchett 2019: 6). Large numbers of case studies have demonstrated the need for complete community input, including the voices of women, young adults, men, and boys, to work with engineers and builders to assure that the facilities being installed are accessible to all, including people with disabilities, while honoring their dignity and health needs. This may include the posting of use and hand-washing instructions that use pictures and drawings, understanding that some members may not be literate. And whatever type of installation is created, locally available maintenance and repair systems should be included with the overall plan and design. These plans and designs must also include medium- and long-term follow-up studies to assure that the facilities continue to be useable, sanitary, and accessible.

CLIMATE CHANGE AND HEALTH

The effects of climate change are recognized and debated in many different sectors in global and national settings; identifying health issues related to climate change is slowly emerging as a priority in this realm of policy and strategy. For example, more extreme weather patterns have been noted around the world; in some areas, floods and devastatingly high levels of rainfall have created extensive loss of

life, food, housing, and productive resources. In other areas, an increase in the number of wildfires, as in the western United States and Greece and other Mediterranean regions, has had an equally devastating effect in loss of life, housing, and injury directly related to the effects of fire. Fires also create human health effects on survivors, including asthma, respiratory diseases, pulmonary inflammation, and immune system reactions.

Climate change is creating a complex of environmental changes and unprecedented disasters that are damaging the health and well-being of people worldwide. Forest fires, like these in Greece, not only destroy homes and important infrastructure, they are also the cause of stress-related illness, respiratory disease, and the destruction of economic resources and distribution systems.

Areas especially hard hit by the effects of climate change and extreme weather patterns are subject to drought and food insecurity. These conditions contribute to the global cycle of forced migration, and all the physical and mental vulnerabilities that are part of the migration experience. Drought and water loss is further implicated in trans-border conflict, as countries dispute control over water sources that serve the needs of an entire region. Advocates focusing on climate change and health challenges stress the importance of engaging political leaders at all levels, but especially at the local and community level to document and publicize the importance of recognizing climate change–related health issues. It is especially important to engage young people in these issues, as they will bear the brunt of the consequences of climate change as they age. Gathering data on a local level is equally important to provide both quantitative and qualitative evidence of these health issues and the necessity for active interventions to protect threatened resources. Recognition of long-term health risks and vulnerabilities can enlighten activists, advocates, policy makers, and politicians to increase their commitment to better understanding, and combating, the health consequences of climate change.

PSYCHOLOGICAL AND MENTAL WELL-BEING

In all countries around the world, mental health challenges are widely distributed among men and women of all ages, and young people and adolescents of all genders. It is estimated by the World Health Organization that "one in eight people in the world live with a mental disorder. . . . People with severe or acute mental disorders die on average 10 to 22 years earlier than the general population" (WHO 2022: xv). This represents a tremendous burden of emotional pain on those who suffer from mental illness, as well as severe stress for their families and communities. The economic consequences of mental health challenges are enormous; accessing scarce sources of care can be exorbitantly expensive if available, and only within reach of the wealthy. Loss of work and income resulting from mental illness compounds its economic impact on those who are ill and their families and caregivers.

BOX 12.2 | Shifting Categories of Mental Disorders: *Diagnostic and Statistical Manual* (*DSM*)

The *Diagnostic and Statistical Manual*, currently in its fifth edition (2013) is published by the American Psychiatric Association. In the United States, it serves as the primary authority for psychiatric diagnoses and treatment recommendations; its use in assigning diagnoses is therefore a critical component of the health insurance industry's reimbursement procedures for people of all ages seeking treatments and therapy for mental disorders.

Each edition of the *DSM* is studied closely by mental health professionals as well as social scientists for changes in diagnostic categories and for the removal of categories. This is particularly significant as it signals changes in society-wide norms about acceptance of behaviors that were once considered mental illness. Famously, in 1973 the diagnosis of homosexuality was removed from the second edition of the *DSM*, leading to the recognition of it as a form of human variation and not illness or pathology. In the current edition, other changes include renaming of "mental retardation" to "intellectual disability" (intellectual development disorder). The fifth edition also includes new categories: gambling disorder and tobacco use disorder.

The *DSM* has been criticized on many different fronts and in the global contexts of mental health, particularly for lacking in cultural diversity and only accepting Western psychological diagnoses and treatments as the norm. Others criticize the reliance on specific diagnostic categories as not acknowledging that mental disorders are usually part of a spectrum shared with normality, and not

a distinct difference from it. Diagnostic labels are often inaccurate in predicting ranges of behavior, and can be socially and medically stigmatizing throughout a psychological client's lifetime.

The World Health Organization developed the Global Assessment of Functioning Scale and then later refined it with its Disability Assessment Schedule 2.0. Known as WHODAS 2.0, this system identifies levels of functioning and levels of disability of sufferers of both mental and physical disabilities. It establishes the International Classification of Functioning, Disability and Health (ICF) system. "The ICF conceptualizes disability as a health experience that occurs in a context, rather than as a problem that resides solely in the individual. According to the biopsychosocial model embedded in the ICF, disability and functioning are outcomes of interactions between health conditions (diseases, disorders and injuries) and contextual factors. . . . It broadens the perspective of disability and allows for the examination of medical, individual, social and environmental influences on functioning and disability" (Ustun et al. 2010). This system is an assessment instrument that provides a standardized method for assessing an individual's self-reporting of functioning at the onset of illness and after interventions. It is therefore believed to be applicable cross-culturally for measuring disorders and the effectiveness of their treatments by assessing the individual's lived experience of their disorder without relying exclusively on diagnostic labels.

Mental health in general is under-recognized as being a critical public-health issue. In most countries it is an under-financed sector of health care; where services are available, there are major gaps in the availability of skilled providers. "Around half the world's population lives in countries where there is just one psychiatrist to serve 200,000 or more people. And the availability of affordable essential psychotropic medicines is limited, especially in low-income countries. Most people with diagnosed mental health conditions go completely untreated. In all countries, gaps in service coverage are compounded by variability in quality of care" (WHO 2022: xv). Low levels of mental health literacy, information, and availability of services are compounded by stigma and taboo, further isolating and exacerbating the marginalization of those who suffer from mental illness. These factors create a public-health crisis, a human rights challenge, and socioeconomic impacts that all justify the necessity for public policy interventions and investment in the mental health sector in all countries around the world.

There is a growing awareness in mental health research that a person's mental health is shaped by social, economic, and environmental factors. "Risk factors for many common mental disorders are heavily associated with social inequalities . . . the poor and disadvantaged suffer disproportionately, but those in the middle of the social gradient are also affected" (Allen et al. 2014: 392). The recognition of these socioeconomic risk factors throughout the lifetime of an individual, a family, and a community provides the potential for developing interventions that recognize mental disorders and address the delivery of relatively low-cost and effective treatments for managing mental issues throughout the lifespan. The World Health Organization proposes a "life course approach" to identifying and monitoring mental health inequalities, which identifies and addresses stressors present in anyone's life that could lead to, or exacerbate, mental health vulnerabilities. This approach helps identify points of intervention in the family and community that alleviate potential stressors; each of the life stages of an individual, including prenatal, early years, working years, and older life stages, creates unique challenges for individuals and families, challenges that can lead to mental health stressors.

For example, the prenatal environment of an unborn child can be a critical period in subsequent mental health. We have already discussed the 1,000 days approach in providing nutritional care and intervention for pregnant mothers and their babies. It is now clear that a mother's mental health is also an important factor in the well-being of her unborn child. A mother's poor health and nutrition can impact the mental development of her child, as can demanding physical work, and tobacco, alcohol, and drug use. "Children of depressed mothers are at a greater risk of being underweight and stunted. Pre-term and low birth weight babies may well themselves develop depression in later life" (Allen et al. 2014: 393). Household-based interventions through family and parenting support, education, and nutritional supplements have shown the potential to improve maternal and child outcomes in economically stressed communities.

In later childhood, schools provide a potential environment for recognizing stress and combating stigma around mental health, as well as communicating with parents and collaborating with care-giving institutions. In the adult work environment, both public- and private-sector employers are increasingly aware of the mental stresses of job and income insecurity. Providing a secure and safe work environment is important to relieving adult and family economic stresses and improving the mental state of employees. This can be supplemented by providing advisory services on health, nutrition, and access to information about drug and alcohol use and abuse. In later life, support services and meeting places can alleviate some of the depression in the elderly by providing physical and mental activities as well as companionship that lessens loneliness and isolation. These interventions should also all be supported by access to primary health services and, when needed, counseling and support. Increasingly these interventions include the use of social media and cell phone technology to provide information as well as the potential for data gathering, appointment and medication reminders, and patient monitoring. These are all practical interventions that can improve the mental state of individuals and communities; their inclusion in local and state policy and budgets ensures their sustainability over time.

COMMUNITY HEALTH WORKER INTERVENTION INITIATIVES

The World Health Organization is now advocating the implementation of "low-intensity psychological interventions" in multiple settings. This approach recognizes the (above cited) scarcity of mental health professionals, especially psychiatrists and psychologists, in countries and communities around the world. This approach is also referred to as **task shifting** in some settings, as it shifts responsibilities for delivering services away from scarce psychiatric and psychological professionals to trained local community members. It mobilizes the potential for paraprofessional interventions, peer support groups, and community volunteers to coordinate basic mental health and informational interventions.

In many parts of the world, **community health workers** are already providing basic medical care in underserved areas; trained midwives and delivery specialists in communities are a critical frontline resource in providing pregnant women and their babies immediate assistance and care. The "Thinking Healthy" initiative provides additional information and training for community health workers to deliver nonmedical psychosocial interventions to help manage perinatal depression in new mothers. Community health workers are trained to recognize depression during pregnancy and breastfeeding, and to engage women and their families in recognizing and mobilizing social support around depressive disorders or illness (WHO 2015). In other settings, community peer volunteers, who have gone through pregnancy and may have experienced postpartum depression themselves, are

task shifting

The shifting of health and wellness service delivery from scarce or unavailable professionals to trained local community health workers.

community health workers

Trained local people, usually women, who provide locally relevant health and mental health services in areas where there is a scarcity of professional practitioners.

trained to facilitate group and family discussions. "In principle, the power of the peer support worker is in sharing her personal struggles, modeling recovery, and offering hope for the future" (O'Hara 2022).

Case Study: "Thinking Healthy Program" in Pakistan—Mobilizing Volunteer Peers

The World Health Organization's Thinking Healthy approach was adapted in a trial program to the needs and resources available for pregnant women in Rawalpindi, Pakistan. The program delivered community-based mental health services to pregnant women in a low-resource setting; in rural Pakistan, it is estimated that the profound treatment gap results in 99 percent of mental issues and challenges going unnoticed and untreated (Sikander et al. 2019: 129). The Thinking Healthy program had two stated goals: to evaluate the effectiveness of trained peer volunteers in delivering psychological care to pregnant women, and to assess the cost-effectiveness of the program in a low resource setting. The program design includes extensive follow-up evaluation and analysis with the peer volunteers and mothers enrolled in the program to evaluate effectiveness, cost, and scalability, that is, the potential to "scale up" the program in multiple settings.

It was determined in preprogram assessments that these communities were already served by community-based health workers, referred to locally as "lady health workers" (LHWs) who provide midwifery services, basic health information, and breastfeeding support to pregnant women in their household settings. It was apparent, however, that the lady health workers were already stretched to the limit in time allocation to provide these services; they were therefore recruited to introduce additional trained peer volunteers into the communities and households in which they currently worked. Pregnant women were recruited to participate in the program if they met certain criteria: "Women aged 18 years or older were eligible to participate if they were in their third trimester of pregnancy, were registered with the local LHWs, and intended to stay in the study area for at least one year" (Sikander et al. 2019: 130).

Women who were eligible to be included in the study were randomly assigned to either the study group or a control group; one group continued to receive care from the LHWs, and the other group received volunteer peer support as well as maintaining their care from the LHWs. The people who were tasked with evaluating project outcomes did not know which group the women were assigned to, creating a "blind" study evaluation to assure that the outcome evaluators were not influenced by knowledge of the participants' intervention status. Extensive baseline data were compiled for each woman enrolled in the program, including data on her physical and mental health indicators and household situations, including presence of domestic violence and substance abuse.

The peer counselors volunteered their services with no financial remuneration. "They were local volunteers; they were married women, around ages 30–35 years who were selected for their good communication skills. All volunteers had children and a similar educational and socioeconomic background as the participants." (Sikander at al. 2019: 131). They were trained in group classroom discussions and received regular supervision and follow-up trainings during the trials. They were regularly assessed for retention of information and their ability to communicate key ideas and concepts. They were also trained in behavioral therapy techniques, such as encouraging women to create narratives of their lives, using pictures and drawings to identify important issues, and in family collaboration to engage family members, including husbands and sons, in information sharing.

Analysis of the outcomes of the project verified that the peer-volunteer-counseling approach is a low-cost, viable strategy that equaled the outcomes of programs involving trained community health workers. Systematic evaluation showed that the most effective outcomes came within the first three months of the program, with "modest" positive effects between three and six months of service delivery. The peer volunteers demonstrated very good retention of information they received during trainings but did require sustained and ongoing training and monitoring. Project participants had positive responses to participating, especially as it provided an opportunity for them to talk about their moods and experiences. The project designers, based on their program implementation and follow-up assessments, see it as a cost-effective system of delivery of psychological services to pregnant women with the potential for providing "front line, first-step intervention, in a stepped up care system or a collaborative care model for maternal depression." The peer-volunteer program did not seem to have a significant effect where cases of severe clinical depression were diagnosed, but they could potentially provide referrals to, and follow-up by, other medical and psychological professionals (Sikander 2019: 137).

Conflict Zones/Migration/Health

The human toll resulting from natural disasters and resource scarcity are exacerbated for migrants and asylum seekers attempting to cross borders to flee these highly dangerous situations. Migrants are especially vulnerable to the physical and mental stresses caused by the uncertainty of their situation. In areas of endemic violence and political conflict, there is a high probability of massive displacement, and the need for displaced people to find safe places, food, clean water and sanitation, and shelter for themselves and for family members. Humanitarian responses are usually not sufficient to accommodate the needs of all migrants, and are often stretched thin by the number of migrants and asylum seekers they try to serve. Women migrants are especially vulnerable to secondary trauma and violence at the hands of traffickers, military personnel and guards, as well as occasionally from other migrants and family members. Large numbers of people in confined spaces immediately creates the risk of malnutrition, diarrheal infections, and the spread of diseases like measles, pneumonia, Covid-19, and malaria. Migrants face unmet needs for mental health services, primary care, and attention to noncommunicable diseases and disabilities.

Humanitarian responses face their own challenges. Migrant camps and transit points, designed to meet temporary needs, in many settings turn into semi-permanent and permanent settlements, without the water and sanitation infrastructure to support long-term residents. Often, calls for humanitarian aid in a crisis setting result in diverse forms of aid and assistance pouring into an emergency setting from multilateral aid organizations, diverse donor sources, and nongovernmental organizations. However, historically, a lack of coordination, communication, and planning among the humanitarian organizations results in duplication of services and waste when these resources don't reach the intended groups.

The Sphere Project was created in 1997 by humanitarian NGOs to improve the quality and accountability of humanitarian responses. The *Sphere Handbook* (Sphere 2021) has been updated with multiple editions, and its users are both practitioners responding to humanitarian crises and the affected people themselves. The *Handbook* contains systematic guidelines for assessing humanitarian crisis settings, particularly by taking into account the diversity of affected populations. Within these settings, demographic characteristics impede some people's ability to access services; women, children, the elderly, people who identify as LGBTQ+, and the disabled require tailored responses to their particular needs for nutrition, shelter, and health care. The *Sphere Handbook* outlines the procedures for, and factors involved in, situation assessment, analysis and prioritization, options and delivery responses, and finally program design based on these assessments. It outlines methods of data collection and service coordination, including the role of private-sector responders, to humanely and equitably distribute the goods and services provided by all the humanitarian responders. It stresses the necessity of integrating the perspectives of affected people in developing a realistic, equitable, and sustainable set of programs in a transparent and effective way. This approach stresses the recognition that each setting is different, and that understanding the unique parameters of each context is key to effective delivery of services. These strategies, when applied systematically and with transparency, have been demonstrated already to be effective in multiple health and wellness settings

SUMMARY

- Despite important successes throughout the twentieth century, a large percentage of the world's population face medical and psychological challenges in obtaining basic resources for a healthy life outcome.

- Gender, sexuality, ethnicity, race, and socioeconomic status play a critical role in health and wellness.

- Poverty is a recognized factor in poor health outcomes around the world.

- Public health perspectives and solutions understand health and wellness as part of social life and community resources. Covid-19 illustrates how different groups in the United States had difference outcomes and impacts resulting from the pandemic.

- Health is now understood as physical, mental, and social well-being, not limited to the absence of illness or infirmity.

- Medical anthropologists are part of public health teams, using their unique methods of social analysis to track disease transmission, and propose sustainable solutions.

- The UN's Sustainable Development Goals (SDGs) are seventeen interconnected global goals supported by all the member states and form a blueprint to achieve a better and more sustainable future for all people and the world by 2030.

- Health disparities are widely documented within and between countries, between regions of countries, and between rural and urban areas.

- LGBTQ+ identity impacts availability of jobs, health resources, and well-being.

- Malnutrition and food insecurity is a global problem that was exacerbated by production and distribution issues during the Covid-19 pandemic.

- Scholars and advocates focus on the documentation of how gender creates multiple physical and mental health challenges. Women and girls are subject to many educational and health-related risks throughout their lives.

- Sanitation, clean water, and closed toilet systems are still unavailable to over 3 billion people worldwide.

- Climate change is increasingly being recognized as a factor in health and nutrition challenges.

- Psychological health and mental wellness is being recognized as a critical factor in global health policy. There is an unmet need around the world for affordable and culturally relevant psychological interventions.

- Pregnant women and their newborn children benefit greatly when postpartum depression is recognized and treated.

- Innovations in mental health programming include training of peer volunteers to facilitate identification and symptom-alleviation strategies of postpartum depression and other psychological challenges in low-resource settings.

- Conflict zones and migration settings are particularly challenging as humanitarian-aid settings. Men, women, and children suffer from a range of physical and mental traumas that go untreated due to lack of resources and political will.

KEY TERMS

biopower, 298
child mortality, 311
community health workers, 318
evidence-based outcomes, 295
human capital, 306
medical anthropology, 297
monitoring and evaluation, 294

randomized controlled studies, 295
structural violence, 300
Sustainable Development Goals (SDGs), 294
task shifting, 318

SUGGESTED READINGS

Davis, Dána-Ain. *Reproductive Injustice: Racism, Pregnancy, and Premature Birth.* New York: New York University Press, 2019.

Based on multiple interviews with women of color and their partners, nurses, midwives, and physicians, this book demonstrates that medical racism impacts the pregnancy outcomes of professional women in the United States. Parents' experiences with neonatal intensive care units (NICUs) reveal pernicious forms of racism as a central factor in premature birth and negative outcomes in minority communities in contemporary urban America.

Farmer, Paul, et al. *Reimagining Global Health: An Introduction.* Berkeley: University of California Press, 2013.

This collection brings together the insights of Paul Farmer, his colleagues and his students, in a series of theoretical and ethnographic essays exploring the challenges of delivering equitable, humane interventions in multiple humanitarian settings.

Skolnik, Richard. *Global Health 101*, 4th ed. Burlington, MA: Jones & Bartlett Learning, 2021.

A highly comprehensive and accessible textbook discussing the critical issues in global health, and featuring detailed case studies in each area to explore the complexities of assessment, program design, and data management.

SUGGESTED WEBSITES

https://www.who.int/

The website of the World Health Organization. Founded in 1948, the WHO is the United Nations agency that promotes global health and safety around the world. The website is easy to navigate and highlights the latest information and studies on epidemics and pandemics, interventions, and emerging health issues. The website also contains data and statistical information by country and region. Information is available in multiple languages for different regions around the world, as well as general information about the agency's activities.

https://www.unicef.org/

The website of UNICEF. This United Nations division works in over 190 countries to protect the lives of children and adolescents through medical, educational, and rights interventions. UNICEF works in humanitarian crisis settings for child protection and survival, and focuses attention on empowering girls and women. The website provides easy access to data and research and background information on particular issues such as discrimination against children with disabilities.

https://www.msf.org/

The website of Doctors without Borders/Médecins Sans Frontières. Doctors Without Borders is an international, independent medical humanitarian organization, providing medical assistance to people affected by conflict, epidemics, disasters, and exclusion. Founded in 1971 in France, the organization's extensive networks of volunteer physicians and health workers provide medical services in conflict areas to all those in need. MSF was awarded the Nobel Peace Prize in 1999 in recognition of its pioneering humanitarian work. The website contains detailed studies of all its intervention sites and activities.

Chapter 13

Living/Working in the Globalized World

Colonialism, Globalization, Migration, and Development

LEARNING OBJECTIVES

- Relate the variations of colonialism and imperialism to contemporary globalization.
- Describe the goals of applied anthropology and the uses of anthropological knowledge in directed change.
- Explain the concepts of development and underdevelopment.

- Document how globalization creates demands for new forms of labor, and the strategies people develop to meet these demands.
- Understand the constellations of family, relationships, and care giving across borders.

IN THE FIRST PART OF the twentieth century, anthropologists generally looked at cultures as if they were static, unchanging entities. Malinowski, who carried out several years of fieldwork among the Trobriand Islanders between 1912 and 1917, recorded his observations without paying attention to the changes taking place before his very eyes. In reality, cultures are constantly undergoing change, but in today's world change occurs at a very rapid rate.

There are numerous and powerful forces for change in the world today. In the nineteenth and early twentieth centuries, colonialism and imperialism were the strongest forces for change globally. There are now a series of postcolonial states whose borders are created by the geographies of colonial empires. Postcolonial nation-states build national cultures in their attempt to integrate the various indigenous groups and ethnicities within their borders, in the same way that, in the past, the nation-states of Europe attempted to forge national cultures with varying degrees of success.

Some scholars make a distinction between **colonialism** and **imperialism**. They are both strategies of domination. Colonialism implies forceful invasion and subsequent control by the invading country, which may be thousands of miles away, over all of its political, economic, and social institutions. Imperialism suggests formal or informal domination, especially in economic, political, and diplomatic functions, particularly over contiguous or nearby territories. Despite political independence, economic interdependency of one-time colonies on former colonial powers, in many places, constitutes **neocolonialism**.

Over several centuries, changes associated with colonialism have greatly altered indigenous economic institutions. These changes include the introduction of cash crops; production and consumption of manufactured goods; exploitation of local resources for export; and the need for labor far away from home. The enormous expansion of cities presents economic and cultural opportunities that attract migrants from rural areas and across borders. When they return to their natal communities, they bring cosmopolitan consumer products and ideas with them. Movers and non-movers are familiar with urban and cross-border norms and technologies.

In many industrializing states, the government's strategies and institutions of economic and social development impact their citizens' everyday life. Developing states adopt agricultural, industrial, educational, health, tourism, and resource exploitation strategies to raise incomes and enhance the quality of lives of their citizens. These development projects, financed historically by Western-dominated multilateral (multistate) lenders and donors, are now increasingly being supported through domestic financial markets and private enterprise.

New forms of credit and institutional lending practices, such as the **microfinance** approach originally developed by Bangladesh's Grameen Bank, provide small-business loans to poor individuals and groups of people who otherwise would not have access to credit. **Nongovernmental organizations (NGOs)** are familiar worldwide as local links to the development resources of national and international donor organizations and information networks. Cell phones, computers, and globally circulated media bring images, ideas, and expertise from urban centers to the countryside. Anthropologists participate in these activities in various

colonialism

Full or partial political and economic subjugation of one country or group of people by another, resulting in multiple forms of social discrimination and resource exploitation.

imperialism

Influence over another contiguous or nearby country or region.

neocolonialism

Economic interdependency of one-time colonies on colonial period elites and on former colonial powers despite political independence.

microfinance

A development strategy that provides small-business loans to poor individuals and groups of people who otherwise would not have access to credit.

nongovernmental organizations (NGOs)

Development organizations that are structurally independent of state institutions.

ways. Some document the experiences of, and resistance to, economic transformation, mass communication, and labor migration; applied anthropologists use their anthropological knowledge to create, initiate, and evaluate the outcomes of development strategies, policies, and interventions.

COLONIALISM, GLOBALIZATION, AND ANTHROPOLOGY

Colonialism and its consequences can be examined at several different levels. **Postcolonial studies** focus on the effects of colonialism on former European colonies; often interdisciplinary, these studies combine the use of historical and literary texts with ethnography. Anthropologists usually focus on the "micro" and "meso" levels in the field: individual perceptions and decision making (micro) and family/community (meso) dynamics. However, they do not study micro- and meso-level dynamics in isolation, but in relation to more inclusive political or "macro" levels, including state and global institutions (Brettell 2003). One focus of anthropologists studying postcolonial states has been on the construction of a national culture and the creation of national identity. States are recognized by other states as sovereign or independent, politically autonomous units; political decisions and economic planning take place at the state level. Consequently, the unit of analysis of economic development is also the state. At a still higher, more inclusive, level of macro-level analysis is the **world system**. This concept, developed by Immanuel Wallerstein (1974, 2004), refers to the historic emergence of the economic interrelationship of the world's states into a global economic system, in which the concept of the division of labor, usually seen as operative in a single society, is projected onto the global capitalist economy.

Wallerstein sees the world system developing after the breakdown of feudalism and the rise of capitalism and entrepreneurship, and with the global influence of the Industrial Revolution. During and after the Age of Exploration, Europeans vastly expanded their search for sources of raw materials and mineral resources, as well as for markets for their manufactured goods. These European countries formed the core of a world system, and the colonies and protectorates that they dominated formed the periphery of the system. The world system now operates according to capitalist market principles, with profits constantly reverting to the investors of capital, who are located, for the most part, in the core. World systems theory focuses primarily on the existence of structures, such as core and periphery, with anthropological research directed toward the examination of the dynamics of the relationship between the smaller, local actors of the system in the periphery and the more powerful actors of the core.

Anthropologists have been particularly interested in the effects of the penetration of the world system on indigenous peoples all over the world and their responses to this penetration. Eric Wolf (1982), in Europe and the People without History, explored this topic, focusing, for example, on how

postcolonial studies

Often interdisciplinary focus on the effects of colonialism on former European colonies.

world systems theory

The historic emergence of the economic interrelationship of most of the world in a single economic system.

the Native peoples of North America responded to the fur trade network set up by the Hudson's Bay Company in the eighteenth century. These responses included transformations of their indigenous systems of production, leadership, and gendered division of labor, creating new economic and political systems to meet the demand of elite consumer markets in Europe for luxury goods.

Within recent years, the term *globalization* has come to signify the multiple rapid transformations in the lives of people in all parts of the world due to "speeding up of the flows of capital, people, goods, images, and ideas across the world, thus pointing to a general increase in the pace of global interactions and processes" (Inda and Rosaldo 2008: 11). There are multiple consequences to this intensification of interaction and connections, including cross-border migration and communication. The impacts of these developments in one part of the world are rapidly felt elsewhere. "All told, globalization can be seen as referring to those spatial–temporal processes, operating on a global scale, that rapidly cut across national boundaries, drawing more and more of the world into webs of interconnection, integrating and stretching cultures and communities across space, and time, and compressing our spatial and temporal horizons" (2008: 11–12).

Globalization has been brought about in part by the development of a worldwide network of finance and capital. This has occurred on a greater scale than ever before, and at an increasingly rapid rate as a result of enormous advances in telecommunications and computer technology. Within various parts of the industrializing world, globalization in the late twentieth century resulted in some economic growth, for example, in South Korea, Malaysia, and India. Many countries in Latin American and Africa are predicted by international economists to be rapidly growing economies in the twenty-first century.

New technologies have not only facilitated globalization, but they have also streamlined resistance against it. Internet and email networks allow those who have access to these technologies to receive and send information reflecting multiple perspectives. This mobilization of concerned individuals and groups facilitated by electronic technologies is seen at the World Trade Organization (WTO) meetings in various cities around the world. The WTO attempts to integrate states into a global economy. At WTO meetings, local citizens regularly demonstrate their resistance to this goal, from various differing perspectives. Some demonstrators are concerned about ecological devastation and global environmental threats. Labor unionists are dissatisfied with changes in tariffs and labor rights, which threaten domestic workers' jobs and deregulate wages and working conditions. Small businesses and entrepreneurs resist the power of multinational corporations to control production and consumption in local markets.

Although globalization seems to be similar to colonialism and the neocolonialism of the latter part of the twentieth century, in reality it represents a quantum leap in the reach, penetration, and power of global capitalism (Appadurai 1996). The anthropologist's role in the study of globalization is in part to examine various contexts where one might say that globalization had its beginnings, and to focus on the contemporary lived experience of people in different communities: to "put human faces on what would otherwise would be anonymous, impersonal statistics" (Orlove 1999: 196). The lived experiences of individuals and communities in globalized settings is increasingly transnational, taking place simultaneously in multiple places, often in different countries. Anthropologists explore the impact of multiple forms of remittances, including money, consumer goods, and information that flow regularly between migrants and "non-movers" in their home communities (Cohen and Sirkeci 2011). Anthropologists study the complexity of relationships and family forms created by migration; this approach uses ethnographic documentation of the diversity of interpersonal relationships created through state policies that regulate migrants' access to residence, marriage, citizenship, and rights (D'Aoust 2022).

Globalization, Production, and Consumption

Factory production, labor, and patterns of consumption are among the variables scholars analyze to document historic changes and local variations associated with globalization. Political-economy theorists and historians make the distinction in American economic history between Fordism and Post-Fordism, referencing the characteristics of Henry Ford's methods of automobile production in the early and mid-twentieth century. **Fordism** refers to assembly-line production systems characterized by mass-production of identical or similar products in "bricks and mortar" factory settings by skilled laborers. These industrial innovations greatly reduced the production costs and increased profitability of Ford's automobiles and other manufactured goods in the early to mid-twentieth century. This mass-production system increased the supply and lowered the cost of manufactured products to consumers, including a new generation of steadily employed and relatively well-paid factory workers who could afford to buy the products they were producing. Despite initial resistance by manufacturers, labor unions made great inroads into organizing factory workers and providing wages and benefits in exchange for increased levels of production. Fordist production contributed to America's post–World War II growth and was the primary economic strategy of industrialization through the 1970s.

Post-Fordism emerged with the shift in the American and other Western economies from manufacturing to service industries, and the

Fordism

The economic, production, labor, and consumer-oriented innovations associated with Henry Ford's twentieth-century assembly-line mass production of automobiles.

Post-Fordism

The production systems associated with contemporary globalization. Products are assembled in multiple sites, using unregulated and low-paid labor often in Free Trade Zones in Southern countries.

One characteristic of contemporary globalization is the re-organization of production systems on a global scale. Production and assembly of finished products takes place in multiple global sites, with manufacturers seeking the most advantageous and inexpensive labor supplies. This has created the "feminization of labor" in many Export Processing Zones around the world, as illustrated by this clothing factory in Vietnam.

simultaneous growth of new information and capital-creating technologies. Cheaper labor supplies abroad, especially in developing countries, quickly replaced domestic factory workers in the United States and other Western countries. Company headquarters are no longer associated with centralized manufacturing facilities, but are instead linked by communication technologies to decentralized globally situated sites of labor, service support (such as the call centers in India), product transportation, and assembly. Reductions in trade barriers and tariffs and the creation of regional and global trading networks facilitate trade, capital transfers, and production. Greatly reduced costs of shipping and air freight quickly link sites of inexpensive labor and product assembly to Northern centers of consumption for consumer goods that are now routinely manufactured and assembled in Asia, Africa, and Latin America.

Many of these products now consumed in Northern markets are produced in **Free Trade Zones (FTZ)** of developing countries, which offer financial incentives and labor regulation concessions to multinational corporations in an effort to attract foreign investment capital. Also known as Export Processing Zones (EPZs), FTZs are usually located in underdeveloped areas of the host country, requiring migration of labor to staff the factories producing garments, electronics, sneakers, and other consumer goods for export. Governments of developing countries create these zones to provide their citizens with employment in the hope of stimulating economic growth and creating jobs. However, concessions made to foreign companies to keep labor costs low include the suspension of benefits and environmental-protection regulations that Northern manufacturers are subject to in their home countries. As a result, laborers do not receive benefits, minimum wage guarantees, secure employment, or healthy working conditions. They can rarely afford to buy the products they labor to produce.

Many ethnographic studies of export production facilities around the world (Ong 1987; Mills 2006; Rothstein 2007; Hewamanne 2008) document the labor inequalities that characterize contemporary globalized capitalism. Scholars and labor advocates note the increasing "feminization of labor" in the globalized economy. Women, often young and unmarried, are targeted as preferred factory workers and "dominate the lowest levels both of pay and authority, whereas men occupy most positions of supervisory and managerial rank" (Mills 2003: 43). The feminization of the globalized labor pool has parallels in the nineteenth-century Industrial Revolution in Europe and the United States, but the contemporary gendered flexible labor practices that characterize late capitalism "encompasses every corner of the globe"

Free Trade Zones (FTZs) (also known as Export Processing Zones)

Areas in developing countries set aside for foreign-owned export-production facilities.

The tragedy of the Rana Plaza Factory fire in Bangladesh that caused the deaths of over 1,000 workers galvanized political awareness and action about worker's rights throughout the country.

(2003: 42). Ethnographic studies of global labor document the social consequences women face by joining the local flexible workforce. By engaging in nontraditional employment requiring travel away from their homes, they may subsequently be deemed "unmarriageable" or "dishonorable" when they return to their home communities, and may be subjected to multiple forms of violence in and around the workplace.

Men are also targeted for labor recruitment based on presumed gendered and ethnic norms. Male labor migrants, particularly those crossing borders in pursuit of employment in mining and fossil fuel–extraction industries,

---

BOX 13.1 | In the Aftermath of Tragedy: Labor Activism, Global Initiatives

On April 24, 2013, in Dhaka, Bangladesh, an eight-story factory collapsed, killing over 1,100 workers and injuring and permanently disabling hundreds of others. Eighty percent of the workers, who stitched garments sold by U.S., Canadian, and European retailers, were young women who earned about 22 cents an hour and were forced to work over 14 hours a day to keep their jobs. The cause of the factory collapse was determined to be shoddy construction and use of substandard materials. This devastation was compounded by inadequate building inspections and lack of basic safety procedures for factory workers. The scope of this factory disaster brought these deplorable working conditions to the attention of the Bangladeshi government, as well as to Western retailers and consumers, prompting global interest in the supply chains producing low-cost clothing and other manufactured goods in EPZs around the world.

Many different forms of labor activism emerged in the aftermath of the Rana factory collapse, representing multiple levels of political and economic actors in the contemporary global system of garment production. The Bangladeshi government, under pressure from millions of factory workers, amended its labor laws to strengthen workers rights and ease some of the roadblocks to forming unions. The United States and the European Union exerted pressure on the Bangladeshi government to enforce labor protection and prevent labor violations by threatening to suspend favorable trade-preference

conditions. The International Labor Organization (ILO) is administering a compensation fund for affected workers and their families, created with contributions from major Western manufacturers and retailers. The names of those organizations that contributed, or were reluctant to contribute, were widely publicized in the global media. Global labor activists in alliance with Bangladeshi labor unions created voluntary accords between European and American manufacturers and retailers that established minimal labor compliance standards for production of their goods, including factory inspection procedures and schedules, transparency about the use of overseas production facilities and contractors, as well as violation penalties. Bangladeshi factory owners, who cite the economic pressures exerted on them by retailers and manufacturers to provide low-cost labor and production facilities, are a significant political force in Bangladeshi politics. They often resist reforms that impinge on what they claim are their already small profit margins.

Activists and journalists who continue to monitor Bangladeshi production facilities say that there have been some modest gains in the support of workers rights and working conditions, but the realization of these goals is a constant struggle. The aftermath of the Rana disaster did, however, create a blueprint for multilevel engagement of stakeholders around the world in improving the labor conditions of workers supplying the global marketplace with inexpensive goods and services.

endure harsh working conditions and discrimination as ethnic and religious minorities (Mills 2003: 52). Dangerous and unprotected work environments are increasingly providing the impetus for laborers to attempt to unionize, often in fierce opposition from government and private enterprises. These labor alliances with domestic and international workers to protect rights and safety are also bringing information to consumers around the world about the working conditions in which their consumer goods are produced.

The Historic Background to Globalization: Many Faces of Colonial Rule

It is important to understand colonial history as the precursor to the flow of labor, capital, and consumer goods today in the globalizing world. Colonialism and imperialism over the course of history has taken many forms, with different effects on the dominated people. There were various reasons for the establishment of colonies. Sometimes, it was the search for raw materials and markets. At other times, colonies were established because of the need to protect the boundaries of an empire from mobilized groups of local people or from other empires. Sometimes, only colonial administrators and people involved in the extraction of resources lived in the colony. In other instances, many people came to the colony as permanent settlers. At the beginning of the colonization of North America, the only contacts that Native American societies had were with explorers and governmental representatives of the British and French colonial empires. Over time, a large and more powerful immigrant population engulfed these societies; new social, economic, and political systems emerged, marked by grossly unequal power over, and coercion of, indigenous groups.

The initial motivation for the establishment of colonies was economic gain, which frequently took the form of exploiting raw materials as well as providing markets for the goods of the colonizing countries. The Industrial Revolution in western Europe led to domestic shortages of resources and the need to find them abroad. Often, a single large trading company, such as the British East India Company, the Hudson's Bay Company, or the Dutch East India Company, held a monopoly on trade; these trading companies eventually attained political control as well.

indirect rule

The system of colonial rule associated with the British Empire by which a small number of administrators controlled large colonial territories by integrating local political leaders and bureaucrats into the administrative system.

direct rule

Colonial strategy involving large numbers of permanent settlers, military personnel, and appropriation of land and resources by the colonial ruler.

There were important differences in the ways colonial powers governed. The British developed the policy of **indirect rule**, which was then applied throughout their extensive empire. A relatively small number of British administrators controlled large colonial territories by integrating local political leaders and bureaucrats into the British-controlled administrative system. In contrast, the French used a policy of **direct rule**, establishing military garrisons and large French populations throughout their empire. The French had a policy of accepting an educated individual from their colonies, who was then referred to as an évolue, as a citizen of France. In contrast, the British integrated educated Asians and Africans into the colonial administration but maintained social and political segregation. Although the indigenous population was usually much larger than the foreign population, power and wealth were both in the hands of the representatives of the colonial power.

Anthropologists studying colonialism document the complexity of the dimensions of colonial life and the reach of colonial powers into the social and political lives of the colonized. These interventions continue to resonate in postcolonial social, political, and religious constructions of identity. (Also see chapter 14.) Colonizers continually enacted policies to define the social boundaries between themselves and the colonized, whose "otherness" was perpetually being redefined. European colonizers had a variety of intentions toward the indigenous populations. Methodist missionaries hoped to turn the indigenous communities of southern Africa into yeoman farmers modeled on the agricultural systems of eighteenth-century England. Other colonizers attempted to transform the existing social organization to create a steady labor force for work in mines and other extractive industries. The social boundaries between the European colonizers and the local population were sometimes eroded by relationships between European men and local women, which produced an intermediate population with an ambiguous identity in the European systems of racial classifications. But colonizers quickly created new classifications and regulations for these relationships and the identities of children resulting from these unions (Stoler 2006).

European missionaries brought various forms and practices of Christianity to the people of New Guinea in the early 1900s.

The nature of initial contact varied from colony to colony. Colonial control was sometimes set up in the form of patrol posts in the native territory. The Australian government used this method to achieve control over indigenous peoples of Highland New Guinea, who were frequently hostile to the colonizers. First contact was sometimes peaceful. Military resistance usually occurred later, as in the case of the Maori in New Zealand, when people realized that they were losing their independence, autonomy, and cultural distinctiveness, as well as their ability to determine their own destiny. Hostilities between British colonizers and the Maori ended with the Treaty of Waitangi in 1840. Under the terms of this treaty, the British Crown received all rights and powers of sovereignty over Maori territory, though the Maori chiefs thought they were giving up only partial rights. In 1996, an official report found that an entire province in New Zealand had been illegally taken from the Taranaki Maori by the Treaty of Waitangi. The report recommended that the Maori be given back the land surrounding Mount Taranaki or equivalent financial compensation.

Different colonial empires had somewhat different policies with respect to the rights of native peoples over their land. Furthermore, these native peoples themselves had a variety of different conceptualizations about land rights. In the Australian case, the colonial government understood the native pattern of land utilization and the claims of various Australian indigenous groups to ancestral homelands, but it chose to ignore them and claim the entire continent as unoccupied wasteland, recognizing neither the land rights nor the sovereignty of the natives.

In America, both the British colonial government and later the new American government, in the Ordinance of 1787, recognized Native Americans' rights to land; these relationships were maintained with Native Americans throughout the nineteenth century. As the immigrant population of the United States grew, and with it the demand for land, the Native American land base began to be encroached on by successive treaties that Native communities were forced to negotiate with the United States government. The fight over land continues today, but the positions are reversed. For example, the Passamaquoddy of Maine have gone to court to lay claim to their traditional land, on the basis of their contention that the United States government illegally broke treaties made in good faith in past centuries.

Exploitation of resources other than land was critical in defining the nature of the colonial experience and can be analyzed from the level of the world system. Western industrial demand for rubber illustrates the way the economic fates of people on three different continents were linked. Natural stands of rubber trees in the Amazon and Congo River basins were exploited by European and American traders during the rubber boom of 1895 to 1910. In both places, indigenous peoples, who had been subsistence agriculturalists, provided the source of labor for the tapping of latex from the rubber trees in the tropical forest. British entrepreneurs took wild rubber plant seedlings from the Congo and Amazon basins and transported them to the British colony of Malaya, where they established rubber plantations, owned and operated by British settlers, to provide a steady source of this raw material. Rubber from these plantations captured the world market, bringing to an end the boom in wild rubber from the Congo and Amazon basins. Subsequently, the Firestone Rubber Company of America developed rubber plantations in Liberia, and this rubber also gained a large share of the world market. Since rubber was Liberia's dominant cash crop, Firestone came to control its entire economy at that time. The discovery of methods to mass-produce synthetic rubber, developed during World War II, signaled the great reduction in importance of plantation-grown rubber and the collapse of these export economies.

Exploitation of resources in colonial areas and their successor states required local labor. This need for labor was met in a variety of ways, which had profound effects on the indigenous peoples, dislocating their economies and their traditional forms of family and social organization. In the earliest period of the colonization of the New World, the demand by the colonizers for a large-scale labor force to exploit resources was satisfied by the enslavement of native peoples such as the Tupi-speaking coastal peoples of Brazil. The Portuguese enslaved them, and their population was decimated as a result of disease and the conditions of slavery. From the sixteenth century to the beginning of the nineteenth century, some eight to ten million enslaved

Africans were brought to North America to furnish labor for the plantations there. As Africans from different cultures speaking different languages were forced to adapt to the new conditions of servitude and to the cultures and languages of their plantation masters, new African-derived languages and cultures were forged in new settings.

With the eventual abolition of enslaving and transporting people against their will, plantation labor was obtained by means of **indentured servitude**, involving long-term labor contracts. This was the case for laborers from South Asia who went to Trinidad, British Guiana, Fiji, and South Africa, creating ethnic communities that continue in these countries today. Local **corvee labor** was the method of the colonial government used in the Congo to force people to work as rubber tappers. In the Pacific, **blackbirding**, as the kidnapping and enslavement of Melanesians was referred to, continued after the abolition of slavery in Europe to fulfill the labor requirement of the sugar plantations on Fiji and in Australia. Violent and coercive forms of labor recruitment eventually gave way to labor contracts and wage labor, which was used to recruit laborers to exploit the mineral resources of southern Africa. In the past, the South African government controlled the flow of domestic workers through Pass Laws, preventing those without a contract from leaving their natal areas for the towns and cities. This migration had left rural areas with greatly reduced male populations, leaving children without fathers and wives without husbands. The earlier organization of the family was undercut and weakened, and women alone raised the children. During the time they worked in the mines, the men became increasingly familiar with urban life, gaining an awareness of labor unions and political rights movements.

When a colonial administration was set up, concerted efforts were made to abolish those indigenous practices that violated the colonizers' moral code; non-Western family forms and marriage patterns were especially targeted for abolition. Anglican and Methodist missionaries among the Haida in northwestern Canada considered the potlatch (described in chapter 2) to be a "heathen" custom, since it was a significant native religious rite that they felt impeded the spread of Christianity among these people. Some missionaries and administrators objected to the accumulation and redistribution practices of the potlatch, which they considered irrational economic behavior. In other settings, missionaries recorded and transcribed languages that existed only in oral forms; the creation of vernacular Bibles was in many cases the first attempt to record and preserve threatened indigenous languages.

NEW IRELAND: A HISTORY OF INCREASING INCORPORATION INTO THE GLOBAL SYSTEM

It is useful to examine the ways in which the variables we have just discussed operated in New Ireland, now part of the state of Papua New Guinea (Rubel and Rosman 2021, 2023). New Ireland is located in the Bismarck Archipelago, close to the equator and east of the much larger island of New Guinea in the Pacific Ocean. The first Western explorer known to have made contact with

indentured servitude

A labor recruitment strategy in which laborers are compelled to agree to long-term and exploitative contracts in exchange for wages or other forms of remuneration.

corvee labor

A system of forced labor associated with colonial plantations.

blackbirding

The term for the kidnapping of Melanesian laborers to work on colonial plantations in Fiji and Australia.

New Irelanders, in 1619, was a Dutch explorer, Willem Schouten (1567–1625). He was searching for trading opportunities in the Pacific outside the geographic area over which the Dutch East India Company had established a monopoly. Schouten tried to exchange beads with the New Irelanders for needed supplies, but the exchange could not be transacted because neither side understood the other. The New Irelanders attacked Schouten's men with slings and clubs; he responded with cannon fire, killing several of them. This violent initial contact with the West was not easily forgotten by the New Irelanders. Over the next two centuries, seven European expeditions sought to replenish their supplies on New Ireland. They offered trade goods, such as beads and cloth, which did not seem to interest the New Irelanders, and consequently they were given little in the way of supplies in return.

During the first decades of nineteenth century, ships began to put in more and more frequently at New Ireland locations. By this time, the New Irelanders knew that the European ships anchoring in their harbors wanted to resupply their ships with coconuts, tubers, and pigs, and the Europeans had become aware of the New Irelanders' desire for iron. Iron hoops, used to hold casks of whale oil together, were given in exchange for supplies. Iron was greatly prized by the New Irelanders to make adzes and axes for gardening. In the early nineteenth century, English and American whalers put in at the bays of New Ireland for fresh water and supplies, in exchange for hoop iron, along with buttons, bottles, strips of cloth, and, later, tobacco. A number of seamen became castaways and settled on New Ireland at this time.

During this period, the island was further enmeshed in the world system when traders came seeking tortoise shell to be sent to Europe for the manufacture of combs and other decorative items, which became the rage of fashionable European elites. Beche-de-mer (sea cucumbers) were also collected and then dried and sold to the Chinese as a food delicacy. By this point, a mutually agreed-upon barter system had been established, and some New Irelanders were able to communicate in Pidgin English. The New Irelanders thus became part of the global system of trade.

The first European trading post was set up on New Ireland in 1880 by the German trader Eduard Hernsheim to purchase coconuts. From his base on Matupi Island in New Britain, Hernsheim set up a network of trading stations, including a number of them on New Ireland. His agents at these stations—Englishmen, Scandinavians, and, later, mostly the Chinese—bought unhusked coconuts (later, only the nuts) from the New Ireland villagers in exchange for tobacco, beads, and ironware from Europe. The price the villagers received for coconuts varied depending on the price of copra (dried coconut meat) on the world market, the price of beads in Europe, and the number of competing traders in the area. These were factors from the world economic system over which villagers on the local level had no control. Hernsheim transported copra on his own ship to be sold in Hamburg, Germany; the success of his business enterprise depended on the world price of copra.

Because the New Irelanders had Big Men, rather than chiefs, there was no one in a position of central political authority with whom traders and later political administrators could make binding agreements and sign treaties. There was no single indigenous political structure that unified the whole island. The alternative for Europeans to the unpredictable supply of copra provided through trading stations was the establishment of a plantation system, which began on New Ireland at the beginning of the twentieth century. Land for plantations had to be purchased by Europeans from New Irelanders. Since land on New Ireland was owned by matrilineal clans, only clan representatives could negotiate such sales.

Labor recruiters began in the 1880s to call at locations in New Ireland to recruit workers for plantations in Fiji and, later, Australia, often resorting to blackbirding, or the kidnapping of laborers. Some of the men tried to escape this forced labor by jumping overboard; the remainder were forcibly taken to Queensland to work as laborers. When they returned home three years later, the recruits brought back boxes filled with Western goods, which they used to maximize their positions in the political arenas of their own villages, becoming leaders and Big Men. Many came back to New Ireland speaking Pidgin English, and this enabled them to deal more successfully with the European traders on the island. The sugar produced in Queensland and the copra from Fiji and Samoa, where the New Irelanders worked, were destined for sale on the world market.

Missionary activity began in New Ireland in 1875 when the Methodist Reverend George Brown, an Englishman, stationed two Fijian religious teachers there, where no colonial administration existed. Fijian teachers were important to the Methodist missionary enterprise because they could more effectively spread the message of Christianity than Europeans. The Methodist missionaries voiced their strong opposition to local habits and tried to eliminate the New Irelanders' customs such as wearing no clothing, ritual dancing—which the missionaries considered lewd—and cannibalism. The progress of missionizing was impeded by the absence of authoritative leadership and the many languages spoken on the island. When a chief converts, as in Fiji, an entire chiefdom converts with him; Big Men do not have the same kind of authority over their followers. Catholic missionaries visited New Ireland in 1882. The Catholic missionary approach involved setting up mission stations run by Europeans to which the local people would come for religious instruction and schooling. There are now many Methodist congregations all over the island led by indigenous religious leaders. The Catholic mission stations of the island are now run by expatriate American priests of the Order of the Sacred Heart, while the diocese of New Ireland for many years was headed by a German bishop.

Although traders of several nationalities were operating in the Bismarck Archipelago after 1880, German companies dominated the area economically. Australia, then a British colony, was concerned about German influence on the island of New Guinea and proceeded to annex the southern half of that island. Within a year an agreement was signed in which Germany took control over northern New Guinea and the Bismarcks and the English were to control the remainder of New Guinea. The German flag was raised over New

Ireland in November 1884. While it had already been tied to the rest of the world economically for several decades, New Ireland now politically became part of the German colonial empire.

In 1900, a government station was established at Kavieng, the present provincial capital, with a German district commissioner. For the first time in its history, the whole island constituted a single political entity, a district within the colony of German New Guinea, instead of many autonomous villages. Former employees of the large German trading companies began to apply for land to establish plantations in such numbers that shortly thereafter the colonial government had to enact regulations to prevent the New Irelanders from losing all their land. A coastal road, stretching for over one hundred miles from Kavieng, was built by means of corvee labor extracted from the villages along its path.

During the German administration, there were efforts to end feuding between local communities and raiding and looting of European trade stations by the New Irelanders. Beyond the retaliatory raids against offending communities by the local native police, organized and led by the Germans, pacification took the form of forced relocation of villages to the coast, where they could be more easily supervised. This movement of inland villagers to the coast tore whole communities away from their ancestral-clan lands, bringing them into the coastal villages as intruders. This left the interior of New Ireland relatively deserted. Headmen, called luluais, not always the traditional leaders, were appointed for each village by the German administration. Sometimes the men who had worked on plantations overseas, learned Pidgin English, and had subsequently become Big Men were appointed luluais.

The Germans were stripped of their colonies, including New Ireland, after their defeat by Great Britain and its allies and colonies in World War I. Australia took over the administration of New Ireland under a mandate from the League of Nations. The Australians expropriated German-owned plantations and sold them at low rates to Australian ex-servicemen, who employed local New Irelanders from nearby villages. In other respects, life for the New Irelanders did not change much when colonial control passed from the Germans to the Australians. When the price of copra rose on the world market in the 1920s, Australian plantation owners became quite successful, but when it fell during the Depression in the 1930s, they lost money. Villagers had to sell coconuts from their own trees to raise cash to purchase trade goods and to pay a newly imposed head tax.

The Australians established patrol posts at various locations over the island and continued to use the luluai system put in place by the Germans. Patrol officers periodically visited almost every village to collect the head tax; adjudicate disputes, particularly over land; examine health conditions; see that labor recruitment rules were adhered to; and conduct censuses. In this way, the colonial bureaucracy increasingly penetrated many aspects of the daily life of the New Irelanders. By this time, Pidgin English had developed as the lingua franca for New Ireland, as well as many other areas of the southwest Pacific. The Europeans used it to communicate with the local people. New Irelanders from different parts of the island, who spoke different languages, used it to converse across linguistic boundaries.

The Japanese occupied New Ireland during World War II, and the primary hardship of the indigenous population arose from Japanese confiscation of pigs and foodstuffs. The Australians returned after World War II to administer Papua New Guinea as a United Nations Trusteeship Territory, with independence as the eventual aim. The Australian owners reopened their plantations, and the economy continued much as it had before the war, though new crops, such as palm oil, began to be grown alongside the coconut palms. In the 1950s, as a first step toward independence, the Australians introduced a system of elected local government councils, which took over some of the functions that had been carried out by patrol officers. The House of Assembly was established in Port Moresby, with representation from districts all over Papua New Guinea. In 1975 the independent nation of Papua New Guinea was established. New Ireland was set up as a province, with its own elected provincial assembly and a provincial government headed by a prime minister.

Since independence, Australian expatriates have been withdrawing from the economic system of New Ireland, though they still own some of the plantations. Some of the plantation laborers are New Irelanders, while others have been brought in from the Sepik River area of New Guinea. The world price for copra has been very low in recent years, and many of the plantations are run at a minimal level since the owners do not wish to take a loss. As plantations are abandoned, they revert to the local villages, which still basically have a subsistence economy of gardening, raising pigs, and fishing. In addition, the local villagers have moved into cash cropping, producing copra to sell to government marketing boards, which then sell these products on the world market. Sometimes villagers have organized themselves into cooperatives to buy and operate a truck or a boat. In recent years, Malaysian and Japanese companies have exploited the timber resources in the interior part of the island; fixed royalties are paid to national and provincial governments and to local people. Rainforest conservation in Papua New Guinea is increasingly becoming the subject of national and international interventions.

The significant social unit for most New Irelanders continues to be their village. Today, although there are still Big Men and matrilineal clans, every village is part of an electoral district, and the majority of New Irelanders participate in provincial and national elections. In contrast to people elsewhere who have become exclusively wage laborers or who depend exclusively on cash crops, New Ireland villagers have resisted being completely absorbed into the global market economy. Many prefer to sell products only when they need cash. However, they are increasingly forced to view themselves in regional terms, as New Irelanders, and in national terms, as Papuan New Guineans. Changes at the world level affect them economically and politically, and they see themselves as necessarily part of the world system. This now includes participating in international systems of tourism, ecological conservation and development, art and artifact production and consumption, commercial fishing, wage labor in the nearby Lahir gold mine, and palm oil production.

DEVELOPMENT HISTORY AND STRATEGIES

After World War II, revolutionary movements led to the establishment of many new states in Africa and Asia. Although the colonial yoke had been thrown off, many newly independent states were crippled economically by policies of resource exploitation and extraction, as well as the legacy of colonial-period suppression of local industries. These states faced wide gaps in wealth and education levels between classes, with growing poverty and health problems among most of its citizens. In comparison to the "developed" world of America and its European allies, now referred to as the Northern states, these Southern states were collectively referred to in development discourse as "undeveloped." The economic underdevelopment of many non-Western countries was recognized as a political threat to Western interests; President Harry Truman, in his 1949 inaugural speech, offered American scientific advances and technology for the improvement of underdeveloped areas of the world as part of his agenda for combating the spread of Soviet communism.

The term Third World came into use in the early 1950s in American and Western European political discourse to designate impoverished, under-industrialized states of Africa, Asia, and Latin America. The term First World referred to the industrialized Western democratic capitalist states and their trading partners and allies; the Second World was the communist bloc and its member states under the domination of the Soviet Union. The terms Northern and Southern states came into use later for First and Third World states, referencing their general distribution above and below the equator as well as the demise of the Soviet Bloc. Later, the term **Fourth World Peoples** collectively designated tribal or indigenous people in nation-states around the world.

Some American economists and social theorists of the 1950s and 1960s believed that underdevelopment was the result of the retention of so-called traditional social and political institutions in independent states that prevented "rational" or Western-style economic transformation. The most influential of these **modernization** theorists, Walt W. Rostow, was the author of the highly influential book *The Stages of Economic Growth: A Non-Communist Manifesto* (1960), as well as a political advisor on the war in Vietnam to Presidents John Kennedy and Lyndon Johnson. Rostow's version of modernization theory hypothesized an evolutionary meta-narrative for economic development, reminiscent of Lewis Henry Morgan's unilineal cultural evolutionary framework. (See chapter 1.) Rostow stated that all countries pass through the same stages of development, and that the ultimate stage of modernization, associated with urbanization and intensive consumer consumption, required the replacement of traditional values and institutions with Western-style technology, economic markets, and political systems. Those states that were not developed into Western-style modern

Fourth World Peoples

Indigenous or original peoples living as minority populations, with varying degrees of state recognition and autonomy in nation-states around the world.

Modernization Theory

The perspective that underdeveloped states should attain modernization by emulating the industrial strategies of Western countries.

industrialization were believed to be stalled at one of the earlier critical stages of transformation and required external inputs to "jump start" their economies into the single proposed trajectory of industrialized development. This unilinear model of development was criticized for a number of its assumptions, particularly its Western bias in articulating one single possibility for development dependent upon the emulation of Western-style capitalism. It was also criticized for its ahistorical perspective. The cause of underdevelopment was explained exclusively by reference to traditionalism within the underdeveloped nation-state, with no reference to the damaging economic relationships between states before and after colonial encounters.

Andre Gunder Frank and other scholars associated with **dependency theory** saw underdevelopment in a different way. They stressed the alliance of interests between elites in underdeveloped countries with those of Western capitalists in the developed countries. Southern countries are dependent upon the Northern capitalist markets, which are consumers for their raw materials and labor; the extraction of these resources benefited a small class of people who controlled the export of resources. Frank and other dependency theorists saw these elites as unwilling to forgo the economic benefits of continuing the dependency of their nation's export economies on Western markets. These export industries generated little significant economic growth or employment opportunity for the majority of the local population, and generally did not create a sustainable or profitable industrial base. Dependency theorists suggested that autonomous national development, free from ties to the world economy, would create significant economic growth and a sustainable development strategy in the national interest, rather than serving the interests only of elites of developing countries.

With the downfall of the Soviet communist system in 1989, **neoliberalism** emerged as the dominant economic and political philosophy driving global economic policy. Neoliberalism harkens back to many ideas about free market capitalism articulated by Adam Smith in his 1776 publication The Wealth of Nations, in which he argued for laissez-faire economics and few governmental interventions in markets and production systems. Neoliberalism in contemporary political discourse actually has much in common with American conservative political strategy, which seeks to greatly limit government controls and interventions in economics, trade, and even the delivery of social services. One example of this perspective in the United States is decentralization and privatization of primary and secondary schools. With its emphasis on privatization, free enterprise, and unfettered competition in the marketplace, neoliberalism is seen by some as facilitating the distribution of globalization's benefits. Proponents encourage unregulated national and regional networks of trade and production between states. Within developing states, this perspective encourages the participation of individual entrepreneurs in the local and national economy through credit schemes, microfinance, and other business incentives. The growth and benefits of developing a robust entrepreneurial economy, they believe, will eventually "trickle down" to all sectors of society. This prediction of growth among

dependency theory

Views underdevelopment as the consequence in former colonies of their economic suppression, coupled with continued economic dependence on colonial-based networks of trade and political alliances.

neoliberalism

The contemporary revival of classic economic liberalism that stresses the role of private enterprise in all institutions of the state and deregulation of markets and trade.

a few eventually trickling down to many has not been realized, as economic growth does not address social and political inequalities.

Development is also seen as replacing "local and rational technologies" with capitalist forms, ignoring local knowledge. Today, local knowledge is seen as crucial, and one must pay attention to it in suggesting any forms of change. Local knowledge means "the culture, values, and social institutions of the place," which are and always have been, in effect, the principal foci for anthropologists. This has also been referred to as "indigenous knowledge" (Sillitoe 2002: 8). There has been a shift in emphasis from "top-down" intervention to a "grassroots" participatory perspective (2002: 2). People at the local level want to share in technological and economic advances, but on their own terms. An example of this strategy is the interaction of First Nations with the Canadian government regarding the resources on First Nations lands. Each Nation has worked out its own agreement. "Various mixtures of this indigenous knowledge with Euro-American approaches have produced some spectacular successes, greatly improving some communities in 25 years" (Croal and Darou 2002: 83).

Over several decades, NGOs have arisen in many countries, facilitating delivery of development, education, and health programs to local communities. Through "participatory development," NGOs try to involve community members in program planning and execution, addressing local priorities and problems (Sillitoe 2002: 8). NGO budgets often derive from either the state or international donor organizations, obscuring the distinction between "governmental" and nongovernmental organizations (Weisgrau 1997: 102–16). NGO organizers may be urban elites of a different social class or ethnic group than the communities in which they work. NGOs introduce development plans and proposals initiated from outside the community, reflecting international or state development priorities (Mosse 2005). Anthropologists are sometimes called in to evaluate program outcomes on behalf of donor organizations that fund NGO projects.

State development initiatives in developing economies often involve the introduction and marketing of tourism. From Highland New Guinea to Bali, tourist dollars have become an important source of income. Mt. Hagen "Sing-Sings" are a "must" stop on tours of Highland Papua New Guinea. The Chimbu in the Highlands have created special dances, utilizing local myths and costumes from a variety of rituals, to perform for tourists. These brief encounters between local communities and tourists, once considered too frivolous for scholarly consideration, are now taken seriously by anthropologists and other social scientists who study their transformative economic, social, and political impacts (Henderson and Weisgrau 2007; Chambers 2010).

Tourism and its related infrastructures dominate the economies of many Southern countries; tourism ebb and flow has serious consequences on labor markets and employment levels. Tourism-oriented transportation infrastructures often privilege foreigners and sidestep the needs of citizens and local communities. Many of the advertising images of tourism brochures and websites market the so-called exoticism of people and destinations with images that perpetuate gender, racial, and ethnic stereotypes as well as historical inaccuracies. Some of the conflicts that arise around tourism strategy are over the degree to which local destinations control their own representations in national and global discourse, and the distribution of economic benefits deriving from tourism enterprises.

Global tourism has a profound impact on countries that adopt a tourism-related development policy. While tourism brings income to governments and multi-national hotel and travel corporations, its benefits usually do not reach local people who are dependent on tourists for income, as in this local market catering to tourists in Port Moresby, Papua New Guinea.

ANTHROPOLOGY AND CHANGE

As we have discussed throughout this chapter, contemporary anthropologists play multiple roles in understanding and documenting the lived experiences of colonialism, globalization, and development. Even before the emergence of anthropology as a discipline, missionaries and government officials were involved in gathering ethnographic information to implement their policies of conquest and conversion. During the colonial period, ethnographic studies were included in the training of government administrators destined to work in colonies all over the world, who instituted many changes in all aspects of life of the people they controlled, as we have documented earlier. They often saw themselves as bringing "progress" to peoples, doing away with "savage" practices such as nakedness and cannibalism, helping to make them "modern"—that is, "civilized," urbanized, and Westernized. The Bureau of American Ethnology, founded in the 1850s, "an early manifestation of anthropology in the United States . . . was created as a policy research arm of the federal government" (Willigen 2002: 23). The people most directly affected did not desire most of the changes that were instituted, but their opinions were rarely sought. This legacy of anthropological involvement in US policy administration has created distrust between some Native American communities and anthropologists.

Anthropologists gathered ethnographic information in the form of policy-focused basic research for the American government during the 1930s on the subject of rural life (Goldschmidt 1947). During World War II, anthropologists put together ethnographic handbooks used to prepare administrators for areas being recaptured from the Japanese, to provide intelligence on the Japanese and other adversaries, and to give the government advice on how to improve national morale (Willigen 2002: 25–29). Many of those involved, such as Margaret Mead, Gregory Bateson, and Ruth Benedict, straddled the academic and applied fields during that time. Ethical questions began to be raised during the Vietnam War, when some anthropologists were involved in providing ethnographic information that suggested the most efficient ways of carrying out local resettlement strategies. These debates continue over the

practicing anthropology

The application of anthropological knowledge and methodologies to the solution of practical problems, direct action and/or development policy.

role of American cultural anthropologists employed by the Department of Defense and working with the American military in Iraq and Afghanistan.

The demand for more involvement by anthropologists in policy research resulted in the development of applied anthropology professionals. Applied anthropologists, also referred to as "**practicing anthropologists**," now work with community leaders, nonprofit institutions, corporations, and governments to create, implement, and evaluate programs and policies, in domestic settings as well as abroad. Applied anthropologists are often hired to do rapid assessment of a particular situation and come to some conclusions regarding a policy or strategy that might be implemented. In that type of situation, collaboration with the local community is critical. Trained to make cross-cultural comparisons and explore cultural diversity, anthropologists are increasingly recruited by corporations to develop international business strategies and personnel training programs. Some academic anthropologists, usually affiliated with a college or university social science department, engage with many of the same subjects as practicing anthropologists, through ethnographic research and writing. They explore the history of ideas about development, local understandings of these concepts, and the often-competing visions expressed by state institutions, international development agencies, and local community members.

The flow of money, expertise, and ideas from the West to underdeveloped countries around the world began after World War II and continues to this day. While originally viewed by some as evidence of Western humanitarianism, this transfer of capital and technology is now recognized to be deeply embedded in what were Cold War geopolitical interests and conflicts. Development as socioeconomic and sociopolitical transformations is analyzed by development anthropologists, who study development theories and histories, and ethnographically document its strategies (Escobar 1995; Weisgrau 1997; Mosse 2005). With the rise of the global development industry and the international bureaucracies that finance and administer it, anthropologists also play roles in shaping and executing development policy and strategy worldwide. As discussed previously, applied or practicing anthropologists, working outside academic settings, are often hired as consultants to facilitate development programs.

public anthropology

The general term for the engagement of anthropologists in important social concerns, and the communication of anthropological perspectives to the general public.

The term **public anthropology** is now used "to describe the engagement of anthropologists in important social concerns, contrasted with traditional academic styles of presentation and definition of problem[s]" (Borofsky 2007). As mentioned above, the work of many prominent anthropologists straddled academic and applied perspectives during World War II and the Vietnam War. Margaret Mead was widely recognized by academics for her pioneering contributions to theorizing gender and her scholarship on childhood and adolescence cross-culturally. She was also a vocal proponent of women's rights, and was a regular contributor to *Redbook* magazine throughout the 1960s and 1970s.

Many in the discipline now understand that there is no such thing as "value-free research." Earlier, during the colonial period, some anthropologists had tried to "increase the fairness and humaneness of various domestic and international colonial systems" (Willigen 2002: 31). However, it became quite clear over time that that was impossible. Value-explicit research meant that anthropologists thenceforth had to clearly define their goals and values for the communities within which they wished to work. These and other ethical issues are often discussed and debated within the discipline; the American Anthropological Association established and continues to reformulate codes of ethical conduct for ethnographic research projects, as discussed in chapter 2. The uses of anthropological field methods and research in nonacademic settings, including those of state policy, development strategy, humanitarian efforts, military operations, and law enforcement, challenge all anthropologists to develop standards, methodologies, and ethics to incorporate the rights and interests of local communities (Morris and Bastin 2004; Whiteford and Trotter 2008).

ETHNOGRAPHY AND DEVELOPMENT

Paige West (2006) documents the interactions between scientists and NGO workers representing an international biodiversity conservation project with communities of Gimi-language speakers in Papua New Guinea. West's ethnography is "multisited and multitemporal" in that it connects diverse sites of the production of knowledge about biodiversity in Papua New Guinea over long periods of time. She explores the connections between consumer markets in New York City and rural, "out of the way" communities near the eastern highlands of Papua New Guinea, where she has conducted several years of ongoing fieldwork projects. She traces the history of ideas about nature, wildlife, and biodiversity management produced in Northern environmental-protection organizations and academic institutions. In this Western "imagining" of Papua New Guinea, its animal and plant life is exotic, threatened, and in need of protection.

To this end, the Crater Mountain Wildlife Management Area (CMWMA) was established in the early 1980s. Funded by the US-based Wildlife Conservation Society, the CMWMA encompassed Gimi-speaking and other communities within its boundaries. The CMWMA was envisioned by the NGOs that created and administered it as a site of economic development and conservation. Their goal was to engage local communities in production and marketing of local products and the development of tourism, while employing strategies of environmental sustainability. "It was imagined that these markets would allow for the flow of cash income to people who live in highly biologically diverse places. In turn, these people would work to conserve the biological diversity on which the markets were based" (West 2006: xii). The NGO workers and conservation planners imagined this undertaking as a social contract between themselves and local community members, which would create income and employment opportunities through sustainable environmental practices that would also attract scientists and researchers to the area.

Throughout the ethnography, West explores the multiple misunderstandings and contradictory visions of development and the environment among the principal actors and participants. To some Gimi, their participation in this project meant access to their vision of the modern, including "medicine, education, technology, and knowledge and wealth, the things they see as development" (West 2006: xiii). Their engagement with their natural environment is meaningful and active; its resources are integral to their physical and cultural lives. The conservationists imagine the "environment" as "existing apart from the Gimi and indeed as being threatened by Gimi practices and social life" (2006: 218). Both sides imagined an appropriate development strategy from their historical, cultural, and practical perspectives; neither side understood the other's perspective. Nor did they understand the role of the American ethnographer in the midst of this contested environment. West's goal in this complicated story that continues to unfold is to "disentangle the connections" and "contradictions" of conservation, development, and commodity production. Her study explores, among other issues, how "the past imaginaries of New Guinea and its nature and culture as untouched, exotic and spectacular drove people who wished to protect it, sell it, explore it, and study it, and that these same imaginaries drive environmental conservation in Papua New Guinea today" (2006: 4).

BOX 13.2 | Migrating Women and the Global Care Economy

"The care economy is growing as the demand for childcare and care for the elderly is increasing in all regions. It will thus create a great number of jobs in the coming years. However, care work across the world remains characterised by a void of benefits and protections, low wages or non-compensation, and exposure to physical, mental and, in some cases, sexual harm" (ILO 2022).

Social justice advocates draw on the lived experiences of women migrants and their challenges in obtaining safe employment and access to transnational financial services. Advocates encourage (but cannot compel) all receiving countries to:

- Record and maintain gender disaggregated statistics on migration and remittances.
- Encourage receiving countries to sign onto bilateral (state-to-state) and global agreements that protect the human rights of migrants to work safely, be paid fair wages, communicate with others during employment, form alliances and labor unions, and terminate their own employment and return home on demand.
- Provide financial literacy and rights training prior to emigration.
- Assure unfettered access to safe and inexpensive methods of opening their own bank accounts and transferring funds as they deem appropriate.

The International Labor Organization (ILO) is in the forefront of these efforts and stresses the importance of open and transparent dialogue on all these issues on a national level in both sending and receiving countries. "It is clear that new solutions to care are needed on two fronts: in regards to the nature and provision of care policies and services, and the terms and conditions of care work" (ILO 2022).

PEOPLE ON THE MOVE

The movement of people from one location to another has characterized the human experience from the earliest times. Fossils and genetic evidence document how our evolutionary ancestors moved out from Africa in wave after wave to populate Asia, Europe, and finally the New World and the Pacific islands. Anatomically modern humans have always been on the move, as we have seen in previous chapters. We have already mentioned that one of the many characteristics of both colonialism and globalization is migration; people move to where labor is required, with varying degrees of autonomy and compulsion. They also migrate as refugees from areas of political conflict, to seek security for themselves and their families. Increasingly, migration is motivated by multiple forms of insecurity caused by environmental changes and disasters. And in the contemporary world, where conflict results from increasingly scarce natural resources, migration may be prompted by a combination of all of the above factors.

Internal Migration

Internal migration refers to population movements within a nation-state. Such migrations have been taking place in America for centuries. The expansion from scattered settlements in Massachusetts to the formation of the thirteen colonies represents a form of internal migration. The nineteenth-century movement of eastern populations westward continued this pattern. At the beginning of the twentieth century, large numbers of African Americans, dissatisfied with life in the segregated rural South, began the **Great Migration** to the northern urban cities where they hoped to find work and freedom from the segregated cultures and economies of the South. This movement continued for many years and ultimately involved the migration of over six million people from the South into the cities of the Northeast and Midwest. During the twentieth century, migration from rural areas to cities represented another significant movement of population. Whereas in the nineteenth century most of the population of the United States lived in the rural areas of the country, increasingly, the urban and suburban populations have since come to dominate. Crop failures, falling prices for agricultural commodities, the mechanization of farming and farm consolidation continue to push farming families to urban centers around the country.

Labor migration, the movement of people to where jobs are available, can also be a form of internal migration. After World War II, many people sought their fortunes in "sunny California," where they saw new employment opportunities. An earlier generation of farmers fled the drought-plagued Great Plains states, such as Oklahoma and Texas, fleeing the Dust Bowl and seeking employment on the West Coast. People have also moved from the urban Northeast to seek employment elsewhere, since the industries of that area were moving to other parts of the country or overseas. Senior citizens, referred to as "snowbirds," whose retirement communities we discussed in

internal migration

Population movements within a state, usually from rural to urban areas.

Great Migration

Early twentieth-century migration of over six million African Americans from southern rural communities to northern and Midwestern urban and peri-urban centers.

chapter 7, move from northern states, with their cold winters, to warmer climates in Florida, California, and the Southwest.

Diasporas

diaspora

A population spread from its original homeland to other countries; group members continue to maintain affiliation with their homeland and each other.

Some migrants maintain their original ethnic identity for centuries and today are known as **diaspora** populations. This term is now applied to populations who have moved to other parts of the world and retained a connection to their actual or imagined homelands. The term *diaspora* was originally applied to the dispersal of the Jewish people after the destruction of the Second Temple in AD 70 and their exile from the Holy Land and subsequent dispersion throughout the Old World and, later, the New World. The term is now applied to diverse migrant groups that settle in countries away from their homelands for a variety of reasons. Some analysts have argued that "the term should be reserved for groups forced to disperse, and whose members conscientiously strive to keep past memories, maintain their heritage and are involved in a survival struggle" (Tatla 1999: 3). Diaspora groups have faced ethnocide-forced cultural integration—or even genocide in the effort to eliminate or exterminate them. Cohen (1997) suggests a number of specific features that all diasporas have in common. First, they all represent dispersal from a presumed homeland. Members of the diaspora always maintain a collective memory about their homeland, including its location, history, and achievements, idealizing their ancestral home. They may have a collective commitment to its maintenance, restoration, safety, and prosperity, and to its re-creation if it no longer exists as a separate political entity. Frequently, a movement to return to the homeland among members of the diaspora becomes important to the group. They may have a troubled relationship with the host country, which does not accept them, and in such situations there is always the possibility that another calamity, a wave of persecution or perhaps another dispersal, will befall the group. In contrast, in some situations in which the host country constitutes a pluralistic society, members of a diaspora may continue to have a distinctive creative life. Diaspora populations also have a strong sense of empathy and solidarity with co-ethnic members residing in other countries (1997: 26).

Sometimes, as with South Asians or Turks, men had to leave families and their homelands, in which employment was scarce, and go in search of work abroad. The Chinese and Lebanese represent the movement of people to other countries in search of trade opportunities (Cohen 1997). "Overseas Indians" migrated to Fiji, East Africa, and the Caribbean during the nineteenth century, mostly as indentured laborers. Their descendants are now well established in these countries and are frequently very successful economically. Their economic and political success may, in some circumstances, put them in conflict with indigenous communities who may resent the successes of these more recent migrants.

Anthropologists are interested in the adaptations diaspora groups make over the generations in different cultural settings and the means by which they create their ethnic identities in new settings. South Asian populations were subject to discrimination in, and eventual expulsion from, Uganda under the rule of Idi Amin, transforming them into a secondary diaspora population. In Fiji, South Asians have been threatened with expulsion and are targeted for political and economic discrimination by native Fijian politicians. Despite their intergenerational commitment to the states in which they reside, some may perceive them as "outsiders." Politicians exploit this perception by claiming "nativist" priorities when attempting to increase their own political power.

MIGRATION AND TRANSNATIONALISM

Some scholars suggest that the term *migration* be replaced with *mobility* in contemporary discussions because "it is a dynamic term that emphasizes the changing, floating and fluid nature of this phenomenon and captures the regular as well as irregular moves of people on the ground regardless of time or destination" (Cohen and Sirkeci 2011: 7). However, the term *mobility* may be too broad a term to capture the multiple aspects and strategies of this phenomenon. The technologies of globalization have dramatically facilitated the ongoing movement of populations around the world. Air transportation has made international travel much faster and easier for many. People relocate more frequently and remain in continuous contact with their homelands, non-migrating relatives and originating communities.

Transnationalism refers to family members who migrate from their homes to another country, and continue to maintain close contact with non-migrating family members, thus forming new kinds of multinational families. Other relatives may follow them, in a pattern of chain migration. These family members maintain a dual identity; they live and work in one country, sometimes even in different cities, but remain strongly connected to members of their families and communities "back home" by sending money, owning property, and sometimes even voting. They may become citizens of their new country of residence and still maintain dual citizenship and close connections with nonmigrants. Transnational families, as we discussed in chapter 6, regularly use email, telephone, social media, and frequent visits as ways of maintaining close contact with people at home.

"Home" however may be a contested location. For example, families of Hindu Punjabi migrants currently living in London originally came from a region of South Asia that, at the 1947 partition of what was then India, became part of the newly created state of Pakistan. At partition, their families crossed the new border between India and Pakistan to settle in cities in northern India, including New Delhi. From New Delhi they migrated to Great Britain, first settling in smaller cities and then relocating to London. In her ethnography of middle-class Punjabis in London today titled Where Are You From?, Raj quotes one informant whose family made these multiple migrations over several decades as saying, "I am from nowhere" (Raj 2003: 55).

transnationalism

Migration with strong economic and social ties remaining with families and communities of origin.

brain drain

The loss of educated professionals from one country as a result of migration to another country.

Migrants from all over the world bring to their new locations skills and forms of professionalism needed in receiving countries to enhance their economies. The **brain drain** refers to the migration of educated professionals originally from and educated in Asian, African, and Latin American countries out of these areas. Their home countries, despite their specialized skills and education, cannot provide them with the wages and lifestyles that they can achieve in countries with stronger economies. While this enhances the quality of life for mobile individuals and their families, it deprives their home countries of the benefits of their professional skills and abilities.

Overseas nationals are now recognized by all states as playing an increasingly important role in the economies and politics of both sending and receiving countries. They contribute significantly to their countries of origin by remitting money to family members and investing capital earned abroad in local communities as well as the national financial markets. They may see themselves eventually retiring to their "home" country, or continuing their transnational identities through maintaining multiple residences in different countries after retirement. This trend toward transnationalism is redefining the concept of "citizenship" as more states acknowledge dual citizenship and recognize the benefits of connections with overseas nationals. Notions of plural societies and multiculturalism in many places now coexist with or replace the idea of a single ethnicity that defines a national or individual identity in both sending and receiving countries.

Transnational Families: Marriage, Partner, and Family Migration

The lived experiences of citizens of one country attempting to form recognized marriages and families with citizens of another country brings into sharp focus the political realities of negotiating immigration and exit policies of sovereign states. The multiple challenges of creating legal marriages and families of people from different countries are now part of American popular culture as illustrated by numerous movies, broadcast television series, and streaming services. Unscripted reality programs like *90 Day Fiancé* and related spinoff programming, follow couples who have met abroad as they negotiate multiple political and administrative hurdles, along with attempts to resolve biases and cultural differences in gender and family norms. All of these stories are supplemented by the aggressive social media presence of many of the parties involved. Their stories are of great interest to social media observers around the world, judging from the viewership of their series and active social media responses.

Stepping back from the engaging individual stories, social scientists see important social and political concepts expressed in these romantic encounters and their outcomes. These diverse narratives raise vital questions about how the right to form a family and live with a partner and children is inevitably determined by multiple and often conflicting state policies that exert power over participation, control, and inclusion. These state policies concerning family-member migration are invariably framed subjectively in terms of risk and security; the outcome of the process of obtaining a legal exit or entry and reentry visa for the purpose of marriage and eventual citizenship in another country invariably turns on an assessment of the individual's risk to the security of the arrival country. These outcomes are not always clear-cut or transparent; "security" concerns can exclude people from migration and immigration on the grounds of racial, religious, ethnic, and sexual identities, as well as political affiliation. States may limit migration on the basis of country of origin, or on the perceived inability of the migrant to work productively and be a financially stable contributor to the economy. The American state demands a demonstration that the proposed marriage is based on love and commitment, and is not only for the convenience of one or both parties. "[T]he state enjoys prerogatives to put conditions on family reunification to protect the public and the immigration system . . . these discourses and practices mobilize and constitute diverse constellations of security-citizenship-rights. They are deployed to different ends, and they are uniquely experienced by a wide range of actors" (D'Aoust 2022: 5).

The challenges that Americans face in attempting to reunite with a fiancée or fiancé from abroad may come as a surprise; we may imagine that as Americans we are free to marry anyone we wish under any circumstances. One particularly outspoken woman on *90 Day Fiancé* (the title references the amount of time allowed to a migrating fiancé or fiancée to legally marry before the visa expires) attempted to reunite in the United States with the husband she married in Nigeria. She exclaimed on camera, "This is the United States. I have a right to marry anyone I want!" She was free to marry in Nigeria, but her husband's migration to the United States was mired in thwarted administrative efforts both here and abroad. Her cross-border engagement and marriage challenged the imagined set of rights she assumed she enjoyed as part of the American democratic process.

Feminization of Migration: Globalized Care and Service Economies

Feminization of migration refers to the global phenomenon that women represent half of the total number of cross-border migrants worldwide. The number of women migrants increases when domestic migration is factored into the statistics. Women move from their homes to other areas within their countries where work is available, and they cross borders to find work in increasing numbers. The primary destinations for women migrants are the service sectors of North America, Western Europe, and Arab states, where Southern women provide indispensable but undervalued labor in female-dominated sectors of manufacturing, care industries, and domestic labor (ILO 2021). Women migrants face multiple forms of vulnerability in employment sectors in the receiving countries; they are often valued for employment because of gender stereotyping, especially in domestic service. In all sectors they are encouraged to be submissive and compliant, despite challenging and sometimes abusive work environments.

Recruitment practices, which begin in their native countries, are often exploitive and increase their vulnerabilities; unscrupulous labor brokers charge enormous fees to their families to provide work, transportation and necessary work permits. Repayment obligates women workers, on behalf of their families, to "work off" the broker fees, despite the conditions of their work environments. It is estimated that 20 percent of all domestic workers globally are international migrants; domestic work exacerbates many of the vulnerabilities facing women migrants because of the isolation employers can enforce. Control by labor brokers or employers of their passports, return airline tickets, and other personal documents increases the pressure on domestic workers to comply with their employers' working conditions.

The determination and resilience of migrant women in light of these challenges is seen in the patterns of remittances, or payment transfers back to their home countries and families. Remittances are a significant form of income directly related to financial services and capital movements of globalization. Women's remittances, resulting from both domestic and trans-border migration and employment, represent a significant percentage of the GNP for many Southern states. It is also estimated that women send larger amounts of remittances to their families than do men, in spite of their incomes invariably being lower than their male counterparts. Transferring the funds they work so hard for can be challenging to women migrants, who may have low levels of financial literacy and lack familiarity with the mechanisms and technologies of cross-border financial transactions. They may also face restrictions on cell phone and internet use imposed by their employers or labor brokers. Domestic migrants may opt to keep their savings as personal belongings, but accumulating cash and traveling great distances also creates risks and vulnerabilities. (See the discussion of transnational families and migration in chapters 6 and 7 for other aspects of globalization, family, and gender.)

"MOVERS" AND "NON-MOVERS": ETHNOGRAPHIC PERSPECTIVES

Anthropologists have explored the ways of life of immigrants living abroad for decades, and have documented different national challenges and strategies for integrating foreign-born immigrants into their new national settings. Contemporary scholars are increasingly shifting their focus away *from* questions of immigrant assimilation and adaptation to new settings and *to* exploring the impacts of transnational families on both migrants and nonmigrants. "The nonmigrating members of the migrant households are critical social actors in the migration process. . . . Non-migrants are often central to the migration decision. And of course, remittances flow from migrants to non-migrants" (Cohen and Sirkeci 2011: 88).

Anthropologist Peggy Levitt (2001) studied both migrants and nonmigrants from the town of Miraflores in the Dominican Republic and their connections with family members who relocated to a Boston suburb. Her analysis focuses in part on the social, cultural, and political impacts of monetary remittances from Boston to Miraflores, and how being part of a transnational village transforms the institutions and expectations of the nonmigrant family members who remain in the Dominican Republic. She documents the important changes that take place in Miraflores as the result of social remittances, "the ideas, behaviors, and social capital that flow from receiving to sending communities. . . . They are the tools with which ordinary individuals create global culture at the local level . . . encouraging them to try on new gender roles, experiment with new ideas about politics, and adopt new organizing strategies" (2001: 11). Exploring social remittances and their impacts on the lives of transnational villagers globally enables an analysis of the dramatic and ongoing impacts of economic remittances in receiving communities. "Once this process has begun, daily life in the village is changed to such an extent, and migrants and nonmigrants often become so dependent on one another, that transnational villagers are likely to endure" (2001: 11).

Transnational communities continue to function, as in Miraflores and Boston, because of the ongoing labor and economic benefits of migration. As Levitt concludes, the money that comes from Boston brings material benefits to Miraflores. When she asked people to describe "how migration had transformed their community, they generally began by pointing out the homes, school, and health center that were built and renovated with money from Boston. . . . They said that most people live better now, with enough money for food and clothing" (2001: 73). But for some households, these benefits come at a high emotional cost. As in many other transnational settings, migration motivated by a search for employment by parents often requires leaving their children at home, in the care of grandparents, aunts and uncles, and older siblings. Despite the efforts of parents living abroad to maintain contact with, and authority over, their children through phone calls, Skype, and visits, the relationship between parents and children living apart is strained and difficult to establish on short visits. Custodial relatives in Miraflores are reluctant to discipline the children and adolescents in their care, who often use absent parents as an excuse to avoid school or doing their chores. Some parents attempt to bring their children to Boston with them and enroll them in schools there; however, this can often be more frustrating and counterproductive for the children who are not fluent in English and feel they are perpetual "outsiders" in both communities.

Some migrants from Miraflores are able to accumulate both capital and professional skills that enable them to return and successfully build businesses that sustain them and their families after migration. But most find that they are not able to accumulate enough capital to create financial stability when they return. The financial benefits for migrants in the long term after return are elusive and transitory. Levitt suggests that the ethnographic information that derives from in-depth studies of the possibilities and challenges faced by both migrants and nonmigrants can provide the basis for effective community organization in both settings, as well as more effective delivery of much-needed social services to support the psychological, emotional, and educational needs for transnational families in multiple settings (2001: 195–97).

Concepts like migration, diaspora, and transnationalism are of some assistance analytically, enabling researchers to have an evolving understanding of life experiences. Ethnographic research illuminates the social and political particulars of individuals and groups in mobile populations. The diaspora population of one generation may identify themselves as a transnational community, while the next generation refers to itself as an ethnic group.

SUMMARY

- Cultures are constantly undergoing change at a very rapid rate in today's world.

- Colonialism, which was one of the strongest forces for change, is all but gone, and in its place is a series of new nationalities, based on the geography of colonial empires rather than on sameness of culture.

- New postcolonial nation-states are industrializing and forming national cultures in their attempt to integrate various indigenous cultures within their borders.

- Globalization has been brought about by the development of a worldwide network of finance and capital. It represents historical continuities with colonialism and the neocolonialism of the latter part of the twentieth century.

- Each example of Western colonial expansion may appear to be different from any other case. Nevertheless, the establishment of a colony and the course of events that followed can be described in terms of a number of variables. These include land policy, resource exploitation, type of labor recruitment, and intensity and type of missionary activity.

- The initial motivation for the establishment of colonies was economic gain, which took the form of exploiting raw materials as well as providing labor and markets for the goods of the mother country.

- The British developed the policy of indirect rule by using the indigenous political structure, which was then applied throughout the British Empire. In contrast, the French ruled directly, establishing military garrisons and large administrative staffs throughout their empire that supplanted local governance institutions and populations.

- Different colonial empires had somewhat different policies with respect to the rights of native peoples over access to land. Furthermore, these native peoples themselves had a variety of different strategies about protecting their access to land and resources.

- Exploitation of resources in colonial areas and their successor nation-states required labor, which was met in a variety of ways. Labor recruitment dislocated traditional forms of family and social organization of colonized populations.

- Applied anthropology, practicing anthropology, and public anthropology are all concerned with the production and application of anthropological knowledge to the solution of contemporary problems.

- Some anthropologists work with the US government and military in conflict areas; many in the discipline recognize that there is no such thing as "value-free research."

- A major characteristic of globalization today is the movement of people across borders for economic, political, and social reasons. Internal migration, transmigration, transnational families, and diaspora populations are some of the categories used to describe contemporary population movements and resettlements.

- Global labor has a pronounced gender component; increasingly, women in the global South migrate to provide service and care in middle- and upper-class countries of the North. This has created a generation of children in Southern countries being raised without their mothers present in their households.

- Stories of migration motivated by love and a desire for marriage, and all its attendant obstacles, is now featured prominently in broadcast media, reality television programs, and social media.

- In studying transnational families, anthropologists are increasingly focusing on the connection between migrants and non-movers through the ongoing circulation of financial and social remittances and the use of digital technologies and social media.

KEY TERMS

blackbirding, 335
brain drain, 350
colonialism, 326
corvee labor, 326
dependency theory, 341
diaspora, 348
direct rule, 332
Fordism, 329
Fourth World Peoples, 340
Free Trade Zones (FTZs), 330
Great Migration, 347
imperialism, 326
indentured servitude, 335

indirect rule, 332
internal migration, 347
microfinance, 326
Modernization Theory, 340
neocolonialism, 326
neoliberalism, 341
nongovernmental organizations (NGOs), 326
Post-Fordism, 329
postcolonial studies, 327
practicing anthropology, 344
public anthropology, 344
transnationalism, 349
world system theory, 327

SUGGESTED READINGS

Eckstein, Susan, and Adil Najam, eds. *How Immigrants Impact Their Homelands*. Durham, NC: Duke University Press, 2013.

Ethnographic essays in multiple settings describe the range of economic, social, and cultural impacts immigrants have on their sending countries.

Flores, Andrea. *The Succeeders: How Immigrant Youth Are Transforming What It Means to Belong in America*. Oakland: University of California Press, 2021.

An ethnographic study of Latino high school students, this book explores how young people with migration histories in their families work out contested ideas about what it means to be an America, through striving for academic success and caring for friends and family.

Walsh, Andrew. *Made in Madagascar: Sapphires, Ecotourism, and the Global Bazaar*. Toronto: University of Toronto Press, 2011.

An ethnography of the Ankarana region of northern Madagascar, focusing on local understandings of the similarities between ecotourism and sapphire-extraction industries.

SUGGESTED WEBSITES

https://www.cwis.org/index.php

The website for the Center for World Indigenous Studies contains multiple links to news and scholarship about indigenous peoples resources and rights around the world.

https://asiasociety.org/education/desi-diaspora

A website exploring the history and current issues in multiple South Asian Diaspora settings.

http://www.history.com/topics/black-history/great-migration

This website explores multiple historical and social issues related to the Great Migration, or the relocation of more than six million African Americans from the rural South to the cities of the North, Midwest, and West from 1916 to 1970.

Chapter 14

States and Identities

Ethnicity, Race, and Nationalism

LEARNING OBJECTIVES

- Understand the various aspects of states and state formation.
- Document how forms of identity can be manipulated by state actors to establish dominant political cultures.
- Distinguish between states, nation-states, and nationalism.

- Describe how religious and ethnic identities have been mobilized by politicians in recent historic events around the world.
- Recognize the various forms of ideology and practice in the United States that mobilize discourses of race, ethnicity, national culture, and cultural assertion.

state

A type of political organization organized on a territorial basis encompassing multiple ethnic, linguistic, and religious groups.

IN TODAY'S WORLD, STATES ARE universally recognized as the sole legitimate political entity; borders are generally respected and maintained by international consensus, treaties, and organizations. In the previous chapter, we discussed the flow of people, ideas, jobs, and capital across borders. In the United States, outsourcing of customer service and data processing is now a familiar aspect of American corporate strategy. Simultaneously, service and care workers from countries in the global South form the majority of people employed in these occupations in the North. Increasingly, state bureaucracies, facing the same financial pressures as private corporations, are outsourcing administrative jobs to reduce administrative costs. Both corporate and governmental outsourcing are generating a backlash by various groups that seek to protect jobs in the United States; legislation has been introduced in some state senates banning the outsourcing of government contracts and reserving government jobs for American citizens. This is just one example of the ongoing conflicts raised by globalization from the perspectives of citizenship and state sovereignty. "[T]he rhetoric of legislation against the flight of jobs abroad seamlessly weaves together national belonging, citizenship, culture, race, state work, and state control. It articulates a fear of the loss of sovereignty to globalization, which in turn presumes a certain understanding of the state and of the state's role in governing a territory and the resources and population within that territory" (Sharma and Gupta 2006: 5).

As we discussed in chapter 9, states are organized on a territorial basis, and invariably encompass diverse groups of people. The term "state" suggests a particular political structure and sovereign territory defined by its recognized borders; nation suggests shared cultural identity that may derive from common ideas about origins, history, family, religion, and language use. Nations are imagined to be composed of one group with shared cultural characteristics, while *state* is the term used to refer to a politically recognized entity, whether it is composed of one or many different ethnic groups. The term *nation-state* is used when nation and state are coterminous. In reality, this is more likely to be a multicultural state with a national identity existing alongside multiple ethnic identities. **Nationalism** is a political movement to claim or reformulate shared ideas about identity among citizens within a state's borders.

nationalism

Political movement to claim or reformulate shared ideas about identity among citizens within a state's borders.

One goal of all newly independent states is to create a national culture incorporating diverse population groups within its borders. The creation and maintenance of a national identity selectively employs myths, symbols, and aspects of history to forge shared sentiments. Competing visions of the past and identities in the present are often the basis of conflict between groups of people in pluralistic states. As suggested above, the discourses of globalization are increasingly being integrated into the cultural framing of national identities. Despite the predictions of some social scientists that the potency of national identity would be reduced by globalism and transnational migration, anthropologists regularly document how cultural ideas about identities, states, nationalism, and citizenship are strengthened and contested in contemporary political settings.

race

A system of classification of groups of people presumed to share biological or genetic characteristics, usually based on phenotypical (appearance) assumptions.

The concepts of ethnicity, ethnic identity, ethnic group, nationalism, multiculturalism, and **race** are among the conceptual tools used by anthropologists and other social scientists. They are also part of the language of media and politics, and are therefore themes in everyday use.

Ethnic groups share some common cultural norms, which may include values, identities, patterns of behavior, and language. Their members recognize themselves as a separate group and are so recognized by others. They may or may not be politicized. Ethnic identity, or **ethnicity**, is based on sentiments that are conceptualized as going back in time and that tie group members to one another intergenerationally. More recently, ethnic identity is recognized by social scientists as a resource or an instrument to be employed in pursuit of economic or political goals. It is therefore understood as situational, invoked by individuals and groups in some contexts but not in others. Ethnic differences may also parallel class differences; in some societies, an economic underclass may simultaneously be a separate ethnic or racial group. Under those conditions, ethnic conflict may be characterized as class conflict (Robben and Saurez-Orosco 2000).

Religion may be one of the important factors serving to distinguish one ethnic group from another. In addition to cultural differences, there may be religious differences between ethnic groups. When religious differences are present, ethnic conflict, although by no means inevitable, may be heightened and intensified in political discourse. Each side finds support in the moral authority of its own religion for continuing the conflict and for using violent action against those whom it characterizes as religious others. Violence in the former Soviet state of Yugoslavia illustrates this very well. The dominant Serbs were an Orthodox population, who viewed themselves historically as Christian martyrs who suffered under the Muslim Ottoman Empire. Bosnians and Albanians, in Kosovo, are Muslims. Croatians are Roman Catholics. Despite similarities in language, culture, and history among these ethnic groups, their religious differences exacerbated ethnic conflict and were used to justify systematic violence against members of the other ethnic groups. Religious and ethnic pluralism continues to be a challenge in the seven independent states that emerged from the former Yugoslavia (Bosnia and Hertzegovina, Slovenia, Serbia, Macedonia, Kosovo, Montenegro, and Croatia) following the fall of the Soviet Union.

Race and racial classifications are also used by states to make distinctions between groups. Many people think of race as a scientific concept based on biological systems of classification; however scientists challenge the genetic basis for claiming that there are separate identifiable races by which all human variation can be classified. The cultural idea persists that racial classifications are discrete, fixed categories to which people can be assigned based on physical appearance and presumed ancestry. In reality, the concept of race differs from one society to another; racial systems are socially constructed over time within specific social and political contexts (Smedley 2007; Goodman 2020).

The cultural construction of racial systems is illustrated by the "one drop of blood" concept in the American system of racial classifications. This social interpretation of identity includes the rule of **hypodescent**, which classifies anyone with any presumed African American ancestry as Black, not White. In comparison, in Brazil, color of complexion forms an element in the conceptualization of status and group; the lighter the complexion, the higher the class status of the individual. Hundreds of different races are recognized in Brazil based on **phenotype**, or physical appearance; as an individual's appearance changes, so does the

ethnic groups

Groups within a state who claim to preserve cultural norms associated with their histories.

ethnicity

Language, history, traditions, and cultural norms with which people choose to affiliate that create groups of shared identity.

hypodescent

A cultural rule that classifies individuals as members of a lower-status group by virtue of their marriage of parents' identity groups.

phenotype

Physical characteristics of a person.

assignment of his or her racial category. Siblings, parents, and children are invariably assigned to different racial groups. In Brazil, race is a continuum and an achieved status; in the United States it is clearly a fixed, bipolar categorization system, and an ascribed status.

RACISM AND CRITICAL RACE THEORY

racism

Discrimination or violence against an individual or group based on presumed shared characteristics.

Racism, discrimination on the basis of presumed or perceived racial categories, is expressed at both individual and institutional levels. Individuals may strive in their dealings with others to reject racist barriers and stereotypes, and attempt a "color-blind" perspective on those around them. But even when individual efforts are successful at removing perceptions of racial categories, prejudices and discrimination are integrated into and perpetuated by the political and social norms of states and communities. The Black Lives Matter movement in the United States and elsewhere (see chapter 7) brought worldwide attention to the systematic police brutality over time against African American young men, which results in their incarceration and involvement with law enforcement at a disproportionately high level. Research around Covid-19 and the delivery of health services during the pandemic revealed clearly how minority groups suffered multiple economic and health-related effects at rates higher than their white middle-class counterparts. Health and nutrition inequalities are linked to residential patterns of communities and neighborhoods of non-White minorities.

critical race theory (CRT)

Interdisciplinary approach to studying the interrelationships between race, racism, identities, discrimination, and political power.

Critical race theory (CRT) is a theoretical and methodological perspective that emerged in legal and academic studies in the United States in the 1970s. The interdisciplinary approach of CRT theorists, scholars, and activists focuses around the relationships between race, racism, and political power. "Unlike traditional civil rights discourse, which stresses incrementalism and step-by-step progress, critical race theory questions the very foundations of the liberal order, including equality theory, legal reasoning, Enlightenment rationalism, and neutral principles of constitutional law" (Delgado and Stefancic 2017: 3). This perspective is informed by understanding racism in all forms as a creation of society, and explores how race, racism, and inequality are produced and reproduced through the structures of society. Its proponents document how racism in all forms impacts lived experiences, with often dramatic and tragic effects on individual lives. The goal of critical race theory is to inspire both scholarship and activism that uncovers and, hopefully, dismantles systems of discrimination and hierarchy.

Contemporary scholars and activists inspired by the critical race theory perspective now include engagement with African American, Asian American, Latino, LGBTQ+, and Muslim/Arab issues. "Latino and Asian scholars study immigration, as well as language rights and discrimination based on accent or national origin. . . . American Indian scholars address indigenous people's rights, sovereignty, and land claims. They also study historical trauma, and its legacy and health consequences, as well as Indian mascots and co-optation of Indian culture. Scholars of Middle Eastern and South Asian background address discrimination against their groups, especially in the aftermath of 9/11" (Delgado and Stefancic 2017: 3–4).

Critical race theory faced a backlash in the United States that began in 2020, associated mostly with conservative politicians and media. Some politicians focused on banning the teaching of CRT in public schools, on the basis, they claim, that it promotes racism against White people. This backlash demonstrates in part how divisive the public discussion of inequality in the United States continues to be. Despite efforts in law, legislation, and policy to address and eliminate racism, it continues to be an unresolved issue that divides some groups, and unites others into action.

In some parts of the United States, racial identities are complicated by patterns of income, property ownership, occupation, political alliances, and religion, all of which cross racial categories. Genetic-identity projects, including the proliferation of commercial enterprises that claim to trace individual ancestry, reify the traditional cultural categories of race and ethnicity through the marketing of individual genomic identity (Jasanoff 2022). "The new molecular biology and its attendant practices of biotechnological intervention are giving race a new lease on life" as social categories with political implications (Abu El-Haj 2007: 284).

Racism and acts of violence against Asians spiked in the United States during and after the Covid epidemic. Asian men and women were erroneously blamed for the epidemic, and became scapegoats for anger and frustration about the epidemic and its effects.

NATION BUILDING

Nation building draws on the idea of the nation defined as a sovereign political state with a presumed single national culture. The development of national cultures involves conscious culture building on the part of the hegemonic group in political control of the state—the goal being the substitution of regional ethnic cultures with a national culture. Anthropological research has revealed the way this process of conscious, national culture building, in contemporary states, utilizes performance and artistic traditions in popular culture, digital media, and all forms of mass media.

Archaeology, the interpretation of the past through material remains, is also utilized in the service of creating national identity. States choose to emphasize one aspect of their archeological past rather than another, in keeping with the messages about the past, which the archaeological results are meant to support. Each state tells its own charter myths about its past. Domestic and foreign tourism, and the information communicated by tour guides at historical sites, is a significant aspect of contemporary nationalism projects. In Israel, archaeology has always served to convey the rights of Israelis out to its national borders. Israel chooses to emphasize archaeological research related to religious rather than secular sites. It concentrates on the periods of the First and Second Temples, that is, the Iron Age through early Roman times, ignoring earlier sites such as the Mount Carmel caves where Neandertal skeletal material was found. Archaeological sites, like that of Masada, are used as widely promoted tourism destinations as well as the locations for national ceremonies to communicate Israeli national values. Emphasis on this particular archaeological information builds a cultural past for Israel that is invoked in contemporary political discourse (Abu El-Haj 2001). Likewise in Pakistan, during the colonial period, Buddhist sites such as Taxila were important locations for archaeological investigation. When the Islamic state of Pakistan was established, there was scant scientific interest in these sites by the Pakistani state, which emphasized only its Muslim historical roots. These are just two examples of how the control of historical discourse is invariably used as a source of legitimization for justification of political control in the present.

The imposed national culture is that of the hegemonic or dominant group. In Great Britain, that meant that the language and culture of the English, the politically dominant group, were to supersede the Celtic cultures and languages of Wales, Scotland, and Ireland. Expression of regional differences were discouraged in favor of standard British English language and culture. The same process occurred in France and somewhat later in Germany as well as throughout the Soviet Union. Despite attempts to impose a national culture emanating from Russia, regional cultural and dialect differences persisted, and Soviet national identity never really fully penetrated the countryside, especially the more remote areas. More recently, in Great Britain, the Scottish people have moved beyond the assertion of their ethnic identity. The establishment of the Scottish Parliament is an expression of their movement to ethnonationalism. Independence from Great Britain, although rejected by the majority of Scottish voters in 2014, continues to be a theme in political discourse. Wales now has its own national assembly, and the Welsh language is taught to youngsters in public schools. The rejection of British participation in the European Community in 2020, the so-called Brexit movement, is widely interpreted as a rejection of economic controls established outside of Great Britain, and an assertion of British autonomy.

CULTURAL IDENTITY: REASSERTED AND TRANSFORMED IN MODERN STATES

In the previous chapter, we saw the way the German colonial government established a single political entity, New Ireland, where previously there had been independent, autonomous villages speaking different languages. The term **tribe** was originally used by anthropologists to refer to these indigenous cultural groupings, each of which spoke its own language or dialect.

tribe

A unit used by colonial powers to refer to groups with a common language and culture.

Some anthropologists see that the concept of the tribe was, in effect, created by colonial governments to enable them to deal more efficiently with groups with a common culture and language and unfamiliar forms of leadership, whose most complex political groupings were villages or bands (Fried 1975). In common usage, *tribal* is often ambiguous and even pejorative, indicating insular ethnic affiliations and kin-based traditions. In contemporary states, the claims of indigenous peoples to maintaining their cultural distinctions and historical access to land and other resources are regulated by state policy.

Most indigenous groups recognize that the introduction of changes from the industrialized world, which is also constantly undergoing change, has had and will continue to have a profound effect on their cultures. Frequently, people accept changes that they perceive as immediately useful, such as access to medical care and education. Sometimes change is forced upon them, and sometimes they forcibly resist it. One form of resistance is to escape, as the Kreen-akore of the tropical forest of Brazil did in running from attempts to contact and pacify them. But you can only run so far and for so long, and eventually even the Kreen-akore stopped running. Other indigenous groups retain their identity and uniqueness through conscious efforts to preserve the traditional and customary and to reject the new. As a Menomini man defiantly said to the former commissioner of Indian Affairs, "You can make the Menomini reservation into Menomini County but you can't make a white man out of me."

An earlier generation of anthropologists, typified by Boas and Malinowski, assumed that the cultures of indigenous societies would not withstand the onslaught of European colonization, industrialization, and globalization; it was inaccurately predicted that they would totally assimilate or would disappear entirely. Throughout North America, Native peoples who formerly practiced hunting and gathering have over time integrated new technologies to carry out subsistence practices. They use rifles, snowmobiles, and modern traps. They have transformed their technology while retaining the cultural meaning and ritual significance of hunting. The distribution of results of the hunt is often carried out according to norms derived in the past. The pattern of distribution after a hunt changes more slowly than its use of technology. For example, the relationship to animals of the Yup'ik-speaking people of Alaska continues in the same manner as in the past. As one Yup'ik informant puts it, "When we bring animals into our houses, we treat them as guests" (Sahlins 1999: xvi). Sahlins states that "they have not lost their cultural identities, not even when they live in white folks' towns" (1999: xvii). The manner in which cultural identity is asserted differs according to the social and political context. As Sahlins states, "I am simply making the point that the [Inuit] are still there—and still [Inuit]" (1999: vii).

When a national identity is being built, political pressure may be applied to suppress cultural differences. Frequently, this pressure has the opposite effect from what was intended and cultural identity may be reasserted. Malaysia has been dominated by Muslim Malay speakers since it gained its independence after World War II. The non-Muslim Iban, who live in Sarawak, part of Malaysia on the island of Borneo, have recently begun to reassert their cultural identity. In the past, the Iban had been headhunters and pirates in the South China Sea. Today, young men leaving home to go to school, search for work, or join the military or the police is seen as symbolically equivalent to the traditional journey into the unknown that an Iban male made as part of his initiation into manhood. The Iban rite of passage from boyhood to manhood is being maintained, but in a new form. Iban politicians talk about preserving their traditional lifestyle while at the same time fighting for a larger share of civil service and other employment in the Malaysian government for their people.

Groups of people develop various ways to assert their continued cultural identity. The ways they separate themselves from the dominant society are known as **boundary maintenance** mechanisms. For example, the Rio Grande Pueblos of New Mexico—Tewa and Keres—who were in contact with the Spanish missionaries and explorers in the seventeenth century, have divided their religious life into two separate domains. The indigenous one, with its katchinas (religious figurines), priests, and kivas (underground religious chambers), are operated in secret, closed off from the outside world, including the village structure of a Catholic church. By preserving their language and much of their ritual structure, Rio Grande Pueblos have been able to maintain their culture and their identity for more than three hundred years, despite some conversion to Catholicism and their integration into the US economy

Revitalization Movements

Often, after changes have taken place in significant aspects of their culture, people recognize that they are in the process of being stripped of their own culture but have not been assimilated into the hegemonic culture. The uncertainty of their position makes them ready to follow a religious innovator who has a more concrete vision of a better future. Out of these conditions, religious cults are born, which have been termed **nativistic movements**, or **revitalization movements**. These religious movements synthesize many traditional cultural elements with some aspects introduced from the dominant society.

An example of such a movement is the Handsome Lake religion of the Seneca, one of the six tribes that constituted the League of the Iroquois. By the end of the American Revolution, the Seneca had suffered partial devastation of their villages, decimation of their population, and the general dislocation of many aspects of their culture. In the 1780s, Handsome Lake, who was a sachem, or tribal leader, of the Seneca, had a series of visions during which he had contact with various Iroquois deities. Through these visions, he foresaw what the life of the Seneca should be like in the future. What he envisioned was an amalgam of older Iroquois traditions and new ideas derived in part from the Quakers and other missionaries. The social organization of the Seneca had been based on matrilineal descent and uxorilocal postmarital

boundary maintenance

The ways in which a social group maintains its individual identity by separating itself from the dominant society.

nativistic movements

Religious cults that develop in periods of drastic cultural change and synthesize traditional cultural elements with newly introduced ones.

revitalization movements

Religious cults that develop in periods of drastic cultural change and synthesize traditional cultural elements with newly introduced ones.

residence. In contrast, Handsome Lake stressed the importance of the nuclear family and deemphasized matrilineages. The Quakers had come as missionaries to the Seneca, and many of their economic values, such as thrift, were adopted by Handsome Lake. At the same time, much traditional Seneca ceremonialism was also maintained. Handsome Lake had many adherents during his lifetime, although there were other political leaders who opposed and competed with him. After his death, his doctrines were written down and formed the Code of Handsome Lake. Though it was revolutionary when it first appeared, over the centuries the Handsome Lake religion, as it came to be called, became a conservative force as new changes were accepted by the Seneca. Today the supporters of the Handsome Lake religion are among the more conservative members of the Seneca tribe living on their reservation in upstate New York. What began as a vision of Seneca accommodation to the culture of a dominant population was transformed over time into a resistance movement.

Cargo Cults

A particular type of revitalization movement in Melanesia is the **cargo cult**. Cargo cults made their appearance early in the twentieth century. However, they proliferated after World War II, which was a period of more intensive contact with outsiders, particularly with the American soldiers who drove out the Japanese and used the islands of Melanesia as a staging base. The Melanesians were astonished by the technological might of the Western world, as represented by the American armed forces. Like all revitalization movements, these cargo cults revolved about a charismatic leader or prophet who had a vision of ancestors rising from the dead. They would arrive in a big ship or plane, bringing an inexhaustible cargo of steel axes, razor blades, tobacco, tinned beef, rice, and rifles. Later, the expected cargoes included transistor radios, wristwatches, and motorcycles. People built piers into the sea, erected huge warehouses, and even prepared landing strips when planes were expected. They neglected their gardening and often killed off their pigs, since the expectation was that they would not have to work anymore after the cargo arrived. Sometimes elements of Christianity were included in the visions of the prophet, so that Jesus Christ was expected to arrive along with the cargo.

Like many other revitalization movements, cargo cults are a synthesis of the old and the new. In a situation of cultural contact in which indigenous peoples find themselves helpless and overwhelmed by the power of the dominant society, a prophet appears who preaches turning to the ancestors to seek their help in acquiring the very things that make the dominant society so powerful. The cargo is seen as the secret of the White people's power. Like all forms of religion that attempt to explain the inexplicable, cargo cults attempt to offer a supernatural explanation of what it is that makes the invaders so powerful. Converts to the cargo cult have faith that the secret of the invader's power, their weapons and consumer goods, will come to them as a result of

cargo cult

A particular type of revitalization movement that first appeared in the early twentieth century in Melanesia and represents a synthesis of traditional beliefs and valuing of the goods and services of colonial or imperialistic powers.

supernatural forces. Cargo cults are religious movements, though many of them are short-lived. At the same time, however, they make statements about power relations; for when the cargo comes, the present power dynamics will be reversed, and the powerless will become powerful. Cargo cults exemplify how the force and emotive power of religious belief can add great strength to a political movement. The particular forms they take not only represent responses to colonialism but also reveal a great deal about the cultures in which these movements originate.

Rebuilding Cultural Identity

Sometimes, a group is forced to surrender its territories but still maintains a sense of its own cultural identity. The Mashantucket Pequot Tribal Nation of Connecticut is such a group. The Pequot were nearly obliterated as a people in the Pequot War of 1637 and stripped of most of their land. However, they were able to demonstrate to the United States Department of the Interior that their tribal existence never ceased, enabling them to receive recognition as a tribe from the American government on October 18, 1983. The introduction of high-stakes gambling in 1992 has made the tribe wealthy and influential and has enabled members to fund events that are part of a conscious attempt to renegotiate their cultural identity. They have approached the task of cultural building or rebuilding on two different fronts. First, they have sponsored Mashantucket Pequot historical conferences, which bring together scholars to discuss topics such as the history of the Indians of New England and the current state of knowledge about Native peoples of New England and their adjustment to the encounter with Euro-Americans. To this end, they have established their own museum, which focuses on Native American culture in general and on Pequot culture in particular. Second, they sponsor a pow-wow, or Schemitzun, translated as "Feast of Green Corn and Dance," which brings together Native American performers from all over the country. The performers are attracted in part by the richest purse offered on the competitive powwow circuit. The Pequots are endeavoring to re-create their own culture by reconstructing their own histories and traditions, as well as creating opportunities for Native American communities to share events and forge new traditions of affiliation. The process the Pequot are now going through, as they construct and enact their cultural identity, is similar to that involved in the fashioning of ethnic identity that is now going on in multicultural America.

Ethnogenesis

ethnogenesis

The creation of a new ethnic group.

Contact and colonialism can produce a process by which a people assert a new ethnic identity and take on a new name. This is known as **ethnogenesis**. William Sturtevant first used the term to refer to the process through which the Seminole historically differentiated and separated themselves from the Creek, the larger group of which they were a part. Nancy Hickerson (1996) has noted that the historic record reveals the disappearance, often quite abruptly, of certain peoples (such as the Mayan Empire) and the sudden appearance of others (such as the Scythians), likening this process to the three-stage sequence that Van Gennep (1960) proposed for rites of passage, discussed in chapter 10. The first phase is separation, the severing of a group's previous loyalties; the second is a liminal phase during which surviving ties wither

away and new ones are initiated; the third is the birth of a new identity, which is affirmed through the adoption of new rituals and a new mythology to validate them. This last phase "may obscure all traces of the earlier history (or histories) of the population and even promote a belief in a miraculous origin or special creation" (Hickerson 1996: 70). Manipulation of the historical past is one of the distinctive characteristics of the process of ethnogenesis. "Ethnogenesis is not merely a label for the historical emergence of culturally distinct peoples but a concept encompassing people's simultaneously cultural and political struggles to create enduring identities in general contexts of radical change and discontinuity" (Hill 1996: 1).

The Green Corn Native American Festival and Powwow in Tennessee, sponsored by the Georgia Tribe of the Eastern Cherokee, invites participation from Native communities throughout the region for a three-day festival of performance and Pan-Indian celebrations.

In the ebb and flow of populations after the arrival of the Europeans in the New World, ethnogenesis occurred many times as groups were physically dislocated from lands they had traditionally occupied. During the sixteenth and seventeenth centuries, Tanoan-speaking people, known as the Jumano, who were bison hunters and traders, occupied an area east of the Rio Grande River in the southern Plains. As a consequence of unsuccessful warfare with the Apache over trade routes and access to trade centers, they appear to have dispersed, many moving north. The use of the name Jumano then declined, but subgroups with their own names continued. The term Kiowa later appeared as the label for these groups, now in their new homeland in the Platte-Arkansas River area. Today, the people of the modern Kiowa Nation have an origin myth that begins with their ancestors' emergence from the underworld in a cold land far north—thought by outsiders to be in the Yellowstone River Valley. The ancestors subsequently moved south and east to their historic territory (Hickerson 1996: 83). Here we see a sequence in which the Jumano identity disappears and a new people, the Kiowa Nation, are created.

Ethnonationalism

The process of ethnogenesis not only is applicable to indigenous or ethnic groups in the New World but also parallels the development of

BOX 14.1 | State Sovereignty and Globalism

State sovereignty in the twenty-first century is sometimes seen as being challenged by the economic and political forces of globalization. There are many arguments that support the observation of the weakening of state autonomy. Proponents of this position cite the rise of multinational corporations, whose often unregulated activities span multiple national boundaries; regional trade agreements that establish conditions for imports and exports; forced deregulation of taxation and wage and labor protection to encourage foreign investment; and the power of global capital to penetrate national economies on its own terms and not those set by national governments or mandated by their citizens. The internet rapidly crosses political boundaries to deliver news, information, products, and new technologies around the world. International organizations like the United Nations promote global rights and economic agendas among its member states.

These arguments emphasize areas where absolute state authority has been weakened; it is, however, necessary to balance this discussion with a reminder of those areas in which state sovereignty and authority remain intact. Countries that claim to be operating their economies and production systems as a free market economy inevitably intervene in this process. Governments incentivize certain domestic industries and products, providing tax, pricing, and cost support for those businesses and raw materials deemed critical to international competition. These domestic interventions inevitably take place despite objections aimed at other countries adopting similar domestic economic strategies. In addition, many state governments routinely block the transmission of internet-based communication flows, using their power to censor or edit domestic media coverage of national or international events.

All states have the power to tax activities within their borders and to regulate the flow of products and resources into and out of their territory. The degree to which they do this is political and strategic. States have the absolute right to tax their citizens and businesses; all states retain the right to approve contracts, license enterprises, and rule on the legality of national or international contracts. States make decisions about, and spend money on, infrastructural development. They make decisions on where and when to build roads, water systems, and airports; deliver and upgrade power grids; and increase internet access. States continue to control the delivery of health care and educational resources to its citizens. The political decisions on development of domestic service sectors often favor regions or localities, targeting some for growth, jobs, and social development at the expense of others. In human rights discourse, states are the duty-bearer of the delivery of rights to its citizens, and therefore have the ultimate authority and responsibility to their citizens in this area.

Most scholars of globalization cite, as one of its primary components, the intensification of the flow of people through internal and cross-border migration. But these processes take place only through the mechanisms, barriers, or incentives that are established by receiving countries, and are often mediated by regulations in sending countries. Passports, visas, and citizenship are the exclusive domain of states that play a major role in determining who is able to migrate where, under what circumstances, for what time period, and with what official status.

Despite the discourse of globalization proponents, state autonomy is an unchallenged principle in international diplomacy. Treaty negotiations, warfare and its cessation, boundaries and borders, and developing its defense infrastructure are among the presumed rights of states. Violations of the sovereignty of one state through border invasion generally results in sanctions of some kind placed on the aggressor state. While ideas about sovereignty in the modern world are being redefined in some domains, the state remains a critical and powerful actor in the complex world of global interactions in the twenty-first century.

ethnonationalism in Europe. When European ethnonationalists took control of the state, they co-opted the use of force, which they now turn to their own nationalistic purposes. Ethnogenesis in Europe has a long history. The French Revolution may be seen as the expression of emerging French national self-identity. Under the banner of "Liberty, Equality, Fraternity," Napoleon brutally brought France's "civilizing principles" to the rest of Europe. Though claiming to spread universal principles, he was actually expanding the scope of French nationalism and hegemony. As often happened throughout history, one group's ethnogenic awakening produced a reaction among that group's neighbors. German ethnogenesis and the movement toward German unification in the latter half of the nineteenth century was a reaction to what was happening in France. This led Germany to develop a sense of its own special destiny.

Ethnogenesis often ignores science in favor of its newly created myths; it manipulates history in order to distort it and control it. French hegemony under Napoleon—that is, nationalism under the guise of universal principles—proved ephemeral. In the same way, Soviet Russian hegemony—Russian nationalism under the guise of universal socialist principles—has also disappeared

Multiculturalism

A multicultural state is composed of several ethnic groups, none of which is officially recognized as dominant. Instead, all are ideologically considered equal. In the nineteenth century, when the United States welcomed large numbers of immigrants seeking refuge from persecution, they became Americans, part of what was later referred to as the "melting pot," in which differences would be weakened and a new amalgamation would emerge. American, as a national identity, was being constructed, and an American culture was developing. However, since the 1960s, we have come to think of ourselves differently. Most of us now view ourselves as a multicultural society. This means a recognition of diversity, highlighting neglected aspects of our social history, particularly the histories and contributions of women, Native peoples, African Americans, and multiple migrant population groups. It also recognizes often-suppressed histories of immigrant discrimination and ethnic exclusion. Multiculturalism is different in theory from the characteristically European situation, in which one ethnic group is the national core identity. In that case, the values of the core group constitute the national culture, politically and religiously, and that group dominates smaller minorities.

As noted above, in Great Britain today, political power and linguistic recognition have now been given to the Scottish and Welsh people. However, those people who migrated to Great Britain from other parts of the commonwealth are recognized in a different way. After World War II, large numbers of migrants from India and Pakistan came to Great Britain to better themselves economically, accepting work that the English no longer wished to do. Although it was originally thought that they would return to their homelands, instead, they sent for their families and settled permanently. Language and religious differences set South Asians apart from the rest of the population. Some of these immigrants were followers of Islam, which provides its adherents with a communal way of life with separate religious institutions—mosques, separate schools, the right to wear their type of clothing, and eat halal meat—all of which maintain their identity. Although the British authorities have made concessions in the direction of multiculturalism, British Muslim activists have been challenging Islamophobia, it has not diminished with time. In fact, since 9/11, Islamophobia in Britain has increased. State support for separate Muslim schools has been an especially thorny issue. Multiculturalism, as currently practiced in Britain, still does not allow for full participation in the society if one chooses a public Muslim identity rather than an accommodation that confines one's Muslim identity to specific domestic and community environments.

Although the political discourse of multiculturalism is publically voiced, Britain has remained essentially a homogeneous, Western, Christian society rather than a pluralist society accepting of people who are of different religions or races. Economic advancement is not the same for the "ethnic population" as it is for British Whites, since a racial barrier exists, and non-Whites, even with PhDs or other advanced professional degrees, find it difficult to find work suitable to their education level. The White British population and British ethnic minorities still lead mostly separate lives, and the "hyphenated" Britons do not feel that they are recognized as part of Britain. The education system is sometimes the only arena that is multiethnic. Links with those "back home" are still maintained by sending remittances and by frequent visits.

ETHNIC DIFFERENCES, ETHNIC VIOLENCE, AND THE NEW NATION OF AFGHANISTAN

Afghanistan provides us with an excellent example of why it is so important to understand the culture, social structures, and political systems of other regions of the world today, particularly regions with which the United States is directly involved. After 9/11, American forces went into Afghanistan to seek out and destroy Al Qaeda and the Taliban, which were governing Afghanistan and providing protection for anti-Western forces. After the Taliban was no longer in control of Afghanistan, Western coalition troops moved in and the international community became involved in nation building in a country with a shallow tradition of "nationhood" and with a mix of many ethnic groups. The Pashtuns are the largest ethnic group in the country. As a result of European colonialism in Asia, the Pashtuns are found on both sides of the Afghanistan-Pakistan border. They number perhaps ten to twelve million people and straddle the highly permeable border between Afghanistan and Pakistan. It is estimated that there are seven million Pashtuns in Afghanistan (Magnus and Naby 2002: 93); the remainder are in Pakistan.

As a consequence of British colonialism and the postcolonial redrawing of state boundaries, Afghanistan includes a large number of other ethnic groups.

To the north are Tajiks, Uzbeks, Turkomen, and Mountain Khirgiz; each group at the present time also has its independent nation-state outside of Afghanistan as a result of the breakup of the Soviet Union. Other ethnic groups are the Hazaras, Baluch, Aimaqs, and Nuristanis, who were non-Muslims in the nineteenth century but later converted. The Pashtuns, the largest ethnic group, had ruled Afghanistan through a monarchy until 1978. Though the Pashtuns dominated the political system and exercised hegemony over Tajiks, Uzbeks, and all the others, they did not try to make them into Pashtuns. The pattern had

In 2021, after several years of military intervention by the United States and its NATO allies in Afghanistan, the abrupt withdrawal of foreign troops coincided with the collapse of the elected government. Taliban officials quickly took control of the government, ending years of state-building efforts by Western-supported interventions.

been set more than two hundred years ago by the great Afghan ruler Ahmed Shah Durrani (1747–1773), who conquered and ruled over an empire that extended from Persia to Delhi in northern India. Over his own people, the Afghans, he ruled as an "elected tribal chief," but over conquered peoples, he exacted tribute (Magnus and Naby 2002: 30).

The porous border between Afghanistan and Pakistan is beyond the control of either state government. It is governed largely by the customary law of the Pashtuns found on both sides of the border. Many are nomadic pastoral peoples. Pashtun nomads move their herds into the Sulayman Mountains of Afghanistan in summer, and back down to the Indus Valley in Pakistan in winter. When they moved with their herds, Pashtun men were always armed—Enfield rifles in the past, Kalashnikovs more recently. This has always been one of the world's most porous borders. When American military forces tried to pin down Al Qaeda forces along this border in Operation Anaconda, they found that the Al Qaeda forces (and Osama bin Laden as well, as was apparent when he was later located and killed) simply crossed into Pakistan. The new Afghan government, with little tax revenue to depend on, tried to collect customs taxes more diligently along this border. However, Pashtuns living there define "freedom" as not being under the yoke of a central government, which collects taxes from them.

The international drug trade has consolidated the power of some warlords in this area. Their access to resources (arms, smuggling, the drug trade) enables them to act as centers of redistribution of resources to their followers, who are predominantly from the same tribe. Barth, who studied Pashtuns of the Yusufzai tribe in Swat, Pakistan, observes that every Yusufzai "chief" had his "men's house." Allegiance to a particular chief is expressed by visiting his men's house and eating the food he provides. These chiefs in Afghanistan are acting as warlords. But they are also are now being designated as "field commanders" by the new central state government. They head armed militias, bound to their leader by Pashtun concepts of loyalty. During conflict, however, the leader may ally himself with one faction or another.

The centralized government of Afghani president Hamid Karzai, a Durrani from the Populzai tribe, was established after the overthrow of the

Taliban regime. Karzai served as president of Afghanistan from 2004 to 2014; his presidency was recognized and supported by the "nation builders" of the West, and rested on a very precarious balance of ethnic and regional groups. Pashtuns historically did not affiliate with a strong central government, and the balance of power inherent in their segmentary lineage structure favors a decentralized political structure. In addition to balancing the forces within the Pashtun political system, it was also necessary to balance political leaders of the various different ethnic groups in the country—especially Tajiks and Uzbeks, with their own array of field commanders and warlords. This is the culture and the underlying social structure that state-building policy continues to cope with in Afghanistan. In 2014, new presidential elections were held; in a contested election that resulted in a series of runoff ballots, Ashraf Ghani, of Pashtun descent, was elected president. His running mate for vice president was General Abdul Rashid Dostum, a prominent Uzbek politician and military leader; his second vice president is of Hazara descent.

The new government, a fragile democracy, was supported by international aid and the continued presence of US and NATO military forces. American military forces were intended to train Afghan police and security personnel, with the intention of eventual withdrawal after the transition was completed. The continued presence, and deaths, of military personnel in Afghanistan proved to be politically contentious in the United States; during his presidency, Barack Obama made several efforts to "draw down" the number of American troops in Afghanistan, but Taliban forces continued their military offensives to gain control of multiple regions. Afghan president Ashraf Ghani negotiated a ceasefire with the Taliban in 2018, but this agreement did not hold. The American government sponsored secret peace talks with the Taliban in 2018 and 2019 that excluded Ghani's Afghan government. Taliban insurgency and violence intensified throughout 2021. Taliban forces overtook the capital city of Kabul, and President Biden abruptly withdrew all remaining American troops in August 2021. Under threat from the insurgency forces, President Ghani and other elected officials fled the country, and the Taliban control of the country was completed.

International observers have called the current state of Afghanistan a humanitarian crisis, with widespread famine, health challenges, dismantling of the educational system, and financial crises. The final withdrawal of American troops was accompanied by a massive wave of out-migration, with its attendant consequences globally. International women's advocacy groups and Afghan expatriates are particularly concerned about the rapid erosion of the educational and health sectors, and the reversal of political gains women had made in the years prior to the final Taliban insurgency. Nongovernmental organizations and advocates both inside and outside of Afghanistan continue to engage with the international community to find ways to actualize transparent governance, peace and security, and the protection of the universal human rights of all Afghan citizens.

EUROPEAN IMMIGRATION AND MULTICULTURALISM IN THE UNITED STATES

As we noted in chapter 1, modern human beings have always migrated from one place to another; in the process, they inevitably confront the cultures and institutions of other groups of people. With the advent of modern states, people crossing borders must negotiate the legal and cultural systems of the receiving state; they are classified and regulated according to the norms and practices of those institutions. Diverse groups within the borders of the United States confront the contradictions of American cultural and political institutions that espouse the rhetoric of equality while simultaneously privileging some groups over others. Restrictions on immigration and citizenship are continuous themes in American history. These debates in different periods of American history illustrate how ideas about race, ethnicity, and multiculturalism are constructed in political discourse and enforced through state law and policy.

According to archaeologists and geneticists, the first settlers of North America started coming across the Bering Strait perhaps as early as 25,000 or 30,000 years ago; migration into North and South America is estimated to have begun sometime after approximately 16,500 years ago (Goebel, Waters, and O'Rourke 2008). In their construction of their cultural past, Kiowa Native Americans view their mythic ancestors as having emerged from places in their native areas. Hence, they have always been in America, which is what their mythology tells them, tying them to the landmarks of their territories from time immemorial. They see the "story," told by scientists of the peopling of the New World by populations originating in Asia and crossing the Bering Strait as an attempt to turn them into immigrants in America. This migration narrative undercuts their hard-won battles with the American state for cultural and territorial autonomy based on claims of indigeneity.

The Europeans who came to North America in the 1600s as colonists identified themselves from their countries of origin, as English, Irish, Scottish, Dutch, Swedish, German, French, Spanish, and Russian. Enslaved people were forcibly brought from Africa by the European colonists to work the plantations that had been established; in that process they were stripped of any ethnic or national origin. An American culture began to develop from an English-Continental base, and earlier national identities merged to become an American identity. In the 1830s, American culture was observed firsthand by French diplomat and historian Alexis de Toqueville. In Democracy in America (first published in 1835) he concluded that nineteenth-century Americans valued entrepreneurship, the "self-made man," personal advancement, individualism, restlessness, and the upholding of biblical traditions. The British had a social structure based on an inherited aristocracy, a monarchy, an official religion headed by the monarch (king or queen), and a class structure. This was clearly different from the American political system, culture, religious organization, and social structure.

As immigration swelled in the late nineteenth and early twentieth centuries, the dominant strategy was that all who came to the United States would be assimilated into the emerging American culture. The picture the United States had of itself was that of a melting pot, as described above, a receiver of people from many different cultures and societies who would learn the language of the country—English—and its culture, and assimilate into the developing American culture and society. Immigrants had chosen to come here because they saw it as a land of opportunity. America was industrializing and expanding. There was a great need for labor, and jobs were plentiful.

The influx of immigrant labor created a backlash, expressed in part through racial and ethnic discrimination. In the late nineteenth and early twentieth centuries the immigration and citizenship rights of Chinese and other Asians were restricted by federal law. One feature of this restrictive policy barred Chinese women from the United States, creating a generation of male-only Chinese immigrants. Immigration from Mexico was subject to increasing scrutiny by border patrols. The Immigration Act of 1924 banned further immigration from most Asian countries. This act restricted the number of immigration visas issued and allocated them on the basis of quotas by nationality. One section of the law, the Johnson-Reed Act, limited total European immigration to 150,000 per year, and limited the number of immigrants by nationality to 2 percent of the total already living in the United States. This had the effect of greatly increasing immigration from Great Britain and other northern European countries, and curtailing immigration of Italians from southern Europe and Jews from eastern Europe.

Italians and Jews of European descent had an ambiguous racial identity in the United States in the early twentieth century. They were "both white and racially distinct from other whites" (Foner 2005: 14, emphasis in original). Under the prevailing racial system, when it came to southern and eastern Europeans "characteristics other than color—believed to be innate and unchangeable—were involved in defining them as separate races" (2005: 14). Racialized discourses of the time referenced presumed facial characteristics of Jews and the complexion of Italians as markers of racial distinction from, and inferiority to, unambiguously White populations of the "Nordic" type from western Europe. "It seems clear that the Johnson-Reed Act was an effort to preserve the racial status quo on the part of those who acted out of a particular sense of white racial consciousness and who saw their privileged position threatened by the changing complexion of America" (Rees 2007: 56).

Many of the immigrants who came from eastern Europe in the middle of the nineteenth century used ethnic terms, rather than terms referring to a nation-state, to identify themselves, demonstrating the weakness of national identity in some places in Europe, like the Austro-Hungarian Empire at this time. These ethnic identities continued to be maintained in the domestic realm and within the community, despite the ideology of the melting pot. Silesians and Kashubians, in the communities they established in Pennsylvania, for example, retained much of their language and culture, as well as their religious affiliation.

Scotch-Irish immigrants were descendants of a Protestant group from Scotland, moved by the conquering English into Ulster County in Northern Ireland. They subsequently immigrated to America in the eighteenth and nineteenth centuries. They came from economically poor areas and moved into equally marginal frontier areas in the United States. The Scotch-Irish retained their ethnic identity in the border areas of Appalachia, providing us with the legends of the feuding Hatfields and McCoys. They also gave us such self-made entrepreneurs as Andrew Mellon, patriots such as Patrick Henry, and five presidents of the United States—Polk, Buchanan, Jackson, Arthur, and Wilson.

American immigration policy underwent transformation again in the 1950s and 1960s. New policies encouraged reunification of immigrants with close family members from abroad, and the immigration of people with professional skills to meet service-oriented and technological labor market demands. The majority of the "**new immigrants**" to the United States came from Caribbean, Latin America, and Asian countries, in contrast to the "old immigrants" who were mostly from European countries (Foner 1987: 2). Among the new immigrants were people from East Asian and South Asian countries, seeking economic and professional opportunities. Dominican and Haitian immigrants were largely motivated by political instability and economic pressures. Vietnamese immigrants left their country due to the impact of war in their country. In the 1980s, large numbers of people from former Soviet republics immigrated to the United States.

As with previous waves of immigration, the influx of new immigrants prompted new formulations of identity categories and new debates over the use of racial and ethnic categories. To cite one example, "Asian" was an option of racial self-identification in the US Census for the first time in 2000, when it was disaggregated from the 1990 category "Asian and Pacific Islander." Proponents of this move argue that it will facilitate more precise data gathering on socioeconomic status, health conditions, and other demographic factors. Those who question its usefulness cite the enormous variation in countries of origin, languages, religions, and ethnicities encompassed in this collective terminology that includes people from South Asia, continental China, other East Asian countries, and the Philippines. The single "Asian" racial category obscures a wide variety of ethnicity and is implicated in generating stereotypes. The label "**model minority**" mythologizes the presumed economic and educational success of "Asian" immigrants. While at first glance complimentary, the model-minority myth, like any other stereotype, is dangerous and misleading on several levels. "[T]he myth is a gross simplification that is not accurate enough to be seriously used for understanding 10 million people. Second, it conceals within it an invidious statement about African-Americans along the lines of the inflammatory taunt: 'They made it, why can't you?' Third, the myth is abused both to deny that Asian Americans experience racial discrimination and to turn Asian Americans into a racial threat" (Wu 2002: 49).

new immigrants

Immigrants to the United States post-1960s resulting from changes in immigration law and policy.

model minority

The mythologizing of the skills and abilities of a minority immigrant community.

Culture Unassimilated, Reiterated, and Renewed in America

As we noted above, in retrospect, the idea of the melting pot was a myth for all Americans. When the founding fathers wrote the Declaration of Independence, the Constitution, and the Bill of Rights, the ideal was having no single dominant ethnic group. In contrast, in other countries, such as Great Britain, France, and Germany, one religion was the state religion and the culture of one group was dominant. However, what was written on paper was not the case in reality. Immigrants who came here learned English, and Christmas was a legal holiday, but not Hanukkah or the Prophet's birthday. Although people conformed to majority norms in the public spheres of work, school, government, and so on, ethnic cultural practices were often retained in the private spheres of life. While **assimilation** was being emphasized, the persistence of ethnic practices in any form was officially ignored and even denied, being revealed only in scholarly articles.

assimilation

Adoption of the language and norms of a new culture.

The United States has recast its image and replaced the melting-pot symbol with that of a multiethnic, multicultural, pluralistic society. Americans are now encouraged to become more aware of and to respect the differing cultural backgrounds of ethnic groups other than their own. All the groups, taken together, are seen to constitute American culture today. The implications of this shift in our image of ourselves from assimilation to multiculturalism continue to reverberate in school curricula, in urban politics, on television, and in films. Now that multiculturalism and multiethnic images occupy center stage, we are also paying more attention to cultural continuities with the past and to ethnic practices that continue from yesterday, in a reworked form. Critics of the multicultural perspective cite its reliance on "food and festival" sharing, while ignoring the political hierarchies and inequalities that continue to characterize American pluralism.

African Americans and African Heritage

The defiant reiteration, strengthening, and redefinition of ethnic identity by various ethnic groups in recent years was a response to the civil rights movement in the 1950s and 1960s, which gave birth to the idea of Black Power—the political empowerment of African Americans—and the conscious construction of African American culture. In the mid-1960s, African Americans proclaimed that "black is beautiful" and strengthened their identity by reiterating their African traditions and constructing their heritage anew.

With today's emphasis on different ethnic traditions, scholars of African American culture are investigating continuities with African cultures in contemporary communities. For example, rural African Americans in southern states such as Georgia, Alabama, and South Carolina had a tradition of cooking, washing, and sharing gossip in swept yards surrounding their houses. This custom is now found only among members of the older generations. Swept yards were the center of family activity during the slave period and after. This use of space has been linked to West African village practices (Westmacott 1992). Cultural continuities with both West African and Central African cultures have been traced in a number of other areas. African American speech, discussed in chapter 3, shows African retentions in verb tense usage and lexicon (Asante 1990). Some words with origins in African languages, like the terms gumbo and goober, are recognized by all American English speakers. Africanisms also survived in various musical traditions including gospel, jazz, and the blues, and are more recently reiterated in performance and rap music.

The strengthening of African American identity involved cultural activism and creativity, increasing the visibility of Black history and experience in mainstream American culture. Alex Haley's television miniseries Roots, which first aired in the 1970s, graphically depicted the epic history of his family, as he reconstructed it, beginning with his West African ancestor who was enslaved and transported to America. All America watched Roots, but it had an especially powerful impact on African Americans and their sense of ethnic identity. Roots served to directly connect African American culture to West African culture. Learning Swahili, wearing Kente cloth, using African greetings, and learning to cook African foods were tied to a cognizance of a Pan-African heritage of historic accomplishments.

This connection to West African culture also stimulated travel and tourism to domestic and African destinations associated with the Mid-Atlantic slave trade and its aftermaths. Anthropologists and other social scientists analyze these tourism sites to document the struggles over the representation of events and their participants in heritage-related travel sites. Leisure destinations that claim educational authority, such as Colonial Williamsburg, present a vision of history as authoritative fact. Behind the scenes, political struggles take place over control of the narratives of American history and the contributions of people of African descent presented in reconstructions, displays of material remains, and tour guide scripts (Gable et al. 1992).

Debates over the representations of the history of the migration of enslaved peoples occur at Elmina Castle in Ghana. The castle and its grounds are a historically significant travel destination for African Americans and others in the Black diaspora worldwide. Elmina Castle was a major site of imprisonment and subsequent disembarkation for African slaves during the height of the Mid-Atlantic slave trade from 1700 to 1850 (Bruner 1996). Tourists from the Black diaspora, particularly African Americans, want to maintain the association of this site with the slave trade, enshrining and commemorating it with this association exclusively. Ghanaians have a more complicated set of historical narratives and references associated with this site. "For Ghanaians, Elmina Castle represents a part of Ghanaian history, from the Portuguese who built Elmina in 1482 primarily to facilitate trade on the Gold Coast, to the Dutch who captured the castle in 1637, to the British who gained control of Elmina in 1872, through to Ghanaian independence in 1957" (1996: 292).

In her ethnography about narratives of slavery-period history in Ghana, Bayo Holsey observes: "I found that the high visibility of the slave trade within the tourism industry stands in sharp relief to its practical invisibility

Three generations of family members light candles together in celebration of Kwanzaa. They wear African produced clothing and jewelry as part of the celebration. Kwanzaa celebrations honor the seven principles of African American unity, self-determination, collective work and responsibility, cooperative economics, purpose, creativity, and faith.

in other arenas of Ghanaian society, where it is rarely mentioned. When I asked local residents whether or not they had ever learned about the slave trade from any sources outside of the tourism industry, from members of their families or other people in their communities, they told me that they had not. . . . Many told me that the castles are just for tourists and expressed little interest in them" (Holsey 2008: 2). These competing visions of this significant period in history form the basis of conflict over the use and control of Elmina Castle's space, and the narratives presented to foreign tourists and Ghanaians, in the castle and on its grounds.

The celebration of the holidays Kwanzaa and Juneteenth is an example of the increasing recognition of cultural practices that draw on African American history and practices. Juneteenth, also known as Freedom Day or Emancipation Day, commemorates the day of the official enforcement of the abolition of slavery in Texas on June 19, 1865. Juneteenth has been recognized as a holiday by some states since 1980; in 2022 it was declared a federal holiday by President Biden. Kwanzaa is widely celebrated today all over the country with the sending of Kwanzaa cards and gift giving. The seven-day cultural festival, held from December 26 to New Year's Day, is observed by African Americans of all religious faiths.

Kwanzaa is particularly associated with the purchase of goods associated with African identity, though these objects are purchased at other times of the year as well. A market has been created, and Africans from West Africa have begun to bring goods from Africa for sale to African Americans. These African entrepreneurs sell in street markets in New York and other cities with sizable African American populations. American businessmen have also found a niche in this holiday market; greeting cards and gifts that represent the African tradition and African American history are exchanged (Stoller 2002: 82). This marketing of Afrocentrism represents an attempt to replicate the signs and symbols of Africa through consumer goods that tie African Americans to their heritage.

As we have discussed previously, the one-drop rule held that "offspring of interracial unions were defined racially as African American, regardless of the racial identity of their other parent" (Daniel 2002: x). Grandchildren, great-grandchildren, and so on, down the generations were also thus categorized. Recently, those of multiracial background have begun to feel that all the backgrounds of their ancestry are important and should be recognized—European, American Indian, and so forth. The US Census now includes categories of self-identification that allow respondents to designate multiple racial and ethnic categories. These new multiracial identity categories are seen by some as undermining the goal of unifying African Americans into a strong

BOX 14.2 | Who Is the Ancient One?

Conflicting narratives of identity and history moved from scholarly journals into contemporary identity politics with the discovery of a skeleton in Kennewick, Washington, in 1996. Dubbed "Kennewick Man" by the archaeologists involved in the case, the remains were accidentally discovered on federal land administered by the Army Corps of Engineers. Scientists who first examined the remains estimated the skeleton to be approximately nine thousand years old and originally classified its cranial features as "Caucasoid." A facial reconstruction of Kennewick Man attracted widespread media attention, due in large part to its similarity to the British actor Patrick Stewart. Historian Vine DeLoria Jr. pointed out striking similarities between Kennewick Man's facial reconstruction and a portrait of Chief Black Hawk painted in 1833 (Thomas 2000: xxv); however, these images did not attract equal media attention.

An alliance of five Northwest Native American communities claimed their rights to the remains. Citing the Native American Graves Protection and Repatriation Act (NAGPRA), the Confederated Tribes of the Colville Reservation invoked their right to claim the skeleton to bury it promptly, consistent with their religious norms for proper handling of the remains of an ancestor. A group of scientists sought access to the skeleton to study it for the important information this unique find could reveal about early human populations in the New World. The battle over control of the remains moved into the American court system. In 2004, a federal appeals court ruled that the Native communities failed to establish the skeleton's cultural identity as American Indian. The remains were moved to the Burke Museum at the University of Washington, where they remained under the control of the Army Corps of Engineers.

In 2015, genetic testing reversed the original identity assigned by geneticists to the skeleton and determined that it was most closely related to contemporary Indigenous Peoples of the Americas (although precise group affiliation could not be determined) and not to Europeans. He was named "The Ancient One" and was returned to the Confederates Tribes of the Colville Reservation for appropriate burial in 2017. This case continues to raise important questions about the rights of possession over human remains and the political uses of science in discourses about race, identity, and history. "[T]he pivotal issue at Kennewick is not about religion or science. It is about politics. The dispute is about control and power, not philosophy. Who gets to control ancient American history—governmental agencies, the academic community, or modern Indian people?" (Thomas 2000: xxvii).

Researchers studying repatriation issues in the United States are now documenting new forms of cooperation and commonality of interests between outside scientists and Native American communities, inspired by NAGPRA's initiatives and successful examples of collaboration. "Indigenous scientists and community-based researchers are leading the way. [A] recent edited volume, *Working With and For Ancestors*, shows how research of all kinds—from oral history work to DNA analysis—has featured prominently in many repatriation cases where researchers sought to work with and for descendent communities. . . . Respectful relationships between institutions and descendant communities must be developed and maintained, the wishes of community partners need to be prioritized, and community control over the disposition of their Ancestors must be respected" (Nichols et al. 2021).

political force. However, as Daniel notes, "The new multiracial identity, rather than imploding African-American identity, can potentially forge more inclusive constructions of blackness and whiteness" (2002: 175). Those who argue for integrative pluralism encourage recognition of cultural and racial diversities as well as commonalities.

DIVERSITY IN AMERICA: CHALLENGES AND DEBATES

Ethnicity was once viewed by social scientists as a perpetuation of cultural traditions from the past. It is now understood as the utilization of symbols of identity that has always involved creativity and inventiveness (Sollars 1989; Stern and Cicala 1991). The question of "authenticity" of "new" customs and traditions is sometimes raised in this context. Scholars, however, recognize that all customs and traditions are invented (Hobsbawm and Ranger 1983) and represent cultural innovations. Ideas about tradition are recognized now to be selective imaginings of the past articulated in the present. Customs and ritual celebrations, invented a century ago or a decade ago, are accepted by group members as authentic representations of their identity; the time-depth of a custom or ritual has nothing to do with its authenticity or relevance to those who partake in it.

Many ethnic groups reassert and reiterate their own ethnic identity and group solidarity by displaying their own cultural traditions in an increasingly public manner. New York City, a receiving destination for immigrants for two centuries, provides a spatial landscape on which to observe the expression of ethnic identity by both "old" and "new" immigrant groups (Foner 1987). Parades along Fifth Avenue in New York, occurring on many weekends throughout the year, reflect the kaleidoscope of groups publicly displaying and reiterating their ethnic identity with floats, bands, costumes, and dignitaries (Rosman and Rubel 2015).

Ethnic parades of the Irish and the Pakistanis in Great Britain symbolize each ethnic group's right to parade through neighborhoods of other ethnic groups. Ethnic parades in the United States make a different symbolic statement. Most of the ethnic groups use the same space—"Main Street" or public thoroughfares for their parades. The participants are proclaiming and celebrating their ethnic identity as hyphenated Americans. In New York City, most ethnic parades use the same routes, either along Fifth Avenue or, for smaller parades, Madison Avenue. Fifth Avenue is lined with major department stores and high-end retail establishments and is therefore an area of everyday commerce. It is also a major tourist-attraction site for visitors to the city; parades will therefore generate large crowds of participants and viewers of all identities. Among the ethnic parades in New York City at different times of the year are the Irish, Greek, Puerto Rican, Scottish, Polish, and German parades. The largest ethnic parade of all in New York City, the West Indian parade, takes place in Brooklyn over Labor Day weekend and attracts a million spectators and participants each year.

There are several features ethnic parades have in common in New York City. Through the selection of floats and grand marshals, and the inclusion of newsworthy politicians and celebrities, they include representations of "ties to the old country, religion, the nature of the connection [of the ethnic group] to the United States, economic success …[and] values of the group" (Rosman and Rubel 2015). As public events, parades take place within contested terrain. Private parade organizers have the power to make decisions about which groups will be allowed to participate and which will be excluded from the parade. Parade participants and audiences frequently interpret the ongoing activity and the symbolism of the parade in different ways. One group of observers may see the accomplishments of an ethnic group and its contributions to and support of American society and values. Another group may see threats to mainstream American control over economic and political processes. For parade participants and organizers, these public events embody the tensions between affiliation of ethnic sentiment and the embracing of American identity and values.

A float representing a local Hispanic social center participates in the annual Columbus Day parade on Fifth Avenue in New York City. For parade participants and organizers these public events may enact the tensions between affiliation of ethnic sentiment and the embracing of American identity and values.

Whether it is Slovenians who settled in Cleveland several generations ago, or Somalis who have recently settled in Lewiston, Maine, or those of Nordic descent who are recapturing the culture of their ancestors, we are becoming more and more aware of the diversity of cultural background of new and old Americans. We are made aware of ethnic celebrations such as the Persian New Year (Nowruz), which is the ancient celebration of the spring equinox, and the distinctive thanksgiving ritual dedicated to the Prophet Elijah, which is celebrated at weddings by the Jews from India, the Bene Israel. The US Post Office has issued postage stamps marking the holidays of Eid, Divali, Kwanzaa, and the Chinese Lunar New Year.

America is a nation based on religious freedom, and from the beginning, attracted religious believers persecuted in their homelands. Despite this, there is a strong streak of religious intolerance in the country, sometimes coupled with racism. Intolerance of African American Muslims, or Native American churches that practice the peyote "cult," or Caribbean "sects" like Santeria, which seeks to carry out animal sacrifice, exemplifies this. The rituals and belief systems of minority religious groups may offend the Judeo-Christian interpretation of morality; these issues are often debated through legal challenges in the courts that seek to eliminate these practices. Muslim Americans of all ethnicities and countries of origin have experienced discrimination, random violence, legal persecution, and religious profiling, sometimes in the name of enforcing national security. During the Covid-19, pandemic Asian

Americans have been wrongfully and violently attacked due to the presumed origin of the virus in one city in China.

How do Americans with mixed ethnic heritages deal with ethnic identity today? Such individuals are now making choices regarding which of several ancestries they want to stress and which they will omit. On the US Census, Americans are increasingly using the multiple options offered for "mixed" and "other" categories to self-describe their identity. People may choose to express their ethnicity situationally, in domestic and ritual settings, or through participation in periodic public events such as parades or annual identity festivals. The United States has always been a multiethnic and pluralist society, although the rights of minorities were ignored for much of its early history. Ongoing contemporary debates regarding how to implement multicultural and diverse curricula in colleges, high schools, and elementary schools reflect our groping for new ways to symbolize and express the multiple aspects of our cultural traditions. We continue to negotiate the ways in which national economic and security interests can be protected, while respecting the rights of all ethnicities, races and religions. These debates in political discourse increasingly focus around the rights of certain immigrant groups to enter the United States and attain full citizenship. Polarized debates over immigration and security have almost eclipsed the consideration of what remains of a shared American culture and value system, which includes religious tolerance and the principles embodied in the Bill of Rights and the Constitution.

SUMMARY

- In today's world, states are universally recognized as the dominant political entity whose borders are maintained by international consensus.

- People, business transactions, and capital flow across borders, especially service providers from the global South to Northern countries.

- States invariably encompass diverse groups of people; the concept of nation suggests shared cultural identity within these borders. Nationalism is the political movement to create a national culture within a state's borders.

- Ethnic groups share common cultural norms, values, identities, patterns of behavior, and language.

- Racial classification systems are political constructs, usually based on culture-specific ideas about phenotype or physical appearance, although many people tend to think of race as a scientific concept of human variation based on biological characteristics.

- Critical race theory is an interdisciplinary perspective that explores how racism and all forms of discrimination are created by state structures, and are experienced by different groups of people in society.

- The building of national identity is always a creative political process that draws on various forms of identities and the use of historical and archaeological interpretation, as well as all forms of traditional and digital media.

- Indigenous peoples in contemporary states around the world have adopted multiple religious and political strategies to resist or accommodate their integration into state systems.

- Multiculturalism is a state policy that, in theory, recognizes cultural differences among citizens. In reality, however, many claim that it does not recognize the political hierarchies of cultural and ethnic diversity, nor does it explore the dominance of a hegemonic culture.

- While the idea of the melting pot was dominant in the United States and assimilation was being emphasized, the persistence of ethnic practices in any form was officially ignored and even denied. However, the United States has recast its image and replaced the melting-pot symbol with that of a multiethnic, multicultural, and pluralistic society.

- In Afghanistan the stability of the central government is challenged by the religious, ethnic, and kin-based affiliations of its leaders and their followers.

- The reiteration, strengthening, and redefinition of ethnic identity by various ethnic groups in recent years was in response to the civil rights movement of the 1950s and 1960s, which gave birth to the idea of Black Power—the empowerment of African Americans—and the conscious construction of African American culture.

- Other ethnic groups also began reasserting and reiterating their own ethnic identity and group solidarity and building their own hyphenated cultures in an increasingly public manner.

- Individuals with mixed ethnic and racial heritages make choices regarding which ancestry and identity they want to stress under different circumstances and situations, especially by choosing among US Census category options.

KEY TERMS

assimilation, 376
boundary maintenance, 364
cargo cult, 365
critical race theory, 360
ethnic groups, 359
ethnicity, 359
ethnogenesis, 366
hypodescent, 359
model minority, 375

nationalism, 358
nativistic movements, 364
new immigrants, 375
phenotype, 359
race, 358
racism, 359
revitalization movements, 364
state, 358
tribe, 362

SUGGESTED READINGS

Brenneman, Robert L. *As Strong as the Mountains: A Kurdish Cultural Journey*. 2nd ed. Long Grove, IL: Waveland Press. 2016.

The history and cultures of the Kurds, the largest ethnic group in the world, whose 30 million people are divided among Turkey, Iran, Iraq, and Syria. Originally pastoral nomads, they are now living in urban centers in states in which their sovereignty and identities are continually challenged by dominant religious and political forces.

Sharma, Aradhana, and Akhil Gupta, eds. *The Anthropology of the State: A Reader*. Malden, MA: Blackwell Publishing, 2006.

Classic theoretical works and contemporary scholarship on states, development, immigration, and citizenship.

Smedley, Audrey, and Brian D. Smedley. *Race in North America: Origin and Evolution of a Worldview*. 4th ed. Boulder, CO: Westview, 2012.

A comprehensive history of the origins and manifestations of racial categories and constructions in North America, traced through intellectual, philosophical, scientific, and migration histories.

SUGGESTED WEBSITES

www.pbs.org/wgbh/pages/frontline/shows/jefferson/mixed/

A website developed by PBS for a documentary on the relationship between Thomas Jefferson and Sally Hemmings, including essays on race, mixed-race categories, and the "one drop of blood rule" in contemporary America.

http://indiancountrytoday.com/

A comprehensive website presenting news, politics, social issues, lifestyle, and advocacy issues among Native Americans as well as indigenous groups worldwide.

https://www.census.gov/history/www/through_the_decades/overview/

An official website of the United States government, this site contains detailed information on the evolution of the census and census categories in use since the first census in 1790. Comparing the categories of identity included in each census shows how the US government has made multiple different efforts at classifying and enumerating groups of people in its population, and documents the changes, additions, and redefinitions of racial and ethnic categories throughout the census history.

EPILOGUE

One of the goals of this book in all its previous editions was to illustrate to students of anthropology that there are many cultures in the world, and that there are multiple perspectives and theories used to explore this diversity. American culture is but one of them; we illustrate the ways in which anthropologists explore cultural differences, demonstrating how cultures are similar in some ways and also how they differ. We have shown how anthropologists study indigenous native societies as well as state-based urban cultures around the world, using historical and linguistic methods as well as fieldwork and participant observation. Anthropologists may focus on groups in their own culture, which may be different from theirs in ethnic and class affiliation.

In more recent editions, we discussed the ways in which globalization significantly impacts our world. The methodologies of anthropology make it well suited to explore how local communities are affected by globalization. The anthropological perspective focuses on the ways people "on the ground" in local communities are affected by, and are reacting to, larger forces beyond their communities, including decentralized production and shifting sites of labor demand. Anthropological methodologies can show: (1) the ways peoples' lives and health are changed in response to the building of new factories locally that are owned by multinational companies; (2) the ways peoples' lives are changed by the availability of new technologies from beyond the borders of their countries; and (3) how family members maintain their ties while living in multiple countries around the world. The local level, where people live their lives, and the way it articulates with regional, national, and international policy and law, are core aspects of the contemporary anthropological approach. One of the central messages of anthropology and of this book is respect for cultural diversity, showing how one community's cultural practices are but one possible way of doing things, and that no one way is the "right way" or "only way."

More recent editions of *The Tapestry of Culture* explore anthropological approaches to widespread ecological shifts confronting all parts of the world. Climate change, drought, and famine are just some of the issues different groups of people around the world face on a daily basis and at all levels of their social lives, from individual decision making about migration, to state and multilateral policy. This eleventh edition of *The Tapestry of Culture* discusses relatively recent forces impacting our contemporary world, including global pandemics and the increasing presence of computers, internet-based information, and social media platforms. We also highlight social movements as they emerge throughout the world, which use traditional media and new forms of communication to spread information and mobilize followers. Their ideas often cross borders and create regional and global movements that mobilize both minorities and dominant groups to communicate their messages and strategies. People on the move motivated by multiple "push and pull" factors are now discussed every day in traditional and new forms of media, as are the many reactions to migration and the presence of new groups within older borders. We document how the lives of migrants globally are shaped by the political categories and requirements for citizenship they control in each new location.

All of these forces are cultural: they are actions and responses embedded with ideas and constructions, often competing and always subject to change and revision. The metaphor of the tapestry of culture, which we use as the framework for this book, relates to the interrelationship, or interweaving, of these various interpretations of cultural institutions. Like the colors and designs of an enormous tapestry, every thread can be thought of as the multiple possibilities of people's activities and individual behaviors as they live out their lives and as contributing to the pattern. However, not even the most elaborate tapestry can approach the splendor and complexity of any single culture. This is only a metaphor. It is an abstraction of how people lead their lives according to cultural norms, about concepts of good and evil, about compliance and transgressions. Members of a community are themselves inevitably in vigorous disagreement over the underlying values of their own culture. Today, the metaphor of the tapestry must be seen in the light of multiple forms of inequality between groups of people in any community, as well as disjunctions that occur on a national level as a consequence of colonialism, postcolonialism, and globalization.

In today's ever-changing world, new strategies are constantly emerging concerning the future direction of particular economic systems, access to education and health resources, and regional networks of production and consumption. Inclusion of formerly marginalized voices in national and global policy is now widely acknowledged as an important right of citizenship. Decisions should therefore be made in consultation with the people most affected, and these should be informed by the realities and complexities of multiple group experiences. The methods, theories, and practice of anthropology can make a contribution in these areas. Anthropologists in partnership with communities ultimately can work in the service of humanity by contributing to cultural recognition and forces of change worldwide.

achieved status   Position in a social structure dependent upon personal qualifications and individual ability.

adaptation   The process in which a population or society alters its cultural norms in reaction to its total environment.

affinal link   Connections between kin groups established by marriage.

African American Vernacular English (AAVE)   Speech patterns and norms adopted in some settings that demonstrate identity and community affiliation.

age grade   Categories of individuals of the same age that are recognized by being given a name and that crosscut an entire society.

agency   Refers to the fact that individuals are active interpreters of and responders to their culture.

age set   A group of individuals of the same age that moves as a unit through successive age grades.

agriculture   Grain cultivation system characterized by permanent use of land, owned and worked continuously. Agricultural production requires access to animal and/or or mechanical traction, use of seeds, fertilizer, and a water delivery system.

alliance   A linkage between kin groups established through marriage for the mutual benefit of the two groups.

allomorph   A variant form of a morpheme.

allophone   A variant form of a phoneme.

animism   A belief in the spiritual or noncorporeal counterparts of human beings.

anthropocene   A term originally introduced from geology to refer to the period in which human cultural behavior had significant impact on the ecology and geology of the earth.

applied anthropology   (also referred to as **practicing anthropology**) The application of anthropological knowledge and methodologies to the solution of practical problems, direct action, and/or development policy.

archaeology   Examines cultures through their material remains.

ascribed status   An inherited position in the social structure.

assimilation   Adoption of the language and norms of a new culture.

authority   An institutionalized position of power.

avunculocal residence   A form of postmarital residence in which the bride goes to live with her husband after he has moved to live with his mother's brother.

band organization   An egalitarian type of social group that may come together annually for a period to carry out joint rituals and economic activities.

barter   An exchange of unlike objects or services, without the use of currency.

Big Man structure   An achieved position of leadership in which the group is defined as the Big Man and his followers.

bilateral cross cousin   Offspring of opposite-sex siblings through both the mother's and father's side.

bilateral societies   Societies with kindreds but without unilineal descent groups.

bilocal residence   A form of postmarital residence in which husband and wife alternate between living with the husband's relatives for a period of time and then with the wife's relatives.

biopower   As articulated by scholar Michel Foucault, the concept of recognizing how institutions and widely held but shifting ideas related to health, criminality, and medical practices are created by state institutions to discipline and control individuals in communities.

bipedal erect locomotion   The emergence of physical and cultural characteristic of anatomically modern humans associated with total upright walking on two legs.

blackbirding   The term for the kidnapping of Melanesian laborers to work on colonial plantations in Fiji and Australia.

blended family   or **stepfamily** A family created by the divorce and remarriage of spouses and the combining of parents, stepparents, stepsiblings, and half-siblings.

boundary maintenance   The ways in which a social group maintains its individual identity by separating itself from the dominant society.

brain drain   The loss of educated professionals from one country as a result of migration to another country.

bride service   A custom whereby the groom works for the bride's family before marriage.

bridewealth   Payments of goods or services made by the groom's family to the family of the bride.

care economy   Delivery of paid and unpaid care in domestic settings and understanding its value, sources, and practitioners.

cargo cult   A particular type of revitalization movement that first appeared in the early twentieth century in Melanesia and represents a synthesis of traditional beliefs and valuing of the goods and services of colonial or imperialistic powers.

chain migration   When earlier migrants attract later ones to the same community, resulting in residential clusters of individuals having long-term social and economic relationships.

chief   The leader of a society with fixed positions of leadership (see **chieftainship**).

chieftainship   A type of political organization in which fixed positions of leadership are present along with a method for succession to those positions.

child mortality   Statistics that measure the rates of infant survival and death usually before the first five years of life.

cisgender   Gender self-identification that corresponds with the sex category assigned at birth.

civil law   The part of a legal system that regulates family and property issues.

civil society   Nongovernmental organizations and institutions that provide opportunities for organizing and creating alliances around particular issues, labor unions, religious organizations, and voluntary clubs and associations.

clan   A social group based on presumed common descent but not necessarily common residence.

clan totem   An animal from which members of a clan believe themselves descended and with whom they enact a special symbolic relationship.

code-switching   The use of one or more languages or speech styles in conversation.

cognate   In linguistics, words in two different languages that resemble one another and demonstrate that the two languages are related to each other.

cognatic descent   A rule of descent in which individuals have the choice of belonging to either their father's or their mother's group, to determine different rights or statuses, or they may have particular rights by virtue of membership in either group.

cognitive science of religion   Examines religious phenomena as a result of how the human brain has evolved over time to process and categorize information.

collateral relative   A relative not in the direct line of descent.

colonialism   Full or partial political and economic subjugation of one country or group of people by another, resulting in multiple forms of social discrimination and resource exploitation.

commensality   Culture-specific rules and meanings related to sharing food and meals with others.

commodity   A product grown or produced for sale in a national or global market.

community   An organized social unit.

community health workers   Trained local people, usually women, who provide locally relevant health and mental health services in areas where there is a scarcity of professional practitioners.

compadrazgo   Ritual godparenthood found in Mediterranean Europe and Latin America.

comparative approach   Comparing societies to uncover similarities and reveal differences.

complex societies   Heterogeneous, culturally diverse societies with regional, class, gender, occupational, religious, and ethnic differences.

consultants (or informants)   Individuals in a community who provide information, insights, and guidance to an anthropologist.

corporate descent group   A kin-based group based upon common descent that owns a form of property collectively.

corvee labor   A system of forced labor associated with colonial plantations.

creationist belief systems   Theories of human history based on interpretations of religious sources.

creole   A stable language resulting from contact situations that is acquired by subsequent generations as the native language.

criminal law   The part of a legal system that determines and punishes criminality.

critical race theory (CRT)   Interdisciplinary approach to studying the interrelationships between race, racism, identities, discrimination, and political power.

cross cousins   Offspring of one's mother's brother and one's father's sister.

Crow-type kinship terminology system   Matrilineal descent system associated with avunculocal residence and extended families.

cultural anthropology   The subfield of anthropology that studies variation in beliefs, understanding, behavior, and ideas in human settings.

cultural appropriation   The adoption of symbols or practices of one group of people by another more dominant group.

cultural evolution   A theory that refers to the patterns of cultures presumed to continually be developing into more complex forms over time.

cultural particularism   Emphasizes uniqueness of individual cultures.

cultural relativism   The emphasis on the unique aspects of each culture, without judgments or categories predetermined by one's own culture.

cultural rules   Internalized norms of behavior covering all aspects of life.

cultural universals   Cultural features that are found in all societies.

culture   The way of life of a people, including their behavior, the things they make, their ideas, beliefs, language use, social organization, governance, and production systems.

culture-bound syndrome   Manifestation of behaviors identified as specific to a culture or culture area.

culture shock   Effect upon the observer of encountering a cultural practice different from one's own.

deity   A spirit perceived as having human characteristics as well as supernatural power.

delayed exchange   The return of goods or of marriage partners between groups; the delay in exchange demonstrates a degree of trust between the exchanging parties.

demonstrated descent   A system of descent in which kinship can be traced by means of written or oral genealogies back to a founding ancestor.

dependency theory   Views underdevelopment as the consequence in former colonies of their economic suppression, coupled with continued economic dependence on colonial-based networks of trade and political alliances.

dialects   Variations within a single language between one speech community and another.

diaspora   A population spread from its original homeland to other countries; group members continue to maintain affiliation with their homeland and each other.

diffusion   The process by which a culture trait that originates in one place spreads to another.

digital divide   Inequality in access to electronic devices and internet resources.

direct reciprocal exchange   A continuing exchange of equivalence between two parties creating relationships over time.

direct rule   Colonial strategy involving large numbers of permanent settlers, military personnel, and appropriation of land and resources by the colonial ruler.

discourse   An institutionalized way of thinking or speaking about a subject that comes to be the normalized and accepted worldview through political processes.

distribution   The manner in which products circulate through a society.

diviners   Part-time religious specialists who manipulate the supernatural to enable people to succeed in specific undertakings.

double descent   The coexistence of matrilineal and patrilineal descent rules in a single society.

dowry   Goods that are given by the bride's family to the groom's family at marriage.

duolocal residence   A postmarital rule of residence in which husband and wife live with their respective kinsmen, apart from one another.

ebene   Hallucinogenic substance used by the Yanomamo.

egalitarian society   A system whereby, in theory, productive resources and positions of status and leadership are available to all members of the group.

ego-oriented group   A kinship unit defined in terms of a particular "ego" as designated on a kinship chart.

embodiment   The perspective that considers the cultural construction of the human body as enacting internalized values that contribute to the lived experience of religion and ritual.

empowerment   The ability of groups or individual to identify and achieve their political, social, and economic rights and goals.

enculturation   The process by which cultural rules and norms are learned and acquired by individuals.

endogamy   A rule requiring group members to marry within their own group.

environmental anthropology   An anthropological specialty that documents the relationships between human communities and their environments.

epigenetics   Genetic changes that take place during an individual's lifetime as the result of environmental influences.

Eskimo-type kinship terminology system   American kinship is an example of this type of kinship terminology system.

ethics   The rules and practices that protect the rights of participants in fieldwork and research.

ethnic groups   Groups within a state who claim to preserve cultural norms associated with their histories.

ethnicity   Language, history, traditions, and cultural norms with which people choose to affiliate that create groups of shared identity.

ethnocentrism   The idea that what is present in one's own culture represents the natural and best way to do things.

ethnogenesis   The creation of a new ethnic group.

ethnography   Written description of an aspect of a community or group of people, usually based on fieldwork, participant observation, and consultant interviews.

ethnohistory   Efforts at reconstructing the histories of societies with limited indigenous records that draw on archaeology, oral histories, or archives.

ethnonationalism   The desire of ethnic groups within a state to have their own nation-states.

ethnopsychiatry   The application of cross-cultural variation to the diagnosis and treatment of mental illness.

ethnosemantics   The anthropological investigation of indigenous systems of classifications.

evidence-based outcomes   Claims of results of health or development initiatives that are based on the objective and verifiable gathering of data.

evolutionary psychology   The application of Darwinian principles of natural selection to attempts at understanding the evolution of cultural norms.

exogamy   A rule requiring group members to marry outside their own social group.

Export Processing Zones (EPZs)   See **Free Trade Zones**.

extended family   Three or more generations living together in a single household.

factionalism   Local groups building support under a powerful individual or idea vying for influence locally and within state systems.

failed state   Term applied when a government is perceived to have no legitimacy to function on behalf of its citizens, nor in relationships with other states.

feminist anthropology   Explores cultural practices and inequities based on gender.

feuding   Hostile actions between people of the same group.

fictive kinship   Social relationships in which unrelated individuals use kin terms to establish and recognize their relationships. Oftentimes, the relationship is established by ritual observances.

fieldwork   The hallmark research methodology of cultural anthropology. When doing fieldwork an anthropologist, to the best of their ability, participates in community activities, explores the material and social environments, and interviews local consultants about their perceptions of an aspect of their lives.

folktales   Stories about fanciful creatures set in indeterminate times that impart morals or lessons.

Fordism   The economic, production, labor, and consumer-oriented innovations associated with Henry Ford's twentieth-century assembly-line mass production of automobiles.

Fourth World Peoples   Indigenous or original peoples living as minority populations, with varying degrees of state recognition and autonomy in nation-states around the world.

fragile state Term applied to a government that lacks legitimacy or capacity to meet security and economic needs of its citizens.

fraternal polyandry A form of marriage in which a woman is simultaneously married to several brothers.

Free Trade Zones (FTZs) (also known as **Export Processing Zones**) Areas in developing countries set aside for foreign-owned export-production facilities.

function The way a particular unit or structure operates and what it does.

functionalism The theoretical position that sees cultures as analogous to living organisms operating to maintain a steady state.

fundamentalism A range of political and religious ideologies generally connoting a set of beliefs accepted as irreducible that forestall further inquiry or debate.

gender The culture-specific set of behavioral, ideological, and social meanings of constructed biological and anatomical differences.

gender stratification The comparative ranking of economic and political activities associated with men and women in any society.

geomancy The interpretation of the future from physical objects.

globalization The worldwide connection between societies based upon the existence of global market connections and the spread of cultural items everywhere; associated with intensive movement of people, goods, capital, technologies, and ideas.

godparents/godparenthood A fictive kinship relationship using marked kinship terms to reflect social privileges and responsibilities.

government The process by which those in office make and implement decisions on behalf of an entire group in order to carry out commonly held goals.

grammar The complete description of a language, including phonology, morphology, and syntax.

Great Migration Early twentieth-century migration of over six million African Americans from southern rural communities to northern and Midwestern urban and peri-urban centers.

Hawaiian-type kinship terminology system A type of terminology system that distinguishes between people by generation and gender only.

headman A leader of a group with no power or authority and with no fixed rule of succession.

hegemony Dominance and influence of one social or political group over another.

heteronormativity Cultural perspective that privileges male and female heterosexual identity in conceptualizing social and family norms.

Hijra In India, communities of individuals born as males who transform their identity into a female gender category.

historical particularism Theoretical approach emphasizing each culture's uniqueness.

hominin In contemporary usage, the group that includes modern and extinct humans and other extinct prehumans such as Australopithecus and its predecessors. The group hominid includes modern and extinct humans and their ancestors, as well as gorillas, great apes, and orangutans and their evolutionary ancestors.

hortatory rituals Exhortations to the supernatural to perform some act.

horticulture A form of cultivation in which crops are propagated in gardens.

human capital The resources, skills, and access to important social and political resources an individual can access to achieve health, education, and economic and political benefits.

human genome The complete set of DNA codes in a human cell.

hypodescent A cultural rule that classifies individuals as members of a lower-status group by virtue of their marriage of parents' identity groups.

imperialism Influence over another contiguous or nearby country or region.

incest taboo Prohibition of sexual relations between certain categories of kin.

indentured servitude A labor recruitment strategy in which laborers are compelled to agree to long-term and exploitative contracts in exchange for wages or other forms of remuneration.

indirect rule The system of colonial rule associated with the British Empire by which a small number of administrators controlled large colonial territories by integrating local political leaders and bureaucrats into the administrative system.

influence The ability to persuade others to follow one's lead when one lacks the political authority or power to command.

informal leadership A type of political organization in which there is no single political leader but rather leadership is manifested intermittently.

informants (or **consultants**) Individuals within a fieldwork setting who provide cultural information and insights to an anthropologist.

informed consent The right of participants in research projects to be fully informed about the nature of the research, potential risks, and liabilities of participation.

innovation The process of bringing about cultural change through the recombination of existing ideas into creative new forms.

Intelligent Design (ID) Theories of speciation and geological history that accept some scientifically proposed evolutionary models but require the presence of deistic agency for the creation of the earth and its diverse life forms.

internal migration Population movements within a state, usually from rural to urban areas.

internet platform A digital service that allows interactions between users

intra-cultural variation Variability within a culture, and within and between cultural groups.

Iroquois-type kinship terminology system A type of kinship system found among the Yanomamo.

joint family A type of extended family in which married brothers and their families remain together after the death of their parents.

kaiko   A lengthy Maring religious ceremony.

kayasa   A competitive period of feasting, including a competitive giving of yams to the chief, and games like cricket among the Trobrianders.

key informants (or **consultants**)   Individuals with whom the anthropologist forms a personal, ongoing relationship and who serve as mentors and cultural consultants.

kindred   A kin group from the perspective of a particular individual, or "ego."

kinship terminology   A system of linguistic designations and groupings for those related, by descent or marriage, to an individual.

kula   An exchange system of the Trobriand Islands—involving one kind of shell valuables moving in a clockwise direction and another kind moving in a counter-clockwise direction—that links the Trobriand Islanders to neighboring islands.

langue   Refers to language and its grammatical rules in contrast to *parole,* which refers to individual speech.

law   A system of conflict resolution and criminalization practice.

legal pluralism   The coexistence of indigenous and postcolonial systems of law.

legends   Stories about heroes who overcome obstacles set in familiar historical contexts.

levirate   A rule whereby the widow of a deceased man must marry his brother.

lexicon   (or dictionary) The complete description of all morphemes and their meanings in a language.

liminal period   The in-between stage in a rite-of-passage ceremony when the individual has not yet been reincorporated into society with their new status.

lineages   Unilineal descent groups in which descent is demonstrated.

lineal relative   A relative in the direct line of descent.

linguistic agency   The capacity of language speakers to make choices about the forms and styles they use in everyday speech.

linguistic imperialism   The imposition by a dominant group of its language on minority speakers of other languages.

linguistic relativity   A point of view that emphasizes the uniqueness of each language and the need to examine it in its own terms.

linguistics   The study of language and the relationship between language and culture.

magic   A system based on the belief that the natural world can be compelled to act in the desired way through human intervention.

markedness   The linguistic process whereby a category (the marked category) is distinguished from a larger, more inclusive category (the unmarked category) by the presence of a single attribute.

market   A place where goods are exchanged for money, or a type of economic system whereby all goods and services are valued by and exchanged for currency.

masculinities studies   Exploration of the variation in what constitutes masculinity within as well as between societies.

matrilineal rule of descent   Unilineal descent rule stating that a child belongs to his or her mother's group.

maximizing   The concept in economic anthropology whereby individuals are seen as interpreting economic rules to their own advantage.

mediator   A third party brought in to resolve conflict between two parties.

medical anthropology   The anthropological specialty that focuses on the social and cultural components of health and wellness, and the distribution of related resources.

mental illness   In anthropological terms, posits normal, expected, and acceptable behavior in a culture as a baseline; deviance from this baseline is abnormal behavior or mental illness.

metaphor   An analytical concept in which one idea stands for another because of some similarity they seem to share.

metonym   The symbolic substitution of one of the constituent parts for the whole.

microfinance   A development strategy that provides small-business loans to poor individuals and groups of people who otherwise would not have access to credit.

model minority   The mythologizing of the skills and abilities of a minority immigrant community.

Modernization Theory   The perspective that underdeveloped states should attain modernization by emulating the industrial strategies of Western countries.

moieties   A grouping based upon descent in which the entire society is divided into halves.

monitoring and evaluation   The evaluation of the outcomes of public health and development initiatives to see if programs and initiatives meet their stated goals.

monogamy   Marriage with only one spouse at a time.

morpheme   The smallest unit of a language conveying meaning.

multisited ethnography   An ethnography that draws on information and informants in various locations, often across borders and over different time periods.

myths   Stories set in the remote past that explain the origin of natural things and cultural practices.

nationalism   Political movement to claim or reformulate shared ideas about identity among citizens within a state's borders.

nation-state   An autonomous state associated with national identity.

Native American Graves Protection and Repatriation Act (NAGPRA)   Federal legislation in the United States requiring the return of human remains and some cultural artifacts to recognized native groups.

nativistic movements   Religious cults that develop in periods of drastic cultural change and synthesize traditional cultural elements with newly introduced ones.

natural selection   In Darwinian evolutionary theory, the concept that genetically based adaptive traits create reproductive advantages over time, thus preserving those traits across generations.

nature vs. nurture   Theories and debates about the influences of inherited and acquired characteristics.

neocolonialism   Economic interdependency of one-time colonies on colonial period elites and on former colonial powers despite political independence.

neoliberalism   The contemporary revival of classic economic liberalism that stresses the role of private enterprise in all institutions of the state and deregulation of markets and trade.

neolocal residence   A rule of postmarital residence in which the newly married couple forms an independent household.

Neo-Marxism   The contemporary study of power relations in the globalized economy, drawing on Karl Marx's theories of class relations, commodification, production, and consumption.

neo-nationalism   The emergence and assertion of newly formed nationalist movements, particularly in new states formed from the former Soviet republics.

New Age Movements   Alternative, small scale, and/or new religious movements.

new immigrants   Immigrants to the United States post-1960s resulting from changes in immigration law and policy.

new reproductive technologies (NRTs)   Manipulation of egg and sperm to create fertilized eggs and viable fetuses through scientific technology; includes the use of surrogate mothers and/or genetic donors.

nomadic pastoralists   Societies dependent upon herds of domesticated animals.

nongovernmental organizations (NGOs)   Development organizations that are structurally independent of state institutions.

nuclear family   A family consisting of a husband, wife, and their unmarried children.

numaym   Cognatic descent group of the Kwakwaka-wala, native people of the Northwest Coast.

office   A recognized political position.

Omaha-type kinship terminology system   Associated with patrilineal descent groups and ignores generational differences in some kinship terms.

pantheon   The population of gods and deities recognized by a society.

parallel cousins   The offspring of two brothers or of two sisters.

parole   See *langue*.

participant observation   The anthropological method of collecting data by living with other people, learning their language, and understanding their culture.

patrilineal rule of descent   A rule stating that a child belongs to his or her father's group.

patron-client relationship   A hierarchical relationship in which the superior (the patron) acts as an intermediary and protector of the inferior (the client) vis-à-vis the national government.

personality   Relatively stable characteristics that form an individual's unique character.

personhood   Culturally constructed concepts of the relationship of individuals to others.

phenotype   Physical characteristics of a person.

phonemes   The smallest units of sound that are distinguished from each other in any language.

physical anthropology   Investigates the physical evolution of the human body and its anatomical and molecular characteristics.

pidgin   A lingua franca that developed when people speaking different languages but no common language needed to communicate with one another.

political ecology   The study of the relationships between political, social, and economic resources and environmental changes.

political economy   The interrelationships of political and economic structures.

politics   The competition for political positions, economic resources, and power.

polyandry   marriage system in which one woman has several husbands at one time.

polygamy   Marriage system with plural spouses, either husbands or wives.

polygyny   Marriage in which one man has more than one wife recognized at one time.

postcolonial studies   Often interdisciplinary focus on the effects of colonialism on former European colonies.

Post-Fordism   The production systems associated with contemporary globalization. Products are assembled in multiple sites, using unregulated and low-paid labor often in Free Trade Zones in Southern countries.

postmarital residence rule   A rule that states where a couple lives after marriage.

postmodernism   Refers to a contemporary point of view that is opposed to making universalizing generalizations in anthropological thinking, and encourages interdisciplinary analysis.

potlatch   A large-scale ceremonial distribution of goods found among the indigenous peoples of the Northwest Coast of North America.

power   The ability to command others to do certain things and get compliance from them.

practice   Individual choices and decision making.

practicing anthropology   See **applied anthropology**.

priests   Full-time religious practitioners who carry out codified and elaborated rituals based on a body of knowledge learned over a lengthy period of time.

primogeniture   A rule of succession whereby the eldest child (usually but not always male) inherits the position of power.

private symbols   Personal symbols related to an individual's unique life history.

production   The process whereby a society uses the tools and energy sources at its disposal and its own people's labor to create the goods necessary for supplying itself.

public anthropology   The general term for the engagement of anthropologists in important social concerns, and the communication of anthropological perspectives to the general public.

public art   Monuments, murals, and other artistic creations on view in public spaces.

public symbols   Symbols used and understood by the members of a society.

queer studies   Theorizes and explores the construction of sexual identities in their cultural contexts.

race   A system of classification of groups of people presumed to share biological or genetic characteristics, usually based on phenotypical (appearance) assumptions.

racism   Discrimination or violence against an individual or group based on presumed shared characteristics.

randomized controlled studies   An objective research method for determining evidence of change as the result of a health or development initiative, comparing groups of people that did and did not participate in the intervention.

reciprocal exchange   A type of exchange system in egalitarian societies in which marriage partners and material goods of equal value continue to be exchanged over generations.

reflexivity   Attention to one's own cognitive framework, assumptions, biases, and privileges as one researches another culture.

religion   The cultural means by which humans interact with the supernatural or extra-human domains.

remittances   Money, consumer goods, and information that flow regularly between migrants and "non-movers" in their families and home communities.

research design   Identifying key research questions and methodologies for fieldwork projects.

revitalization movements   See **nativistic movements.**

rites of intensification   Communal rituals celebrated at various points in the yearly cycle.

rites of passage   Communal rituals held to mark changes in status as individuals progress through their culturally patterned life cycle.

ritual   Patterned or repetitive performance that symbolically communicates values and ideas to both participants and observers.

sagali   A large-scale funerary ceremonial distribution among the Trobriand Islanders.

salvage anthropology   In Boas's time, the term applied to the gathering of ethnographic information about disappearing and threatened cultural practices.

science   A system of knowledge based on empirically determined connections between aspects of the natural world that will regularly result in predictable outcomes.

segmentary lineage system   A descent system, typically patrilineal, in which the largest segments are successively divided into smaller segments, like branches of a tree.

self   An individual's own sense of identity and self-awareness.

serial monogamy   The practice of marrying a series of spouses, one after the other.

sex   Biological and anatomical composition of genitals and related secondary sexual characteristics.

sexualities   Erotic desires and the practices associated with them.

shaman   Part-time ritual specialist who, depending on the cultural context, diagnoses and cures illness, causes illness, and divines the future.

shifting cultivation   A type of horticulture in which new gardens are made every few years, when the soil is exhausted.

sister exchange   A marriage pattern in which two men marry each other's sisters, perpetuated across generations.

social capital   Relationships, skills, and resources enabling an individual's or group's maximal participation in society.

social media   The multiple forms of electronic communication, expression, and creativity.

social organization   Behavioral choices that individuals make in connection with the social structure.

social role   The behavior associated with a particular social status in a society.

social status   The position an individual occupies in a society.

social structure   The pattern of social relationships that characterizes a society.

society   An organized social grouping characterizing humans and other social animals, often differentiated by age and gender.

sociolinguistics   The study of aspects of language that express status and class differences as understood through language use and practices.

sorcery   The learned practices of magic, usually for negative purposes.

sororal polygyny   The marriage of a man to several sisters.

sororate   The custom whereby a widower marries his deceased wife's sister.

sovereignty   The ability of a group to determine their own laws and practices that will be recognized by other groups.

speech community   A group of people that interacts and speaks frequently with one another.

spirits   The general term for those that populate the supernatural realm.

state   A type of political organization organized on a territorial basis encompassing multiple ethnic, linguistic, and religious groups.

stem family   A two-generation extended family consisting of parents and only one married son and his family.

step family   See **blended family**.

step immigration   Process by which a younger generation of immigrants reunites with their relatives in their new countries of residence.

stipulated descent   A social unit, such as a clan, in which all members consider themselves to be related, though they cannot actually trace the genealogical relationship.

structuralism   Theoretical approach emphasizing the relationship between cultural elements.

structural violence   Multiple forms of violence and exploitation that are the consequences of societal norms and institutions that regularize discrimination throughout society.

structure   A description of parts or elements of a culture in relationship to one another.

style   A characterization of the component elements of art and the way those elements are put together.

Sudanese-type kinship terminology system   A terminology system in which each category of kinship is distinguished from all others by the use of different terms.

Sustainable Development Goals (SDGs)   The United Nations goals and priorities aimed at eliminating global poverty and inequality by 2030.

swidden   See **shifting cultivation**.

symbolic anthropology   Theoretical approach emphasizing the interpretation of cultural symbols.

symbols   Words, objects, actions, or concepts recognized within a group suggesting other concepts and often invoking strong sentiments.

syncretism   The integration of ideas and newly adopted practices in cultural practices.

syntax   That part of grammar that deals with the rules of combination of morphemes.

task shifting   The shifting of health and wellness service delivery from scarce or unavailable professionals to trained local community health workers.

technology   That part of culture by means of which people directly exploit their environment.

terms of address   The kinship terms used when talking to a relative.

terms of reference   The kinship terms used to refer to a relative when speaking to someone else.

terrorism   Acts of violence perpetrated against property and civilian populations, usually by non-state actors, designed to destabilize and demoralize perceived enemies.

thick description   A methodology whereby culture is viewed as a text to be read, analyzed, and interpreted, associated with the scholar Clifford Geertz.

total social phenomena   Large-scale rituals that integrate all aspects of society—economic, political, kinship, religion, art, etc.

totemic animal   See **clan totem**.

trance   An altered state of consciousness associated with the performance of ritual.

transgender   A form of self-identification indicating gender affiliation different than sex assigned at birth.

translation   The multiple forms of explaining the meaning of words, ideas, symbols, and norms from one cultural setting to another.

transmigration   Populations who migrate from their homelands to other parts of the world.

transnationalism   Migration with strong economic and social ties remaining with families and communities of origin.

tribe   A unit used by colonial powers to refer to groups with a common language and culture.

tribute   Presentation of objects of value by people of lower status to those of higher status.

trickster   A common motif in folktales cross-culturally, an animal character that is conniving and sneaky, and occasionally but not always outsmarts others.

unilineal descent group   A kin group, such as a clan, in which membership is based on either matrilineal or patrilineal descent.

universal human rights   A doctrine that emphasizes inalienable rights of the individual over the cultural norms of the community.

urban legends   Stories about contemporary events purporting to be factual that circulate widely and with variation.

urigubu   A Trobriand harvest gift given yearly by a man to his sister's husband.

uxorilocal residence   A rule of postmarital residence whereby the newly married couple resides with the relatives of the bride.

virilocal residence   A rule of postmarital residence whereby the newly married couple resides with the relatives of the groom.

virtuality   Collective activities that have been normalized through digital technologies.

vision quest   The search for a protective supernatural spirit through rituals that may involve starvation and deprivation.

warlord   A militarized Big Man; he and his followers are structurally similar to a faction.

witchcraft   A form of magic or manipulation practiced by individuals presumed to be born with this ability.

world systems theory   The historic emergence of the economic interrelationship of most of the world in a single economic system.

REFERENCES

Abotchie, Chris. *Social Control in Traditional Southern Eweland of Ghana: Relevance for Modern Crime Prevention.* Accra: Ghana Universities Press, 1997.

Abu El-Haj, Nadia. *Facts on the Ground: Archaeological Practice and Territorial Self-Fashioning in Israeli Society.* Chicago: University of Chicago Press, 2001.

———. "The Genetic Reinscription of Race." *Annual Review of Anthropology* 36 (2007): 283–300.

Abu-Lughod, Lila. "Do Muslim Women Really Need Saving? Anthropological Reflections on Cultural Relativism and Its Others." *American Anthropologist* 104, no. 3 (2002): 783–90.

Adair, Joshua C., and Amy K. Levin, eds. *Museums, Sexuality, and Gender Activism.* New York: Routledge, 2020.

Alexander-Frizer, Tamar. *The Heart Is a Mirror: The Sephardic Folktale.* Detroit: Wayne State University Press, 2008.

Allen, Jessica, et al. "Social Determinants of Mental Health." *International Review of Psychiatry* 26 no. 4 (2014): 392–407.

Al-Issa, Ihsan. "Culture and Mental Illness in Algeria." In *AI-Junun: Mental Illness in the Islamic World.* Ihsan Al-Issa, ed. 101–20. Madison, CT: International Universities Press, 2000.

Alsharekh, Alanoud, ed. *The Gulf Family: Kinship Policies and Modernity.* London: The Middle East Institute, SOAS, 2007.

Andrews, Edmund L. "A Turkish Clan Labors, Bound by Its Grieving." *New York Times,* August 22, 1999. http://www.nytimes.com/1999/08/22/world/a-turkish-clan-labors-bound-by-its-grieving.html. Accessed May 8, 2016.

Appadurai, Arjun. *Modernity at Large: Cultural Dimensions of Globalization.* Minneapolis: University of Minnesota Press, 1996.

Asante, Molefi Kete. "African Elements in African-American English." In *Africanisms in American Culture.* E. Holloway, ed. Bloomington: Indiana University Press, 1990.

Atkinson, Jane Monnig. "How Gender Makes a Difference in Wana Society." In *Power and Difference: Gender in Island Southeast Asia.* Jane Fishburne Collier and Sylvia Junko Yanagisako, eds. Stanford, CA: Stanford University Press, 1990.

———. "Shamanisms Today." *Annual Review of Anthropology* 21 (1992): 307–30.

Atkinson, Michael F. *Tattooed: The Sociogenesis of a Body Art.* Toronto: University of Toronto Press, 2003.

Atkinson, Quentin D., and Russell D. Gray. "How Old Is the Indo-European Family? Illumination or More Moths to the Flame?" In *Phylogenetic Methods and the Prehistory of Languages.* Peter Foster and Colin Renfrew, eds. Cambridge: Short Run Press, 2006.

Azhar, M. Z., and S. L. Varma. "Mental Illness and Its Treatment in Malaysia." In *AI-Junun: Mental Illness in the Islamic World.* Ihsan Al-Issa, ed. 163–86. Madison, CT: International Universities Press, 2000.

Bacchilega, Cristina. *Legendary Hawaii and the Politics of Place: Tradition, Translation, and Tourism.* Philadelphia: University of Pennsylvania Press, 2007.

Baker, Philip, and Peter Muhlhausler. "Creole Linguistics from Its Beginnings, through Schuchardt to the Present Day." In *Creolization: History, Ethnography, Theory.* Charles Stewart, ed. Walnut Creek, CA: Left Coast Press, 2007.

Baldwin, Dare, and Meredith Meyer. "How Inherently Social Is Language." In *Blackwell Handbook of Language Development.* Erika Hoff and Marilyn Shatz, eds. Oxford: Blackwell, 2007.

Banks, Marcus, and Andre Gingrich. "Introduction: New-Nationalism in Europe and Beyond." In *NeoNationalism in Europe and Beyond: Perspectives from Social Anthropology.* Andre Gingrich and Marcus Banks, eds. New York: Berghahn Books, 2006.

Barlet, Oliver. "Bollywood/Africa: A Divorce?" *Black Camera* 2, no. 1 (2010): 126–43. http://www.jstor.org/stable/10.2979/blc.2010.2.1.126. Accessed February 3, 2016.

Baron, Robert. "Sins of Objectification? Agency, Mediation, and Community Cultural Self-Determination in Public Folklore and Cultural Tourism Programming." *Journal of American Folklore* 123, no. 487 (2010): 63–91.

Barrett, Louise and Gert Stulp. "Evolution and Human Behaviour: Helping to Make Sense of Modern Life." In *Genes and Behaviour: Beyond Nature-Nurture,* David J. Hosken et al., eds. Hoboken NJ: John Wiley & Sons, 2019.Barth, Fredrik. *Political Leadership among Swat Pathans.* London: Athlone Press, 1959.

Belcher, Stephen. *African Myths of Origin.* New York: Penguin Books, 2005.

Bhatt, Rakesh M. "World Englishes." *Annual Review of Anthropology* 30 (2001): 526–50.

Biber-Klemm, Susette, Thomas Cottier, Phillippe Cultel, and Danuta Szymura Berglas. "Rights to Plant Genetic Resources and Traditional Knowledge: Basic Issues and Perspectives." In *Rights to Plant Genetic Resources and Traditional Knowledge,* Susette Biber-Klemm and Thomas Cottier, eds. Wallingford, UK: CABI Publishing, 2006.

Boas, Franz. *Primitive Art.* New York: Dover, 1955.

———. *Kwakiutl Ethnography.* Helen Codere, ed. Chicago: University of Chicago Press, 1966.

Boellstorff, Tom. "Queer Studies in the House of Anthropology." *Annual*

Review of Anthropology 36 (2007): 17–35.

———. "Rethinking Digital Anthropology." In *Digital Anthropology*. H. Horst and D. Miller, eds. London: Berg, 2012.

Boesch, Christophe, Josephine Head, and Martha M. Robbins. "Complex Tool Sets for Honey Extraction among Chimpanzees in Loango National Park, Gabon." *Journal of Human Evolution* 56 (2009): 560–69. http://www.ncbi.nlm.nih.gov/pubmed/19457542. Accessed May 17, 2016.

Bolin, Inge. *Growing Up in a Culture of Respect: Child Rearing in Highland Peru*. Austin: University of Texas Press, 2006.

Borofsky, Robert. "Defining Public Anthropology a Personal Perspective." Center for a Public Anthropology, 2007. http://www.publicanthropology.org/public-anthropology/. Accessed May 8, 2016.

Bourguignon, Erika. "Suffering and Healing, Subordination and Power: Women and Possession Trance." *Ethos* 32, no. 4 (2004): 557–74.

Boyer, Pascal. *Religion Explained: The Evolutionary Origins of Religious Thought*. New York: Basic Books, 2001.

Brasch, Walter M. *Brer Rabbit, Uncle Remus and the "Cornfield" Journalist: The Tale of Joel Chandler Harris*. Macon, GA: Mercer University Press, 2000.

Brasher, Brenda. *Give Me That Online Religion*. San Francisco: Jossey-Bass, 200l.

Brass, Paul R. *The Politics of India Since Independence*, 2nd ed. Cambridge: Cambridge University Press, 1994.

Brettell, Caroline. *Anthropology and Migration: Essays on Transnationalism, Ethnicity, and Identity*. Walnut Creek, CA: Altamira, 2003.

Briggs, Jean. "Conflict Management in a Modern Inuit Community." In *Hunters and Gatherers in the Modern World: Conflict, Resistance, and Self-Determination*. Peter P. Schweiter, Megan Biesele, and Robert K. Hitchcock, eds. New York: Berghahn Books, 2000.

Brittan, Arthur. "Masculinities and Masculinism." In *The Masculinities Reader*. Stephen M. Whitehead and Frank J. Barrett, eds. 51–55. Cambridge, UK: Polity Press, 2001,

Bromley, David G. "New Religious Movements." In *Encyclopedia of Religion and Society*. William Swatos, ed. Walnut Creek, CA: AltaMira/Sage, 1998.

Brown, Julie V. "Afterword." In *Madness and the Mad in Russian Culture."* Angela

Brintlinger and Ilya Vinitski, eds. Toronto: University of Toronto Press, 2007.

Brown, Michael E., and Sumit Ganguly. *Fighting Words: Language Policy and Ethnic Relations in Asia*. Cambridge, MA: MIT Press, 2003.

Brown, Roger. "The Language of Social Relationship." In *Social Interaction, Social Context, and Language*. Dan Slobin, Jule Gerhardt, Amy Kyratzis, and Jiansheng Guo, eds. Mahwah, NJ: Lawrence Erlbaum, 1996.

Bruner, Edward M. "Tourism in Ghana: The Representation of Slavery and the Return of the Black Diaspora." *American Anthropologist* 98, no. 2 (1996): 290–304.

Brunvand, Jan Harold. "Urban Legends." In *What's So Funny: Humor in American Culture*. Nancy A. Walker, ed. Wilmington, DE: Scholarly Resources Books, 1998.

———. *The Truth Never Stands in the Way of a Good Story*. Urbana: University of Illinois Press, 2000.

Buch, Elana D. "Anthropology of Aging and Care." *Annual Review of Anthropology* 44 (2015): 277–93. https://doi.org/10.1146/annurev-anthro-102214-014254. Accessed January 14, 2016.

Buckley, Thomas, and Alma Gottlieb. *Blood Magic: The Anthropology of Menstruation*. Berkeley: University of California Press, 1988.

Cai, Hua. *A Society without Fathers or Husbands: The Na of China*. New York: Zone Books, 2001.

Cairncross, S., R. Muller, and N. Zagaria. "Dracunculiasis (Guinea worm disease) and the Eradication Initiative." *Clinical Microbiology Reviews* 15, no.

2 (2002): 223–46, 2002. https://doi.org/10.1128/CMR.15.2.223-246.

Campion-Vincent, Veronique. *Organ Theft Legends*. Jackson: University of Mississippi Press, 2005.

Caren, Neal, Kenneth T. Andrews, and Todd Lu. "Contemporary Social Movements in a Hybrid Media Environment." *Annu. Rev. Sociology* 46, no. 443–65 (2020).

Carrillo, Jo. *Readings in American Indian Law: Recalling the Rhythm of Survival*. Philadelphia: Temple University Press, 1998.

Carsten, Janet. *After Kinship*. Cambridge: Cambridge University Press, 2004.

Chagnon, Napoleon. *Yanomamo: The Fierce People*. New York: Holt, Rinehart and Winston, 1983.

———. *Yanomamo*, 4th ed. New York: Harcourt Brace Jovanovich, 1997.

Chambers, Robert. *Native Tours: The Anthropology of Travel and Tourism*, 2nd ed. Long Grove, IL: Waveland Press, 2010.

Chirot, Daniel. *Contentious Identities: Ethnic, Religious, and Nationalist Conflicts in Today's World*. New York: Routledge, 2011.

Chivers, C. J. "A Big Game." *New York Times Magazine*, August 25, 2002. www.nytimes.com/2002/08/25/magazine/a-big-game.html. Accessed May 8, 2016.

Chomsky, Noam. *On Language*. New York: The New Free Press, 1998.

———. *New Horizons in the Study of Language and Mind*. New York: Cambridge University Press, 2000.

Choubisa, S. L. "Fluoride Distribution in Drinking Groundwater in Rajasthan, India." *Current Science* 114, nos. 9–10 (2018).

Choubisa, S. L., et al. "Dracunculiasis in Tribal Region of Southern Rajasthan, India: A Case Report." *Journal of Parasitic Disease* 34, no. 2 (2010): 94–96.

Clark, Gracia. *Onions Are My Husband: Survival and Accumulation by West African Market Women*. Chicago: University of Chicago Press, 1994.

Clerk, Christian. ""That Isn't Really a Pig': Spirit Traditions in the Southern Cook Islands." In *South Pacific*

Oral Traditions. Ruth Finnegan and Margaret Orbell, eds. 161–76. Bloomington: Indiana University Press, 1995.

Clifford, James. "Introduction." In *Writing Culture: The Poetics and Politics of Ethnography.* James Clifford and George Marcus eds. Berkeley: University of California Press, 1986.

Coates, Jennifer. *Women, Men and Language: A Sociolinguistic Account of Gender Differences in Language*, 3rd ed. New York: Longman, 2004.

Cohen, Jeffrey, and I. Sirkeci. *Cultures of Migration: The Global Nature of Contemporary Migration.* Austin: University of Texas Press, 2011.

Cohen, Robin. *Global Diasporas: An Introduction.* Seattle: University of Washington Press, 1997.

Collins, Thomas W. "Introduction." In *Communities and Capital: Local Struggles against Corporate Power and Privatization.* Thomas W. Collins and Charles Wingard, eds. 1–4. Athens: University of Georgia Press, 2000.

Colloredo-Mansfield, Rudi. "The Handicraft Archipelago: Consumption Migration, and the Social Organization of a Transnational Andean Ethnic Group." *Research in Economic Anthropology* 19 (1998): 31–68.

Connell, Raewyn. *Masculinities.* Cambridge: Polity, 1995.

Cook, Scott. *Understanding Commodity Cultures: Explorations in Economic Anthropology with Case Studies from Mexico.* New York: Rowman & Littlefield, 2004.

Cowan, Douglas E. "Online U-Topia: Cyberspace and the Mythology of Placelessness." *Journal for the Scientific Study of Religion* 44, no. 3 (2005a): 257–63.

———. *Cyberhenge: Modern Pagans on the Internet.* New York: Routledge, 2005b.

Coyne, Michael. *The Crowded Prairie: American National Identity in the Hollywood Western.* New York: I.B. Tauris, 1997.

Craver, Amy. "Household Adaptive Strategies among the Inupiat." In *Complex Ethnic Households in America.* Laurel Schwede, Rae Lesser Blumberg, and Anna Y. Chan, eds. New York: Rowman & Littlefield, 2005.

Croal, Peter, and Wes Darou. "Canadian First Nations' Experiences with International Development." In *Participating in Development: Approaches to Indigenous Knowledge.* Paula Sillitoe, Allan Bicker, and Johan Pottier, eds. London: Routledge, 2002.

Cutler, Cecelia. "Hip-Hop, White Immigrant Youth, and African American Vernacular English: Accommodation as an Identity Choice." *Journal of English Linguistics* 38, no. 3 (2010): 248–69.

D'Aoust, Anne-Marie, ed. *Transnational Marriage and Partner Migration Constellations of Security, Citizenship and Rights.* New Brunswick, NJ: Rutgers University Press, 2022.

Daniel, G. Reginald. *More than Black? Multiracial Identity and the New Racial Order.* Philadelphia: Temple University Press, 2002.

Dasgupta, Jyotirindra. "Language Policy and National Development in India." In *Fighting Words: Language Policy and Ethnic Relations in Asia.* Michael Brown and Sumit Ganguly, eds. Cambridge, MA: MIT Press, 2003.

Davis-Floyd, Robbie. *Birth as an American Rite of Passage*, 2nd ed. Berkeley: University of California Press, 2003.

De Bose, Charles E. "Codeswitching: Black English and Standard English in the African-American Repertoire." In *Readings in African American Language: Aspects, Features and Perspectives*, vol. 2. Nathaniel Normant Jr., ed. New York: Peter Lang, 2005.

Deegan, Chris. *Village Study on Water Use and Perceptions and Statistical Profile on Treated/Reported Guineaworm Patients and Villages.* Udaipur: UNICEF, 1990.

Delgado, Richard, and Jean Stefancic. *Critical Race Theory: An Introduction*, 3rd ed. New York: New York University Press, 2017.

DeSilva, Jeremy. *How Upright Walking Made Us Human.* London: William Collins, 2021.

Diamond, Jared. "The Worst Mistake in the History of the Human Race." *Discover Magazine* (May 1987): 64–66. https://www.discovermagazine.com /planet-earth/the-worst-mistake-in -the-history-of-the-human-race. Downloaded March 27, 2023.

Diesendruck, Gil. "Mechanisms of Word Learning." In *Blackwell Handbook of Language Development.* Oxford: Blackwell, 2007.

Dissanayake, Wimal. "Globalization and the Experience of Culture: The Resilience of Nationhood." In *Globalization, Cultural Identities, and Media Representations.* Natascha Gentz and Stefan Kramer, eds. Albany: State University of New York Press, 2006.

Dombrowski, Kirk. *Against Culture: Development, Politics, and Religion in Indian Alaska.* Lincoln: University of Nebraska Press, 2001.

Douglas, Mary. "Witchcraft and Leprosy: Two Strategies of Exclusion." *Man* 26, no. 4 (1991): 723–726.

Droschel, Yvonne. "Queering Language: A Love That Dare Not Speak Its Name Comes Out of the Closet." In *Language, Sexualities and Desires: Cross-Cultural Perspective.* Helen Sauntson and Sakis Kyratzis, eds. New York: Palgrave Macmillan, 2007.

Dubin, Margaret. *Native America Collected: The Culture of an Art World.* Albuquerque: University of New Mexico Press, 2001.

Dunak, Karen M. *As Long as We Both Shall Love: The White Wedding in Postwar America.* New York: NYU Press, 2013.

Dundes, Alan. "Into the Endzone for a Touchdown: A Psychoanalytic Consideration of American Football." *Western Folklore* 37 (1978): 75–88.

Durkheim, Emile. *The Elementary Forms of Religious Life.* 1915. Reprint. Translated by Joseph W. Swain. New York: Free Press, 1965.

Earle, Timothy. *Bronze Age Economics: The Beginnings of Political Economies.* Boulder, CO: Westview, 2002.

Eisenlohr, Patrick. "Language Revitalization and New Technologies: Cultures of Electronic Mediation and the Refiguring of Communities."

Annual Review of Anthropology 33 (2004): 21–45.

Eller, Jack David. *From Culture to Ethnicities to Conflict: An Anthropological Perspective on International Ethnic Conflict.* Ann Arbor: University of Michigan Press, 1999.

Ellin, Abby. "Burden of Paying for Wedding Bells Shifts." *New York Times*, April 4, 2010: ST12. http://www.nytimes.com/2010/0404/fashion/weddings/04FIELD.html?_r=0. Accessed September 22, 2015.

Engels, Frederick. *The Origin of the Family, Private Property, and the State.* 1884. Reprint. New York: International Publishers, 1972.

Erikson, Erik H. *Gandhi's Truth: On the Origins of Militant Nonviolence.* New York: W. W. Norton, 1969.

Escobar, Arturo. *Encountering Development: The Making and Unmaking of the Third World.* Princeton: Princeton University Press, 1995.

Ewing, Katherine. "Consciousness of the State and the Experience of the Self: The Runaway Daughter of a Turkish Guest Worker." In *Power and the Self.* Jeannette Marie Mageo, ed. New York: Cambridge University Press, 2000.

FAO, IFAD, UNICEF, WFP, and WHO. *In Brief to The State of Food Security and Nutrition in the World 2022: Repurposing Food and Agricultural Policies to Make Healthy Diets More Affordable.* Rome. 2022. https://doi.org/10.4060/cc0640en. Downloaded July 2, 2022.

Fedorova, Elena G. "Mansi Female Culture: Rules of Behavior." In *Identity and Gender in Hunting and Gathering Societies.* Ian Keen and Takako Yamada, eds. Osaka: National Museum of Ethnology, 2001.

Ferguson, R. Brian. *Yanomami Warfare: A Political History.* Santa Fe, NM: School of American Research Press, 1995.

———. *Chimpanzees, War, and History: Are Men Born to Kill?* New York: Oxford University Press, 2023.

Ferreira, Luana. "This Heavy Metal Band Is Hell-Bent on Saving an Endangered Language." https://getpocket.com/explore/item/this-heavy-metal-band-is-hell-bent-on-saving-an-endangered-language. Downloaded September 13, 2022.

Foner, Nancy. *New Immigrants in New York.* New York: Columbia University Press, 1987.

———. *In a New Land: A Comparative View of Immigration.* New York: New York University Press, 2005.

Foster, Robert. "Commoditization and the Emergence of 'Kastom' as a Cultural Category: A New Ireland Case in Comparative Perspective." *Oceania* 62, no. 4 (1992): 284–93.

Foucault, Michael. *Archaeology of Knowledge.* New York: Pantheon, 1972.

Frank, Russell. "*Caveat Lector*: Fake News as Folklore." *Journal of American Folklore* 128, no. 509 (2015): 315–32.

Fried, Morton. *The Notion of Tribe.* Menlo Park, CA: Cummings Publishing, 1975.

Fry, Douglas. *The Human Potential for Peace: An Anthropological Challenge to Assumptions about War and Violence.* New York: Oxford University Press, 2006.

Gable, Eric, et al. "On the Uses of Relativism: Fact, Conjecture and Black and White Histories at Colonial Williamsburg." *American Anthropologist* 19, no. 4 (1992): 791–805.

Gampel, Yolanda. "Reflections on the Prevalence of the Uncanny in Social Violence." In *Cultures under Siege: Collective Violence and Trauma.* Antonius C. G. M. Robben and Marcelo M. Suárez Orozco, eds. Cambridge: Cambridge University Press, 2000.

Geertz, Clifford. "Deep Play: Notes on the Balinese Cockfight." *Daedalus* 101 (1972): 1–37.

———. "From the Native's Point of View: On the Understanding of Anthropological Understanding." *Bulletin of the American Academy of Arts and Sciences* 28, no. 1 (1974): 26–45.

Gerken, Lou Ann. "Acquiring Linguistic Structure." In *Blackwell Handbook of Language Development.* Erika Hoff and Marilyn Shatz, eds. Oxford: Blackwell, 2007.

Gerry, Aaron. "Can Indigenous Language Comics Save a Mother Tongue?" *Sapiens*16, September 2021. https://www.sapiens.org/language/indigenous-language-comics/. Downloaded September 13, 2022.

Gettler, Lee T., et al. "Broadening Perspectives on the Evolution of Human Paternal Care and Fathers' Effects on Children." *Annual Reviews of Anthropology* 49, nos. 141–60: (2020).

Ginsburg, Faye D. *Contested Lives: The Abortion Debate in an American Community.* Berkeley: University of California Press, 1989.

Gmelch, George. "Baseball Magic." *Trans-Action* 8, no. 8 (1971): 39–47.

Goebel, Ted, Michael R. Waters, and Dennis H. O'Rourke. "The Late Pleistocene Dispersal of Modern Humans in the Americas." *Science* 319, no. 5869 (2008): 1497–1502.

Goldschmidt, Walter. *As You Sow: Three Studies in the Social Consequences of Agribusiness.* Glencoe, IL: Free Press, 1947.

Goleman, Daniel. "Making Room on the Couch for Culture." *New York Times*, December 5, 1995. https://www.nytimes.com/1995/12/05/science/making-room-on-the-couch-for-culture.html?searchResultPosition=1. Accessed September 12, 2022.

Goodman, Alan. "Race Is Real, but It's Not Genetic." *Sapiens*, March 13, 2020. https://www.sapiens.org/biology/is-race-real/. Downloaded August 13, 2022.

Gottlieb, Alma. "Afterword." In "Special Issue: Blood Mysteries: Beyond Menstruation as Pollution." *Ethnology* 41, no. 4 (2002): 381–90.

Gottschall, Marilyn. "The Mutable Goddess: Particularity and Eclectism within the Goddess Public. In *Daughters of the Goddess: Studies of Healing, Identity and Empowerment.* Wendy Griffin, ed. Walnut Creek, CA: AltaMira Press, 2000.

Gregg, Gary S. *The Middle East: A Cultural Psychology.* Oxford: Oxford University Press, 2005.

Gregor, Thomas. *Anxious Pleasures: The Sexual Lives of an Amazonian People.* Chicago: University of Chicago Press, 1985.

Gutmann, Matthew C. "A (Short) Cultural History of Mexican Machos." In *Gender Matters: Rereading Michelle C. Rosaldo.* Alejandro Lugo and Bill Mauer, eds. Ann Arbor: University of Michigan Press, 2000.

Hanchett, Suzanne. The Toilet: Infrastructure Technology of Critical Importance to Women and Girls. Conference Paper 2019. https://www.researchgate.net/publication/331813357_The_Toilet_Infrastructure_Technology_of_Critical_Importance_to_Women_and_Girls. Downloaded July 2, 2022.

Hanna, Bridget, and Arthur Kleinman. "Unpacking Global Health Theory and Critique." In *Reimagining Global Health: An Introduction.* Berkeley: University of California Press, 2013.

Hansen, Karen Tranberg. "Commodity Chains and the International Secondhand Clothing Trade: Salaula and the Work of Consumption in Zambia." In *Theory in Economic Anthropology.* Jean Ensminger, ed. Walnut Creek, CA: AltaMira Press, 2002.

Harding, Nick. *Urban Legends.* Harbenden, UK: Pocket Essentials, 2005.

Harrison, Simon. "The Past Altered by the Present: A Melanesian Village after Twenty Years." *Anthropology Today* 17 no. 5 (2001): 3–9.

Hauser, Marc D., et al. "The Mystery of Language Evolution." *Frontiers in Psychology* 5, article 401 (2014): 1–12. http://journal.frontiersin.org/article/10.3389/fpsyg.2014.00401/fullE. Accessed May 17, 2016.

Hawley, C. John. *Postcolonial, Queer: Theoretical Intersections.* Albany: State University of New York Press, 2001.

Hayslip, Bert, and Julie Hicks Patrick. *Custodial Grandparenting: Individual, Cultural and Ethnic Diversity.* New York: Springer, 2006.

Hefner, Robert W., ed. *Market Cultures, Society and Morality in the New Asian Capitalisms.* Boulder, CO: Westview Press, 1998.

Henderson, Carol E. "Virtual Marketing: Making Heritage, Marketing Cyberorientalism? In *Raj Rhapsodies: Tourism, Heritage and the Seduction of History.* Carol Henderson and Maxine Weisgrau, eds. Aldershot, UK: Ashgate, 2007.

Henderson, Carol E., and Maxine Weisgrau. *Raj Rhapsodies: Tourism, Heritage and the Seduction of History.* Aldershot, UK: Ashgate, 2007.

Henderson, Mary. *Star Wars: The Magic of Myth.* New York: Bantam Books, 1997.

Henrich, Joseph, S. J. Heine, and A. Norenzayan. "The Weirdest People in the World?" *Behavioral and Brain Sciences* 33 (2010): 61–135.

Hewamanne, Sandya. *Stitching Identities in a Free Trade Zone.* Philadelphia: University of Pennsylvania Press, 2008.

Hewitt, Kim. *Mutilating the Body: Identity in Blood and Ink.* Bowling Green, OH: Bowling Green State University Popular Press, 1997.

Hickerson, Nancy P. "Ethnogenesis in the South Plains: Jumano to Kiowa." In *History, Power, and Identity: Ethnogenesis in the Americas 1492–1992.* Jonathan D. Hill, ed. Iowa City: University of Iowa Press, 1996.

Higgins, Rylan, Emily Martin, and Maria D. Vesperi. "An Anthropology of the COVID-19 Pandemic." *Anthropology Now* 12, no. 1 (2020): 2–6. https://doi.org/10.1080/19428200.2020.1760627.

Hill, Jonathan D. "Introduction: Ethnogenesis in the Americas, 1492–1992." In *History, Power, and Identity: Ethnogenesis in the Americas, 1492–1992.* Jonathan D. Hill, ed. Iowa City: University of Iowa Press, 1996.

Hitchcock, Robert K., and Megan Biesele. "Introduction." In *Hunters and Gatherers in the Modern World: Conflict, Resistance and Self-Determination.* Peter P. Schweitzer, Megan Biesele, and Robert K. Hitchcock, eds. New York: Berghahn Books, 2000.

Hobsbawm, Eric, and Terence Ranger, eds. *The Invention of Tradition.* New York: Cambridge University Press, 1983.

Hodgson, Dorothy L. "'Once Intrepid Warriors': Modernity and the Production of Maasai Masculinities." *Ethnology* 38, no. 2 (1999): 121–50.

———, ed. *Rethinking Pastoralism in Africa: Gender, Culture & Myth of the Patriarchal Pastoralist.* Oxford: James Curry, 2000.

———. *Once Intrepid Warriors: Gender, Ethnicity and the Cultural Politics of Maasai Development.* Bloomington: Indiana University Press, 2001.

Hogbin, Ian. *The Island of Menstruating Men: Religion in Wogeo, New Guinea.* Prospect Heights, IL: Waveland Press, 1996.

Holodynski, Manfred, and Wolfgang Friedlmeier. *Development of Emotions and Emotion Regulation.* New York: Springer, 2006.

Holsey, Bayo. *Routes of Remembrance: Refashioning the Slave Trade in Ghana.* Chicago: University of Chicago Press, 2008.

Hosken, David, et al., eds. *Genes and Behaviour: Beyond Nature-Nurture.* Hoboken NJ: John Wiley & Sons, 2019.

Howell, Signe. *Kinning of Foreigners: Transnational Adoption in a Global Perspective.* New York: Berghahn Books, 2006.

Hrdy, Sarah Blaffer. *Mothers and Others: The Evolutionary Origins of Mutual Understanding.* Cambridge, MA: Harvard University Press, 2009.

Hume, Lynne, and Jane Mulcock. "Introduction: Awkward Spaces, Productive Places." In *Anthropologists in the Field: Cases in Participant Observation.* Lynne Hume and Jane Mulcock, eds. New York: Columbia University Press, 2004.

Humphrey, Caroline. *The Unmaking of Soviet Life: Everyday Economies after Socialism.* Ithaca, NY: Cornell University Press, 2002.

Humphrey, Caroline, and David Sneath. *The End of Nomadism? Society, State and the Environment in Inner Asia.* Durham, NC: Duke University Press, 1999.

Huntsman. Judith. "Fact, Fiction and Imagination: A Tokelau Narrative." In *South Pacific Oral Traditions.* Ruth Finnegan and Margaret Orbell, eds. 124–60. Bloomington: Indiana University Press, 1995.

ILO (International Labor Organization). *ILO Global Estimates on International Migrant Workers—Results and Methodology*, 3rd ed. Geneva: International Labor Office, 2021.

ILO. https://www.ilo.org/global/topics/care-economy/lang--en/index.htm. Downloaded November 1, 2022.

Inda, Jonathan X., and Renato Rosaldo. "Tracking Global Flows." In *The Anthropology of Globalization: A Reader*, 2nd ed. Jonathan Inda and Renata Rosaldo, eds. Malden, MA: Blackwell, 2008.

Ingraham, Chrys. *White Weddings: Romancing Heterosexuality in Popular Culture*. New York: Routledge, 1999.

Inhorn, Marcia C., and Daphna Birenbaum-Carmeli. "Assisted Reproductive Technologies and Culture Change." *Annual Review of Anthropology* 37 (2008): 177–96. https://doi.org/10.1146/annurev.anthro.37.081407.085230. Accessed May 12, 2015.

Issac, Gwyneira. *Mediating Knowledges: Origins of a Zuni Tribal Museum*. Tucson: University of Arizona Press, 2007.

Jasanoff, Maya. "Ancestor Worship." *New Yorker*, xcviii:11, May 9, 2022.

Jellison, Katherine. *It's Our Day: America's Love Affair with the White Wedding, 1945–2005*. Lawrence: University of Kansas Press, 2008.

Jenike, Mark R. "Nutritional Ecology: Diet, Physical Activity and Body Size." In *Hunters and Gatherers: An Interdisciplinary Perspective*. Catherine Panter-Brick, Robert H. Layton, and Peter Rowley Conwy, eds. Cambridge: Cambridge University Press, 2001.

Joshi, P. "Herbal Drugs Used in Guinea Worm Disease by the Tribals of Southern Rajasthan." *International Journal of Pharmacognosy* 29 no. 1 (1991): 33–38,

Juillerat, Bernard. *Children of the Blood: Society, Reproduction and Cosmology in New Guinea*. New York: Berg, 1996.

Kaeppler, Adrienne. "Structure Movements in Tonga." In *Society and the Dance*. P. Spencer, ed. Cambridge: Cambridge University Press, 1985.

Keesing, Roger M. "New Lessons from Old: Changing Perspectives on the Kula." *Finnish Anthropological Society Transactions* 27 (1990): 139–63.

Kehoe, Alice Beck. *Shamans and Religion: An Anthropological Exploration in Critical Thinking*. Prospect Heights, IL: Waveland Press, 2000.

Kelly, Raymond C. *Warless Societies and the Origin of War*. Ann Arbor: University of Michigan Press, 2000.

Kendall, Laurel. *Getting Married in Korea: Of Gender, Morality, and Modernity*. Berkeley: University of California Press, 1996.

———. "The Cultural Politics of 'Superstition' in the Korean Shaman World: Modernity Constructs Its Other." In *Healing Powers and Modernity—Traditional Medicine and Science in Asian Societies*. Linda H. Connor and Geoffrey Samuel, eds. Westport, CT: Greenwood, 2001.

Kenin-Lopsan, M. B. *Shamanic Songs and Myths of Tuva*. Los Angeles: International Society for TransOceanic Research, 1997.

Kimmel, Michael S. "Masculinity as Homophobia: Fear, Shame, and Silence in the Construction of Gender Identity." In *The Masculinities Reader*. Stephen M. Whitehead and Frank J. Barrett, eds. Cambridge: Polity Press, 2001.

Kinoshita, Yasuhito, and Christie W. Kiefer. *Refuge of the Honored: Social Organization in a Japanese Retirement Community*. Berkeley: University of California Press, 1992.

Klass, Morton. *Ordered Universes: Approaches to the Anthropology of Religion*. Boulder, CO: Westview Press, 1995.

Klass, Morton, and Maxine K. Weisgrau, eds. *Across the Boundaries of Belief: Contemporary Issues in the Anthropology of Religion*. Boulder, CO: Westview Press, 1999.

Koch, Klaus-Friedrich. *War and Peace in Jalémó: The Management of Conflict in Highland New Guinea*. Cambridge, MA: Harvard University Press, 1974.

Kochanek, Stanley A. *Patron-Client Politics and Business in Bangladesh*. Newbury Park, CA: Sage, 1993.

Kolbert, Elizabeth. "The Terrible Teens What's Wrong with Them?" *The New Yorker*, August 31, 2015. https://www.newyorker.com/magazine/2015/08/31/the-terrible-teens. Downloaded March 17, 2023.

Koven, Mikel J. *Film, Folklore, and Urban Legends*. Lanham, MD: Scarecrow Press, 2008.

Kuhn, Steven L., and Mary C. Stiner. "The Antiquity of Hunter-Gatherers." In *Hunter-Gatherers: An Interdisciplinary Perspective*. Catherine Panter-Brick, Robert H. Layton, and Peter Rowley-Conwy, eds. Cambridge: Cambridge University Press, 2001.

Kurtz, Donald. *Political Anthropology: Power and Paradigms*. Boulder, CO: Westview Press, 2001.

Laidlaw, James. "Introduction." In *Ritual and Memory: Toward a Comparative Anthropology of Religion*. Harvey Whitehouse and James Laidlaw, eds. Walnut Creek, CA: AltaMira Press, 2004.

Lamb, Sarah. *White Saris and Sweet Mangoes: Aging, Gender, and Body in North India*. Berkeley: University of California Press, 2000.

Lang, Sabine. *Men as Women, Women as Men: Changing Gender in Native American Cultures*. Austin: University of Texas Press, 1998.

Larkin, Brian. "Indian Films and Nigerian Lovers: Media and the Creation of Parallel Modernities." *Africa: Journal of the International African Institute* 67, no. 3 (1997): 406–40. http://www.jstor.org/stable/1161182. Accessed March 6, 2016.

Lasswell, Harold. *Politics: Who Gets What, When, How*. New York: McGraw-Hill, 1936.

Layton, Robert H. "Hunter-Gatherers, Their Neighbours and the Nation-State." In *Hunter-Gatherers: An Interdisciplinary Perspective*. Catherine Panter-Brick, Robert H. Layton, and Peter Rowley Conwy, eds. Cambridge: Cambridge University Press, 2001.

Lee, Sang M. "Information Technology and Economic Development Strategy." In *Globalization and Change in Asia*. Dennis A. Rondinelli and John M. Heffron, eds. Boulder, CO: Lynn Rienner Publisher, 2007.

Lefkowitz, Mary R. *Women in Greek Myth*, 2nd ed. Baltimore: Johns Hopkins University Press, 2007.

Lepowsky, Maria. "Big Men, Big Women and Cultural Autonomy." *Ethnology* 29, no. 1 (1990): 35–50.

Lett, James W. *Science, Reason and Anthropology: The Principles of Rational Inquiry.* Lanham, MD: Rowman & Littlefield, 1997.

Levin, Betty Wolder. "COVID in New York City: Looking Upstream to Find Truth, Power and Responsibility for Disease and Death." Unpublished paper, 2021.

Levine, Nancy E. "Fathers and Sons: Kinship Value and Validation in Tibetan Polyandry." *Man* 22, no. 2 (1987): 267–86.

———. "Alternative Kinship, Marriage, and Reproduction." *Annual Review of Anthropology* 37 (2008): 375–89. https://doi.org/10.1146/annurev .anthro.37.081407.085120. Accessed May 12, 2015.

Levine, Robert A., and Karin Norman. "The Infant's Acquisition of Culture: Early Attachment Reexamined in Anthropological Perspective." In *The Psychology of Cultural Experience.* Carmella C. Moore and Holly F. Mathews, eds. Cambridge: Cambridge University Press, 2001.

Lévi-Strauss, Claude. *Tristes Tropique.* New York: Atheneum. 1961.

———. "The Structural Theory of Myth." In *Structural Anthropology.* New York: Basic Books, 1963.

Levitt, Peggy. *The Transnational Villagers.* Berkeley: University of California Press, 2001.

Lewis, Eshe. "How Black Caribbean Communities Are Reviving an Ancestral Dance Tradition." *Sapiens Anthropology Magazine* 29 (April 2021). https://www.sapiens.org/culture /bele-martinique/. Downloaded April 30, 2022.

Lewis, I. M. *Arguments with Ethnography: Comparative Approaches to History, Politics and Religion.* New Brunswick, NJ: Athalon Press, 1999.

LiPuma, Edward. *Encompassing Others: The Magic of Modernity in Melanesia.* Ann Arbor: University of Michigan Press, 2000.

Lizot, Jacques. "Words in the Night: the Ceremonial Dialogue—One Expression of Peaceful Relationships among the Yanonami." In *The Anthropology of Peace and Non-Violence.* Leslie E. Sponsel and Thomas Gregor, eds. Boulder, CO: Lynne Rienner Publishers, 1994.

Lowe, Kathy. "Gendermaps." In *Gender in Early Childhood.* Nicola Yelland, ed. New York: Routledge, 1998.

Luhrmann, T. M., R. Padmavati, H. Tharoor, and A. Osci. "Differences in Voice-Hearing Experiences of People with Psychosis in the USA, India and Ghana: Interview-Based Study." *British Journal of Psychiatry* 206 (2015): 41–44. http://bjp.rcpsych.org/. Accessed December 3, 2015.

Lukanuski, Mary. "A Place at the Counter: The Onus of Oneness." In *Eating Culture.* Ron and Brian Seitz, eds. Albany: State University of New York Press, 1998.

Lynch, John. *Pacific Languages: An Introduction.* Honolulu: University of Hawaii Press, 1998.

Macdonald, T., et al. "The Fourth Delay and Community-Driven Solutions to Reduce Maternal Mortality in Rural Haiti: A Community-Based Action Plan." *BMC Pregnancy and Childbirth* 18 (2018): 254.

Mackey-Kallis, Susan. *The Hero and the Perennial Journey Home in American Film.* Philadelphia: University of Pennsylvania Press, 2001.

Mackie, Jamie. "Business Success among Southeast Asian Chinese." In *Market Cultures: Society and Morality in the New Asian Capitalisms.* Robert W. Hefner, ed. Boulder, CO: Westview Press, 1998.

Macklin, Audrey. "Epilogue: Love Triangle: Nation, Spouse, Citizen." In *Transnational Marriage and Partner Migration Constellations of Security, Citizenship and Rights.* Anne-Marie D'Aoust, ed. New Brunswick, NJ: Rutgers University Press, 2022.

Magnus, Ralph, and Eden Naby. *Afghanistan: Mullah, Marx and Mujahid.* Boulder, CO: Westview Press, 2002.

Mahan, Jeffrey H. *Media, Religion and Culture: An Introduction.* New York: Routledge.

Malinowski, Bronislaw. *Coral Gardens and Their Magic.* New York: American Book Co., 1935.

———. *Argonauts of the Western Pacific.* 1922. Reprint. New York: E. P. Dutton and Co., 1961.

———. *Magic, Science and Religion and Other Essays.* London: Souvenir Press, 1974.

Marchant, Jo. "The Awakening." *Smithsonian*, January–February (2016): 80–95.

Marshall, Yvonne. "Transformations of Nuu-chah-nulth Houses." In *Beyond Kinship: Social and Material Reproduction in House Societies.* Rosemary A. Joyce and Susan D. Gillespie, eds. Philadelphia: University of Pennsylvania Press, 2000.

Mascolo, Michael, and Jin Li. "Editors' Notes." In *Culture and Developing Selves: Beyond Dichotomization.* San Francisco: Jossey-Bass, 2004.

Mashal, Mujib. "Vice President Turns Back to His Warlord Roots." *New York Times*, August 19, 2015, A10. http://www.nytimes.com/2015/08/19 /world/asia/afghanistan-. Accessed August 24, 2015.

Mason, Mary Ann. "The Modern Step Family: "Problems and Possibilities."" In *All Our Families: New Policies for a New Century.* Mary Ann Mason, Arlene Skolnick, and Stephen D. Sugarman, eds. New York: Oxford University Press, 1998.

Mauss, Marcel. *The Gift.* [1925]. Reprint. Translated by Ian Cunnison. London: Cohen and West, 1954.

McClenon, James. *Wondrous Healing: Shamanism, Human Evolution and the Origin of Religion.* DeKalb: Northern Illinois University Press, 2002.

McKnight, David. *People, Countries, and the Rainbow Serpent: Systems of Classification among the Lardil of Mornington Island.* New York: Oxford University Press, 1999.

McLoughlin, Moira. *Museums and the Representation of Native Canadians: Negotiating the Borders of Culture.* New York: Garland Publishing, 1999.

McWhorter, John H. *Defining Creole.* New York: Oxford University Press, 2005.

Mead, Margaret. *Sex and Temperament in Three Primitive Societies.* [1935]. New York: Mentor Books, 1950.

———. *Coming of Age in Samoa.* [1928]. New York: Morrow Quill Paperbacks, 1961.

Merry, Sally Engle. "Rights, Religion and Community: Approaches to Violence against Women in the Context of Globalization." In *Law and Anthropology: A Reader.* Sally Falk Moore, ed. Malden, MA: Blackwell, 2005.

Meshorer, Hank. "The Sacred Trail to Zuni Heaven: A Study in the Law of Prescriptive Easements." In *Readings in American Indian Law: Recalling the Rhythm of* Survival. Jo Carrillo, ed. Philadelphia: Temple University Press, 1998.

Meyer, Stephen. "Work, Play and Power: Masculine Culture on the Automotive Shop Floor, 1930–1960." In *Boys and Their Toys: Masculinity, Technology and Class in America.* Roger Horowitz, ed. New York: Routledge, 2001.

Miller, Daniel, et al. *How The World Changed Social Media.* London: UCL Press, 2016. www.ucl.ac.uk/ucl-press.

Mills, Mary Beth. "Gender and Inequality in the Global Labor Force." *Annual Review of Anthropology* 32 (2003): 41–62.

———. *Thai Women in the Global Labor Force: Consuming Desires, Contested Selves.* New Brunswick, NJ: Rutgers University Press, 2006.

Mintz, Sidney. "Food at Moderate Speeds." In *Fast Food/Slow Food: The Cultural Economy of the Global Food System.* Richard Wilk, ed. New York: AltaMira Press, 2006.

Mirchandani, Kiran. "Practices of Global Capital: Gaps, Cracks and Ironies in Transnational Call Centres in India." *Global Networks* 4, no. 4 (2004): 355–73.

Moore, Mignon R. *Invisible Families Gay Identities, Relationships and Motherhood among Black Women.* Berkeley: University of California Press, 2011.

Moore, Sally Falk. "General Introduction." In *Law and Anthropology: A Reader.* Sally Falk Moore, ed. Malden, MA: Blackwell, 2005.

Morcom, Anna. "Terrains of Bollywood Dance: (Neoliberal) Capitalism and the Transformation of Cultural Economies." *Ethnomusicology* 89, no. 2 (2015): 288–314. http://www.jstor.org/stable/10.5406/ethnomusicology.59.2.0288. Accessed June 3, 2016.

Morgan, David. "Family Gender and Masculinities." In *The Masculinities Reader.* Stephen M. Whitehead and Frank J. Barrett, eds. Cambridge: Polity Press, 2001.

Morris, Barry, and Rohan Bastin. *Expert Knowledge: First World Peoples, Consultancy and Anthropology.* New York: Berghahn Books, 2004.

Morris, Ewan. *Our Own Devices: National Symbols and Political Conflict in Twentieth- Century Ireland.* Dublin: Irish Academic Press, 2005.

Mosse, David. *Cultivating Development: An Ethnography of Aid Policy and Practice.* London: Pluto Press, 2005.

Nagata, Judith. "Beyond Theology: Toward an Anthropology of 'Fundamentalism.'" *American Anthropologist* 103, no. 2 (2001): 481–98.

Nanda, Serena. *The Hijras of India: Neither Man Nor Woman,* 2nd ed. Belmont, CA: Wadsworth, 1999.

———. *Gender Diversity: Crosscultural Variations.* Prospects Heights, IL: Waveland Press, 2000.

Nardi, Bonnie. "Virtuality." *Annual Rev. Anthropol* 44 (2015): 15–31.

Nash, Stephen F. and Chip Colwell. "NAGPRA at 30: The Effects of Repatriation." *Annual Rev. Anthropol* 49 (2020): 225–39.

Nasser, Latif. "Do Some Cultures Have Their Own Ways of Going Mad?" *Boston Globe,* January 6, 2016. https://www.bostonglobe.com/ideas/2012/01/08/some-cultures-have-their-own-ways-going-mad/fSuwCngcHbTpMZdBzSFagI/story.html. Downloaded March 17, 2023.

Nathanson, Paul. *Over the Rainbow: The Wizard of Oz as a Secular Myth of America.* Albany: State University of New York Press, 1991.

Nelson, Robin G. "Beyond the Household: Caribbean Families and Biocultural Models of Alloparenting." *Annual Review of Anthropology* 49 (2020): 355–72.

Newport, Frank. Polling Matters. April 6, 2020. https://news.gallup.com/opinion/polling-matters/307619/religion-covid-virus.aspx.

Nichols, Katherine L., Chelsea H. Meloche, and Laure Spake. "Repatriation Has Transformed, Not Ended, Research. *Sapiens,* November 16, 2021. https://www.sapiens.org/archaeology/repatriation-effects/. Downloaded November 1, 2022.

O'Brien, Kevin A. "Privatizing Security, Privatizing War? The New Warrior Class and Regional Security." In *Warlords in International Relations.* London: MacMillan, 1999.

O'Hara, Michael. "Peer-Delivered Psychotherapy for Postpartum Depression: Has Its Time Come?" *Journal of Clinical Psychiatry* 83, no. 1 (2022): 21com14209.

Ong, Aihwa. *Spirits of Resistance and Capitalist Discipline: Factory Women in Malaysia.* Albany: State University Press of New York, 1987.

———. "Corporate Players, New Cosmopolitans, and *Guanxi* in Shanghai." In *Frontiers of Capital: Ethnographic Reflections on the New Economy.* Melissa S. Fisher and Greg Downey, eds. Durham, NC: Duke University Press, 2006.

Onishi, Norimitsu. "Nigeria's Booming Film Industry Redefines African Life." *New York Times,* February 19, 2016, A1. http://www.nytimes.com/2016/02/19/world/africa/with-a-boom-before-the-cameras-nigeria-redefines-african-life.html. Accessed March 2, 2016.

O'Reilly, Karen. *Ethnographic Methods.* New York: Routledge, 2005.

Orenstein, Catherine. *Little Red Riding Hood Uncloaked: Sex, Morality and the Evolution of a Fairy Tale.* New York: Basic Books, 2002.

Orion, Loretta. *Never Again the Burning Times: Paganism Revived.* Prospect Heights, IL: Waveland Press, 1995.

Orlove, Benjamin. "Working in the Field: Perspectives on Globalization in Latin America." In *Globalization and the Rural Poor in Latin America.* William

M. Loker, ed. Boulder, CO: Lynne Rienner Publishers, 1999.

Otterbein, Keith F. *How War Began.* College Station: Texas A&M University Press, 2004.

Oxfam America. Annual Report 2021. https://www.oxfamamerica.org/explore/research-publications/annual-report-2021/. Downloaded March 18, 2023.

Pader, Ellen J. "Spatiality and Social Change: Domestic Space Use in Mexico and the United States." *American Ethnologist* 20, no. 1 (1993): 114–37.

Panter-Brick, Catherine, Robert H. Layton, and Peter Rowley-Conwy, eds. *Hunter-Gatherers: An Interdisciplinary Perspective.* Cambridge: Cambridge University Press, 2001.

Parkin, Robert. Kinship: *An Introduction to Basic Concepts.* Malden, MA: Blackwell, 1997.

Parrenas, Rhacel Salazar. *Children of Global Migration: Transnational Families and Gendered Woes.* Stanford, CA: Stanford University Press, 2005.

Patel, Reena. *Working the Night Shift: Women in India's Call Center Industry.* Stanford, CA: Stanford University Press, 2010.

Paugh, Amy L., and Kathleen C. Riley. "Poverty and Children's Language in Anthropological Perspective." *Annual Review of Anthropology* 48 (2019): 297–315.

Peletz, Michael G. "Transgenderism and Gender Pluralism in Southeast Asia since Early Modern Times" *Current Anthropology* 47, no. 2 (2006): 309–340. http://www.jstor.org/stable/10.1086/498947. Accessed January 16, 2016.

———. "Gender Pluralism: Muslim Southeast Asia since Early Modern Times." *Social Research* 78, no. 2 (2011): 659–86. http://www.jastor.org/stable/23347194. Accessed January 16, 2016.

Pennycook, Alastair. *Critical Applied Linguistics: A Critical Introduction.* Mahwah, NJ: Lawrence Erlbaum, 2001.

Perlez, Jane. "Aboriginal Art, from an Isolated Part of Australia, Resonates Far." *New York Times*, March 23, 2016, A7. http://www.nytimes.com/2016/03/03/world/australia/australia-aboriginals-tiwi-islands.html?_r=0. Accessed March 31, 2016.

Peters, John F. *Life among the Yanomami: The Story of Change among the Xilixana on the Mucajai River in Brazil.* Peterborough: Ontario: Broadview Press, 1998.

Potenza, Alessandra. "Insult or Honor?" *New York Times Upfront Magazine* (September 1, 2014): 6–7.

Powdermaker, Hortense. *Life in Lesu.* [1933]. Reprint. New York: W. W. Norton, 1971.

Price, T. Douglas, and Ofer Bar-Yousef. "The Origins of Agriculture: New Data, New Ideas" *Current Anthropology* 52:S4: 163–74.

Purkiss, Diane. *Troublesome Things: A History of Fairies and Fairy Stories.* London: Penguin Press, 2000.

Rabbens, Linda. *Brazil's Indians and the Onslaught of Civilization: The Yanomami and the Kayapo.* Seattle: University of Washington Press, 2004.

Raj, Dhooleka S. *Where Are You From? Middle-Class Migrants in the Modern World.* Berkeley: University of California Press, 2003.

Ramirez, Rafael I. *What It Means to Be a Man: Reflections on Puerto Rican Masculinity.* New Brunswick, NJ: Rutgers University Press, 1999.

Rapp, Rayna. "Reproduction and Gender Hierarchy: Amniocentesis in America." In *Sex and Gender Hierarchies.* Barbara D. Miller, ed. Cambridge: Cambridge University Press, 1993.

———. *Testing Women, Testing the Fetus: The Social Impact of Amniocentesis in America.* New York: Routledge. 2000.

Rappaport, Roy A. *Pigs for the Ancestors: Ritual in the Ecology of a New Guinea People*, 2nd ed. New Haven, CT: Yale University Press, 1984.

Reddy, Gayatri. *With Respect to Sex: Negotiating Hijra Identity in South India.* Chicago: University of Chicago Press, 2005.

Rees, Richard W. *Shades of Difference: A History of Ethnicity in America.* New York: Rowman & Littlefield, 2007.

Ricento, Thomas. "Theoretical Perspectives in Language Policy: An Overview." In *An Introduction to Language Policy: Theory and Method.* Oxford: Blackwell, 2006.

Rich, Paul B. "Introduction." In *Warlords in International Relations.* Paul B. Rich, ed. London: Macmillan, 1999a.

———. "The Emergence and Significance of Warlordism in International Politics." In *Warlords in International Relations.* Paul B. Rich, ed. London: Macmillan, 1999b.

Rickford, John R. "Suite for Ebony and Phonics" *Discover* 18, no. 12 (1996): 82–91.

———. "The Anglicist/Creolist Quest for the Roots of AAVE: Historical Overviews and New Evidence from the Copula." In *Studies in Contact Linguistics: Essays in Honor of Glenn G. Gilbert.* Linda L. Thornburg and Janet M. Fuller, eds. New York: Peter Lang, 2006.

Riekse, Robert J., and Henry Holstege. *Growing Older in America.* New York: McGraw-Hill, 1996.

Robben, Antonius C. G. M., and Marcelo M. Suárez-Orozco. *Cultures under Siege: Collective Violence and Trauma.* New York: Cambridge University Press, 2000.

Rogers, Richard A. "From Cultural Exchange to Transculturation: A Review and Reconceptualization of Cultural Appropriation." *Communication Theory* 16 (2006): 474–503.

Rogoff, Barbara. *The Cultural Nature of Human Development.* Oxford: Oxford University Press, 2003.

Rohter, Larry. "An Intrusion of Soldiers Threatens Amazon Tribe." *New York Times*, October 1, 2002, A12. http://www.nytimes.com/2002/10/01/world/a-new-intrusion-of-soldiers-threatens-an-amazon-tribe.html. Accessed May 8, 2016.

Romero, Mary. "Who Takes Care of the Maid's Children? Exploring the Costs of Domestic Service." In *Feminism and Families.* Hilde Lindemann Nelson, ed. 151–69. New York: Routledge, 1997.

Roscoe, Will. *Changing Ones: Third and Fourth Genders in Native North*

America. New York: St. Martin's Press, 1998.

Rosman, Abraham. "Social Structure and Acculturation among the Kanuri of Bornu Province, Northern Nigeria." *Transactions of the New York Academy of Sciences* 21, no. 7 (1959): 620–30.

Rosman, Abraham, and Paula G. Rubel. "Nomad-Sedentary Interethnic Relations in Iran and Afghnistan." *Journal of Middle East Studies* 7 (1976): 545–70.

———. "Structural Patterning in Kwakiutl Art and Ritual." *Man* 25 (1990): 620–40.

———. "'I Love a Parade': Ethnic Identity in the United States and Israel." In *Toward an Anthropology of Nation Building and Unbuilding in Israel.* F. Markowitz et al., eds. Lincoln: University of Nebraska Press, 2015.

Ross, Marcus R. "Who Believes What? Clearing Up Confusion Over Intelligent Design and Young-Earth Creationism." *Journal of Geoscience Education* 49, no. 1 (2005): 30–35.

Rostow, Walt W. *The Stages of Economic Growth: A Non-Communist Manifesto.* Cambridge: Cambridge University Press, 1960.

Rothstein, Frances. *Globalization in Rural Mexico: Three Decades of Change.* Austin: University of Texas Press, 2007.

Rowley-Conwy, Peter. "Time, Change and the Archaeology of Hunter-Hatherers: How Original Is the 'Original Affluent Society'?" In *Hunter-Gatherers: An Interdisciplinary Perspective.* Catherine Panter-Brick, Robert Layton, and Peter Rowley-Conwy, eds. Cambridge: Cambridge University Press, 2001.

Rubel, Paula G. *The Kalmyk Mongols: A Study in Continuity and Change.* Indiana University Publications, Uralic and Altaic Series, vol. 64. Bloomington: Indiana University Press, 1967.

Rubel, Paula G., and Abraham Rosman. *Your Own Pigs You May Not Eat.* Chicago: University of Chicago Press, 1978.

———. *Collecting Tribal Art: How Kwakiutl Masks and Easter Island Lizard Men Became Art.* West Conshohocken, PA: Infinity Publishing, 2015.

———. *Aliens on Our Shores: An Anthropological History of New Ireland, Papua New Guinea 1616–1914.* Suzanne Hanchett, ed. Pasadena, CA: Development Resources Press, 2021.

Ruffini, Julio L. "Disputing over Livestock in Sardinia." In *Law and Anthropology: A Reader.* Sally Falk Moore, ed. Malden, MA: Blackwell, 2005.

Sahlins, Marshall. "What Is Anthropological Enlightenment: Some Lessons of the Twentieth Century." *Annual Review of Anthropology* 28, 1999.

Salaff, Janet W. *Working Daughters of Hong Kong: Filial Piety or Power in the Family.* New York: Columbia University Press, 1995.

Saler, Benson. *Conceptualizing Religion: Eminent Anthropologists, Transcendent Natives, and Unbounded Categories.* Leiden, Holland: E. J. Brill, 1993.

Schatz, Edward. *Modern Clan Politics: The Power of "Blood" in Kazakhstan and Beyond.* Seattle: University of Washington Press, 2004.

Scheper-Hughes, Nancy, and Philippe Bourgois. "Introduction: Making Sense of Violence." In *Violence in War and Peace: An Anthology.* Nancy Scheper-Hughes and Philippe Bourgois, ed. Malden, MA: Blackwell, 2004.

Schiefenhovel, Wulf, and Ingrid Bell-Krannhals. "Of Harvests and Hierarchies: Securing Staple Food and Social Position in the Trobriand Islands." In *Food and the Status Quest: An Interdisciplinary Perspective.* Polly Wiessner and Wulf Schiefenhovel, eds. Providence, RI: Berghahn Books, 1996.

Schieffelin, Bambi B., and Elinor Ochs. "The Microgenesis of Competence: Methodology in Language Socialization." In *Social Interaction, Social Context, and Language.* Dan L. Slobin, Julie Gerhardt, Amy Kyratzis, and Jiansheng Guo, eds. Mahwah, NJ: Lawrence Erlbaum, 1996.

Schröder, Ingo W., and Bettina E. Schmidt. "Introduction: Violent Imaginaries and Violent Practices." In *Anthropology of Violence and Conflict.* Bettina E. Schmidt and Ingo W. Schröder, eds. New York: Routledge, 2001.

Schwede, Laurel, Rae Lesser Blumberg, and Anna Y. Chan. *Complex Ethnic Households in America.* New York: Rowman & Littlefield, 2005.

Scott, Eugenie C. "The Creation/Evolution Continuum." *National Center for Science Education Reports* 19, no. 4 (1999): 16–25.

Seligmann, Linda J. *Women Traders in Cross-Cultural Perspective: Mediating Identities, Marketing Wares.* Stanford, CA: Stanford University Press, 2001.

Sharma, Aradhana, and Akhil Gupta. "Introduction: Rethinking Theories of the State in an Age of Globalization." In *The Anthropology of the State: A Reader.* Aradhana Sharma and Akhil Gupta, eds. Malden, MA: Blackwell, 2006.

Sharp, Lesley A. "The Commodification of the Body and Its Parts." *Annual Review of Anthropology* 29 (2000): 287–328. https://doi.org/10.1146/annurev.anthro.29.1.287. Accessed May 2, 2016.

———. "Commodified Kin: Death, Mourning, and Competing Claims on the Bodies of Organ Donors in the United States." *American Anthropologist* 103, no. 1 (2001): 112–33.

Shay, Anthony. *Dancing across Borders: The American Fascination with Exotic Dance Forms.* London: McFarland & Company, 2008.

SIDA. *SIDA Pilot Project: The Example of SWACH.* 1998. https://www.irc-wash.org>files>822-INRA98-15353. Downloaded July 12, 2022.

Sikander, S., et al. "Delivering the Thinking Healthy Programme for Perinatal Depression through Volunteer Peers: A Cluster Randomised Controlled Trial in Pakistan." *Lancet Psychiatry* 6 (2019):128–39.

Sillitoe, Paul. "Participant Observation to Participatory Development: Making Anthropology Work." In *Participating Development: Approaches to Indigenous Knowledge.* Paul Sillitoe,

Alan Bicker, and John Pottier, eds. London: Routledge, 2002.

Sinnott, Megan. 2010. "Borders, Diaspora, and Regional Connections: Trends in Asian 'Queer' Studies." *Journal of Asian Studies* 69, no. 1 (2010): 17–31. https://doi.org/110.1017/S0021911809991586. Accessed January 16, 2016.

Siskind, Janet. "The Invention of Thanksgiving." *Critique of Anthropology* 12, no. 2 (1992): 167–91.

Smedley, Audrey. *Race in North America: Origin and Evolution of a Worldview*, 3rd ed. Boulder, CO: Westview Press, 2007.

Sollars, Werner. *The Invention of Ethnicity*. New York: Oxford University Press, 1989.

Sphere. *Humanitarian Standards Matter Strategy 2021–2025*. Geneva, Switzerland: Sphere 2021. https://spherestandards.org>English. Downloaded August 1, 2022

Stammler, Florian. *Reindeer Nomads Meet the Market: Culture, Property, and Globalisation at the End of the Land*. Munster: LIT Verlag, 2005.

Stern, Stephen, and John Allan Cicala, eds. *Creative Ethnicity: Symbols and Strategies of Contemporary Ethnic Life*. Logan: Utah State University Press, 1991.

Stoler, Ann Laura. *Haunted by Empire: Geographies of Intimacy in North American History*. Durham, NC: Duke University Press, 2006.

Stoller, Eleanor P. "Informal Exchanges with Non-Kin among Retired Sunbelt Migrants: A Case Study of a Finnish American Retirement Community." *Journal of Gerontology: Social Sciences* 53 B (1998): S287–S298.

Stoller, Paul. *Money Has No Smell: The Africanization of New York City*. Chicago: University of Chicago Press, 2002.

Stone, Lyman. Institute for Family Studies, n.d. https://ifstudies.org/blog/pro-natal-policies-work-but-they-come-with-a-hefty-price-tag. Downloaded March 21, 2023.

Straight, Bilinda. "Gender, Work, and Change among Samburu Pastoralists of Northern Kenya." *Research in Economic Anthropology* 18 (1997): 65–91.

Suarez-Orozco, Marcelo M., and Antonius C. G. M. Robben. "Interdisciplinary Perspectives on Violence and Trauma." In *Cultures under Siege: Collective Violence and Trauma*. Antonius C. G. M. Robben and Marcelo M. Suarez-Orozco, eds. Cambridge: Cambridge University Press, 2000.

Sullivan, Maureen. *The Family of Woman: Lesbian Mothers, Their Children, and the Undoing of Gender*. Berkeley: University of California Press, 2004.

Tambiah, S. J. "Animals Are Good to Think and Good to Prohibit." *Ethnology* 8, no. 4 (1969): 423–59.

Tannen, Deborah. *You Just Don't Understand: Women and Men in Conversation*. New York: Quill, 2001a

———. *Talking from 9 to 5: Women and Men at Work*. New York: Quill, 2001b.

Tatla, Darshan Singh. *The Sikh Diaspora: The Search for Statehood*. London: UCL Press, 1999.

Taussig, Michael. "Culture of Terror-Space of Death." In *The Anthropology of Politics: A Reader in Ethnography, Theory, and Critique*. Joan Vincent, ed. Oxford: Blackwell, 2002.

Thaddeus, S., and D. Maine. "Too Far To Walk: Maternal Mortality in Context." *Social Science & Medicine* (1982): 38:8.

The Knot. "Real Wedding Survey 2014." https://www.theknot.com/content/average-wedding-cost-2014. Accessed September 23, 2015.

Thomas, David H. *Skull Wars*. New York: Basic Books, 2000.

Thomas, Wesley. *Two-Spirit People: Native American Gender Identity, Sexuality, and Spirituality*. Urbana: University of Illinois Press, 1997.

Thompson, Charis. *Making Parents: the Ontological Choreography of Reproductive Technologies*. Cambridge, MA: MIT Press, 2005.

Thornton, Thomas F. *Being and Place among the Tlingit*. Seattle: University of Washington Press, 2008.

Tongue, Nancy E. "I Live Here and I Stay There: Navajo Perceptions of Households on the Reservation." In *Complex Households In America*. Laurel Schwede, Rae Lesser Blumberg, and Anna Y. Chan, eds. New York: Rowman & Littlefield, 2005.

Townsend, Joan B. "Shamanism." In *Anthropology of Religion: A Handbook*. Stephen D. Glazier, eds. Westport, CT: Greenwood Press, 1997.

Turino, Thomas. "The History of a Peruvian Panpipe Style and the Politics of Interpretation." In *Ethnomusicology and Modern Music History*. S. Blum, P. Bohlman, and D. Neuman, eds. Urbana: University of Illinois Press, 1991.

Turner, Victor. *The Forest of Symbol: Aspects of Ndembu Ritual*. Ithaca, NY: Cornell University Press, 1967.

Tylor, Edward B. *Primitive Culture: Researches into the Development of Mythology, Philosophy, Religion, Language, Art and Custom*, 2 vols. London: John Murray, 1871.

Ueno, H., and M. Ives. *New York Times*, April 14, 2022. https://www.nytimes.com/2022/04/14/world/asia/japan-toddler-tv-show.html.

UNICEF. *Project "Clean": The Swach Experience in Rajasthan*. Jaipur: UNICEF Rajasthan, 1994.

———. *Levels and Trends in Child Mortality Report 2021*. New York, 2021. https://data.unicef.org/resources/levels-and-trends-in-child-mortality/. Downloaded July 25, 2022.

UNICEF South Africa. *First 1000 Days: The Critical Window to Ensure That Children Survive and Thrive*. 2017. https://www.unicef.org/southafrica/media/551/file/ZAF-First-1000-days-brief-2017.pdf. Downloaded July 3, 2022.

UNWater. "World Toilet Day 19 November." https://www.un.org/en/observances/toilet-day. Downloaded July 20, 2022.

UNWomen. "A Toolkit on Paid and Unpaid Care Work: From 3Rs to 5Rs." New York: UNWomen, 2022. https://www.unwomen.org/en/digital-library/publications/2022/07/a-toolkit-on-paid-and-unpaid-care-work. Downloaded August 10, 2022.

USAID. *Multi-Sectoral Nutrition Strategy 2014–2025*. US Agency for International Development. https://www.usaid.gov/nutrition-strategy. Downloaded July 23, 2022.

Ustun, T. B. et al. *Measuring Health and Disability Manual for WHO Disability*

Assessment Schedule WHODAS 2.0. Geneva: WHO Press, 2010.

Van Gennep, Arnold. *The Rites of Passage.* [1909] Reprint. Translated by Monika B. Vizedom and Gabrielle Caffee. Chicago: University of Chicago Press, 1960.

Venkataraman, Vivek V. "Women Were Successful Big-Game Hunters, Challenging Beliefs about Ancient Gender Roles." *The Conversation,* March 10, 2021. https://theconversation.com/women-were-successful-big-game-hunters-challenging-beliefs-about-ancient-gender-roles-153772. Downloaded October 16, 2022.

Verkaaik, Oskar. "The Captive State: Corruption, Intelligence Agencies and Ethnicity in Pakistan." In *States of Imagination: Ethnographic Explorations of the Postcolonial State.* Thomas Blom Hansen and Finn Stepputat, eds. Durham, NC: Duke University Press, 2001.

Walker, Roslyn Adele. *O˘ló>wè> of Isè:> A Yoruba Sculptor to Kings.* Washington, DC: National Museum of African Art, Smithsonian Institution, 1998.

Wallerstein, Immanuel M. *The Modern World System: Capitalist Agriculture and the Origins of the European World Economy in the Sixteenth Century.* New York: Academic Press, 1974.

———. *World-Systems Analysis: An Introduction.* Durham, NC: Duke University Press, 2004.

Walsh, Andrew. *Made in Madagascar Sapphires, Ecotourism and the Global Bazaar.* North York, Ontario: University of Toronto Press, 2012.

Ward, Charlotte. "Reconciling His History: How Revisiting the Memory of Cook's Visit Facilitated a Process of Reconciliation within the Cooktown Community from 1998 to 2019." *Aboriginal History* 44 (2020): 3–20.

Watt, Lisa J. "Today's American Indian Tribes and Their Museums." In *American Indian Nations: Yesterday, Today, and Tomorrow.* New York: AltaMira Press, 2007.

Watters, Ethan. "The Americanization of Mental Illness." *New York Times Magazine,* January 10, 2010. https://www.nytimes.com/2010/01/10/magazine/10psychet.html?searchResultPosition=1. Accessed June 3, 2022.

Weiner, Annette. *The Trobrianders of Papua New Guinea.* New York: Holt, Rinehart and Winston, 1988.

Weinhouse, Beth. "The Mental Weight of COVID-19." *Columbia Magazine* (Fall 2021). https://magazine.columbia.edu/article/mental-weight-covid-19. Downloaded July 2, 2022.

Weisgrau, Maxine K. *Interpreting Development: Local Histories, Local Strategies.* Lanham, MD: University Press of America, 1997.

Wellings, Peter. "Joint Management: Aboriginal Involvement in Tourism in the Kakadu World Heritage Area." In *Tourism and Protected Areas: Benefits beyond Boundaries.* Robyn Bushell and Paul Eagles, eds. Oxfordshire: CAB International, 2007.

West, Paige. *Conservation Is Our Government Now: The Politics of Ecology in Papua New Guinea.* Durham, NC: Duke University Press, 2006.

———. *From Modern Production to Imagined Primitive: The Social World of Coffee from Papua New Guinea.* Durham, NC: Duke University Press, 2012.

Westmacott, Richard. *African-American Gardens and Yards in the Rural South.* Nashville: University of Tennessee Press, 1992.

White, Merry. *The Material Child: Coming of Age in Japan and America.* Berkeley: University of California Press, 1994.

Whiteford, Linda M., and Robert T. Trotter II. *Ethics for Anthropological Research and Practice.* Long Grove, IL: Waveland Press, 2008.

Whitehead, Stephen M., and Frank J. Barrett. "The Sociology of Masculinity." In *The Masculinities Reader.* Stephen M. Whitehead and Frank J. Barrett, eds. Cambridge: Polity Press, 2001.

Whitehouse, Harvey. *Arguments and Icons: Divergent Modes of Religiosity.* Oxford: Oxford University Press, 2000.

Wierzbiecka, Anna. *Emotions across Languages and Cultures: Diversity and Universals.* Cambridge: Cambridge University Press, 1999.

Willigen, John Van. *Applied Anthropology: An Introduction,* 3rd ed. Westport, CT: Bergin and Garvey, 2002.

Wilson, Monica. *For Men and Elders: Change in the Relations of Generations and of Men and Women among the Nyakyusa-Ngonde People 1875–1971.* New York: Africana Publishing, International African Institute, 1977.

Winkelman, Michael. *Shamanism: The Neural Ecology of Consciousness and Healing.* Westport, CT: Bergin and Garvey, 2000.

Winzeler, Robert L. *Latah in Southeast Asia: The History and Ethnography of a Culture-Bound Syndrome.* Cambridge: Cambridge University Press, 1995.

Woodbury, Anthony C. "A Defense of the Proposition, 'When a Language Dies, A Culture Dies.'" *Texas Linguistic Forum* 33 (1993): 1–15.

Workman, Lance, and Will Reader. *Evolutionary Psychology: An Introduction.* New York: Cambridge University Press, 2004.

World Health Organization (WHO). *Thinking Healthy: A Manual for Psychosocial Management of Perinatal Depression* (WHO generic field-trial version 1.0). Geneva: WHO, 2015.

———. *10 Facts on Ageing and the Life Course.* http://www.who.int/features/factfiles/ageing/ageing_facts/en/. Accessed January 20, 2016.

———. *World Mental Health Report: Transforming Mental Health for All.* Geneva: World Health Organization, 2022.

Wu, Frank H. *Yellow: Race in America beyond Black and White.* New York: Basic Books, 2002.

Yékú, James. *Cultural Netizenship: Social Media, Popular Culture, and Performance in Nigeria.* Bloomington: Indiana University Press, 2022.

Yuen, Sun, Pui-Iam Law, and Yuk-ying Ho. *Marriage, Gender, and Sex in a Contemporary Chinese Village.* Armonk, NY: M.E. Sharpe, 2004.

Ziolkowski, Jan M. *Fairytales from before Fairy Tales: The Medieval Latin Past of Wonderful Lies.* Ann Arbor: University of Michigan Press, 2007.

367 Matt Hamilton/Chattanooga Times Free Press via AP

371 AP Photo/Ebrahim Noroozi

378 © Jupiter Images

381 Marmaduke St. John / Alamy Stock Photo

INDEX

Page numbers followed by *b* refer to boxes and *f* refer to figures and photos.